THE GREAT TUDORS

Edited by
KATHARINE GARVIN

1935
IVOR NICHOLSON & WATSON
LIMITED   LONDON

First Published in 1935

Printed in Great Britain by
Hazell, Watson & Viney, Ltd., London and Aylesbury.

THE
GREAT TUDORS

CONTENTS

CONTENTS

INTRODUCTION

THIS book has no unity in the accepted sense, for it was imagined by one person, planned by another, and executed by forty-one more, each in his individual mood. Yet it has the unity in variety of any large and loose design whose effect depends upon the massing and interrelation of several entities. An impression of shadowy and patchwork grandeur emerges from the collection of forty essays dealing with a critical period of English history; but the rhythm is sustained just as in a folk-dance where the dancers, sometimes as many as forty, step through a series of figures until gradually, apparently almost by accident, they act out the complete sequence of the music. But here every man danced as it seemed to him fit. The only connecting links were the length of the article, and the links of time, nationality, and interconnection between the different subjects. Various characters appear again and again in more than one essay, and they do not, as they would not in life, always appear in the same light. In some cases, these reappearing figures also have an essay to themselves, Queen Elizabeth, Shakespeare, Marlowe; in others, "little Bilney," Bishop Bonner, they are treated only incidentally for their influence on others. From the whole some idea of the Tudor dispensation emerges.

"Is it to be a learned or a popular book?" someone asked rather pretentiously, clinging to a commonly used but radically false division between historical sheep and goats: as if a book must necessarily be either wantonly scholarly or grimly popular! This one is neither, but a blend of both—just as a good work of art is both classical and romantic. It was designed for a general public in whom some scholars are included; and it was written by a band mainly composed of professional scholars into whose august company some lively or illuminating general writers have, by invitation, intruded. A miserly hugging of expert knowledge will make that knowledge as useless as a diamond blinded in a safe—or as a light hidden under a bushel. Scholars who are sincere in their ends must feel pleasure in addressing themselves comprehensibly to the general reader. Research is essential, but so, as a historical reviewer lately remarked, is interpretation. "I

vii

can see a church by daylight," boasted Beatrice, but afterwards she found that human feeling could illuminate the church perhaps more truthfully than could the sun.

History is not only, what Foxe called it, " the glasse of times," for a mirror records equally the unimportant with the important. The humanistic study of the past should be carried on as nearly as possible through scientific methods, but it should lead to self-knowledge, self-discipline, and ultimately to a higher philosophy. It must, to be of any use, be an art, and the Greeks wisely placed Clio among the Muses. This is why the amusing side of history, its attractiveness, its loveliness, should never fall into neglect. Its function is like that of tragedy, deepening our experience of life by appealing to our sense of pity and terror and resolution. We can learn something from the living example that we cannot learn from fiction; and the faithful but imaginative record in stimulating language can do as much to civilise and shape the mind as can the prejudiced historian to brutalise and warp it, by means, for example, of a false Aryan doctrine. In this noble function of history there is as much room for groups of essays centred round particular people as there is for massive and sustained volumes. The several points of view have the value of concentrating upon personality, and the collection gives the idea that an age is in fact made up of a multitude of separate characters; it is not a fixed and unified circle.

We have become, in the modern world, too apt to think fatalistically that one virtue must necessarily exclude another. If a book is interestingly presented and lucidly written, some people are inclined to think that it must be inaccurate, and if it is well documented, another set of people is inclined to be sure that it must be dull. Hence has arisen the usage of dividing books loosely into learned and popular. Both words are misleadingly used. A Sir Walter Raleigh, a W. P. Ker, an Alfred North Whitehead brings years of patient study, discipline, and experience to his work so that his final utterance seems so devastatingly simple and complete that an intelligent and unlearned person might possibly grasp the message more quickly than a trained scholar. The truth is that professional scholars who spend their lives in dealing with original records and in painfully reconstructing a whole from amassed details have an advantage in the interpretation of truth that is similar to the priest's advantage over the layman in the practice of holiness. The scholars who combine speculative imagination and a fine style with humility and diligence and accuracy are among the richest and rarest of writers. On the other hand, no one would be so mistakenly worshipful of authority as to suppose that a greater saint might not be found outside the scholarly priest-hood, and that a finer historical imagination might not inspire someone who had not the opportunity to spend his life in research, who must to a certain extent accept his facts at second-hand. The real test of good history—allowing always for the different intentions of various historical styles—is not in the relative learning or popularity but in the integrity and vision of the writer. An honest concentration on the subject and an urgent anxiety to express it are cardinal virtues. Shakespeare lacked historical equipment; yet he can give a profoundly illuminating flash. He presents the whole of a historical mood in *Richard III*, for instance, bringing a redemptory idea out of misery and horror and treachery. It is a true historical touch to have imagined backwards and seen the turmoil of an out-of-date baronial system, to have contrasted this with the sober dignity that was the foundation of Tudor greatness with its care for the individual, its respect for Parliament, its encouragement of the middle class. And people less wise than Shakespeare, Charles Kingsley in *Westward Ho*, Charles Reade in *The Cloister and the Hearth*, Dumas the elder in *Ascanio*, Virginia Woolf in *Orlando*, Marjorie Bowen in *The Viper of Milan* (all novels dealing with the period of this book or those contiguous to it) give a quicker feeling of history, a broader and clearer sweep than many a textbook.

Therefore the authors in this book are a varied company. When we were thinking who could do the various subjects, we found ourselves proceeding as if we were casting a great play. People were invited to interpret characters whom they would most thoroughly understand, and with whom they could sympathise, although the sympathy need not always be an amiable or sentimental one. An actor must understand Iago in order to make him credible; but that is not to say that he must condone him. The essays are not all panegyrics. Miss Marjorie Bowen, for instance, strips Mary Queen of Scots of a false romanticism. When you have read her article, you are at liberty to agree or disagree with her final judgments, but she has performed a very salutary service in reducing Mary's problem to historical perspective and to its true political and human value. In other essays, we attempted to stress, through our choice of author, the human or the political element where each was predominant, and the articles touching on religion we tried to entrust to writers who understood the depth and peculiar colour of religious belief in that age. This was more difficult than might appear, partly because religion is no longer the matter of course that it was in the sixteenth century, and religious enthusiasm is to-day being forced, in a great many cases, into secular channels. There was no question of " becoming a Catholic " in Tudor England, but, on the other hand, it is difficult nowadays to realise fully the fortitude that enabled people to break away from a Church that held the keys of Heaven and Hell. It is the more fortunate that Mr. Ellis Roberts should have brought out so sensitively the para-doxical sincerity of Cranmer, that Professor A. W. Reed should have shown so clearly the almost detached pains-takingness of Tindale in a religious cause; that Mr. Hugh Massingham should have described with such warm and delicate understanding the loftiness of the Puritan spirit, now too often misinterpreted; that Mr. Christopher Hollis should have stressed the holiness of the Jesuit martyr Campion, and that Miss M. Theodora Stead should have so well portrayed the wholly English combination of rectitude and thoroughness in Archbishop Parker.

We leave religion and turn to other enthusiasms: Mr. Peter Fleming has the magical vision of a traveller—something of the extended " realms of gold " excitement of Marlowe—and he has appreciated the boundless aspiration of Gilbert, even when it is least sensible. Mr. Wynyard Browne has drawn a novelist's perspicacious and subtle sketch of Raleigh, the individualist in a somewhat gregarious age. The late Sir Nigel Playfair wrote on Burbage more in the style of conversational musing than of formal essay. He approached his subject from the point of view of a practical actor, and his comments upon the ephemeral fame of great actors, their devotion, their hardworkingness, have gained in memorableness since his death. The Very Reverend Charles L. Warr, Dean of the Chapel Royal, Edinburgh, a Scot and a divine as well as a man of immense learning, is particularly qualified to write on John Knox; while John Bell, High Master of St. Paul's School, writes of his founder with the resources of tradition and the enrichment of association, as well as with careful learning.

A number of writers have distilled the work of a lifetime into the short space of the five-thousand word essay. The articles on Sir Thomas More by Professor R. W. Chambers, on Sir Francis Walsingham by Professor Conyers Read, on Henry VIII by Professor A. F. Pollard, on Cardinal Wolsey by Professor E. P. Cheyney, are all, in different ways, remarkable for concentration, condensation, and unobtrusive knowledge. For Shakespeare, the most difficult to do of all, two great scholars have joined together—it was their own idea—and Professors J. Dover Wilson and A. W. Pollard have written together a joyful, quick-moving essay with apparently easy but actually complex erudition.

There are those writers also among our contributors who are not so much specialists on a particular person as connoisseurs of the general background of the Tudor age. Miss Muriel St. Clare Byrne could not have written so sympathetically and convincingly on Mary Tudor if she were not immersed in the social life of the century, and if she had not been able to illustrate Mary by comparison with her greater sister. Mr. Harold Child on Cardinal Pole and Dr. G. B. Harrison on Elizabeth could not have presented so sanely and so fully the contrary influences of the age, if they were not so familiar with the whole epoch.

The period covered is an exceptionally long one, beginning with medieval England tired from the Wars of the Roses and established in peace with the victory of Henry VII, and ending at least with Elizabeth's death. It lasts from 1485 to 1603, and is carried beyond that date, almost into parliamentary England, by the later lives of Raleigh, Bacon, and Ben Jonson. Five reigns show the rise and extinguishment in death of a great dynasty. The period was so complex, so many sided, that it seemed wise to abandon the alphabetical arrangement of the *Great Victorians* and other companion books in order to adopt a chronological scheme. The birthdates have not been taken as a chronological basis, for they are rarely important, and men do not leave their mark on public life at ages corresponding equidistantly to their births. But their years of activity and influence not infrequently, in so violent and autocratic a period as the Tudor one, precipitate their deaths, and we have arranged the characters in this book successively according to their deaths, except in the case of the reigning monarchs. These, Henry VII, Henry VIII, Mary I, and Elizabeth, were seldom important until their accessions, and the terminal dates of their reigns governed and characterised the destinies of lesser men. They have been placed in the sequence of the book so that those who died in their reigns come after them. The method is far from being perfect or wholly consistent, but it seemed to work best, in the present case, because it enables those readers who know little about the general outlines of the Tudor period to follow it coherently. We begin with Henry VII and end with Ben Jonson, whom Dr. Enid Glen shows as the last of great Tudor characters, an almost philosophical product of Tudor ideas.

Two obvious phenomena weld the long and diverse period into a whole. The first, in history, is the reigning dynasty that held England together, in whose time England accomplished its coming of age. The second, in the present, is a reflection in the public mind revealed by the recent flood of Tudor works of every sort. Tudor Street, Tudor hotels, inns, and restaurants with waitresses dressed in pseudo-Elizabethan dress, with baronial panelled halls and massive furniture, these all indicate something of the permanent popular charm of the Tudors. Of late there has been a special burst of increased enthusiasm. The new interest is many sided, producing many scholarly studies of Tudor institutions and persons as well as romanticised biographies of the greater men and women. The film on Henry VIII, crude and inaccurate, it is true, attempts to bring out some of the essential Englishness that people find most plainly expressed in the Tudors. Henry's wives have been the subjects of wellnigh innumerable plays and biographies; so has his daughter Elizabeth, until she is now almost headline stuff. In her case it is natural, for she is that most fascinating and tantalising of all subjects, a personal enigma and a clear political force. Mary Stewart has also been the subject of plays and stories, and we have even had our dramatised William Shakespeare. The British Broadcasting Corporation has thought it worth its while to broadcast upon a subject so highbrow as *Queen Elizabeth and her Subjects*. Altogether, for several years past, England has been Tudor mad.

The reasons are speculative and complex. Some of the key essays in this book characterise the Tudor period in broad terms that give some indication of the colours of the whole period. They give an occasional clue to the reasons for this popularity. Professor R. W. Chambers notices with admirable, shrewd insight how and where the age falls into two parts, medieval and modern. The break becomes most clear at the Dissolution of the Monasteries. That is one thing, then—our taste for the sixteenth century is comparable with our taste for Victorians. We are intrigued and puzzled by the gradual emergence of a type similar to ourselves, gradually breaking the parental bond. The age has the beginning of something that we prize. Professor A. F. Pollard gives us another facet; he says that the modern affection for Tudors is an innocuous expression of that spirit of nationalism that expresses itself fascistically in other nations.

Certain obvious characteristics of the Tudor age make it picturesque, appealing to the imagination and as " romantic " as the period of the French Revolution. Many features immediately fire the fancy. The Renascence itself has always attracted popular attention. The stress, the division between old and new, the novel theories about statesmanship, peace, freedom, and education, the evolution of a new type of woman, the re-discovery of the classics, the splendid and ornate dress, all these are direct magnets to an age like ours that has too little leisure, generally speaking, and too little pageant and splendour. But in one way, we do not think of Tudor England as a Renascence period, although it was so. Renascence France and Italy have their own character, but in spite of the work of the humanists in England, in spite of their enormous influence, Tudor England seems something special and apart from the general Renascence, something more active and exciting, less meditative and removed. This is partly because it was a critical period when national consciousness was almost forced upon her by the necessity for her taking her place among the nations as a major force and a formidable power.

Another, perhaps more deeply seated, cause of attraction is the religious question. England, as Mr. Hilaire Belloc says in his essay on Burghley, is Protestant " to the marrow." We feel that the spirit of religious stubbornness has always flourished in Christian England, even in the mind of the devout and orthodox Chaucer. But this independent mood is not crystallised until this period when Shakespeare glorified the monster John as a pre-Protestant and reproached, in the same play, the papal legate, for his pious reproofs to a bereft, distracted mother, with the pertinent remark " He speaks to me who never had a son." This Protestantism, the almost fortuitous means by which it came about, is attractive. After the separation from Rome, accomplished by a monarch who was Catholic in ritualistic sympathy, the persistent and indomitable struggle of the upright spirit of Protestantism, rising from below, is deeply moving and even thrilling. There are few who could not be excited by the indefatigable work of Tindale in translating the Bible, his editions and subsequent re-editions, the new translations until the final appearance, after Elizabeth's death, of the magnificent Authorised Version, a triumph for the Reformed Religion and also for the English Language.

Professor C. H. Williams has shown forcibly how the power of the Renascence in England, and indeed everywhere, depended upon money. Henry's accumulations, the rising prosperity and increased importance of the money-getting class is not to be despised or contemned. Napoleon, it is fabled, sneered at the English as a nation of shopkeepers. The sneer was ill-advised, for it is difficult to see why power from armed force or from tyranny is more respectable than power from commercial transactions; and Mr. G. K. Chesterton in one of his early books has shown the spiritual contribution of commerce in remarking how much poetical genius has in this country come from behind the counter. The gibe, taken seriously, is a true observation. Although the English merchants had thriven before, and though much of England's greatness comes from the merchant class, it was not until this Tudor period that the sober, dignified and decent merchant class comes into its own, in life, in manners, in stage and portraiture. The dignity of humble trade is seen in *Ralph Roister Doister*, and the ideal portrait of a rich bourgeois shines as the one instance of spiritual integrity in the *Merchant of Venice*. In spite of its tyranny and its grandeur, we feel that Tudor England was the ancestor of democratic England, of the nation that to-day, from the humdrum of its armchair, flings itself by wireless, but with whole-hearted romance, into the glorious spectacle of a royal and international wedding.

This craving for pageant and splendour was largely exploited by Henry VIII. Professor A. F. Pollard shows the

gorgeous king spending his father's legacy, and developing
Parliament—the latter not while the great autocrat Wolsey
(more obstinately aristocratic in his grand attitudes than
anyone merely nobly born could be) was in power, but
afterwards.   For other sides of the picture there is the record
of the grievances of the poor in Mr. Robert Randall's essay
on Robert Kett, the echo in Edward's reign of the effect of
the Dissolution of the Monasteries on land tenure and on
economics generally.   In the time of the early Tudors, as
Mr. W. H. Auden has said in his essay on Skelton, the working, self-denying middle class were operating even through
the Wars of the Roses.   They were building solid stone houses
in Gloucestershire and seamen's churches in East Anglia
with spires as beacons at either end, and commissioning
austere and lovely brasses to put on their tombs.   The glory
of Henry VIII's court increased until the English spectacle
could compete successfully with Genoese and Venetian display, and consolidation and prosperity rose until Edward's
reign, and from that time onwards, so that after the first
Reformation had taken apparent effect—actually misleading the persons who wished for absolute simplicity and life-
by-conscience and Biblical accuracy—steadily and gradually
the voices of the working classes became audible.   John
Foxe speaks for the people in Mary's reign.   He does not, it
is true, deal with economics, but indirectly he shows that the
humble people had not yet come into their own.   Miss
Byrne shows how the eldest Tudor heir, Mary, in spite of her
attempts to enforce laws dealing with heresy which by the
very nature of things must be out of date for Henry's
daughter, gradually increased the orderliness of England in
repairing roads, and augmented the sense of justice and individual responsibility in the law courts.   The steps forward
on behalf of the common folk were not always in the same
direction, for sometimes they bore on religion, sometimes on
economics, sometimes on education, but all the time steady
progress was being made towards individualism.   To the
eye of the lay observer, there is a steady development in the
actions of the monarchs, a growing change in the conception
of monarchy, and the nature of this change shows why a
development of freedom, of upright and independent fear-
lessness should have been possible under an absolute
monarchy.   Henry VII took on a chaotic nation with a
small but coherent bourgeois nucleus.   His aims were chiefly

relative to the establishment of his dynasty. But where he was merely a family man, coming short in this of the popular idea of a hero, his son identified himself with his country. Henry VIII *was* England. He was the autocrat, the epic hero, who put all his energies into advancing the combined interests of himself and the land that he ruled. In the child Edward's time there was an apparent recurrence of the lawless polyarchy of pre-Tudor days. The appearance might have become reality if it had been given longer time; but the people, having learned their conception of kingship from the temper of the times, redeemed the young Edward by relying on him as their friend as against the barons. It was, in the people's mind, the king and the people against the oligarchy or squirearchy. The change becomes evident with Mary. She had a real sense that her duty was to her people rather than to her land. Even her fanaticism shows that it was her responsibility to the individual that concerned her. She was no longer England itself, and her mistaken benevolence was due to her belief in the necessity of redemption for the English people, not that of England herself. She no longer thought of an abstract state but in terms of single people. It was a woman's quality, and she had a woman's defects. Elizabeth, so different from her in many ways, was like her in this understanding of the individual, but more thorough. Elizabeth as sovereign no longer thought of her land as her own attribute, she thought of it as a collection of individuals for whose welfare she was trustee. It was Tudor England with its advanced political and religious sense of the value of the unit that found the ideas of the Scottish kings, James and Charles, out of date. It was the example of Elizabeth that prompted the removal of Charles's head.

The desire for expansion, the breaking of the medieval bounds of the known world, the yearning for a larger world as a larger experience, the braving of danger for the sake of plunder, all these touch the financial aspect of the period on one side, but on another they touch upon man's eternal desire for adventure. It is infinitely more exciting to hear of the discovery of a new world than to hear of an Atlantic record, or a speed limit broken. Both contain an overleaping of the bounds of imagination, the unfolding of the vistas of an unexplored and beautiful land. A child's vision and desire is in some ways the most abiding guide that man keeps through life, and many of our notions of right and wrong, of beauty and ugliness, of aspiration and victory, derive from our childish conceptions; and this passion, the childish wonder allied with danger, is always with us. Our love for the Tudors matches our desire for mental and spiritual expansion. The outward spreading nearly always goes with, and is an expression of, the inward emancipation of the spirit. The best emigrant is one who cannot possess his soul in peace at home. Goethe's remark, that America is within you, is incomplete; America is never within, is capable neither of envisagement nor of attainment until it has been realised as an almost subconscious and external ideal. The adventurous personal character, the heroism, the commercial and imperial motives of sixteenth-century seamen, pirates, warriors, and merchants, is not so important to the modern public mind as their unconscious symbolism of a universal desire. These were the men who broke the chains of Western Europe and exposed an illimitable view of the World. Physical exploration led directly to the conception of man's own infinity, his variety, his incalculability. The profound satisfaction of annoying Spain was of ephemeral importance compared with the enlarging of the horizon. It is important that the Tudor age was greatest, with the Cabots, Drake, Hawkins, Frobisher, Gilbert, and Grenville, in its action.

The arts, flourishing in this England, partly expressed the cardinal enfranchisement and partly restricted it. England became self-conscious about the arts in a way that she was not about her explorations and active achievements. She was, we are told, better known on the Continent for her music than for her literature. This is not at all surprising, although it is difficult to prove, for in music she adhered to and perfected a tradition while in literature she created a new tradition. Literature is a swift-winged art that speeds ahead of the times; or else it follows after and reflects them; and it is wayward and whimsical and eccentric in either case. It is the only art that expresses conscious and logical thought. It very often, for that reason, ceases to be an art at all, failing to conserve the purity and abstraction of mood necessary for a work of art. Yet this peril itself and by its nature frees literature from the impediment of tradition. Where early Tudor literature trod a previously unmarked way, as it did in works of criticism and instruction, the later writing compensated by concerning itself with the immediate past, with a reflection of the yesterday of memory that is hardly to be distinguished from the future. The literature that is usually styled as Elizabethan really belongs, in its greatest aspect, to the age after Elizabeth. The greatest of the plays, philosophical in conception and as great in character as in reflection, *Hamlet, King Lear, The White Devil*, these come towards the end of the Elizabethan period or else they come after it altogether. Even the great comedies date after the climax of the reign, the execution of Mary, and the triumph over the Armada. But it is not the excellence of drama that is so revealing of the age as its development and multiplicity; and for the record of social background, for the image of the reflected mood we must look to the lesser writers, Nicholas Udall, John Lyly, *George à Greene, the pinner of Wakefield*, and the development of the theatres generally, their extensive patronage by the court, and the whole desire of Elizabethan England for dramatic expression.

This was in fact a dramatic age. People felt and acted dramatically. The greatest of the achievements of the age was spectacular and memorable. The last fight of *The Revenge*, the execution of Mary of Scotland, the singeing of Philip's beard, or earlier, the trial of Queen Catherine, the death of Wolsey, or the Field of the Cloth of Gold—these are all scenes. People were absorbed in direct action, and they had little time in which to reflect. There was a great deal of noble gesture and of fine religious enthusiasm, but little inward mysticism; though the exceptions to this generalisation are rare and sweet. It is astonishing, with all that we know about Elizabeth, how little we know of her personal musings. The clues as to her private feelings, such as her remark that " The Queen of Scots is mother of a fair son," are reported only and of doubtful authenticity. But her speeches, those of Peter Wentworth, of Mary Stewart, of Raleigh, the superb gesture of the dying Sidney, these are all dramatic, acted out before people so that they would sound natural inserted into a play as they stand. The written records are not only unusually full, they are also astonishingly expressive. Soon after the coming of the Stewarts, this spontaneous and sincere sense of dramatic gesture vanishes. The Elizabethan dramatists show England in an epic mood, a heroic temper, and the sovereigns were, or tried to be, the outward manifestation of the national hero. It was a heroic age, in the throes of a national emancipation; and this suits our modern taste very well. We may no longer be able to identify ourselves readily with the epic ideal, we may have lost the primitive simplicity of aggregate emotion, but we feel the need still for losing ourselves in a larger whole, and to this craving the Tudor age ministers.

Marlowe, in the drama, together with the best of Shakespeare and of Ben Jonson, is somewhat out of tune with the prevailing mood. He is lyrical and inward, and his plays can be better understood through inward brooding than through outward viewing. It is the knowledge within man's mind, the inward conflict, the quick and full absorption in a diamond that inspires Marlowe. Tamburlaine's actual battles are far less important than his desire to make himself one with the map. The obvious aspirations that urge the heroes of his plays merely provide starting-points for a revelation of the soul. Even his most objective poem, *Hero and Leander*, is concerned with internal and sacramental truth. When it is time to proceed with plain narrative, Marlowe stops, and Chapman continues in a critical vein.

The great exception to the prevailing temper was Spenser, as unique in his kind and as ill-fitting as Milton in the Restoration. Professor W. L. Renwick has finely illustrated his lack of self-confidence and, to our thinking, this is an indication that his genius was not really in character with the times. He evokes a last vision of the Middle Ages; he breathes of the Renascence spirit; but in spite of his adoption of Arthur, it is not the English Renascence that he typifies. We do not recall many of the great English figures when we read him, but Plato and Pico della Mirandola ; just as in music Byrd recalls St. Gregory and Palestrina. This inward mysticism in Spenser is what more than anything else has obscured his poetical greatness. He tried to put his ideas into a sixteenth-century scene of English adventure; but in his deep absorption in the moment, his realisation of spiritual truth, he almost strips adventure of action. Those who would love him best for his real accent are often put off by his frame of knightly adventure, and his insistence upon action, while those who would like the adventurous frame are disappointed because he lingers in description. The essential Spenser speaks most clearly in the *Fowre Hymnes*, in the *Epithalamion*, and in the philosophical passages in the *Faerie Queene*. There is nothing epic about him, but he wrote an epic because it was an epic age and epic was what the public wanted.

Inwardness was not in place in Tudor England, and the same thing comes out again in the lyric poetry. Poetry was much less universally good than is often assumed and commonly repeated. Everyone, it is true, or almost everyone, tried to write verse, and almost everyone succeeded. The same is true of to-day. We never know whom we shall find bursting into verse in the Sunday papers. But such generality is apt to breed imperfection. To-day our lyrists often lack music and concentration; in Elizabethan England they often lacked depth and significance. No one can avoid being struck by the healthiness of Elizabethan poets; their poetry was the normal addition to a well-rounded active life. Poetry was not so much a product of thought and feeling as expressed action. The lyrics are more or less conventional. They often take their frame from a well-known dance step or from a popular musical air. Lyly's *Cupid and Campaspe* is almost a dance. Drayton's exquisite small picture:

> " *Clear had the day been from the dawn,*
> *All chequered was the sky,*
> *Thin clouds like scarfs of cobweb lawn*
> *Veil'd heaven's most glorious eye.*
> *The wind had no more strength than this,*
> *That leisurely it blew,*
> *To make one leaf the next to kiss*
> *That closely by it grew* "

is a pure poem in the absorption and detachment of its expression; but it is an outward not an inward poem, descriptive not emotional or thoughtful; and the same poet's *Since there's no help, come let us kiss and part*, is in itself a drama. The songs of the age, it is no detriment to them to say so, are not true lyrics, for they express not the original mood of the individual but the general fashion of feeling in a suitable and often passionate form. Peele's *His golden locks Time has to silver turned*, deeply meditative, and exquisitely progressive in movement, belongs less to the lyric than to the elegiac mood. On the whole, the men who wrote poetry in the Tudor age, always excepting the greatest, were untroubled by inward conflict. Exceptions are Wyatt and Sidney (sometimes) and Raleigh; and it is significant that the authors who write on them here, Mr. Paul Chadburn, Mr. C. Henry Warren, Mr. Wynyard Browne, all make the exceptional claim for their subjects that they wrote intimately and sincerely. Mystical and introspective poetry could be freely found in Tudor England; but its exponents were not the most successful nor the most typical. What we take for granted in the seventeenth-century poets, in the soldier poets as well as the divines, we accept as a comparative rarity in the century preceding.

The untroubled and conventional accomplishment of the lyric is echoed by its great sister, music. The accompaniments of the songs, such as *Come, live with me and be my love* and *Have you seen but a white lily grow*, complete, and are almost inseparable from, the words they express. Mr. Anthony Standen, in an article in *The Gramophone* for December 1934, has traced how beautifully and poignantly the notes of William Byrd's *Lullaby my sweet little baby* intensify the meaning of the words, how accurately and smoothly the melody follows the poetry. It was a pity that St. George's singers, in the gramophone performance of this carol, could not record all four beautiful verses. Here is what Byrd said himself about the musical inspiration of divine words : " illis ipsis sententijs (vt experiendo didici) adeo abstrusa atque recondita vis inest ; ut diuina cogitanti, diligenterque ac serio peruolutanti ; nescio quonam modo, aptissimi quique numeri, quasi sponte accurrant sua."

This was England's greatest period in music, and a period of change whose first-fruits in the newer Italianate secular school appear in the splendid crop of later Elizabethan composers. To the earlier period, Henry VII's and Henry VIII's reigns, are attributed such a moving ballad as *The Three Ravens* and such a gay dance as *Sellenger's Round*. The great church composers produce steadily from about 1550 onwards. England was famous for her music abroad, she bred musicians as she did lyrists, and we are reminded until it is a commonplace that the Elizabethan gentleman could play and read his music at sight ; that music was essential to a full education ; and that the Elizabethans sang naturally and spontaneously. The quality of the singing is something we do not so well know, for William Byrd says that " the benefit of a good voyce " is a gift " so rare as there is not one among a thousand, that hath it; and in many, that excellent guift is lost, because they want Art to expresse Nature." It was no matter ; the madrigal books were left about in barbers' shops as the *Bystander* is to-day. Henry VIII could play the flute ; and a manuscript in the British Museum contains thirty-three of his pieces (Add. MS., 31,922). Elizabeth and her sister Mary both learned to play the virginals, and Elizabeth was proud of her accomplishment. Music is also a universal taste to-day ; but there is a vast difference between our appreciation and theirs. We listen more and more to our gramophones and we patiently accept whatever the wireless offers. The Elizabethans had the craftsman's love for the art, because they were all potential performers. Shakespeare scattered musical references through his plays, apparently sure that they would be comprehended. Many of his similes and metaphors depend upon a knowledge of music. He mentions " broken music " ; he uses the themes of folk-songs to intensify emotional situations ; but the main point about all his references and all the music of the period is that it was traditional enough to serve usefully as a background and accompaniment to a theme. It was still somewhat akin to folk music, common and not individual property, of universal appeal, and still allied to words and dancing.

The composers of the age are just at the stage when they express individualism, but only by a deeper and sincerer interpretation of the universal formula. When they write musical pieces, for their own sake, pieces such as Byrd's *The Bells*, they are pleasant enough, but they lack the resolved crisis and the exaltation of the true autonomous art. This follows from Byrd's own view, perhaps a general one, that " There is not any Musicke of Instruments whatsoeuer, comparable to that which is made of the voyces of Men." The conventional patterns were infinitely refined until they were able to express intricate subtleties of feeling delicately and finely ; but the musical character of the age was not so much stamped with great musicians as it was saturated with general knowledge and appreciation.

It is difficult for us, the average modern public, to have the music by heart as easily as we have the verbal lyrics because, in the first place, we have to wait upon public performances, and in the second place, there is not a little Tudor music still unedited. Private performers, with their lutes, recorders and voices, are still comparatively few, although they are increasing in numbers. The dozen or so of Tudor gramophone records, admirably chosen and executed though they be, cannot seriously represent the vast body of Tudor composition ; and in spite of the amount of research that has been done in the past thirty odd years, we must not forget that its results are not readily available to many people of limited time and expense. From the composers that we know something of, we can feel the austerely English quality and the joyful control. Thomas Tallis' short service is still used in the Church of England ; its dignity still fittingly accompanies the solemnity of the *Book of Common Prayer*, and what we know as *Tallis' Canon* (All praise to Thee, my God, this night) is one of our most familiar and beloved hymns. Lesser composers strengthen our impression of finish and charm. Giles Farnaby, for instance, wrote many slender pieces of exquisite grace ; one of the most delicate and final is *His Rest*. Perhaps the greatest of many composers was William Byrd. He was, if not excelling in all types of music, more excellent than anyone else in composing many kinds. They thought of him in his time as the " Father of Musick," and he published the first English madrigal in the year of the Armada. His madrigals, his motets, and his three Masses show something of the roundness of the later type of composer. The religious works, and the *Gradualia* especially, have a deep and moving serenity and sincerity. It is remarkable that nearly all the great musicians—the noted exception is Orlando Gibbons—still clung to the Roman Faith ; and the greatest works in music belong to the ancient ritual. The inspiration of the music was, therefore, different from that of the literature. It is as if music were so reflective and so echoing that it is often a step or two behind the age ; in this period there was no robust and discovering pioneer spirit, but a perhaps more valuable, certainly more flawless, raising of formality to final perfection. This is not to decry Byrd and his compeers. What they did with their medium is beautiful and solemn, and Byrd's grave pavane for the Earl of Salisbury is completely satisfying. But when the composers of this age are compared with Bach or Mozart, or even Debussy, they appear to be composing in a different and less self-reliant and comparatively light medium. Music was still not so much an art for itself as it was a means of accompaniment.

The other arts were equally a background to the social life, and only when they are utilitarian arts are they native. For his tomb Henry VII imported an Italian who designed the beautiful chapel in Westminster Abbey. Wolsey encouraged institutional architecture in his various foundations, and we see the perpendicular arch, square and sturdy, as a fitting frame for perpendicular kings and prelates. It is no frame for the prayers of the ascetic and austere. Church architecture decreased in suggestive spirituality, but domestic architecture showed a definite and sudden progress. Houses began to be designed for comfort and social life rather than for fortification and defence. The stately homes of England date from the Tudor period. They were filled with furniture that showed a duplicity of motive and ideal. The tables were long, beautifully proportioned, and massive; the chairs were solid and could easily accommodate a padded doublet or a huge farthingale; but they, like much of Tudor Gothic, show a confusion of two principles, that of line and that of ornamentation. The greatest medieval workmen evidently understood, as we can judge from their work, that sculpture and carving were subservient to cleanness of line, and the carving actually underlines the essentially clear and sweeping shape. The flowing lines of medieval design give way in the Tudor age to static and finite patterns which not infrequently detract from the massive dignity of the object they adorn, chairs or tables or beds. Even the panelling, so fine in the great halls, so sombre and impressive, somewhat distracts the eye from the great bare lines by the multiplicity of its squares. It was a grand bluff age, but its foible was decoration and elaboration. It is fortunate that most of the portraiture was at first done by foreign artists. Holbein was the greatest painter and draughtsman of the period, and the plainness and honesty, as well as the consummate skill, of his representations makes his gallery of portraits an invaluable letter of introduction to the period as well as a unique contribution to the body of art. We must feel more dearly for More when we see the faces of his daughters; and the paintings of Erasmus and others give a knowledge of the period that the written record could not give unaided. After taking the trouble to look at the face of Mary Tudor, at her reposeful position, her resolute shoulders, her suffering and enduring face, with its steady eyes, we could not dismiss her as a cold sanguinary. But as the vogue for portraiture becomes more and more adopted by English performers, the austerity of the Tudor portrait gives way to the inevitable display. We can only perceive Elizabeth's character by carefully averting the eye from her dress and pomp. It is true that she enjoyed every frill and every jewel of her costume ; but the painting of these details takes up too much of the canvas so that the austerity of the face can have too little of our attention. The same is true of nearly all the later portraits ; Sidney's portrait, Leicester's portrait, tell us more about stuffs and fashions than about the people. This is not a failure in the intrinsic excellence of the subject but a fault in technique and taste. The fault is originally in the fashion of the age ; but something also is owing to the mediocrity of painters who were misled and trapped by the fashion into obscuring the faces and postures of their subjects. Art, in domestic as well as abstract forms, does not really become simple again until the time of Cromwell.

These are varied impressions of Tudor England. It was a contradictory and multifarious age, and it is held together by the dynasty that came as a saviour at the crucial moment. Henry VII was the necessary male establishing a firm monarchy. Henry VIII and Wolsey rudely established a Continental idea of England's independence and weighty value; Henry and Anne Boleyn accomplished a Protestant Church, and in their reign the English had thrown off the bonds of authority with adolescence. Edward, by his minority and feebleness, had allowed for the expansion of popular ideas; and Mary underlined and emphasised all the things that the new England most hated. It was left for Elizabeth, great-granddaughter of a Lord Mayor, granddaughter of a Welshman and of an Irish noblewoman, daughter of the Defender of the Faith and of a partly bourgeois adventuress, sister to the Reformed young Edward as well as to the fanatical Mary, sister-in-law to Philip of Spain—it was left for her to summarise and glorify Tudor England. She drew all these diverse threads together, and she brought England safely into the path of adult development. After she had reigned, the greatest and most absolute of the sovereigns (though she had enough wisdom and wit to dissemble her absolute will), the cause of independence and empire was safe.

" What security, what dignity, what glory could a female give to a nation of men ? " This is the pertinent (and impertinent) query of a recent book on Henry VIII. The secret of Elizabeth's success lies not in her capacity, exceptional in a female, but in her very female nature itself.

It was doubtless as well that Catherine of Aragon never had a son. What could a half-Spaniard have made of the England of this moment? The consistent and logically Spanish Mary failed, and there is little reason to think that a brother of hers might have done better. The inconsistent, dissembling, half-Celtic and wholly British Elizabeth was the woman for the hour. She was so great a sovereign because she was the right person at the right time. Undoubtedly her very disabilities turned into advantages under her skilful control. On all sides the new woman, the typically Renascence woman, was controlling or meddling with politics. There was Catherine de Medici, Mary of Guise, Mary Stewart; but these contemporary rulers were not altogether such as to give people confidence in female rulers. They were also, and this is by the way, all married, and acquiesced in the medieval ideal of woman. A newer type was developing. Elizabeth, without her Tudor splendour, even, as she said herself, in her shift, would have been competent and noticeable anywhere. She represented less the royal woman of her time than the common women, the educated and sensible women. Something of the prejudice against petticoat government was undoubtedly removed by the Renascence insistence upon male and female equality. But apart from this a Tudor woman was actually better fitted for rule than a Tudor king.

Miss Byrne in one of her books has pointed out that the derisive phrase " a public virgin " is true of Elizabeth in no scornful sense. In the new national religion, Elizabeth did sublimate the worship of woman that had previously found outlet in the devotion to the Blessed Virgin. Woman in her period became a monument rather than a figure. But the office of government was developing and a radical change came when all streams of influence combined to heighten the importance of each man. People no longer regarded themselves as appendages of their sovereigns, for they began to regard their sovereign as their representative. In this form of government with the welfare of others put first and with a strong but sympathetic guiding hand, a woman could be the most successful experimenter. It is woman's function, one of her major functions, to care for the needs of others. She knows the technique of humouring people. The care for individual liberty, sympathy with all persons' affairs, that dependence upon keeping people in an agreeable mood, is part of woman's training through the ages. Her job is to manage households and to second men's interests. Her position in life depends upon her art of sympathy and good management, and for this reason women are said erroneously to be more unselfish than men, whereas it is only that in this matter their technique is more finished. Their interest, unlike that of men, which is usually abstract and mentally creative, is practical, domestic, tangible, and realist. The woman's virtue is seen in Elizabeth's devotion to her people and in her national domestic economy, derived from her grandfather but in a feminine form.

She *was* a realist; we can never realise Elizabeth unless we remember Mistress Quickly, the tangential and inconsequential ancestress of a long line of women including Jane Austen's Miss Bates, innumerable women in Dickens, and Miss Dorothy Sayers' Miss Climpson. Mistress Quickly is the best of them, together with her forerunner, Alice of Bath. She almost forgets the main issue in her realisation of the circumstances of it. She remembers that Sir John promised to make her Lady Falstaff (a treat we should have enjoyed) less well than she remembers that Mrs. Keech came in at the time of the proposal for a mess of vinegar and a dish of prawns. And when Sir John dies, she deduces his approaching death from his nose, " sharp as a pen," his fumbling with sheets and playing with flowers, his babbling of green fields. This is circumstantial evidence; it shows absorption in reality and the present moment. It is a uniquely feminine quality. It very often prevents women from being governed by a larger end, from concentrating and subordinating the means to the end. But if it is combined, as it rarely is, with the domination by a large thought, common in men, it produces rare genius. It adds richness and proportion to concentration, and it is one manifestation of intuition often giving women a measure by which to judge rightly on a first impression. They have registered almost unconsciously so many little details of conduct and physiognomy. The fitness of Elizabeth for her complicated and energetic England is partly produced by her kinship with the realism and irrelevance of Mistress Quickly. She retained the normal, the commonplace, the homely sense of life along with her greater, more conspicuous qualities. We find her recompensing a carter who commented upon the womanly indecision, the involvement in the moment, the forgetfulness of the future; we find her springing to bind the wound of an ambassador; we find her boxing Burghley's ears, and seeing through Essex's flattering letters.

The unselfishness, the sense of reality, these were common female attributes. Alone they would have been useless and might have been harmful. She differed from the majority of women in envisaging a larger and finer end; while she differed from the majority of great women, broadly speaking, of the masculine type, in realising that the equality of women with men is based not upon total similarity but upon a fundamentally different way of approaching life, combined with an intellectual evenness of brain and equipment. She realised the virtue of singleness not in the spirit of commercial virginity of a Pamela, but following the example of the Church, in the laws laid down, in wisdom, for its priests. She seemed to understand that a husband was politically dominant and that a lover was apt to sap woman's common sense, reducing her to the primitive. Whether Leicester was her lover or not, the madness was passing, and she recovered herself, allowing the greater principle to rule her. " I have always so behaved myself," she said, " that under God, I have placed my chiefest strength and safeguard in the loyal hearts and goodwill of my subjects." That is the reliance of a good nurse upon her charges' goodwill; or of a priest upon the affection of his flock. Elizabeth's outspoken dislike of, and unwarrantable prejudice against, the marriage of the clergy may have been due to a simple but subconscious fact, that she followed the celibate rule for the good of her people, and she disliked seeing her priests comfortable and married.

Tudor Elizabeth may have been coarse and vain in the sense that, denied more abiding comforts, she fed upon her people's love, but she was unselfish, single-minded, self-controlled. In her whole-hearted grasp of England's necessity, in her resolute furtherance of it, she was as much a national saint as Joan of Arc. But her great usefulness was feminine; the abstract ideas were plentiful in Tudor England; she left them to Drake and Burghley and Walsingham and Parker, concerning herself with the management of the talent.

Choosing the forty characters who should together give the truest picture of the age involved great difficulty of distribution. It was not easy to apply the same principles of selection to the different reigns and also to the rough categories of characters. We did attempt to give groups representative of statesmanship, the Church and the arts, in the earlier and the later periods, and we have tried, a little, to balance the proportion of adventurers, bishops, poets, courtiers, and dramatists. It was of course obligatory to include the sovereigns Henry VIII, Mary, the permanent importance of whose reign is not lessened by its transience, and Elizabeth. We preluded the book with an excellent essay on Henry VII, because although he is far less well known as a popular figure than the other three, it seemed to us that he was probably of greater historical significance, and that he must be understood in order to understand any Tudor. Some characters of indisputable greatness step into the book as obviously as the three sovereigns. They are John Colet, Cardinal Wolsey, Sir Thomas More, Thomas Cromwell, Thomas Cranmer, Cardinal Pole, Matthew Parker, Sir Philip Sidney, Sir Francis Walsingham, Christopher Marlowe, Sir Francis Drake, Lord Burghley, Edmund Spenser, William Shakespeare, Sir Walter Raleigh. A further group consists of people who might have been omitted, but who roughly belong to very representative types. John Fisher was a great personality, and he was included in place of the many other distinguished and important bishops of the period, both good and bad, Gardiner, for example, Warham, Jewel, Bonner, and many others. The translation of the Bible is of the utmost importance, and Tindale was chosen among a host of translators. Sir Thomas Wyatt, illustrating the earlier poetry with Italian influence, was preferred to Surrey because, in our opinion, he was intrinsically a better poet. For the Marian martyrs Latimer is representative; Father Campion shows the other side of the picture, a Jesuit martyr, preferred to Father Parsons because of his more lovable personality. Of the lesser, or rather less popularly known adventurers, Sir John Hawkins was chosen as an example of an industrious and competent Navy man, Sir Humphrey Gilbert for exactly opposite qualities, vision, romance, attractive personality, and naïvety. Sir Richard Grenville appears in preference to Martin Frobisher because Mr. J. A. Williamson, who is perhaps the greatest living authority on Tudor seamanship, preferred to write upon him. It was a fortunate choice, because he has presented him in a way which brings back an almost legendary figure in an honest and careful presentation. John Lyly appears as a representative of the earlier dramatists, deriving from the Renascence classical and Italian influences and leading on towards the mature and formal high comedy of Shakespeare's middle period. Essex is interesting as a type of the young and foolhardy courtier, with flamboyant manners and military ambitions; while Burbage, a little late for the period, represents the practical side of the Elizabethan stage. Another set of figures in this book is conspicuous not so much for the loftiness of the individual as for his expression and summing-up of a side of Elizabethan life. Peter Wentworth shows the importance of parliamentary development, and Sir Thomas Gresham that of commerce. Robert Kett, the obscure Norfolk gentleman, shows in his career the sombre current of the affairs of the smaller people all over the English country. John Foxe speaks for the humble people again, dealing with their religious development; and two things, the fact that his book was in every church along with the Bible, and the picture of contemporary rustic manners in that book, make him an invaluable study for the undertones of the period. Richard Hooker, so much an individual, yet shows the increase in intellectual thought in the Anglican Church, and in fact leads on to the autonomous attitude of the seventeenth-century divines.

Others are included who might have been omitted and to whose inclusion critics may take exception. John Skelton, though not a great poet, is important as an early poet and for his odd versification and reflection of the times. Mary Queen of Scots, it may be objected, was not English. But she was Tudor as well as Guise, and her claim to the English throne, together with her religion and her political troubles made her seriously affect the trend of Elizabeth's policy With her, both influential and representative as well a intensely interesting as a man, comes John Knox. Finally Francis Bacon and Ben Jonson were included after judicia consideration, although they are usually regarded as Jaco bean, and did their greatest work after Elizabeth's deatl They died late; but they were Tudor bred, and certain qual ties of their work both illuminate and conclude Tudo England. There are several obvious omissions for a fu picture of the period. Hans Holbein would have shov something of the art of the early period; but he was a foreigner, and there was no sufficiently pre-eminent Engli artist. Erasmus was also a foreigner, and More and Co sufficiently show the humanist culture. William By would have been an excuse for treating Elizabethan music; but he was left out for several reasons, the chief being that he was not so much proportionately greater than Tallis, Dowland, Morley, Orlando Gibbons as to warrant his inclusion. A great deal of his characteristic work was done after Elizabeth, though much also before. Furthermore, theoretical criticism of music is always difficult and inadequate, especially for a general public. Finally, John Dee, the Queen's Astrologer, would have made an attractive subject for an essay, but there was no room for him. We did actually keep Byrd and Dee in reserve, sometimes half hoping that somebody would fall out so that one of these might fall in.

It was a great age. And this is a good representative selection of its greatness. We have not added bibliographies either here or with the individual essays. The main purpose of the book is not educational. The standard works on the period concerning politics, music, painting, literature, are well known, and it would verge on the platitudinous to cite such landmarks and beacons as the works of Professors A. F. Pollard and Conyers Read and Sir Edmund Chambers, Sir Richard Terry and Dr. E. H. Fellowes. Nor do specialists need to be told where they can find the first-hand sources. The value of the book is in its literary and personal criticism, and its whole vitality depends upon its successful transmission of original and individual feeling, based in greater or less degree upon facts. Here we must close with a caution that this introduction is to be taken, not referentially and reverentially, as a portent, but in the spirit in which it is meant, as a discourse expressive of personal opinion. Our opinions are valueless except as a record of personal experience, but as this they may possibly stimulate others.

K. G.

HENRY VII

1457–1509; *reigned* 1485–1509

By

C. H. WILLIAMS

" . . . The minds of posterity, whose homage is craved by the ambitious man, will probably have very false conceptions of his thoughts and purposes. What they will call by his name will be, in a great measure, a fiction of their own fancy, and not his portrait at all."—G. SANTAYANA, *The Life of Reason*, I, 247.

I

HENRY VII

by C. H. WILLIAMS

OF all the achievements of Henry VII, that which was most significant has received least notice. He was the creator of a legend. From the early years of his reign he seems to have been determined to impose upon his contemporaries a picture of what he wanted them to think he really was. He was not wholly unsuccessful.

The first full-length description of him, in nervously phrased, forceful prose, will be found in the funeral sermon preached on May 10, 1509, by Bishop John Fisher, who had been Henry's trusty adviser. In it Henry was depicted just as he would have wished. He is the ideal king compounded of all the virtues; singularly wise in the practice of politics, with a quick and ready wit, a pithy intelligence, and a good memory; a man of wide experience, deliberate in action, wise in counsel, fluent in several tongues, attractive in person, the father of a charming and accomplished family, the ally and equal of European monarchs, a king feared by foes, obeyed by subjects, powerful not only because of his virtues but also because of his incomparable wealth. It is true that we are listening to a *Nunc dimittis*; but, as we shall see, some of the qualities here delineated were precisely those that Henry strove most strenuously to persuade contemporaries he possessed.

This was the legend as it passed into history to be appropriated by a master artist. When Francis Bacon had worked his will on it, literature was the richer by an essay in biography that fixed for all time the main outlines of the first Tudor monarch. Bacon put it into final shape in 1621, in the year of his disgrace, when he had turned for relief from his anxieties to a subject that could give him pleasure. He had long been drawn towards Henry VII, because he saw in him one of the best sort of wonders, a wonder for

3

wise men. As a portrait, his Henry bears the same relation to Fisher's as a Rembrandt does to an Italian primitive. The lights are deftly exploited. There are more shadows to throw them into relief. This is a king " sad, serious, and full of thoughts," suspicious, capable of employing " flies and familiars " to ferret out plots, studious rather than learned, not much given to pleasure, a man of action (" what he minded he compassed "), a dispenser of justice save where the King himself was a party, merciful, " but the less blood he drew the more he took of treasure," for his mind was set on accumulating it. That strain of avarice, Bacon says, was variously interpreted by men, for some thought it was done to keep his subjects low, others that he wished to leave his son a golden fleece, some that he had designs on foreign parts, " but those perhaps shall come nearest the truth that find not their reasons so far off, but rather impute it to nature, age, peace, and a mind fixed upon no other ambition or pursuit."

There is no gainsaying the mastery of the portrait. But while we read it with pleasure, we shall do well to accept it with caution, remembering that Bacon was writing nearly one hundred and twelve years after Henry's death when the materials at his command, though varied, were not altogether reliable. So, with all his sources before him, Bacon was nearer the legend than he was to Henry. What he had portrayed others copied, and as is ever the case, the likeness became fainter in the process. The colours lost their original freshness, the drawing fell out of perspective, caricature crept in, until at last, when Bacon had become for most men only a name, the popular conception of Henry was that of a petty, mean-spirited skinflint, lacking all those qualities of kingliness that make impressive, though not always attractive, the other members of his house.

This was a dreary end to the legend Henry had cultivated with so much care; but it had done its work ere ever Bacon wrote. The historian cannot afford to ignore it, since the problem that it sets him is one that seems wellnigh impossible to solve. It is the baffling one concealed in the question, What kind of a man was this King?

Now, if anyone under-estimates the difficulty of that question, let him explore the limits within which Henry's biographer has to work. The paucity, in some cases the complete absence, of those types of manuscripts that are the especial preserve of the biographer (letters, diaries, speeches, may be suggested as examples) make it extremely difficult to bring out the human qualities of the personalities of the period. On the other hand, there is much material on which the biographer can draw. It is, admittedly, not the kind that lends itself to speedy results: much of it is not prepossessing; but its very nature dictates to some extent a biographer's methods. For it consists in the main of documents containing entries of receipts and expenditure, of account-books, memoranda made by royal officials, and warrants authorising government agents to make payments. Such records yield rich stores of facts, and joined to the shrewd comments made by foreigners, hidden away in the diplomatic correspondence of the reign, they make up the materials on which biographer and historian must work.

It is necessary to realise the nature of this historical evidence, because it affects the question of Henry's biography, and shows why his real personality seems doomed to be for all time something of a mystery. It is as though one were to take away from the biographer of a modern statesman, all, or nearly all, his subject's intimate papers, and were to leave him to compile his memoir from a handful of bills, and the stubs of a few cheque-books. The result would be an unconvincing sketch, lacking life, and conveying but a feeble impression of what the living man must have been. So with Henry VII. It is not possible to reconstruct the subtleties of his psychological equipment, for we have too few intimate revelations on which to work. We can only use the accomplished facts of his policy to suggest the paradoxes of his character, and to show that he was—as seems extremely likely—a far more complex piece of human mechanism than some of his more dogmatic biographers have appreciated. To return to the analogy of painting, modern portraits of Henry must be impressionistic, rather than copies in the grand traditional manner. A sentence from an ambassador's letter will now and then supply a dash of bright colour, an entry in an account book may suggest a line here or a curve there, a warrant for payment will sometimes supply an unsuspected shade. The colours on the palette may be good in quality, but they will be limited in quantity, and Henry's personality will have to be suggested rather than depicted in detail. And yet, some of the results that might be achieved by methods such as these show that, useful as Henry found his legend, there were several features in it which did not, apparently, correspond to the facts.

The bronze effigy of Henry, by Pietro Torregiano, which is on his tomb in Westminster Abbey, suggests—that is, if it can be taken as a model—a slender man of little more than average height, and the clean-shaven features bear some resemblance to the portrait of Henry, now in the National Portrait Gallery, painted by an unknown Flemish artist. In the latter, the face is that of a strong, serious, mildly whimsical, man. The stern set mouth gives more than a suggestion of meanness. There are reserves of forcefulness in the firm chin, and the eyes look out a little sadly, as though the trials of his early adventurous years and the responsibilities of kingship had left him disillusioned and weary of the strenuous search after security. It is likely that the strain left its mark on his physique. Quite early in his reign the legate Giglis wrote to Innocent VII that the King, on account of ill-health, needed a dispensation authorising him to eat meat on fast days. Certainly, throughout the reign a group of doctors and apothecaries found Henry lavish in his payments for gifts and wages, and in the accounts there are repeated references to expenditure on heavy quantities of medicines, spices, " and other apotecary " for the King's use. Indications of a premature old age were not missed by those who observed Henry critically: " Old for his years, but young for the sorrowful life he has led," said Ayala the Spaniard: " Henry," wrote an observer in 1499, at the time when Ralph Wilford, son of a London cordwainer, was hanged for trying to turn into reality his dreams that he was a royal prince, " Henry has aged so much during this last two weeks that he seems twenty years older." There comes a pathetic flash of self-revelation in a letter of uncertain date written by the King to his mother. What the " most humble and loving son " touched upon in that document is obscure business that need not be our concern. It is the postscript that illuminates and wins our sympathy.

" Madame, I have encumbered you now with this my long writing, but methinks that I can do no less considering that it is so seldom that I do write, wherefore I do beseech you to pardon me, for verily, madame, my sight is nothing so perfect as it has been, and I know that it will appayre daily wherefore I trust that you will not be displeased though I write not so often with mine own hand, for on my faith I have been three days or I could make an end of this letter."

"On my faith" (it was Henry's favourite oath), this is no man of destiny to stride with ringing footsteps down the corridors of time.

Whatever may have been the physical obstacles in Henry's way, he was determined to surmount them in order to leave an impression of his kingliness upon contemporaries. What could be done by the wearing of rich clothes, by an ostentatious display of jewels, by insistence upon formal ceremonialism, by lavish hospitality and wise expenditure, all this should be done. To his interest in fine clothes and jewels his account books bear eloquent testimony. Some of the documents we meet read like the lading bills of a firm of wholesale drapers. Here is one, drawn from a warrant authorising the payment of £550 4s. 2d. (no small sum in modern money) for cloth supplied by a Florentine for the King's use. The details are set out at length: one piece of white cloth of gold, twenty-five and three-quarter yards long; one of green cloth of gold, thirty-seven yards long; a piece of crimson cloth of gold, thirty-one yards long; another forty-three and a half yards long; a piece of red cloth of gold, seventeen and a quarter yards long;—all at thirty-six shillings and eightpence the yard; a piece of purple cloth of gold, fifteen and a half yards long, at ten marks the yard; a piece of crimson satin, thirty-two yards at twenty shillings the yard; sixteen pieces of tawny satin at eleven shillings the yard; twenty yards of black satin and another piece of thirty-two yards; twelve and a quarter yards of tawny velvet, and seventeen yards of black velvet; a dozen pieces of "Bukram" at six shillings and eightpence the piece. . . . The list goes on, but this will be sufficient for most readers! Not infrequent are orders to deliver in all haste for the King's use such things as a riding gown of nine yards of tawny velvet trimmed with black fur, six hats of different colours, and three bonnets. The King's hat-band might, apparently, cost him four shillings in the money of the time, and he was capable of spending thirty pounds on a collar of gold for himself. Nor was it only of his own appearance that he

was mindful. " Our derest wyf the Quene " is constantly
receiving presents of cloth or fur, his children and members
of his household likewise have their gifts. Even the royal
buckhounds were dressed to the part, witness an order to
recoup the yeoman of the buckhounds for money spent " in
buying eight colers of silk garnished with Crowns, Roses,
floures de luys, and other our bagieux [badges] for our said
buckhounds, price the piece of the said colers three shillings
and four pence."

Such hints of Henry's expenditure, illustrating his love of
fine things, find corroboration in the more specific descriptions of his ostentation which sometimes occur in the comments of foreign observers. Now and again an ambassador
will speak of a royal reception, sketching the King, as he
leans against a tall gilt chair covered with cloth of gold, in
a small hall hung with very handsome tapestry. Henry
wears a violet-coloured gown lined with cloth of gold, and
a collar of many jewels, in his cap a large diamond and a
most beautiful pearl. Or again, he gives an audience to the
Milanese ambassador, standing by a royal seat adorned with
cloth of gold.

> " Beside the multitude of nobles and gentlemen, six
> bishops, the Cardinal of Canterbury, and the Spanish
> ambassador were also present. . . . His Majesty, in
> addition to his wonderful presence, was adorned with
> a most rich collar, full of great pearls, and many other
> jewels, in four rows, and in his bonnet he had a pear-
> shaped pearl which seemed to me something most rich ! "

" There is no country in the world," writes a Spaniard,
" where Queens live with greater pomp than in England,
where they have as many court officers as the King ":
while Puebla describes how he " went at an unexpected hour
to the Queen whom we found with two and thirty companions
of angelical appearance, and all we saw there seemed very
magnificent and in splendid style."

This magnificence was not reserved for ambassadorial
receptions alone. Henry never spared expense for festivities, and during his reign all opportunities were taken for
making the most of such occasions. Notes of expenses for
royal christenings, coronations, marriages, festivals like St.
George's Day, Saint David's Day, and Twelfth Night, appear

regularly in the accounts. Here it is a payment of forty pounds for " thordeyning and preparing of disguysings for oure disporte ayenst the fest of Cristemas " ; there the Queen " oure most dere wyf" receives forty marks to spend on celebrations; now it is a bill for provisions, or a sum to be spent on the equipment of the royal barges with banners and streamers in readiness for a pageant on the Thames. On such occasions there was no stint of hospitality. The author of the *Italian Relation* was impressed by what he saw:

> " Though frugal to excess in his own person (Henry) does not change any of the ancient usages of England at his court, keeping a sumptuous table, as I had an opportunity of witnessing twice that your Magnificence dined there, when I judged that there might be from six to seven hundred persons at dinner. And his people say that His Majesty spends upon his table £14,000 sterling annually . . . and it is possible that his own personal expenses, those of his Queen and of his children, and the military escort who compose his guard, and are from 150 to 200 in number, besides the many civilities that he pays to foreigners, may amount to £20,000 sterling as it is said they do."

On the eve of the arrival of the Spanish princess, Catherine, in England, someone writes:

> " In Flanders many a Spaniard has died from starvation. But I tell you that as many as like may come with the Princess of Wales, and none of them will die of hunger. If they die it will be from too much eating. Such a stock of provisions is laid in that nothing will be wanting."

These descriptions will be enough to belie the traditional belief that Henry was a skinflint. If they were not, there would be another way of disproving the accusation. Not a little of the contempt with which men have viewed him, has arisen from the knowledge that he had the bourgeois habit of making a careful note of his day-to-day petty cash expenses. The mere thought of such a thing damns him for ever in the eyes of those who would have kings move in splendid isolation, freed from the niggardly considerations and economic cares that darken their own lives. But such a view is far too superficial. It is not the keeping of accounts that is really significant. It is the nature of the entries themselves that is revealing. And Henry's show a king by no means in keeping with the legend. They are worth a glance, even though we cannot here do more than provide a few specimens.

Some of the entries mirror him, for instance, as a king who had his pleasures—though he took them seriously. He liked to chance his luck as well as his skill, and when he lost he made a note of the fact. So the entries read—" lost at the buttes (archery) to my lorde Marques, £1 " ; " for the kinges loss at chess 13 shillings and fourpence." When he was at Taunton engaged in crushing Warbeck's rebellion he seems to have relieved his mind from the burdens of politics by heavy plunging, " for the kinges losse at cardes at Tauneton £9 ". He would lose anything from thirty shillings to seven pounds fifteen at dice play. His games of tennis were not cheap nor were his shots, it would appear, always accurate— " item for the kinges losse at tenes twelve shillings ; item for losse of balles there three shillings." He was generous, too, in his rewards to the stream of entertainers who helped the members of the royal household to enjoy themselves. To his minstrel troupe, " to one that tumbled before the king " ; " to one that joculed before the king " ; " to a woman that singeth with a fidell " ; " to a little maiden that danceth " ; " to Newark for making of a song " ; to Morris dancers, to John English, Edward Maye, Richard Jakson and John Hamond, " lez pleyers of the Kinges interludes "—these are only a few of the many entries that throw a light on the amusements of which the King was fond. The royal family was musical. The King often bought musical instruments for the children. His son Henry was an expert performer on lute, organ, and harpsichord, while he was also trained in the theory of music, so that in youth he composed songs of quite considerable merit. Judged by his tips, Henry's musical tastes were catholic. He would reward equally lavishly trumpeters, wandering musicians who performed before him on the violin, the organ, the harp—even the noise of bagpipes was not too much for him to show his gratitude to those who perpetrated it !

While such recreations passed away evening hours and

festivals in the royal household, Henry's real passion was
for outdoor sport of a more serious kind. Like the Emperor
Francis Joseph, with whom he would seem to have much in
common, Henry was an enthusiastic lover of field sports,
and many are the hints which reveal his keenness. By no
means all his time was spent in the business of kingship, and
it is indicative of his love of country life that he spent much
of his time at his hunting lodge at Sonning, or in Windsor
Forest, Enfield Chase, the New Forest, or Woodstock.

There is not much evidence on which to base an estimate
of Henry's attitude to things intellectual. True, he was not
a man on the left wing of the new intellectual movement
that was stirring during his reign. He was a most loyal son
of the Church, whose piety and superstitious belief in relics
and miracles rivalled that of the most orthodox. (Those
he cherished most were a piece of the Holy Cross brought
from Greece, and the leg of his favourite Saint George,
which had been captured by Louis of France at the siege
of Milan. These Henry left in his will to the altar before
his tomb.) But there is evidence enough to show that he
was not wholly out of touch with the age. It was one of life
in things of the mind. Those who think that the glories of
the English Renaissance came only after Henry's death are
mistaken. It was in 1499 that Erasmus, the great humanist,
gave his impressions of the England of Henry VII in words
that deserve to be quoted. To Robert Fisher in Italy he
wrote from London:

"Well! you will say 'how does our dear England
suit you?' If you have any confidence in my word at
all, dear Robert, pray believe me in this, that nothing
ever pleased me so much. I found the climate here
so very mild and healthful, and so much refinement
and erudition, not of the trite and commonplace, but
of the abstruse, accurate, and classic, both in Latin and
Greek, that now I no longer sigh for Italy except to
visit it simply. When I hear my friend Colet I seem
to be listening to Plato himself. Who does not admire
in Grocyn his absolute mastery of the sciences? What
judgment more acute, more lofty, or more penetrating
than that of Linacre? Has nature ever created a
gentler, sweeter, or happier character than that of
Thomas More? But why need I go over the rest of

the catalogue? It is wonderful to say what a wide-spread and dense crop of classical literature is flourishing here. . . ."

This, be it remembered, was the England of Henry VII, and these were the men with whom the King and his family came into close contact. It may be true that Henry himself, immersed in the cares of his lifework, had little time or inclination to be in the van of the movement, but he was not ranged on the opposite side. Thanks possibly to his mother, the Lady Margaret, a lover of culture and founder of colleges, whose influence upon him was great, Henry allowed his children to benefit from what was going on in English education. They were given teachers like Bernard André, poet and historian, Giles d'Ewes, the Poet Laureate Skelton. They were brought into touch with the best of the court personnel. There are little sketches that tell us much. There is the Milanese ambassador's account of the King's eldest son, Arthur, Prince of Wales, " about eleven years of age, but taller than his years would warrant, of remarkable beauty and grace, and very ready in speaking Latin." There is Erasmus's description of how Thomas More took him to see the royal children, the nine-year-old Henry, and his sisters; how More presented the young Henry with some writing; how Erasmus was angry because he had nothing to offer, not having been warned it would be expected, " especially as the boy sent me a little note, while we were at dinner, to challenge something from my pen "; and how he went home, and " in the Muses' spite from whom I had been so long divorced, finished the poem within three days." The royal accounts, too, give brief hints that have point—here a note of payments for books and binding, or alterations in the royal library, of which Quintin Poulet was librarian. We know of patronage to Wynkin de Worde, and the printer Pynson, while Peter Artois, a native of Savoy, was given the office of King's stationer, with licence to import books both printed and manuscript, and to sell them free of customs dues. In a word, the England of Henry VII was the England of the Renaissance, and the King was no stranger to the movement. If he was not a great intellectual leader, he had his place in the changes; and one art, at any rate, found in him a steady patron. There can be no doubt about his keen interest in architecture. He was always ready to respond to the demands of his clerk of the works, Richard Doland, for money and materials for building, repairs, rebuilding, additions, at his palace of Westminster, at the Tower of London, the manors of Sheen, Greenwich, and Eltham. It was on January 24, 1503, that the foundation was laid for the lady chapel at Westminster Abbey which bears Henry's name, one of the most perfect buildings ever erected in England. True, it was not completed until 1519, but it is only necessary to glance at Henry VII's will to realise how completely the inspiration for it was his. And when the guide-books link Henry VIII's name with it, it is to ask visitors to try to imagine what the splendours of this superb building must have looked like between 1519 and 1540, that is, between the year of its completion and the time when the destructive forces of the Reformation were let loose on English church art.

Now these random gleanings, although only suggestive, will serve to indicate that there was a Henry who was incompatible with the legend. Obviously, the caricature of him which still exists in some minds may be ignored, for Henry was infinitely more than a shabby moneygrubber. But that does not mean that the more flattering form of the legend ought not to be taken seriously. It had very important historical consequences.

Look at Henry as he appears in it. He had sought to establish himself in men's minds as a serious-minded, practical, deliberate, prudent, wise, and stern ruler, whose government, while benevolent, rested on force—force that would be ruthlessly used against any subject daring to intrigue against his king. In some respects that impression was a fair estimate of the King, and Henry succeeded in imposing this view of himself upon contemporaries. Even in those points where the impression was not wholly accurate, the mere fact that an attempt was made to assert it as truth is of significance, since here lies a clue to Henry's policy. Contemporaries conceded the gravity and the wisdom: " a most sage king and well advised "; " this most sage king " ; " the king's wisdom whereof everyone stands in awe "; " most prudent "—these are some of the expressions contemporaries used in describing him, when writing to foreign courts. They show that Henry's studied demeanour impressed those coming into contact with him, and through them, influenced continental princes who had to come to a decision as to the kind of man with whom they were negotiating.

This was of great importance. It affected materially Henry's position. He had come to the English throne at a time when kingship had suffered an almost incredible debasement. From being an office of divine delegation it had become the possible perquisite of any adventurer with some brains (a drop of royal blood in his veins was desirable, but not essential), and a sufficiently resolute will, backed by a strong enough force, to make good his claims against those of others no better equipped. The feuds of Lancaster and York turned the succession problem into a gambler's sporting chance, and it is not surprising to find that foreigners could only make logic of English politics by concluding that in matters relating to the royal succession there was in this island no established constitutional principle. As one of them said, here in England the succession to the kingship was settled, not by election, but by battle, and he who lost the day lost the kingdom.

In 1485 the only difference between Richard III and Henry VII was that Henry proved successful. The claims of each were equally dubious, and after Bosworth had been won, Henry was much too shrewd to place any great reliance upon his hereditary claims. What would be much more to the point than vague statements of divine right or legal quibbles, would be to convince men that he stood secure, that no intrigue could shake his throne. It was to this end that he deliberately magnified his own importance. Thereby he did something that was greater than he probably knew. For he brought into Tudor politics a new idea. It was that of a king who, in relation to his nobles, was not a first among equals, but a being apart from them, a majesty lifted high above, yet dominating their little lives. To Henry VII it seemed that only thus could the recurrence of fifteenth-century conditions be avoided. A king who was a paragon of virtue, raised high above the remnants of a turbulent aristocracy, was an unanswerable argument to family intrigues. To Henry's successors this idea appealed as one rich in possibilities. Both Henry VIII and Wolsey saw that it could be exploited so as to make the Tudor monarch greater than Henry VII had ever dreamed. Their success explains the Tudor period. That the " new monarch " of the sixteenth century became an institution rather than a person was due in the main to Henry VII's lead. His legend was the inspiration of the dynasty he had founded.

In foreign affairs, too, this ideal had its place. Henry won recognition abroad—though not without a hard struggle —and he owed his victory in no small measure to the skill with which he developed his reputation for kingliness. Only a detailed study of the diplomatic history of the fifteenth century could reveal the richness of that achievement, or bring out the precariousness of Henry's position in the European world at the opening of his reign. For about half a century England had counted for less than usual in foreign politics. She was not more than a fourth-rate Power (when she was a Power at all!). The rehabilitation of the kingship worked wonders, enabling the country to rise again to a respectable position, and giving Henry the satisfaction of a marriage alliance with the rising house of Spain. A marriage between his son Arthur and Catherine was his most cherished ambition and he achieved it. Whether England might not have been better off if he had failed, it is for historians of Henry VIII's reign to decide. For us the fact remains that he would not have succeeded if there had been no legend.

And yet, was Henry quite successful in creating his legend? It is difficult to free oneself entirely from some persistent doubts. For there were contemporaries who seem to have been sceptics. They broke through Henry's elaborate defences. "Henry," wrote one of the Spanish ambassadors early in the reign, "likes to be much spoken of, and to be highly appreciated by the whole world. He fails in this because he is not a great man." Is this, perhaps, the clue to his perplexing personality?

Here the real Henry comes to our rescue. For the more clearly we see him as a man the more easily we can break through the myth. It really was most fortunate for England that Henry was not as great as he would have liked men to think. Had he been a grand original, an idealist, an enthusiast fighting for a cause, even a soldier with a real love of war, he would very probably not have been King of England for more than a few months. For the country was not yet ready to be put to the test of staking everything on an idea or a principle. Men were emerging from a period when enthusiasms had grown cold, beliefs had been strangled

by scepticism, politics had been turned into disillusi[on].
Before there could again be enthusiasm for a cause [or]
loyalty to a principle, faith and confidence had to be
kindled.   In such circumstances the narrow field of Hen[ry's]
vision, his lack of inspiration, and the somewhat e[c]-
centric selfishness of his outlook were a positive advant[age].
His policy, simple in conception, and making no high [de]-
mands upon his subjects, gave them a respite in whic[h to]
restore their exhausted spirits.   Henry had no far-reac[hing]
designs.   He knew the goal he wished to attain, and it [was]
not very far away.   He was content to carry through to [the]
logical conclusion what his predecessors, especially [the]
Yorkists, had dreamed of doing, and had failed because they
lacked the moral stamina that was essential.   In Henry's
policy as expressed in his legislation there are few novelties,
and—save for one important exception to be touched upon
later—he was not a revolutionary administrator.   What he
succeeded in introducing into government was indeed a
novelty for England, but it was the hall-mark of the small
mind, for it was the policy of " thorough," and genius more
often than not seems to be a definite incapacity for taking
pains.   Content with limited ambitions, he succeeded in
getting things done, and some of them were things that
badly needed doing.   He took no chances and—as a contemporary said—he liked always to be on the winning side.
What he aimed at was selfish, but it was at any rate clear-
cut, and capable of attainment.   Security for himself and
a heritage for his family was what he most desired, and in
the achievement of these aims he allowed nothing to stand
in his light.   Above all else he realised the surest means
whereby security could be achieved.   It was not by the
ruthless repression of rebellion, though that would count.
It was not by rigorous punishment of those who disturbed
the peace, or used their superior estate to bully the poor and
the weak, though this too might be an important factor.
It was not by threatening wars of aggression, though Henry
showed that threats of war, rightly handled, might be made
to pay.   All these means might be drawn into the service
of his policy, but none was the vital factor.   The real
solution of his difficulties lay elsewhere.   Characteristically enough, Henry was not the first to discover it.   Every
politician who had sought to diagnose what was wrong with
fifteenth-century England agreed about the remedy.   None

put it more succinctly than did Sir John Fortescue, in his *Governance of England* written about 1476. His words will bear quotation. "But we most holde it for undoubted that ther may no reaume prospere or be worshipfull vndere a poure kynge." Henry, after a youth passed in the exile of foreign courts, had been given too many opportunities for learning that lesson to need a reminder from Fortescue.

Those who allow their interests in the Tudor period to centre on the literary and artistic developments are apt to be impatient with Henry VII. They dismiss him as a man whose mind was engrossed with money, and presumably they imagine that the world of letters ought not to be concerned with these things. Let them cherish their illusion; but they will not understand the Tudor period if they do not understand the mind of the age. It was one that was not unresponsive to the enticements of wealth. Even literature heard the call. There is an interesting manuscript, written in a late fifteenth-century hand, which contains a poem inspired by such thoughts. It is a song in twenty-four-line stanzas with a four-line refrain. It begins:

> " *Above all thing thow art a kyng*
> *And rulest the world over alle* ";

and the refrain runs:

> " *Money, Money, now hay goode day*
> *Money where hast thou be*
> *Money, Money, thou gooste away*
> *And wyllt not byde wyth me.*"

There is the authentic note for the period!

It is a mistake to think that the England of Henry VII was prostrate after the Wars of the Roses. True, the country had suffered under the aimless faction fights of a feudal nobility struggling for they scarce knew what; but their noisy brawls ought not to distract attention from the real fifteenth-century scene. While swaggering gangsters wore the shirts of rival parties and terrorised civilians, a hard-headed, energetic, enterprising middle class was scouring land and sea for trade. While the nobility were squandering fortunes on the upkeep of soldiers, that same middle class was amassing the wealth that would purchase for its children position and power in sixteenth-century England. These men of trade wanted peace and good government, and they saw that they might get them from Henry VII. For he was a king after their own hearts, in spirit (and despite the legend) a real bourgeois king. Like his subjects he knew that money was king.

As in so many problems of Henry's reign, his work in the sphere of high finance is only beginning to be understood, and it will be some time before any satisfactory generalisations will be possible as to the effect of his efforts. For here again legend and truth are inextricably blended. Legend sees him as a miser. Truth acquits him of this vice. Legend fostered the impression that at his death he bequeathed to his son vast sums of gold and silver. Even in his lifetime rumour said that it amounted to some £1,800,000. Truth denies that he left in chests such stores of silver and gold, but it adds that he left very considerable resources, largely in the form of papers. The qualification is important. Those papers were recognisances and obligations. They bore witness to transactions whereby subjects had been bound to the King to perform certain promises, default being followed by the forfeiture of heavy sums of money. Despite what has been said to the contrary, most of these pledges were not the result of extortionate practices on the part of the King or his agents. They were rather symbols of Henry's devices for good government. They represent the means he adopted to gain a hold over lawless subjects who could not be adequately dealt with even by his re-shaped court of star chamber, which he was using to force the great nobles to keep the peace. They were a means of raking in money; but they were also a guarantee of security and peace.

They do not represent anything like the whole of his work in finance. For in such matters Henry deserves a reputation greater than he has yet been given. In this field he was an innovator, and the result of his application to the work of financial reform it is hardly too much to call revolutionary. Before the end of his reign he had overhauled the whole of the machinery of financial administration, and he left it completely modernised, so much so that we may say that the main outline of our present-day system of finance was blocked out by him. He enjoyed the work, had a flair for it that was the nearest approach to genius Henry ever revealed. By close application he so equipped himself for this task that before the end of his reign he was virtually his own chief financial officer. Day by day he went carefully through his official accounts, annotating them, scrawling his big initial H in bold strokes across the pages, mastering their contents, and using that knowledge to institute reforms in financial administration. That is why experts see in his scientific reorganisation of the exchequer and the departments of the household and the chamber, the work which must stand out as the really constructive contribution Henry made to the transition from mediæval to modern England.

For those of us who find it difficult to follow these technicalities, that verdict by the experts must suffice. We shall have to look elsewhere for our impression of this king. Shall we find it in the legend? Or shall we watch that pen tracing with difficulty the sentence so instinct with human frailty: " For verily, madame, my sight is nothing so perfect as it has been "?

HENRY VIII

1491–1547; *reigned* 1509–1547

By

A. F. POLLARD

HENRY VIII

by A. F. POLLARD

A PHILOSOPHER has said that "to popularise philosophy is at once to debase it." That, no doubt, is true of every kind of truth, but history runs a greater risk than most. Philosophy, like physical science, is the perquisite of experts; but history is the happy hunting-ground of the novelist, the playwright, the film-producer, and the correspondent who writes to the Press about things he admits he did not even learn at school. The "taste for Tudors" is less a taste for history or even for biography than for the common things which make the great akin to little men. The age of heroes and of hero-worship concentrated on the distinguishing features which raised men up above their fellows : democracy dotes on the defects which bring them down to a common level understanded of the people. If we cannot share the greatness of men, our self-esteem seeks fellow-feeling in their foibles. Some of the Tudors are immune from this ignominious popularity : even Shakespeare wrote no play about Henry VII, who would paralyse any film ; for he merely conducted the most successful foreign policy in English history and established a throne on foundations invisible to opera glasses. Edward VI died at fifteen, disqualified by disease and early death from admission to the school for scandal, while Mary was too conscientious or too plain. Elizabeth was anything but either, and Lytton Strachey's book *Elizabeth and Essex* were better named *Elizabeth and her Sex*. Martin Hume was more polite in his *Courtships of Queen Elizabeth* than in his *Wives of Henry VIII*, and it is Henry's wives who qualify him for posthumous popularity. The grave and right reverend Bishop Stubbs did, indeed, confess (while he was only a professor) that the portraits of those wives "were, if not a justification, at least a colourable occasion for understanding the readiness with which he put them away." But the more wives he put away, the more they cling to his memory.

Marriage was doubtless—though murder was not—one of the matters the Apostle had in mind when he counselled moderation in all things. The morality of the problem is obscure. Six mistresses would have been no news at a royal court; they would have eluded the film altogether, like the forty-five debited to Henry of Navarre or the unspecified number George II had in mind when he protested in tears to his dying Queen that he could not bear the thought of marrying again. Mere mistresses might, perhaps, have cast over Henry VIII the meretricious halo which now adorns the brow of that prince of profligates, Charles II. Even four wives might not have mattered: Henry's last queen, Catherine Parr, had four husbands without leaving a stain on her character; his brother-in-law the Duke of Suffolk had four wives and his sister Margaret Tudor, Queen of Scotland, three husbands. Six seems to have been the limit which divided the silly sheep from the giddy goats. The gravamen of the charge against Henry is not that he seduced the ladies of his court, but that he married them. The Papal Curia itself was lenient to mistresses; it was, indeed, as Mr. Hilaire Belloc has noted, " a common practice " for his " greater ecclesiastics " of that time to take a mistress, and Anne Boleyn only encountered Papal censures when Clement VII discovered that Henry really meant to marry her.

Henry could have had, if he wanted them, as many mistresses as Francis I without raising a ripple on the surface of English history. He had at least one, Bessie Blount the mother of the Duke of Richmond, and almost certainly another, Mary, the elder sister of Anne Boleyn—both before he was thirty years of age. If there were others they have entirely escaped the records, his correspondence, and the chronicles of the time; not one has ever been named, and a hundred thousand contemporary documents can be searched in vain for any reference to a child of Henry's other than the Duke of Richmond, Edward VI, Mary, and Elizabeth. There was no secrecy about any of these, and total silence with regard to others is fairly conclusive proof that they never existed.

The King, indeed, was not in search or in need of a mistress, or even of a wife, so much as of a son to succeed him,

carry on the Tudor succession, and avert a recrudescence
of the Wars of the Roses. That was his engrossing problem
throughout almost the whole of his reign; and it was only
solved in the end by an Act of Parliament, to the terms of
which—in spite of religious passions and rival claims—
England stood staunch so long as a Tudor remained to fulfil
them. Catherine of Aragon, whom he had not chosen
himself, failed him : one miscarriage or still-born child
succeeded another, and in 1514, after five years of parental
misfortune Henry—or Wolsey—petitioned Leo X to annul
the marriage with his brother's wife which another pope had
sanctioned, doubting the validity of his own dispensation.
Then in 1516 came Mary, who was welcomed, not for her
own sake, but as an earnest of the son to follow. No
woman had yet reigned in England, and Henry VII had
secured the throne, not only by ending a civil war, but by
excluding from the throne his mother, from whom he
derived whatever hereditary right he possessed. The
expected heir never followed Mary, and by 1527 it was
certain that Henry VIII would have no legitimate son so
long as Catherine remained his wife. He ceased to cohabit,
though not to live, with her from that date, and fell a victim
to the one grand passion of his life. It might provide a
better hope for the succession than the *mariage de convenance*
with Catherine. He was the second English king to marry
for love and nothing else, and its ripe and refreshing fruit
was Queen Elizabeth. But for five years he waited ; the
child must be legitimate, and a divorce from Catherine was
confidently expected from Clement VII in 1529. It was
refused : if, wrote the Pope's secretary, it is granted, " The
Church cannot escape utter ruin, as it is entirely in the power
of the Emperor's servants." Charles V's armies had almost
turned Italy into a province of Spain; Catherine was his
aunt, and Mary his cousin whose succession to the English
throne he was bent on securing.

The Papacy was immovable: so was Henry on the
question of the succession to his throne. So, too, was the
Queen: her honour was involved, the legitimacy of her
child, that child's prospects of a crown, and the Spanish
alliance of which they were the emblems and the agents.
The women of England supported her on the grounds of
morality and sentiment; their husbands opposed on those of
national policy. It was not yet a question of religion or the

faith: the Lutherans and Tyndale, the Protestant martyr, denounced the divorce; and, could Clement VII have been constrained or persuaded to grant it, there might have been no immediate breach with Rome and no Act of Supremacy. France, for the sake of the English alliance and her ambitions in Italy, supported Henry, and the diplomatic struggle raged for three years. But, meanwhile, the Reformation Parliament assembled in November 1529 and gave voice to the anti-clerical tide which Wolsey had dammed for fifteen years. It overflowed, swept away some of the more notorious privileges and abuses, and enabled Henry to extort from the Church itself a reluctant admission of his supremacy. Warham died, protesting in vain, and Cranmer became Archbishop of Canterbury, while Cromwell succeeded to Sir Thomas More's and Stephen Gardiner's place in Henry's counsels. The Act of Annates robbed the Papacy of its revenues from English benefices, and the Acts of Appeals made England independent of its jurisdiction. Henry married Anne Boleyn about the end of January 1533, in the confidence born of her pregnancy, and on September 7, she gave birth to the future queen, Elizabeth. Finally, in 1534, the Royal Supremacy was enshrined in a Parliamentary statute, where it has remained ever since, save for Mary's Catholic reign and the Puritan regime a century later.

Never was revolution more skilfully draped as reform; it was made respectable, like treason, by success. Its path had, indeed, been prepared by centuries of struggle between Church and State, in which the Church had grown weaker and the monarchy stronger through the decline of ecclesiastical unity and the rise of secular nationalism; and the Church in England had already proved too weak to resist the royal demand that it should become the Church of England. Nevertheless, Henry VIII was the parent of what Lord Acton justly termed " a new polity." Hitherto there had been no " State " in England, but various Estates, of which the ecclesiastical were subject to papal, and the secular to royal, sovereignty. The Act of Supremacy brought all under one Sovereign and created out of them a single, novel State which also claimed to be an Empire, independent alike of Holy Roman Emperor and Holy Roman Pope; and, what was more, the emancipator became dictator and the father of all the Fascists in the world. The Middle Ages passed away in child-birth, and its child was what Michelet calls " le nouveau Messie, le Roi."

Happily, the Middle Ages had also left in England another child, born before the decadence and still surviving, though threatened in England and doomed elsewhere; and, with equal good fortune, Parliament found in Henry a foster-father who did not, like other Fascists, strangle the off-spring left by the Middle Ages on the doorstep of modern despots. He nursed it, because he discerned its promise as a sure shield and weapon for his own defence and that of the realm. " He has always fortified himself by the consent of Parliament," wrote the Emperor's ambassador with an envious wish that Charles V could do the same. Of all the legends about Henry VIII, the most extravagant is that he sought to weaken Parliament. In truth he gave it and its acts a prestige and authority they had never possessed before; he enhanced its power and extended its sphere of authority; and critics in 1540 were jeering at " this new-found article of our creed, that Parliament cannot err." All his great acts were Acts of Parliament, and they fill in the statute-book more space than all the earlier Acts of Parliament put together.

This invitation to Parliament to share his work and strengthen his hands constitutes Henry's chief claim to statesmanship. It may be that he had no choice, and that Parliament was the only means at hand adequate to his purpose. But that implies that Parliament was the dominant factor in the situation, and that is a view which is not easily reconcilable with the decline of parliamentary institutions elsewhere or with the disdain in which they were held by Wolsey and even by Henry VII. It is truer to say that Henry VIII felt the national impulse, discerned possi-bilities which were not yet explicit, and saw in Parliament the means of effecting his own particular objects. Only a national legislature could effect the breach with Rome, eradicate foreign jurisdiction, and make England the exclus-ive and common property of Englishmen. Wolsey's gaze was riveted on Rome; Henry's after 1529 on what he called his little island. That did not mean that he could not see beyond it. England herself was not an island; Wales and even Calais were brought within its Parliamentary system, and during his later years most of his attention was devoted to Ireland and Scotland: England for the English was to be expanded into Britain for the British.

But England was the core of the situation when theological dissension was rending Europe and precipitating it into a century of Wars of Religion. So long as she was united, said Henry, anticipating Shakespeare's words in *King John,* she could not be conquered; the problem was to keep it united and English Catholics and Protestants at peace with one another. His last speech to Parliament, a lay sermon on charity, summed up Henry's position. He denounced Catholics for calling Protestants heretics and anabaptists, and Protestants for calling Catholics papists, hypocrites, and pharisees, and asked " how can poor souls live in concord when you preachers sow amongst them in your sermons debate and discord? " Not that the laity were much better, and he was " sorry to hear how unreverently that most precious jewel, the word of God, is disputed, rhymed, and jangled in every alehouse and tavern." The balance he strove to maintain and the *via media* he sought to follow could only be achieved by supporting now the one and now the other disputant. In his breach with Pope and Emperor he had to rely on the Reformers, and Thomas Cromwell used the European situation to press him nearer to German Lutheranism than he liked. Catherine's death and the restoration of Mary to her place in the succession to the throne removed the grievance of Charles V, while Cromwell's unfortunate speculation on Anne of Cleves destroyed the German attraction. Cromwell fell, and Henry seemed bent for the rest of his life on showing that Catholicism was safer in essence but more capable of practical reform under his royal supremacy than under papal jurisdiction. It was a position which history showed that none but he could maintain.

But it had a profound effect on English politics. A critic has recently declared that in England " we have our rationalists and our free-thinkers, but only out of Continental soil can there spring the anti-clerical." It may seem odd to attribute this distinction to Henry VIII; but he had relieved the Church of the obloquy under which it suffered by reason of its privileges, wealth, control over laymen's lives and beliefs, and immunity from secular punishment for its crimes. It had enjoyed exclusive jurisdiction over heresy; when a layman was accused of heresy there was no benefit of clergy, no sanctuary, no *habeas corpus*, and no trial by jury; and men were charged with heresy for merely refusing to pay "mortuaries"—a sort of ecclesiastical death-duty—on the death of infants who had no property. Such were some of the irritants, rather than any legitimate question of faith, which fomented the anti-clerical spirit. More tolerable evils were the unlimited number of benefices the favoured clergy might hold, their consequent absence from their livings, their lack of learning, their immersion in secular pursuits, and the extortionate charges for proving wills over which the ecclesiastical courts had exclusive jurisdiction. The worst of these evils were curbed by Henry's legislation, so far as they angered the English people; but Catholic countries in Europe had for the most part to wait till grievances festered into the fever of revolution; even after 1789 Spaniards attributed their sufferings at Napoleon's hands to the neglect of their duty to God in not burning heretics. Anti-clericalism thus became associated with Revolution rather than Reformation. Henry VIII did not succeed in eliminating religion from English party-politics by subjecting the clergy to English common law, but by so doing he helped to relieve them of the bitterness which the survival of clerical privilege fomented on continental soil.

That was no disservice to the Church in England, however obnoxious it might seem to the Church abroad. But Henry was a nationalist and therefore a schismatic; Popes and Councils having failed in their efforts at reform, he determined to attempt it himself in his own dominions, hoping that others would follow suit. So far as England is concerned, his anti-ecclesiastical character has been exaggerated. He secured the concurrence of Convocation in all his measures; and instead of exasperating the mediæval conflict between Church and State, he brought it to an end. Whatever might happen elsewhere, he was determined that England should be united, self-sufficient, and independent. Within its borders there was to be no jurisdiction to rival that of the Crown in Parliament. But he did not contemplate the purely secular modern State: he was himself Head of the Church and a theologian of no mean learning; he took his unction at coronation seriously, and composed anthems still occasionally sung in our cathedrals. To the end of his reign bishops sat in his Privy Council and he had ecclesiastics as his Secretaries of State and chief diplomatists; even Convocation was still regarded as a " house " of Parliament. The royal head and the Parliamentary body were still supported by two legs, and stood on one foundation: Convocation as well as Parliament declared that England was an empire of itself; and the modern " taste for Tudors " is a comparatively innocuous expression of the spirit of nationalism that has gone to the heads of younger nations less experienced in the manners and methods of self-government which depend upon self-control.

This national reconciliation under the Crown in Parliament substituted a single for a dual control of the life and liberty, the faith, the law, and property of English people. It imposed upon them self-reliance; henceforth they could look to no appeals at Rome, to no papal censures or excommunications to remove a tyrant or chastise an heretical king. They must seek their remedies at home and realise that they were responsible for their own government. Some sought a remedy in rebellion, and the Pilgrimage of Grace was the first forcible protest against the new Tudor polity; it was followed by others which have been alleged as proofs of its unpopularity. The fact that they always failed points to a different moral. The rebellions were all against Parliament as well as against the Crown; and, while Parliament might rebel with success against the Crown, no rebellion against Parliament in England has ever succeeded. If the English had been taught to look to themselves for their own remedies, they had also learnt that remedies were not to be found by means of force imposed upon their own representatives. While other European countries were dispensing with representative systems and falling into the arms of despots or the abyss of civil war, Henry VIII wound round his royal carcase and the Tudor State a garment more effective than coats of armour. Had his constitution of Church and State been overthrown, Parliament would have died before becoming the mother of Parliaments scattered all over the world, upon whose vitality depends to-day the freedom of mankind. The New World would have been a mere replica of the Old, and government of the people, for the people, by the people, might have perished from the earth.

Man is often said to be greater than his work. It is hard to believe that of Henry VIII; his failings as well as his capabilities exceeded the measure of common humanity. His egotism was immense, and his people conspired to make it worse. The only apparent bulwark against a recrudescence of the Wars of the Roses, embittered perhaps by religious strife, his person was sacrosanct and his security the foundation of public peace. " These bishops," wrote his French ambassador in 1540, " make of him not only a king to be obeyed, but an idol to be worshipped "; and the worship of man as a god is apt to make him a devil. Henry had some redeeming graces: he was apparently sincere in the Catholic faith he professed, and was at least scrupulous in his religious observance. He showed no personal animus against the victims of his statecraft, but he was a pitiless *étatiste*; the more eminent and the more conscientious the objector, the more needful to make him an example: the King was no respecter of persons. Men might argue a bill as much as they liked, but a law they must not impugn or resist. Bishop Gardiner relates the story of a dispute between him and Cromwell in Henry's presence whether the King's will should be the law, in which Cromwell maintained that it should, while the bishop held it better that the King should make the law his will. Henry chose the latter part, and no one was put to death in his reign except by due process of law or Act of Parliament; he was not in person the supreme court of his country for a single hour.

That does not, of course, exhaust the argument. Few kings of England have been in a better position to make their will the law. But that was not due to force of arms : his standing army consisted of a hundred yeomen of the guard, and for his defence against rebellion he depended on the good will of his people. When he grumbled about them, it was not on the ground of their disloyalty, but on that of their dissensions among themselves. Provided that national unity was preserved, he was not scrupulous over the means of preserving it, nor perhaps very particular about the shade of orthodoxy which England presented abroad; German or Scandinavian Protestants were as welcome allies, in case of need, as Catholic France or Spain. Against foreign foes he relied partly on fortifications which monastic masonry helped him to provide, but more on the English Navy, which was to him, from the earliest years of his reign, a plaything, a weapon, and almost a passion. He was an expert in shipbuilding and in artillery, and the Navy he founded enabled him to steer his national course without serious molestation from Catholic Europe. It was for the sake of that Navy that Philip II married Mary Tudor and proposed to Elizabeth; and it was by its means that Scotland was rescued from the clutches of France, and England was saved from the Spanish Armada.

Early in Henry's reign Erasmus described him as " a universal genius." The courtly remark indicates no more than the wide range of his interests and intelligence; but his learning was remarkable in a king, and although he confessed that writing was to him " somewhat tedious and painful," there survive pages and pages of diplomatic instructions, drafts of statutes, and plans of fortification written in his own hand. His immense vitality expressed itself on fields as divergent as sport and statesmanship, and the sport impressed itself most on the popular mind. But the only sphere in which he was really great was in state-craft. Fortunately, perhaps, he was no soldier, and so was not tempted to follow Henry V in his criminal folly of trying to annex France. But his understanding of English mental-ity and European politics was profound, and his bluff and hearty appearance concealed an intellect as subtle as Machiavelli's and as lithe as a panther's body. His phrases give an occasional glimpse into the workings of his mind; " three may keep counsel if two be away "; " if I thought that my cap knew my counsel, I would cast it into the fire "; " the opinion of the world is often stronger than truth." But, while he kept his own counsel, he exacted all that others could give. His theological conclusions were only reached after conference with both Catholics and Pro-testants: when a book of note appeared, he would tell one of them to read it, then give it to the other with similar injunction, and finally make them debate the crucial points in his presence. He was always the King in Council and not the monarch alone, and he organised his Privy Council, with its regular sittings and formal minutes, out of the more fluid and less business-like Council of the Middle Ages. So, too, in spite of the disappearance of abbots from the House of Lords, attendance at its meetings grew steadily fuller, until in 1540 the clerk of the Parliaments began to note the absences instead of the daily presence of peers, as being the less laborious method.

Facts speak louder than words, and the fact that, so long

as Henry and his three children were available, England would tolerate no one else on the throne is eloquent testimony to the impress he made on the minds of his people; so, too, was Elizabeth's public avowal at her accession that she intended to follow in his footsteps. Phrases like Cromwell's and Warwick's, which passed from mouth to mouth, to the effect that he was " the light of all the kings and princes in Christendom " and " the father of wisdom of all the world " may properly be discounted, though they were amplified by an Italian after Henry's death. But critical ambassadors at his court were hardly less emphatic: "he has no respect or fear," writes Charles V's, " for anyone in the world "; and, while Francis I's remarks that " this King, as all the world knows, is far from reckless," he adds, " when he decides on anything he goes the whole length." But the most remarkable testimony comes from Cardinal Pole, who had more reason than any other living man to loathe Henry VIII on personal, political, and religious grounds; for the King had proscribed the Cardinal, executed his mother and his brother, and extirpated the papal jurisdiction to which the Cardinal was heart and soul devoted. Yet, says Pole, writing from Rome to Protector Somerset two years after Henry's death, " he was the greatest King who ever ruled that realm."

JOHN COLET

1466–1519

By

JOHN BELL

JOHN COLET

by JOHN BELL

A SERIES of lectures on the epistles of St. Paul, begun in 1496 or 1497 and delivered without fee by a young man of thirty with no theological degree, first brought the Old Faith into direct contact with the New Learning in England. For centuries, theologians had regarded the Bible as a store-house of disconnected texts, and the learned scholar had busied himself with the subtleties of the School-men; Duns Scotus and Thomas Aquinas held the stage. To hear reasoned and detailed expositions of *Romans* and *Corinthians*, treated in their historical settings, astonished an audience completely ignorant of the life and circumstances of the Roman Empire of the first century; many believed that the Scriptures had been written in the Latin of the Vulgate, and regarded Greek with the greatest suspicion. "*Cave a Græcis, ne hæreticus fias.*"

The New Learning in Italy had already shown a pagan bias, which filled the orthodox with horror. This young man, by name John Colet, had spent some years in Italy; he had no doubt sat at the feet of the Platonist, Marsilio Ficino; he had listened to the sermons of that dangerous firebrand, Savonarola. His friend Erasmus tells us that—

> "While in Italy, he devoted himself to the study of the sacred writers. He had previously, however, roamed with great zest through literature of every kind, finding most pleasure in the early writers, Dionysius, Origen, Cyprian, Ambrose, and Jerome. . . . At the same time he did not omit to read Scotus and Thomas, and others of that stamp, if the occasion required."

While an undergraduate at Oxford, "he had eagerly devoured the works of Cicero, and diligently searched into those of Plato and Plotinus (in Latin translations); while there was no branch of Mathematics that he left untouched."

Yet the learned Doctors of Oxford, the Abbots and other dignitaries flocked to hear him; they listened without open protest to his attacks upon abuses in the Church :

> "O priests! O priesthood! O the abominable impiety of those miserable priests of whom this age of ours contains a great multitude! . . . Abandoned creatures! on whom the vengeance of God will one day fall the heavier, the more shamelessly they have intruded themselves into the divine office."

Whatever may have been the effect upon his audience, Colet was not officially considered a dangerous influence, for within eight years he had been admitted to the degree of D.D. and appointed Dean of St. Paul's. During those years he had gathered around him a band of friends of whom Grocyn, Linacre, William Lily, and Thomas More, among Oxford men, and Erasmus from the Continent were the most celebrated. The Oxford Reformers, as they were known, were enemies of pedantry, superstition, and bigotry; Grocyn and Erasmus in particular did their utmost to spread a knowledge of Greek, which had brought back to the light of day the long-forgotten masterpieces of the ancient world, both sacred and secular. Philosophy, History, Poetry, and the New Testament itself might now be read in the original by those who could learn Greek, for the invention of printing had made it possible for thousands to read what had hitherto been confined to the few.

Colet himself was never a fluent Greek scholar, but he did all that was possible to ensure that the key to unlock the treasure-house of antiquity should be in the possession of those who came after him. He determined to devote the fortune which came to him on the death of his father in 1505 to the foundation of a school in which "good litterature both laten and greke" should be taught. And so, some years after his appointment as Dean, as he tells us in his own words, still preserved in his own handwriting in the Statutes of St. Paul's School :

> "John Colett, the sonne of henry Colett Dean of paules desyring nothing more thanne Educacion and

bringing upp children in good Maners and litterature in the yere of our Lorde 1512 bylded a Scole in the Estende of Paulis Church for 153 [1] to be taught fre in the same."

It was fitting that the son of a Lord Mayor of London should choose a site in the heart of the City for his school. The Colet family had for many years been connected with Bucks, and their home lay near Wendover; but Henry was sent up to London as a young man to be apprenticed as a mercer, and, after rising to wealth and prosperity and holding office as alderman and sheriff, was elected Lord Mayor for the first time in 1486, the year of the marriage of Henry VII with the heiress of the House of York. He had married, about 1465, Mistress Christian Knyvet, of Norfolk, who survived her eldest son John, the only one of her twenty-two children, eleven boys and eleven girls, who did not die in infancy. John is said to have been sent to the school of St. Anthony's Hospital in Threadneedle Street, and to have gone thence to Magdalen College; but of this there is no positive evidence. St. Anthony's was one of the few distinguished London schools of the time, educating, we are told, Sir Thomas More and Archbishop Whitgift. Colet's name is not found in any extant register of Magdalen, though one or more of his surname are alleged to have been at the College at the time of his Oxford residence. There is no doubt that he completed the usual course of University study, lasting seven years, but little is known of this period in his life, beyond the statement of Erasmus that "he diligently mastered all the philosophy of the Schools, and gained the title expressive of the knowledge of the seven liberal arts."

It has been suggested that Colet merely enlarged and re-endowed a school already in existence at the Cathedral. That a school had for centuries been attached to the Cathedral is certain, but it is no less certain that Colet regarded his school as a new foundation. Hitherto, all schools in England had been under ecclesiastical control; but Colet broke with tradition, by placing his school in the hands of laymen. As Erasmus says:

[1] It has been long supposed that this number was chosen to correspond with the 153 fishes caught in the miraculous draught (St. John xxi. 11); but Colet himself gives no reason for his choice. Scholars of St. Paul's School still wear a silver fish on their watch-chains.

"Over the revenues and the entire management of his school he placed neither priests nor the Bishop, nor the Chapter, nor noblemen, but some married citizens of established reputation. And when asked the reason, he said that, while there was nothing certain in human affairs, he yet found the least corruption in these."

In Colet's own words:

"The honourable Compeny of Mercers of London that is to say the Maister and all the Wardens and all the assistence of the feloshipp shall have alle the Cure and charge rule and governaunce of the Scole."

This care and charge has been in the hands of the Mercers' Company for upwards of four centuries, and at no period have the Dean and Chapter had any say in the management of Colet's school. It is inconceivable that any Dean, however high-handed, who had merely re-endowed the existing Cathedral School would have been permitted to remove it from the control of the Chapter; and, in fact, there is evidence in plenty to show that the Cathedral School continued its separate existence after the foundation of Colet's school.

It has been claimed that St. Paul's was the prototype of the reformed grammar school, and it is interesting to observe the aims of Colet in providing for the education of "children of all nacions and counties indifferently." In his Statutes he tells us:

"I wolde they were taught all way in good litterature both laten and greke, and goode auctors suych as have the veray Romayne eliquence joyned withe wisdome specially Cristyn auctours that wrote theyre wysdome with clene and chast laten in verse or in prose, for my entent is by thys scole specially to increase knowledge and worshipping of god and oure lorde Crist Jesu and good Cristen lyff and maners in the Children."

There follows a list of books to be studied, including—

"above all the Cathechyzon [Catechism] in Englysh ... and thenne ... auctours Christian as lactancius [1]

[1] Some of these writers were still being read when John Milton was at St. Paul's School, about 1620–4.

prudentius and proba and sedulius and Juvencus and Baptista Mantuanus and suche other as shalbe tought [? thought] convenyent and moste to purpose unto the true laten spech, all barbary all corruption all laten adulterate which ignorant blynde folis [fools] brought into this worlde and with the same hath distayned and poysenyd the olde laten spech and the varay Romayne tong which in the tyme of Tully and Salust and Virgill and Terence was usid . . . that fylthynesse and all such abusyon which the later blynde worlde brought in which more ratheyr may be callid blotterature thenne litterature I utterly abbanysh and Exclude oute of this scole and charge the Maisters that they teache all way that is the best and instruct the chyldren in greke and laten in Redyng unto them suych auctours that hathe with wisdome joyned the pure chaste eloquence."

It is evident that he did not consider it wise that boys of school age should read the heathen " classical " authors, for those whom he prescribes are all Christian poets, ranging in date from the fourth century to contemporary Italy ; and there was as yet little prospect that Greek authors might become available for young students. In fact, it was doubtful if a master could be found capable of teaching Greek, and Colet was fortunate in being able to appoint, as his first High Master, William Lily, who had learnt Greek in Rhodes and afterwards at Rome. Lily was one of his own Oxford circle, a Magdalen man, a pupil of Grocyn, and a close friend of More, and no better choice could have been made. Though he died in 1522, he sent out from the school a number of men destined to rise to eminence in the later years of Henry VIII, no less than three of whom were included among the executors of the King's Will.

Colet himself drew up an " Accidence," or elementary Latin Grammar, for the use of the boys, which was augmented by Lily and continued in use for over three centuries, being authorised by a Royal proclamation in 1540 as the only Latin Grammar to be used in schools ; and Erasmus was persuaded to prepare other textbooks, including his *Institutum Christiani hominis* and a Latin phrase-book.

The Statutes laid down the method of appointing the High Master, Surmaster (Second Master), and Chaplain ; and the Mercers' Company, as governors, are empowered to alter and amend them as time and circumstances shall suggest. "The children" must pass an entrance examination; they may "bring no mete nor drink nor botellis nor use in the Scole no brekefastys nor drinkingis in the tyme of lerninge in no wyse."

> "In noo tyme in the yere they shall use talought [tallow] candill in noo wyse but allonly wexcandill at the cost of theyre ffrendes." [1]
>
> "I will also they shall have noo remedies [holidays]; yff the maister graunteth eny remedies, he shall forfeit forty shillings, Except the Kyng or a archebisshopp or a bishopp presente in his owne persone in the Scole desyre it." [2]

The affection Colet bore to his school is shown by the letter which he sent to Lily with the final draft of his Accidence, and the language of the preface is characteristic of one who, as Erasmus says, "took a delight in the purity and simplicity of nature that is in children":

> "I praye God all may be to his honour and to the erudicyon and profyt of children my countre men, Londoners specyally, whom dygestynge this lytel werke I had alwaye before myn eyen. . . . Wherefore I praye you, al lytel babys, al lytel chyldren, lerne gladly this lytel treatyse, and commende it dylygently unto your memoryes. Trustynge of this beynnynge that ye shal procede and growe to parfyt lyterature, and come at the last to be grete clarkes. And lyfte up your lytel whyte handes for me, whiche prayeth for you to God: to whom be al honour and imperyal majeste and glory: Amen."

The subjects of instruction in the new school may not appear to us to mark a new epoch; but we can realise that they broke fresh ground in many directions, when we compare them with the stereotyped curriculum in vogue in the mediæval schools. This consisted of the "trivium," Dialectic, Grammar, and Rhetoric. Hitherto, Dialectic had been

---

[1] Wax candles were expensive, and found only in wealthy households, which seems to prove that Colet did not intend his to be a "charity" school.

[2] This last Statute is still in force; but elsewhere Colet laid down that there should be 153 holidays and half-holidays in each year.

supreme in the schools; disputations upon themes of little interest to boys, and logical quibbles based upon the verbal subtleties of the Scholastic philosophers, had overshadowed Grammar. Before the invention of printing, it was impossible to provide many textbooks or editions of authors for reading, and much of the instruction was necessarily oral. Consequently the study of Latin as a literary language was at a low ebb; yet Latin was still very much alive; it was the universal medium of conversation between educated men of all nations; it was, and continued to be, the language of diplomacy. That it had sunk into a dreary jargon may be inferred from Colet's " blotterature "; and it was a task worth attempting, to restore the grace and " eloquence " of Classical times. By the importance he assigned to Grammar, Colet shows that he was interested chiefly in this attempt. Rhetoric, or the ability to use Latin as a spoken and written language with accuracy and fluency, would follow in due course from the study of good authors.

That one who had been greatly influenced by Plato should wish his scholars to be taught Greek is not surprising; but it is probable that Colet's real purpose was to enable them to read the New Testament in the original, and in this respect, the publication by Erasmus of the Greek Text in 1516, soon after the foundation of St. Paul's School, set the seal upon the work begun by Colet in his Oxford lectures twenty years earlier. St. Paul's claims to be the only English school in which Greek has been taught without a break for over four hundred years.

To provide for instruction in the " cathechyzon in Englysh," Colet drew up a Catechism which formed part of the volume containing his Accidence. The Articles of the Faith, a section upon the Seven Sacraments and a series of " Precepts of Living " are followed by the Apostles' Creed and the Lord's Prayer, in Latin, and by two Latin prayers composed by Colet, one of which is still in regular use at the school.[1]

It cannot surprise us that conservative opinion was suspicious of, or antagonistic to, the new foundation. In a letter to Erasmus, Colet writes that a certain bishop had called it in public " a useless, nay a mischievous institution;

[1] It is worthy of note that Colet dedicated his school to the " boy Jesus and his blessed Mother Mary," not to St. Paul, and a mosaic of the young Christ sitting among the Doctors in the Temple occupies the place of honour in the Great Hall of the school.

nay, a very home of idolatry." "No wonder," wrote More to Colet, "your school raises a storm, for it is like the wooden horse in which armed Greeks were hidden for the ruin of barbarous Troy." In truth, the New Learning threatened established traditions, and when joined with the moral fervour and hatred of hypocrisy which Colet never concealed, was abhorrent to vested interests in the Church, always eager to detect and punish anything that smacked of heresy. The Bishop of London, FitzJames, was a particular enemy of Colet, and on more than one occasion laid charges against him before Archbishop Wareham; but the Archbishop, so far from upholding them, showed his sympathy with Colet by appointing him to preach before the meeting of Convocation in February 1511–12.

This famous sermon, it has been said, deserves to be called the overture in the great drama of the English Reformation. More than a century had passed since Wyclif and his disciples had denounced scandals and abuses in the Church, and now again there came forward one who, though no "Protestant," was equally fearless and in a position of greater authority. Convocation had been summoned by order of the King, to vote money for the war in defence of the Pope against Louis XII, and also to take into consideration measures for the extirpation of heresy. Bishops, deans, abbots and priors from the whole province of Canterbury were present, among them, no doubt, Thomas Wolsey, Dean of Lincoln, now rapidly coming to the fore. To speak plainly before such a congregation demanded courage; Colet was not found wanting. Taking as his text [1] the words of St. Paul (Romans xii. 2):

> "Be ye not conformed to this world: but be ye reformed in the newness of your understanding, that ye may prove what is the good will of God, well pleasing and perfect,"

he divided his sermon into two main heads, Conformation to the world and Reformation.

> "By the world," he said, "the Apostle means the worldly way and manner of living, which consists chiefly

[1] The sermon was delivered in Latin, but an early translation has been preserved, possibly made by Colet himself. I have modernised the spelling.

in these four evils, that is to say, in devilish pride, in carnal concupiscence, in worldly covetousness, in secular business."

Of pride, he said:

" How much greediness and appetite of honour and dignity is nowadays in men of the Church? How run they, yea almost out of breath, from one benefice to another, from the less to the more, from the lower to the higher? "

Of " carnal concupiscence ":

" Hath not this vice so grown and waxen in the Church . . . that there is nothing looked for more diligently in this most busy time of the most part of priests than that that doth delight and please the senses? They give themselves to feasts and banqueting; they spend themselves in vain babbling; they give themselves to sports and plays; they apply themselves to hunting and hawking; they drown themselves in the delights of this world."

Of " covetousness ":

" This abominable pestilence hath so entered in the mind almost of all priests, and so hath blinded the eyes of the mind that we are blinded to all things but only to those which seem to bring us some gains. For what other thing seek we nowadays in the Church than fat benefices and high promotions? "

Of " secular business ":

" Therein priests and bishops nowadays do busy themselves, the servants rather of men than of God: the warriors rather of this world than of Christ."

He proceeded to turn the tables upon the heresy-hunters by declaring that no heresy was so pestilential and pernicious to the people as the vicious and depraved lives of the clergy, quoting St. Bernard, who considered perverse living a greater and more dangerous heresy than perverse doctrine. In treating of " Reformation," he demanded no new measures but the enforcement of existing laws. His attack was made, not upon heretics, not upon laymen, but upon those very dignitaries of the Church who sat before him. Reformation should begin with the bishops themselves:

" You spiritual physicians, first taste you this medicine of purgation of manners, and then offer us the same to taste."

" First let those laws be rehearsed that do warn you fathers that ye put not over soon your hands on every man or admit unto holy orders . . . thereof springeth and cometh out of the people that are in the Church both unlearned and evil priests. . . . It is not enough for a priest, in my judgment, to construe a collect . . . but much more a good and pure and holy life, approved manners, some knowledge of the Sacraments; chiefly and above all things the fear of God and love of the heavenly life."

" Let the laws be rehearsed that command that benefices of the Church be given to those that are worthy."

" Let the laws be rehearsed that command personal residence of curates in their churches . . . the laws that forbid clerks to haunt taverns . . . that command soberness and measureableness in apparel."

" Above all things, let the laws be rehearsed that concern you, my reverend fathers and lord bishops . . . for because prelates are chosen often more by favour of men than by grace of God, therefore have we not a few times bishops full little spiritual men, rather worldly than heavenly."

" Let the laws be rehearsed of the residence of bishops in their diocese . . . that they show themselves in their churches at the least on great holy days."

" If you reform first your life to the rules of the Canon laws, then shall ye give us light, that is to say, the light of your good example . . . if ye will have the lay people to live after your wish and will, first live yourselves after the will of God."

And finally:

" There are the things, reverend fathers and right famous men, that I thought should be said for the reformation of the Church; I trust ye will take them of your gentleness to the best. And if peradventure it be thought that I have passed my bounds in this sermon, forgive me, and ye shall forgive a man speaking of very zeal, a man sorrowing for the decay of the Church. . . . Suffer not, fathers, this your so great a gathering to depart in vain; truly ye are gathered often times together . . . yet I see not what fruit cometh of your assemblying . . . to the Church."

Did this great gathering depart in vain? We cannot tell, but it may be that Colet's words brought a cynical smile to the lips of the Dean of Lincoln. Reformation, when it came, was brought about by more drastic means and from less disinterested motives than those suggested in this sermon.

To beard the assembled leaders of the Church demands a stout heart, but still greater courage is needed to confront a young king, eager to lead his army against England's hereditary enemy, France. More than once, Colet was reported to Henry for " pacifist " utterances, but the King, in the words of Erasmus, " privately encouraged him to go on without restraint, and improve by his teaching the corrupt morals of the age." At last, in the year of Flodden and the Battle of the Spurs (1513), upon Good Friday, Colet—

" preached a noble sermon before the King and his court on the victory of Christ, exhorting all Christians to war and conquer under the banner of Him, their proper King. For they, he said, who through hatred or ambition were fighting, the bad with the bad, and slaughtering one another by turns, were warring under the banner not of Christ but of the Devil. At the same time, he pointed out to them how hard a thing it was to die a Christian death; how inconsistent it was that a man should have that brotherly love without which no one would see God, and yet bury his sword in his brother's heart. Let them follow, he added, the example of Christ as their Prince, not that of a Julius Cæsar or an Alexander. Much more to the same effect he gave utterance to on that occasion, so that the King was in some apprehension lest the soldiers, whom he was on the point of leading abroad, should feel their courage gone through this discourse."

Colet was summoned to Greenwich, where he had an audience with Henry in the monastery garden adjoining the palace. He might have expected some signal mark of the King's displeasure; but—

> " the courteous young prince bade him be covered and converse with him without ceremony, himself beginning in these terms: ' To spare you any groundless alarm, Mr. Dean, we have not sent for you hither to disturb your sacred labours, which have our entire approval; but that we may unburden our conscience of some scruples, and with the help of your counsel may better discharge the duties of our office.' "

The audience lasted an hour and a half, during which Colet's enemies waited in the palace in high spirits, gloating over the disgrace and danger in which they believed him to be involved; but in fact Colet won the King's entire approval of all he said and—

> " not only set the King's mind at rest, but even increased the favour in which he stood before. On returning to the palace, the King had a wine-cup brought to him, and pledged Colet in it before he would let him depart. . . . As the throng of courtiers was now standing round, eager to hear the result of the conference, the King in the hearing of all said, ' Let every man have his own doctor, and every man follow his liking; but this is the doctor for me.' Thus they departed, like the baffled wolves in the adage, nor did anyone from that day forward venture to molest Colet."

Whatever Henry may have become in later life, this incident is a proof of his generous and unprejudiced nature as a young man; and if Colet had not died prematurely of the sweating-sickness, at the age of fifty-three, the course of Church history in England might have been very different.

A few more quotations from Erasmus [1] may be added to throw light upon Colet's character.

> " I never saw a more highly-gifted intellect. . . . His opinions differed widely from those commonly

---

[1] In his letter to Julius Jonas, Erasmus has left character-sketches of the French Franciscan, Vitrier, and of Colet, which form the main authority for the details of Colet's career.

received, but he showed a remarkable discretion in adapting himself to others, so as to avoid giving offence. Among friends and scholars, however, he would express himself with the utmost freedom."

" Though no one approved of Christian devotion more warmly than he, he had yet but little liking for monasteries. . . . The gifts he bestowed upon them were either none or the smallest possible. . . . The reason was not that he disliked religious orders, but that those who took them did not come up to their profession. It was in fact his own wish to disconnect himself entirely from the world, if he could only have found a fraternity anywhere really bound together for a gospel life." [1]

" As Dean, he restored the decayed discipline of the cathedral body and—what was a novelty there—began preaching at every festival in his cathedral."

" The Dean's table, which in former times had ministered to luxury under the guise of hospitality, he brought within the bounds of moderation."

" He could not endure any slovenliness ; so much so as not to tolerate even an ungrammatical or illiterate mode of expression."

" He set a very high value on the Apostolic epistles, but he had such a reverence for the wonderful majesty of Christ that the writings of the Apostles seemed to grow poor by the side of it."

The relations between Colet and Erasmus would indeed form a subject for a separate study. In a brilliant but critical life of Erasmus, a recent writer [2] has said of Colet :

" A lover of the Renaissance, he was determined that it should be a Christian Renaissance, and if Erasmus gave his genius to the affairs of religion rather than, like so many of his Italian contemporaries, to the rediscovery of merely pagan antiquity, the influence which led him to this was Colet's."

The gravest charge that one who has no love for Erasmus can bring against Colet is that he " misunderstood and

[1] It was Colet's intention to retire to the Carthusian monastery at Sheen, near Richmond; but " death forestalled him."
[2] Christopher Hollis, *Erasmus.*

underrated the mediæval mind." It is true that he had no sympathy with the Scholastic philosophy; but Aristotle had enjoyed so long a reign, that it was high time that Plato should come into his own again, even at the cost of some hard knocks; and in the battle of the philosophies, Colet is certainly to be found on the side of Plato.

Once again, in 1515, Colet was called upon to preach on a great public occasion, the installation of Wolsey as Cardinal in Westminster Abbey. In his early years, Wolsey had been a schoolmaster at Magdalen College School, and his interest in education was maintained throughout his career, as is shown by his foundation of a great school at Ipswich and of Cardinal College (Christ Church) at Oxford; there were grounds for sympathy between the two men, although their careers were so dissimilar.

Twelve Archbishops and Bishops, the heads of the great abbeys and all the officers of State attended the ceremony, the climax of Wolsey's rise to fame. Colet's sermon was worthy of the occasion; he alluded to " the many divers and sundry virtues that he hath used, which have been the cause of his high and joyous promotion to all the realm "; and, having dwelt upon the honour and dignity of the title of Cardinal, addressed these words to Wolsey himself:

" Let not one in so proud a position be puffed up by its greatness; remember that our Saviour said to his disciples, 'I came not to be ministered unto but to minister.' . . . My Lord Cardinal, enforce yourself always to execute righteousness to rich and poor, with mercy and truth."

Had Shakespeare chosen to dramatise the earlier years of Henry VIII's reign, what a scene he might have made of this! The " top-proud fellow " had some fifteen years of power before him; within four, Colet himself was in his grave. The year of his death, 1519, was the year of Luther's breach with the Church. Had Colet lived, his influence would have been on the side, not of revolutionary change, but of true Reform. The leaders of the Reformation had much in common with him; in their sincerity, their hatred of superstition, their denunciation of papal and clerical scandals, they possessed something of his spirit. But, had he lived, we may well believe that he would have been ready to go to the block with his friend More, rather than renounce his allegiance to the Church. "Fide et literis" was his motto, as it is still the motto of his School; throughout his life, Faith and Learning were his guiding principles, and his dearest wish was ever that those for whose education he made such generous provision should direct their steps in the same path.

JOHN SKELTON

Circa 1460–1529

By

W. H. AUDEN

JOHN SKELTON

by W. H. AUDEN

TO write an essay on a poet who has no biography, no message, philosophical or moral, who has neither created characters, nor expressed critical ideas about the literary art, who was comparatively uninfluenced by his predecessors, and who exerted no influence upon his successors, is not easy. Skelton's work offers no convenient critical pegs. Until Mr. Robert Graves drew attention to his work some years ago, he was virtually unknown outside University-honour students, and even now, though there have been two editions, in the last ten years, those of Mr. Hughes and Mr. Henderson, it is doubtful whether the number of his readers has very substantially increased. One has only to compare him with another modern discovery, Hopkins, to realise that he has remained a stock literary event rather than a vital influence.

My own interest dates from the day I heard a friend at Oxford, who had just bought the first Hughes edition, make two quotations:

> *"Also the mad coot*
> *With bald face to toot"*;

and

> *"Till Euphrates that flood driveth*
> *me into Ind,"*

and though I should not claim my own case as typical, yet I doubt if those to whom these lines make no appeal are likely to admire Skelton.

Though little that is authentic is known of Skelton's life, a fairly definite portrait emerges from his work: a conservative cleric with a stray sense of humour, devoted to the organisation to which he belonged and to the cultural tradition it represented, but critical of its abuses, possibly a scholar, but certainly neither an academic-dried boy or a fastidious highbrow; no more unprejudiced or well-informed about affairs outside his own province than the average modern reader of the newspapers, but shrewd enough within it, well read in the conventional good authors of his time, but by temperament more attracted to more popular and less respectable literature, a countryman in sensibility, not particularly vain, but liking to hold the floor, fond of feminine society, and with a quick and hostile eye for pompositas in all its forms.

Born in 1460, he probably took his degree at Cambridge in 1484, and was awarded a laureate degree by Cambridge, Oxford, and Louvain, which I suppose did not mean much more then than writing an essay prize on the Newdigate would to-day, became tutor to the future Henry VIII, was sufficiently well known socially to be mentioned by Erasmus and Caxton; took orders at the age of thirty-eight, became Rector of Diss, his probable birthplace, about 1500; began an open attack on Wolsey in 1519, and died in sanctuary at Westminster in 1529. Thus he was born just before Edward IV's accession, grew up during the Wars of the Roses, and died in the year of Wolsey's fall and the Reformation Parliament. In attempting to trace the relations between a poet's work and the age in which he lived, it is well to remember how arbitrary such deductions are. One is presented with a certain number of facts like a heap of pebbles, and the number of possible patterns which one can make from them are almost infinite. To prove the validity of the pattern one chooses, it would be necessary first to predict that if there were a poet in such and such a period he would have such and such poetical qualities, and then for the works of that poet to be discovered with just those qualities. The literary historian can do no more than suggest one out of many possible views.

Politically Skelton's period is one of important change. The Plantagenet line had split into two hostile branches, ending one in a lunatic and the other in a criminal. The barons turned their weapons upon each other and destroyed themselves; all the English Empire in France except Calais was gone; the feudal kind of representative government was discredited and the Church corrupt. The wealth of the country was beginning to accumulate in the hands of the trading classes, such as wool merchants, and to be concentrated in the cities of the traders. Traders want peace which gives them liberty to trade rather than political liberty, secular authority rather than a religious authority which challenges their right to usury and profit. They tend therefore to support an absolute monarchy, and unlike a feudal aristocracy with its international family loyalties, to be nationalist in sentiment. Absolute monarchies adopt *real politik* and though Machiavelli's *Prince* was not published till 1513, his principles were already European practice.

Skelton's political views are those of the average man of his time and class. A commoner, he had nothing to lose by the destruction of the old nobility; like the majority of his countrymen, he rejoices at royal weddings and national victories, and weeps at royal funerals and national defeats. With them also he criticises Henry VII's avarice.

" *Immensas sibi divitias cumulasse quid horres?* "

Like a good bourgeois he is horrified at the new fashions and worldliness at Henry VIII's court, but cannot attribute it to the monarch himself, only to his companions; and hates the arrogance and extravagance of Wolsey, who by social origin was no better than himself.

In religious matters he is naturally more intelligent and better informed. Though Wyclif died in 1384, his doctrines were not forgotten among the common people, and though Skelton did not live to see the English Reformation, before he was fifty Luther had pinned his protest to the church door at Wittenberg, and he lived through the period of criticism by the Intelligentsia (*The Praises of Folly* was written in 1503) which always precedes a mass political movement.

The society of Colet, Grocyn, Linacre, and More was an intellectual and international one, a society of scholars who, like all scholars, overestimated their capacity to control or direct events. Skelton's feelings towards them were mixed. Too honest not to see and indeed in *Colin Clout* unsparingly to attack the faults of the Church, he was like them and like the intelligent orthodox at any time, a reformer not a revolutionary, that is to say, he thought that the corruptions of the Church and its dogmatic system were in no way related; that you could by a " change of heart " cure the one without impairing the other; while the revolutionary, on the other hand, attributes the corruption directly to the dogmas, for which he proposes to substitute another set which he imagines to be fool-proof and devil-proof. Towards the extremists he was frightened and hostile.

> " *And some have a smack*
> *Of Luther's sack . . .*
> *And some of them bark*
> *Clatter and carp*
> *Of that heresiarch*
> *Called Wickleuista*
> *The devilish dogmatista.*"

His difference from the early reformers was mainly temperamental. He was not in the least donnish and, moving perhaps in less rarefied circles, saw that the effect of their researches on the man in the street, like the effect on our own time, for example of Freud, was different from what they intended.

He has been unjustly accused of opposing the study of Greek; what he actually attacked was the effect produced by the impact of new ideas upon the average man, never in any age an edifying spectacle.

> "*Let Parrot, I pray you, have liberty to prate*
> *For aurea lingua greca ought to be magnified*
> *If it were cond perfitely and after the rate*
> *As lingua Latina, in school matter occupied*
> *But our Grekis, their Greek so well have applied*
> *That they cannot say in Greek, riding by the way,*
> ' *Ho, ostler, fetch my horse a bottel of hay.*' "

As a literary artist, it is difficult to escape the conclusion that Skelton is an oddity, like Blake, who cannot be really fitted into literary history as an inevitable product of the late fifteenth century. There is every reason for the existence of Hawes or even Barclay as the moribund end of the Chaucerian tradition; it is comparatively easy to understand Elizabethan poetry as a fusion of the Italian Renaissance and native folk elements; but the vigour and character of Skelton's work remains unpredictable.

One may point out that the Narrenschiff influenced the *Bouge of Court*, that Skeltonics may be found in early literature like the Proverbs of Alfred,

> *"Ac if þu him lest welde*
> *werende on worlde.*
> *Lude as stille*
> *His owene wille,"*

or that the style of his Latin verses occurs in Goliardic poetry or Abelard.

> *"Est in Rama*
> *Vox audita*
> *Rachel fluentes*
> *Eiolantes*
> *Super natos*
> *Interfectos."*

But that a writer should be found at that particular date who would not succumb to aureate diction, and without being a folk writer, should make this kind of rhythm the basis of work, would seem, if it had not occurred, exceedingly improbable.

Excluding *Magnificence*, Skelton's poetry falls naturally into four divisions: the imitations of the " aureate " poetry of Lydgate and similar fifteenth-century verses, such as the elegy on the Duke of Northumberland and the prayers to the Trinity; the lyrics; the poems in rhyme royal such as the *Bouge of Court* and *Speke Parrot*; and those like *Elinor Rumming*, *Philip Sparrow*, and *Colin Clout*, written in skeltonics.

Of the first class we may be thankful that it is so small. The attempt to gain for English verse the sonority of Latin by the use of a Latinised vocabulary was a failure in any hands except Milton's, and Skelton was no Milton. It was dull and smelt of the study, and Skelton seems to have realised this, and in his typically ironical way expressed his opinion.

> *"For, as I to love have said*
> *I am but a young maid*
> *And cannot in effect*
> *My style as yet direct*
> *With English words elect. . . .*

"Chaucer that famous clerk
His terms were not dark
But pleasant, easy and plain
No word he wrote in vain.

"Also John Lydgate
Writeth after a higher rate
It is diffuse to find
The sentence of his mind
Some men find a fault
And say he writeth too haut"
(PHILIP SPARROW);

and in the *Duke of Albany* he rags the aureate vocabulary by giving the long words a line a piece:

"Of his nobility
His magnaminity
His animosity
His frugality
His liberality
His affability," etc. etc.

As a writer of lyrics, on the other hand, had he chosen he could have ranked high enough. He can range from the barrack room " 'Twas Xmas day in the workhouse " style of thing, to conventional religious poetry like the poem " Woefully arrayed " and the quite unfaked tenderness of the poem to Mistress Isabel Pennell, and always with an un-failing intuition of the right metrical form to employ in each case. Here is an example of his middle manner, Fancy's song about his hawk in *Magnificence*.

"Lo this is
My fancy y wis
Now Christ it blesse!
It is, by Jesse.

"A bird full sweet
For me full meet
She is furred for the heat
All to the feet:

> *"Her browès bent*
> *Her eyen glent*
> *From Tyne to Trent*
> *From Stroud to Kent. . . .*

> *"Barbed like a nun*
> *For burning of the sun*
> *Her feathers dun*
> *Well favoured, bonne! "*

Skelton's use of Rhyme Royal is in some ways the best proof of his originality, because though employing a form used by all his predecessors and contemporaries and at a time when originality of expression was not demanded by the reading public, few stanzas of Skelton's could be confused with those of anyone else.

The most noticeable difference, attained partly by a greater number of patter or unaccented syllables (which relate it more to a teutonic accentual or sprung rhythm for verse) lies in the tempo of his poetry. Compare a stanza of Skelton's with one of Chaucer's:

> *" Suddenly as he departed me fro*
> *Came pressing in on in a wonder array*
> *Ere I was ware, behind me he said ' BO '*
> *Then I, astoned of that sudden fray*
> *Start all at once, I liked nothing his play*
> *For, if I had not quickly fled the touch*
> *He had plucked out the nobles of my pouch."*
>
> (SKELTON.)

> *" But o word, lordlings, herkeneth ere I go:*
> *It were full hard to finde now a dayes*
> *In all a town Griseldes three or two*
> *For, if that they were put to such assayes,*
> *The gold of hem hath no so bad aloyes*
> *With brass, that though the coyne be fair at ye,*
> *It would rather breste a-two than plye."*
>
> (CHAUCER.)

In Chaucer there is a far greater number of iambic feet, and the prevailing number of accents per line is five; in the Skelton it is four.

Indeed, the tempo of Skelton's verse is consistently quicker than that of any other English poet; only the author of *Hudibras*, and in recent times Vachel Lyndsay, come anywhere near him in this respect.

It seems to be a rough-and-ready generalisation that the more poetry concerns itself with subjective states, with the inner world of feeling, the slower it becomes, or in other words, that the verse of extrovert poets like Dryden is swift and that of introvert poets like Milton is slow, and that in those masters like Shakespeare who transcend these classifications, in the emotional crises which precede and follow the tragic act, the pace of the verse is retarded.

Thus the average pace of mediæval verse compared with that of later more self-conscious ages is greater, and no poetry is more " outer " than Skelton's.

His best poems, with the exception of *Speke Parrot*, are like triumphantly successful prize poems. The themes— the death of a girl's sparrow, a pub, Wolsey, have all the air of set subjects. They may be lucky choices, but one feels that others would have done almost equally well, not, as with Milton, that his themes were the only ones to which his genius would respond at that particular moment in his life; that, had they not occurred to him, he would have written nothing. They never read as personal experience, brooded upon, and transfigured.

Considering his date, this is largely to the good. Pre-Elizabethan verse, even Chaucer, when it deserts the outer world, and attempts the subjective, except in very simple emotional situations, as in the mystery plays, tends to sentiment and prosy moralising. Skelton avoids that, but at the same time his emotional range is limited. The world of " The soldier's pole is fallen" is not for him :

> " *We are but dust*
> *For die we must*
> *It is general*
> *To be mortal* "

is as near as he gets to the terrific. This is moralising, but the metre saves it from sententiousness.

The skeltonic is such a simple metre that it is surprising that fewer poets have used it. The natural unit of speech rhythm seems to be one of four accents, dividing into two half verses of two accents. If one tries to write ordinary conversation in verse, it will fall more naturally into this scheme than into any other. Most dramatic blank verse, for example, has four accents rather than five, and it is possible that our habit of prefacing nouns and adjectives by quite pointless adjectives and adverbs as in " the *perfectly priceless* " is dictated by our ear, by our need to group accents in pairs. Skelton is said to have spoken as he wrote, and his skeltonics have the natural ease of speech rhythm. It is the metre of many nursery rhymes.

> " *Little Jack Horner*
> *Sat in a corner* " ;

or extemporised verse like the *Clerihew* :

> " *Alfred de Musset*
> *Used to call his cat pusset* " ;

and study of the Woolworth song books will show its attraction to writers of jazz lyrics :

> " *For life's a farce*
> *Sitting on the grass.*"

No other English poet to my knowledge has this extempore quality, is less " would-be," to use a happy phrase of D. H. Lawrence.

It makes much of his work, of course, quite unmemorable—it slips in at one ear and out at the other; but it is never false, and the lucky shots seem unique, of a kind which a more deliberate and self-conscious poet would never have thought of, or considered worthy of his singing robes :

> " *Your head would have ached*
> *To see her naked.*"

Though much of Skelton's work consists of attacks on people and things, he can scarcely be called a satirist. Satire is an art which can only flourish within a highly sophisticated culture. It aims at creating a new attitude towards the persons or institutions satirised, or at least at crystallising one previously vague and unconscious. It presupposes a society whose prejudices and loyalties are sufficiently diffuse to be destroyed by intellectual assault, or sufficiently economically and politically secure to laugh at its own follies, and to admit that there is something to be said on both sides.

In less secure epochs, such as Skelton's, when friend and foe are more clearly defined, the place of satire is taken by abuse, as it always is taken in personal contact. (If censorship prevents abuse, allegorical symbolism is employed, e.g. *Speke Parrot*.) If two people are having a quarrel, they do not stop to assess who is at fault or to convince the other of his error: they express their feelings of anger by calling each other names. Similarly, among friends, when we express our opinion of an enemy by saying " so and so is a closet " we assume that the reasons are known:

> " *The Midwife put her hand on his thick skull*
> *With the prophetic blessing, ' Be thou dull,' "*

is too much emotion recollected in tranquillity to be the language of a quarrel. Abuse in general avoids intellectual tropes other than those of exaggeration which intensify the expression of one's feelings such as, " You're so narrow-minded your ears meet," or the genealogical trees which bargees assign to one another.

Further, the effect on the victim is different. Abuse is an attack on the victim's personal honour, satire on his social self-esteem; it affects him not directly, but through his friends.

Skelton's work is abuse or flyting, not satire, and he is a master at it. Much flyting poetry, like Dunbar's and Skelton's own poems against Garnesche, suffer from the alliterative metre in which they were written, which makes them too verbal; the effect is lost on later generations, to whom the vocabulary is unfamiliar. The freedom and simplicity of the skeltonic was an ideal medium.

> " *Dundas, drunken and drowsy*
> *Scabbed, scurvy and lousy*
> *Of unhappy generation*
> *And most ungracious nation!*
> *Dundas*
> *That drunk ass*

64

That rates and ranks
That prates and pranks
Of Huntly banks
Take this our thanks:—

" *Dundee, Dunbar*
Walk, Scot,
Walk, sott
Rail not too far! "

Later literary attempts at abuse, such as Browning's lines on Fitzgerald or Belloc's on a don, are too self-conscious and hearty. Blake is the only other poet known to me who has been equally successful.

" *You think Fuseli is not a great painter; I'm glad*
This is one of the best compliments he ever had."

With his capacity for abuse Skelton combines a capacity for caricature. His age appears to have been one which has a penchant for the exaggerated and macabre, and he is no exception. His description of a character is as accurate in detail as one of Chaucer's, but as exaggerated as one of Dickens's. Compared with Chaucer he is more violent and dramatic; a favourite device of his is to interpolate the description with remarks by the character itself.

" *With that came Riot, rushing all at once*
A rusty gallant, to-ragged and to-rent
As on the board he whirled a pair of bones
Quarter trey dews he clattered as he went
Now have at all, by Saint Thomas of Kent!
And ever he threw and cast I wote n'ere what
His hair was growen through out his hat. . . .

" *Counter he could O lux upon a pot,*
An ostrich feather of a capon's tail
He set up freshly upon his hat aloft:
' *What revel rout!* ' *quod he, and gan to rail*
How oft he had hit Jenet on the tail,
Of Phillis featuous, and little pretty Kate
How oft he had knocked at her clicket gate."

This has much more in common with the Gothic gargoyle than with the classicism of Chaucer; *Elinor Rumming* is one of the few poems comparable to Breughel or Rowlandson in painting. The effect is like looking at the human skin through a magnifying glass.

> " *Then Margery Milkduck*
> *Her kirtle she did uptuck*
> *An inch above her knee*
> *Her legs that ye might see*
> *But they were sturdy and stubbed*
> *Mighty pestles and clubbed*
> *As fair and as white*
> *As the foot of a kite*
> *She was somewhat foul*
> *Crooked-necked like an owl;*
> *And yet she bought her fees,*
> *A cantel of Essex cheese,*
> *Was well a foot thick*
> *Full of maggots quick:*
> *It was huge and great*
> *And mighty strong meat*
> *For the devil to eat*
> *It was tart and pungate.*"

All Skelton's work has this physical appeal. Other poets, such as Spenser and Swinburne, have been no more dependent upon ideas, but they have touched only one sense, the auditory. The Catherine-wheel motion of Skelton's verse is exciting in itself, but his language is never vaguely emotive. Indeed, it is deficient in overtones, but is always precise, both visually and tactually. He uses place-names, not scientifically like Dante, or musically like Milton, but as country proverbs use them, with natural vividness:

> " *And Syllogisari was drowned at Sturbridge Fair.*"

Naturally enough the figures of classical mythology which appear in all mediæval work (just as the Sahara or Ohio appears in modern popular verses) occur in Skelton also, but he is never sorry to leave Lycaon or Etna for the Tilbury Ferry and the Plains of Salisbury. The same applies to the Latin quotations in *Philip Sparrow*; not only have they dramatic point, but being mainly quotations from the Psalter, they make no demands upon the erudition of his audience, any more than would " Abide with me " upon a modern reader.

Of Skelton's one excursion into dramatic form, *Magnificence*, not much need be said. It is interesting, because he is one of the few dramatists who have attempted, and with success, to differentiate his characters by making them speak in different metres, thus escaping the tendency of blank verse to make all the characters speak like the author; which obliged the Elizabethans to make their comic characters speak in prose; for the future of poetic comedy it may prove important. Its fault, a fatal one in drama, is its prolixity, but cut by at least two-thirds it might act very much better than one imagines.

Skelton's reputation has suffered in the past from his supposed indecency. This charge is no longer maintained, but there are other misunderstandings of poetry which still prevent appreciation of his work. On the one hand, there are those who read poetry for its message, for great thoughts which can be inscribed on Christmas calendars ; on the other, there are admirers of " pure " poetry, which generally means emotive poetry with a minimum of objective reference. Skelton satisfies neither of these : he is too carefree for the one, and too interested in the outer world for the second.

If we accept, and I think we must, a distinction between the visionary and the entertainer, the first being one who extends our knowledge of, insight into, and power of control over human conduct and emotion, without whom our understanding would be so much the poorer, Skelton is definitely among the entertainers. He is not one of the indispensables, but among entertainers—and how few are the indispensables—he takes a high place. Nor is entertainment an unworthy art : it demands a higher standard of technique and a greater lack of self-regard than the average man is prepared to attempt. There have been, and are, many writers of excellent sensibility whose work is spoilt by a bogus vision which deprives it of the entertainment value which it would otherwise have had; in that kind of pride Skelton is entirely lacking.

CARDINAL WOLSEY

Circa 1475–1530

By
EDWARD P. CHEYNEY

CARDINAL WOLSEY

by EDWARD P. CHEYNEY

A SEVENTEENTH-CENTURY antiquarian, advising Lord Clarendon on his collection of portraits of great Englishmen, chooses Cardinal Wolsey, with Walsingham, Leicester, Raleigh, Pole, and Sir Thomas Smith as his six " polititians." To no one of these is the adjective great more suitably applied than to Wolsey. He had a certain native and essential greatness, quite apart from any position he attained. It impressed his contemporaries, and has not failed to obtain recognition from his later biographers. It extorted the reluctant admiration of hostile Norfolk in *Henry VIII.*

> "*There's in him stuff that puts him to these ends,*
> *For, not being propped by ancestry,* . . .
> *The force of his own merit makes his way,*
> *A gift that Heaven gives.* . . ."

His earliest biography is entitled *The Negotiations of Thomas Wolsey, the Great Cardinal.* To the diarist already quoted he is " the great cardinal," " the magnificent cardinal "; to another contemporary he is " that great man." Even when his oppressions are complained of, he is " the great tyrant." This greatness doubtless meant different things to different men, but to all it was something characteristic of Wolsey. It was intensified no doubt by the contrast between the obscurity of his origin and his later fortunes. Son of a butcher or cattle dealer of Ipswich, well-to-do but certainly plebeian, the boy, evidently gifted, was put to school to rise in the church, through which alone a boy of the lower classes could rise in the fifteenth century. A " boy bachelor " at fifteen, fellow and schoolmaster of his college, Magdalen, at Oxford, his first appointment was as tutor to the sons of the Marquess of Dorset. He soon became chaplain to a bishop, then to a court official, upon whose death he was taken into the service of Henry VII. He was the ablest of the group of servants that Henry bequeathed, along with his fortune, his secure title, and his political problems, to his son Henry VIII; but there was nothing yet to indicate his pre-eminence. "This Ipswich fellow," one of the nobles still calls him.

It was with the new king that the life, the work, the rise and fall of Wolsey were inextricably bound up. Seldom have a king and his minister been more closely united. So long as Wolsey retained the confidence and affection of the King, the foundations of his power and influence were firm and he was practically ruler of England. So long as Henry entrusted the principal control of government to his minister he was, if not always wisely, at least ably and on the whole devotedly guided.

This was no narrow policy for either king or minister. The problems of English government in State and Church extended widely, the personality of Wolsey was restless and his ambition soaring, the possibilities of power of a gifted and trusted minister of an almost autocratic king were great beyond previous English experience. *Ego et rex meus*, as he was charged by his critics with writing to foreign rulers, in good Latin order, if bad constitutional form, had endless possibilities of achievement. It is principally with the manifold and varied activities of Wolsey in this relation that we are concerned. He was not one of those statesmen whose personality is lost in their achievements. Few men indeed who have occupied such an influential position have left so little impression on the subsequent course of events. He was not a planet, exerting as it revolved in its orbit a steady and measurable effect on history, but a meteor, swinging in a long and brilliant arc across the sky, extinguished at last in the obscure mists of the horizon.

His political career was a long one. Appointed king's almoner and a member of the Privy Council in November 1509, only six months after the King's accession, he began to exert a visible influence over him almost immediately. He was eighteen years older than the King; in the prime of life and vigour, handsome, witty, vivacious and adaptable, easy-mannered, yet shrewd and infinitely capable and industrious. His obvious skill and energy in organising the expedition by which Henry entered the continental struggle in 1512 strengthened the King's appreciation of his abilities, and by the end of that year he had won Henry's complete confidence. From that time on for eighteen years, until 1529, he was Henry's principal adviser, frequent companion, and, so far as that is possible between a king and a subject, an intimate friend. His more ignorant or prejudiced opponents called this influence wizardry, but there is no mystery in the sway he obtained over the mind of the easy-going, pleasure-loving, yet intelligent and appreciative young king, coming at eighteen into the inheritance of a crown and a fortune, the diversions of a court, the freedom of absolute rule, and the exhilaration of unbounded popularity. For Henry's political, social, and intellectual needs Wolsey could provide with unusual facility, and it was only natural that his influence should supersede that of all other ministers. In 1516 he became Lord Chancellor, and thus in form as well as in fact the principal minister of the King ; the varied powers and duties of the Lord Chancellorship in the sixteenth century giving a precedency that under an indulgent king was almost unlimited.

Wolsey's dependence for the sum-total of his power was, however, almost as great upon the Pope as upon the King. It is true that some minor Church positions and the deanships of Lincoln, Hereford, and York he owed to his college or to private patrons, and his nominal but lucrative possession of the bishopric of Tournai was his reward for his share in the English victories in France in the campaign of 1512. But even for these he needed papal dispensations for absence and pluralism, and for his appointments in 1514 as Bishop of Lincoln and Archbishop of York and the possession *in commendam* of the Abbey of St. Albans he needed both provision and dispensation from the Pope. As he was promoted, also, to more lucrative bishoprics as they became vacant, from Lincoln to Bath and Wells and then to Winchester, he needed and received in each case from the Pope a bull for his translation.

More direct was his appointment in 1515 as cardinal, and in 1518 as papal legate and its extension from time to time in period and in power until he was given the appointment for life and with authority scarcely less than that of the Pope himself, if he had been in England. The cardinalate and the legateship were the results of intrigue by Wolsey at Rome and of letters from Henry to the Pope; the price paid for the influence of the English minister and the English king in the Pope's favour in the complicated diplomatic and military contests in progress in Italy.

The culmination of this series of promotions would naturally have been the election of Wolsey himself to the papacy. It was more than once considered. Three vacancies occurred during his period of greatness. The first, when Julius II died, in 1513, was before Wolsey had been made a cardinal and therefore eligible. At the second, when Leo X died in 1521, not only did Wolsey urge his own election, through his correspondents at Rome, write long letters to the cardinals in his favour, signed by the King, secure the support alternately of the French and Spanish kings, but he is said to have proposed a Spanish military expedition, of which he would himself bear the expense, to force the cardinals in conclave to elect him. He was unpopular at Rome; but his name appeared on the ballots at the conclave once, when he received seven votes out of thirty-nine. He could force the hand of the Pope to grant him his desires; he could not force the hand of the cardinals.

Adrian VI, who was then elected, lived only a year and a half, and again in 1523 Wolsey secured promises, illusory as it proved, that made him feel sure for a while of his election. But he received no votes. The fact is, the papacy had become an Italian principality; almost all of the cardinals were Italians, and it was hardly to be expected that they would put its powers into the hands of a foreigner; especially a native of a distant country, strong in the government of that country in State and Church, and already showing an inclination to make use of the papacy for English purposes. So another Italian, a Medici, was elected, who took the name of Clement VII.

Once more, in January 1529, when there was a rumour of the death of Clement, Wolsey set in motion all the old plans, stressing his claims as the only one of the cardinals who could be trusted to rescue the Holy See from its dangers, and offering to release many Church positions, if he were elected, to the use of those who favoured him. Both Wolsey and Henry had special need at this time for the Cardinal's elevation, for the King's divorce was now at its most critical stage, and Wolsey as Pope could give the decision which the Spanish-controlled Clement was unable or unwilling to give. But the rumour was a mistake, and Clement outlived his would-be successor.

For a long time already Wolsey had been hoping to impose his will and that of the King upon Clement in the matter of the divorce. Before taking up the "King's matter," however, it is necessary to consider the use the cardinal made in the English Church itself of his episcopal and legatine powers. His bishoprics gave him control of a vast number of minor appointments; he exercised also, by virtue of his power as legate, the right of appointment to all positions in the gift of vacant sees, and of Salisbury, Worcester, and Llandaff, held by foreign bishops whose only interest in them was the receipt of a certain sum in commutation of their revenues. He reintroduced the practice of papal provisions for minor Church appointments, long given up by the popes themselves, and in many cases intruded his own nominees into such positions against the possessors of the rights of patronage and in violation of the old statutes of provisors. Unwelcome as these extensions of his powers were to English lay and ecclesiastical patrons, his claims of jurisdiction, right of visitation, the probate of wills and the summons of convocations, all by virtue of his position as legate, were a vexation and a burden to the English Church. He collected four per cent. on the annual income of every benefice visited and exacted regular fees for the probate of wills, not only in his own archdiocese of York, but in that of Canterbury. He appointed English bishops as his commissaries for carrying out under his legateship much jurisdiction they felt to be their own, and placed his agents and officers through all England, interposing in affairs the archdeacons and lower clergy felt were in their sphere.

Much of his power over the English Church was excused to himself as to others by the anticipation that it was to serve reform. He talked to the Pope, to the King, and to Convocation vaguely about being able, with his legatine power, " to accomplish some good in the Lord's vineyard and to be profitable to all Christendom." He obtained a papal commission to negotiate a peace among Christian princes and to launch a crusade against the Turks. He was given authority to reform both the monastic and the secular clergy in England. His powers were quite sufficient for carrying out a general reform.

But little was accomplished or even entered upon. He had obtained the means, but made no attempt to employ them. It was as if instinct made him grasp at all obtainable power, but left him satisfied with its possession without its use. Such of his plans for the reformation of the Church as can be discovered, the higher education of the clergy, an increase in the number of bishoprics, the regulation or dissolution of many of the monasteries, a commutation of annates, commended themselves at the time to More and Erasmus and certain enlightened English bishops as embodying some of the ideas of the humanists, and to some modern students as correcting the weaknesses of the Church that would have precluded the Reformation. But there was no driving force behind them.

There is no evidence that Wolsey had any religious sentiments, probably few if any thought-out beliefs, certainly no devotion. He was a churchman, and performed the customary services regularly in private and frequently in public, but there is no indication that they were more to him than official forms. A hundred times he was the central figure in some great religious ceremony, but such prominence and conformity was too common among purely worldly prelates to consider it any evidence of a devout spirit. He valued his Church positions for the authority they gave and the income they brought to him. He was never in any one of the bishoprics he held, except for a few days before his death, just within the confines of the archbishopric of York. He never saw any one of the cathedrals from which his titles and much of his income were drawn.

His indifference to religion may have been the cause of his lenience to heretics. The period of his administration of the affairs of the Church in England was a welcome oasis between the burnings that took place under the old Lollard laws before 1518 and their resumption after his fall. Many recusants were disciplined by penance or imprisonment, or forced to abjure; but so far as is known, no person suffered death for nonconformity in religion while Wolsey was in control of the ecclesiastical and civil courts.

It is always hard to separate Wolsey's desire for personal distinction from his interest in reform. He would endow a new college at Oxford for the training of secular clergy, but it must be larger and richer than any of the other colleges; it must bear his name; the cardinal's hat must be its emblem. Its feeder should be another college, in his native town of Ipswich. His interest in these two colleges was genuine and continuous. For their endowment he dissolved, with the agreement of the King and the Pope, some twenty small monasteries and nunneries, diverting their property to the new foundation, except for a scanty support, in some cases none at all, left to the dispossessed monks and nuns. He prepared their course of study and plan of discipline.

To contemporary observers much of Wolsey's greatness lay in his magnificent way of life. His " gentleman usher," Cavendish, describes his career as if it were one long pageant interspersed with scenes of special and dramatic brilliancy. He enumerates the officers and servants of his dining-hall, kitchen, stable, garden, pantry, barge, chapel, " sixteen singing men," " twelve singing children," " sixteen chaplains to say daily mass before him," a physician, an apothecary, four minstrels, " four counsellors learned in the laws of the realm," and so through a household which must have numbered almost a thousand. Four hundred and twenty-nine members of his household were assessed for the subsidy in 1529. The two great silver crosses and two pillars of silver regularly carried before him, and the great seal and his cardinal's hat on state occasions, the train of noblemen and gentlemen that followed him, were the outward and visible sign of his " official " greatness. The Field of the Cloth of Gold was an occasion of universal show, as its traditional name indicates. The Archbishop of Canterbury and two dukes were there. Each of these had some seventy attendants; Wolsey had three hundred. There were numberless other scenes of show or pride. When in 1515 the papal prothonotary brought Wolsey his red hat as emblem of his appointment as cardinal, a bishop and an earl met the messenger at Blackheath, the mayor, aldermen, and gilds accompanied the procession as the hat was borne through the city to Westminster Abbey, where, at the ceremony of its presentation on the succeeding Sunday, three archbishops, eight bishops, and eight abbots took part in the service, and eighteen noblemen, including the Dukes of Norfolk and Suffolk, acted as attendants on the new cardinal. Among the many dramatic scenes that have taken place in the choir of Amiens, there can have been few more picturesque than the occasion when Wolsey, as priest, cardinal, and papal legate, said Mass and gave the sacrament to the Queens of France and Navarre, then knelt by the King of France to receive it himself. The chroniclers, with characteristic Tudor love for a show, revel in the gorgeousness of these scenes. In their accounts, his regular movements as chancellor and councillor became glittering processions.

Building is traditionally a temptation to the wealthy and the great. In addition to his two colleges, Wolsey rebuilt York House, the later Whitehall, begged the ground and built the palace of Hampton Court, then gave it to the King, though he continued to occupy it till his fall, and built his two country houses, The More, "handsomer than Hampton Court," and Tyttenhanger. He rebuilt, from fines received there, the Star Chamber, and even after his downfall began the repair of the dilapidated buildings of his archbishopric of York.

For his princely way of life and for these expensive operations Wolsey needed and possessed a princely income. The Venetian ambassador in 1519 estimated it at 42,000 ducats, which would amount in modern value to £80,000 a year or more; his successor in 1531 declared that just before his fall it had been 150,000 ducats, or some £300,000 a year in modern value. These statements can be confirmed with some accuracy. He was far richer than any noble in the kingdom, and his income was second only to that of the King. Even after his fall from office and departure for his archbishopric he claimed he needed at least £4,000 a year, some £40,000 of modern value, to live in his diminished estate.

As one turns from all this getting and spending to Wolsey's work as Lord Chancellor it is a more attractive figure that appears. He is still in full dress it is true, and domineering to the limit of tyranny, but he is now concerned with abstract principles of justice, with the equal application of the law to rich and poor in Star Chamber, with social order in the Court of Requests, especially with the protection of the poor from the aggression of the rich; applying his great mental powers and his unwearied industry to the astonishing variety of subjects that engaged the attention of Tudor government.

Apart from all his public activities Wolsey had a more personal and private life, relegated by the rules of the

Church and the conventions of the time to concealment, yet not entirely unacknowledged. About the time he became a member of the King's council, probably in 1511, he entered into an uncanonical marriage relation with the daughter of a man named Lark, possibly an inn-keeper at Thetford, not far from Wolsey's original home. By the time he was a cardinal he had a daughter and a son. The daughter, named Dorothy, became a nun at Shaftesbury, and survived to become a pensioner of the Crown when that convent was dissolved ; she died in 1553. The son, named Thomas for his father, and known as Thomas Wynter, sometimes spoken of by Wolsey and others as his son, sometimes, according to the euphemism of the time, as his nephew, was brought up carefully as a wealthy man's son and educated by private tutors in England and at the universities of Louvain, Padua, and Paris.

Offers of service to him came to his father, at one time or another, from Erasmus, Lupset, a papal secretary at Rome, the French ambassador in London, Cromwell, and Henry himself. There was indeed much in his early career similar to that of the Duke of Richmond, Henry's illegitimate son, nearly of the same age. While still a boy Thomas Wynter took minor orders, but never proceeded to higher clerical degrees. He had intellectual interests, and spent most of his life travelling on the Continent. His mother was married during Wolsey's lifetime to a well-to-do landowner named Lee, of the county of Chester, with the cardinal's consent and provision of a dowry. It is evident that bigamy was a question of canon law, not of morals, to Wolsey as to his master.

Whatever may be said of Wolsey's paternity of Thomas Wynter, there is an abundance of scandal in his provision for his support. It shows nepotism and the secularism of the Church at their worst, and an effrontery that is almost incredible. When the boy was ten years old he was given a parish. When he was thirteen, at Wolsey's request the canons of Wells elected him to the deanship of that cathedral. When he was fourteen he was made Provost of St. Peter's, Beverley, Archdeacon of York and Richmond, and Chancellor of Salisbury. The next year he was given five prebends in various cathedrals and two rectories, one in Ipswich, his father's birthplace. He never appeared in any of these places, and dispensations had to be obtained from the Pope for non-residence, pluralism, and illegitimacy of birth. Later grants and his father's suggestion to the King that he should be appointed to the vacant bishopric of Durham may well go unrecorded. The total value of his Church preferments was estimated at £2,000, perhaps £20,000 in modern terms. All of this went through the cardinal's hands, and, as it was supposed, was given his son in the form of an allowance on which to live. On Wolsey's downfall Wynter lost many of his Church positions, but retained enough for his support on his travels, and through the influence of Cromwell was even given an archdeaconry later. He disappears from view about 1543.

Wolsey's long career had given opportunity for the accumulation of much antagonism. He had many dependents, some admirers, but few friends. The price of greatness was, as always, isolation. Among the higher classes he had no party, large or small. Parliament had met but once during fourteen years and he had utilised that meeting only to extort a large grant for an unpopular war. With the common people he had little to do. The wide chasm which separated him from the class from which he sprang he never tried to close or even to bridge. For a statesman of the Tudor period and a native of a seaboard town he was strangely uninterested in commerce, and dragged England in 1528 into a war with Charles V, although it bade fair to destroy all English trade with the Netherlands and the home industry that depended upon it. His effort to secure for the government a loan of one-sixth of the people's property in 1525 stirred the anger of all classes to the very verge of rebellion. Threats were heard in Kent, that if the people could get hold of him they would send him to sea in a boat with holes bored in it.

Wolsey cared little, probably, for popular approval or disapproval so long as he had the confidence of the King. A contemporary satirist remarks that the cardinal " carryeth a kyng in his sleve, yf all the worlde fayle." But if he had had less self-confidence he might have seen evidence as early as 1528 of a diminution of even the King's trust. There had always been something excessive in it, and observers, if not Wolsey himself, watched for its decline. How soon his un-popularity, the intrigues of his enemies, the difficulties in his foreign policy and the increasing participation of the King in affairs of government would have of themselves brought about the fall of the cardinal from power there is no means of judging, for in 1527 a new factor entered; Anne Boleyn came on the scene. So far as Wolsey was concerned the failure of the King's marriage with Catherine to produce an heir to the throne was an old political problem, and a divorce in order to arrange a new marriage was advocated as early as 1514. Again in 1526 a divorce was suggested in order that closer relations might be established with France by means of a marriage between Henry and a French princess. Even when the increasing tenderness of Henry's conscience and the certainty that Catherine would have no more children brought up the question of a divorce again in 1527, Wolsey hoped that the remarriage of the King might be with the sister of the King of France.

Such was not Henry's idea. He had fallen in love with Anne Boleyn and wanted to marry her and have a legitimate heir by her. Wolsey might have given the necessary divorce by virtue of his legatine powers, and there were times when the Pope himself expressed a wish that he would do so and relieve him of responsibility. But Wolsey himself, convinced of his ability to persuade the Pope and anxious for its acceptance by other Governments, referred the matter to Rome.

There followed two years of tortuous diplomacy and, on the whole, consistent efforts on the part of Wolsey to secure from the Pope the decision which would alone satisfy the King and preserve his own ascendancy. At last the question was before Wolsey and his brother cardinal Campeggio at Blackfriars in London in what was destined to be the last of that long line of brilliant spectacles in which his scarlet cardinal's gown almost outshone the robes of sovereigns, nobles, and court functionaries. The course of events was too powerful even for the great cardinal. The divorce question was settled not in England nor in court, but in Italy and on the battle-field. The long Italian struggle between France and Spain was settled in favour of the latter; the Pope, who would willingly have given to Henry the customary permission to crowned heads to arrange their own marriage relations, accepted at the Treaty of Barcelona, June 29, 1529, the suzerainty of the King of Spain, against whose interest it was that the Pope should grant favours to England; the appeal of Catherine from the Blackfriars court to Rome was accepted by the Pope, July 23, and Wolsey recognised that he had failed Henry in his dearest wish. His failure left him defenceless before his enemies.

The steps in the alienation of the minister from his sovereign were taken slowly through the summer of 1529. The King's acts were dictated by his determination to take other measures to obtain his divorce, not by anger or hostility to Wolsey, which in fact he never showed even to the end. Positive action when it came emanated from the group of members of the privy council—Norfolk, Suffolk, Sir Thomas Boleyn, perhaps Sir Thomas More, who had long been hostile to him. When the blow fell it was sudden and crushing. On October 9, as Wolsey took his seat as Chancellor in Westminster Hall, on the other side of the Hall, before the judges of King's Bench, the Attorney-General indicted him for the offence of præmunire. On October 30 his sentence was announced; for in the meantime he had acknowledged the long series of charges made in the indictment and had thrown himself on the mercy of the King. He was declared guilty, and in accordance with the old law his lands and goods were declared forfeited to the King and his person put out of the King's protection. The procedure was rather a political than a judicial one. The statutes which created the offence of præmunire were passed, not to be applied, but to prevent the exercise of papal power in England except by consent of the King. That consent had frequently been given, and in the case of Wolsey had been given by Henry fully and in writing. But it was ill contending with a Tudor king. Moreover, Wolsey had reason to believe, or at least to hope, that this was only a disciplinary action on the part of the King, and that in good time he would be restored to office and to favour, and have his property returned.

It is true that the King immediately took possession of York House with all its contents, and habitually used it afterwards as one of his palaces, and ordered the seizure of all the rest of the fallen minister's property. On the other hand, he was allowed to retain his archbishopric of York with all its emoluments and a pension of £1,000 yearly from his bishopric of Winchester. He was also given about £7,000 in money and plate as part value of all his other possessions taken by the King. He was allowed to retire to Esher, a comfortable house formerly belonging to him as Bishop of Winchester, with a considerable household. The King also sent him messages of comfort and assurances of his continued kindly feelings. But he must give up the chancellorship, which was given to Sir Thomas More.

His old opponents were not so compassionate. When Parliament opened in November a committee of both Houses was appointed and drew up a long statement of the offences of the late minister. The flood of accusations reduced themselves to forty-five, and left few fields of Wolsey's activity untouched in their bitter complaints, and few of his sins unremembered and uncondemned. It was not in the form of an impeachment or a bill of attainder; it only asked the King that Wolsey " be so provided for that he never have any power, jurisdiction, or authority hereafter to trouble, vex, or impoverish the commonwealth."

The fall from such a height as Wolsey had attained, so complete a reversal of his policy, the condemnation of such a series of violations of law and charity as in his pride he had allowed himself to commit could hardly have occurred with less loss to dignity and consideration than it did. It would have been well for him if he had remembered that when such as he falls, " he falls, like Lucifer, never to hope again." But there remained a year of restless hoping and scheming for a return to power, with how much loyalty or disloyalty it is impossible to tell. Intrigues and suspicious actions reached the ears of the King and his councillors, and brought about Wolsey's banishment to his distant See of York. For a while it would seem that his restless spirit might find sufficient satisfaction in the unexpectedly cordial welcome given him by the people of his archdiocese, in the kindly services he was able to do them, in the repair of his neglected Church buildings, and in his religious duties. But his secret negotiations came to include the French and Spanish ambassadors, incriminating correspondence was seized, he awakened suspicion by calling a convocation at York for November 7, 1530, and issuing a general appeal for attendance by the gentry, clergy, and common people of the north, the old region of rebellion, at his enthronement as archbishop in the cathedral which he would see for the first time that day.

Without waiting for that day, at Cawood in Yorkshire, November 4, he was arrested for treason, and began a wearisome journey, the end of which would have been the Tower of London. But he was old, by the standards of that day—fifty-eight; he fell sick, and travelled only with difficulty and interruptedly. He lay ill at Leicester Abbey from November 26 to 29, and died on that day. He was buried in the abbey church early the next day and the unfinished tomb he had ordered in the days of his magnificence was turned over to the uses of his royal master.

The "native greatness" of Wolsey had been wasted in achieving an external greatness of ostentation, of wealth, of power, all for its own sake and without any serious object. There was a curious purposelessness in all he did: expenditure for the sake of expenditure, show for the sake of show, grandeur for the sake of small and momentary ends. He made no great acquirements for his king, his country, or even for himself, beyond such as were exhausted in the acquisition.

> "*Like little wanton boys that swim on bladders* . . .
> *This many summers in a sea of glory.*"

His foreign policy was opportunist. His greatest pupil, the King, reversed all his plans. His colleges, his proposed reforms in the Church and the law courts, which gave greatest promise of permanency, were founded on sand, and fell in the storm in which he fell. The biographer is baffled by the problem of the sterility of the career of so great a man.

JOHN FISHER
1469–1535

By

DOUGLAS WOODRUFF

JOHN FISHER

by DOUGLAS WOODRUFF

KING HENRY VII, who can claim on so many grounds
to be among the three or four in the first rank of our
post-Conquest sovereigns, wrote to his mother in the year
1504 that he was well minded to promote Master Fisher, her
Confessor, to a Bishopric

> " for none other cause but for the great and singular
> virtue that I know and see in him, as well in cunning
> and natural wisdom, and specially for his good and
> virtuous living and conversation. And by the pro-
> motion of such a man [he continued] I know well it
> should encourage many others to live virtuously, and to
> take such ways as he doth, which should be a good
> example to many others hereafter. Howbeit, without
> your pleasure known I will not move him nor tempt
> him therein. And therefore I beseech you that I may
> know your mind and your pleasure in that behalf,
> which shall be followed as much as God will give me
> Grace. I have in my days promoted many a man
> unadvisedly, and I would now make some recompense
> to promote some good and virtuous man, which I doubt
> not should best please God, who ever preserve you in
> good health and long life."

King Henry nominated and Pope Julius confirmed the
nomination, and John Fisher found himself Bishop of the
smallest and poorest but by no means the least important see
in England, that of Rochester, in Kent. He remained its
Bishop for over thirty years. Normally the see was a
stepping-stone, and his six immediate predecessors had all
been translated to grander Bishoprics, but Fisher refused any
further promotion. In the Rochester diocese was the palace

of Greenwich, the birthplace and favourite residence of the young King Henry VIII, and to the love of poverty which marked his private life the Bishop had this further motive for abiding at Rochester, that he felt bound by a special tie to the royal house, and had been specially charged by the mother of Henry VII to make her grandson's welfare his peculiar care. Fisher, who preached the funeral sermons for both Henry VII and his mother, owed much to the house of Tudor. His earlier life had been along a track well beaten by the feet of many men, the holy, the naturally able, the ambitious, who had made learning their ladder. He had gone to Cambridge as a tradesman's son from Beverly in Yorkshire. He had taken his degree in 1487, two years after Bosworth field; and while the first Tudor was by cautious steps consolidating the English monarchy, Fisher was advancing by steady progression till he was one of the leading men in the then diminished academic world of Cambridge which the royal bounty was through his offices to enlarge. In 1494, as Senior Proctor of Cambridge, he went to court for the first time, and the Proctors' Book has his entry of his expenses, with his statement, " I dined with the lady mother of the King." It was some years later, and Fisher had become master of his College (it was Michael House, later absorbed into Trinity) and Doctor of Divinity and Vice-Chancellor, that he became the Lady Margaret's confessor and began to turn the stream of her liberality towards his University. Christ's College and St. John's College, and the Lady Margaret chairs of divinity are the living monu-ments to the piety of that remarkable woman and to the zeal and Cambridge spirit of her confessor, who was no sooner established in her favour than he found himself elected Chancellor of Cambridge, year after year from 1504 onwards and finally for life. The Lady Margaret died in the same year as her son, 1509, when only the first steps had been taken in the foundation of St. John's. It was Fisher, as her executor, who carried the great work through in the next seven years, and Cambridge to-day by many a statue and portrait attests his position among the greatest of her benefactors.

Fifteenth-century Cambridge had been a poor shrunken place, its library no more than 330 books. No Greek lectures were given until 1511, and the heathen Latin poets were not much studied. The motive of Fisher and Henry

and Margaret was not at all the motive of contemporary
Renaissance scholars, the establishment of pagan learning.
Their aim was to maintain a supply of instructed and virtuous priests. Other men were great promoters of learning;
three generations of the royal house, Wolsey, Fox, all in
these years were making foundations at Oxford and Cambridge. The new foundations were one side of the new progress, but even before modern America learnt the lesson, it
had been found much easier to arrange for buildings and
endowments than to produce real scholars.

Fisher was the collector of what was said to be the best
private library in Europe. His enormous reading lay in all
the centuries of the Christian era, mainly of course in Latin.
He seems to have acquired, not a mastery of Greek, but a
working knowledge, for the reading of Erasmus' New Testament, and some Hebrew. What Greek he had, Fisher
acquired comparatively late in life, when he was nearing
fifty. The Greek lectures which Erasmus gave at Cambridge
were not well attended. His health was bad and there was
an outbreak of plague, but his appointment to the Lady
Margaret chair and a pension of a hundred florins a year
were tangible benefits for which he had to thank the
Chancellor Bishop. " A true Bishop and true theologian,"
he calls him, and writes, in 1510, " either I am greatly mistaken or Fisher is a man with whom no one in our time can
be compared, either for holiness of life or greatness of soul."

When Erasmus stayed with Fisher at Rochester, he wrote
to a friend that he had more than ten times regretted his
promise to make a ten-day stay, and there was more holiness
of life than he cared for at such close quarters. By a fortunate chance we can know very well how Fisher lived at
home in his own see, among the estuary marshes of Kent.
His palace overlooked the river, and Erasmus has no doubts
as to its unwholesomeness.

" I shrewdly suspect," he wrote to Fisher in 1525,
fifteen years after that visit of his own which he had
regretted, " that the state of your health principally
depends upon your situation. The near approach of
the tide, as well as the mud which is left exposed at every
reflux of the water, renders the climate unwholesome.
Your library, too, is surrounded with glass windows,
which let the keen air through the crevices. I know

how much time you spend in the library, which is to you a very paradise. As to me, I could not live in such a place three hours without being sick."

Apart from his books, Fisher had few possessions. Even a small bishopric, with but £300 or £400 a year, like Rochester, had other houses, one on the Surrey side of the Thames as a London residence, three in the country in Kent, and a considerable household, for a mediæval Bishop could not help being a considerable personage. Rochester was an unimportant place (in Elizabeth's reign it had but 144 houses inside the walls), and the household at the Palace was largely self-supporting. There are extant the inventories taken after the Bishop's committal to the Tower, and we can go through the rooms of the Palace as it was, and gain a vivid impression of its sparse and ascetic furnishing, a few leather-backed chairs, benches, trestles, shelves for books, with boxes and glasses of syrups, stilled water, and boxes of marmalade as the only things that could be considered luxuries, unless as luxuries be classed also the painted altar cloths that hung in the gallery and " a great looking-glass broken " in the little chamber next the Great Chapel. In this house he lived for thirty years, only varied by his necessary visits to Cambridge, to the Court, and to the outlying parts of his small diocese. His chief food was a thin pottage and he ate meat little and rarely, but he provided good and plentiful fare for his household and guests. He gave alms and food daily at the gate of his Palace, and used to watch the distribution himself after his own dinner. He recited his breviary daily with extreme care and devotion, " so that he seemed," says his earliest biographer, " a very devourer of heavenly food, never satiate nor filled therewith."

He was as ascetic over sleep as over food, spending much of the night in prayer and never sleeping for more than four hours at a stretch. He continually exhorted his household to frugality and thrift, and made his brother his steward, with the single injunction to keep him out of debt. The diocesan revenues and his other income he divided into three parts, one for the upkeep of his Cathedral, one for the relief of poverty and support of scholars, and the third for his household and the buying of books " whereof he had great plenty."

When a Carthusian praised to him his books against the

new heresies, " he said that he wished the time had been spent in prayer, knowing that prayer would have done more good and was of more merit."

His sermons, of which a good number remain in print—among the earliest sermons printed in English, and the forerunners of the torrents of centuries—are full of homely metaphor clothing the greatest earnestness. They are not at all the compositions of a Cambridge academic leader, but of a devout parish priest. At a time when men like Wolsey were gaily collecting Church offices, bishoprics, and livings, each of which was the undertaking of a serious responsibility towards the inhabitants of a particular district, Fisher was a reproach to worldly Churchmen, equally by the moderation of his own appetite for preferment and by the solemn piety with which he fulfilled his charge. He was particularly grieved by the low state into which preaching had fallen, and the prevalence of a slack custom of reading. Some of the greatest sermons have been read from a preacher's own manuscript, but the practice of reading from the compositions of other men can be the most lifeless and dreary performance. Fisher's writings in the vernacular are still extraordinarily alive. The reader of his series on the seven penitential Psalms of David finds his attention at once arrested by the intensity of the preacher, reaching across the centuries with the most searching doctrines of the Christian faith. The language has acquired a mellowed sweetness with the passage of time, but modern editors need make but a short glossary and very little alteration in spelling and punctuation, for men to read with ease what was being preached in the Rochester diocese four hundred and thirty years ago.

"All our life here we be sprinkled with the dust of sin, and peradventure some sinner will say, ' I perceive nor feel any weight in myself, do I never so many sins.' To whom we answer that if a dog, having a great stone bound about his neck, be cast down from a high tower, he feeleth no weight of that stone as long as he is falling down, but when he is once fallen to the ground he is burst all to pieces by reason of that weight. So the sinner going down towards the pit of Hell feeleth not the great burden of sin, but when he shall come into the depths of Hell he shall feel more pain than he would."

The imagery is direct and vivid, and the balance is held between the two dangers to the Christian, reckless presumption and reckless despair.

> " Nothing is more profitable to the sinner than to have a just moderation of them both. And nothing is more perilous than leaning more to the one than to the other. For the which thing St. Gregory compareth hope and dread unto two millstones wherewith meal is made. So it is, one millstone without a fellow made meet can do no good; but if the one be made fit with the other, that is to say, the overstone turned downward, and the nether contrariwise against it upward, with a due proportion of both, then shall the wheat put in the midst between them be shortly broken into many small pieces and in conclusion to meal. Likewise it is with sinners when hope is mixed with dread and dread with hope . . . so that, although the certainty of forgiveness be never so great, yet a remembrance be ever had of the fear of Almighty God, never to put it out of mind."

The men of his generation were more tempted to presumption, to the excessive reliance on mechanical and easily bought satisfaction without true contrition, or at the other extreme, to the rising Lutheran doctrine of justification by faith alone. There is in Fisher's preaching that note of the saints which makes them, from a kind of courtesy or good manners, refuse to risk belittling what he terms " man's unkindness to Almighty God," and while he will quote answers to Socrates or Demosthenes, and use Plato's division of the parts of the soul to explain his points, he makes more use of St. Jerome and St. Augustine, for their great love of penance, and dwells much on King David, whose repentance had given to the Church the Psalms which were her penitential prayers.

It is against this background of deep personal holiness and a ceaseless round of the works of mercy to which a Bishop is appointed, that the figure of the Bishop of Rochester must be seen as the main current of political history turns and gathers him into its course with the emergence of the King's divorce as the dominating question of the day. He began in high favour with the King. He rode with him to the Field of the Cloth of Gold in 1520. Henry and Fisher combated the first approaches of Lutheranism together. When in 1524 the King wrote his book against Luther and in defence of the Sacraments, it was Fisher who replied to Luther's counterblast. He wrote copiously in the years following Luther's final breach with the Church in 1520, and his books remained standard quarries for later generations of controversialists. In these books he was very soon concerned with the teaching authority of the Church and with the position of the Pope, not only as supreme guardian of revealed doctrine, but as the spiritual head of Christendom. The Turks, led by the great Sultan, Solomon the Magnificent, were sweeping onward. Rhodes fell in 1521, and the Knights of St. John were driven westwards to find a new island base at Malta. From many expressions Fisher shows how he felt Christendom to be besieged, driven back into a small corner of Europe with all Africa still waiting to have the Gospel preached there. He had no illusions about the need for a thorough reform of the Papal Court. He wrote, after replying to Luther:

" I do not however say this as if I were unwilling that the Pope or his Court should be reformed, if there is anything in their life divergent from the teaching of Christ. The people speak much against them, I know not with what truth. Still, it is constantly repeated that things are so. Would then that, if there is anything amiss, they would reform themselves, and remove the scandals from the souls of the weak. For it is greatly to be feared, unless they do so quickly, that Divine vengeance will not be long delayed. It is not, however, fitting that the Emperor or Lay Princes should attempt such a matter, and reduce them to a more frugal mode of life."

But he was not in any doubt about the primacy and jurisdiction of the Pope, and here was the matter where he was to incur the enmity of the King.

Early in 1527 Wolsey and Warham, as Papal Legate and Archbishop of Canterbury, asked for the opinions of the other bishops, whether the Pope could lawfully give a dispensation for a man to marry his brother's widow, or was such a marriage one of the things prohibited by the divine law and therefore beyond a dispensation? Fisher replied that, after fully weighing the matter, he had no doubts. " So that I am now thoroughly convinced that it can by no means be proved to be prohibited by any Divine Law that is now in force, that a brother marry the wife of his brother deceased without children." In any doubtful question, he continued, " the theologians of both sides grant that it belongs to the plenitude of the pontifical office to interpret ambiguous places of Holy Scripture, having heard the judgement of theologians and priests . . . and so," he wrote to Wolsey, " from these premisses no scruple or hesitation remains in my mind about the matter. I wish your Eminence long life and happiness." A vain wish, for Wolsey was to be a dead and ruined man within four years through the same question.

Wolsey stayed with Fisher during that summer of 1527, and sounded him to find out if Queen Catherine had been in touch with him, as she had. Fisher did not really come into the divorce till the end of the following year, when Cardinal Campeggio arrived in England with power to grant a new dispensation so that Henry's scruples might be set at rest, and he might continue, as he was still professing in public he ardently wished to do, with Catherine as his lawful wife. The Legate Campeggio was to sit with Wolsey and try the question. Queen Catherine asked for counsellors, and Fisher was her obvious choice. Campeggio, therefore, sought Fisher out and endeavoured to make him use his influence with Catherine to persuade her to become a nun, with the idea that such a course might make the annulling of a doubtful marriage feasible. It was not a scheme with much to recommend it to the Queen and her counsellors, nor was Fisher the man to give advice lightly. When he was asked later how many books (or, as we might now say, dissertations) he had prepared on the divorce question, he replied, " I am not certain of the number, but I think seven or eight. The matter was so serious, both on account of the importance of the persons concerned, and on account of the injunction given me by the king, that I devoted more attention to examining the truth of it, lest I should deceive myself and others, than to anything else in my life."

When the trial took place, in the Chapter House of Blackfriars (*The Times* office now covers the site), Fisher came forward with a boldness very irritating to Henry, and declared on his life and the salvation of his soul that he would stand by the validity of the marriage, and he alluded pointedly to John the Baptist, "who had thought it impossible to die more gloriously than in the cause of marriage." For a long time now the Bishop had kept in his private chapel at Rochester an image of the head of the Baptist. Henry was angered to the point of writing an answer, full of unbridled abuse against the Bishop. The King made one telling point in his answer, that it was Fisher's duty "as a religious and obedient prelate to acquiesce in the sentence of his holiness, who had sent judges here, admitting the necessity of the case, rather than thus accuse the Pope of levity, as if the cause which he had remitted here for decision was so clear, easy and obvious, that it was folly to call it in question."

To the margin of the MS. of this address is Fisher's comment: "It is not obvious to all, but only to those who are compelled to study it."

The attempted trial came to nothing, and Pope Clement recalled the case to Rome. The failure of Wolsey led to his disgrace, and at the end of the same year a Parliament was called and the royal attack on the clergy began. They were made to buy, for a huge sum, pardon for having acknowledged Wolsey as Legate, against the old statute forbidding the exercising of legatine authority. The laity, who had been equally guilty, were pardoned, and the clergy gained nothing by their instant submission, for they were required to acknowledge the King as supreme Head of the Church of England. When this demand came before Convocation in 1531, Fisher heartened them to resist, but Henry threatened and cajoled, and with a face-saving formula "as far as the law of God allows" the declaration was made. At first the clergy were thinking in terms of their jurisdiction and its supersession by that of the King's courts, and the question of the Pope's authority did not arise till the following year. Fisher accepted the saving clause and the new title for the King, but with great reluctance and misgivings. He was the leader among the Bishops of those who stood by Queen Catherine and so against the new legislation. He preached in favour of the Queen in June 1532, and spoke against Henry's Acts forbidding appeals to Rome in 1533.

But the divorce would wait no longer, for Anne Boleyn's child, the Princess Elizabeth, was nearing birth. Henry had to get a declaration from the clergy that he was free to marry Anne, and he had only a few months in which to get it. He bullied Convocation, and only Fisher stood out against him. So in April 1533, that he might be out of the way during the divorce of Catherine and marriage to Anne, Fisher was arrested and sent to the Tower, " which is a very strange thing," wrote the Ambassador of Charles V, " as he is the most holy and learned prelate in Christendom." After the coronation of the new Queen, he was released, in June. In July the Pope annulled everything that Cranmer had done, and issued his censure against the King and the new Queen. Fisher, according to the letters of the Imperial Ambassador, wanted the Emperor Charles to take up his niece's cause. Catherine, too, was convinced that if Pope and Emperor acted firmly, Henry and the Boleyn party could be brought to reason. Most of the English, said the Ambassador, were of the same opinion as the Bishop of Rochester, and were only afraid the Emperor would not listen. In the same way were appeals to be made a hundred and fifty years later, by those who hated James II, to bring a nephew in at the head of an army. Unlike those who invited over William of Orange, Fisher was a prominent theologian, consistent and logical, and his obedience to the King was ultimately a conditional obedience owed by a Christian man to a Christian King, but no longer owed if the King should violate his coronation oaths, and become the oppressor instead of the protector of religion. Charles did not act. He had his hands full with the Lutheran Princes in Germany, and the Turks and the French King on his frontiers, and Henry and Cromwell went forward with their policy of making the King supreme over the Church. An attempt was made at the end of 1533 to involve Fisher with the Holy Maid of Kent, an ecstatic who was prophesying evil to come to the King. She was executed with the priests around her, but Fisher was able to show that he had neither encouraged nor concealed her sayings. He was very ill throughout this winter, and only anxious to withdraw from the public scene.

It was in the April of 1534 that he was summoned to take the oath recognising Anne's children as successors to the throne, an oath in which the King's new claims to ecclesiastical supremacy were inserted. Fisher left Rochester for the last time, with little expectation of ever seeing it again.

He declared that he could not take the oath, and was sent to the Tower. The same treatment was meted out to Sir Thomas More, and the two illustrious prisoners were lodged on different floors of the Bell Tower. Fisher's prison was cold, and he lived in it in extreme poverty for over a year, paying, as was the custom, very large sums to his jailers for the barest necessities of life. During his imprisonment, the break with the Papacy was carried to its full lengths. When in 1533 the Papal Nuncio reproached Henry with reminders of what he had himself written on the side of the Pope's authority in his book against Luther, Henry replied that deeper study had convinced him he had been wrong, and added that it was possible yet more profound research might bring him round to his original view, it all depended on how the Pope behaved. The clergy had placed themselves at the King's mercy by their earlier acts of submission, and with Fisher in the Tower had no clear-sighted and courageous leader among the Bishops. Step by step they were made to renounce the Pope and to preach against him. But these startling changes were arousing growing hostility, and More and Fisher, as men of great reputation for holiness of life, learning, and incorruptibility, were a serious and potential danger to the King. As soon as they were imprisoned fears for their lives were entertained, but every effort was made to win them over to the King's side. Fisher was repeatedly visited by his fellow-bishops, who had accepted the Royal Supremacy. When these efforts were seen to be vain, he was arraigned for high treason, an Act being passed making it high treason to refuse to take an oath acknowledging the supremacy. Under this Act the prior of the London Carthusians, and some others, were executed in May 1535.

In the same month the new Pope, Paul III, named Fisher as a cardinal. When he was told how this angered the King, Paul declared that he had thought to give particular pleasure to Henry VIII. The new Cardinals were being elected with a view to the summoning of the General Council which met afterwards at Trent, and there was no man in Europe better qualified than Fisher to take part in such a General Council. It is equally possible that it was hoped that the honour would prove an added protection. In fact, it made him more formidable, and Henry, egged on by the Boleyn faction, resolved on immediate death. He was brought to a typical Tudor trial in the middle of June, and every attempt was made to produce witnesses to say that, while in the Tower, he had denied the King's supremacy. He was at the time too sick to ride from the Tower to Westminster Hall and was carried much of the way by water. He was easily found guilty and condemned to the usual death at Tyburn for High Treason, but this was changed, of the King's goodness, to beheading on Tower Hill. The sentence of June 17 was carried out on the 22nd, before a great concourse of people, who were horrified at the emaciated figure which emerged when his garments were stripped from him. He had been too weak to walk to the scaffold, but his usual high courage shone through all the final actions of his long life. He was not permitted to say much, and only explained that he was dying because he would not deny one of the articles of the Catholic Faith, and asked for the prayers of the bystanders " that at the very point and instant of death's stroke, I may in that very moment stand steadfast, without fainting in any one point of the Catholic faith, free from any fear." It is related that the procession from the Tower had halted a few minutes at the outer precinct, till it was ascertained that the Sheriffs were already at the scaffold, and that the Bishop opened the New Testament which he was carrying, and prayed, saying : " O Lord, this is the last time that ever I shall open this book, let some comfortable place now chance unto me, whereby I, thy poor servant, may glorify thee in this my last hour," and, opening the book, read in the seventeenth chapter of St. John's Gospel : " Haec est autem vita æterna. . . . This is life eternal, that they may know thee the only true God, and Jesus Christ whom thou hast sent. I have glorified thee upon earth, I have finished the work that thou gavest me to do."

Politically, however, the execution of More and Fisher was a successful stroke. It was now doubly plain that no one was safe who should oppose the royal will. The execution of a Cardinal, after the French King had specially pleaded for his life, showed that neither rank nor influence would avail the King's subjects. The policy of ruthlessness and of the strong hand succeeded, and Henry made himself master of the clergy, not only over their property, but over the doctrines they were to teach.

Fisher was cast in the mediæval mould, a bishop of the old order of Christendom, a man who would have been well at home contending at Clarendon with Henry II for the rights of the spiritual order. The destruction of Wolsey, who was a symbolical figure, representative of the worldly side of mediæval churchmanship, summing up in himself with his assembled powers and revenues the strengths and weaknesses of his order, prefigured the coming fall of the clergy at whose head he stood. Fisher represents another tradition of a quieter and nobler sort. He is in the succession to Anselm and Hugh of Lincoln and Edmund of Abingdon, men who were the counsellors of kings, but who also withstood them because Kings had no claim to absolute obedience. With him, the great company of the saintly bishops of mediæval England close their tremendous record on the high note of a voluntary death.

SIR THOMAS MORE

1478–1535

By

R. W. CHAMBERS

SIR THOMAS MORE

by R. W. CHAMBERS

FROM his own day to ours, Sir Thomas More has always appeared to the practical Anglo-Saxon mind as a paradoxical figure.   When we learn, in our schooldays, of the lawyer who was decapitated because he could not tell a lie, we are moved by feelings of respect, tempered by astonishment; like the little American girl when she read the story of the boy who stood on the burning deck, we are inclined to say, " I think he was very good; but he wasn't very smart."

A boy grows into a man, and a man on rare occasions into an eminent historian, into a Froude, or an Acton, or a Creighton.   The respect for More remains; and though the grounds for the perplexity may have shifted, the perplexity remains also.   To our great historians More is either an incomprehensible riddle, or else, as he is described in the forefront of a biography published last year, " a bundle of antitheses."

From those who adhere to the faith for which More died, he has generally received a tribute of complete and understanding sympathy.   Elsewhere, however (and sometimes even among those of his own faith), More is regarded as a daring innovator, who somehow or other became one more example of " the lost leader," one more example of the Triumphs of the World:

> " *Behold*," she cries, " *so many rages lull'd,*
> *So many fiery spirits quite cool'd down.*"

As to the cause of this change, historians are not agreed. Some eminent writers put it down to the bad influence of Henry VIII.   More allowed his sentiments to be moulded by the official theology of the court, till under that sinister influence he was changed from a " liberal " into a " pseudo-liberal." Creighton and Acton had their little quarrels, but upon this estimate of More they are in complete agreement. Froude also agrees, except that his respect for Henry VIII will not allow of that monarch retaining the part of More's misleader, a rôle which in Froude's pages has to be undertaken by the Roman Catholic Church: it was that which turned the " genial philosopher " into the " merciless bigot."

Thirty years ago, the great English biographer and organiser of English biography, Sidney Lee, expressed the traditional English view of More:

> " None who read the *Utopia* can deny that its author drank deep of the finest spirit of his age. There is hardly a scheme of social or political reform that has been enunciated in later epochs of which there is no definite adumbration in More's pages. But he who passes from the speculations of More's *Utopia* to the record of More's subsequent life and writings will experience a strange shock. Nowhere else is he likely to be faced by so sharp a contrast between precept and practice, between enlightened and vivifying theory in the study, and adherence in the workaday world to the unintelligent routine of bigotry and obscurantism. By the precept and theory of his *Utopia* More cherished and added power to the new light. By his practical conduct in life he sought to extinguish the illuminating forces to which his writing offered fuel.
>
> " The facts of the situation are not open to question . . . Sir Thomas More's career propounds a riddle which it is easier to enunciate than to solve."

Yet one thing is clear. There is no sixteenth-century Englishman as to whom there exists more intimate information. If we wish to solve the " riddle of his career," there is no one whose motives we can learn to appreciate so fully. More's son-in-law, William Roper, " knowing at this day no one man living, that of him and of his doings understood so much as myself," wrote, in Queen Mary's reign, his deeply understanding notes on More's life. Nicholas Harpsfield, in the same reign, wrote a careful official biography. An even more elaborate biography by More's nephew, William Rastell, has been lost, but some priceless fragments remain. Had it not been for Rastell, much of More's written work might have been lost also. The reminiscences of the young people who had lived with More in the Great House at Chelsea were collected by yet a fourth biographer. The family tradition did not finally work itself out till a fifth biographer and a sixth (Cresacre More, More's great-grandson) had told the story.

Even more important are More's own writings. In *Utopia* More expressed the hopes and fears for the world which moved the humanist circle surrounding Erasmus and himself. More's defence of the things for which he most cared is extant in his voluminous controversial and devotional writings. And, in his letters, we can trace his thoughts (especially during his last months of imprisonment) in a way which is possible with only very few of the great characters of history.

Yet, abundant as this material is, much of it has only been made easily accessible during the past eight years, and much of it is not easily accessible even now. The misunderstanding of More is chiefly due to neglect of what he has himself written, and also in some degree to neglect of what his biographers tell us.

Let us take a single paragraph from Roper's *Life*, and see what we can get from a study of it.

As an example of the " fruitful communication " which he "had ofttimes with his familiar friends," Roper records a conversation in which More told him of the three great wishes of his life:

" So on a time, walking with me along the Thames' side at Chelsea, in talking of other things he said unto me : ' Now would to our Lord, son Roper, upon condicion that three things were well established in Christendom, I were put in a sack, and here presently cast into the Thames.'

" ' What great things be those, Sir,' quoth I, ' that should move you so to wish ? '

" ' Wouldst thou know what they be, son Roper ? ' quoth he.

" ' Yea, marry, with good will, sir, if it please you,' quoth I.

" ' In faith, son, they be these,' said he. ' The first is, that where the most part of Christian princes be at mortal war, they were all at an universal peace. The second, that where the Church of Christ is at this present sore afflicted with many errors and heresies, it were settled in a perfect uniformity of religion. The third, that where the king's matter of his marriage is now come in question, it were to the glory of God and quietness of all parties brought to a good conclusion.' Whereby, as I could gather, he judged that otherwise it would be a disturbance to a great part of Christendom."

We can date this conversation pretty exactly—it must have been after the King's marriage had come in question, but before the peace of Cambrai, in which More took a big part, and by which England secured the only long-continued cessation from foreign warfare which this country enjoyed during the troubled reign of Henry VIII. More, when he spoke these words, was a man of fifty, and was shortly to become Lord Chancellor. He could look back on a life of public service. Born of a family of London lawyers, he was taught the ways of the great whilst still a boy, by service in the household of Cardinal Morton. He was subsequently trained as a lawyer at Lincoln's Inn, after a short spell of education at Oxford. This was a combination which, though it may seem natural enough to us to-day, was rare in More's time—but it is typical of More's two great interests. Oxford, with its theological training, led to the secular priest-hood or the cloister—a calling which throughout his life had a great attraction for More. Lincoln's Inn and the Law led to the political career which, after a period of hesitation between the Church and the Law, was to be More's vocation. Like some great modern statesmen, More came to political life after an apprenticeship in the service of his city. For nearly eight years he had been one of the two Under-Sheriffs of London. The post was then a very important one, for the Sheriffs had to perform legal duties for which, being men of business rather than lawyers, they had not usually any special qualifications, and their permanent legal officials conse-quently carried a considerable responsibility. Then More left the service of the city for that of Henry, and for nearly a dozen years had been rising in political life when this con-versation with his son-in-law took place.

The passion for universal peace was one which More shared with his humanist friends, and above all with Colet and Erasmus. During the twenty years of Henry's reign England had been plunged into one futile campaign after another, till the accumulated wealth of Henry VII had been wasted, and the resources of the country so exhausted as to make for a time any further war impossible. No danger had been averted and no advantage gained; historians have been puzzled to find any justification or even explanation of Henry's wars. There was comparatively little fighting, but the waste of treasure was enormous. All these useless wars More detested. Yet his ideal was anything but a policy of selfish isolation for England. It is because he cares for Europe, not because he ignores Europe, that More is a lover of peace. The humanists were hoping for a Reformation by reason and argument, not by violence. If this was to be brought about, it could only be in an atmosphere of European peace. The humanists were an international body, very closely knit together. Their greatest danger lay in the rising passions of nationalism. We may take Erasmus as their great example. To Erasmus, Europe was one great State. For Holland, as the country of his birth, he had a certain love, combined with a feeling that it was rather a provincial backwater, remote from the real centres of civilisation. His feeling towards his country was very much what an Englishman long resident in London, where he has grown eminent, might cherish towards a remote county of agriculturists and fishermen in which he happened to have been born and bred, and where poor relations still lived. Erasmus has a sentimental combination of affection and dislike for Holland, but Europe is the country which demands his allegiance.

More's feelings are much more complicated: he is a thoroughly loyal Englishman. But we can never understand More if we allow ourselves to forget the Great Turk. The threat to the whole of Christian civilisation from the marauding bands of Asia was a very real thing to him. That Christian princes should be struggling one against another whilst Belgrade and Rhodes were falling, and whilst all the chivalry of Hungary perished on the field of Mohacz, till the Turk reached the gates of Vienna, seemed to More to be treachery to the common cause. There were pacifists in More's day, who held that the Turk was a divinely appointed scourge, and that Christians should allow themselves to be enslaved and butchered without offering resistance. More disagrees, and (in language which has found an echo in later ages) he complains that these pacifists are so pugnacious. But More feels that war between Christian princes is detestable. The wars of Christendom are, to him, civil wars.

This balance and combination of loyalties brings More very closely into touch with problems of to-day. To More, the whole question cannot be entirely settled by allegiance to a king, or loyalty to the country in which a man happens to have been born. Yet he would have been the last to deny the binding power of these obligations.

Few in these days will censure More for his longing for peace among the states of Europe; there will in some quarters be less sympathy for his second aspiration, that whereas the Church is afflicted with many errors and heresies, it were settled in perfect uniformity. More was very frank as to his hatred of heretics. The accusation that he was himself a bitter persecutor can be refuted; but the fact remains that he believed it necessary to prohibit " the sowing of seditious heresies "; and he believed that, in extreme cases, it was right to punish with death those who defied this prohibition.

Seditious heresies. Emphasis must be laid upon the adjective. To those who were in any kind of doubt or spiritual trouble, More was always the gentlest of counsellors. His son-in-law, Roper, had in his youth a violent bout of Lutheranism. More and he lived together in the same house, and argued together constantly, but Roper records that he never knew More lose his temper: never knew him " in a fume." People in spiritual difficulties, troubled with " vehement and grievous tentations of desperation," would come to More for advice. At the time when More was Chancellor, and at the height of his controversy with the Lutherans, a distinguished Lutheran scholar, Simon Grinæus, needed to come to England to consult manuscripts of Plato and commentaries thereon, in the College libraries of Oxford. More entertained him hospitably, and gave him every possible assistance, only insisting on a promise that his guest would not spread his heresies during his stay in England. Grinæus acknowledged More's kindness by dedicating his work, when published, to More's son John. Rather naïvely, Grinæus emphasises the enormous personal trouble More took, accompanying him everywhere, and, when that was not possible, sending as escort his secretary, a young scholar, John Harris. Grinæus would have been pained had he known that, in fact, More had very little belief in the value of any heretic's promise. We know from John Harris himself that he was instructed to see that Grinæus issued no pernicious propaganda; if Grinæus had done so, More would have bundled him out of the kingdom unceremoniously. But, so long as he behaved, More showed him untiring generosity and kindness. And also, amid all the cares of office, More spent many hours in a vain attempt to bring Grinæus back into the fold, first by discussion in his home, and later by correspondence. Nor was this merely the freemasonry of scholarship. More would have been even gentler with a poor and ignorant heretic than with a learned one. "Little rigour and much mercy should be showed," he said, "where simpleness appeared, and not high heart or malice." More argued eloquently that the whole Bible might be suffered to be spread abroad in English among the laity. His sense of discipline was too strong to allow him to press this claim against the opinion of the bishops; but under episcopal supervision, at any rate, translations of the Bible should be issued, he thought, and even issued, where necessary, gratis. But it must be an authorised translation, made by the most responsible scholars. At a time when civil war might break out over the interpretation of a biblical text, More denied the right of Tyndale or any individual to issue his translation of the Bible on his own authority. The public and deliberate defiance of authority in matters of religion was, to More, sedition; and, like other forms of sedition, might, in extreme cases, merit the death penalty. But the trial and definition of heresy were matters for the bishops, not for him, a layman.

Why should More be blamed for holding views which everybody held in his age, and many people in a much sterner and more cruel form than he? Because, it is answered, he had shown, a dozen years before, in *Utopia*, that he knew better.

More has suffered the fate of many pioneers, in that he has been interpreted in the light of those who have followed him. *Utopia* has been followed by a long series of "Ideal Commonwealths," often written in direct imitation. Francis Bacon in the *New Atlantis*, and William Morris in *News from Nowhere*, have drawn pictures of the world as they would like to see it. So *Utopia* has been christened an "ideal commonwealth." The citizens of Utopia are not depicted as insisting on any dogma except in the existence of God and the immortality of the soul. Therefore, it has been argued, More believed the vague deism of the Utopians more " ideal " than the Catholic faith of his own day. And it is certainly the case with the romance of William Morris, that it represents the writer's ideal—the world as he would have it, if he could shatter it to bits and remould it nearer to the heart's desire. But if we want to understand *Utopia* or *News from Nowhere*, we must think of the first as published in 1516, and the second as published in 1890.

More's education was Mediæval; and the Middle Ages recognised many kinds of law: canon law and common law, the law of God and the law of nature. In 1516 one of the most burning questions of the day was whether, apart from revelation, nature and philosophy taught that the soul was immortal. Three years before, this question had led to an important decision of the Lateran Council. By that decision teachers of philosophy were put in their place. They were instructed to point out the difference between the merely philosophical and the Christian view as to the immortality of the soul.

More's contribution to the discussion is to depict a Commonwealth based entirely upon the law of nature and on philosophy, the Commonwealth of Utopia. But the views of the Commonwealth, as to what philosophy can teach regarding the immortality of the soul, are actually stricter than those of Christians. So far is the Utopian Commonwealth from having any doubts about immortality, that the man who does not accept the immortality of the soul is not allowed to rank as a citizen, or even as a man. The Utopians cannot believe that a man who holds that the soul perishes with the body can be anything but a potential criminal, restrained from felony only by his cowardice, " and thus he is of all sorts despised, as of an unprofitable and of a base and vile nature." And then comes the sentence upon which are based the many laudations of the toleration of Utopia: " Howbeit, they put him to no punishment." No punishment, indeed! It is a mere mistranslation, as More's critics might have seen, if they would have referred back to the Latin original.

In Utopia, as in ancient Sparta, where all life was lived in common, to be sent to Coventry was a living death. What More really wrote was that the unbeliever is not put to any bodily punishment. The Utopians do not threaten him with violence, to make him dissemble his disbelief. He may, in private, with learned men, even argue in defence of it. On the same principle More, whilst silencing Simon Grinæus publicly, was willing to spend long hours in trying to convert him privately. So the Utopian disbeliever in immortality is not allowed to counter the public odium by defending himself *publicly* in argument. And nobody, in Utopia, is allowed to argue vehemently or violently about religion. If he does so, he is punished with bondage. If still recalcitrant, the bondsman is punished with death.

An inhabitant of Utopia has little liberty, as little as a warrior in the Spartan State, or an inmate of a monastery, although the Utopian has an easier life than either. Utopia is indeed modelled on the Spartan and the monastic disciplines, with the austerities of both alleviated. That God exists, and that in an after-state vice is punished and virtue rewarded, are the only Utopian religious dogmas. But there is a Utopian State religion—a kind of greatest common measure of all the different religions prevalent among the Utopians. In their dark churches an elaborate ritual is practised with music, vestments, incense, and candles. The Utopian priests are inviolate. And the Utopians believe in miracles, which happen among them very often. It is odd that, a year before Luther began his attack by fastening the Ninety-five theses to the church door at Wittenberg, More should have singled out so many things which the Protestants were later to impugn. More makes them part of the State religion of Utopia—a religion based upon reason, and containing nothing that any reasonable man can object to, More thinks.

More is very careful to point out that the Catholic Church has many practices to which a man would not be led by his unaided reason. From his early manhood to the day before his death, More from time to time wore a hair shirt, and followed other ascetic practices. Reason, the Utopians hold, would not lead a man to such austerities, " unless any goodlier opinion be inspired into man from Heaven." There are celibate ascetics in Utopia; the Utopians would ridicule them if they based their austerities on reason; but as they base them on religion, the Utopians honour them.

But what comes out most emphatically in Utopia is the prophetic fear which More, the humanist reformer, felt of the violent reformer. Any man who, in Utopia, *attacks* any established religion, even though it be idolatrous and super-stitious, in the interests of his own purer and more spiritual religious outlook, is liable to be punished with bondage, and, if still recalcitrant, with death. It is one of the weak points of Utopia, that any kind of reformation is impossible. More has guarded his citizens so strenuously against violence, that they seem to have nothing before them but a monotonous eternity of the benevolent despotism of their patriarchal constitution. No man may use contentious rebuking or inveighing against any of the recognised religions of Utopia upon pain, first of bondage, and then of death. But con-tentious rebuking and inveighing was the stock-in-trade of the Protestant Reformer. As More said of the Reformers, " In railing standeth all their revel." A Protestant Reformer in Utopia, who publicly derided miracles, vest-ments, music, incense, candles, the inviolability of the priest-hood, and salvation by works, would soon have sighed for the toleration of England in the days of Chancellor More.

More's third wish, as he walked along the Thames, side by side with Roper, was for a settlement, to the satisfaction of all parties, of the question of Henry's marriage with Catherine of Aragon, because otherwise he saw that it would be a disturbance to a great part of Christendom. Many reasons combined to make More long for this good conclusion : firstly, his sympathy and friendship with Catherine. He had hailed her with enthusiasm when, some twenty-seven years before, he watched her entering London as Prince Arthur's bride. " There is nothing wanting in her," he had said, " which the most beautiful girl should have." Since that time she had been his gracious hostess many and many a year : she and her consort had so enjoyed More's company that they had asked him, when the day's routine was done and after the Council had supped, to be merry with them. This happened so fre-quently that not once in a month could More get leave to go home to his wife and children.

But, apart from the personal question, the separation of Henry from Catherine meant a quarrel between England and the Emperor Charles ; yet, on the friendship between those two, in More's view, all hopes of permanent European peace and stability rested. But the threat to European unity was more deadly even than that. If the Emperor

opposed the divorce, and the Pope would not grant it, then
Henry had his own solution. So far as England was concerned, Henry would be King, Emperor, and Pope all in
one; he would be Supreme Head of the English Church, and
his Archbishop of Canterbury should declare him to be still
a bachelor.

Wolsey's failure to achieve any solution on less drastic lines
led to his fall, and More was commanded to fill Wolsey's
place as Chancellor. More tried to avoid the dangerous
honour. Already the King had consulted him on the
divorce question, and he had been unable to accept the royal
view. But when Henry had promised More that in prosecuting the matter of the divorce he would use only those
whose consciences were persuaded, while those who thought
otherwise he would use in other business, More had no
excuse for refusing office. The judicial side of his office he
transacted with a dispatch and incorruptibility which,
together with his reputation as a jester, made him one of the
most popular figures of sixteenth-century tradition.

Otherwise his short Chancellorship was a succession of
disappointments and humiliations. The business of the
divorce went on, and with it the King's claim to be Supreme
Head of the Church of England. Finally, on May 15, 1532,
came the event which, if there be any one such event, must
mark the beginning of modern England. The clergy of
England made their submission to the King. It is here that
we should make, if we make it anywhere, the division
between Mediæval life and our Modern life. The fact that
this division cuts into the middle of a dynasty and of a reign
is all to the good, because it emphasises the fact that you can
mark no deep gulf between Mediæval and Modern history.
The deepest is here. Within ten years every Abbey in
England had been dissolved, and they were in rapid process
of conversion into gentlemen's country mansions. The
epoch which had begun with the landing of St. Augustine
and his monks in 597 had come to its close. In the Refec-
tory of (shall we say) Northanger Abbey, in 1530, St.
Augustine, the Venerable Bede, Thomas Becket, and
Thomas More might all have felt at home. Nothing except
some slight differences in the pronunciation of their Latin
would have prevented them from understanding each other
perfectly. Ten years after More's death, Northanger Abbey
has just been adapted out of the old monastic remains by

5   113

Master Tilney, of the Court of Augmentations. Imagine Jane Austen paying him a visit. . She would soon have got used to the archaic fashions and archaic English of her host, and, as he showed her with pride the remodelled kitchens, where every invention had been adopted to facilitate the labour of the cooks, she would have remarked to him that " his endowments of that spot alone might at any time have placed him high among the benefactors of the convent."

On May 15 the clergy made their submission. On May 16 More resigned the Chancellorship. His public career, then, had fallen entirely within what we may call the Monastic or Mediæval Period of English history. Mommsen has remarked that, when an age is passing away, Destiny seems to allot to it one last great figure, so that it may not pass without honour and dignity. More is the last great hero of Mediæval England.

What followed is among the best-known episodes of English history.

For a time, More was permitted to live quietly in his Chelsea home, carrying on his controversy with the heretics. But his refusal to be present at the coronation of Anne Boleyn embittered the quarrel, and an attempt was made to involve him in the matter of the " Holy Maid of Kent." His proved innocence saved him, but on April 13, 1534, he was summoned before the royal commissioners at Lambeth. Roper tells us that he would not allow his wife and children to follow him, as they usually did, to the riverside, " but pulled the wicket after him, and shut them all from him, and with a heavy heart, as by his countenance it appeared, with me and our four servants there took his boat toward Lambeth. Wherein sitting still sadly a while, at the last he suddenly rounded me in the ear, and said: ' Son Roper, I thank our Lord the field is won.' " More was quite willing to swear the oath recognising Elizabeth as heir to the throne, for that was a matter on which he considered himself bound by the decision of Parliament. But, in the form in which the oath was tendered, he could not take it without renouncing the spiritual authority of the Pope, and that he would not do. More was sent to the Tower, attainted, and all his goods confiscated. Subsequently an Act was passed making it high treason maliciously to attempt to deprive Henry of his titles, one of which was Head of the Church. More took refuge in silence, but the Solicitor-General, Rich, was prepared to swear that More, in conversation with him in the Tower, had said that Parliament could not make the King Supreme Head of the Church. More denied this, and there is no doubt that Rich was lying. But More was found guilty, and sentenced to death. After condemnation he felt it his duty to speak out, stating that England " might not make a particular law, disagreeable with the general law of Christ's Universal Catholic Church, no more than the City of London might make a law against an Act of Parliament to bind the whole realm." After some friendly words to his judges, he was taken back to the Tower. On the way, his daughter Margaret, " pressing in among the midst of the throng and company of the guard, that with halberds and bills went round about him, hastily ran to him, and there openly in the sight of them all, took him about the neck and kissed him." On the fifth day after, he was executed on Tower Hill. A depressed Winchester man, obsessed by " very vehement and grievous tentations of desperation," had in old days found comfort from his advice. As More passed to execution, " he thrust through the throng and with a loud voice said, ' Mr. More, do you know me? I pray you for our Lord's sake help me : I am as ill troubled as ever I was.' Sir Thomas answered, ' I remember thee full well. Go thy ways in peace, and pray for me : and I will not fail to pray for thee.' " More made (according to Henry's wish) only a brief speech from the scaffold, stating that he suffered " in and for the faith of the Holy Catholic Church," and that he died " the King's faithful servant, but God's first."

More's claims to distinction are very various. He was a member of that earliest group of Greek scholars, with whom English humanism begins. He was High Steward of Oxford and Cambridge, an educational pioneer, particularly enthusiastic about the education of women. As a writer of English prose, his position is specially important. It was not till long after his day that anyone could rival his mastery of many different types of English : dramatic dialogue and rhetorical monologue, narrative and argument combined in a style at once scholarly and colloquial. More's *History of Richard III* remained a pattern of historical writing unequalled for a century. His death as a martyr " for the faith of the Catholic Church " was at the same time a protest against the claim of the civil power to dictate religious belief, and should make him the hero of all who care for religious liberty. For over twenty years he exercised important judicial functions of different kinds, and it was his promptitude and incorruptibility as a judge that most impressed his countrymen. It is as " the best friend that the poor e'er had " that his fellow Londoners remembered him, in the old play of *Sir Thomas More*. Swift had learnt from *Utopia* many of the things which make *Gulliver's Travels* remarkable, and he repaid his teacher by giving him the magnificent testimonial, of being the person " of the greatest virtue this kingdom ever produced."

WILLIAM TINDALE

1495(?)–1537

By

A. W. REED

WILLIAM TINDALE

by A. W. REED

ONE of the difficulties of writing of William Tindale is that while he lived in England he was an obscure man and that the rest of his life—the last twelve years—was spent abroad in concealment. His first biographer, Foxe, to whom he was " the apostle of England in this our later age," knew no more of his early life than that he was born " about the borders of Wales "; that he graduated at Oxford, where he read privily " some parcels of divinity " with certain students and fellows; that " spying his time " he moved to Cambridge, and that he left Cambridge to join the household of " Master Welch, a knight of Gloucestershire." He left Cambridge to return to his native county.

He was born of yeoman stock in the lowlands by the Severn Estuary about the year 1495. Even More knew nothing of his parentage; but he had two brothers: Edward who became under-receiver of crown-rents for the lordship of Berkeley and was described in 1533 by the Bishop of London as " brother to Tindale, the arch-heretic," and John, a merchant of London who was fined in 1530 for assisting William in circulating his New Testament. As if to add to the difficulties of his biographer, Tindale described himself as late as 1528 as " William Tindale *alias* Hychins," and it is under the name Hychins that he appears in the Registers of Oxford. His college, Magdalen, held the advowson of the rectory of Slymbridge (his birthplace), and assigned, according to legend, the Slymbridge tithes to the maintenance of the May Day singing from the College Tower. It was as Hychins that in July 1515 he was admitted Master of Arts.

In a way, Tindale's Oxford days fell either too early or too late. Earlier he might have been directly inspired, as Erasmus was in 1499 at Oxford, by the new impulse that

Colet was giving to the study of the Bible by his lectures on the Pauline Epistles. Later he would have had the company of a select band of young humanists surrounded by books of the classical revival gathered by Fox for his new college of Corpus Christi. On the other hand, had he spent at Cambridge the years he spent at Oxford, he would have met Erasmus, who was then dividing his time (1509–14) between Cambridge and London.

Before Tindale reached Cambridge, Erasmus had completed his New Testament, and by 1516 had seen it through the press. It was the first edition of the Greek Testament to appear in print; but it was much more than that. Together with the Greek were Erasmus' own Latin translation and his annotations. It was dedicated to Leo X; and a Papal brief commending it appeared in the second edition of 1519. It is important to realise the impetus which the humanism of Erasmus gave to the movement in which Tindale was to play his part. It is not less important to recognise that it was Colet and the English humanists who had inspired Erasmus to do for the New Testament what had already been done for the Greek classics. Nor was it in the mind of Erasmus that he was working for scholars only. " I wish," he wrote in his prefatory *Exhortation* to the second edition, " that the Gospels and the Epistles of St. Paul were translated into all languages of all people. . . . I wish that the husbandman may sing parts of them at his plough and the weaver at his shuttle, and that the traveller may with their narratives beguile the weariness of the way "; words that were afterwards to be closely echoed by Tindale. Five editions of his New Testament appeared in the lifetime of Erasmus, and with each edition his annotations grew in volume, interest, and frankness. At the same time he issued companion volumes of commentaries under the title of *Paraphrases*. In fact, he was giving to the question, " What is the New Testament ? " the answer of a humanist; and he found a northern printer, Froben of Basel, to work with him. He had not to take his work to the Italian printers of Greek texts. Yet a larger question, " What is the Bible ? " had already as early as 1502 been put as a central problem to his new University of Alcalá by its founder, Cardinal Ximenes; for to it he had assigned the task which Aldus had not attempted, of printing the whole Bible in its original languages. Indeed, the printing of the Greek Testament had been completed at Alcalá before Erasmus left England, but the sheets had to lie idle until the Old Testament was set up. The death of Ximenes in 1517 doubtless delayed this work, and it was not until 1522 that the great Polyglott Bible reached Erasmus. It has been necessary to say so much of Erasmus and the other pioneers because it is easy to exaggerate the historical importance of Tindale's later undertakings. The door had, in fact, been opened at which he was to push.

If Foxe's words, "spying his time," mean anything, they suggest that Tindale escaped from an environment at Oxford in which he was not comfortable to a more agreeable atmosphere at Cambridge. It must be supposed that there he met Bilney, an ardent evangelical reformer who attributed his conversion to " the New Testament set forth by Erasmus " (1516). Presumably also he met Latimer and other converts of little Bilney. And at Cambridge these Erasmophiles would hear of Luther's challenge at Wittenberg in 1517; and would follow with interest the progress of his revolt up to his excommunication in 1520. Up to this point Erasmus himself had sympathised with Luther; but after Luther's burning of the Bull and his condemnation at the diet of Worms, he saw schism looming ahead; and Erasmus stood loyal, working for a healing of the schism rather than with the extremists of either side.

We leave the Cambridge days, vague and undocumented, and pass to Gloucestershire, where Tindale, now in orders, became chaplain and " schoolmaster " to a wealthy Cotswold landowner, Sir John Walshe of Little Sodbury. At Walshe's table he met, according to Foxe, distinguished churchmen from the neighbouring religious houses, and when talk turned, inevitably, on Erasmus, Luther, and the Scriptures he irritated them by his insistence on plain scriptural evidence. To satisfy, it may be, his master and mistress, and confound his opponents, he translated a moral handbook—the *Encheiridion Militis Christiani*—to which Erasmus had recently added a new Preface (1518), trouncing the obscurantists who had attacked his New Testament. But, not content with the discomfiture of " great beneficed doctors " at the hospitable table of Sir John and Lady Walshe, Tindale preached in the neighbouring villages to the plowmen, weavers, and wayfarers, and his teaching " savoured sometimes so shrewdly (of heresy) that he was

5*

once or twice examined thereof, but glosing his words with a better sense," he escaped with a warning. It was at this period, according to Foxe, that Tindale became convinced that the Pope and the whole organisation that he controlled was that *Antichrist* of whom St. John speaks in his First Epistle: " Little children, it is the last time: and as ye have heard that antichrist shall come, even now are there many antichrists; whereby we know that it is the last time." It was to this period also that Foxe assigns Tindale's determination to do for the common people what Erasmus had done for scholars, by giving them the Scriptures in their own language.

In 1523 he left Little Sodbury for London, determined to translate the Scriptures into English; and there he must soon have learned, if he did not already know it, that in 1522 Luther had translated the New Testament into German. He carried with him letters of introduction to Sir Henry Guildford, Master of the Horse, and, as evidence of his competence in Greek, a translation of an oration of Isocrates. Guildford advised him to approach Tunstall, Bishop of London. Tindale applied to the Bishop for a chaplaincy in his household, but it is not related whether he spoke of his proposal to translate the Scriptures. " My lord answered me," said Tindale, " his house was full, he had more than he could find (keep); and advised me to seek in London where I could not lack a service." It appears that he preached a number of sermons at St. Dunstan's in the West, and that these were attended by a wealthy draper, Humphrey Monmouth, a merchant who did a considerable foreign trade in cloth. Monmouth took him into his own house, as a chaplain, where, he said, he lived a studious, quiet and abstemious life, " like a good priest."

" There was not only no room in my Lord of London's palace to translate the New Testament," Tindale wrote a few years later, " but also no place to do it in all England." Accordingly, with the help of Monmouth and his friends, he went to the Continent, arriving in Hamburg probably in May 1524. Nor is it surprising that he was not allowed to do his work in England. The Lutheran schism had been exercising the disciplinary powers of the bishops since 1520, and particularly of Tunstall, whose diocese contained the port of London as well as the printing and publishing houses. In 1521 Luther had been declared a heretic and his books burnt at Paul's Cross. The King had written his *Defence of the Seven Sacraments* and had had the title conferred upon him, *Fidei Defensor*. In the same year as his translation of the New Testament Luther had published a scurrilous treatise against Henry, and to this More, under the pseudonym of Rosseus, had replied. In 1524 Tunstall had had to warn the booksellers of London against the sale of Lutheran books, and it is difficult to see how he could at this juncture have found a place in his household for a translator with a dubious record.

According to More, Tindale went straight to Luther at Wittenberg, accompanied by another Englishman, Roye, and there translated his New Testament. A year later he reported at Hamburg, where he received remittances from Monmouth that enabled him to make arrangements for printing with Peter Quentel of Cologne. Precautions were taken to ensure secrecy, and ten sheets were printed off without interruption when an order from the Senate stopped further progress. The secret was out. A priest named Dobneck (Cochlæus), a vigorous anti-Lutheran writer, had left Frankfort during the Peasant Rising in 1525 and found an asylum in the Catholic city of Cologne, where he sent a work that he had on hand to Quentel's press. He became familiar with the printers and overheard them boast that England would soon be Lutheran in spite of the King and the Cardinal; and that two Englishmen, learned and skilled in languages, were hiding in the city. Failing to find the strangers, he asked some of the printers to his inn and, having warmed them with wine, learned from one of them in confidence that three thousand copies of the Lutheran New Testament, translated into English, were in the press. Further, he was informed that funds were being freely supplied by English merchants, who meant to import the work into England and disperse it surreptitiously before King or Cardinal could discover or forbid it. Dobneck feigned great admiration, but he reported his discovery to a senator, who not only obtained an order from the Senate to forbid the printing, but sent a report of the affair to Henry and Wolsey. Presumably the printer had been paid in advance, for the two Englishmen carried off the printed quires, and made their escape by boat up river to Worms. Copies of this unfinished quarto edition of 1525 were sent to England, and a single copy, complete up to the twenty-second chapter of St. Matthew, of which a reproduction in facsimile was edited by Dr. A. W. Pollard in 1926 with a full introduction, survives to-day in the Grenville Library at the British Museum.

At Worms Tindale made a fresh start with a new printer, Schöffer, on an edition not in quarto but octavo; the difference in form being probably due to the fact that in the new edition he omitted his marginal glosses. This important modification was not congenial to Tindale, for, like Luther, he used his translation as a weapon in controversy, the glosses being a means by which they might direct the attention of their readers to their own doctrines. Schöffer's octavo edition, without glosses, reached England soon after Quentel's quarto; and both alike were condemned by the authorities. That the translation was unauthorised brought it under the penalties of the Constitutions of Arundel of 1408, a code elaborated first when the Wycliffite translation was being circulated, and by which Tunstall and the bishops were bound to act. Further, Tindale had invited condemnation not only by his glosses and his Prologue, but also by the significance of some of his renderings. For certain familar words he substituted others that had in them a note of challenge. The *church* became the *congregation, priests* became *seniors, penance* became *repentance, grace* became *favour,* and *charity, love.*

The authorities not only destroyed such copies as they were able to seize, but also attempted through their foreign agents to buy up copies in Antwerp, a plan that must have pleased Tindale's English merchants. Over £60 is known to have been spent in this way by the Archbishop of Canterbury; and Tindale boasted to one of Tunstall's agents that the money that was coming to him in this way would both pay his bills and enable him to correct and reprint his translation. So, says the chronicler Hall, " The bishop had the books, Packyngton (the agent) had the thanks and Tindale had the money."

In order that he might continue his work in greater safety, Tindale left Worms for the congenial seclusion of Marburg, where in 1527 a new university had been founded by the Landgrave of Hesse, a disciple of Luther's more gentle colleague, Melanchthon. Here, beyond the reach of English agents, the printing press of Hans Luft enabled him to continue the work of converting his native land to Lutheranism. And here in 1528 he published two highly polemical and provocative works. *The Parable of the Wicked Mammon,* a treatise on justification by faith, is based on the

Parable of the Unjust Steward. As Christian morality there is much in it that is admirably urged; but this is set in a vigorous defence of Lutheran doctrine and vitiated by its conception of the " common known catholic church " as antichrist. The second work, *The Obedience of a Christian Man ; and how Christian Rulers ought to govern*, is Tindale's answer to the charge brought against the reformers that they promoted insurrection, disobedience, and social unrest. He defines the attitude of the " congregation " to kings and rulers, who, whether they be good or evil, are a gift of God, a blessing or a scourge. It is a sign of the wrath of God if kings are evil. His doctrine is one, therefore, of passive resistance or thankful acquiescence. It was not the reformers, but antichrist who organised resistance to the temporal power. The Pope and the clergy demanded a law for themselves, and even in the smallest parish governed a worldly kingdom of their own. If the story in Foxe is true, Anne Boleyn's copy of the *Obedience* came to be read by Henry VIII, and he declared, " This book is for me and all kings to read."

Meanwhile in London Tunstall had determined that other measures than those of confiscation and burning must be adopted to counteract the influence of heretical literature. He therefore formally invited Sir Thomas More, then chancellor of the duchy of Lancaster, to undertake the task of " publishing in English something that would expose, even to simple lay folk, the subtle malice of the heretics "; and he gave a formal licence to him to read the heretical books. A year later, in the month of June 1529, More published a " Dialogue . . . wherein are treated divers matters, as of the veneration and worship of images and relics, praying to saints and going on pilgrimage; with many other things touching the pestilent sect of Luther and Tindale, by the one begun in Saxony and by the other laboured to be brought into England." But, as More said in the opening words of the *Dialogue*, " It is an old-sayd saw that one business begetteth and bringeth forth another." His defence of Catholic unity and tradition and his attack on the schismatic works of Luther and Tindale provoked an *Answer* which in its turn compelled him to write his *Confutation of Tindale's Answer*; and by the time the *Confutation* was in print More had resigned the Great Seal, Cranmer was Archbishop, Thomas Cromwell was in power, Henry had married Anne Boleyn, and his breach with Rome was imminent.

In the most virulent of Tindale's attacks on the ecclesiastical authorities, *The Practice of Prelates*, he denounces the Pope as antichrist and the whore of Babylon, his clergy as robbers of the laity, and the religious orders as caterpillars, horse-leeches, drone-bees, and draff; but the arch-fiend is Wolfsee, amongst whose other enormities he alleges the appointment of his friend, the Bishop of Lincoln, to be the King's confessor that he might be informed of the King's secrets. Even the promotion of the divorce was only another instance of the prelatical practice of tampering with the law of God; an argument that was not likely to please Henry.

Tindale's work at Marburg, however, was not confined to invective. In the month of January 1531 Hans Luft printed his second great work of translation, the Pentateuch. He had had opportunities of continuing his Hebrew studies both at Worms and at Marburg, and there is no reason to doubt his competence in the language of the Old Testament. The translation is prefaced by a challenging Prologue in which he goes over a good deal of old ground, insisting, for example, that his motives in translating the New Testament had been that unlearned lay folk might possess the simple literal sense of the Word " whose light the owls could not abide "; and he relates his early troubles and tells of his interview with Tunstall. Each book also has its own Preface, and he returns to his first practice of adding marginal glosses, often very provocative in tone. Thus, against the verse in the story of Balaam, " How shall I curse whom God curseth not and how shall I defy whom the Lord defyeth not ? " we read in the margin " *The Pope can tell you how.*"

In 1531, after the publication of the Pentateuch, Tindale left Marburg and went to Antwerp, where a curious attempt was made by a sympathetic protégé of Cromwell's to induce him to return to England under promise of a safe-conduct. Tindale, naturally, refused; but he went so far as to arrange a meeting with Vaughan outside the walls of the city ; a bold step for a man to take who was in great danger of arrest. What Cromwell's motives were one cannot say, but Henry was indignant when he read Vaughan's report of his interview with the " arch-heretic," and he instructed Cromwell to inform his agent that Tindale had a " malicious, perverse, uncharitable, and indurate mind," that he saw in him no hope of reconciliation, and that he was " very joyous to have his realm destitute of such a person." The sequel to these unofficial overtures was that Tindale addressed to England in the Prologue to his Book of Jonah such a call to repentance as he deemed the prophet to have addressed to the Ninevites.

And this was followed by an extremely polemical *Exposition upon the first Epistle of St. John*, which was duly sent to England by the bewildered Vaughan. Sir Thomas Elyot, the ambassador to the Emperor Charles V, was now commissioned to work for Tindale's apprehension. But as the promotion of the king's divorce had greatly displeased the nephew of Catherine of Aragon, in whose dominions Tindale was a refugee, it was not likely that the Emperor would take steps to hand over to Henry a man who was so effectively disturbing the peace of England. The money, therefore, that Elyot disbursed among the imperial servants was wasted; and while Elyot was trying to catch him, Tindale published a lengthy exposition on the *Sermon on the Mount*, in the course of which he repeats his old, false charge against More that his defence of orthodoxy was lucrative. " *Covetousness* blinded the eyes of that gleering fox more and more and hardened his heart against the truth, with the confidence of his painted poetry, babbling eloquence and juggling arguments . . . grounded on his unwritten verities, as true and authentic as his story of Utopia."

In Vaughan's dispatches several references had occurred to a companion of Tindale's, a young scholar, John Frith, who had joined him at Marburg in 1528 and been much in his company for four years. In July 1532 Frith returned to England on what appears from Tindale's letters to have been a special mission in which the elder man was greatly interested. It almost seems as if Tindale hoped that the qualities that he himself lacked, attractiveness of personality, charm, wit, and good humour, qualities that distinguished Frith, might win for his cause a hearing in England. Such, at least, seems to be the significance of the following passage from one of his letters: " God has made me evil-favoured in this world and without grace in the sight of men, speechless and rude, dull and slow-witted; your part shall be to supply what lacketh in me."

The letter from which this extract is taken followed Frith to England, but it reached him in the Tower; and in Tindale's last letter to him before Frith's death at the stake (July 4, 1533), he writes grimly: " Fear not threatening, neither be overcome of sweet words; with which twain the hypocrites shall assail you. Neither let the persuasions of worldly wisdom bear rule in your heart; no, though they be your friends that counsel. Let Bilney be a warning to you!"

During the next two years the situation in England underwent a radical change. The Papal jurisdiction was abolished, and Tindale's opponent, More, after fifteen months' imprisoment, was executed on July 6, 1535. During this period Tindale was revising his New Testament, a task to which he devoted himself with great closeness. There were cogent reasons why he should no longer postpone the publication of a revised text. No fewer than four reprints of his original translation had been issued (without his authority) by the Dutch printers for sale or distribution in England. A fifth reprint was on foot for which the printers had engaged an English " corrector," George Joye; and not only did they catch the market by getting this edition out early, but Joye, thinking in his conceit to improve on Tindale, tampered with his text. In particular he replaced the word " *Resurrection* " by the phrase *the life after this*, a most improper impertinence in a proof-corrector, for Joye did not offer the translation as his own. He excused himself on the grounds that Tindale's dilatoriness had driven the printers to act without him, and that his opinions on the doctrine of the resurrection of the body were confused. The truth is, as Dr. Pollard has said: " Joye had grossly misused his position as the proof-corrector of a translation by a much better scholar than himself, to make changes at his own pleasure, and he was too muddle-headed and too conceited to realise the greatness of his offence or the seriousness of the consequences it might have for Tindale."

The revised New Testament appeared in 1534. Tindale had acquiesced reluctantly in 1526 in the removal of his marginal glosses, and these now reappear. He also permitted himself a larger kind of gloss in the form of an extended general Prologue. But in spite of these excrescences the revision was a very great achievement, marked by the closest attention to significance of cadence, selection of emphasis and effectiveness of rhythm. It attains what is almost verbal finality. To Tindale it was indeed the very Word of God that he was transmitting; and this Word was to be preached to the common people of England. It is an entirely English idiom, therefore, that he uses; the English idiom of his own day. He tells us himself that he found both the Greek idiom and the Hebrew nearer to the English than the Latin, and he often departs very far from the traditional rhythm of the Vulgate. As an example of the closeness with which he did his work of revision we may take the familiar verse from the Sermon on the Mount, " Let your light so shyne before men that they maye se youre good workes and glorify youre Father which is in Heven." In the Cologne quarto of 1525, this read, " Se that youre light . . . "; but by securing the alliteration of *let* and *light*, and replacing the weak *se that* by the emphatic *Let*, he secured that the main emphasis shall nevertheless fall on the word *glorify*.

In Dr. Pollard's facsimile edition of the 1525 quarto he sets out in a form convenient for comparison a portion of the Sermon on the Mount as given by (*a*) Tindale, in his last revision, (*b*) the Great Bible of 1539, (*c*) the Geneva Bible of 1560, (*d*) the Bishops' Bible of 1572, (*e*) the Rheims (or Jesuit) Bible of 1582, and (*f*) the Authorised Version of 1611. The conclusion that he himself draws from this evidence is that " Tindale set a model for the translation of the Bible into English which (even in the Jesuit version) was respectfully followed by his successors, so that the authorised version of 1611, which still holds its place in the affection of English-speaking Christians, alike in language, rhythm and cadence, is fully 90 per cent. his."

It is significant of the change in England that no sooner had Tindale published his revised New Testament than he set to work on a second revision. It is also significant that this was published *without* marginal glosses. But before the 1535 edition appeared Tindale was the prisoner of the Emperor Charles V in the castle of Vilvorde.

Although in a great part of the Emperor's German dominions the reformers were dominant, his laws against heresy were in force in the Low Countries. Tindale had been protected in Antwerp by the English merchants, who enjoyed privileges and immunities there similar to those enjoyed by the Hanse merchants of the Steelyard in London. At the time of his arrest Tindale was living in the house of an English merchant, Thomas Pointz, where apparently he was quite safe, particularly as the city of Antwerp asserted privileges for its own citizens and resident merchants which were not accorded to Lutherans in other parts of the Low

Countries. Foxe's story is that a certain Henry Philips cultivated the acquaintance of Tindale in Antwerp and won his confidence. While Pointz was away on business, Philips invited Tindale out to dinner, and had him arrested by officers from Brussels as he was leaving the house. He was interned on May 23 or 24, 1535, about six weeks before the execution of More ; and, from the account of the expenses incurred during his imprisonment it has been calculated that he was a prisoner for a year and a hundred and thirty-five days. He was executed on October 6, 1536. Attempts were made from England to save him, but the relations of the King and the Emperor were not favourable to these overtures. Pointz particularly did everything that he could to rescue his friend, even to the extent of being himself imprisoned.

The last effort to save him seems to have been made by the optimistic Vaughan, who, writing from Antwerp in April 1536, said : " If now you send me but your letter to the privy council (of Brabant) I could deliver Tindale from the fire: see it come by time or else it will come too late." It is reported by Foxe that Tindale's last words were: " Lord, open the King of England's eyes." " Whether Henry's eyes were ever opened to anything but what he considered his own interests may be doubted "—the words are Dr. Pollard's—" but while Tindale yet lived the King was slowly veering round to the policy of permitting (for a time even of enforcing) the circulation of the Bible in English, and within seven years of Tindale's martyrdom a Great Bible had been set up in every parish church in England."

A year after Tindale's death his chief benefactor, Humphrey Monmouth, died, having nominated in his will Bishop Latimer and three other evangelical divines to preach a series of memorial sermons in his parish church " to the lawde and prayse of Almighty God and to the setting forth of the Prince's godly and hevenly purpose to the utter abolishing and extincting of the usurped and false feyned power of the busshop of Rome." And that they might protect the said preachers, he bequeathed to Sir Thomas Cromwell and the Lord Chancellor (Audeley) each a silver cup of the value of £10. The work of the translator had been made possible by Monmouth and his friends, and it is perhaps not inappropriate that this short account of Tindale should close with this reference to his chief backer.

THOMAS CROMWELL
Circa 1485–1540

By
DAVID MATHEW

THOMAS CROMWELL

by DAVID MATHEW

IT is difficult even to indicate the wide ramifications of the influence of Henry VIII's vicar-general on the subsequent development of English life. For Cromwell possessed an outlook on the new Europe, a sense of the State, which was perhaps not shared by any contemporary English leader, while the complete uprooting of the monastic system was a tribute to his power of administrative destruction. The life of Thomas Cromwell was well planned, balanced, and singularly successful, hazardous, passionless, and great in achievement. The mask-like features of the Holbein portraits confirm the impression derived from his vast mass of correspondence, the type of the bureaucrat statesman had at last arrived. The lesser functionary had been long familiar ; but Cromwell's contemporaries had yet to experience the lay bureaucrat in supreme office. Here was a man upon whom hatred would concentrate, the enemy of all vested interests with which he was not identified, with a public life very open to attack and a mind beyond his enemies' comprehension. In a brief study it is probably simplest to consider his position in the last months before his fall, and thus to gain an impression of his significance from the moments of his greatest power.

On April 17, 1540, when the Easter festivities were over and a new Parliament had lately met, the Lord Privy Seal, as Cromwell was generally styled from his chief office, was created Earl of Essex and made Great Chamberlain of England. In connection with this Parliament an important service was required of him, a further exercise of his capacity for rendering the Houses first pliable and then generous in their money grants. Cromwell was already vicar-general and vicegerent of the King in spirituals, and the promotions of this April marked the culminating point of a career characterised by a highly developed sense of politics, a clear grasp of statecraft, a controlled but unremitting power of acquisition, and a rapid, tortuous, supple mind. A list of some of the other appointments and posts which he held at this time will provide a reflection of his predominance. He was Chancellor of the Exchequer and a Knight of the Garter, Chancellor and High Steward of the University of Cambridge, Warden and Chief Justice in eyre north of Trent, Governor of the Isle of Wight, Recorder of Bristol, a Privy Councillor of course and, rather surprisingly for so anti-clerical a layman, Dean of Wells. His post of visitor-general of the monasteries, absorbed in higher office, had become a sinecure, since the work of the total suppression of the religious houses had been carried through with smooth efficiency and was now almost completed. He had, indeed, deserved well of his sovereign.

It was, however, the very successful completion of his work which made Cromwell's position now precarious. He had become less necessary, and a man so hated could not survive once he had become unnecessary to his master. And Henry VIII was painfully accessible, desperately open to gusts of influence. The King might not be prepared to sacrifice anything of importance, but he would sacrifice an unprofitable servant.

Cromwell in this April was already fighting a losing battle. The days of his first secure period of office were behind him. He was fifty-five and had been for seven years the most powerful factor in English politics. Each year his responsibilities had increased and with them his pensioners and beneficiaries and, of course, his enemies. He had long been an isolated man with a too-great knowledge of his world. His personal contacts were numerous and unexpected : many were valuable, some were painful, none was entirely frank. The obvious detail can be filled in rapidly. Twenty years of private trading in wool and woollen cloths, the inheritance of a fulling mill at Putney, the transition from established commerce to the service first of Cardinal Wolsey and then of the King, this certainly forms a most respectable background. But there was always the more private side to his financial transactions. It is difficult for a moneylender to grow old gracefully.

Besides, Cromwell had first appeared in a rather menial capacity in the service of the Marquis of Dorset, and he had not the protection of the Church to make his rise to power less unacceptable, for he always remained a layman. His great position in the State had made the lords and the churchmen approach him humbly and obsequiously. They were determined that Cromwell should one day pay for their obsequiousness.

The dissolution of the monasteries had come to the courtiers as an unhoped-for piece of good fortune and, once they found the easy terms on which these great areas of well-developed property were obtainable, they had entered with serene calculation upon this golden age of the English landed interest. They reaped great profits without labour. Cromwell, on the other hand, carrying through his own plans, concentrated the opposition upon himself. Whatever little odium might attach in Court circles to the executions of the abbots of Colchester and Glastonbury was centred upon him. He received the blame for all the acts of oppression which were required before the monastery lands in the kingdom could be parcelled out at moderate prices. The anger of the country people rose against Cromwell as the type of the New Man about the King. The shouts of " Cow Crummock " left the Lords in little doubt as to who was marked out to be their Jonas.

At the same time other causes had embittered the feelings of the Court circle against Cromwell. The separation from Rome was already of some six years' standing, and the memory of More and Fisher had perhaps grown faint; but there had been more recent executions, Exeter and Montague, Neville, Fortescue, Carew. The peers who had been compelled to carry through the treason trials of their friends and relatives did not forgive the plebeian minister who had arranged them. And in the background there was the great body of the bishops, careful men, some timorous, most diplomatic, all Court-appointed. They knew that Cromwell had an intimate and unfriendly knowledge of their careers. Their innate conservatism and the remnants of their pride revolted against this layman who held all the damaging and closely detailed information possessed by a financial go-between. Few of the bishops could rest easy in the presence of the King's Grace's vicegerent in spirituals. Still, these hatreds weighed little in the balance as against his successful administration in home affairs, and Cromwell would perhaps have remained invulnerable but for his failing foreign policy. And with his line of action in this matter the King's marriages were intimately linked.

The wives of Henry VIII have provided a pleasantly diversified chess-board for the amusements of romantic history. Yet their real personal influence in politics was at most intermittent. The King was probably not susceptible of this influence in connection with the broader lines of policy; but anyone who lived in daily contact with him, on terms of such intimacy as the Tudor might permit, possessed the power of occasional destruction. Most despotic sovereigns are prepared to learn that they have been ill-served by their closest intimates and, if suspicion is an almost inevitable concomitant of tyranny, the vein of naïve suspiciousness in the King's character would be the natural reaction of a buoyant temperament seldom thwarted and rarely openly opposed.

A brief objective account of Cromwell's relations with the Queens of England with whom he had to deal will provide the setting for one aspect of his fall. To Queen Catherine and the strongly Catholic Party he had been an open enemy; but the enmity of her Imperialist supporters only strengthened him. Cardinal Pole had compared Cromwell to the demoniac in the tombs in the Gospel, and the hatred of the King's enemies thus stood him in good stead. With Anne Boleyn and Jane Seymour the case was different. Both were connected, one intimately, the other more, remotely, with those Court circles which were to provide the most tenacious and astute of Cromwell's enemies. Their daily access to the King, their relationship to the wealthy entrenched councillors who hated him, made these Queens potential sources of danger. Both marriages were in the eyes of a statesman unfortunate, without dignity or even personal wealth, subject alliances which could not aid the sovereign and would inevitably trammel his action. It is not surprising that the Privy Seal had maintained a passive attitude towards Jane Seymour, an unfriendly, a minatory passivity towards Anne Boleyn.

The two years of Cromwell's greatest security covered the period between the death of Jane Seymour in September 1537 and the close of the King's eligible widowerhood in the first days of 1540. But during 1539 the Privy Seal had unwisely allowed himself to become the supporter of a particular royal marriage in the development of general foreign policy. It was a cardinal error of judgment for one whose links with his sovereign were purely utilitarian to allow himself to be involved in the complicated reactions of the King's emotional life. The opposition to Rome had hardened, and Cromwell was thus encouraged to seek support for his policy in Germany. He had the pliability of indifference in the matter of formularies of Faith and an alliance with the new Lutherans would seem a commonplace of political prudence, if France and the Empire should unite against England. The possibility of an effective Franco-Imperial alliance appeared to be increasing, and he had used this as a lever to induce the King to negotiate with the supporters of the new religion. But it had been a mistake to use any lever where the King's very tender theological conscience was concerned. Cromwell had, perhaps, seen this and withdrawn; for the marriage with Anne of Cleves was in effect the support of a compromise candidate, one whose family was not fully committed to the Reformation. The plan was therefore moderate and cautious; so cautiously drawn up, in fact, that the high contracting parties slipped through Cromwell's fingers. The Duke of Cleves abandoned King Henry politically, the King was moving to a determination to discard the new Queen Anne, and the Privy Seal's position was undermined.

This was the state of affairs when Cromwell received his last promotion. With these forces against him it is extraordinary how weak were the supports which he could count on. Among the great officers of State he had one constant friend, the Archbishop of Canterbury, Cranmer. They were very different in character, poles apart in cast of mind, but agreed on policy. In any case Cranmer had serious disadvantages as an ally in extremity; for he was not ruthless, he became timorous at a crisis, he was sincere about tiresome religious detail. Beyond the Archbishop there was not one among the leaders at the Court whose falsetto expressions of devotion towards the Lord Privy Seal could be held to express a true opinion. In the consciously elaborate phrasing of his colleagues' letters one element recurs, an irony, sometimes detached, more often bitter, always present.

Still, difficult as was his position, Cromwell was bound to go forward. An organisation of dependants and agents had grown up about him, cumbrous and inescapable. A constant influence on policy made it necessary to be well-informed; there was no question of a quiet withdrawal.

Besides, in this April it was manifest that the King had need of him. During the period that his services were required, some change in the attitude of the foreign Powers could perhaps develop, or his enemies in England might yet play into his hands. For at the moment Cromwell was engaged on the perfecting of an important financial service to the Crown, the carrying through of the suppression of the hospitals of St. John of Jerusalem in England, and until these plans were completed he seemed safe.

A brief reference to this suppression will indicate something of the general nature of his work in liquidating the religious orders; for it required an experienced technique in manipulating surrenders, in calculating and arranging pensions, and in securing the transfer of the buildings and landed property in good condition. There was also always needed that element of delicate personal negotiation in which the vicegerent in spirituals excelled. A not wholly serious correspondence between the English Government and the Grand Master in Malta had been carried on over two years. The fullest value as a political factor had been extracted from the Grand Master's imprisonment of an English knight, and the matter was by now reduced to the question of the minimum figure at which the necessary pensions must be fixed. The Lord Prior in England, Sir William Weston, had proved most amenable to all the suggestions of the Government. That in the past had been an advantage; but in consequence he was now unfortunately in a position to press for a substantial sum. Cromwell, however, had private information: he was aware of the Lord Prior's decrepit physical condition, he saw that he could prudently make extensive promises. The negotiations for surrender were eased by the grant of an annual life-pension of £1,000 to the Lord Prior, who signed the necessary documents, and then died on the very day of the dissolution of the Order. The whole of the considerable sum was thus saved for the Treasury. It is only a minor instance, but the last, and in some ways the most typical, example of Cromwell's methods.

But such methods, when applied through an unemotional balanced judgment unbiased by any personal sympathy, left Cromwell isolated. Each such successful operation carried through with his cold skill removed him farther from the general track. He was always the New Man, self-made, the servant of that new State which his contemporaries could only understand imperfectly. Around him were grouped the courtiers with their consciousness of good birth or sound connections. They in a sense were all united and, acting in their respective stations, negligently, obsequiously, or furtively made their fortunes in that grave financial scramble which gave its tone to the late Henrican Court. It was true that it was their own class, the courtiers and rich squires, which benefited chiefly by this well-founded speculation, but the Privy Seal received no more gratitude from his clients than any other large-scale financier.

In his great new house whose gardens pressed against the crowded city dwellings, he went through this business, through the mass of correspondence which the summoning of a fresh Parliament always brought him and the despatches of the envoys and of his agents. The plainness of his dress would only emphasise the ostentatious and costly fittings of his chambers, the " ball of astronomy " upon its tripod on the Flemish carpet, and the " great muros or looking-glass of steel gilted." The cushions on the corner seats were worked with the rose gules which formed a part of the Privy Seal's armorial bearings, and the wall space above was hung with an elaborate tapestry on green and red serge, the history of Susanna. It must have been a luxurious set of rooms, but certainly not homely and probably not reassuring for a man in crisis. A sense of value was evidenced by the hangings and the paintings and the inlaid Italian tables, but this was possibly the merchant's flair. The rooms at any rate were overcrowded, and in the midst of this accumulation of predominantly sacred art there moved the bourgeois Cromwell household, the young unmarried daughters and the dull son Gregory. It was eleven years since his wife had died, and Thomas Cromwell had not remarried. A certain frost lay on his relations. Save through his son's recent wedding to Elizabeth Seymour he had no marriage links with the great families. It was a marked contrast to such an intimate domestic circle as Thomas More's, with its wide range of outside friendship; for the tolerably pleasant wit of Cromwell's middle life does not seem to have survived his years of office. Those who like Stephen Vaughan had been his friends were now his servants. He was too " great " and perhaps his knowledge of private affairs was too intricate for the survival of friendship. Similarly his generosity to his relatives was hardly of a nature to provoke intimacy; it was rather a businesslike and unrespectful affection. He settled his relations in a moderate station and paid the expenses involved. For instance, there was a bill of some pounds to be met which his sister Mrs. Wellyfed had owed to her maltster. He could deal proudly with his dependent clan, but could hardly expect support from them. Like all the bourgeois ministers who were in time to serve the monarchies, he stood inevitably in isolation drawn from his own class by the very intimacy of his State service.

In his earlier years he had made efforts and had taken part in that formal hunting which gave consistency to the routine of the courtier's country life. But he was now grown elderly for such exertion, and he no longer needed proof that the gentry who paid the interest on his loans were also prepared to entertain him. His earldom placed him far beyond such questionings. The high title of Essex with its half-royal associations had passed from Mandeville to Bohun and Bourchier: the great chamberlainship also had descended through equally exalted generations. Both had come recently to Thomas Cromwell. With his acute perception of all worldly values each aspect of these advantages stood out clearly, painfully clear, since it was so doubtful if he could hold them. Everything depended on his ability to ride out the storm without assistance.

The French Ambassador de Marillac summed up accurately this stage of the last conflict. " Cromwell," he wrote on April 24 to Paris, " is in as much credit with his master as ever he was, from which he was near being shaken by the Bishop of Winchester and others." In these French despatches a fair description is given of how he was dogged by his enemies, especially his ecclesiastical enemies. If only he could leave churchmanship behind and concentrate on pure politics it must have seemed that he might yet save himself. He had been to Parliament in his new robes, the crimson velvet furred with miniver of his earldom, that symbol of a future security; but a constant straining political effort paid for this magnificence. On April 31 he was due at a Chapter of the Garter, where it was his duty as Earl of Essex to offer up the banner of the Earl of Shrewsbury, just deceased. This was perhaps his line of safety, if he could have become securely the great lay lord and shake off the religious aspect of his work, the vicegerency in spirituals and all that it implied. The monasteries were dissolved, and a whole section of his life was finished. For six years he had been dealing with aspiring monks zealous for promotion, and now at last they had been hustled from the scene. But it was his ecclesiastical enemies who pursued him. Perhaps his calm indifference in religion made the *odium theologicum* more difficult to counter.

The idea of religion in the sense of rival theologies appears to have been quite alien to a mind open to that world system which the growth of the State's power would soon embody. For Cromwell seems to have possessed a clear conception of the meaning of sovereignty at last untrammelled from the old feudal concepts and the dualism of the Empire and the Papacy. Taking for granted the heavy leavening of a prudent self-interest, the Privy Seal's more general intention was to serve the new State and bring it to perfection. For him religion seems to have been protective colouring, an attitude well marked by traditional bequests for Masses in middle life and by strong attacks on Rome in his last years. Cavendish has a story of Cromwell, at the time of Wolsey's fall, standing in the window embrasure of the great hall at Esher reading Our Lady's Matins. Such public prayer was an accepted custom, and it was manifestly imprudent for a statesman to wreck his future by some singularity of personal conduct. But by misfortune Cromwell's service of the " Prince " had led him into immediate dependence on a sovereign whose cast of mind was theological in the extreme. Eighteen years separated King Henry's *Assertio Septem Sacramentorum* from his enactment of the Six Articles in which adherence to the doctrine of Transubstantiation was enforced. It was within this space of time that Cromwell's public action was enclosed. The King sought constantly, and it would seem successfully, to satisfy a curious, but very exacting and rather mediæval, conscience. His boisterous sanguine temperament reflected one of the types of the innately religious nature. But with this outlook Cromwell had no points of contact. Relieved as he was at the decrease of the Church's power, he seems to have been utterly without interest in all purely theological positions. This would alone explain consistently his long practice of accepted religious custom, his doctrinally rash support of the Reformers, and his final declaration of adherence to the King's conception of the Catholic faith.

What with the King was an inevitable lack of sympathy became hostility where the bishops were concerned. But it appears that Cromwell's opposition concentrated on a strong political objection and not on any strictly religious matter. He was opposed resolutely and with a Latin clarity to the strong ecclesiastical corporations, to that long tradition of English administrative churchmanship of which Bishop Gardiner of Winchester remained the chief defender and exponent. In Cromwell's scheme of values it was clear that the " Prince " must be obeyed directly and implicitly, and served with an efficiency inevitably ruthless. The traditional line of bishop-chancellors would soon be swept away by the new State. Yet in spite of attachment to these general views it would seem to accord with Cromwell's character that he was always forced to fight as an opportunist. The King aided his minister in the development of the practice of absolute sovereignty rather than in its theory. The Lord Privy Seal was always forced to strive to muzzle rather than to extinguish his opponents and to stave off such accidents as might destroy his foreign policy. Thus one small episode was transiently useful to him at this crisis.

A report of a new menace to Calais came to hand. The French King had placed falconet cannons on the walls of Ardres and had ordered the town ditch of that frontier place to be made " the depth and the breadth of the ditch of Therouanne." Any sign of hostility to England tended to produce in King Henry's outlook a reawakening of sympathy towards the disintegrating Lutheran alliance. But such a matter, unless reinforced by future action, must have small weight. In actual fact the submission of Cleves to the Emperor and the increasing friendship of Charles V and the King of France led, not to an offensive league against England, but to further offers of alliance. Such peace upon the Continent by tending to include England in its scope was bound to render more difficult the position of the minister, whose only external policy was based on anti-Imperial and anti-Papal action.

The Lutherans alone stood out from this new (and to Cromwell) dangerous harmony. But in spite of the favours that the Privy Seal had obtained for those who were so clearly pledged to maintain an anti-Roman policy the King had never been induced to tolerate these German tenets. It is remarkable how the theocratic trend of King Henry's thought gave a religious colour to such divergent policies as those of Cromwell and the older courtier grouping of Norfolk and Southampton. To describe the Privy Seal as Protestant, in so far as the term could then exist, and Norfolk as consciously Catholic would seem a misreading. For the old Court party was not so much Catholic as traditionalist, holding to a standpoint not in any way original, predominantly secular in their outlook, not quick, but very shrewd. Such were perhaps the marks of that whole range of English life which centred on the ruling class under the early Tudors. And opposed to them was Cromwell intent upon a synthesis of the State, with a mind more rapid in its action, clear defined, and logical. It is necessary to stress the secularism of these opposing factions, for in the last round of the duel they both made use of religious counters.

Owing to the increasing pressure brought to bear against him Cromwell now attacked the opposition; for, if he was vulnerable through his German Lutheran allies, they might be accused of sympathy with the Roman Pontiff. In May a charge of " relieving certain traitorous persons who denied the King's Supremacy " was brought against one of Gardiner's chief supporters, the Bishop of Chichester, who was thereupon thrown into the Tower. " A trustworthy personage," wrote de Marillac on June 1, in regard to this affair, " says he heard from Cromwell there were still five bishops who ought to be treated thus; whose names however cannot be learned unless they are those who lately shook the credit of ' Maistre Cramvel,' so that he was very near coming to grief. Things are brought to such a pass that either Cromwell's party or that of the Bishop of Winchester must succumb." This appears an accurate impression and, besides, there would seem to be no situation in which the Privy Seal was so little at home as the theological or so remote from the King's sympathy.

During May, too, charges against Lord Lisle, the Governor of Calais, and his chaplain had occupied attention; for they were accused of secret dealings with Cardinal Pole's agents. Since anti-Roman patriotism was the Privy Seal's strong suit, all rumours of treachery would serve to assist him. But these were merely passing diversions and the ominous lull in his enemies' activities must only have borne in upon Cromwell the sense of his own grave danger. He was surely too isolated a man not to be most fully conscious of the new set of the tide. In his great hall the Marquis of Dorset's arms would serve to remind him of his earlier service, the gilded mantecor and the unicorn. But he could not rely upon those who were now his fellow-nobles. The Italian pictures hung beyond his windows, the Pietà and the painting of the Passion and the Rape of Lucrece; while below, in his strong room, "the silver plate, crosses, chalices, and other spoils of the Church"[1] had been collected. These were hardly reassuring treasures. Spread along the wall in the parlour was the carved woodwork of the King's arms and the Queen's with an eagle and a white greyhound; and on the King all depended.

It was on June 10 that the blow fell: Cromwell was arrested at the Council Table and taken to the Tower. A bill of attainder was introduced, and he was attainted of heresy and high treason. Even in the Tower his services, so long valuable to the State, were needed. The King having finally decided on the dissolution of his marriage with Anne of Cleves, the evidence of his former minister became of material importance. This was provided with all Cromwell's accustomed cogency and skill. On July 28 he was beheaded on Tower Hill. For the moment the old Court Party alone held power, the great lords and the bishops. There is some truth in Hall's remark in his *Chronicle* that Cromwell "could not abide the snoffyng pride of some prelates"; but it was something deeper than anti-clericalism. His conceptions were to find favour in a later period. It would seem that Cromwell had looked far beyond to the great State, where his high talent played freely, secure beyond the trammels of religion and its restrictions and the hot emotions; down the centuries, past the Puritans, to an untheological England.

[1] *Cal. Letters and Papers, Henry VIII*, vol. XV, No. 804. The details mentioned in regard to Cromwell's life during these months are to be found in this volume, *passim*, in the Cromwell Papers, *ibid.*, pp. 511–25, and in the documents printed in R. B. Merriman's *Life and Letters of Thomas Cromwell*, vols. I and II.

SIR THOMAS WYATT

1503–1542

By
PAUL CHADBURN

SIR THOMAS WYATT

by PAUL CHADBURN

I

ANYONE of whom it could be claimed, however wildly, that he had commenced the reformation by a *bon mot* and planned the fall of Wolsey by an apposite story must have been something of a personality. There is no doubt that Wyatt did leave a very strong impression on his contemporaries. Whatever he did, he did well—and there was not much he did not turn his hand or brain to. One of the finest jousters at Henry VIII's court; an adept at all sports —tennis, bowls, hunting. Something of a gambler—reckless, generous. A lover with all the courtly graces—wit, poetry, lute-playing, looks. One who could inspire deep friendship, not only in men of such a different type to himself as Thomas Cromwell and King Henry, but, it appears, in women also; Anne Boleyn was one of them, and Elizabeth Darrell, the mistress of his later years, was perhaps another. Then Wyatt was a scholar: he translated Plutarch (the *Quyete of Mynde*) for Catherine of Aragon. As a " meterer " he introduced the sonnet form into England, worked on the Chaucerian five-foot line, prepared the way for blank verse. Together with all this Wyatt was an active diplomat, entrusted by Henry with one of the most important missions of his reign, conciliating the Emperor Charles, whose aunt Henry had divorced.

All these accomplishments, all this achievement suffice to make Wyatt an outstanding figure, but still there were contemporaries of his who were not far behind Wyatt as courtier poets, Surrey notably, and such all-round types as Lord Rochford, Thomas Lord Vaux, and Lord Thomas Howard.

But there is more to Wyatt than this: a passionate sincerity which caused the comparative failure of his professional life, the rare power of his poetry. Where others had a formal code of manners, Wyatt had a fiery belief—belief in an ideal that had informed a social structure which was breaking up, whose passing is the theme of his friend Surrey's two finest poems.

The poem Surrey wrote when he was a prisoner in Windsor Castle, where he had spent his adolescence with Henry's natural son, the Duke of Richmond, is more than an elegy on his dead friend; it is a lament for the heyday of a society, select, exclusive, brilliant, a society whose justification—the conception of hereditary service—was failing. This conception is the keynote of Wyatt's life and poetry:

> " It is not now but long and long ago
> I have you served as to my powre and myght,
> As faithfully as any man might do,
> Clayming of you nothing of right, of right."

When Surrey was writing in Windsor Castle, where he had composed his first courtly verses, under whose walls he had once jousted and hunted the deer, called up betimes by the lusty song—

> " The Hunt is up! the Hunt is up!
> And it is well nigh day;
> And Harry our King is gone hunting,
> To bring the deer to bay "—

when Surrey wrote his elegy only a decade or so later much of the splendour had passed. The old hereditary aristocracy was being superseded by a new class of officials, political power was no longer vested exclusively in a brilliant set of knights: it was passing more and more to the clever, pushing, unprincipled representatives of the middle-class, politicians of Machiavelli's mind. Mediæval Christendom was falling, Erastian states were rising, the fabric of feudal society was in collapse, broken through at all points by the new politics, by the new religion, by the sweep westwards of the new learning; the entire economic basis which had sustained the former pageant at Windsor was shifting.

Much as Wyatt and Surrey owed to the new, both of them were at heart representatives of the old order. The impulse of their best poetry derives from it. Both were conservative in the feeling of their poetry while experimenting with the new forms. Their intellects were Renaissance intellects, receptive, eager, ranging: Surrey extraverted, Wyatt introverted; Surrey anticipating the Elizabethan extension of the poetic field, Wyatt the spiritual intension of the seventeenth-century religious poets. Yet with all this the two of them, and especially Wyatt, were rooted in the society which had formed them.

So that the other of Surrey's elegies—that on Wyatt himself—is also, in a wider sense, an elegy on a defunct society. The poem is a portrait of Wyatt; it shows the type in its highest aspect, the type of Castiglione's *Courtier* before it had degenerated into the type formulated in Chesterfield's letters to his son:

> " *A hed, where wisdom mysteries did frame,*
> *Whose hammers bet still in that lively brain,*
> *As on a stythe; where that some work of fame*
> *Was daily wrought, to turn to Britain's gain* . . .

> " *A hart, where dread was never so impressed*
> *To hide the thought, that might the truth advance.*"

Surrey's conception of Wyatt is borne out by the painting in the National Portrait Gallery. It shows up in striking contrast to the portraits which surround it, pictures, for the most part, of formularised Tudors, ruffed, puffed, square-jowled, meaty—the hunting, jousting, high-living, hard-fighting aristocracy, men like the Duke of Suffolk who " twice committed bigamy and was three times divorced; began by marrying his aunt and finished by marrying his daughter-in-law "; or pictures of the new intellectual class, those who rose to power on the trend of the Tudor kings' policy, their faces lined and hardened by endless machinations for position. The portrait of Wyatt—whose family had acquired its standing through service to the Tudors—shows the virility of the one class, the intellect of the other. The bared neck is the neck of a fighter, a man of outstanding physical strength; the bottom of the face, shown in profile, is thickly grown over by the " stern " black beard; the upper part is delicate, earnest. The effect is of manliness and refined sensibility combined, as Surrey put it:

> " *A valiant corpse, where force and beauty met.*"

The portrait contrasts with that of Surrey, volatile, gay-witted, haughtily choleric, where Wyatt is earnest, passion-ate, ironic. Pictures of Sydney and Raleigh, the Eliza-bethan court poets, hang opposite. They do not show that latent power, ungratified in action, love, in courts, study, anywhere, that set Wyatt's mind on its restless interrogatory of the soul, gave the " deep-witted " quality to his poetry, the " *sæva indignatio* " to the famous prose Defence (against accusations of treason); that animates the protest ringing through all Wyatt's work:

> " *What shulde I say,*
> *Sins Faithe is ded,*
> *And truth awaye*
> *From you ys fled?*
> *Shulde I be led,*
> *With doblenesse?*
> *Naye, naye, mistresse.*"

II

The greatest mistake is to think of Wyatt's poems as " airs and madrigals that whisper softness in chambers." The titles —*The Lover Professeth Himself Constant, The Lover Beseecheth His Mistress, The Lover Who Cannot Prevail Must Needs Have Patience*—do suggest that Wyatt is exclusively a poet of the formal exigencies of love. But the titles were put in later by the laborious anthologist Tottel in 1557, when he com-piled his collection of lyrics, *The Miscellany*. They are mis-leading titles, as Tottel's text of Wyatt—that preserved in most anthologies and subsequent editions—is misleading. For Tottel imposed on Wyatt's original metres all the refine-ments which had been introduced into English versification by Surrey and his followers. He tried to match Wyatt's metre with the undisturbed heart-beat of a formal lover; he put in syllables; he took from Wyatt's original, in the interests of the easy and the obvious, many sharp accents of irony, subtle undertones, hesitations of a spirit doubting, recollecting, suddenly protesting. In the words of E. K. Chambers: " The sophisticator failed to appreciate Wyatt's free syllabic handling of iambic metres; the ready substitu-tion of an anapæst in any foot, the occasional trochees, the frequent omission of an unstressed syllable."

Tottel did not see that Wyatt's was far too profound a

nature to find fulfilment in writing madrigals to his mistress's hand, in mere experiment with metre and verse forms, attempting to capture the sweetness of Italian models. This sort of thing Wyatt did do to some extent; he might have done it much better, as well as Surrey, Gascoigne, and others, had it not been that what he had earnestly to say cannot be expressed in smoothly flowing numbers. The true musical quality in Wyatt's best poetry does not come out fully until his meaning is understood. There is a sinewy contention between the intellect and the soul's projected complement, the ideal, which often breaks the surface rhythm, intact in the pretty lilt of courtly love songs. This is well shown in one of Wyatt's most famous poems, " They fle from me, that sometyme did me seke," where an erotic episode—the most particularised of any in Wyatt's poetry—is used to express a world of experience, not only, not primarily in bedchambers:

1

" They fle from me, that sometyme did me seke
With naked fote, stalking in my chambr.
I have sene theim gentill, tame, and meke,
That now are wyld, and do not remembr
That sometyme they put theimself in daunger
To take bred at my hand; and now they raunge
Besely seking with a continuell chaunge.

2

" Thancked be fortune it hath ben othrewise
Twenty tymes better; but ons, in speciall,
When here lose gowne from her shoulders did fall,
And she me caught in her armes long and small,
Therewith all swetely did me kysse
And softely saide: ' Dere hert howe like you this? '

3

" It was no dreme: I lay brode waking;
But all is torned, thorough my gentilnes
Into a straunge fasshion of forsaking;
And I have leve to goo of her goodness:
And she also to use new fangilnes;
But syns that I so kyndely am served,
I wold fain know what she hath deserved."

If this is compared with Tottel's version, it will be found that, in the *Miscellany*, the significant breaks have all been filled in to make a swinging Tennysonian effect; the hesitancy of recollection, the sigh, the bitter smile, have been strummed away—" That now are wild, and do not *once* remember," " It was no dream; *for* I lay broad awaking," " But since that I *un*kindly so am servèd." So with many of the other poems, the gold rifts in Wyatt, just those parts which distinguish him from his contemporaries, have been plastered over.

This distinguishing accent comes from Wyatt's deep identification with the ideal of service. As a feudal conception applied to vassalage to a lady, early French poetry is permeated with the idea, welded with platonism, larded with scholastic conceits, it informs Italian poetry from Guinicelli to Petrarch—all sources which Wyatt used abundantly. Though with Wyatt the conception runs on naturally into the nationalistic current of the times : " My Kyng, my Contry for whom alone I lyve," at bottom the feeling in his poetry is feudal and platonic, too. Into the courtly forms, artificial, cold, Wyatt presses passion and drama—at his best, for sometimes he is as coldly conceited as anybody. At times he is cynical; no doubt he indulged with the rest in the facile gratifications the court went in for. He can write about woman's inconstancy : " It is their kind, and hath been long "; of love, " For tyger like, so swift he is in passing "; and he can even chime in with Panurge in Rabelais, egging on the Lady of Paris to lie with him, using the most materialistic arguments. Wyatt was sensible to Renaissance influence, but his finest poetry does not come from it. His scene is one that had been set long since, the protagonists are the conventional ones. But Wyatt's whole-hearted participation, at the nerve centre of Europe, in the tussle of contending forces, the passing of one age, the coming into being of a new, quickens the puppets to life, lends them an altogether novel significance. The woman in his poetry is not just the ideal woman handed down from one poet to another; she is the personification of a society into which new values were coming; an avowedly realistic society, one which, because it was freer intellectually, had less spiritual integrity. The plaint in Wyatt's poetry, the sharp accent of protest, is drawn from him by the " falsèd faith " of his friends and his sovereign, by unrewarded service, disdained loyalty. The famous poem beginning:

>  " *Fforget not yet the tryde entent,*
> *Of such a truthe as I have ment,*
> *My great travayle so gladly spent,*
> *Fforget not yet* "

acquires its force as a love poem from the synthesis of experience it expresses, experience only a small part of which is erotic, being mostly the result of Wyatt's professional life. The poem is so moving because Wyatt's nature, receptive and profound, brought all experience to an archetypal model. Wyatt, while he was lively, restless, sociable, observant (" As much wit to remember and remark everything he seeth as any man in England," writes a contemporary), possessed at the same time a quality of introversion, transforming what was practice and formality in other courtiers to a mode of feeling. While he borrows his forms —sonnet, rondeau, terza rima—he strikes a note no English poet then, not many since, have been able to manage. While others at best acted, Wyatt also felt in courtly forms. Faith and truth were really in his heart.

The most direct expression of Wyatt's lifelong affirmation comes in the *Defence*, where he answers the paltry, scheming priest, Bonner, who accused him of treason. " Ye," he writes, " and when ther is anye (treason) towarde my maister within thys harte, a sharpe swerde go thether with all." More measured, more reflective, the creed is given in one of the eight-line epigrammes:

> 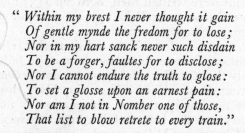 " *Within my brest I never thought it gain*
> *Of gentle mynde the fredom for to lose;*
> *Nor in my hart sanck never such disdain*
> *To be a forger, faultes for to disclose;*
> *Nor I cannot endure the truth to glose:*
> *To set a glosse upon an earnest pain:*
> *Nor am I not in Nomber one of those,*
> *That list to blow retrete to every train.*"

Again, in one of the extant letters to his son, Wyatt writes: " I hauve nothing to crye and cal apon you for but honestye, honestye."

Such is the affirmation in Wyatt's work; the reverse side, as it is bound to be with any idealist, is the Protest. The Protest is effective because of Wyatt's integrity, his belief, his values that would not crumble, his passionate cry for honesty in life, justice in love.

III

Wyatt, who married when he was sixteen, died before he was forty. The body—by no means pigmy—was soon fretted to decay. One has only to compare the portrait in the National Portrait Gallery with Holbein's sketch done a few years before to see how the Spanish ambassade had shattered him. He lived dangerously, as did all courtiers and politicians at that time, but also with seriousness and intensity, qualities which must have broken up the most powerful physique in a reign of such ruthless reverses as was Henry's. One had to be unscrupulous, hardened, to bear the bumps of the " slipper-wheel of Fortune " as it revolved in that century. If Wyatt's integrity of character just saved his neck after his recall from the Emperor's court, his own sensitiveness, a sharp sword piercing inward, weakening his physical resistance, soon afterwards substituted for the axe that had lopped off the heads of so many of his contemporaries: a chill, caught when he was riding to Falmouth on the King's business, killed Wyatt in a few hours.

The period when Wyatt was at the very centre of European affairs, bearing the entire responsibility of Cromwell's policy towards the Emperor, coincides with his maturity as a poet; his best poems were written then, between 1537 and 1540; and his prose *Defence* and religious poems were composed as a result of that unhappy ambassade.

Wyatt, it seems, undertook the mission with reluctance. It was a mission, for one thing, foredoomed to failure. It was not likely that Charles would ever become reconciled to his aunt being divorced and his cousin, Mary, losing the succession to the English throne. Intimations of marriages between Mary and the Infant of Portugal, between Henry himself and Christine of Milan, sounded hollow enough when set against Cromwell's coquetting with the Lutheran princes and his panderous negotiations for Anne of Cleves as Henry's fourth wife. They were not calculated to prevent Charles and

Francis getting together with the Pope and " casting Henry out at the cart's tail." The nervous strain must have been very great for anyone with Wyatt's hatred of failure. Wyatt was not altogether suited for diplomatic work; he confesses as much in his *Defence*. Though he was shrewd and observant, and though he saw exactly how the land lay and was a great personal favourite with the Emperor (so close that Catholics feared his Lutheran influence, and plotted to submit him to the Inquisition); while he had all this to commend him in his ambassade, Wyatt, who served his master as faithfully as ever Wolsey or Cromwell did, could not shake off adherence to a creed that went beyond allegiance to King and State. Then there was in him a restless need to be active all the time, that unquiet spirit which Surrey writes of in his epitaph, " Wyat resteth here that quick could never rest," the spur that goaded him on to so many activities, searching after knowledge, hammering and filing at his metric, discussing theology with the nuns at Barcelona; that drove him at last into retreat and self-examination. The languid movement of Spanish affairs, " the painful patience in delays " maddened him. And Wyatt always longed for England. It was from the court at Madrid that he wrote:

> " *My song, thou shalt ataine to fynd that plesent place*
> *Where she doth lyve, by whom I lyve; may chaunce to have this*
> *grace:*
> *When she hath red, and seen the dred wherein I serve,*
> *Bytwene her brestes she shall thee put, there shall she thee reserve.*
> *Then tell her that I come. . . ."*

The lines about his return are exuberant:

> " *Tagus, fare well, that westward with thy stremis,*
> *Torns up the grayns of gold alredy tryd:*
> *With spurr and sayle for I go seke the Temis,*
> *Gaynward the sonne that showth her wealthi pryde,*
> *And to the town which Brutus sowght by dremis,*
> *Like bendyd mone doth lend her lusty syd;*
> > *My Kyng, my Contry for whom alone I lyve:*
> > *Of myghty Love the winges for this me gyve.*"

A joyous outburst, and Wyatt's last on that note. Almost immediately on his return he was sent out to the Netherlands, whither the Emperor had removed his court. When he was finally recalled he was put into the Tower, accused of treason against his king and country. Wyatt's mission had failed, and, partly because of this, partly on account of Henry's revulsion for Cromwell's choice for him, Anne of Cleves, Cromwell had fallen. Wyatt's remorse bit deep. He felt responsible for his friend's death. Forgetting his own plight, he writes in a sonnet:

> " *The pillar parished is wharto I lent:*
> *The strongest staye of myne unquyet mynde."*

Henceforth he must be condemned: " . . . I my self, always my self to hate."

After Cromwell's fall, Wyatt's enemies had got busy. There were two of them, Haynes, a mere tool, and Edmund Bonner, afterwards Bishop of London, the man who figures as a notable slaughterer of Protestants in Foxe's *Book of Martyrs* (Bonner charges Wyatt, incidentally, with being a papist).

Bonner was not without his points. His rôle in the *Book of Martyrs* is certainly exaggerated, and anyone who could get the reputation for being the most unpopular man in London must have had some good in him. Although he allowed himself a certain latitude for religious vacillation, he did end his days in Marshalsea prison, because he would not take the Oath of Supremacy; and reports of his disregard for court etiquette in his missions among kings (Francis I nearly had him killed for his churlishness) show that Bonner was something of a character.

Bonner's accusation against Wyatt reveals a quaint, humourless dogmatism, an almost childish plaint, like a baby boy, blubbering out that his elder brother won't play with him. The serious charges are that Wyatt was heard publicly to pronounce disrespectful words against his master, Henry, and that he had conspired with Cardinal Pole, the Pope's Legate.

The accusation dated back some years to a most crucial period in Wyatt's diplomatic career. In 1538 a meeting took place at Nice between the Pope, Francis, and the Emperor. Wyatt's business was to see that an alliance did not result against England. He had also to keep a watchful eye on the movements of Cardinal Pole, who, it was thought, might work dangerously against Henry's interests. Wyatt was ultimately the victim of chicanery, an agreement being made while he was on his way back to consult Henry.

Before this happened, at a time when affairs were most critical at Nice, Bonner and Haynes arrived to strengthen the English ambassade. Wyatt was in a state of nervous tension:

> " *Such hammers work within my hed*
> *That sound nought els unto my eris. . . .*"

" I trotted continually," he writes in his *Defence*, " ap and downe that hell, throughe heate and stinke, from Councelloure to Embassator, from on frende to an other." Bonner's prying and coarseness got on his nerves. Wyatt was resentful that such a man had been sent out, for Bonner's behaviour can have done no credit to English manners. Wyatt was as courteous as he was able, gave his guests the best apartments in the galley in which he was living, paid for nearly everything. But he preserved an ironical aloofness. Bonner remembered.

> " I cannot commend Mr. Wyat," he writes in his quaint, priggish way, " that at the departing of Mr. Haynes and me he would so strangely do, neither to bring us forth of the town, nor yet to lend us of his horses, which to harlots (meaning low roistering fellows) he refuseth not to lend. . . . And he, regarding neither the King's honour or his honesty or ours, suffered us to ride on such spittal jades as I have not seen."

There is much more in this vein of petty reprimand.

Wyatt, after demolishing the main charges, takes up the trivial ones, turns them brilliantly against his accusers. " I know no man that did you dishonour, but your unmannerly behaviour, that made ye a laughing-stock to all men that came into your company, and me sometimes to sweat for shame to see you." To Bonner's accusation of immorality with the nuns at Barcelona Wyatt replies simply, " I graunt I do not professe chastite: but yet I use not abomination." Then comes the invective. The passage shows Wyatt's flair for the dramatic, his relish of a Boccaccian situation. One can see him engineering the scene he afterwards described with so much irony—sitting apart, courteous, grave, yet sparkling inwardly at the fun.

"Yf ye knowe yt," Wyatt goes on, referring to Bonner's statement about his immorality, " tell yt here, wyth whome, and when. yf ye harde it, who is your autor? have you sene me have anye harlet in my companie? dyd you ever see woman so myche as dyne or suppe at my table? none, but for yowr pleasure, the woman, that was in the gallye; wch I assure ye may be well seene, for (before you came) nether she, nor anye other came above the masts. but, bycawse the gentell men toke pleasure to see you intertayne her, therfore theie made her dyne and suppe wyth you; and theie leked well yowr lokes, yowr carvinge to Madonna, yowr drynking to her, and yowr playing under the table. aske Mason [Wyatt's secretary], aske Blage . . . yt was a playe to them, the kepinge of yowr bottels, that no man myght drink of but yowr self; and that ' the lyttel fat prest were a jollye morsell for the Signora.' "

Wyatt was pardoned; as a mark of his complete rehabilitation Henry gave him considerable property. But Wyatt could not forget. He writes to his friend Bryan from the Tower:

> " *Mallice assaulted that rightiousness should have,*
> *Sure I am Brian, this wounde shall heale agayne,*
> *But yet, alas, the scarre shall styll remayne.*"

Wyatt was thirty-seven now. He had known all that had seemed so magnificent to him as a young man—the splendour of court life, the confidence of his sovereign, power in the direction of his country's fortunes, learning, love. The fiery spirit feeding on these things had sent off their essence in poetry. But the achievements themselves were ashes. The gust of passion was still in his soul, the instrument perfected through twenty years' experiment was ready to hand. But it is not tuned for love, but for the accompaniment:

> " *Of stormy sighs, deep drafts of his decay.*"

Wyatt still served his master, died in his service, but the courtier-poet is dead, his epitaph " scarred " deep in the heart:

" In Court to serve, deckèd with freshe aray,
Of sugred meates felyng the swete repast;
The life in bankuets and sundry kindes of play,
Amid the presse of lordly lokes to waste,
Hath with it joynde oft times such bitter taste,
That who so ioys such kinde of life to holde
In prison ioys fettred with cheines of gold."

Some years before, probably after a short term of imprisonment in the Fleet, due to a quarrel with the Duke of Suffolk, Wyatt had written three satires on the court, but they are comparatively genial, they are more in the nature of eulogies on the country life. It is not the country as such that allures now, not Wyatt's dogs and his reading, his epicurean leisure. The impulse to retreat is a much deeper one—the necessity for self-renunciation, self-knowledge, repentance. The inwit of the Reformation has begun to bite. The pomp, formalities, emptiness of court life are paralleled with the outward show of catholicism. In renouncing the one Wyatt comes naturally to reject the other, probing down to confront that fiery particle in his soul which had eaten its way through all the trappings of the times. The vital impulse no longer worked outwards, no longer spurred the body to action, the mind to political intrigue; turned inward, it needed solitude to identify itself, not now with a courtly ideal, but beyond, with an ultimate cause. The dread is upon Wyatt of being one,

"That knowen is to all, but to himself, alas,
He dieth unknown, dasèd with dreadful face."

Wyatt's paraphrase of the seven penitential psalms of David, however, does not represent his best work. There is more poetry in the first two lines of the introduction than in all the rest:

"Love to gyve law unto his subject hartes
Stode in the Iyes of Barsabè the bryght . . ."

The conception of service is shifted from King and country to God, from courts to the soul's solitudes, but the distinctive note has left his poetry. Though Wyatt could not help but be sensitive to the infiltration of new ideas, and though his nature was particularly adapted to receive Lutherism, yet he had been so formed by heredity, upbringing, and natural accomplishments for the rôle of courtier, he had become so set in the chivalrous, feudal mould, that his poetic experience could never become disaffected. A century was to pass before the religious experience which so profoundly affected Wyatt found complete expression in English poetry.

IV

The restless intellect at grips with the protean shapes of love—a strong, resourceful wrestler twisting and shifting to bring down love, to resolve it to a simplicity intuitively grasped, a simplicity which can only be achieved by the mind's surrender, this is the animating theme of Wyatt's poetry and this is what puts him with Donne and the early Shakespeare. Wyatt differs from them in that it is not the Renaissance senses, but the chivalric sentiments with which the intellect struggles. Whereas the lists with Shakespeare and with Donne are in the open, outward, physical, " on sweet bottom grass and high delightful plain," with Wyatt they are far down in the " hertes forrest." There is no question of a sensual victory. Following the platonic precept, the sensual element in the soul's trinity " becommeth full and wholy most obedient to reason, and ready to turn unto her all his motions, and follow her where she lust to lead him, without any resistance, like a tender lamb that renneth, standeth and goith always by the ewe's side."

A sonnet of Petrarch's, translated by both Surrey and Wyatt, states the chivalric convention. Love has made a bold advance, has showed itself on the lover's face as physical desire. The lady is displeased. So Love retreats, " leving his enterprise with payn and cry." The courtly code leaves no doubt what the lover, or servant of Love, must do in the circumstances:

> "What may I do when my maister fereth,
> But in the feld with him to lyve and dye?
> For good is the lif, ending faithfully."

The very reverse of the courtier Donne's conclusion:

> "So must pure lovers' souls descend
> To affections and to faculties,
> Which sense may reach and apprehend,
>   Else a great prince in prison lies."

With Wyatt the betrayal is in the heart, the residence of faith and truth.　Guided by its faith, the heart of the lover surrenders to its mistress of its own free will.　" Where two love one another," writes the Italian platonist, Ficino, " each of them departeth from himself to draw near unto the other, and dieth in himself to revive in the other."　It is the other's betrayal and putting to death of this faith and truth which is inconceivable to the intellect, which kindles the passion and creates the drama in Wyatt's best poetry :

> *"Ys yt possyble*
> *That so hye debate,*
> *So sharp, so sore and off suche rate,*
> *Shuld end so sone that was begone so late,*
> *Is it possyble!*

> *"Ys yt possyble!*
> *So cruell intent*
> *So hasty hete and so sone spent,*
> *Ffrom love to hate, and thens ffor to relent,*
> *Is it possyble! "*

Wyatt could never understand how truth and faith could be so buffeted about.　Not only in his love, but in his life generally he had as bitter proofs as anyone that they could. It is Wyatt's achievement, what made him so eminent both as man and poet, that he affirmed to the end, would not admit defeat.

ROBERT KETT

d. 1549

By

ROBERT RANDALL

ROBERT KETT

by ROBERT RANDALL

THERE are many accounts of Kett's Rebellion, yet there is little to be found about the character of Kett himself or his relation to the neighbouring gentry. Even his birth and his age at the time of the rising must be left to conjecture. Kett was of Norman ancestry, a landowner and a tanner, and his brother William, who was also hanged after the Rebellion, is described as a butcher as well as a landowner. At the beginning of the thirteenth century, when Philip Augustus captured Gournai from King John, the ancestors of Robert Kett settled in Repton Hall, Norfolk, where their first recorded name is Le Chat. From the earliest time the family seems to have been attached to the more important house of Gurney, which, after the coronation of William the Conqueror, took over responsibilities in Norfolk as well as in Normandy. Until the Rebellion in 1549 the Ketts lived, increasing their estates as a result of the dissolution of the monasteries, without attracting much attention to themselves. At his death Robert Kett was possessed, besides of Wymondham, of four or five small properties in Norfolk, which were taken from his family and granted as a reward to Thomas Audeley, a chief opponent in Norwich. Contemporary historians pay little tribute to the idealism of the Ketts, but it may speak something for the spiritual background of their home that in later generations they intermarried with the family of William Penn in Buckinghamshire.

Robert Kett grew up in times which were restless. The rare combination of capacity, gallantry, and rashness he displayed as a leader may be attributed to a limited experience of the world. " Periods of revolution," writes Froude, " bring out and develop extraordinary characters: they produce saints and heroes, and they produce also fanatics, and fools, and villains; but they are unfavourable to the application of the plain principles of right and wrong to everyday life." We do not know what kind of an education Kett had or whether he had visited London before Thomas Audeley brought him there to be tried. Albeit we may assume, from the ready manner in which the rebels accepted his leadership, that his duties as a landowner and his work as a tanner were conscientiously carried out. These, together with the unprecedented quantity of new reading then in circulation, must have left him with very little leisure or inclination to understand the ways of court life.

It was a period when promotion and disgrace followed as rapidly upon one another as the night upon the day. Shame and indignation were aroused by the arrogance, injustices, and luxury of the nobles, the superstition and corruption of the Church; and there was a new and earnest idealism, the prospect of a commonwealth in which every man could be a self-respecting unit. The rough picture of society, created in Kett's imagination as an outcome of his reading and activities, could scarcely have been of a more precise nature than this conflict. For we shall note that in his leadership he displayed the executive ability of one who knew well the merits and shortcomings of those who worked under him and about him; but of the powers and subtleties which are the resources of higher responsibilities Kett, in spite of his being a landowner, seems to have known little or nothing.

The Norfolk labourers and Norwich workers whom Kett led existed in the wake of a flood of ignorance and superstition such as remains now in Europe only among peasants of the Far East. When abuses of religion are being laid bare and superstitions exposed, it follows that the private passions of men are deeply aroused: fears, hatreds, hopes, and faiths strive with one another in a welter of aimless confusion. Reforms had been carried out in the Church, the onsets upon maladministration and debauchery had been successful. The abuse of penance and the fantastic worship of images so alien to the development of national character were fast disappearing with the approval of the central authority. Although prophecy, witchcraft, conjury, and divining had not lost their grip upon popular imagination, there were arising those who were willing to attack such misuse of human frailty, and the sway of necromancy and magic was on the wane. The prospect of a new era more natural to the development of dignified character could plainly be discerned, and there were signs enough of success to intoxicate the headstrong and to spread among the ignorant an irresistible temptation to be dangerously self-confident. Yet the people could have no pause in which to dwell upon their successes; it fell to their unhappy lot to bear with the shortcomings of the times without the power to look ahead and measure the great benefits which would befall later generations. As changes took place nobles became no less arrogant, and even more luxurious; while distresses affecting the lives of the poor were multiplied by harsh times and gaps created in the distribution of charity by the disorganisation of the Church.

The confidence vaguely arising among the people that their growing ideals of right and wrong would eventually be defined and prevail was not the only outcome of the dissolution of the monasteries. In material matters of everyday existence the dissolution affected the poor with a series of very real grievances. Some monks had undoubtedly committed and permitted acts which were disgraceful or which could not be approved in a time of changing manners. Nevertheless as a class the monks had been careful and kindly landlords, considerate and pleased to attend to the needs of their poorer neighbours. In good times their charity would have been missed; but, as will be shown, the times were bad and unprecedented. It has never been the policy of monasteries to force high rents: it has always been the way of monks to purchase where necessary in the local markets, to minister to the poor and sick, and to attend to whatsoever grievances are brought to them by those who do not know how to manage their own affairs. The interests of new landlords in the estates granted to them during the Reformation were soon discovered to be foreign to any such traditional goodness. They were a type mainly of rising gallants in pressing need of money to maintain themselves in ambitious circumstances connected with court life, adventure, and foreign wars. Their new estates were therefore administered with a view to increasing their wealth and freedom in another world to that of their tenants. Living mainly in London, they were for the most part lacking in local affections and obligations, and there was no need for them to purchase goods for their households from poor tenants and distressed neighbours. Thus in a time of stress there was often no one to perform good offices for the poor and needy. Men found themselves friendless, neglected, and deserted in circumstances more hopeless than ever they had been brought up to expect.

Far more important for the seditious of East Anglia, who rallied whole-heartedly to Kett's standard than this one aspect of changing national life were the alterations in the conditions of the people following upon the trend of events all over the Western world. The basis of commerce was shifting from the Mediterranean Sea to the Atlantic, from agriculture and riches from the East to manufacture and plenty from the West. At home it was a time of vagabonds and pirates, when beggars were to be found loitering in every street and common ground, ready to serve anyone who might claim loyalty in the interest of rebellion or authority. Though blame might be attached to their old masters, it was not with the masters that the fault lay. The wonders of the New World, in the form of gold, precious stones, and metals, were brought back to Europe in ships destined, not for our own ports, but for the ports of other countries. So much new wealth in the chests of foreigners reduced the value of our own coinage in its relation to the coins of other countries. Thus it was made difficult or impossible for our impoverished merchants to purchase from abroad. At home the new discoveries had their peculiar bearing upon shops and markets. Commodities which could be exported to other lands increased in value to a point which in home commerce placed them beyond the purse of all but the richest citizens. In 1548 an order had to be issued to prevent the further export of leather, and many a fellow must have then been shoeless for the first time. Clothes were at a premium for the poor. Wool commanded very high prices from foreign manufacturers, and that which had before been made into garments to be worn at home was no longer sold in England, but sold to manufacturers in Flanders prepared to pay a much higher price. As a consequence of foreign fashions the elegant clothes of the rich became even more conspicuous. To meet the profitable foreign demand for wool at high prices, ploughed land was hastily being turned into pasturage, and common lands were being wrongfully enclosed. It seemed that there could be no point at which this chain of evil circumstances and contrasting conditions could end. For with the claiming of agricultural land for sheep the price of wheat soared up, and bread became dearer, while wages remained much as they were. With town and country labourers out of work and unprovided for, the quick profits made by the enterprising led to speculation in house owning and building and a general rise in rents. The woollen trade in London and Norwich, the business of manor life and farming had been caught up in a turmoil of incoherent and endless upheaval.

Moreover, a man's apprehension of insecurity by no means ended with effects of changes taking place in foreign trade. The hired mercenaries and soldiers who fought at Boulogne and Pinkie had somehow to be paid. There was no other way to pay them but by following the example set by Henry VIII in debasing the coinage. A Bristol shilling that was worth a shilling to-day might be worth nothing to-morrow.

Thus, to aggravate the upsets which befell the poor and steady-going, there was always harassing them a medley of pertinent contrasts. Open to all eyes was the spectacle of the gallants, daily growing richer and more offensive, to whose adventurous natures the changing circumstances were propitious. "Is there not reigning in London," asked Latimer, "as much pride, as much covetousness, as much oppression as there was in Nebo?" "In times past," he lamented, "when any rich men died in London they were wont to help the poor scholars of the universities with exhibitions. When any rich men died they would bequeath great sums of money towards the relief of the poor." When nothing has a fixed value, it is with the selfish and un-scrupulous that wealth lies. Men spend their money on themselves, uncertain of what may become of them when a day or two has passed, and often not knowing how to care for institutional life and the well-being of others from whom they receive no benefit and towards whom they feel no gratitude.

Popular printing was still a novelty. There were a few men, nevertheless, who stood out, determined that wisdom and learning should no longer remain the monopoly of those who read Latin. Their deeds and words were ready to expose injustice and to set forth ideal remedies in a way which would appeal to one of Kett's temperament and stand-ing. In the sermons of Latimer and Gilpin there were eloquent illustrations drawn from the hardships of everyday life. These preachers were fearless in their rebukes and downright in the searching methods by which they tried to formulate a higher conception of inward character in the imaginations of their audiences. The radical pamphlets of Simon Fish, Henry Brynkelok, and Robert Crowley had spread the idea of a new commonwealth, an ideal state in which the middle classes should hold greater riches and share all responsibilities: " they not only wished," says Professor Pollard, " to reform enclosures, but to reform the House of Lords as well." In the cause of these new ideals the lame John Hales, member for Preston, one who had not been educated at Oxford or Cambridge, introduced into the House of Commons bill after bill, returning again and again to the attack after bitter debates and lonely defeats. The courage, honourable bearing, forthrightness, and pertinacity shown by these men must have moved Kett by example. We may suppose him possessed of an imagination ahead of his time and inspired by a romantic and lonely puritan idealism.

The year 1549, it will be gathered, was one in which what we would now term " drastic action " was demanded. Yet there was no policy which the Government could pursue with general approval. Distress was too great and passions ran too high. Alarm concerning the future of property and fine manners had created another political alignment besides that already growing on account of religious differences. Those who thought with Somerset and possibly with the King were influenced by Hales and Latimer; they wished the people to understand that their grievances were recognised by the central authority and were receiving persevering attention. But Warwick, Paget, and most of the rest of the Council were of another frame of mind. They feared for their property and suspected the ability of the people to conduct their own affairs.

The rebelliousness shaped itself by concentrating upon two sets of symbols, enclosures and church images. In both cases the Government was forced to define a line of policy and to take action by issuing a proclamation and appointing a commission: the Lord Protector " gaping after the fruitless breath of the multitude and more desirous to please the most than the best," comments Sir John Hayward. The new measures were unpopular as well as popular. The gentry who " improved the Lands they enclosed by three parts at least " and the Roman Church Party, together with many others, " who esteemed the Beauty of their Churches," took offence at them.   Every device was mustered in order to subvert the report of the Commission on Enclosures, and the friends of the Lady Mary were suspected of instigating every petty riot.   Warwick led a shameful attack on John Hales, who had been appointed one of the Commissioners. Strype's account is : " Some of them got means for their servants to be sworn on Juries that they might be more favourable to them.   And in some part where the commissioners went, such were the numbers of the retainers to the great men (who were the chief enclosers) that it was not possible to make juries without them.   Some men threatened to be put by their holds if they presented, and others had no certainty of their holds, which were wont to be let by copy for lives, or otherwise for years, so that their landlords might have them upon the bank at any time, nor in anything to offend them.   And some were indicted because they presented the truth.   And many shameful sleights were used to blind the commissioners and the presenters and to baffle the good work they were upon."   But the ice was cracking. By their industry and example the Commissioners gave authority to one set of standpoints, causing fierce resentment among those who held another.

That year the summer was hot, and restraint became impossible.   Revolt first broke out in Cornwall, where a Mr. Body, a commissioner, was stabbed while pulling down an image.   Rebellion spread all over the South-west of England and as far North as Oxford.   The provocations, it seems, were chiefly religious, enclosures playing their part after the revolts had begun.   The rebels were encouraged by the time-gaining policy of the Council and the leniency of Somerset.   The city of Exeter fell into their hands.   But the seditious were for the most part a rabble, without order or determination.   They fought hard and sometimes repulsed the gentlemen who were under the leadership of Lord Grey of Wilton.   But the revolters could not resist pillage, while lack of direction made their eventual defeat certain.   Unfortunately, before the Rebellion was under way, or news of its defeat could reach Norfolk, circumstances had arisen to encourage Kett to lead a revolt in his own county.

There had been smoulderings of an alarming kind in the neighbourhood of Wymondham for many years before Kett's rebellion. Bitter local feeling had arisen on account of an outrage committed upon the Priory Church, and leading to a private feud between the families of Kett and Sergeant Flowerdew of Heathersett.

Attached to the dissolved monastery of Wymondham was a church very much esteemed for its beauty by the inhabitants of the village. In 1531, the parishioners organised by the Ketts, who feared that the church would be destroyed because it was no longer needed for services, petitioned that they might buy the bells, the roof, and the choir in order to preserve them in their own parish church. The Crown appears to have sanctioned their request, and may also have paid the money for the purchase. The good intentions of the neighbourhood were thwarted by the abrupt action of Sergeant Flowerdew, who stripped the lead from the roof and carried away the bells. Whatever may have been the cause of Sergeant Flowerdew's strange action, it cannot be supposed that the peasants thought any the better of the gentry on account of it. For a number of years bad feeling between the peasants and the gentry, the Ketts and the Flowerdews, awaited an outlet for expression. The Ketts and Flowerdews, like other gentry in the neighbourhood, had, moreover, seized chances to augment their land and riches by means of the new opportunities opened by sheep grazing and enclosing.

An opportunity came when the annual play in honour of Thomas à Becket was given at Attleborough. The assembled villagers were smarting under the new grievances, poverty, their loss of common land, unemployment in ploughing and tilling. Earlier in the year they had thrown open land enclosed by John Green of Wilby by digging up the surrounding hedges. On this occasion the rioters attempted to overturn the fences at Heathersett belonging to Sergeant Flowerdew. Perhaps against Flowerdew the peasants may have had no just grievances. At any rate he retorted that his neighbour, Robert Kett, had enclosed land at Fairstead, and that if they would throw down his hedges he would pay them forty pence. So the mob made their way to Fairstead, where Kett was told by the rabble that his enemy had bribed them to pull down his fences. To their amazement the rioters found themselves made welcome. Kett set to with them and manfully helped to free his own enclosures. Fired by his eloquence, by the words with which he declaimed the covetousness of the surrounding gentry, and by his assurance of his readiness to lead a revolt and stand by it with " body and goods," they returned to Heathersett to pursue their original intention of pulling down all the fences of the out-witted and furious Sergeant Flowerdew.

Kett was joined by his brother William, a hardy butcher at Wymondham. Within a few days the news of the revolt had spread among the neighbouring poor and out-of-work farm hands, servants, and vagabonds, and there being nothing left to destroy in the district, the band proceeded to Cringleford and Boethorpe. Here they were encountered by Sir Edmund Windham, the High Sheriff of Norfolk, who courageously called the rebels to order and commanded them to go back to their homes. But they would have none of him, and the Sheriff was forced to ride as quickly as a good horse would carry him to Norwich, the rioters following, doing damage on the way and pulling down the fences of the Town Close. Outside Norwich, Kett, the number of whose followers very soon mounted to sixteen thousand men from all over the county, found quarters on Mousehold Heath.

The Mayor of Norwich at once sent to London for help. There was fighting and some plunder, but there seems to have been very little panic. The Mayor had his duties to carry out and Kett and his followers had their sense of how a rebellion should be run. Kett's men had to be fed and armed. Their need to revenge themselves upon the landlords whom they believed had oppressed them must be given some outlet. There was respect for Christian principles. The enemy was the gentry, and the rebels did everything in the King's name, appointing themselves his friends and deputies. No gentleman was murdered, but many of them were brought to Mousehold Heath to be tried. At this stage Kett's leadership ensured that the progress of the rebels was well directed and humane. Near the camp was the famous Oak of Reformation. Beneath its leafy boughs Kett held his councils, addressed his followers, and sat in judgment upon the gentlemen who were brought to him. Courts were set up and services were held. The Mayor was constrained to accept an invitation to sit in judgment with Kett. Sermons were preached and the pulpit was thrown open to those not in sympathy with the revolt. Matthew Parker, at one time during the rebellion in Norwich, attempted from the Oak of Reformation to persuade the mob to return to their homes, and, when his appeal failed, begged of them to behave with restraint.

The idealist leaders of the rebels set to work to give their rebellion practical shape in the form of changes in the policy of government and the law of the land. Under the guidance of Kett, the seditious from twenty-two hundreds in Norfolk and one in Suffolk set down their grievances in the form of a Petition forwarded to London and presented to the King. " We pray," they complained in words that will always be remembered, " thatt all bonde men be ffre for God made all ffre w^t his precious blode shedding." Their petition, although it contained a clause concerning teaching cate-chism and some clauses related to vicars and priests, was not concerned at all with religious disputes. The appeals were addressed to the alleviation of poverty and the safe-guarding of the common man against the Norfolk gentry, relentlessly pressing home the advantage of superior resources and cunning at a time of duress. The petitioners invited the King to intervene to prevent high rents and dear wool, to protect common lands and the profit from them, called for the exposure of false weights and measures, and asked that river fishing be made free and that some profits from sea-fishing should be secured to sailors. A few of the demands were impractical or ahead of the times; but most were related to questions of policy upon which it would stretch no one's imagination to suppose that a Tudor monarch would not be prepared to identify himself with the wishes of his people.

In London the news of Kett's good leadership gave place to alarm at the size of the rebellion. Although the Pro-tector had some sympathy with the rebels' case, most of the Council was in favour of strong measures. The temper of the gentry and their way of looking at the seditious may be gathered from Sir John Hayward's description of Kett's conduct and rhetorical manner:

" He told them with vehement voice, how they were overtop'd and trodden down by Gentlemen, and other good Masters, and put out of responsibility ever to recover Foot; how whilst Rivers of Riches ran into their Landlords coffers, they were par'd to the quick, and

fed upon Pease and Oats like Beasts; how being fleeced
by these for private benefit, they were stay'd by publick
Burthens of the State, wherein whilst the richer Sort
favour'd themselves, they were gnawn to the very
Bones; how the more to terrify and torture them to their
Minds, and wind their necks more surely under their
Arms; their tyrranous Master did often plead arrest
and call them into Prison, and thereby consume these
to worse than nothing; how they did palliate them
Pillories with the fair pretence of Authority and Law.
Fine Workmen I warrant you, who can so closely carry
their Dealings that then men only discover them; how
harmless Counsels were fit for tame Fools but for them
who had already stir'd there was no hope but in
adventuring boldly."

Kett's law court and the preaching under the Reformation
Oak he described as " Actions cover'd and disguis'd with
Mantles, very Usual in a Time of Disorder.   They aimed,
not at ambitious Ends, their rude Earthly Spirits were never
seasoned with any manly adventurous Thought, and therefore they were content with a licentious and idle Life,
wherein they might fill their Bellies with Spoil, rather than
by Labour."

The King and Somerset replied to the Petition on July 21.
The risings in the west were still in progress.   There could
be no point in forcing matters.   The rebellion was one thing,
the claims the people were pressing were another.   Time
was needed to gather forces to move against Kett: nothing
better than to make a direct attack upon the enemy by
assuming sympathy with their demands.   " Seeing he was
ready to rèceive and relieve the quiet complaints of his
subjects," the King's reply began, " he marvelled much that
upon opinion either of necessity in themselves or of injustice
to him, they should first put themselves in arms as a party
against him, and then present him with their bold petitions."
The King then proceeded to deal one by one with most of
their complaints.   He reminded them that he had recently
issued a proclamation relating to the price of victuals, and
that orders had been issued and a commission appointed to
deal with enclosures.   He would charge his commissioners
to hear complaints and take steps to reduce the high farm
rents.   He suggested some remedies for dealing with the

price of wool. Parliament he promised would sit in October, and the County of Norfolk should appoint four or six from its number in order to present bills to deal with other grievances. The answer was soft enough; but in fact it promised very little change, and in the case of wool its proposals were no better than specious.

In the camp at Mousehold Heath the tone, alas, had deteriorated between the despatch of the Petition and the arrival of the King's Herald with an answer. Good food and plunder had made their impression upon persons unaccustomed either to responsibility or plenty. Neither Kett nor the dignitaries of Norwich could now hold the men back; the imprisoned gentlemen were exposed to insult and torture and those who had fled from Norwich in order to keep care of their wives and children were vindictively termed traitors by the rebels and maltreated. Yet after the Herald had read the King's reply and announced the Free Pardon to all accompanying it, there was a warm demonstration of loyalty and a readiness to accept so generous an answer. Kett albeit was not of the same mood as his followers. He may have feared for his own head. It was, however, his superior intelligence, I dare say, which enabled him to discover before the others how little in fact had been gained to the rioters by the King's reply. He had no true imagination of what might be won in a practical way. He had not the foresight to see how weak would be his forces in the face of a fully equipped and well-led army. His heart was in the rebellion, but his mind had no conception of the difficulties he had to overcome. He guessed aright the power he himself had acquired over his followers. Standing out in the face of the people, rendered humble by the apparent generosity of their King, kneeling, shouting, and giving thanks, Kett made bold answer: "Kings are wont to pardon wicked persons, not innocent and just men: they for their part have deserved nothing." His speech ended, the Herald called Kett a traitor, charged him with high treason, and commanded a sword-bearer to arrest him; the Herald's ill-considered change of front confirmed the suspicions of Kett in the minds of the multitude. Thereupon the mob rallied to him again, and the Herald was forced to leave the camp and enter into the city.

After this affair Kett set to work to strengthen his position upon Mousehold Heath and in relation to the city of Norwich. His guns when first fired at the city from a hill nearby did no damage, either on account of their position or because the skilled men needed to fire them, not being of the rebels' mind, shot up into the air. So Kett moved his artillery to lower ground, and from there was able to dominate Norwich by force as well as by terror of the multitude, and the Mayor and chief citizens were captured.

Kett was fortunate in the character of the first military commander sent against him by orders from London. As the Council would not permit Somerset to lead, William Parr, Marquis of Northampton, was appointed to raise the siege. He was a courtier rather than a soldier, a good-natured man of some integrity, who excelled in negotiation, but had had no experience of command. He had at his disposal an army consisting not of regular soldiers but of the personal retinues of the lords and gentlemen of the neighbourhood; about 1,500 horsemen and a band of Italian mercenaries.

Upon his approaching the city the magistrates went out to meet him and join forces. Northampton, however, had not been many hours in Norwich before his army was betrayed by his own bad generalship and lack of control over his men. Some of the gentlemen went out at once to examine the battlefield and discover for themselves how Kett's forces were disposed and what condition his men were in. These appear to have been attacked by the rebels. For a short time the Italian mercenaries coming to their rescue displayed their skill as trained soldiers so well that it looked as if the tide might be turned against Kett at once. But Northampton had been surprised by the swift onslaught of the rebels, and was not yet ready with a plan or with his whole forces. He permitted rebels by mere numbers to press upon the Italians, and at the moment when the Italians should have been strengthened, they were forced to retire fighting in a circular formation, very frightened that Kett's men would surround them and cut them off entirely. Kett was unable to encompass them, and in the gallant fighting one of the gentlemen was captured whom the angry mob " spoiled of his Armour and Apparel and hang'd over the Walls of Mount Surry."

Believing that he had an advantage, Kett tried to press it home. Northampton, instead of at once taking up a position which he could defend and from which he could use the superior quality of his troops to advantage against the attack of the rabble, kept his tired men in Norwich, lighting fires in every street and walking to and fro in their armour, alert against a surprise attack. This came about midnight, when Kett brought the full force of his artillery into play. Northampton then attempted to place some of his divided troops at the ramparts and at the gates. At this point Kett began a new attack before Northampton had consolidated his position on the outside of the city. The new assault failed, and it appears Kett did not capture the city until the next morning, after Northampton, severely shaken and with many wounded, had by means of a herald, made another offer of Free Pardon . . . rejected by the confident rebels, who swarmed up the walls and captured the ramparts. Northampton, his ranks depleted, fled hastily from the city in order to save the lives of his fellow gentlemen and to retain the small force of mercenaries with which he had set out. The gentlemen had suffered losses in the street fighting. " Lord Sheffield's Horse fell with him into a Ditch, whereby he fell into the power of the seditious, and as he pulled off his helmet to show them who he was, a Butcher slew him with a stroke of a club." Thirty other gentlemen were captured by the rebels and taken to prison, " where they were visited alike with Scarcity and Scorn."

In London news from all quarters pointed to the need to take decisive measures. Many of our fortified positions in Scotland had to be abandoned. The French had been successful at Boulogne. New rebellions had broken out in Yorkshire. Word came of the successes of Russell in the west and of the failure of Northampton against Kett. The hearts of the Council hardened in their policy not to permit Somerset to go to Norfolk. They determined to send a soldier, and John Dudley, Earl of Warwick, finally was chosen. In him Kett had an opponent very different from Northampton. Warwick was a man of the world and a man of action. He had distinguished himself in the wars with Scotland, where he had been regarded as the hero of Pinkie. He was a stout defender of enclosures, and showed no sympathy with the rabble. " He had the art," says Froude, " of gaining influence by affecting to disclaim a desire for it." His first concern was to keep Northampton's forces together, and he not only refrained from criticising Northampton's generalship, but went so far as to praise him for the manner in which he had extracted himself from a difficult position. Thus Warwick moved slowly towards Norfolk, collecting together all the forces he could, and stopping at Cambridge, where he discussed the position with some of the chief citizens of Norwich, who there joined him. At Alwood he took council with Sir Thomas Gresham. When he arrived at Norwich, on August 23, he had made up his mind how to proceed against the rabble. With him were 6,000 footmen and 1,500 horsemen, cannon, and gunmen, upon whom he could rely.

Warwick's first move was to send out a herald to make an overture to the other side. Kett met the herald, and being aware of the man who was against him, allowed him to make his proclamation throughout the streets of Norwich, himself securing the safety of the herald by accompanying him. Misfortune now pursued Kett. He was never permitted to meet Warwick and to discuss terms with him. When the herald was offering his pardon, " a lewd Boy turn'd towards him his naked Breech, and used words suitable to that gesture; one standing by mov'd by this barbarous Behaviour discharg'd a Harquebus upon the Boy, and Stroke him with a shot above the Reins." This unhesitating reply on the part of the King's men incensed the crowd who, filled with a fear of what might happen to them if they accepted a pardon, resolved to defend their own rights. Although Kett had learned how to face a changed situation, the rabble had learned nothing new. They were back in the mood of suspiciousness Kett had stirred in them at the arrival of the first herald. Kett's eloquence and authority, which before had been able to stir the crowd to fight, was this time without avail in persuading them to peace. He did not desert his followers, but decided to prepare them for a desperate battle.

Warwick took possession of Norwich, which had been in Kett's hands since the defeat of Northampton. This he did by capturing the gates and placing his cannon there, himself taking up quarters in the market-place. The sixty prisoners made in the first skirmishes he put to death without delay under martial law. But so fierce was the fighting of the rabble that Warwick found himself without men at his disposal with which to guard the entry of his ammunition and baggage.

Thus Kett was able to secure an important advantage by cutting off a large proportion of Warwick's stores and driving or detracting them to Mousehold Heath. Encouraged by new plunder and fresh ammunition with which to fire off their cannon, Kett's men began to make great advance. With Warwick in Norwich, his forces divided in the streets, his cavalry useless against the rebels perched on Mousehold Heath, his cannon without shot, many among his followers tried to persuade him to retire and to await the arrival of Russell's lanzknechts coming victorious from the rebellion in the west. But his honour as a general was at stake and his mind was made up. Better than his followers Warwick knew the strength of his position and the weaknesses of the enemy. Weariness, he foresaw, or an error of judgment might at any moment place the victory in his hands. On one vital point he had been successful. He had stopped all roads by which victuals could be supplied to the camp on Mousehold Heath. He would give Kett no fresh opportunity to learn more lessons, and the rabble no chance to re-hearten themselves for fresh attack after a second victory. So he gathered his gentlemen together, and in an elegant soldierly custom of the time bad them kiss one another's swords, swear loyalty, and take courage.

Within a few days important changes had taken place. Warwick's reinforcements had arrived, and among his opponents demoralisation had set in, his calculations proving true. The men at Mousehold Heath were growing hungry and desperate. Superstition began to grip them, a foolish prophecy took hold of them. It may be that it was spread by men in Warwick's pay or it may have been an expression of their apprehension that defeat was inevitable and further extensive effort futile. Kett's chosen position on Mousehold Heath, from which his guns overlooked Norwich, where Warwick's horse were useless, had enabled him always to maintain his full strength in face of the enemies' weakness. Kett probably understood this very well. But he could not restrain his supporters, who were influenced by an old saying,

> " *The country Knapps, Hob, Dick, and Hick,*
> *With clubs and clouted shoon,*
> *Shall fill up Dussendale*
> *With slaughter'd bodies soon.*"

The strange saying, if it had any meaning at all, might just as well refer to their own bodies as to those of the King's army. But this ambiguity was passed over. Kett, alas, was forced to give way to superstition. Under the cover of smoke from their cannon and from the blaze they had made of the burning cabins, built since July, the rabble came forward to the fields and meadows of the low ground at the foot of the hill.

The Earl of Warwick had scarcely to fight in order to drive home his new advantage. The rebels marshalled the whole of their great number on the flat ground, exposed to any form of attack Warwick might care to select. In the forefront Kett had placed the captured gentlemen, using their bodies to ward off the attacks of the enemy. Warwick began by sending out a messenger, offering, not a general pardon, but a pardon to everyone except the leaders. But the rebellion was not to end without deaths. The men refused to accept the terms, to abandon Kett, or the hideous prospect of their own slaughter. They opened battle by making a great demonstration, firing off their cannon and striking down the Royal standard. The lanzknechts replied by shooting straight into the assembled mass, Warwick leading his horsemen into their midst. The field was soon covered with dead bodies. Those alive fled and others stood on and awaited the advent of further slaughter. Three thousand five hundred it is said were slain. Warwick again offered a pardon; but the men, not believing him, refused, saying they would rather die fighting than give up their leaders or be slaughtered without weapons. Warwick, victorious, would not parley; the lanzknechts lifted their matchlocks, and before this sight the people threw down their arms and surrendered. The Earl of Warwick, having no further use for violence, restrained his followers from killing those ringleaders who were left upon the field. So easy had been the victory that the skilled soldiers had won without slaughtering one of their friends imprisoned in the forefront of the enemies' ranks.

When it became certain that complete failure awaited the rebels, Kett and his brother took horses, attempting to flee disgrace and punishment. Kett was possessed of a swift horse, which on the first day got him as far as Swannington. But on the next day a party of Warwick's soldiers captured him in a barn together with his brother William. Twenty horsemen were allocated to convey the brothers in charge of Thomas Audeley to London. Of those who remained in Norwich it is related that nine of the principals were hanged on the Tree of Reformation, " of whom two were seducing prophets, a third was a most excellent Cannonier, whose good will evilly employed did much to endanger the Forces of the King."

In London Robert and William Kett were kept guarded in the Tower for some months. It was not until November 25, when the rebellion had died down, that the Constable was commanded to bring the brothers for trial at Westminster. There they pleaded guilty to a charge of treason, " not having God before their eyes, but seduced by diabolical instigation." According to custom they threw themselves on the King's mercy. As a result of their pleading it was determined that Robert Kett and William Kett " be led by the aforesaid Constable of the Tower as far as to the said Tower and from there be drawn through the midst of the City of London straight to the gallows at Tyburn, and on that gallows be hanged, and while yet alive, that they be cast on the ground, and the entrails of each of them be taken out and burned before them, while yet alive, and their heads be cut off, and their bodies divided into four parts; and that the heads and quarters of each of them be placed where our Lord the King shall appoint." Such a judgment was meant to strike terror into the hearts of the defeated multitude by words as well as deeds. The two traitors were in the end conveyed back to Norwich. There on November 29 they were handed over to the Sheriff. " Robert Kett was hanged in Chains upon Norwich Castle," Sir John Hayward relates, " his Brother William in like Sort was executed upon Wymondham Steeple, but not without some murmuring that that Church, dedicated to the Service of God, and which is polluted by death, should be made a place of publick Execution."

MARY I

1516–1558 ; *reigned* 1553–1558

By

M. ST. CLARE BYRNE

MARY I

by M. ST. CLARE BYRNE

THE Popular Mind—also known as "Little Arthur"—still refers to Mary Tudor as Bloody Mary. No less a representative Englishman than Charles Dickens declared that "as Bloody Queen Mary this woman has become famous, and as Bloody Queen Mary she will ever be remembered with horror and detestation." In vain have a majority of our historians, Protestant and Catholic, male and female, endeavoured that justice should be done to her character. Little Arthur may not be quite sure whether it was Mary or her sister Elizabeth who cut off the head of Lady Jane Grey; but he is quite sure that Elizabeth's reign was spacious and honourable, long and victorious, happy and glorious, and that Mary's was brief, inglorious, and dishonourable, and that consequently Mary was . . . Bloody Mary—as much a part of the English legend as Bluff King Hal or Good Queen Bess. And whatever else Little Arthur successfully forgets, he generally remembers in his prime that Mary burnt the Protestants and died with Calais written on her heart—vaguely disgraceful, this loss of the last of our English possessions abroad. He has memories of Edward III, the Black Prince, Crécy, Poictiers, and Agincourt—all lost. What they ever stood for he is not quite sure, but each was a famous victory, and it was very unpatriotic of Mary to lose Calais. At his shrewdest he knows that Henry VIII and Elizabeth were great and successful, and that he must therefore accept the religious persecution and bloodshed of their reigns in a totally different spirit from that in which he condemns the Smithfield burnings. He may not be quite sure how to explain away the execution of Sir Thomas More; but he knows that Henry VIII virtually created the English navy. Henry and Elizabeth understood the English temperament. They were great personalities, symbols, figureheads—popular, successful, creative—belonging to and creative of a new world. Mary was not successful, and she was not a great personality. There is nothing to balance Smithfield. So " Bloody Mary " let it be.

By their Tudor inheritance Mary took after her father, and Elizabeth after her grandfather. Mary had much of the bull-obstinacy and childlike transparency of Henry VIII, Elizabeth the tenacity and the evasive caution of Henry VII. Like the latter, Elizabeth was favoured by the circumstances of her upbringing : such inborn caution as each possessed was sharpened by years of adversity. Of family life and affection Elizabeth knew next to nothing—less, even, than the average child of royal or noble birth in those days, when the family was a social and political rather than an emotional unit. Mary's childhood, however, was in many ways exceptional. She was the first child of Henry and Catherine of Aragon to survive infancy, and throughout her early years every circumstance conspired to make her realise that she was dear to her parents and to the English people, that she was the heiress of England, and one of the most important persons in Europe. Until the age of twelve she was the object of Henry's genuine affection and continual solicitude for her well-being. Not only was she " the pearl of his kingdom " : she was also the baby daughter in her nurse's arms whom the proud father could show off to the Venetian ambassador, boasting that she never cried ! Catherine herself supervised her education, and taught her Latin till the age of ten. It was Catherine, too, who asked the great scholar Vives to draw up his famous scheme for Mary's education, and who could find time in 1528, when the troubles of the divorce were gathering thickly about her, to implore Vives to come to England to teach the Princess. Isabella of Castile, Catherine's mother, may have regarded her numerous offspring as nothing but material for potential alliances : but Catherine of Aragon's letters to Mary, in the last years of her life, are the letters of a mother to a dearly loved daughter.

In her third year Mary was betrothed to the Dauphin. They dressed her in cloth of gold, and in the presence of her father and mother, Wolsey, and the chief dignitaries of the two kingdoms, they slipped a very small ring set with a very large diamond on to her baby finger. The next year she knew enough of what was expected from a betrothed princess to welcome messengers from her future husband " with most goodly countenance, proper communication, and pleasant pastime in playing on the virginals." In 1522, aged six, she was reft from France and betrothed to the Emperor Charles V, her grave young cousin of twenty-three, ruler of the greater part of Europe. At twelve she was to marry him, and promises were given that she should be fitted for her future position as the Emperor's wife by being brought up like a Spanish lady, under the personal care of her mother. At the age of nine she sent Charles an emerald ring, symbol of constancy, and her " assured love." Charles replied with the proper messages, and then a few months later found it convenient to marry a Portuguese princess. England replied with negotiations for her to marry James IV of Scotland, and later, Francis I, the dissolute thirty-two-year-old King of France. Heaven alone knows what the precocious child-mind made of it all; but it must have impressed upon her for life the importance of a grand European matrimonial alliance.

At the age of ten Mary was sent as Princess of Wales to keep her court at Ludlow, and administer justice on the Welsh border. Her establishment numbered over three hundred, amongst them many persons of " gravity and distinction." Margaret Pole, Countess of Salisbury, was her Lady Governess. Her Chamberlain was John Dudley, who as Duke of Northumberland was afterwards to try to rob her of the throne. Orders from the King in Council provided that she was " to use moderate exercise for taking open-air in gardens, sweet and wholesome places, and walks." Music, Latin, and French were to be studied, with the proviso " that the same be not too much, and without fatigation or weariness." She was to dance, and her diet was to be well-prepared and served, " with comfortable, joyous, and merry communication." Even " the cleanliness and well-wearing of her garments and apparel," and the sweetness and cleanliness of her chambers, were matters of concern to the Council. It makes an extraordinarily vivid contrast to the well-known account of Elizabeth's childhood, in which her governess points out that the unfortunate royal infant is practically destitute of clothing !

Mary was about fourteen or fifteen before the troubles of

her mother's divorce began to affect her. She must always have looked back to her childhood as the one really happy period of her existence. Nothing, so far, had touched her security; she was always the King's " dearest, best beloved, and only daughter." She was allowed to indulge discreetly in the pleasures of the court, where she appeared in masques and dances. She was an accomplished musician and a good scholar—" ripe in the Latin tongue " before she was twelve. By order of the King she was herself consulted by her own Council at Ludlow when they met to discuss her well-being and education. Life was padded, appreciative, pleasant, safe. Nothing had ever happened to make her realise that everything in which she believed, the very fabric of her existence, might crumble, and that life was a dangerous, frightening, cruel thing. At fifteen her sister Elizabeth engaged in a tussle of wits with the Privy Council over the affair of the Lord Admiral Seymour. Separated from her friends, bullied and badgered in daily interviews where a single slip might involve her in the charge of treason, Elizabeth at fifteen had won, and bent the Council of England to her will and her vindication. By fifteen life had turned Elizabeth into a shrewd, cool-headed young diplomat. It had kept Mary wrapped in cotton-wool.

The first repercussions of the divorce meant that between 1528 and 1530 Mary was hardly ever allowed to visit her parents. But she was still Princess of Wales in 1530. In 1531 she was separated from her mother, and even letters were forbidden. Henry had started in earnest to overcome the opposition of wife and daughter, and although Catherine lived until January 1536, Mary never saw her mother again.

The methods of Henry's attack make nasty reading. His Privy Purse expenses reveal that when Mary was sixteen he spent upon her in one year just a fifth of what he was accustomed to lavish upon Anne Boleyn in one day. In 1532 he sent no Christmas presents to Catherine and Mary, and none to the ladies of their households. He also forbade the Council to send them any presents. In 1533 he took away Mary's title, and sent her to live in a thoroughly unhealthy dwelling. When Anne's daughter Elizabeth was born he declared Mary illegitimate, and had her deprived of the succession by Act of Parliament. At the end of the year her household was dissolved, and she was separated from the Countess of Salisbury, who had been a second mother to her since the day she carried her to the font. Worst degradation of all, she was sent to the household which had been formed for the infant Elizabeth, accompanied only by two attendants, and herself regarded and treated practically as an attendant on the new heir. Well might Catherine write to her daughter, counselling submission to Henry's will, and concluding, " We never come to the kingdom of Heaven but by troubles."

The story of the next two years is a miserable one. Henry is reported to hold her still in his affections, but to be determined to break what he calls her " Spanish pride." There are rumours that Anne Boleyn, certainly her bitter enemy, means to compass her death. Poison is hinted at. She is not even allowed writing materials. She is penniless, almost destitute of clothes. There is petty persecution. She is not allowed to be served with breakfast in her own chamber: if she wants food she must eat at the common table with the ladies attending on the Princess Elizabeth. Her health breaks down. Catherine, ill herself, implores the King for permission to nurse " his daughter and mine." " Say to his Highness," she begs the Emperor's ambassador, " that there is no need of any other person but myself to nurse her; that I will put her in my own bed where I sleep, and will watch her when needful." Even this is refused. And all the time Mary is driven to tragi-comic shifts to assert her dignity. When the household moves to Greenwich Mary *will not* follow the litter of " the Bastard "; but is tricked into the ignominious second place as they leave. She pushes ahead, therefore, as fast as she can ride, so that she is the first to enter on arrival! At last, in 1536, Catherine of Aragon dies.

Follows, the final breaking of Mary's pride. Anne Boleyn was not alone responsible for Mary's ill-treatment. In vain, after Anne's death, did Mary send letter after letter, couched in the most humble and supplicating terms, begging to see her father. All remained unanswered; until eventually Cromwell, rating her roundly as " the most obstinate and obdurate woman, all things considered, that ever was," wrung from her the submission that Henry demanded. She was forced to acknowledge the King as Supreme Head on earth of the Church of England, and to agree that she would " utterly refuse the Bishop of Rome's pretended authority, power, and jurisdiction within this realm heretofore usurped." Last bitter acknowledgment—" the marriage heretofore had between his majesty and my mother . . . was by God's law and man's law incestuous and unlawful."

Her mother was dead ; and her cousin the Emperor, whom she regarded as her only adviser and protector, recommended her to yield. Mary signed. So honour was satisfied, and " Spanish pride " broken at last. Mary was allowed to see her loving parent again, and a modest household was once more provided for her. At New Year she received handsome presents from the King, Queen Jane Seymour, and minister Cromwell. For the rest of the reign, when not at court, she spent most of the time living quietly at one or other of her country residences. Her days, however, were not yet free of the shadow of tragedy and personal loss. In 1540 her old tutor, Dr. Featherstone, and her mother's chaplain, Abell, were both burnt at the stake for refusing to subscribe the Oath of Supremacy. Worst blow of all was the attainder of the Pole family in 1539. The Countess of Salisbury, her oldest friend and guardian, then aged seventy, was imprisoned in the Tower. The eldest son, Lord Montague, and his relative the Marquess of Exeter—both descendants of Edward IV, and therefore possible claimants to the throne—were beheaded without trial. The Marchioness of Exeter, another of Mary's closest friends, was imprisoned with her young son Edward Courtenay; and in 1541 the Countess of Salisbury was beheaded in a manner almost unsurpassed for horror.

Apart from such tragic happenings, however, Mary's life for the remainder of her father's reign seems to have settled into the normal routine of any Tudor lady's. Her Privy Purse Expenses give us a delightful picture of the quiet round of her days. She plays cards, loses twenty shillings, forty shillings, borrows twenty-two and sixpence from my Lady Sussex during a game, and gives the child Elizabeth presents of money to stake at play. She has her own minstrels to make music : Heywood, the dramatist, brings his Children of the Chapel to play an interlude before her. Every now and again she herself has some lessons on the virginals. She stands godmother to innumerable infants, gentle and simple. There are presents and tips for everybody—to one to christen his child, to another for the burying, to Harry the Shoemaker for his daughter's wedding. She gives her small step-brother Edward an embroidered coat: Elizabeth has a pomander, a brooch, and pair of beads, and when she is seven years old Mary buys her five yards of yellow satin to be made into a kirtle. For Edward's christening she buys herself a kirtle of cloth of silver. A few days later she is the chief mourner at his mother's funeral. There are illnesses: and she pays forty shillings to have a tooth drawn. She keeps greyhounds: and someone sends her a parrot. She is lavish with gifts of jewellery to all her relatives, friends, and attendants; and receives all the neighbourly and friendly presents that any Tudor lady had the right to expect—offerings of strawberries and cream, pheasants, swans, cheese, butter, eggs and bacon, apples, cakes, puddings, fish, and pigs! There are clocks to be mended, virginals to be repaired, alms for the London prisons, or for the poor, and the purchase, on one occasion, when she was to appear at court, of a hundred pearls at thirteen and fourpence apiece. But perhaps the two most interesting things about the whole manuscript are the facts that Mary herself corrected her accounts throughout in her own hand, and that, in spite of her father's bastardising of her half-sister, Mary still persists in describing her as " my lady Elizabeth's grace."

At the death of Henry VIII Mary, though not acknowledged as his legitimate daughter, was left heiress of England, in the event of her brother's death without issue. Her chief troubles, during Edward's reign, were caused by the Privy Council, who tried to demand religious conformity and to force her to give up the Mass. When the Lord Chancellor and other members visited her in person her final answer was, " Rather than use any other service than that ordained during the life of my father, I will lay my head on the block." They could imprison her officers, but " if ye leave your new comptroller within my gates, out of them I go forthwith, for we twain will not abide in the same house." In no way intimidated, her parting thrust was a complaint that, since they had robbed her of her comptroller, she had been forced to do her own accounts: " Have I learned how many loaves of bread be made of a bushel of wheat? I wis my father and mother never brought me up to brewing and baking; and to be plain with you, I am a-weary of mine office! " Nor were persuasion and menace any more effective under the Northumberland régime. Mary simply ignored the Council and wrote to the King, reminding him that in their last argument upon the subject she had desired him " to take her life " rather than deny her the practice of the religion in which she had been brought up. " Death shall be more welcome than life with a troubled conscience," was the conclusion of her complete refusal to conform.

In July 1553 Edward died, and Northumberland made his bid for power by forcing the Council to proclaim his daughter-in-law, Jane Grey. Mary was to be lured to London by a forged message from her already-dead brother. She was warned while on her way, and promptly fled for refuge to her own house of Kenninghall, in Norfolk, from which she wrote in spirited terms to the Council, promising a general amnesty if they proclaimed her at once. Their reply told her in round terms that she was illegitimate, and advised her to submit. And then Mary took a step as wise as it was venturesome. She had no money and no armed forces; and the Emperor, watching affairs, saw no chance for her. But with her personal attendants, mostly women, and the Norfolk tenants of Sir Henry Bedingfield and Sir Henry Jerningham who had rallied to her, Mary went straight to the fortress town of Framlingham, one of the Howard strongholds. There she hoisted her standard, and proclaimed herself Queen. Courageous and resourceful, Mary announced to her subjects, " The Queen is not fled the realm, nor intendeth to do, as is most untruly surmised."

It was a characteristic Tudor gesture, and the nation responded, rallying to the support of the rightful heir. The Council proclaimed Mary at Paul's Cross, deserting Northumberland, who was arrested as a traitor. Finally, on August 3, 1553, she entered London in triumph as Queen, restored to the throne by the will and loyalty and affection of the English people.

Michele, the Venetian ambassador, sent his Government an extremely interesting account of the impression Mary made upon her contemporaries. In appearance she was " of short stature, well made, thin and delicate, and moderately pretty." Though very short-sighted " her eyes are so lively that she inspires reverence and respect and even fear, wherever she turns them." " Her voice is deep, almost like that of a man." He considered her " endowed with great humility and patience, but withal high-spirited, courageous, and resolute; having during the whole course of her adversity been guiltless of any of the least approach to meanness of comportment; she is, moreover, devout and staunch in the defence of her religion." Her own account books help to add the simpler and more intimate details, presenting her to us as a careful but generous woman, kind, hospitable, and charitable.

Nor were the simpler pieties of her life put by after she came to the throne. Godchildren were still provided for, poor people's children were apprenticed at the Queen's expense. Most significant detail of all was her habit of visiting poor men's houses in disguise, to see for herself the conditions of their lives, and to see that they were not victimised by officials acting in the name of the Queen. Jane Dormer, one of her Ladies of the Bedchamber, gives an account of these expeditions:

> " And being at Croydon, for her recreation, with two or three of her ladies, she would visit the poor neighbours, they all seeming to be the maids of the Court. . . . She would sit down very familiarly in their poor houses, talk with the man and his wife, ask them of their manner of living, how they passed if the officers of the Court did deal with them, as such whose carts and labours were pressed for the Queen's carriage and provisions."

It is not quite the kind of story they tell of Elizabeth. It is human, admirable, of a touching simplicity, even; but of the simplicity that is not for princes.

For her success as a ruler there was much promise inherent in her character. A strong sense of justice was one of her rooted virtues, which even the weary years of her father's injustice had never sapped. Shortly after Anne Boleyn's disgrace and death Mary wrote to Henry, " My sister Elizabeth is in good health, thanks be to our Lord, and such a child toward, as I doubt not but your Highness shall have cause to rejoice of in time coming." Mere human feeling must still have been sore and resentful at the suffering meted out to her simply on account of the fact of the infant Elizabeth's existence; but in the twenty-year-old granddaughter of Isabella of Castile justice could conquer lesser emotions. It was in Mary's reign that witnesses for the subject were first allowed to be heard in cases brought by the

Crown; and her charge to her judges admonished them " to sit as indifferent judges between me and my people," and to administer justice " without respect of persons."

Like her sister Elizabeth Mary had courage, both moral and physical. She could keep a cool head in an emergency, as witness her conduct during Northumberland's rebellion. When Wyatt's mob had almost reached the palace doors she was the one undaunted figure amidst the chaos of alarmed and despairing attendants; and her long speech to the citizens at the Guildhall, exhorting them to stand firm against the rebels, was a magnificently spirited outburst: " I am come unto you in mine own person. . . . Now, loving subjects, what I am you right well know. I am your Queen." It was downright Tudor, as was the conclusion. " As good and faithful subjects pluck up your hearts, and like true men stand fast with your lawful prince against these rebels. . . . Assure you that I fear them nothing at all."

She has been described by a modern historian as a monarch " who for the wrongs done to her personally showed almost unexampled clemency." To traitors she was more lenient than either Henry or Elizabeth. Only three of the Northumberland plot conspirators were put to death, and then only when pressure had been brought to bear upon the Queen. Where Henry executed hundreds of the rebels implicated in the Pilgrimage of Grace, and Elizabeth some eight hundred after the rebellion of the Northern Earls, hardly more than one hundred suffered under Mary for Wyatt's rebellion. And in spite of the unexampled severity with which the laws against heresy were applied during the Marian persecution, at the beginning of the reign ample opportunity to seek refuge abroad was given to the extreme Protestants who were not prepared to conform—an opportunity which was taken by many, though not by Latimer and Cranmer amongst others.

On the day of her entry into London as Queen all State prisoners of the two previous reigns then in the Tower—Catholic and Protestant alike—were released by Mary in person, who embraced them with tears in her eyes. To all of them their rank and possessions were at once restored. Like Elizabeth, on her accession Mary remembered and rewarded all who had been faithful to her during her misfortunes. Unlike in so many ways, Mary and Elizabeth could both give and win unfaltering personal loyalty. But there were other loyalties, however, in Mary's heart—debts to the past, which were to prove her undoing. Circumstances, and her own nature, made Elizabeth look forward to the future; and by the time she came to the throne she had had her sister's reign in which to learn something of the strength of English national feeling. Mary came to the throne weary and prematurely aged. Inevitably she looked back, and saw in the past, in the days of her own childhood and youth, the picture of security and happiness, when her first duty as a woman was to be a devout daughter of the Church, and the first duty of a princess a dynastic marriage. Hence the twofold mistake which foiled so much promise, and made her reign a failure—her concentration upon the spiritual rather than the national welfare of her people, and her marriage with Philip of Spain, son to the Emperor.

Tudor obstinacy and Spanish inflexibility had produced in Mary a mind altogether too rigid, too direct and unsubtle, for the difficult time of transition into which she was born. That she must marry was as obvious to her as to her male advisers. When they urged her to choose an English husband, however, not only was she faced with the fact that there was no eligible candidate, but the whole past rose up to tell her that princes matched with princes, realm with realm. She turned for advice to the Emperor, who offered his son. Her Spanish blood, her feeling for her mother and her mother's family, sentiments of gratitude to the Emperor, friend and protector of her distressed youth—these, and a handsome picture, caught her heart for Philip of Spain. Her English subjects had loved and revered her Spanish mother. National independence, the succession, questions of regency—every conceivable point was guarded for the English interest in her marriage treaty. Philip did his conscientious best to make himself agreeable to England. How was Mary to understand her subjects' hatred, or to realise that even if Philip's credentials had included a passport for the kingdom of heaven they would have been utterly useless without an English birth-certificate? Insular feeling, jealousy of Spain's trading monopoly in the New World, and the belief that Spain beyond all other European countries was identified with the Papacy, rendered whatever he did suspect. It made no difference that during part of the reign Philip was at war with the Pope. The anti-Spanish feeling that, within a week of the signing of the marriage treaty, had declared itself in Wyatt's rebellion grew steadily in intensity. And as Mary's devotion to Philip and his interests became more and more apparent, so her own unpopularity came almost to equal his.

It was the same with her religious policy. Brought up as she had been, how was the daughter of Catherine of Aragon to understand that these illogical English, who considered it a wicked shame and scandal that her good mother should be divorced, took at the same time the attitude that they would be damned if any Pope of Rome was going to tell the King of England he could not divorce his wife if he wanted to? Mary and her advisers knew that the greater part of the country was ready to welcome a restoration of the religious compromise of her father's time. To them this meant that the people as a whole still held to the Catholic faith, and to Mary's limited, logical, and devout mind a Catholic was *ipso facto* a good Catholic. A clear-cut issue between those to whom Rome meant the Holy Father and their opponents who shouted Scarlet Woman, she could understand, and this was the situation with which she thought she was dealing. What she could not understand was that, actually, the majority of her subjects were neither good Catholics nor good Protestants, but simply illogical Englishmen, who nourished a conservative affection for the older form of worship, at the same time as they regarded the Pope as a damned foreigner, of whose interference in English affairs they had been resentful for centuries.

Until the beginning of 1555 Mary's reign can be described as one in which the constitutional rights of the subject were both restored and protected; and in her first Parliament legislation was carried through which should have made it famous in popular history. All the new treasons created since the time of Edward III and all new felonies since the accession of Henry VIII were abolished, which meant a wholesale restoration of the ancient liberties of the English people. The popular mind, however, knows only two outstanding events—the loss of Calais, and the burning of the Protestant martyrs, for which latter it holds Mary responsible, though sometimes linking with hers the names of Philip, Gardiner, Bonner, and Cardinal Pole.

The approximate truth, in this matter of ultimate responsibility, is probably best deduced from a series of complementary statements. In the first place, it is a mistake to assume that Mary, as a ruler, wielded anything approaching the same power as Henry VIII or Elizabeth. She was limited both by her own character and by circumstances. The attitude of her advisers was that of the average man of the Tudor period towards the idea of a woman ruler, and needs neither description nor comment. There is no doubt that the " monstrous regiment " of Elizabeth was much helped, psychologically, by the fact that she was not the first queen-regnant. In the matter of her own marriage Mary's wishes overrode those of her Council and Parliament; but we know that in various other matters of vital importance to her, their wishes overrode the Queen's. We know, for example, that the Royal Supremacy was peculiarly distasteful to Mary, and that she did her utmost to have it rescinded by her first Parliament—but without avail. Perhaps the most definite sign of the control of Council and Parliament, however, is their continued refusal to crown Philip. Relying on her love and devotion, Philip went so far as to apply pressure by removing his suite and refusing to return to England, unless Mary could persuade Parliament to crown him. But not all the grief and hurt of his desertion and continued absence could teach Mary to bully like her father or manage like her sister, and Philip was never crowned. Whether or not she wished to do so, Mary ruled as a constitutional monarch.

Philip and the Spanish influence have been absolved by all reasonable historians of any responsibility for the burnings. Contemporary opinion naturally blamed him; but the documents show that, from motives of policy, dictated by the Emperor who knew something of the English temperament, Philip and the ambassador Renard kept aloof, and even urged mildness on the Council. Cardinal Pole is generally held to have been opposed to persecution, by temperament and policy; and however much weight his views carried with Mary he was never a real power in the land. Bonner was not a member of the Privy Council, and therefore not one of the originators of the policy, though more of the executive responsibility for the carrying out of the sentences seems to belong to him than to anyone else, in spite of the fact that on one occasion he was rebuked by the Council for his lack of zeal. Gardiner undoubtedly believed that the persecution would effectively stamp out heresy in a short time; but it must be remembered that he died in

November 1555, and that at least two-thirds of the burnings were carried out after his death. The idea that it all happened simply because Mary was a cruel woman who really enjoyed shedding blood is, of course, ridiculous. It is likely, indeed, that death itself may not have seemed to her a very big thing, or very terrible. She had seen the friends of her youth, and the great of the land, innocent and guilty alike, tread the bloody path to the scaffold. She herself had faced the possibility of dying for her faith; and in the sufferings of her mother, and of friends such as Margaret Pole, it is possible that her spirit had tasted something more bitter than death. Nor are she and her advisers convicted of more savage minds than their contemporaries because they restored a penalty that had been enforced throughout the reign of Henry VIII. Catholic and Protestant alike still envisaged the death penalty as naturally applicable to cases of heresy.

No one mind, in fact, was alone responsible for the persecution. What happened was that a Privy Council, representative of the statecraft and mentality of the time, found in Mary's third Parliament a body of representative Englishmen who were prepared to restore to the statute book the act *de hæretico comburendo*. This gave back to the ecclesiastical courts the power to judge heresy that had been taken from them by Henry VIII. Whether Parliament guessed how this power would be administered cannot be determined. What they expected, perhaps, was some dozen victims a year, preferably clerical; but they knew that the ecclesiastical courts were bound to pronounce sentence of burning in every case declared guilty. At best, they were the stupid accessories of the men in power. At worst, having passed legislation to secure to their lay owners the lands and property looted from the Church, to colour their " reconciliation " with the see of Rome they then gave the Church unlimited power over men's consciences in matters of faith. Behind them, endorsing their action, and believing in it as a part of her duty as a daughter of the Church, stands the woman who still bears the odium of responsibility for the holocaust that followed. But that Mary's sole will and religious conviction could have forced the Privy Council into initiating such a policy, had they been unwilling, and then forcing it through an unwilling Parliament, is an impossible conclusion. The English preference for political rather than religious or moral rights, functioning through Council and Parliament, sanctioned the whole atrocious business. Then, faced with the logical results of its action, the English temperament discovered that it did not like what it had asked for. Three hundred martyrs in less than four years showed the nation that its humanitarianism, such as it was, would no longer permit wholesale execution. Nationalism and Protestantism were thrown into each other's arms, Catholicism and cruelty were identified, and condemned together as foreign.

Discontent grew apace, and men's hopes began to turn towards Elizabeth. Fifteen-fifty-eight began with the loss of Calais—a loss which Mary felt as bitterly as did the English pride of her subjects. In September the Emperor died. Reginald Pole lay sick to death at Westminster. And Philip of Spain delayed in the Netherlands, sending messages and a ring to his dying wife, whom he did not intend to see again. Little could either of them have guessed then of the significance of the loss of Calais. Neither could look forward to that September night, just thirty years later, when Philip's great Armada was to anchor in the French roadstead and harbour of Calais, in order to tranship his conquering army. They could not see Drake's fire-ships, and the panic and destruction wrought amongst the Spanish galleons—prelude to the destruction of the world's mightiest fleet, and the freeing of England at last from the menace that had been Spain. But it is easy to see now that the loss of Calais marked fitly enough the end of the old order which died with Mary. The future of England did not lie in Europe and European alliances: it lay in the New World, not the Old.

Mary died on November 17, 1558. Her will directed that the body of her mother was to be brought from Peterborough and interred beside her own. Consistent to the last, she also directed that she herself was to be buried, not in robes of state as a queen, but in the habit of a religious order. It is unnecessary to dwell on the personal tragedy of her life. The Crown brought her little but stern duties, cares, and frustrated hopes, after years of injustice, humiliation, suffering, loss, and ill-health. Even the passionately longed-for moment, when she and her kingdom were received back into the Roman communion, was rendered incomplete by the nation's refusal to make restitution of its

Church spoils. Her marriage was a tragedy in itself. It lost her the trust and affection of her people, and committed her to loving with all the strength and intensity of her nature a cold-hearted would-be dynast, who deserted her when she was a disappointed dying woman. Her continued delusion, during her last illnesses, that she was going to bear a child, the Tudor prince who should mend all, was the final bitterness; and she died with the grim knowledge that all she had worked for had failed, or would be brought to nothing by her successor.

Mary was a good woman, naturally pitiful, conscientious, honest in word and deed, and the one passionately devout member of her family. These were not the qualities needed by a Renaissance prince. All the Tudors have a number of judicial murders sticking on their hands, but Mary, the only one of them who executed for principle and not for expediency, is popularly singled out as the only Tudor tyrant. A failure to understand that national feeling and the desire for national unity could matter more than religion made the blunders of her reign inevitable; but without them it is probable that both the religious compromise and the national triumph of Elizabeth's reign would have cost much more in blood and tears. Mary belonged to one of those difficult periods of transition between the old order of things and the new, when only genius succeeds. She was not a genius; and she and her advisers all belonged to the older generation that had come to its maturity under Henry VIII. For Mary the times were out of joint—victim of the hour that was not hers, but was appointed for the last and greatest of the Tudors.

HUGH LATIMER

Circa 1485–1555

By
BRIAN LUNN

HUGH LATIMER

by BRIAN LUNN

AT the beginning of the sixteenth century the fashionable enthusiasm for the New Learning had spread from Italy to the countries north of the Alps. Its more eminent exponents were sought for by princes and potentates as passionately as a rare tulip a century later. The aim of the leaders of the movement was simple—to introduce men to the actual works of the great writers of antiquity instead of to their commentators, and to criticise current institutions by the light of these works. This principle came to be applied, not only to the works of profane writers, but also to the Sacred Canon, and thus the religious movement known as the Reformation grew out of the literary renascence which had preceded it. The man who completely embodied the connection between the two movements was Erasmus, who pervaded Europe almost as much with his person as with his writings.

In 1510 Erasmus paid his second visit to Cambridge. Hugh Latimer was an obscure but promising divinity student, probably in his twenty-third year—the date of his birth is uncertain. His father, a yeoman, whose circumstances, owing to the economic tendencies of the time, were no longer as easy as they had been when he " tilled so much as kept half a dozen men and kept hospitality for his poor neighbours," had incurred the censure of his neighbours for his extravagance in sending his son Hugh to the University. Before Erasmus had left Cambridge the young student silenced the criticism of his father's neighbours by his election to a fellowship in Clare Hall, even before proceeding to the degree of Bachelor.

It was his proficiency in the traditional learning of the schoolmen which had gained this distinction for Hugh. The presence of Erasmus at Cambridge affected him not at all. Of the religious question he was hardly aware, except that he had a healthy dislike for Lollards, natural in a young man who was pleased to relate when preaching before Edward VI how he " buckled his father's harness," when Hugh senior went to his king's aid against the Cornish rebels, and in another sermon urged the same king to see that the justices did their duty in carrying out Henry VIII's Acts for the promotion of archery.

> " Men of England in times past were wont to go abroad in the fields a shooting. But now it is turned into bolling, glossing, gulling, and whoring within the house. . . . My father was as diligent to teach me to shoot as to teach me any other thing. He taught me how to draw, how to lay my body in my bow, and not to draw with strength of arms, as other nations do, but with strength of the body: I had my bows bought me, according to my age and strength, for men shoot never so well except they be brought up in it; it is a goodly art, a wholesome kind of exercise, and much commended in physic."

The effects of the visit of Erasmus to Cambridge became more apparent after the great scholar had left, especially when his new edition of the New Testament found its way to the University. As the interest in the new ideas grew, Latimer's zeal as a defender of traditional belief increased, and he continued his progress through the degrees of academic distinction without showing any sign of infection with heterodox notions, until in 1522 he had the honour on ceremonial occasions of carrying the University cross, for sixteen pence, the equivalent of nearly a pound to-day. Although he was strictly orthodox, Latimer already attracted the attention at Cambridge of men who saw more in him than the conventional theologian. Like others who have launched a new religious movement, he was distinguishing himself for his zeal in attacking the movement of which he was to be a prophet. In the meantime the secret adherents of the German and Swiss reformers had been growing in numbers. There had been a public burning of Luther's works, but this only gave a fresh impetus to the movement. Distinguished amongst these earnest young men was one Thomas Bilney, who has related his conversion after tasting despair like Luther's, in his attempt to find spiritual comfort in the observances of religion.

They had exhausted both his health and his pocket, he being

> "of nature but weak, with small store of money; and they appointed fastings, watchings, buying of pardons and masses; in all which things they sought rather their own gain than the salvation of my sick and languishing soul. But at last I heard speak of Jesus, even when the New Testament was first set forth by Erasmus. . . . At the first reading I chanced upon this sentence of St. Paul (Oh most sweet and comfortable sentence to my soul): 'It is a true saying, and worthy of all men to be embraced, that Christ Jesus came into the world to save sinners, of whom I am the chief and principal.' This one sentence did so exhilarate my heart: being before wounded with the guilt of my sins, and being almost in despair, that immediately I felt a marvellous comfort and quietness, insomuch that my bruised bones leaped for joy."

"Little Bilney," as Latimer always used to call him in later life, was touched by the moral earnestness, the astringent humour of the preacher Latimer. He saw in Latimer a brand to be plucked from the burning. He went to Latimer's rooms and desired Latimer "for God's sake to hear his confession." He confessed how he had found comfort through ignoring the priests and reading the Bible, and asked whether Latimer would drive him back to the remedies which had nearly brought him to despair. Latimer was touched by his sincerity and unassuming manner. He had always thought of these heretical Scripture students as unpleasantly conceited young men, who affected to despise the ordinances of the Church, and made much of their own personal religious feelings, while they were actually ill at ease. Latimer procured a New Testament for himself, and as he studied it, such morbid fears as had occasionally troubled him during his forty years of life were dissipated. "I have thought in times past," he wrote later, "that if I had been a friar and in a cowl, I would not have been damned nor afraid of death, and I have been minded many times to have been a friar when I was sore sick and distressed."

The effect of his conversation with Bilney did not cause any violent change in Latimer's manner of life. He remained a priest in the Church in which he was ordained. In order to understand the careers not only of Latimer, but of the kings Henry VIII and Edward VI as well as of Cranmer and his fellow reformers, it is necessary to bear in mind that these men lived before western Europe became roughly divided into Catholics and Protestants. In the period between the fall of the Byzantine empire and the rise of the Protestant churches the Roman Catholic Church substantiated the claim to be the Church Universal. Throughout these two or three centuries there were men and women in the Church who consumed their lives criticising practices and even doctrines without ever thinking of questioning her supremacy. A citizen of the Union of South Africa may question certain imperial institutions while at the same time maintaining unimpaired his loyalty to the empire. If the empire should split into two parts, Australia and South Africa recognising a president at Cape Town, the other Dominions a monarch at Ottawa, all Britons would feel they must call themselves either monarchists or republicans. For Latimer Christendom was still a unity.

About this time Cardinal Wolsey, feeling that Oxford needed assistance from the other University, drafted twelve of the more eminent exponents of the new learning from Cambridge to his new college at Oxford. These men were all members of the same group as Bilney and his friends. Their departure left Latimer, who was now about forty, pre-eminent amongst the reformers.

Latimer was not slow to preach the new doctrine from the pulpit. He had acquired his new truths from another without passing through any acute spiritual crisis himself. His moral earnestness rather than any profound religious emotion had been kindled. He addressed himself therefore to those practices which seemed to him to conflict with the ethical teaching of the Gospels rather than to any recondite questions of Catholic dogma.

Restitution, he said, was more important than acts of penance, which could be no substitute for it. Acts of charity availed more than pilgrimages or creeping to the cross. He began to throw doubts upon the efficacy of buying masses for the souls in purgatory. It is noteworthy that widely as Protestant sects have differed on other questions, they have never varied in attacking the doctrine of purgatory. This has been the first doctrine which those Anglicans who call themselves Catholic have attacked, the last with which they have been reconciled. And yet it is no less marvellous than the doctrine of a physical hell or of a millennium which feature so prominently in many Protestant Confessions. It can easily be supported by Scriptural texts, and it affords comfort to those who feel that, without any further purgation, their state at death would qualify them for hell rather than for heaven.

The reason is a practical one. Remission of the pains of purgatory has always opened the richest treasures to the Power of the Keys. The force of the appeal does credit to the heart of humanity. It is to relieve or shorten the sufferings of the dear departed that most of the money for masses has been given. The appeal to self-sacrifice has always been more potent than that to self-interest.

It was not long before complaints about Latimer's forthright sermons were made to his diocesan, West, Bishop of Ely. The Bishop paid a surprise visit to the University Church on a day when Latimer was due to preach, and entered in the course of the sermon. When the Bishop and his retinue were seated, Latimer calmly said: " A new audience, especially of such rank, deserves a new theme." He proceeded to preach from the text of Hebrews " Christ being come, a High Priest of good things to come," and enlarged upon the carelessness of pastors whether priests or bishops which was the great scandal of the day. West sent for Latimer, and sagaciously thanked him for an excellent sermon, adding, " If you will do one thing at my request, I will kneel down and kiss your feet for the good admonition that I have received of your sermon." He asked that Latimer should preach in that place one sermon against Martin Luther. To this Latimer answered: " My lord, I am not acquainted with the doctrine of Luther, nor are we permitted here to read his works. . . . Sure I am that I have preached before you this day no man's doctrine, but only the doctrine of God out of the Scriptures. And if Luther do none otherwise, there needeth no confutation of his doctrine."

To which the Bishop: " Well, well, Mr. Latimer, I perceive that you somewhat smell of the pan: you will repent this gear one day."

The Bishop inhibited Latimer from preaching in the diocese, but Latimer, taking advantage of the Roman administration, preached from the pulpit of his friend Dr. Barnes, whose monastery, like many religious houses, was exempt from episcopal jurisdiction.

At the same time Barnes preached a heretical sermon in Cambridge in which he attacked Cardinal Wolsey savagely. Brought before the Cardinal, Barnes made an abject recantation, and in due course performed on Sunday morning the ominous ceremony of carrying a faggot, walking at dawn through crowded streets to Old St. Paul's, where he " declared that he was more charitably handled than he deserved, his heresies were so horrible and detestable."

Latimer's oratory at this time was mainly directed to ethical teaching in straightforward, homely language : " He spake nothing but it left as it were certain pricks or stings in the hearts of his hearers." But the activities of Barnes had compromised him, and in due course he was summoned to an interview with the Cardinal,

" ' Is your name Latimer? ' asked Wolsey. ' Yea, forsooth.' ' You are of good years, nor no babe, but one that should wisely and soberly use yourself . . . yet it is reported to me that you are much infected with this new fantastical doctrine of Luther . . . that you do very much harm among the youth.'

" ' Your grace is misinformed, for I ought to have some more knowledge than to be so simply reported of, by reason that I have studied in my time both the ancient doctors of the Church, and also the school-doctors.'

" ' Marry that is well said. Mr. Doctor Capon, and you Mr. Doctor Marshall, say you somewhat to Mr. Latimer touching some question in Duns.'

" Whereupon," the report continues, " Dr. Capon propounded a question. Mr. Latimer, being fresh then of memory, and not discontinued from study as those two doctors had been, answered very roundly ; somewhat helping them to cite rightly. . . .

" The Cardinal, perceiving the ripe and ready answering of Latimer, said : ' What mean you, my masters, to bring such a man before me into accusation? I had thought that he had been some light-headed fellow that never studied. . . . I pray thee, Latimer, tell me the cause why the Bishop of Ely and other doth mislike thy preachings; tell me the truth, and I will bear with thee upon amendment.'

" Quoth Latimer, ' Your Grace must understand that the Bishop of Ely cannot favour me, for that not long ago I preached before him in Cambridge a sermon from this text, *Christus existens pontifex*, etc., wherein I described the office of a bishop so uprightly as I might, according to the text, that never after he could abide me, but hath not only forbidden me to preach in his diocese, but also hath found the means to inhibit me from preaching in the University.'

" . . . The Cardinal, nothing at all misliking the doctrine of the Word of God that Latimer had preached, said unto him, ' Did you not preach any other doctrine than you have rehearsed? '

" ' No, surely,' said Latimer.

" . . . The Cardinal said unto Mr. Latimer, ' If the Bishop of Ely cannot abide such doctrine as you have here repeated, you shall have my licence, and shall preach it unto his beard, let him say what he will.' "

On the next holiday Latimer read the Cardinal's licence from the pulpit in Cambridge.

This remarkable interview, so critical for Latimer, was crucial for the future of the Church in England. It may be called the starting-point of the Church of England. Wolsey had acted as an enlightened newspaper magnate might do towards an editor (the Bishop) who had mistakenly suppressed the work of a brilliant contributor, as being contrary to the policy of his employer.

Like Talleyrand, if less consciously, Wolsey was pre-eminently concerned for the glory of his country. He was aware in Latimer of a new quality which was emerging, the English character. It was this quality which lit the subtle sympathy that governed the surprising course of the interview, with the result that for a quarter of a century Latimer worked as a reformer within the Church instead of becoming a rebel outside it.

Latimer made generous use of the Cardinal's licence. He was attracting dangerous attention again by his unorthodox sermons, when Henry VIII's first marriage difficulty became acute. After processes and negotiations which had lasted for over two years, Pope Clement VII had finally refused to acquiesce in the view that the King's marriage to his brother's widow was an infringement of God's fundamental law which no papal dispensation could contravene.

Latimer was known to share the King's opinion regarding the validity of the marriage, on which doubts had been cast some years before by the French ambassador. The fact that of several children whom Catherine had borne only one had survived, and that one a female, suggested that, by marrying Arthur's widow, Henry had incurred the curse in Leviticus, " They shall be childless." In the complicated political situation at the time the question was submitted to the universities of Christendom. Henry had little difficulty in securing the verdict he desired from the foreign univer-sities. In his own kingdom he found more opposition, perhaps because he would not condescend to bribe his own subjects. At Oxford he had frank recourse to intimidation, saying that if they insisted on " playing masteries, they should soon perceive that it was not wise to irritate hornets." At Cambridge it was agreed that the question should be decided by a committee of Masters. Latimer was appointed, and assisted his colleagues in arriving at the decision which the King was awaiting.

Not long after the universities had given their decision Latimer was summoned to preach before the King. There is no record of this sermon; but its effect was favourable, for Henry stopped Latimer in the gallery and " did most familiarly talk " with him. Latimer took the opportunity to ask and obtain the royal pardon for a woman convicted of murdering her own child. Latimer and Bilney had both believed the woman innocent. The child had died during the harvest when, as Latimer recounted in the course of a sermon preached towards the end of his life before Katharine, Duchess of Suffolk,

> " every man was in the field. The woman, in an heaviness and trouble of spirit, went, and being herself alone, prepared the child to the burial. Her husband coming home, not having great love towards her, accused her of the murder. . . . In the mean season that same woman was delivered of a child in the tower at Cambridge, whose godfather I was. But all that

time I hid my pardon, and told her nothing of it, only exhorting her to confess the truth."

After the child was born, the woman, still ignorant of the pardon which Latimer had in his pocket, asked that she should be purified before her execution.

> " Where Master Bilney and I told her that that law was made unto the Jews, and not unto us; neither is purification used to that end, that it should cleanse from sin; but rather a civil and politic law, made for natural honesty sake. . . . To that end purification is kept and used, not to make a superstition or holiness of it, as some do; which think that they may not fetch neither fire nor any thing in that house where there is a green woman. . . . For women be as well in the favour of God before they be purified as after."

Were there not so many recorded instances of Latimer's generosity and human sympathy, this story might convict him of callousness. It is rather an example of a moral toughness, more characteristic of that age than of our own. And we are left with the impression that Latimer withheld the pardon, not only because he wished to be free of any doubt of the woman's innocence, but also because he wished first to establish in her a right attitude towards moral truth.

His remarks on purification ceremonies, so reminiscent of Hindu customs described in *Mother India*, illustrate the driving force which governed him as a religious reformer. He had not, after spiritual conflict, achieved any new vision of the profundities of religious truth. Such experience had been another's; but Bilney had imparted to him something of a spiritual enlightenment comparable to Luther's, and Bilney's experience had liberated Latimer's rugged moral common sense for attacking with the fervour of the less poetic prophets of Israel the abuses and superstitions of his day.

It was not long before Latimer became involved in doctrinal difficulties with the authorities. During the vicissitudes of that talented but somewhat arbitrary theologian Henry VIII, few ecclesiastics who held views at all definite, avoided altogether doctrinal conflict in one direction or another. The surprising fact is that so few Catholics were executed as traitors for refusing to take the oath recognising Henry as " sole protector, only sovereign Lord . . . of the English Church " while so few others went to the stake under Henry's sometimes very savage heresy laws. The explanation lies in the characteristically English reluctance to confer or to incur martyrdom. Distrust of religious emotionalism is older than the eighteenth century, when the word " enthusiast " was so effectively used by Anglican divines to denote their distaste and suspicion of any manifestation of personal religious experience. In the early Church prelates used their influence to cool the ardour of Roman maidens ambitious for the martyr's crown.

It is not surprising, therefore, that Latimer, typical Englishman, even to the Christian name with its suggestion of Norman gentle blood on the distaff side, should have exerted his influence to dissuade Bilney from paying the extreme penalty for holding heretical views. It was Bilney's second incarceration. He had already been arrested once, and had borne his faggot and spent some weeks in a condition of utter dejection after an ignominious recantation. Then, determined for the last time to bear steadfast witness, he left his weeping friends to go to London, saying, " I must needs go up to Jerusalem."

Latimer was shattered by Bilney's death at the stake. He preached certain sermons which the authorities could not ignore, and he had some very active enemies on the episcopal bench. He spent some weeks in prison.

First he was examined before Bishop Stokesley, and we have his own account how he detected that a clerk was hidden in the chimney to take down his words: " ' I pray you, Master Latimer,' said he (Stokesley), ' speak out, I am very thick of hearing.' I marvelled that I was bidden to speak out, and began to misdeem, and gave an ear to the chimney. And there I heard a pen walking in the chimney behind the cloth. They had appointed one there to write all my answers, for they made sure work that I should not start from them. . . . A subtle question, a very subtle question. . . . But God which alway hath given me the answer helped me, or else I could never have escaped it ; and delivered me from their hands."

Twice he appeared before Convocation. On the first occasion he was required to sign fifteen articles to prove his orthodoxy in such questions as purgatory, masses for the dead, invocation of saints, pilgrimages, celibacy, the seven sacraments. Through his influence at Court, especially with Cromwell, who was now rising into power, Wolsey having fallen, Latimer was required to subscribe only two articles, approving Lenten fasts and that the crucifix and images of saints should be kept in churches as memorials. But when Latimer had signed these two articles the reactionary bishops persuaded their colleagues to defer his release, and eventually to insist upon his signing all the articles. This he did, and acknowledged on his knees that whereas previously he had confessed only to committing errors of discretion, he now, having searched his acts more deeply, acknowledged that he had erred also in doctrine.

Not long after this humiliating surrender Latimer went to see the reformer Bainham who had been flogged at the Tree of Troth in Sir Thomas More's garden, and had been racked in the Tower until he was almost lame, while More stood over him. Latimer asked Bainham on what charges he had been condemned. Bainham said he had called Thomas à Becket a traitor. " That," said Latimer, " is no cause at all worthy for a man to take his death upon." Whereupon Bainham explained that he had also spoken against purgatory and the sale of masses, as being matters on which he must go to his death to maintain his opinions.

> " Marry," said Latimer, " in these articles your conscience may be so stayed that you may seem rather to die (think you ought to die) in the defence thereof, than to recant. . . . But yet beware of vain-glory; for the devil will be ready now to infect you therewith, when you shall come into the multitude of the people."

Bainham went to the stake, and Latimer returned to his west country parish. We may suppose that the loss of his friend spurred him to greater activity. His reforming sermons roused the neighbourhood. Bristol, always an excitable city, was in a ferment. The Catholics of Bristol, Latimer tells us, procured " certain preachers to blatter against him." One of these, Hubbardin,

> " ordinarily rode in a long gown down to the horse's heels, all bedirtied like a sloven, as though he were a

man of contemplation. His sermons consisted of tales and fables, dialogues and dreams. He would dance and hop and leap, and use histrionical gestures in the pulpit. At which he was once so violent, stamping so much, that the pulpit brake, and he fell down, and brake his legs, whereof he died."

Latimer, for his part, was preaching the doctrines of reform as energetically as before his recantation. But in the meantime the political situation had changed. Henry was in the first flush of his second marriage; Latimer was personally popular with Anne Boleyn; the King was beginning to lay hands on the treasures of the smaller monasteries; his friend Sir Thomas More, the man Henry loved most in his life, had resigned the Chancellorship on the question of the Act of Supremacy. In 1535 Latimer was back in London. More was awaiting the verdict of the Commissioners in a garden shed at Lambeth when, as he wrote to his daughter, he had a glimpse of Latimer walking in the garden with several doctors and chaplains. "And very merry I saw him: for he laughed, and took one or twain about the neck so handsomely that if they had been women, I should have weened he had been waxen wanton."

Not long after More met his martyr's death Latimer was consecrated Bishop and appointed to the see of Worcester, which at that time comprised as well the united diocese of Gloucester and Bristol. In a short essay it is impossible to say much of his work during the three years and nine months of his episcopate. He worked assiduously at carrying out the principles of reform, at raising the standard of education amongst the clergy and seeing to it that they studied and expounded the Bible. He was *ex officio* Cromwell's instrument for the suppression of monasteries in his diocese; he became the advocate of innumerable heads of houses against the oppression of Cromwell's commissioners. Neither did he forget to support the interests of those whose tie with him was more personal. In November 1537 he writes to Cromwell, " I am in a faint weariness over all my body, but chiefly in the small of my back; but I have a good nurse, good Mistress Statham, which, seeing what case I was in, hath fetched me home to her house, and doth pymper me with all diligence: for I fear a consumption." In the following June he wrote, " God prosper you with good remembrance of Mistress Statham's suit." What the suit was is not known.

About the time of Jane Seymour's death Latimer visited London. He was now the leading preacher of the day. And when he preached before the King he was as outspoken as ever, telling him that the lands of abbeys should not be used to pasture the royal stud. The disastrous affair of Henry's fourth marriage to the German Protestant Princess Anne, the marriage which was to be the crowning point in Cromwell's career, but which terminated in the King's statement, " I have left her as good a maid as I found her," gravely imperilled the cause of the Reformers. Cromwell was in disgrace and the King was under the influence of Gardiner, who later re-established Catholicism in England under Mary. Cromwell told Latimer that it was the King's wish that Latimer should resign his bishopric. Cromwell had no authority for his statement. Latimer resigned, and in the course of the resignation both he and the King realised that the resignation was due to Cromwell's presumption. But owing to the pride of Henry and of Latimer the resignation stood. Latimer never again had a diocese. Cromwell was kept alive to write a letter which should assist Henry in establishing his second nullity, the grounds this time being entirely physical, and he was then executed. It is not unreasonable to impute the King's cynical treatment of Cromwell to his resentment at the wound which he had suffered in his personal relations with Latimer.

It is recorded that when Latimer disrobed " he gave a skip on the floor for joy, as he put off his rochet." It was certainly easier to resign his office than to remain a bishop under Gardiner.

Latimer never resumed his rochet. After an uneasy period during Henry's fifth marriage, he felt that danger was behind him when the King married a lady who had once been called Latimer. When the King died, Latimer became the preacher both of the people and of the new King. It is to the four-hour sermons which he preached before Edward VI that we are indebted to so many of the facts of his life. When he preached in churches accessible to the public, the throng was so great that the woodwork suffered, as we know from certain quaint accounts for repairing damages to pews after Latimer's sermons.

The accession of the daughter of Catherine of Aragon left

the way perfectly clear for Latimer without vain-glory to follow, " Bilney, little Bilney, that blessed martyr of God," as he had used to speak of him during the reign of Edward VI. He did so with commendable fortitude, and he was more fortunate than his fellow heretic, Dr. Ridley. Kindly ladies used to supply gunpowder to speed the end, as during the war they gave cigarettes to German captives. Latimer had barely uttered the words, " Be of good comfort, Master Ridley, and play the man. We shall this day light such a candle, by God's grace, in England, as I trust shall never be put out," when the keg under his faggots exploded.

Dr. Ridley's powder was damp.

THOMAS CRANMER
1489–1556

By

R. ELLIS ROBERTS

THOMAS CRANMER

by R. ELLIS ROBERTS

I

WHEN Thomas Cranmer, in the late autumn of 1529, was summoned by Henry to attend him at Greenwich, he was already in his forty-first year, and a man of no particular note, except in University circles. His was a time when men reached maturity of mind and character very often before they were out of the twenties; and this slow development of Cranmer gives us certain indications of his nature. He was, we may safely conclude, an unambitious man, and he came of an unambitious family; he was also a man who was slow, in his earlier years, to take up with new ideas, and the rapidity with which, after he had become Archbishop, he changed his opinions, argues in his temperament a kind of delayed intellectual adolescence. It is true that he stated in a famous discourse in 1534 that he had for many years prayed against the power of the Pope in this country; but a national anti-Papalism was no new thing in the history of English Catholicism, and in the sixteenth century, as in the century of the anti-Popes, need argue no more than a pious impatience at the trickery of Italian politicians and the corruptions of the Papal Court. Cranmer, who all his life was a tolerant man—this is admitted both by friends and enemies—was also an easy one. I think this is shown clearly enough by the story of his two marriages. Ralph Morice, in his brief memorial of his master's life—he was Cranmer's secretary—speaks of them in almost identical terms. As soon as Cranmer had proceeded to his master of arts degree " it chawnced hym to marye a wif," who died a year after in child-birth. When in 1532 Cranmer was sent on an embassy to the Emperor and was staying in Nuremberg,

" being by this meanes both well acquaynted and enterteynid emongs lernyd men there, it was his chaunce to mary a kyniswoman of one of theirs, this his laste wif, whome he secretlie sente home into Englande within one yeer of his placing in his dignitye."

I can see nothing in either of these stories to justify the romantic language of modern biographers who say that Cranmer " fell in love " with Joan of the Dolphin Inn, or became attached to Margaret, the niece of Osiander. If we consider his character as it develops, I think we shall conclude that the young graduate was probably the victim of pitiful affection, rather than of passion; and that the middle-aged man of forty-three was argued into a match which was inconvenient and illegal—for in 1532 Thomas Cranmer had been for many years in priest's orders. Nothing in his history, nothing in what we know of his few permanent convictions about the laws of Church and State, would lead us to believe that he would, unless his kindness were vehemently appealed to, have so flouted the prejudices of his royal master as by this second marriage.

I have stressed these facts in Cranmer's life, because I believe they give us, far more than his originally unenquiring and his subsequently fluid theological opinions, the key to his character. Cranmer had kindness and charm: he hated to persecute—his Protestant friends who delated obstinate Catholics to him complained bitterly of this; and he hated to say " No " when his kindness prompted him to say " Yes." It is far too simple a solution of his success with Henry to picture Cranmer as a pliant tool whom King Harry chose because he could do what he would with him. Though Cranmer was always ready with scriptural arguments in favour of the divine right of kings, and though he certainly was sincere in producing those arguments, what weighed far more with him was the fascination he felt for, the fascination he exercised over that turbulent monarch. After all, Henry was Elizabeth's father, and he could exercise when he would the same arrogant Tudor attraction that was so unscrupulously used by his daughter. But Henry was, in a sense, softer than Elizabeth. When Cranmer and he met, the King had many tools, many good servants; but he had few men whom he could at once respect and love. Something was growing in him which repelled the finer spirits of his age; but Cranmer, who was liked and trusted by the man, worshipped the King; he evoked in Henry the affection which his own nature roused in nearly all who met him, and the trust which springs from love. He became the man's friend as well as the King's servant. There was no man to whom Henry was more lenient, or allowed to approach him with greater freedom—Cranmer, we must not forget, pled with Henry for the sake of Mary Tudor, and tried his best to help Fisher and More when they were under that royal and maleficent displeasure; and it was Cranmer who knelt by the King's death-bed and whose hand the King held—" the archbishop, speaking comfortably to him, desired him to give him some token that he put his trust in God through Jesus Christ, according as he had advised him; and thereat the king presently wrung hard the archbishop's hand, and soon after departed."

Cranmer, in short, was a man who inspired and felt affection; and whose opinions were more governed by his personal relationships than one may think any theologian's or ecclesiastic's should be. For that which had been a solace and a source of joy to him—though it led him into some awkward circumstances and some strange inconsistencies—became in the end the faggots and the fire of his burning and, worse than that, the foul smoke of the shame which he so gloriously burnt away in his martyrdom. Loving the poor young Edward as he did his father—in mourning for whom he suffered his beard to grow—he could remain through that child's brief reign of distraction and destruction, buoyed up and heartened by his belief in the divine right of royalty. And then comes Mary. Mary whom he, more than any man, had helped to bastardise; Mary whose religion he had scorned and done his best to destroy; Mary in whom no man or woman found any charm; Mary who threatened England, not only with the Papacy, but with the secular power of Spain; Mary who loathed his name and his deeds and his apostasy. For months Cranmer strove to remain faithful to his one constant doctrine (outside the beliefs common to all Christians, Papist or Protestant), the divine right of princes. His struggle was dreadful—and for a brief time it looked as if Cranmer's unnatural principles would win against his conscience, that he would go the way of bully Northumberland,

and renounce all which he had advocated at such dangerous cost—and it is to Cranmer's immortal credit that at the end he could not swear obedience to the idol he had set up. He renounced, by what sudden illumination we shall never know, the right of princes to dictate to their people how they should worship God. In his martyrdom and in his final perseverance Catholic as well as Protestant can rejoice. If Cranmer had kept to the repudiation of his own past, he would have died obedient to an opinion which is fatal, not merely to Catholicism or Protestantism, but to any kind of Christian doctrine. He would have died proclaiming the supremacy of the God-State, that ancient mask of Mammon which the Tempter assumed when he swept Jesus Christ into the holy city and set Him on the pinnacle of the Temple.

II

Cranmer was born on the festival of the Visitation of Our Lady in the year 1489. He was the second son of his father, who lived at a small hamlet, Aslacton, in Nottinghamshire. The family was modest enough; though in Tudor times, so rich in opportunity for jumped-up men, there was in the new nobility a fine appetite to pretend to ancient lineage; and Cranmer in later life was pleased to argue that he came of a family whose ancestor had travelled here with the Conqueror. He was, as was customary with second sons, destined for scholarship and the Church, and proceeded to Cambridge. Though it was the old, lazy Cambridge, it was also the Cambridge of Erasmus who, high in his tower-room at Queen's, was engaged on his edition of the Greek New Testament. Cranmer was a student of theology, and it was as a theologian he became one of the first fellows of Jesus College, a new and poor foundation on the site and with the endowments of a derelict Augustinian nunnery. For a time the regular course of Cranmer's academical career was broken by his marriage; but on his wife's death his college took him back again, and it is evidence of his academical distinction that he was urged to go as a fellow to Wolsey's great new college at Oxford, an offer which " he utterlie refused." I think this refusal of a position which might have changed the course of Cranmer's life may fairly be ascribed to his sense of gratitude—the sense which was to lead him into such difficulty and danger. At Cambridge he remained, and, as far as we know, led the ordinary life of a college fellow of that period. Morice says that he began to read the works of the new men—Erasmus and Luther especially—who were seeking to reform the Church. How far he sympathised with any of the new doctrine is uncertain—for we cannot rely too much on his own later recollections of his youthful convictions; but that he was of the party of reform, so far as Church discipline was concerned, is certain. Cranmer had all the scholar's impatience, all the honest and unambitious man's detestation of carelessness, ignorance, and incompetence.

It was by an accident that he came into the confused business of the divorce. He was at Waltham, in the house of one Cressy, with two pupils, Cressy's sons. They had journeyed there to avoid the plague. To Waltham also came the King: and with him were Stephen Gardiner, afterwards Bishop of Winchester, and Edward Fox, afterwards Bishop of Hereford. They were also lodged at Mr. Cressy's: they were all Cambridge men, and their familiar talk was how to rid Henry of Catherine. Cranmer was asked for his opinion. He pleaded his ignorance of canon law; but suggested that the King had better appeal to the universities of Europe. The suggestion had been made before; but Henry, about whose conscience the only certain fact is that it always counselled dilatoriness, had not acted. Why he acted now we do not know. Possibly Gardiner, his secretary, had felt Cranmer's charm, and conveyed an impression of it to the King. Anyhow, a few months later the fatal meeting at Greenwich took place, and Cranmer became the King's man.

If at this time Cranmer had any difficulty in reconciling the claims of Church and king, his doubts vanished at his first contact with King Harry. His position then and throughout the rest of his life might be summed up in the epigram of a Roman Catholic poet of the next century:

> " *All we have is God's and yet*
> *Cæsar challenges a debt;*
> *Nor hath God a thinner share*
> *Whatever Cæsar's payments are:*
> *All is God's, and yet 'tis true*
> *All we have is Cæsar's too.*
> *All is Cæsar's: and what odds*
> *So long as Cæsar's self is God's?* "

There is no reason to suppose that Cranmer was in the least dishonest in his belief that Henry's marriage with his brother's widow was invalid; and if he had any doubts about the wisdom or the propriety of the proposed union with Anne Bullen, they disappeared when he grew to know and to love that determined lady. Nor does it matter whether in 1532 Cranmer was made Archbishop of Canterbury in order to pronounce the King's divorce, or because Henry was sure that he would do so. Cranmer's opinion was well known; and he would shrink, not from expressing it, but from a position of authority which was certain to be troublesome and dangerous, and which would prevent him from making the slightest public recognition of his own recent matrimonial error. What is certain is his feeling for Anne; whether or no he were her chaplain, he was her friend for her own sake as well as for the King's—but his love for her must yield if she were faithless to Henry. When she was committed to the Tower on the charges which led her to her death, Cranmer wrote to the King, May 3, 1536:

> " I am in such a perplexity, that my mind is clear amazed; for I never had a better opinion in woman than I had in her; which maketh me to think that she should not be culpable. And again, I think your highness would not have gone so far, except she had surely been culpable. Now I think that your grace best knoweth, that next unto your grace I was most bound unto her of all creatures living."

Some have condemned Cranmer bitterly because, after Anne had been found guilty, he acted as judge in the divorce action which Henry, for reasons quite inscrutable, ardently desired. Such criticism means only that the critic despises the whole of Cranmer's ecclesiastical position, as he is entitled to do; but one is not entitled to scarify this action as particularly cowardly or dishonourable. He had, under the King, accepted the responsibilities of the Pope; and he could not retreat from that acceptance because of personal affection, without falsifying his past. I detest Cranmer's theory of the King-God; but I do not think I or any man can say what was the nature of his interview with Anne, when he drew from her the confession that there had been some impediment to her marriage with the King. All we know is that the cause was " not yet set down otherwise than that they were declared *just, true, and lawful impediments* of marriage." Anne's admission was made, not to a confessor, but to a judge; and if we think it unfortunate that a man should act as judge in a case which so nearly concerned him and on one who had befriended him, Cranmer is not the first man to be thrust into such a position.

Cranmer was not unassailed. Slow as he had been in working for the reformation, he was inconveniently rapid directly he was in a position of responsibility. Tolerant though he could be to individuals, his language about the Pope and the Papacy has all the extravagances and virulent excess of the day. Here he had Henry with him; but, except on the question of the Papal authority, Henry remained a moderate Catholic—true he plundered the religious houses, and, under Anne Bullen's influence, was lenient to certain reforms on minor matters of devotion, but other Catholic sovereigns, before and since, have gone as far as Henry. Cranmer wished to go much farther. Already obsessed by the vision of the Papal power as Anti-Christ, he dreamed, before Henry's death, of a Church purged from all the business of Babylon. It is hardest to forgive his wholehearted assistance in the pillaging and suppression of the monastic orders; hardest to forgive, and hardest to understand. That some reform of the religious, men and women, was needed was granted on all sides; but here Cranmer sided with those who wished not to reform but to destroy, and whose wish, when it was not based on fanatical ignorance, sprang from motives of greed and secular wickedness. It is possible that Cranmer was confused. So many of his supporters, and of the stoutest advocates of reform, were men of the new families who were made rich and, for a time, secure by their theft of monastic property that he feared to alienate them by any suggestion of discretion in that evil work of destruction. It is more likely that, with the King worshipped by him as his Pope, Cranmer saw the King's men as God's men, and had a fantastic dream that to take from the monks and give to the new capitalists was to take from Anti-Christ and to give to God. It is true that Cranmer's own jurisdiction, and that of all the bishops, was suspended during Cromwell's visitation in 1535; but he made no protest against that monstrous Vicar-General and his creatures, as he might have done had he felt strongly on their methods or their aims. He cannot be acquitted from his share in an action which, according to Professor Pollard, " from the point of view of education and of provision for the sick and poor . . . was a waste of one of the most splendid opportunities in English history."

It was not his support of the dissolution that gained Cranmer powerful enemies. Men find it easy to shut their eyes to evil with fingers to which the loot sticks. Cranmer earned opposition through his genuine effort to make some reform, and by his hasting on the road to continental Protestantism far faster than the majority of his old friends, and at a pace which altogether outran the commons of England. I see no reason to suspect his honesty, only his intelligence; it passes the wit of man to follow Cranmer's mental tergiversations about the doctrine of the Real Presence. It can only be pled in his excuse that some of the stoutest defenders of transubstantiation upheld the doctrine with words formally heretical, and did so un-rebuked by authority. One wonders whether these fellows had ever read in the great Doctor's works that Christ is not in the sacrament, *quasi in loco*; that by Aquinas' theology the Real Presence is not a local presence.

Henry while he was alive would not budge from Catholic doctrine nor from Catholic devotion and practice, unless it benefited his power or his purse. He had not made him-self Pope to have his religion otherwise altered. So in the Articles, in the two books known as The Bishops' and The King's there is a general adherence to the Catholic religion. There was nothing un-Catholic in the tentative permission to have prayers in the vernacular, nor in the encouragement of Bible-reading. The efforts made to prejudice Cranmer in the King's eyes failed because, in the last event, Cranmer always gave way to the King. This seems monstrous to us. It is wholly repugnant to our feelings that an archbishop and a theologian, in subscribing a paper defining his opinions on certain disputed questions of religion, should declare

> " This is mine opinion and sentence at present, which nevertheless I do not temerariously define, but refer the judgement thereof wholly unto your majesty."

Yet to Cranmer, who believed in the King's divine authority, this seemed as natural as a modern Papist finds his submission to the Encyclical on the Inspiration of Scripture. Cranmer submitted his opinions to the King, not because he necessarily agreed with the King's views, but because he believed he owed implicit obedience to him who was Head of the Church. There is something extraordinarily pathetic in " this is mine opinion at present "; for Cranmer not only was ready to forgo his own opinions at the King's bidding, he was also by this time well aware that the opinion of December might have melted away in May.

After Henry's death, and with the temporary triumph of the Protestant Party, Cranmer's last vestige of Catholicism began rapidly to disappear. Here we must remember again what he was. An obscure country boy, a shy, diligent scholar, a capable unassuming don—what experience had he had of popular religion, of what was needed to keep alive the devotion, the interest, the colour of the people's devotion? Snatched out of Cambridge into the strange hothouse of the Tudor Court; muddled by his task of resolving Henry's matrimonial tangles; befriended by the vehement Protestants of the Continent; leaning on the support of those who robbed and misgoverned the country under Edward VI; meeting only—unless he were judge in some heresy trial—ecclesiastics, politicians, time-servers and enthusiasts—he knew nothing, we can well think, of the religion of the people of England. He was a typical example of a kind of bishop who was to be fatally prominent in the Church of England—the bishop who has never said or attended a mass at a parish church since he was a child, whose knowledge of the people's religion is gained from reports, forms, statistics, visitations, and what-not. How clearly this is seen from his tedious, academic answer to the rebels of the West of England who rose against the Prayer Book of 1549. For a pastoral staff he had a ferule; it is the college cap, not the mitre, on his head; and he speaks, standing angrily, from his desk, not seated on the metropolitical throne.

He trips up those Cornishmen, he confutes them, traverses their direct requests with scholastic arguments, enjoying himself hugely in the art of academic disputation—continually answering what they have said, not what they meant; and insisting that, when they complain they had no English, they had as small knowledge of Latin—a fact of which he

227

could not have had trustworthy knowledge. It was here Cranmer failed most miserably. He was separated monstrously from the people, understood neither their needs nor their grievances; it was in bitter recognition of this that an anonymous scribbler wrote:

" For bribery was never so great, since born was Our Lord,
And whoredom was never less hated, since Christ harrowed hell :
And poor men are so sore punisht commonly through the world
Thus would it grieve any one that good is, to hear tell.
For all their homilies and good books, yet their hearts be so quel,
That if a man do amiss with mischief they will him wreck.
The fashion of these new fellows, it is so vile and fell;
But that I little John Nobody dare not speak."

No one now supposes that the English reformation was due to popular feeling or intended to promote freedom in matters theological or religious. In London and a few other centres—but especially in London, where notable foreign Protestants had their places of worship—there was some popular force behind the new religion; but in the country generally it met with either hostility or indifference. The terror felt at the idea of freedom, of free enquiry, is shown sufficiently by the fact that in 1547 even the licensed preachers were forbidden to preach anything but the official Homilies; argument too clearly disclosed the popular disagreement with the Government's policy. No one doubted —except perhaps a few quiet mystics—that the authorities had the right to dictate the religion of the people. The only questions were: Who had authority? and which religion? Not yet did the world know of that one great alternative to the Catholic body of theology, the system to be known as Calvinism. Men—and at their head Cranmer—wavered between the subjective and emotional theologies of Luther and Zwingli. In the late forties Luther was already discredited; and Ballinger could confuse Luther's doctrine of the Blessed Sacrament with transubstantiation, a confusion from which Cranmer himself was not free in his later years. The extraordinary fluidity of his theological opinions earned for him the contempt of other Protestants, as well as the mockery of the Catholic Party. When Joan Butcher, who held a private heresy about the Incarnation, was tried and con-

demned in 1550 she taunted her judges with the martyrdom
of Anne Askew, burned under Henry for denying transubstantiation; and indeed there seems no reason to suppose
that Cranmer, had he lived, might not have journeyed from
Zwingli to Servetus, just as he journeyed to Zwingli from
Luther. It was the death of King Edward, and the subsequent tragic and transient return of the country to
Catholicism, which stabilised the opinions of Thomas
Cranmer.

III

Cranmer, let us remind ourselves again, was a don. He
was as remote from the ordinary needs, the ordinary desires,
the ardent and ignorant aspirations of most church-going
people as are some of our modern bishops—there is more
than one on the bench to-day—who progress to the episcopate from a position in a great public school or a university.
Such men have never, in the plain sense, even " been to
church." As schoolboys they worshipped in the school-
chapel, and at school they were confirmed as part of the
school routine; as schoolmasters or dons they worship in
school or college chapel; on holidays they go, as Cranmer
went, abroad; they may then have a quiet decade in a
cathedral close, and so come to the rule of a body of country
clergy of whose difficulties they know as little as they do of
the ways of the country people. Their idea of religion is
always decent and often dull; sometimes scholarly, generally impracticable. Cranmer's opinions about public worship finally flowered in the Prayer Book of 1552—a book
never enforced in the Church, nor authorised by it, and
probably in use only for a very short time.

Yet Cranmer, with all his strange misunderstandings, performed one incomparable work. He gave us the English of
the Book of Common Prayer.

This is not the place to argue on the comparative merits
of a vernacular and a non-vernacular liturgy. The obvious
argument in favour of a vernacular liturgy is that it is more
easily understood by the ignorant; the argument in favour
of a special, hieratic language is that, while the vernacular
will change, the hieratic language may remain constant.
Whatever our views, no one can read the Litany, the
Collects, or Cranmer's other liturgical essays and refrain
from saluting a genius in English prose second only to

Shakespeare's. His rhythm, his cadences, the profound equanimity of his sentences are part of the heritage of English literature: there was his real work, there his genius was at home, and in happiness—a genius no less great because it was for the most part a genius for translation. The supremacy of his achievement can be easily estimated if we compare his work with that of those who have come after him, whether Caroline or later. He gave to English men and women a language in which to approach God; and he showed incomparable art in the making of prayers in which exaltation and supplication were gloriously at one.

Looking at that work, one is loath to enter into the dusty and uninviting regions of his interminable controversies, theological or ecclesiastical. In them he showed no originality, no greatness of thought: he was no better than his lesser opponents, Gardiner and Pole; and could only combat their scholasticism with a scholasticism equally narrow, and unsupported by the body of doctrine to which they could appeal.

Cranmer's development was at first gradual and slow, then tragically rapid; so his end, at first terribly protracted, came at last swiftly with his run through the rain to the faggots piled in Broad Street, at Oxford.

When Edward VI lay dying, his supporters and the partisans of the Reformation were gravely apprehensive. Under the will of King Henry, the next successor of the throne was Mary; and these men could expect no favour from the daughter of Catherine of Aragon. So they agreed on a plot, devised by that Duke of Northumberland who during Edward's brief reign had made himself one of the most unpopular tyrants who ever robbed and harried the people of this country. He determined that the next sovereign should be Lady Jane Grey, a granddaughter of Henry VII, and that this girl should be his daughter-in-law. Mary and Elizabeth, as bastards, were to be excluded from the succession. Now the claims of King Harry's two daughters were secured not only by Henry's will, but by an Act of Parliament; so Northumberland had chosen a difficult piece of illegality in his efforts to justify his position. How could he contrive to have his way?

First he attacked the King, and secured Edward's consent by insisting on the grave danger in which true religion would be, did Mary succeed. Then having the King, he bullied the lawyers into conniving at a plan—whether they agreed or refused, they risked trial for treason; after the lawyers he overpersuaded the Council. His greatest trouble was with Cranmer.

Still Cranmer remembered, with reverence and respect, his master Henry VIII. How could he go against that master's wishes? How could he perjure himself? He asked to see the King; and he was allowed to, though only in the presence of Northumberland and Darcy. In spite of his opponents' anger, Cranmer spoke plainly to the King; but Edward was now set on his minister's plan, and argued that, as it was a King's natural right to devise the crown, any action to the contrary taken by his father was invalid. Sad and unconvinced (he afterwards pled his ignorance of the shifts of lawyers) Cranmer signed. And signed once again his own death-warrant, first delivered when he had assisted at the bastardising of Catherine's child.

The plot failed. Never was sovereign of England more whole-heartedly acclaimed than Mary Tudor. She would have been carried to the throne, even if Northumberland had pretended to be of her party. With the wicked Duke as her enemy, she had no other. A little more than a month after he had celebrated the obsequies of Edward VI, Cranmer was sent to the Tower, in September 1553. He was tried for treason: for treason he could not be executed with any show of justice. For he was less guilty than others of Northumberland's signatories; and the new Government was faithful to its own principles which forbad it to proceed against a cleric still in possession of the privileges which his sacred orders gave to him.

So began the long agony of his imprisonments, in London and at Oxford, his disputations, his recantations, his degradation and the final scene in St. Mary's. He wrote to the Queen and asked for his life; his petition was in vain. Even if Mary could have forgiven his action against her mother, he had ruined his chances by a vehement tract against the Mass, written shortly after Edward's death, and broadcast in Cheapside as an antidote to the shameless repudiation of Protestantism by Northumberland.

Meanwhile Mary had already modified the enthusiasm with which she had been acclaimed. There was Wyatt's rebellion to make her uncertain; and she had not wit to see, or anyone with the courage to advise her, that to pardon Cranmer would be the best blow she could strike in her own defence. She was determined that he should die. In March 1554 he was transferred to Oxford, and in April he, with Latimer and Ridley, was in Bocardo prison. He was forced to argue with Romanist theologians; he was being kept until the country was reconciled to the Papacy, until the anti-Papal legislation was repealed. So in January 1555, when that was accomplished, Cranmer was held a prisoner, not on a charge of treason, but of heresy. Followed the tedious business of delating him to the Pope, the appointment of a commission to hear the case, and Cranmer's sentence of deprivation and degradation. The sentence was carried out on February 15, 1556. But the end was not yet. It was desired ardently that Cranmer should recant as well as die; and we need not think that this desire sprang from mere malice. It was not unnatural to think that a man whose opinions had been so fluid, a man who had been so ready to obey his sovereign in matters of religion, should once again change with a sincerity at least equal to that which inspired his old convictions. It looked as if the Queen and Pole might have their way. Cranmer, with that nimble mind of his, began to see two sides to the disputed doctrines. After all, he had always held that there was nothing really wrong in religion except over-definition; had he not perhaps erred by defining too nicely, and rejecting too roughly, the definitions of others? So he began to hedge, to equivocate. And then his enemies committed the greatest act of cruelty in the whole tragic business. Cranmer was released from prison.

He left the narrow confines of Bocardo and was lodged in the Deanery of Christ Church. There he walked freely, talking with the canons and students, playing bowls, sharing the college meals, a guest and not an unhonoured one. How the years must have rolled away! Here once more the good scholar, the man who had chosen the life of the academy, was home again in the circumstances of his youth and maturity.

After all, how unreal were the squabbles of theologians, the ambitions of ecclesiastics, the ardours of politicians, beside this considered life of the intellect, this companionship of fellows, in the lovely House, whose meadows stretched down to the Isis.

He remembered, no doubt, that he had refused to be a fellow of this great foundation when Wolsey's zeal and ambition first ordered it. Was it too late? Here he might be allowed to stop, untroubled and untroublesome, talking and writing, and remembering. Could it have been this that Bishop Brooks hinted at when he told Cranmer that " whereas you were Archbishop of Canterbury and Metropolitan of England, it is ten to one that ye shall be as well still, yea, even better."

So his life would come full circle, and he would end as he began, a humble student, remote from affairs and alarums.

The prospect was heavenly; and Cranmer rid himself of that recent past and its burdens. He recanted wholeheartedly. Luther, Zwingli, and the rest—they were nothing beside this sudden recognition that his real life was here.

Then he was taken back to Bocardo.

They believed that they had secured what they wished. Northumberland's recantation of his past Protestantism had been a help; but, after all, who respected Northumberland? Now that Cranmer had consented to forswear the work of all those years under Henry and Edward, it must mean not only his own salvation but the salvation of the Catholic cause in England. Cranmer had never been a firebrand like Latimer, or a hot-headed, rather pedantic fanatic like Hooper. He was sober, except in his theological aberrations, he had tried to be tolerant, he was still a greater friend to England than to the foreigner, he was honoured by many of the middling people, and though men rightly suspected his judgment and his theological ability, they did not suspect him of ignoble ambitions. If Cranmer repudiated the Reformation, it would mean that thousands of people, all over England, would turn, a little wearily perhaps, and sigh : " You see, the Archbishop himself admits that he was wrong. This thing has gone too far. We have lost the faith, and with that loss something else has gone, something incalculable. Now it shall be returned to us."

Had Mary been able to forgo her revenge, had a pardon of Cranmer preluded a general cessation from the bloody work of persecution, those who were anticipating a return to Catholicism would probably have had their confidence justified. Protestantism, of the Swiss or French or German variety, could never have become the religion of England.

It never has been her religion; but the return to a kind of Catholic order was to be made laboriously painful by Mary's unswerving bitterness against Cranmer.

We do not know whether any man ever promised him his life in return for his recantation. We have no doubt that he believed he had saved it. We do not know when Cranmer realised that the Queen's determination was fixed; we do not know certainly whether he was aware of his unalterable doom, even on that rainy day in March when he was taken to St. Mary's Church to hear Dr. Cole's sermon, and to read his recantation in public.

It was March 21. In the early morning Cole came to Cranmer, assured himself of the Archbishop's constancy in his recantation, and gave him some money to distribute to the poor: this must have made Cranmer suspect that his doom was fixed. As the rain was incessant the sermon and the ceremony of recantation were to be in church instead of in an open place. There is an account of what then happened written two days after the martyrdom by a Roman Catholic gentleman in a letter to a friend. This account is of extraordinary value for two reasons. It shows how kindly were the thoughts of some of the Catholic Party to their fallen enemy; and it disposes altogether of the view, encouraged by some modern historians, that our sixteenth-century ancestors were brutal, bloody-minded people, not to be understood by or comparable to ourselves. J. A.— we only know his initials—begins by expressing his pity at " the unfortunate end and doubtful tragedy, of T. C. late bishop of Canterbury . . . I little pleasure take," he declares, " in beholding of such heavy sights. And, when they are once over-passed, I like not to rehearse them again; being but a renewing of my woe, and doubling of my grief." The great University Church was packed: there " was prepared over against the pulpit, an high place for him, so that all the people might see him. And when he had ascended it, he kneeled him down and prayed, weeping tenderly: which moved a great number to tears, that had conceived an assured hope of his conversion and repentance." Cole's sermon was free from the virulent bitterness then too customary in addresses to heretics, and he excused Cranmer from the burden of responsibility for Henry's divorce; but, had Cranmer any hopes of a reprieve from his sentence, they were now vanished. All Cole could do was to urge him to pray God, who would " either abate the fury of the flame, or give him strength to bear it," and to promise that prayers should be made for him in every church in Oxford. Then J. A. writes:

> " When he had ended his sermon, he desired all the people to pray for him: Mr. Cranmer kneeling down with them and prayed for himself. I think there was never such a number so earnestly praying together. For they, that hated him before, now loved him for his conversion, and hope of continuance. They that loved him before could not suddenly hate him, having hope of his confession again of his fall. So love and hope increased devotion on every side. . . .
> " I shall not heed, for the time of sermon, to describe his behaviour, his sorrowful countenance, his heavy cheer, his face bedewed with tears; sometimes lifting his eyes to heaven in hope, sometimes casting them down to the earth for shame; to be brief, an image of sorrow: the dolour of his heart bursting out at his eyes in plenty of tears; retaining ever a quiet and grave behaviour. Which increased the pity in men's hearts, that they unfeignedly loved him, hoping it had been his repentance for his transgression and error. I shall not need, I say, to point it out unto you; you can much better imagine it yourself.
> " When praying was done, he stood up, and, having leave to speak, said Good people, I had intended indeed to desire you to pray for me; which because Mr. Doctor hath desired, and you have done already, I thank you most heartily for it. And now will I pray for myself, as I could best devise for mine own comfort, and say the prayer, word for word, as I have here written it. And he read it standing; and after kneeled down, and said the Lord's Prayer; and all the people on their knees devoutly praying with him."

When he had finished praying, using words which he has taught, in the Prayer Book, to all English people after him, he began his confession. There is a story that Cranmer came to his final scene with two documents. It has been suggested that, as these two papers were, almost certainly, the formula of recantation agreed on, and the form with

Cranmer's own ending repudiating his recantation, the Archbishop had come to St. Mary's with a faint hope that the Queen would at the last relent, and spare him; that, if Cole had then pronounced the royal mercy, Cranmer would have recited the document he had signed. This is just possible; but highly improbable. I think his heart was now fixed. He was no longer slave to the divine king: there was now only one sacrifice his conscience would allow him to make on any altar, the sacrifice of his life. He brought the agreed parchment so that it, with the hand which had subscribed it, might be first in the flames; an offertory to be made before the ultimate satisfaction: and the Venetian ambassador says it was held in that testifying hand. His sermon was an injunction that men should be free from the love of the world which is hatred against God; that they should be loyal to the King; that they should love the brotherhood ; and that they should be charitable to the poor—" for if ever they had any occasion to shew this charity, they have now at this present, the poor people being so many and victuals so dear. (For though I have been long in prison, yet I have heard of the great penury of the poor.) "

So he arrived at the great business of that day, the confession of his faith. As he spoke, in sudden and complete repudiation of his recantation, the men of the old religion and those of the Queen's party cried out on him. He was allowed to utter his denial of the Pope's authority: he began to assert his case against Gardiner about the Blessed Sacrament of the altar, and then he was stopped speaking, and was hurried away out of the church to the burning-place outside Balliol College.

" Coming to the stake with a cheerful countenance and willing mind, he put off his garments with haste, and stood upright in his shirt: and a bachelor in divinity, named Elye, of Brazen-nose college, laboured to convert him to his former recantation, with the two Spanish friars. And when the friars saw his constancy, they said in Latin one to another, *Let us go from him; we ought not to be nigh him: for the devil is with him.* But the bachelor in divinity was more earnest with him: unto whom he answered, that, as concerning his recantation, he repented it right sore, because he knew it was against the truth; with other words more. Whereby the lord Williams cried, Make short, make short. Then the bishop took certain of his friends by the hand. But the bachelor in divinity refused to take him by the hand, and blamed all others that so did, and said, he was sorry that ever he came in his company. And yet again he required him to agree to his former recantation. And the bishop answered, (shewing his hand,) This was the hand that wrote it, and therefore shall it suffer first punishment.

" For when the fire was put to him, and pretty while before the fire came to any other part, he stretched out his right hand, and thrusted it into the flame, where it was seen of every one sensibly burning, crying with a loud voice, ' This hand hath offended.' As soon as the fire got up, he was very soon dead."

REGINALD POLE

1500–1558

By

HAROLD CHILD

REGINALD POLE

by HAROLD CHILD

FOR a man who came very near to being King of England and very much nearer to being Pope, Reginald Pole has little fame among his fellow-countrymen in general. Royal in blood, a scholar and humanist of European reputation, and one of the most renowned and respected statesmen of his age, he was a greater man than scores whose names are more commonly known. But the twenty-two years of his mature power were spent out of England. When he came home, he had only four years to live, and he gave them to the losing side, the side which has ever since been the unpopular side; and the hatred which has hung over the memory of Queen Mary has inevitably shadowed the memory of her kinsman, friend, and adviser. One other reason there is why Cardinal Pole should not be as famous as he was great. His achievement was never worthy of his powers. Again and again he was, in the event, ineffectual. And the capital question about him is, whether it was strength or weakness, greatness or littleness, that made him thus ineffectual; whether he met circumstance with its own weapons and was beaten, or whether he was too high above the battle to fight it as lesser men would fight it.

His royal blood went for a good deal in those days. He was the son of Margaret Plantagenet, Countess of Salisbury, the grandson, therefore, of "false, fleeting, perjured Clarence," and great-nephew of Kings Edward IV and Richard III. On his father's side he was connected with the mother of King Henry VII. He was, therefore, a member of the houses of both York and Lancaster, and intimately related to King Henry VIII. It was as a princeling that he was educated by the Carmelites, first at Sheen and then at Oxford, where he took his degree from Magdalen College;

as a princeling that he was made, at eighteen, Dean of the collegiate church of Wimborne; as a princeling that he went, at twenty-one, to study at Padua. There he lived in great state on the handsome means allowed him by King Henry; and his Italian friends have left a rather droll and charming record of the shy, austere young Englishman—" of singular modesty and few words," "endowed with marvellous modesty, and also prodigiously taciturn," who was yet very gracious and very hospitable. They saw the prince in him; they saw also the scholar. He was the "most learned" as well as the "most virtuous" young man then in Italy. There is plenty of evidence that in that age of humanists Pole was one of the best; but one piece should suffice. At the age of sixty-eight, Leonicus, who had taught him Greek, sent the preface of his "Commentaries" to Pole, aged twenty-four, with the request that he and another Englishman, Lupset, aged perhaps twenty-six, no prince, but a tradesman's son, should rewrite, add, or cut out, according to their pleasure.

To the prince and the scholar one more trait must be added, the devoted friend of King Henry VIII. "The greatest enemy I had in the world, who was that King whom I had loved above all other men . . ." [1]—it must have been very easy to love Henry in those early years; and Pole, as his lifelong love for Alvise Priuli helps to show, was capable of ardent friendship, a virtue which the Renaissance valued very highly. Henry, on his side, loved Pole well in his own way, and his love survived for a time even Pole's direct defiance. Henry's defection and the turning of his love into hate were wounds in Pole's heart that never healed. And he was well aware of the change they wrought in him.

> "The hatred with which the King pursued me, acted on me as the ploughman's furrows on the earth, that the seed he sows may grow and increase, sending me to the deeper study of the theological virtues that the seeds of faith, hope, and charity might take deeper root."

At the age of twenty-seven the scholar-prince came home, to be made Dean of Exeter though not even in minor orders, and well equipped and prepared to be an ornament to the

[1] The quotations in this paper are all taken either from the *History of the Life of Reginald Pole* (by T. Phillips, 1767), or from the *Life of Reginald Pole*, by Martin Haile (2nd edition, 1911).

learning of his native land. He looked forward, perhaps, to the sort of life which Thomas More, his friend at Oxford, had wished for, with the study of theology occupying his maturer years, when scholarship and philosophy should have been duly served. John More and the law had first diverted the course of Thomas More. What was destined to divert Pole's course was politics. Like More, he would have concerned himself with politics as little as possible; and like More he had politics forced upon him by a King who wanted his own way and the world's approval at the same time. A clumsy attempt of Cromwell's to hook him with a coarse fly out of Machiavelli only made Pole shyer of politics than before; and after a little more than two years at home, seeing that the matter of the King's divorce and what lay behind it left no room for him to serve England in his own way, he got leave to go to Paris to study. To Paris politics, at the King's instance, pursued him. He all but evaded them; but he could not evade the King. And the moment came when the King found that he could not evade Pole—the essential truth of the man with whom he was trying to play a game of pretence.

On the pretext that he had helped forward the cause of the divorce, Pole was summoned home for reward. Wolsey fallen and dead, he was offered the throne of either York or Winchester. He declined both. To please his family and friends, he spent a month in labouring to find a solution of the problem of the divorce which should satisfy both the King and his own conscience. He believed that he had succeeded. He took his report to the King. And face to face with his friend in a private gallery of the palace, he was suddenly inspired. He had come to bless, and he could but curse. " I found, oh, good providence of God! that my tongue was hampered, my lips refused to move, and when at last, recovering myself, I began to speak, I uttered every argument most opposed to the theory I had come to defend." Henry was so taken aback that for once he was struck dumb. His hand went to his dagger; but all he could say was that he would consider Pole's opinion and reply to it; and he went out, slamming the door. Pole was left alone, in tears.

It was not only a decisive moment in Pole's life: it was also perhaps the only one in which this man of patience equal to his wisdom, and of fine feeling informing both, was effective, so to speak, at short range. For once, he asserted himself in person, and even King Henry went down before him. What the effect on the history of Europe might have been if Pole had done the like by the Emperor Charles V is one of the many speculations which the period tempts its students to play with.

After that, there could be small question of Pole's staying in England. For the last time the King gave proof of his love and respect by letting him go abroad again on his old allowances. He went back to Padua, within the sphere of that Venice where alone in the Italy of those days men could live and study at peace. And there, and at Priuli's scholar-haunted villa at Treville, he became one of a circle which included, not only classicists like Bembo, but also such men as Sadoleto, Bishop of Carpentras, Contarini, the Venetian Ambassador at Rome, and Giberti, Bishop of Verona—all, like Pole, like More, like Erasmus, fit and willing to help the reform of the Church from within, if politics had not forbidden.

For such work Pole had been preparing himself in peace for about two years, when the pertinacious King of England, now Supreme Head of the Church in his realm, and shortly to execute More and Fisher for denying it, once more tried to win support from Pole, or perhaps to force him into enmity that should give excuse for reprisals. He asked him for an opinion on the Supremacy. This was the occasion of Pole's greatest work, the treatise commonly called the *De Unitate*. He took fourteen months to write it; and while he was about it he made it as thorough and as sound as all his learning could. He kept it very secret, showing it only to Priuli and to Contarini. He kept it even from the Pope, because he disliked the idea of revealing to any but his intimates the sins (as he considered them) of his friend and cousin. On May 19, 1536, Anne Boleyn's head was cut off. Then, the chief obstacle to the reunion of King Henry with the Church having been removed, he sent his treatise to the King. So tremendous an attack was not, indeed, for all eyes. Pole's invective was ruthless; but in the last of the four books there is ruth enough. All Pole's love for his friend pours out anew, and he pleads as earnestly as he had thundered. The King's reply was a request that he would come to England to discuss certain points. His mother and his brother wrote to the same effect. With Cromwell still in power, Pole knew what that meant. For one thing, he was a more marked man than before. The young Duke of Richmond being dead and the Boleyn marriage discredited, the Princess Mary's position was greatly advanced, and Pole was still talked of as a likely husband for her. He knew, as More had known, that his attitude of no compromise must throw his family into danger. He knew, therefore, what men might say if he avoided his own danger by staying in Italy. And here, as on some later occasions, there is a choice between seeing Pole as timid and seeing him as too high-minded to care what his actions looked like. For, having been often and in vain invited, he had now been peremptorily summoned to Rome by Pope Paul III. Already on his way when the King's summons came, he was for turning back. Cardinal Caraffa, Giberti, Sadoleto, and others who had been summoned to Rome with him, pointed out where his duty, as they saw it, lay. He must choose now between Rome and England. In England he knew he could do nothing. To Rome he went.

In Rome Pope Paul III, now some two years on the throne, wanted him, at Contarini's suggestion, to join the commission on the internal reform of the Church which was to prepare for the summoning of a General Council. But the internal reform of the Church, and very much else, was so tangled up in politics, in the rivalries and wars between the Empire and France and the quarrels which that enmity induced in Italy, that there was small practical scope for disinterested wisdom and sincere goodwill like Pole's. He had been but a few weeks in Rome when, much against his will, he was made Cardinal. His attainder in England and the persecution of his family by a now savagely vindictive monarch followed as matters of course; and so long as King Henry VIII lived, Pole was in constant danger of assassination. Then, early in 1537 (too late to take advantage, in the Church's interest, of the Pilgrimage of Grace), he was sent north as Papal Legate, partly to see what could be done for England, and partly to try to make peace between the Emperor and King François I. This was no work for Pole. All the humbug of diplomacy, the saying Peace, Peace, where there was no peace and no honest desire for peace, only confused a man whose vision was long and simple. So it was again when he met the Emperor at Nice in 1538, and again at Toledo in 1539. At politics he was no match for an astute old hand like Charles V; and since there was no personal love nor zeal for the soul of a dear friend to fan his power to flame, such temporary successes as he may have won were only failure in disguise.

Fortunately the Pope had better employment for him. Quietly and persistently he went on working at reform within the Church, especially for more and better preaching, and for the residence of prelates in their own places. He concerned himself less with heresy; and his dislike of compulsion—especially his disapproval of the establishment of the Inquisition in Rome—earned him both the suspicion of being himself a heretic, and an estrangement from Cardinal Caraffa which was later to have grave effects. At Ratisbon in 1541 the preparatory labours of the Commission and all Contarini's skill in mediation had failed. Another attempt at the reconciliation of Church and Protestants by reform and definition was to be made; and Pole was one of the three Legates sent by Paul III in 1542 to prepare for it. It was a task worthy of him; but in that Europe there was no scope for moderates. While the Council, summoned at last, was sitting at Trent in 1545, Pope and Emperor together were defeating the Protestants of Germany in the battlefield, and there was no hope of adjustment. Pole—in speech and in writing the principal moderator (as he might well be called) of the Council—left Trent in 1546 and went to Padua, a sick man. It was said—and it is still said by some—that at heart he was on the Protestant side about justification by faith, and that therefore he ran away and pretended illness. It is more likely that the certain failure of all his labours broke his health.

He worked best when he worked as adviser, behind the scenes. His English shyness had not forsaken him; and he had besides the very English—very " public school "—sort of pride, which at once refines and impoverishes certain noble natures, because it sees self-assertion as self-seeking, and brings reluctance to assume authority. On November 10, 1549, Pope Paul III ended his long and vigorous life. And Pole was within an ace of being elected to succeed him. In effect, he was elected. He had merely to assume the office. He deferred his answer through a scruple, and he lost the election. Once more, it is tempting to speculate. A Pope of Pole's wisdom, of his gentleness, of his piety and purity of life; a Pope of royal blood yet with no family intrigue to foster, nor territorial ambition to fatten—and what might have been the future of Europe and of the Church?

But what, meanwhile, of the future of England? Perhaps even dearer to Pole's heart than the reform of the Church was the reconciliation of England; but in an age when Catholics could be found making war on the Pope and Protestants fighting in his defence, no direct course was possible; and at indirect courses Pole was not good. Long ago Tunstall had told him that in Rome his " simplicity would be imposed on." " The answer I made was, that if I acted with integrity, I could not be the loser; and, if I did not, I deserved to bear the punishment." Such a man was easily tangled up in political manœuvrings. All other means having failed, he would, if he could, have organised a league against the England which had proclaimed him a traitor; but the dissensions of the other powers kept King Henry secure. Reform the Church, Pole later told Pope Julius III, and these dissensions will cease; but in the world as it was, he had no chance of exercising his influence on affairs in England. In January 1547, King Henry VIII died; and for the first time for years Pole could bring himself to write the name of his friend and enemy— " Henry." The Emperor was then at loggerheads with the Pope, and had more than he could do to protect the interests of his cousin, the Princess Mary; and the aged Pope, apparently despairing of England, kept the Cardinal of England busy on other work. Pole's attempts to get into touch with the Privy Council and the Protector were rebuffed; and it is posterity, not the young King and his England, that has reaped the benefit of the letters that Pole wrote, and especially of the letter, noble in thought and in feeling, that he wrote to King Edward VI himself.

On July 6, 1553, King Edward died; and nine days later Queen Mary was firmly seated on the throne of England.

It is not hard to see in imagination the new world that opened then before Pole's eyes. The vision must have had its personal allurement, which it would be disingenuous to overlook. Not counting Edward Courtenay (and poor Edward Courtenay very soon showed that he was not worth counting), Pole was now the Queen's nearest English male relative. He was fifty-four years old to her thirty-seven, and he had long been talked of as a possible and suitable husband for her—his minor orders offering no insuperable obstacle to marriage. For the third (and last) time, it is impossible not to speculate—on what might have happened if Pole could have married his cousin and shared the throne of England : a King of world-wide respect, renowned for his wisdom and moderation, free from political entanglement, willing and able to be friend and mediator to Pope, Emperor and King of France. But Queen Mary had another cousin, on her mother's side ; and that cousin had a father, the Emperor. And that part of Pole's life which gave his power the freest play in the highest spheres of practical achievement showed him also most tragically frustrate.

Yet, whatever part he might have to play in it, the future for England must have looked to Pole very bright. Freed from the heavy hand of King Henry VIII, the reformers had gone too far for the nation, which was very ready to return to the old faith and allegiance. Both Catholics and Protestants seem to have looked to Pole as the one man who could guide the nation wisely. On July 25, 1553, not three weeks after Queen Mary's accession, the Pope had appointed him Legate to England. It was November 20, 1554, before he landed, and by that time the mischief was done.

Pole, having characteristically first suggested that the Pope could find someone better, had been eager to be gone.

> " My manner of living, which, for the most part, has been to retire often to my studies, and not thrust myself into action, or to shew any desire of those employments which lead to the busy scenes of life, might easily induce a person who was a stranger to me, to imagine, either that I am very lazy, or that I make more account of myself than of the public ; or that I am of their opinion, who persuade themselves, that God being sufficient to compass every thing by his power and providence, all they have to do is to wait till he puts them in action."

Cardinal Morone, to whom the letter is addressed, is told that he should have known Pole better. Now that he thought he knew what he had to do, he hastened north. But he had reckoned without the Emperor. Charles was determined that the Cardinal Legate should not set foot in England before the Imperial design was fulfilled. Pope Julius III, now out of heart with government, suggested that Pole should, once more, try to make peace between Empire and France. Queen Mary now bade him come and now bade him wait. His time and strength and patience were wasted in journeys necessarily fruitless, negotiations deliberately false. The simple-minded man, trusting as usual to his integrity, was once more the sport of politics. Four months before Pole was rapturously received at Dover, King Philip of Spain had been less rapturously received at Southampton, and was married to the Queen.

The influx of Spaniards—suspect in a newly self-conscious England both as foreigners and as firm adherents of the Papal Supremacy—gave new power to the reformers, whom Mary's clemency had already emboldened. To restore the Papal Supremacy in England was now a far more difficult task than it would have been a year before. Pole's wisdom and moderation shone out all the more clearly for this and other difficulties; but even at the outset of his work the Spanish marriage hampered him by stirring up national feeling against the side which he represented. Another capital difficulty was the restoration of Church lands. Pope Julius III had issued a Bull permitting their retention. It was permissible to give what might not be sold; and " if it was lawful to alienate the goods of the Church for the redemption of captives, it were even more so to redeem a kingdom, and for the welfare of so many souls." Pole, himself of opinion that such retention was wrong, bowed to the Pope's decision, and left it to the conscience of each holder. The Queen's conscience forbade her. She insisted on making reparation. And Pole approved and aided her. It was a serious political mistake, since it induced uneasiness in a great many powerful holders of Church lands, who feared that the Queen's example might be forcibly imposed on others. In this way and in that, the opposition was sharpened into conspiracy and turbulence, until the safety of the throne as well as of the Church seemed to demand such forms of repression as Pole had consistently set his face against, and even King Philip's own Spanish chaplain had condemned from the pulpit.

At first things went fairly smoothly. Early in 1555 the Bill of Reconciliation was passed; Convocation declared its loyalty to the Legate, and Pole's decree about the Church lands and other thorny matters had set many minds for a time at rest. Thereafter the weather grew heavier and heavier. On March 23, 1555, Pope Julius III died. On May 1, 1555, his successor Marcellus II—to all appearance the Pope for whom Europe and the Church had too long been waiting—died also. He was succeeded by Pope Paul IV, whom we have met as Cardinal Caraffa. It was an unfortunate event for one who was sincerely and cautiously labouring to make peace in Europe and to accomplish the delicate task of reconciling England to the Church. The trouble did not declare itself at once. The Synod opened by Pole at Westminster in November 1555 produced the decrees which regulated the Church in England and may have served as model for the later decrees of the Council of Trent. On Gardiner's death the same month, the Pope very earnestly proposed Pole for the Archbishopric of Canterbury, and Pole, in spite of his strong views on the duty of a prelate to live and work in his own place, undertook the charge in addition to his labours as Legate and as adviser of the Queen. At last, moreover, he had succeeded, in the Truce of Vaucelles, in patching up a peace between France and Spain. And then, in the summer of 1556, Pope Paul IV's hatred of Spain broke loose. By the beginning of 1557 there was war between them. Pole was now suspect at Rome as a friend of Philip, suspect in Spain as a friend of the Pope. French intrigues made the government of England even harder than it had been before. England, hating Spain, was dragged into war on the Spanish side, and fought only to her own disgrace and the loss of Calais. And Pole, deprived of his legateship and named a heretic by the angry Pope, now indeed " *gran persecutore di Polo*," was robbed of prestige and authority just when he most needed both. With a " sword of anguish " in his heart, and strong only in the love and respect which he had won in England for himself, he went on labouring for peace in Europe and for the Church in England during the last eighteen heavy months of his life. On November 17, 1558, his unhappy friend, cousin, and Queen died; and a few hours later he followed her.

He was fortunate, no doubt, in the time of his death. His work was unfinished, and it was destined to be swept away. The four years of his rule were to take on the appearance of an interruption, a gap, in the development of modern England. Yet he cannot be said to have failed. One of England's wisest, gentlest, noblest, he did more than the mere facts of history can record to hold her steady in turbulent waters.

ELIZABETH

1533–1603; reigned 1558–1603

By
G. B. HARRISON

ELIZABETH

by G. B. HARRISON

POETS, said Sir Philip Sidney, disdaining the subjection of other arts and lifted up with the vigour of their own inventions, do " grow in effect another nature, in making things either better than Nature bringeth forth, or quite a new, forms such as never were in Nature "; and this can be well seen in their praises of Queen Elizabeth, whom they celebrated in many guises, as Diana, or Luna, or Eliza, the Fairy Queen of the Shepherds. Sometimes even they spoke of her in terms more fitting the Godhead, as when Sir John Davies wrote in the second of his *Hymns to Astræa*:

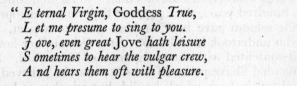

> " *E ternal Virgin*, Goddess *True*,
> *L et me presume to sing to you.*
> *J ove, even great* Jove *hath leisure*
> *S ometimes to hear the vulgar crew,*
> *A nd hears them oft with pleasure.*

> " *B lessed* Astræa, *I in part*
> *E njoy the blessings you impart;*
> *T he Peace, the milk and honey,*
> *H umanity, and civil* Art,
> *A richer dower than money.*

> " *R ight glad am I that now I live,*
> *E ven in these days whereto you give*
> *G reat happiness and glory;*
> *I f after you I had been born,*
> *N o doubt I should my birthday scorn,*
> *A dmiring your sweet story.*"

Often in such devotions Loyalty walked hand in hand with Hope and Expectation; and the Queen herself delighted in

them. At the great entertainment given on her progress
to Elvetham by the Earl of Hertford, there was a song in
her honour, sung by certain young women representing the
Fairy Queen and her maids, who danced around a garland,
chanting this ditty:

> " *Eliza is the fairest Queen*
> *That ever trod upon this green.*
> *Eliza's eyes are blessed stars,*
> *Inducing peace, subduing wars* ";

and more to the same effect. This so pleased the Queen
that she caused it to be sung twice over and rewarded the
singers with largess. She was then in her fifty-ninth year.

Such extravagances, offered to a Princess, young and
beautiful (as was the Princess Elizabeth, King James's
daughter), might be allowed to poetical enthusiasm; but
when the goddess is a woman well advanced in middle age,
notable for her shrewdness, parsimony, and temper, they
smack somewhat of insincerity. Nor had the race of poets
peculiar reason to be grateful to her. Though the generosity
of critics has given " Elizabethan " to the literature of nearly
a hundred years, the arts owed little to her encouragement.
She seldom gave bone or kind word to a poet. Spenser,
who undertook his laborious *Faery Queen* in her honour, was
ill-contented with the meagreness of his reward. She commanded Shakespeare (if the story may be believed) to show
Falstaff in love, which he did, but whether to her satisfaction or his own, it is not recorded. Her company of players
was of second rank and disbanded through insufficiency.
She did indeed tolerate a court poet, one Thomas Churchyard, a poor foolish creature even amongst court poets.
Moreover, the best of the work of the poets of her time
(apart from Spenser) was written in the reign of her
successor.

Nevertheless, poets continued to praise the virtue and
beauty of the Virgin Queen, without any sense of im-
propriety; and it is notable that her virginity was most
hymned when it had long ceased to be the anxious care of
statesmen. Fashions of compliment change, and the leaves
are mostly fallen from the divinity that once hedged kingship. No mode is more dead than the pastoral, but, however quaint the expression, this zeal for the Queen was

unfeigned and came from the heart. Nevertheless, for a true character of Queen Elizabeth, as Nature framed her, the poets are hardly to be trusted.

Her first education in kingship was brutal, for after her mother, Queen Anne Boleyn, had been beheaded, she was declared illegitimate; but though the lawfulness of her birth was much in question, she was always more than a royal bastard. On the death of her father, King Henry the Eighth, she was brought up by his widow Catherine Parr, who had married the Lord Admiral Seymour, but died soon afterwards. Hereupon the Lord Admiral would have sought her hand in marriage, for which he lost his head, and brought her into some danger. Yet, although still little more than a girl (she was in her fifteenth year), she answered all examinations so boldly that her name was cleared. In these early years she was much given to study, and before her eighteenth year she understood well the Latin, French, and Italian tongues, and something also of the Greek, as well as music, for she could sing sweetly and play handsomely on the lute, so that she was very greatly admired for her learning amongst the princes of her time.

Upon the death of her brother, King Edward the Sixth, she became heir to the throne, and was thus in that same unhappy state which afterwards befell Mary, Queen of Scots. For she had been brought up a Protestant, and although under the new order she openly professed herself a Catholic, her sister, Queen Mary, was suspicious of her sincerity. Zealous Catholics were as clamorous for her death as thirty years afterwards the Protestants bayed for the blood of Mary, Queen of Scots. After the rebellion of Sir Thomas Wyatt she was imprisoned in the Tower, and it was generally expected that she would be put to death, but though the rebels were very strictly examined no proof could be found that she had in any way fostered or countenanced them. She was therefore released from the Tower and allowed to retire into the country, until, on the death of Queen Mary, whose Spanish marriage and religious zeal had by this time made her reign generally odious, she was joyfully brought to the throne on November 17, 1558.

She was thus for the space of ten years constantly in peril of her life, and being a young woman of more than ordinary understanding, she learnt in this hard school many lessons in statecraft which would not have come her way in more

settled times. She learnt that in extremity she could trust
only in God and herself, so that she always kept her own
counsel and never confided her inmost thoughts. She learnt
never to commit herself to any irrevocable course if it could
by any means be avoided, which was a principal reason why
she never married. She learnt also that men will always
turn their faces to a rising sun and their backs on the setting.
She was naturally stout-hearted, of good health for the most
part, and very sparing in her diet, so that she slept well and
was not overgiven to broodings. She had few theories of
politics or large and distant plans, for which indeed perils
at home and abroad gave small opportunity, but she trusted
rather to her own instinct upon every occasion, which seldom
betrayed her. From her grandfather, King Henry the
Seventh, she inherited a keenness in money matters (which
some condemn for discreditable parsimony and others praise
as wise husbandry) and ability to choose faithful and discreet ministers, such as Cecil and Walsingham, who served
her loyally to the end of their days.

The later years of her reign were the greatest, when she
was freed from the dangers of Mary, Queen of Scots, and
no longer vexed by the controversies of marriage. She had
by this time outlived most of those councillors and nobles
who were older than herself, and her ability as a ruler was
unquestioned, except by a few malcontents. Nevertheless,
Nature exacted a price, as often happens with ageing
spinsters, and especially those who must be for ever acting
a great part before applauding multitudes. It cannot be
denied that in many ways she was very fantastic, in her
dress, language, and manners, as was noted by foreign
ambassadors and especially by M. de Maisse, who was sent
by Henri IV in the autumn of 1597 to discover for his
master her mind and intention, a task far beyond any man's
power. At his first coming into her presence she received
him in her nightgown, alleging, as excuse for some delay,
that she had been ill, when, he notes—

> " she was strangely attired in a dress of silver cloth,
> white and crimson, or silver ' gauze,' as they call it.
> This dress had slashed sleeves lined with red taffeta,
> and was girt about with other little sleeves that hung
> down to the ground, which she was for ever twisting
> and untwisting. She kept the front of her dress open,

and one could see the whole of her bosom, and passing low, and often she would open the front of this robe with her hands as if she was too hot. The collar of the robe was very high, and the lining of the inner part all adorned with little pendants of rubies and pearls, very many, but quite small. She had also a chain of rubies and pearls about her neck. On her head she wore a garland of the same material and beneath it a great reddish-coloured wig, with a great number of spangles of gold and silver, and hanging down over her forehead some pearls, but of no great worth. On either side of her ears hung two great curls of hair, almost down to her shoulders and within the collar of her robe, spangled as the top of her head. Her bosom is somewhat wrinkled as well as one can see for the collar that she wears round her neck, but lower down her flesh is exceeding white and delicate, so far as one could see.

" As for her face, it is, and appears to be, very aged. It is long and thin, and her teeth are very yellow and unequal, compared with what they were formerly, so they say, and on the left side less than on the right. Many of them are missing, so that one cannot understand her easily when she speaks quickly. Her figure is fair and tall and graceful in whatever she does; so far as may be she keeps her dignity, yet humbly and graciously withal."

Of her vanity much has been written, and to the last year of her life she affected a greed for compliment and a liveliness more becoming to a young girl. When in 1601 the Duke Orsino Brachiano came to visit her, she danced before him, for she would have all men know her proficiency in that art; as also in her music, so that her courtiers took care that foreign ambassadors should, as it were, surprise her when playing upon the virginals. At another time when the young Duke of Stettin Pomerania visited the court, to impress him with her might she ordered some of her Councillors to approach, and they were obliged to remain on their knees all the while she spoke to them. She sent word also that the Duke might kiss her hand, but he was so great a booby, or so overawed by her majesty, that he dared not appear before her.

She loved flattery always, but was not always deceived

by it, as Essex found. In the time of his last disgrace he wished her to renew his grant of the taxes on sweet wines, and accordingly began to ply her with court holy water, until she observed to Bacon that she had received some dutiful letters and had been moved by them, but when she took it to be the abundance of his heart she found it to be but the preparation to a suit. But Essex was ever an unskilled courtier; he could not utter flatteries with an air of truth. At other times she could be pleased by honest boldness. When Sir Roger Williams once came with some suit into her presence wearing new boots, she said, " Foh, Williams, how your boots stink," to which he had the wit to reply that it was not his boots but his suit that stank.

After her own manner she was very religious, though she had small patience with churchmen, and did not hesitate to rebuke or to interrupt them in their sermons when they preached unpalatable doctrine. Indeed, she despised the subtleties so prized by theologians. She told M. de Maisse that if there were but two Princes in Christendom who had good will and courage, it would be easy to reconcile the differences in religion; for there was but one Jesus Christ, and one Faith, and all the rest that they disputed about but trifles—an opinion more acceptable to common sense than to theology. Nor did she persecute either Catholics or Puritans without good cause, for the former laboured to stir up her subjects to rebellion, and the latter, or at least the extremer among them, proclaimed that the Church of England (of which she was Head) was anti-Christian, and that their assemblies had the right to depose any prince who refused to subject himself to their will. In her time Englishmen had not yet learned that politics have nothing to do with religion.

Nevertheless, she had a great faith in God, regarding herself as His vicegerent on earth and believing herself to be under His especial Providence. This she would constantly declare in her public speeches and private conversation and sometimes even in her proclamations. Pious men indeed will trace the finger of God in her many escapes from perils, and even men with less faith cannot but recognise that among the gifts bestowed by Nature upon great men the most valuable is a peculiar kind of good luck. Nor could she have continued so long and so prosperously had she not been sustained by a belief in this Providence and in her own judgment.

Her variableness and irresolution were notorious, especially in matters which concerned charges; which once moved Walsingham (then ambassador in Paris about her marriage) to write a very straight letter, wherein he rebuked her for irresolution and parsimony, saying that if she continued in her sparing and improvident courses there was not one of her Councillors but would rather wish himself in the farthest part of Ethiopia than enjoy the fairest palace in England.

Nevertheless, her parsimony which has been so much condemned was one of the principal causes of her greatness, for she knew that nothing would more quickly destroy the love of her subjects than to tax them without good and necessary cause, as her successors soon found. It had also this good result, that when her necessities were greatest her Parliaments gave her money the more willingly. She kept a tight hold over the expenses of her service, knowing full well that her officers would cheat her when they could and if they dared; for the public services were very corrupt, especially in the administration of the army, and above all in Ireland. Such husbandry was very galling to her commanders, and not least to Essex, who was openhanded and generous with honours and rewards, and so by natural consequence greatly indebted to his creditors. On his return to court after his great victory at Cadiz in 1596, he was not greeted by the Queen with favour and commendation, but with a demand for a strict account of the money spent and received, for she was very angry when she perceived that, owing to the embezzlement of the loot, the expedition had cost her more than she would receive.

As for her love affairs, many gross scandals were spread about during her reign, but chiefly by those who had no chance of learning the truth. Nor for the most part are they worthy of any credence, for in all ages the private morals of a prince, the less they are known, the more are they scandalised. Yet it must be remembered that she was the daughter of Henry the Eighth and Anne Boleyn, and therefore not naturally inclined to the cloister; and she encouraged familiarities from her favourite courtiers, which were fuel for scandalmongers. If she gave herself to any man, then it would seem to have been Leicester, whom she

certainly loved at one time; and this is noteworthy, that
shortly before his death, which was sudden and unexpected,
he sent her a letter of compliment, upon which she wrote in
her own hand the words, "his last letter," a rare mark of
private feeling in one who seldom recorded it. But the
truth of this, as of many other tales about her, was never
revealed by those who knew it. She chose servants who
said less than they saw; nor in those days had Councillors
of State, and great ladies, discovered that of all the fruits of
office the most lucrative is to sell the secrets of greatness to
the gaping vulgar.

Of her many suitors, the one who seemed likeliest to become her husband was the Duke of Alençon, afterwards
Duke of Anjou, whom she called familiarly her " Frog with
the little fingers," and who was for several years enticed
with promises of marriage. At one time it appeared that
she had at last consented, for she gave him a ring before
witnesses, but that evening, when she returned to her
private apartments, her ladies made such weeping and
lamentation at this dangerous decision that she lay awake
all night, and in the morning changed her mind.

Her irresolution was shown on many occasions, particularly in this matter of her marriage and in the affair of
Mary, Queen of Scots, about which there are many opinions.
Few acquit her of cowardice and duplicity. She openly
wished Mary dead, and she signed the warrant for Mary's
execution, and yet when the Council caused it to be carried
out, she bitterly upbraided them, sent Davison, her Secretary,
to the Tower, and wrote to the King of Scots lamenting the
" unhappy accident." Even her most fervent apologist of
modern times can offer no further excuse than that she thus
sought to shift upon others the blame of Queen Mary's
death, which caused great disgust in the courts of Europe.
The truth seems to be that at the last she never intended the
sentence to be carried out. Either way was perilous. She
was in great danger of murder or rebellion so long as Mary
lived, but by executing Mary she justified her enemies in
seeking her own death. She had moreover a great sense
of the divinity of kingship. Nor is it strange that in different moods she should have uttered contrary opinions,
for the decision was as terrible in itself as has ever befallen
a sovereign. Though historians and other penmen (who
are rarely called upon to play any part in great affairs) are

wont to denounce bold, constant, and resolute judgments against the lives of princes long dead, it was less easy for one who always shrank from irrevocable dooms, knowing from experience that even the greatest dangers had often passed away by themselves. Though she did indeed sign the warrant for Mary's death, she was overcome with horror when she learnt that (unknown to her) it had been put into effect; and the truth of the matter, insomuch as she ever had any fixed intention, seems to have been shown in her words to the French ambassador that she had signed the warrant to satisfy her subjects, but had never intended it to be carried out, except in case of foreign invasion or insurrection at home, and that her Council, supposing that they acted for her welfare and safety, had played a trick upon her.

She was naturally merciful. Four times she revoked the sentence on Norfolk before she could be persuaded to allow it to proceed. When Essex rebelled there were but five put to death, though he had attempted by force of arms to raise the City of London, to break into the palace, to remove her ministers and to force her to do his will—an example of clemency not paralleled in the treasons of our times.

In her judgments and decisions she was independent, yet dependent upon her ministers at home and abroad, for, except from the reports which came through them, and especially through Burghley (and after his death through Robert Cecil, his son), she had small means of knowing what was happening abroad. She was not one to employ spies upon her own servants. Few men had secret or private access to her, and she did not consult her women in State affairs. The Cecils for this reason were much courted and well hated as the reputed cause of all unpopular actions. Nevertheless, though she trusted in the loyalty of her servants, she took care to ensure it; and she was endowed with natural authority, which is compounded part fear and part love; for it is no disadvantage for a ruler to be somewhat uncertain in the temper.

This was well observed by Sir John Harington, who wrote, some three years after her death:

"I marvel to think what strange humours do conspire to patch up the natures of some minds. The elements do seem to strive which shall conquer and rise above the other. In good sooth, our late Queen did enfold them all together. I bless her memory, for all her goodness to me and my family; and now will I show you what strange temperament she did sometimes put forth. Her mind was often like the gentle air that cometh from the westerly point in a summer's morn; 'twas sweet and refreshing to all around her. Her speech did win all affections, and her subjects did try to show all love to her commands; for she would say, 'Her state did require her to command, what she knew her people would willingly do from their own love to her.' Herein did she show her wisdom fully: for who did choose to lose her confidence; or who would withhold a show of love and obedience, when their Sovereign said it was their own choice, and not her compulsion? Surely she did play well her tables to gain obedience thus without constraint: again, she could put forth such alterations, when obedience was lacking, as left no doubting whose daughter she was."

She was wont, Sir John continues,

" to soothe her ruffled temper with reading every morning, when she had been stirred to passion at the Council, or other matters had overthrown her gracious disposition. She did much admire Seneca's wholesome advisings, when the soul's quiet was flown away; and I saw much of her translating thereof. By art and nature together so blended, it was difficult to find her right humour at any time. Her wisest men and best councillors were oft sore troubled to know her will in matters of State: so covertly did she pass her judgment, as seemed to leave all to their discreet management; and, when the business did turn to better advantage, she did most cunningly commit the good issue to her own honour and understanding; but, when aught fell out contrary to her will and intent, the Council were in great strait to defend their own acting and not blemish the Queen's good judgment. Herein her wise men did oft lack more wisdom; and the Lord Treasurer [Burghley] would oft shed a plenty of tears on any miscarriage, well knowing the difficult part was, not so much to mend the matter itself, as his mistress's humour: and yet he did most share her favour and goodwill; and to

his opinion she would oft-time submit her own pleasure
in great matters. She did keep him till late at night,
in discoursing alone, and then call out another at his
departure, and try the depth of all around her sometimes. Walsingham had his turn, and each displayed
their wit in private.

"On the morrow, everyone did come forth in her
presence and discourse at large; and, if any had dis-
sembled with her, or stood not well to her advisings
before, she did not let it go unheeded, and sometimes
not unpunished. Sir Christopher Hatton was wont to
say, ' The Queen did fish for men's souls, and had so
sweet a bait, that no one could escape her network.'
In truth, I am sure her speech was such, as none could
refuse to take delight in, when forwardness did not
stand in the way. I have seen her smile, sooth with
great semblance of good liking to all around, and cause
everyone to open his most inward thought to her; when,
on a sudden, she would ponder in private on what had
passed, write down all their opinions, draw them out
as occasion required, and some time disprove to their
faces what had been delivered a month before. Hence
she knew everyone's part, and by thus fishing, as
Hatton said, she caught many poor fish, who little
knew what snare was laid for them."

She possessed that other necessary quality of a prince,
which is courage. Though she would procrastinate and
falter in her decisions when the event was doubtful, in face
of danger she was unafraid. It was no mere flourish when
she reviewed her soldiers at Tilbury at the time of the
Armada, and in her later years, when she went constantly
in danger of murder, she never faltered or hesitated to show
herself on all public occasions. At the time of Essex's rebellion, when a false report was brought that the City had
revolted to him, she went on with her dinner without any
sign of fear or distraction, merely saying that He which had
placed her in that seat would preserve her in it; and she
could hardly be prevented from going out in person to see
if ever a rebel of them all durst show their faces against her.
She could be strangely tender, both to men and also to
her own sex. When news came that Sir John Norris had
died of his wounds in Ireland, she caused a letter of sym-

pathy to be written to the Lord and Lady Norris, his parents, and at the top, in her own hand, she wrote, as one woman of understanding to another, " Mine own Crow, harm not thyself for bootless help; but show a good example to your dolorous yokefellow." At another time, when the Earl of Huntingdon died at York, his Countess being then at Court, the Queen sent twice to prepare her for the ill news, and at last came herself to tell her that he was dead. Yet when the Lord Keeper Egerton seemed to grieve somewhat heavily at the death of his wife, she sent to comfort him but to remind him also that the public service must be preferred before private sorrow.

Towards old Lord Burghley, though at times she rated him soundly, she could be very considerate. On her last progress to the University of Oxford, whilst making a speech to the Heads of Houses, she noticed that he was standing for want of a stool, nor would she proceed with her speech till he was seated. When he died, she sorrowed so greatly that for months afterwards she would not have his name mentioned lest her grief should be renewed.

At all times she could win men's hearts by gracious acts. When old William Lambarde was made Keeper of the Records in the Tower, he made a digest of them which he would have presented to her by the hands of the Countess of Warwick. But the Queen said, " If any subject of mine do me a service, I will thankfully accept it from his own hands." So she sent for him, and for a long while encouraged him with the liveliest interest to speak of his labours, and at length dismissed him with great commendations, a favour rarely shown to scholars by those in great places.

Her commanders in the field found her hard to please, so that her praises, when they came, were the sweeter. Mountjoy, who succeeded Essex in Ireland and there brought order out of chaos, complained bitterly that he was ill-supported at home, and treated like a scullion. Hereupon she wrote a letter to him with her own hand beginning, " Good Mistress Kitchenmaid " and ending " Your Sovereign that dearly regards you." At another time she wrote,

" My faithful George, how joyed we are that so good event hath followed so troublesome endeavours, laborious cares and heedful travails, you may guess, but we best can witness, and do protest that your safety hath equalled the most thereof. And so God even bless you in all your actions."

She spoke often of the love of her people both in her public speeches and in conversation with foreign ambassadors. It was truly very dear to her, for she fed on their applause, unlike King James, who withdrew himself from crowds; but the Queen was expert in the art of popularity, and on her progresses which she made every summer and in the capital she won all by apt and kindly compliment. But she would brook no rival in popular affection. Most of those whom she favoured, such as Leicester or Raleigh, were odious to the people at large. Only Essex was loved by the common people, and this, more than any other, was the cause of his downfall.

But she could not escape the twin penalties of kingship, which are responsibility and loneliness, both more burdensome to a woman who had neither husband nor child to succeed her. She was indeed wedded to her kingdom, and so long as she retained the affection of her people she laboured for them incessantly; but in her last days she could trust no one. Her nobles and councillors were treating underground with her successor, and she knew it well. At last, when she felt that as well as the loyalty of her court she was losing the love of her subjects, she lapsed into melancholy and died on March 24, 1603, in the seventieth year of her life and the forty-fifth of her reign. Such were her times that, had she not been a great Queen, she would have died sooner.

JOHN KNOX
1505(?)–1572

By
CHARLES L. WARR

JOHN KNOX

by CHARLES L. WARR

I

IT was at Easter, 1547, almost a year after the murder of
Cardinal Beaton, that John Knox emerged from a
previous obscurity. Suddenly he strode, a portentous and
volcanic figure, into the arena of Scotland's tempestuous
affairs.

Of his earlier life we are largely ignorant, and he has left
little of autobiographical interest to enlighten us. There is
no certainty as to the year of his birth. It may have been, as
was long accepted, in 1505, or it may not have occurred until
some eight years later. His birthplace was either the ancient
town of Haddington, whose influential abbey constituted
one of the strongholds of Catholicism, or somewhere in the
adjacent neighbourhood of Gifford. He came of modest
farming stock, and, according to his own account, his grandfather, father, and many of his relations served under the
forbears of the Earl of Bothwell, husband of Mary, Queen of
Scots. His mother, whose maiden name was Sinclair, seems
to have died in his infancy, and his father, William Knox,
took to himself a second wife. The boy was in all likelihood
schooled by the priests and monks of Haddington, and
probably at its highly reputed Grammar School. Afterwards he proceeded to the University, where he came under
the influence of the redoubtable John Major. Whether it
was at the University of Glasgow or at that of St. Andrews
that Knox sat at the feet of this fearless and trenchant
theologian is uncertain, but the probabilities are strong that
it was at the latter.

Whatever else the teachings of John Major may have
effected, they must certainly have caused his students to
prick up their ears. For he tiraded endlessly against the

corruptions of his fellow-clergy, as well indeed he might, since, taken as a whole, they were the most debauched and degenerate in Europe. Moreover, he was wont to enunciate the most heterodox opinions regarding the prerogatives of the people and the limitations of the rights of earthly rulers. He held the view, for instance—and, for these days, a very startling view—that princes had their institution from the people, and that on the people the royal power depended. In one mind, at least, this seed found fruitful soil, and that same opinion, some decades later, was passed on by Knox to Mary, Queen of Scots. When he had completed his studies, Knox entered the priesthood of the Roman Church, and between the years 1540 and 1543 we hear of him as an ecclesiastical notary. On an extant document we have his signature: "John Knox, minister of the Sacred Altar, of the Diocese of St. Andrews, notary by Papal authority."

By this time, the Reformation troubles in Scotland were growing to dimensions quite sufficient seriously to disturb the ecclesiastical authorities. Though Knox had remained immune from their contagion, the Lutheran doctrines had infected a considerable number of the clergy, lairds, and better-educated burgesses. We must not exaggerate its strength as yet, but religious discontent had rapidly increased from the year 1528, when Patrick Hamilton, a youth of outstanding intellectual gifts who had studied in Germany, and the scion of a noble house, paid for his dissemination of the new teachings by being burned to death at St. Andrews. During the next decade the fires were rekindled on several occasions. A number of heretics were banished or fled the country. But tracts, pamphlets, and copies of the English New Testament were pouring in from the Continent through the eastern sea-ports. Matters advanced to a graver stage when some images were broken, and a monastery or two were plundered. A movement was obviously on foot which showed every sign of becoming dangerous, and the Government, roused to action, took strong repressive measures.

But Church and State seemed quite equal to the occasion. A hunting of heretics resulted in some suspects, men and women, being burned alive or hanged; and things in general seemed so far satisfactory to Cardinal Beaton, Archbishop of St. Andrews, that in 1544 he gave it as his considered view that heresy in Scotland was dead. This judgment, as events were soon to show, was very wide of the mark. The

Protestant movement, it was true, had for the moment been driven underground. Moreover, with many sympathisers it had become discredited owing to its unfortunate association with the ambitions of Henry VIII, who since 1542 had been savagely using fire and sword to secure for himself the suzerainty of Scotland. In this attempt he was treacherously abetted by a company of the Scots nobility. These rapacious knaves, having seen what the dissolution of the monasteries had meant to their *confrères* in England, and having as a consequence espoused the Protestant cause for reasons connected more with their pockets than their souls, had not scrupled to covenant with the English King to betray their country in his interests. The mass of the Scottish people were ignorant, superstitious, and largely irreligious. They had little love for or interest in the Roman Church, sunk in its slough of dreadful corruptions, and carried with a sullen resentment the crushing economic burdens which its colossal and demoralising wealth laid upon their shoulders. But the Roman Church and Cardinal Beaton stood, as against Henry's pitiless encroachments, for Scottish independence and the old French alliance; and the Scots hated England with a traditional and inveterate detestation. In the early forties, lifted on the wave of an anti-English revulsion, Catholicism by its appeal to the patriotic instinct seemed to have won for itself a new lease of life and Protestantism to have suffered an eclipse.

II

There was still at large, however, a gifted young preacher called George Wishart, who, having studied abroad, had returned to Scotland determined to carry the Lutheran challenge into the camp of Catholicism. He was intimately associated with those Scottish nobles who were the henchmen of Henry, and was almost certainly aware of the activities of a number of them who were engaged in a plot to murder the Cardinal. In January 1546, having preached to great crowds in Dundee, Montrose, and in the West, Wishart came to the Lothians. There he was the guest of a group of these Protestant and Anglophile lairds—Douglas of Longniddry, Cockburn of Ormiston, and Crichton of Brunstan—while from his Castle at St. Andrews, Beaton kept a watchful eye upon his movements. It was while on this visit that

Wishart met John Knox, who was acting as tutor to the sons of Douglas and Cockburn. For the next few weeks Wishart and Knox were constantly together, and their association, proving to be the crisis and turning-point of Knox's life, was destined to be fraught with tremendous consequences for Scotland and the world at large. Knox accompanied Wishart when he preached at Haddington and at various places throughout the neighbourhood. As many another had done before him, he fell completely under the preacher's spell. For long periods they would converse together—Wishart, with glowing eyes and impassioned voice, expounding, exhorting, persuading, convincing; Knox, literally at his feet, drinking in his teachings and exposition with amazement and avidity. Soon he was singled out by Wishart—a signal honour indeed—to bear the sword which it had been found necessary to carry in front of the young Reformer ever since a Catholic priest had tried to assassinate him in Dundee.

But the Cardinal at St. Andrews was moving stealthily but surely. The blow fell ere long. One night a troop of Government cavalry surrounded Ormiston House, where Wishart was staying. He was seized, hurried to Edinburgh, and carried thence to St. Andrews. A month later, on March 1, he was burned to death outside the archiepiscopal castle. Cardinal Beaton, sitting at a window, watched the horrible scene, callous, cynical, and triumphant.

Beaton may now have congratulated himself that heresy in Scotland was dead indeed; but the brutal execution of Wishart was soon to loose terrible forces. Among the victim's associates the passion for revenge was raging like a madness. They were no longer concerned with the assassination of Beaton as an obstacle in the path of the King of England, but were out for his blood as the murderer of their friend. On May 8, a dozen of them succeeded by a subterfuge in gaining admittance to the Castle of St. Andrews. They butchered the Cardinal with unrestrained ferocity, hung his mutilated body out of a window as an object-lesson to the citizens, and barricaded themselves within the massive walls. There followed a farcical siege. The Government appealed for help to Catholic France, and the rebel garrison to Protestant England, and the weeks dragged into months. The Castle, feebly invested by in-effective Government troops, which were able neither to force an entrance nor to prevent the garrison from going and coming as freely as they chose, became a rendezvous for all sorts and conditions of disaffected men and women. Those who felt themselves under suspicion of Church or Government made for its protection like rabbits scudding to their holes. The majority were depraved and vicious persons who soon were successful in turning the Castle into a cockpit of squalid immorality. Within the garrison, however, was an earnest-minded group, sincere adherents of the Lutheran movement, and at their head was a man of deep piety, John Rough, who later was to perish as a martyr in the fires of Smithfield. Their presence constituted the Castle the first organised stronghold of Protestantism in Scotland.

At its gates, one day, arrived John Knox. The new archbishop, acutely mindful of his close association with Wishart, had for almost a year been seeking to effect his arrest, and Knox at last had fled to the comparative security of St. Andrews.

III

There now appears before us the man of destiny. Knox had no sooner arrived at the Castle than the Protestant group recognised that in this hitherto obscure priest they had found their leader. The exigencies of the hour, like steel on flint, seemed suddenly to ignite powers within him which hitherto had found no opportunity for expression. Chief among these was a capacity for public speech, terrific in its overwhelming strength. Wishart had been a preacher of outstanding gifts, but his oratory paled before the cataractal vehemence of this gaunt and passionate zealot who seemed like John the Baptist come to earth again. Compared with that of Wishart, the scholarship of Knox was markedly inferior. His intellectual capacities were not of the same order. But more urgent at the moment than any such equipment was a voice which could lash men to enthusiasm, stiffen them to endurance, compel them to obedience, and put the fear of God into their hearts. That such was the voice of Knox was evident from the moment he took a hand with John Rough in attacking the debaucheries of their fellow-refugees. Rough not only recognised his master, but saw at once that here was the man to head the Protestant crusade in Scotland. Very earnestly he entreated Knox to come to definite decisions. The times were far too critical to halt any longer between two opinions. Knox must publicly take upon himself the office of a preacher of the Protestant Faith. To such an office, urged Rough, he was most obviously called by God.

But Knox himself was not so sure, and the suggestion seems to have startled him considerably. It was one thing to be genuinely sympathetic with the new Lutheran doctrines, but quite another irrevocably to repudiate the Catholic priesthood, buttressed as it was by the tradition and accepted orthodoxy of a thousand years. No man could be expected lightly to dissociate himself from this spiritual past. Knox's perplexities as he faced this proposition were very great. It involved an adherence to an entirely revolutionary conception of the source of authority, of the doctrine of the Church, of holy orders, of the sacraments, and of man's personal relationship to God, which, however it might and could be justified by a dispassionate study of Christian origins and Holy Scripture, ran profoundly counter to an established and agelong tradition of Catholic Christendom. Great indeed must be his care not to " run " where by the divine will he was not sent. Was he really called by God to do this thing? Did the truth lie in such a course, and was everything as clear as Rough and his friends made it out to be? And, even if it were, how could he, Knox, be certain that, bereft of the support of an infallible Church, he was fitted to declare to men " the whole counsel of God "? There were other considerations, too. He was not overstrong, and a man would require to be physically strong to endure the unavoidable hardships and probable sufferings attendant on one who accepted the dangerous calling of a Protestant minister. It was all very difficult indeed.

Moreover, no mortal man could fail to hesitate before the obvious personal dangers which such a course of action would inevitably involve. What, for instance, had happened to Wishart, only a year ago, and just a few yards away, as the result of a similar temerity? What was likely to be the fate of any man who put his hand to the Reformation plough in Scotland? And there was in Knox's character, as well as a perfervid religious enthusiasm, a marked element of enervating timidity. It is a form of moral weakness not uncommon among men of highly imaginative temperament

and forceful aggressiveness of disposition. Ultimately he
conquered it, but it was in evidence on more than one
crucial occasion in the course of his turbulent career. At
this present juncture, adding further disturbance to a profound spiritual uncertainty, it caused him to hedge and
hesitate as he grappled with a critical and awesome issue.
Eventually he fought his way through the dilemma. Partly
through genuine conviction, and partly compelled by force
of circumstances which he was not able to resist, he took the
tremendous step. To the Castle garrison he dramatically
declared that he felt himself called by God to the ministry of
the Protestant Faith. Then, having crossed the Rubicon, he
threw himself, with all the headstrong impetuosity of his
nature, into the advancement of the new movement he had
now definitely and publicly espoused.

The siege of the Castle, as we have seen, was quite fantastic. The garrison wandered without let or hindrance in
the city of St. Andrews, and to the pulpit of the parish
church Knox now betook himself to conduct violent disputations with the Catholic clergy. To awed and bewildered crowds he thundered and declaimed, attacking the
iniquities of the Papacy and the corruptions of the Roman
Church. Alarmed by the disturbing influence of this extraordinary preacher, the Catholic clergy ineffectually endeavoured to counter his anathemas. But their efforts were
of little use against these torrential denunciations. The city
was moved to a feverish excitement, which was destined,
however, soon to be cut short. One day French galleys
arrived in the bay and turned their cannon on the Castle
walls. The garrison were forced to surrender. Knox, and
the ringleaders, shipped aboard, were carried captive to the
shores of France.

IV

For nineteen hideous months Knox toiled as a galley-slave.
In after years he was reluctant to speak of the torments he
endured; but his physical sufferings must have been appal-
ling, and they left their mark on him for the remainder of his
life. The manner in which he bore them was characterised
by a patient spiritual dignity, and also by a gentleness and
resignation which we never find in him again. His captivity
ended in the spring of 1548, when, owing to the special

pleading of Edward VI of England, the exhausted prisoner was set at liberty. Having made his way to London, he placed his services at the disposal of Archbishop Cranmer, who, now that the death of Henry VIII had released ecclesiastical affairs from his contaminating grip, had got the English Reformation well in hand. A most appropriate field was awaiting Knox's peculiar powers. What the English Reformation needed most was preachers, and it soon became apparent that in all the length and breadth of England there was none who could preach like Knox. The Protestant leaders, fully alive to the value of their new ally, set themselves to use him.

Soon after his arrival in London, Knox was a licensed priest of the Church of England and appointed to Berwick-on-Tweed. It was a dour and obstinate stronghold of Catholicism, whose granite resistance only a voice like that of Knox could blast. There he met Marjory Bowes, whom he afterwards married. Two years later he was translated to Newcastle and appointed a Chaplain to the King. By this time his name was widely known and his influence was very great. He had achieved an enormous reputation as a preacher, and, as Cranmer was soon to discover, was a force to be reckoned with. In 1552 the English archbishop felt the extent of the Scotsman's power. At the very last moment, after the book had been sanctioned by King and Parliament and ordered to be put into general use, Cranmer, at the peremptory dictation of Knox, was forced to insert into the Second Prayer Book of Edward VI the famous rubric anent kneeling for the reception of the Holy Communion. On this addition Knox had insisted, and, so great was his influence, Cranmer was compelled to yield. On Knox's part the rubric was intended as a definite, unequivocal, and decisive repudiation of the doctrine of Transubstantiation, and the repercussions of this episode were heard in the debate on the Prayer Book in the House of Commons only a year or two ago.

Knox, to whom increasing power was bringing an increasing confidence and self-assertiveness, was by now a leader in the Church of England, and soon he had the chance of high preferment. He was offered the bishopric of Rochester. His refusal of this office can hardly be accepted as evidence that he had no desire for episcopal honours. When a little later he declined the incumbency of All Hallows', London, he himself was perfectly frank in giving his reasons. His refusal was based on "foresight of troubles to come." This doubtless was also his reason for refusing the see of Rochester. What these troubles were it is not difficult to guess. Edward VI, sickly and ailing, was obviously nearing the end of his brief unhappy pilgrimage, and Mary Tudor, his heir, was a fanatical Catholic. Both Rochester and All Hallows' were dangerously near the sphere of the royal activity, and Knox, who had so recently returned from the galleys, is not unlikely to have felt that, for the moment, he had had enough of persecution. As it happened, his foresight of troubles to come was accurate. In 1553 Edward died, and by the beginning of the following year the Roman Church was again established throughout England. Cranmer and Latimer were thrown into the Tower. The Protestant Party was in imminent danger, and the fires were being prepared for the extermination of recalcitrant heretics. Knox sailed from Newcastle, and, reaching Dieppe, placed the Channel between himself and Mary Tudor.

For eighteen months or more his lot was cast abroad. He resided in Geneva, in Zurich, and in Frankfort-on-Main. His recent taste of power in England had gone to his head like wine. Since his release from the galleys he had become steadily more dictatorial, impatient of contradiction, confident in his own infallibility. And thus his association with his fellow-Protestants on the Continent was not always harmonious. But, as was his wont, he gave whole-hearted and disinterested service, according to his lights. Forceful, determined, consumed with a restless energy, he was a dynamic if sometimes disturbing influence among the Protestant communities. Yet, on one occasion at least, he appeared in the unusual rôle of an apostle of moderation, and at Frankfort for a time held the balance in a liturgical dispute which was growing unpleasantly embittered. It was while he was in Geneva that Knox studied with admiration the doctrinal system and ecclesiastical organisation which were stamped with the genius of Calvin. To Knox they went home with an urgent and direct appeal. Rigid, logical, clear-cut, and dogmatic, Calvinism to him seemed infinitely stronger than the compromises of Lutheranism. Thus it was to the City of Calvin that the Scottish Reformation later looked for its inspiration in the remoulding of ecclesiastical doctrine and polity.

In the autumn of 1555 Knox ventured to pay a visit to his wife at Berwick, and while there received encouraging news of the progress of the Protestant cause in Scotland. Crossing the Border, he made his way to Edinburgh to see for himself at first hand how things were really shaping in his native country.

V

Knox arrived in Edinburgh in September 1555, and things immediately began to move. Since the surrender of the St. Andrews' garrison, Protestantism had been largely subterranean and doctrinaire. Its adherents had avoided any overt rebellion against the established order. They still went to hear Mass, and, however among themselves they might repudiate its doctrine and authority, outwardly observed the obligatory religious duties of the Roman communion. But Knox, on his arrival, at once prepared to force an issue, and the Protestant Party in Edinburgh, faced with his masterful self-assurance, seem without demur to have accepted his supremacy. Though with no great enthusiasm, they acquiesced in his plans to stiffen up the movement. One or two pleaded the wisdom of expediency, but Knox would have none of it. Hesitancy would lead them nowhere, and a challenge had to be made. Those who adhered to the Protestant position were no longer to go to Mass, and were to cease to attend the ordinances of the Roman Church. The Protestant Party, with some trepidation, surrendered to the domination of Knox and bowed to his decision. They now began to absent themselves from the services of the Church, and the ecclesiastical authorities, quite alive to the implications of this, prepared for possible eventualities.

Knox began to preach, though secretly, among the wynds of Edinburgh in the houses of his co-religionists. Then, relying for protection on those nobles who had committed themselves to the cause, he went farther afield and publicly conducted services in Ayr and several other places in the safer provinces. Soon he grew bolder, and took the more serious step of actually celebrating the Holy Communion after the Reformed usage with which he had become familiar on the Continent. The ecclesiastical authorities now determined that the time was ripe to make an example of him, and he was summoned to appear in Edinburgh before a convention of the Catholic clergy. Some curious hitch occurred in the proceedings, and the summons was withdrawn; but everyone knew that whatever lull there was could only be of brief duration. The Protestant nobility now hurriedly endeavoured to secure themselves and their associates against future contingencies, and sought from the Queen-Regent an assurance that the Protestant preachers should be protected from molestation. Mary of Guise received the petition with angry scorn. The skies were darkening. If Church and Government still stayed their hands it was only to await a moment when they could strike with even more deadly force. It was a time of breathless and anxious suspense, and the Protestant Party braced themselves for the outburst of the storm.

And then, one day in the summer of 1556, they received the shattering news that Knox was on the point of leaving them. In utter consternation they heard the amazing excuse. He had been called to be minister of the little congregation of English exiles which lived and worshipped in the tranquil security of Geneva. Bewildered, they impressed upon him the magnitude of the crisis which confronted them. Great was their need of his leadership and counsel. It was largely owing to him that they were in their present position. Was it not he who had insisted on abstention from the services of the Church, and who had forced the grave issue between Protestantism and the established order which had now, and at whatever cost, to be settled one way or another? Surely it was his duty to God, and to the convictions which they held in common, to stay and see this crisis through? Anyone could shepherd that handful of English folk, safe and unthreatened in Geneva; but the Scottish Protestants were in jeopardy. Faced by rising danger, they indeed required their leader. They pleaded with him—Argyle and the others—but it was no use. In the month of July he made off for Geneva, just as the withdrawn summons was again re-issued. He was condemned *in absentia* as a heretic, and his effigy was ordered to be publicly burned at the Mercat Cross of Edinburgh. This act of desertion has been, and will continue to be, widely argued; but when the last word has been said in defence of Knox, it remains an unpleasant episode. Impartial history can hardly avoid the inevitable conclusion.

VI

With the flight of Knox, affairs in Scotland settled down to a stalemate. The Queen-Regent was watchful and alert, but on more than one occasion the attitude of the Protestant nobility, by now a powerful body, warned her that caution was advisable. Moreover, she knew that she might yet need their assistance in furthering both her domestic and foreign policies. The new movement spread, without the assistance of Knox, and in defiance of secular and ecclesiastical threat and censure. Small groups or congregations organised themselves in ever-increasing numbers, and their baronial supporters, whose wide territorial power alone prevented their extermination, became known as the Lords of the Congregation. They were, on the whole, quite typical specimens of sixteenth-century Scotland's perfidious nobility, and in many cases their manner of life was scandalous. To most, if not all, Protestantism meant little more than an alluring if complicated gamble, in which the glittering prizes were political power and the vast endowments of the ancient Church. With the Church's fall, these endowments would be open for the strongest to seize. But associated with them, and committed to the Protestant cause for very different reasons, were a considerable number of preachers, mostly ex-priests of the Roman Church. These, despite their baronial leaders, impregnated the movement with a spiritual power and reality, and associated it in the minds of the common people with the truth of the living God.

In March 1557 the Lords wrote to Knox appealing to him to return. Calvin added his influence, and declared to him that it was his obvious duty and the clear call of God. Knox, however, thought otherwise, and delayed for six months before sending a reply. When at last he decided to accept the invitation, he was informed that the Lords had changed their mind. The following December the fight in Scotland began in dead earnest. The First Covenant was signed in Edinburgh, and the ordinals of the Roman Church were cast aside by the Protestant Party, who adopted instead the English Prayer Book of Edward VI. The Lords boldly demanded of the Queen-Regent liberty of private and public worship, and that the Gospel should be preached and the Sacraments administered in the vulgar tongue of the people. The Roman ecclesiastics, thoroughly alarmed at the obvious and unexpected strength of the Protestant movement, tried to temporise, and set themselves, though rather late in the day, to deal with the gigantic evils of their degenerate Church, which was as lifeless as a rotten tree. The months dragged by. The Queen-Regent hesitated wholly to break with the Lords of the Congregation. Attempts towards compromise were made, but failed dismally. The public tension grew more and more acute. Beneath the outward crust of negotiation passions were seething and ready to burst into volcanic flame. Here and there, at Perth, at Stirling, and at sundry other places, threatening outbreaks occurred. And at last the Queen-Regent decided on action. Discarding further negotiation or concession, she took drastic steps. In May 1559 all Protestant preachers were declared outlaws and rebels, while any who had association with them were to be held guilty of high treason. It was now clearly to be a fight to a finish. The Protestant and Catholic supporters organised themselves for battle. And at this moment of crisis, John Knox reappeared in Scotland.

The death of Mary Tudor and the accession of Elizabeth had meant the return of the Protestant exiles in Geneva to their native England, and as a consequence Knox's congregation disappeared. He found himself on the horns of a dilemma. Geneva was emptied of his English co-religionists; France was perilous owing to a threatened revival of persecution; England was closed to him as a result of that extravagant and fanatical document which he had written not long before, and which had roused the blazing indignation of Elizabeth. Knox must now have seriously regretted that he had ever penned the scorching pages of *The First Blast of the Trumpet against the Monstrous Regiment* (*government*) *of Women*. The anger of Elizabeth was a serious blow to him. In the Church of England he had had a great, if brief, career; and now, secure in the Protestant restoration, he could have had a greater still. Once before he had been offered a bishopric, and he had still many friends in London whose influence was powerful. Who could say where a man like Knox would end if given his chance amid the crowding opportunities of this glorious hour of Protestantism triumphant in England? But Elizabeth would not have him in her realm, and there was no circumventing that royal blockade.

Gloomy and depressed, he hung about Dieppe, and eventually made up his mind to return to his native Scotland.

The diplomatic but unwilling toleration which, from political expediency, the Regent had been exercising towards the Scottish Protestants, possibly misled Knox as to the state of affairs which he would find on his return. But if he expected to find religious toleration he was rudely awakened; for he arrived in Edinburgh in the month of May, just when the Regent had bared her teeth and struck her first savage blow. Finding himself a rebel and an outlaw, he hurriedly made his way to Dundee, one of the strongholds of the Protestant cause.

VII

Whatever resentful memories may have lingered with the Protestant nobles regarding Knox's inexplicable departure from Scotland in July 1556, his return was hailed with exultant jubilation. His peculiar gifts and capacities were now most urgently needed, and whatever was past was forgotten and forgiven. Once again, as in 1555, he stepped, as by natural right, into the place of leadership. But from now until the end of his days there was never any further suggestion of cowardice or defection. Just as the conditions of the St. Andrew's crisis had called forth from him unsuspected forces, so now the fierce and threatening atmosphere of battle, the stirring tension of armed forces awaiting the clash of desperate conflict, the final disappearance of any further possibility of compromise or postponement, and the grim inevitability of a struggle to the death, purged Knox of nervous vacillation and hardened him to adamant resolution. The storm had broken about his head. From the situation in which he found himself, there was now no retreat. Caught up into the maelstrom of a warfare from which there could be no discharge, he was confirmed in an indomitable purposefulness.

In this transformation of character there is presented to us no odd or obscure psychology. His back, this time, was to the wall, and the man who formerly had never been wholly master of his nerves, now reacted to a tremendous urgency and turned in wrath upon his foes. He became the genius, the spirit, the incarnation of the Protestant cause. More clamant and commanding than any trumpet call became his voice. Wrapping about him the sombre mantle of the prophet, he inspired the Protestant camp by his confident assurances of the favour and protection of the Almighty, and of the terrible retributions which Heaven held in store for those who opposed their will. He was as a figure of flame and thunder, an avenging spirit, an ambassador of judgment. His turbulent and passionate energy, his tempestuous oratory, his contemptuous disregard of whatever conflicted with his views, his capacity for organisation and initiative, his imperious assumption of infallibility, no less than his genuine abomination of the evils and decadence of the corrupted Roman Church and the blazing sincerity of his conviction in the righteousness of the crusade in which he was engaged—these were undoubtedly the forces which carried the Protestant Party to their victory. The Protestant nobility, serving the Reformation for their own ends, and by their very nature incapable of realising its significance as a mighty and tremendous upheaval of the human spirit, could supply the armed retainers. But it was Knox who saved the fight from becoming a mere expression of successful local force. He lifted it up from the slough of political and financial pitch-and-toss, and revealed it as a terrific and epoch-making religious issue in which men stood responsible to the God who made them.

The struggle was not long, and was ended before a year was out. It affected only a section of Scotland, for the vast Highland area, still largely Catholic, stood traditionally aloof from Lowland affairs. Mary of Guise hastily called French troops to her aid, but this move was countered by Knox who successfully engineered an agreement between the Lords of the Congregation and Protestant England. Elizabeth may have hated Knox, but since the whole Catholic world regarded her as a bastard usurper, and Mary Stuart as the rightful Queen of England, the establishment of Protestantism in Scotland was a matter of more moment than her personal detestation of the author of *The First Blast of the Trumpet*. English troops and English warships hastened to the aid of the Scottish Protestants; in the supreme hour of crisis the Queen-Regent died; the French, whose armies were urgently required elsewhere, were glad enough to sign a Treaty early in 1560; and the Protestant forces were left in control of the Scottish situation. John Knox was appointed minister in charge of Edinburgh, and soon was preaching in St. Giles'.

Speedily the Protestants set to work. In August 1560 Parliament met, and Knox, with the aid of a committee of ministers, drafted a Confession of Faith which Parliament immediately ratified. Although the works of Calvin were there to draw upon, it was a remarkable document to have been completed in four days. Acts were passed abolishing the jurisdiction of the Pope within the realm of Scotland. The Roman Church was disestablished, and the Mass and all religious ceremonies, practices, and observances which conflicted with the Protestant doctrine were abolished. Those who still adhered to them were to be subject to the severest penalties. All this having been successfully carried through, the next step was the drawing up of a constitution for the Protestant Church, and to this task Knox, assisted by five ex-priests of the Roman Church, now energetically addressed himself. In it the episcopate was swept away, and the ecclesiastical system, appealing to the order of the primitive Church, was reorganised on a presbyterian basis which, however, retained something of episcopacy in the office of the Superintendent. The laity, in the form of " elders," were given a voice in general administration and parochial supervision. Forms of worship were simplified, and the great doctrines of Christendom were extricated from the mass of superstitious and unscriptural accretions which had grown up like choking weeds about them. There was also defined a system of national education on which many a modern educationist looks with admiration and envy. With the presentation of this comprehensive and singularly able document to the Privy Council in January 1561, the troubles of Knox began.

VIII

They began, and until his death in 1572, they never ceased. He found his dreams and ambitions blocked by the rapacity and greed of the Protestant nobility. If Knox, fighting his way towards the establishment of a Protestant regime, had cherished dreams, as he did, of a Scotland Protestant and free, of a purified and reorganised Church, swept clean of its gross corruptions, strengthened by the enlistment of the laity into its government, lifting a demoralised nation from superstition and spiritual indifference into a robust and enlightened religious faith and practice; if he had racked his brains to produce, as he did, a superb educational programme which was to embrace the entire Scottish nation; if he visualised an educated, efficient, and energetic ministry planted throughout the country, modestly but sufficiently supported from the ancient ecclesiastical patrimony, and bringing culture no less than religion to a rude and barbarous society; if such were his dreams, he was soon roughly awakened to the fact that his noble friends had not such elevated ideas. They had not carried through the Reformation to divert the rich endowments of the Roman Church towards the better provision of Universities and schools and the payment of the stipends of the Protestant clergy, but to transfer them to their own pockets. Knox, who was not easily bluffed, soon knew exactly where he stood with them. The First Book of Discipline was never passed by Parliament, and Knox was driven bitterly to confess that among the Lords of the Congregation there was not one honest man.

But his angry determination was only reinforced by his bitter disillusionment. He urged the Kirk, whatever the State might do, to put the provisions of the Book into operation, and the Kirk, despite its weakness, resolutely responded. While the nobility wove their squalid schemes, planned their devious political intrigues, and pilfered, like common thieves, the rich ecclesiastical patrimony, the Kirk, headed by Knox, struggled out of its dire poverty to carry through its ambitious educational policy; while its ministers, unable to secure any support from the ancient endowments—held fast in the grip of the Lords of the Congregation—existed on what charity their people chose to give them. The Protestant cause, moreover, was in serious danger. In August 1561, Mary arrived, a Catholic Queen, to rule over a Protestant Kingdom. The Protestant nobility, time-serving and unreliable, again trimmed their sails to suit the wind, and, hungry for royal favours, showed themselves by no means anxious to carry into execution the edicts issued against the adherents of Catholicism. Large tracts of the country were still Catholic to the core. The Reformation was but insecurely established. The Protestant acts and edicts still technically lacked the force of law, as Mary had refused to ratify them.

The years that followed were full of turmoil and anxiety, intrigue and perfidy, violence and confusion; and the

Queen, no less than Knox, grew to estimate rightly the Lords who formed her Council and by whom she was surrounded. To M. du Croc, the French ambassador, accustomed as he was to the aristocracy of the Continent, these Scottish noblemen presented a bewildering study. Coarse, avaricious, and traitors to a man, they knew no loyalties and accepted no code of honour. To them both religion and politics were a game in which each played for his own hand. Cabals were made and dissolved at the dictates of personal advantage. The loyalty of the individual to his fellow-conspirators inevitably terminated whenever such loyalty ceased to pay, and a man's friend of to-day might be his assassin of the morrow. Mary, trustful, young, and gracious, loaded them with benefits; and in return they each and all of them betrayed her, and betrayed her again and again. Even Moray, her half-brother, who owed everything to his royal sister's lavish bounty, was consistently in the secret pay of Elizabeth of England. Knox himself was under no illusions, and knew that he could rely on them only when it suited their interests.

IX

The eventual triumph of the Reformation in Scotland was largely the work of Knox. It is for this that he is enthroned in the grateful honour of his countrymen, for Scotland, perhaps more than any nation, appreciates to the full the significance of that triumph. Whatever were his failings, his utter disinterestedness in the Protestant cause has never been questioned. Surrounded by powerful enemies, and thwarted and opposed by those who professed to be his friends, he ploughed a lonely furrow, but he ploughed it unswervingly to the end. It is foolish to invest him with the glamour of an unreal romanticism, or to estimate his character in terms of our own days. He was the child of his age, and shared its limitations. His theology and attitude of mind were inelastic, bigoted, and stern, and were derived from Horeb rather than from Galilee. His assertiveness has been described as " almost boundless in character," and even if the New Testament could be shown as contradicting his opinions, he did not hesitate to assert that it was not himself, but the Apostles, who lacked the inspiration of the Holy Ghost. He lived in a barbarous society which recog-

286

nised calumny, the forged paper, the perjured oath, and assassination as the legitimate methods of diplomacy, and of the latter as a means of the removal of opposition he seems cordially to have approved. " God had raised up " the murderer of Rizzio, and over the bloody end of Cardinal Beaton, Knox gloated with unseemly hilarity.

Though he was not responsible for the iconoclasm which, in the early stages of the Reformation, destroyed a number of Scotland's noble buildings, his æsthetic sense was dim and his cultural reactions weak. In many ways he was harshly illogical, and denounced in others what he permitted to himself. He could be vindictive and uncharitable, defamatory and cruel. Yet, withal, during these twelve tumultuous years from 1560 to 1572 he stood head and shoulders above his contemporaries as an embodiment of virtues which few could boast, and the principles of Protestantism and democracy which he thundered from the pulpit of St. Giles' have gone out to the ends of the earth. In his advocacy and furtherance of the Protestant cause he was wholly incorruptible, and, surrounded as he was by adventurers and opportunists, not even his bitterest enemies could accuse him of ever seeking personal gain. His loyalty to his friends was unshakable; his concern for the salvation of the souls of his fellow-men (provided they were of his way of thinking) was profound and sincere; and, alone among the statesmen of his era, he had a great heart for the poor and oppressed. His private and domestic life were stainless, and to both the women whom he took to wife he showed himself a devoted and affectionate husband.

His bitter antagonism to the hapless young Queen was not justified by her personality and character; for she was generous to a fault, warm-hearted, and friendly, and was the most tolerant of any of her race. It may have been that Knox, who was unusually susceptible to feminine influence, strove thus to save himself from weakening in purpose before the peril of her charm. " I could wish," wrote Maitland to Cecil, " that he would deal more gently with her," and had he done so, history might have taken a different turn. Before she left France for Scotland, Mary told Throgmorton that she meant to constrain none of her subjects, and later she repeatedly emphasised by proclamation that she did not intend to force the conscience of any person, and hoped for a similar toleration towards herself in return. Badgered by the Papacy and the Catholic Powers, she admittedly wrote much in another strain to the Courts of Rome, Spain, and France, but on a dispassionate estimate the contents of these letters must in large measure be estimated as composed at the dictates of political expediency. During her years of power, Mary made no attempt to subvert the Protestant Church. It may be argued that since her power depended on what support she received from her territorial nobility, of whom only one-third was Catholic, she could not have done so even had she wished; but her character, temperament, and utterances witness to a real consideration for the peace and welfare of her subjects and to religious persecution being wholly alien to her nature. Her highest interests, and especially her English interests, were deeply interwoven with her attitude to Protestantism, and it was one of the tragedies of her unhappy life that Knox, with his hectoring and rasping tongue, always seemed to rouse her to angry reactions. There is no reason to suppose that, had she been allowed liberty of worship after her own fashion, she would have sought to interfere with the religious liberty of her Protestant subjects. Towards the close of her reign she consented to be married to Bothwell according to the Protestant form, and had that marriage not ended in immediate disaster it almost certainly would have effected, if still not in theory, at least in practical results, the Protestantising of the Crown. For Bothwell was a determined anti-Catholic, and knew how to enforce his will.

But from start to finish, from the point of view of Knox, harassed and threatened on all sides, the situation with the Queen was impossible. The times were too serious for risks to be endured, and Mary's undoubted devotion to the Catholic Faith was in his eyes a constant menace to the Protestant cause. There was, moreover, no common bond between them. Mary stood for the divine right of the ruler, and Knox for the divine right of the people, and these two rival theories no syncretism could bridge.

It was not until the abdication of Mary in 1567 that Protestantism was made definitely secure. In December of that year the Regent Moray, in a legally constituted Parliament, ratified the Protestant Confession of Faith and enactments which Mary had consistently refused to sign, and the Protestant Church became established by law. But on the part of the nobles, the plundering of the ancient endowments went on. In 1572, in order to check this process, and at the same time to secure for the Kirk a voice in Parliament, the Church leaders entered into an agreement with the secular power to restore the episcopate and the ancient dioceses. This experiment, with its temporary abandonment of Presbyterianism—it lasted but eight years—was to prove a miserable failure, and only played the better into the grasping hands of the nobility; but it was an attempt, though a misguided and unsuccessful attempt, to preserve for the Kirk the last remnants of a rapidly vanishing patrimony which, though scandalously diverted, belonged to it by right. The provisions were submitted to Knox, who, seeing more clearly than did his fellow-clergy in whose interests such a concordat was likely to work out, gave to them his grudging and apprehensive approval. Towards the close of the year, though in feeble health, he journeyed to St. Andrews to preach the sermon at the consecration of John Douglas to its revived archbishopric; and shortly afterwards, gravely concerned as to the future of events, his stormy spirit took leave of this world.

He left affairs not as he would have wished them, and the Kirk, of which he had been the supreme formative influence, still involved in struggle with secular treachery and avarice. But the storm clouds of the graver dangers which for so long had threatened the Reformation by now had passed away, and his dying eyes looked out on the new Scotland as he had largely made it—Scotland Protestant and free.

MATTHEW PARKER

1504–1575

By

M. THEODORA STEAD

" Matthew, by the providence of God, Archbishop of Canterbury, Primate of all England. . . ."

Mundus transiit et concupiscentia ejus.—Parker's Emblem.

MATTHEW PARKER

by M. THEODORA STEAD

IT is a great tribute to Matthew Parker, as Archbishop, that the Elizabethan Church Settlement, of which he was the master builder, is so much clearer to the public mind than the man himself. He did not seek office: it was thrust upon him; but, being Primate, he laboured earnestly to make safe the bulwarks of the Church. The proposal that he should enter on the See of Canterbury, vacant by the opportune death of Cardinal Pole, he refused with a sincerity inspired, not only by genuine modesty, but by a perception of the immense difficulty of the task. The first suggestion came from Nicholas Bacon, the Lord Keeper, a Norwich man like Parker himself, the second from Cecil, Elizabeth's Secretary of State, and both these invitations he refused.

The work of the new Archbishop would indeed be difficult. He would have to guide and discipline a Church of which the form alone was settled. Mary's desperate attempt to recall England to the Roman obedience had decided that England would be Protestant. Rather than face a return of the fires of Smithfield, the people would accept the Royal Supremacy and welcome the return of Edward VI's Prayer Book; but the authority the Archbishop was to wield and the practices of the Church he was to rule would have to be defined. It would be his duty to secure reverence and uniformity in the services and to recruit and discipline the clergy. He would have to deal with the returned Protestant exiles, fresh from the heated controversies of Geneva or Frankfort, who saw in Elizabeth's accession the opportunity to remould the Church in England to the patterns they severally approved. The " unruly flock of the English people " would tax the watchful care of their Primate. Many of them were still of the Roman obedience; and the

Queen, politically and intellectually a Protestant, was yet in temperament Catholic enough to raise the hopes of the Papal Party. The revenues of the Church were attacked, both by Elizabeth, whose Treasury was empty and whose needs were pressing, and by her courtiers, true successors of the rapacious Protestants of Edward VI's reign, of whose greed Martin Bucer wrote,

"It is nothing but sacrilege and lessing the revenues of the Crucified Lord."

Was it surprising that Matthew Parker, now over fifty, after years full of change and anxiety, should be reluctant to take up such a burden? He protested to Cecil,

"I should be inwardly heavy and sorry that his [Bacon's] favourable affection should procure me anything above the reach of my ability, whereby I should dishonest myself, and disappoint the expectation of such as may think *that* in me, which I know is not; but specially I might clog and cumber my conscience to Godward."

In no weak recoil from office, he added,

"If I might be bolder with you . . . of all places in England I would wish to bestow most my time in the University. I pray you, either help I be quite forgotten, or else so appointed that I be not entangled of new with the concurre of the world."

After a visit to London early in 1559, when he preached at Paul's Cross, he wrote to Bacon :

"concerning a certain office you named to me, [clearly the Archbishopric] God grant it chanceth not on arrogant man, neither on fainthearted man nor on covetous man. The first shall both sit in his own light, and shall discourage his fellows to join with him in unity of doctrine, which must be their whole strength. . . . The second man would be too weak to commune with the adversaries, who would be the stouter for his pusillanimity. The third man not worth his bread, profitable for no estate in any Christian commonwealth to serve it rightly."

Humility, courage, indifference to wealth are indeed qualities worthy an Archbishop. He went on, almost playfully,

> "Except ye both moderate and restrain your over-much goodwill to me-ward, I fear, in the end, I shall dislike you both."

Then, more seriously, he wrote of his physical unfitness for the task,

> "Sir, I am in body so decayed, *coram Deo non mentior*, that whatever my ability were, either of worldly furni-ture or inward quality, and though my heart would right fain serve my sovereign lady the Queen's Majesty, in more respects than of my allegiance, not forgetting what words her Grace's mother said to me of her, not six days before her apprehension; yet this my painful infirmity will not suffer it. . . . Flying in a night, from such as sought me to my peril, I fell off my horse so dangerously, that I shall never recover it."

It is to be regretted that he did not tell us what Anne Boleyn said about the baby Elizabeth, or what were the circumstances of his hurried flight in Mary's reign. At the end of the letter, he apologised for "so many words in a case private to myself," which he had, with a queer carefulness, put up in book form, that Bacon might dip into it at his leisure.

Why, in spite of his continued refusals, his "oft relucta-tion," did the Queen and her ministers persist in their choice? To Elizabeth, the fact that he had been Anne Boleyn's chaplain, and, later, Henry VIII's, was of im-portance; and he had, moreover, belonged to that group of Cambridge scholars, whence her two tutors, Ascham and William Grindal, had come. Henry VIII, nominating him as Master of Corpus Christi College, had described him as "a man as well for his approved learning, wisdom and honesty, as for his singular grace and industry in bringing up youth in virtue, very hard to find the like."

Cecil and Bacon, in their Cambridge days, had known him as conspicuously learned, even in that age of learning, and moderate, when mildness was a rare virtue. His steadfastness in the Protestant faith had been tested in the

" school of affliction," and Cecil, whose politic suppleness had allowed him to conform under Mary, could yet value rightly the moral courage which made Parker defy her persecution. He had lived in hiding in England, and so was untouched by the foreign controversies in which so many learned Protestants were involved, remaining " mere English " in his experience and his outlook. All these, a distinguished past, profound learning, uprightness, were weighty arguments for his appointment, but, beyond these, there was that " inward quality " of deep personal religion and of priestliness, easier to discern than to describe. So the end of all Parker's protests was a letter from Bacon, conveying the Queen's order to " make his indelayed repair " to London to receive the office, " knowing none so meet, indeed I should prefer you before others." He abandoned his dream of a peaceful life as Master of Corpus, and set himself to serve God in a place he had not sought. His wife, Margaret, took up her part of the burden, and prepared to order his household, that he might be free for weightier matters.

It is noticeable that, in the course of this correspondence, no one referred to the fact of Parker's marriage. He was devoted to his wife, and he had written a defence of the marriage of the clergy. The Queen's policy on this question was anxiously awaited. In April 1559 Sandys, later Bishop of Worcester, wrote bitterly to Parker:

> " Nothing is decided about the marriage of the clergy, but it is, as it were, left in the air. The Queen's Majesty will wink at it, but not stablish it by law, which is nothing else but [to] bastardise our children."

This meant that the position of the wives of the clergy would be difficult indeed, the Queen doing nothing to make it easier. The law of Edward VI sanctioning clerical marriage was not re-enacted, and, when Margaret Parker died in 1570, her brother, not her husband nor her son, was legally her heir. The Visitation Articles of 1559 allowed the clergy to marry, provided that they obtained the approval of the bishop and two justices of the peace for their choice. This question of clerical marriage was, later, the cause of a serious dispute between Elizabeth and her Archbishop. It was also to produce her less than graceful thanks to the Archbishop's wife, after entertainment at Lambeth Palace:

" Madam, I may not, Mistress, I am ashamed to call you, but I thank you for your hospitality."

Yet, in 1559, knowing Parker to be married, the Queen insisted on his entering upon " that so high and chargeable office."

Archbishop elect, he took up his duties at once, both as defender of the Church and as spiritual adviser to the Queen. He protested against her scheme for the wholesale confiscation of Church property, ultimately persuading her to a settlement, which, if unduly favourable to her, yet left the bishops with a reasonable income for the discharge of their responsibilities. With the support of some bishops-elect, of whom the most notable was Jewel, he admonished Elizabeth for maintaining a crucifix and candles on the altar of the Chapel Royal. Sandys wrote of this interview: " God, in whose hands are the hearts of Kings, gave us tranquillity instead of a tempest and delivered the Church of England from stumbling-blocks of this kind."

Possibly in connection with this admonition, Parker sent her a petition against the use of images in churches, forti-fying his argument with many quotations from the Fathers, in whose works he was deeply read. He set his face, with courtesy, but with unshakable firmness, against an attempt to bestow a benefice on a child of fourteen, an abuse very profitable to the nobility, but destructive both of the honour and of the efficiency of the Church. He would seek right-eousness first, and not be " too weak to commune with adversaries."

Another side of his character was shown in his dealings with the aged Bishop Tunstall, of Durham, who had refused the Oath of Supremacy, and who, in accordance with Elizabeth's practice, was committed to the custody of the Church. Parker persuaded the Council, determined on harsh measures—if he will not conform himself, " he must receive the common order of such as refuse to obey laws "—that he saw hope of Tunstall's conforming, until the old man had died peacefully in his house. He had not only the moderate man's objection to persecution, a quality unusual enough in his time, but a passionate hatred of it, dating from the tragedy of his friend, Thomas Bilney. They both belonged to the group of Reformers who met regularly for discussion in Cambridge, and Parker knew and loved him well. He had seen him go up to London to face a charge of heresy, and had been witness of his two years' remorse after, under pressure from Wolsey, he had abjured the mildest of Protestant doctrine. He had known also with what liberation of spirit Bilney had "set his face to Jerusalem," going out to preach in Norfolk and court arrest and the horrible death of a relapsed heretic. He was taken and burned at Norwich in 1531. Foxe records that Parker was present at the burning and testified to Bilney's steadfastness. This terrible experience left its mark on him, and its impression was deepened by his own peril "in those hard years of Mary's reign." And so, again and again, he interposed his authority to prevent harsh measures; for example, in 1563, he forbade the Bishops to offer the Oath of Supremacy a second time, when refusal entailed the penalties of treason, without his express permission, and in 1565 he reminded Cecil that clergy were not to be punished by deprivation for disobeying the Articles.

The Archbishop's hatred of persecution chimed well with the Government's policy of including all "God's creatures our subjects" in the national Church. The modifications of the Prayer Book, in 1559, had aimed at avoiding offence, and the title of "Supreme Head," so great a stumbling-block under Henry VIII, had been abandoned. Elizabeth could justly write:

"We never had any meaning or intent that our subjects should be troubled or molested in any matter of their faith . . . as long as they shall show themselves quiet and conformable."

She remained consistent in this; Catholic and Protestant suffered at her hands, but for breach of the civil laws: no comfort admittedly to the sufferers, but a relief to the Archbishop, who was free to deal with matters of faith without a royal demand for persecution.

The power of the Archbishop in relation to the Crown was worked out, in practice, during Parker's sixteen years in the See of Canterbury; but at the threshold of his office, he showed how firmly he would base his authority on Canon Law. He drew up the order of Rites and Ceremonies to be observed at his consecration, and deposited it with Cecil as part of the archives of England, to prevent future doubt of the continuity of the Church or of the canonical regularity of the service. He was one in a line of Archbishops of Canterbury, going back through St. Augustine to the Apostles, but he was the first who would receive no Papal sanction, and so he appealed to the law and tradition of the Church, which were older than the Papacy. He meant so to rule the Church in England " that that most holy and godly form of discipline, which was commonly used in the primitive Church, might be called home again."

This strong historical sense set him apart from the extremer Protestants, who, attacking the abuses of Rome, destroyed along with them many practices older than the Roman authority, and so cut themselves off from a continuity of Christian experience. Parker was a Reformer, but he was not a revolutionary. He was prepared to take the Oaths of Supremacy and Allegiance, for that was to render to Cæsar the things that were Cæsar's; but he was determined to render to God what is God's. To Elizabeth and her ministers the Church in England might seem a department of State—did she not permit herself to direct Parker to use the French Ambassador with all courtesy, " not meaning thereby that you should neglect the place you hold in *our* Church? "—but to the Archbishop it was the Church of Christ, in which, conscious of his many infirmities, he would work for the glory of God. He wrote in his journal, after the consecration on December 17, 1559:

" I am come into deep waters. . . . O Lord, strengthen me with thy free spirit."

Established in his office, he must busy himself with Church affairs, of which the most urgent was the institution of bishops to vacant sees. Sixteen were instituted within a few months, and a diverse group they were. Jewel took his eminent learning to Salisbury; Cox, with his sturdy independence, went to Ely; Parkhurst in Norwich was a difficult problem, with his Puritan zeal and his lax administration; while Nicholas Grindal in London proved incapable of decisive action and given to constant appeal to Parker and to the Queen. Rarely can an Archbishop have been called to guide so untried a bench of bishops. All, including Parker, lacked diocesan experience. His rule of Colleges, the suppressed Stoke-by-Clare, and Corpus, had been invaluable training in handling men, and he had played his part in public affairs; but the problems of Church administration were new to him, and he had to create the technique for dealing with them. In those critical years, the " arrogant man " against whom he had warned Bacon would indeed have "shivered them asunder"; but Parker succeeded in asserting the authority of the bishops and maintaining the tradition of the English Church. The ideal unity of all the English people was beyond human compassing, but that so great a measure of unity was actually attained was due to the wisdom and statesmanship of Matthew Parker. When the Bishops had been instituted, clergy had to be found; there were hundreds of ordinations, and a temporary order of lay "readers" was set up, to provide for parishes without priests. They must wait until men of learning could be trained, for Parker would not lower the standard necessary for Orders. Pastors must be men fit to guard their flocks against ignorance and loss of faith. He believed in the goodness of heart of the people, but held also that they must be under authority :

"God keep us from such a visitation as Knox has attempted in Scotland, the people to rule all."

His attempts to supply the Northern provinces with bishops and priests were thwarted by Elizabeth, still in need of money, though he warned her that unshepherded and untaught congregations were potential rebels :

"Whatever is now too husbandly saved, will be an occasion of further expense, in keeping the people down."

His foresight was justified by the rebellion which broke out in 1568, when the arrival of Mary, Queen of Scots, stirred the already troubled waters.

"The coals were kindled here; but the bellows which gave the wind lay at Rome and there sat he which made the fire," as Jewel observed. The rebellion having borne the character of a Catholic crusade, the Government afterwards ordained that the people of Northern England should be instructed by "some discrete preachers in open sermons," and demanded that Parker should prepare a "Homily against Wilful Rebellion." As he did so, he must have reflected that no need for it would have arisen, if instruction by discreet preachers had been given ten years earlier.

The Visitation of the whole English Church undertaken in 1561 showed that "things were far out of order in matters of religion." Many clergy were absent from their parishes; some were busy, profitably to themselves, at the Court of Arches; few clergy could preach, at a time when preaching was vital, and there were those who maintained Romish practices. The fabric of the churches was badly damaged and finance generally chaotic. The Universities, whence future clergy must come, were both of them unsatisfactory; Oxford, a stronghold of the Papal Party, and Cambridge, zealous for Reform, but moving towards Puritanism. There was much to be done before the Church should become a true school of piety; but the Visitation stirred up the conscience of the clergy and people. The reports of the Visitors showed that the majority of the people accepted the Protestant settlement.

There was need for a translation of the Bible to be set up in churches. The " Great Bible," based on the work of Tyndale and Coverdale, had been " set out by the diligence of that godly father, Thomas Cranmer," but the copies had generally disappeared in Mary's time. In 1560 there appeared the " Geneva Bible " translated from the Hebrew and Greek by an English exile, Whittingham; and comparison showed how inaccurate the " Great Bible " had been. The Gospels and Epistles and the Psalms in the Prayer Book remain in Coverdale's beautiful English, and in them the traces of his Vulgate original are evident. The " Geneva Bible " was comparatively small, and had notes of a definite Calvinist tendency, so that it could not suitably be chained in parish churches. Parker therefore planned a careful revision, " with more light added, partly in the translation and partly in the order of the text," and divided the books among various readers for correction. Their notes were to illustrate the text and eschew controversy. He invited Cecil, " if you could spare so much leisure," to be " one of the builders of this good work in Christ's Church "; but Cecil did not accept. Parker bore the main burden of the work, not only editing it, but revising many books, including the Gospels of St. Matthew and St. Mark; yet he did not regard it as the only possible translation, heartily approving the renewal of Bodley's licence to publish the " Geneva Bible "; " it should nothing hinder, but do much good, to have diversity of translations and readings."

His prefaces, to the Old and the New Testament, in the " Bishops' Bible," as it was called, are interesting in their emphasis on the " open Bible ":

" Search ye the Scriptures. . . . These words were first spoken unto the Jews by our Saviour, but by Him in His doctrine meant to all, for they concern all, of what nation, of what tongue, of what profession soever any man be: for to all belongeth it to be called unto eternal life. . . . No man woman or child is excluded from this salvation. . . . Antichrist therefore he must be that under whatsoever colour would give contrary precept or counsel to that which Christ did give unto us. Search, therefore, good reader (on God's name) as Christ biddeth thee, the holy Scripture."

This care for the ordinary man to whom Latin was not, as it was to himself, a second language, had been foreshadowed by the English metrical version of the Psalms with which he "eased his heart" in Mary's reign. The verse is rarely more than pedestrian;

> " *Lift up your gates, you heades and states*
> *Ye lasting dores aryse:*
> *In at this house Kyng glorious*
> *Wyll enter princely wyse.*"

and again:

> " *Lo come and see how God (in wrath)*
> *great mervayles aye hath wrought:*
> *What landes to nought he scatred hath*
> *how low their Idols brought* ";

but the language of the collects, following each Psalm, is magnificent, for example, after Psalm 102:

> " O Lord, most mercifull protectour of all them that be in trouble, who in thyself art God everlasting, shew thy mercy upon us so frayle and transitory as we be, that we may rejoice in thy saving health, through Christ. Amen."

His work on the Prayer Book was mainly administrative; the revision of the Articles of Religion, ultimately the familiar Thirty-Nine, the restoration of the full Calendar of Saints, where in 1559 only the "red letter" Holy days had appeared, and the addition of the Table of Kindred and Affinity, intended to free the English Church from the Roman abuse of traffic in marriage dispensations. More than this he did not add; but he bent his energies to secure the celebration of the services decently and in order.

Parker's chief literary interest was the collection of materials for English history. Agents scoured England to save what they might from the wreck of the monastic libraries; and scholars, among them Foxe, were employed in reading manuscripts and preparing them for printing. Parker's edition of Ælfric's Homilies was designed to show the agreement in doctrine of the Elizabethan and the Anglo-Saxon Church; but such other books as Asser's *Life of Alfred* and Matthew Paris were printed because he believed that a nation should be acquainted with its origins. He was reputed to be better pleased by an old book than by any other gift.

He might seem absorbed in scholarly pursuits, and be so quiet and modest in company that he appeared negligible, but both Elizabeth and Nicholas Bacon found him valiant to defend righteousness. The Queen, affronted on one of her frequent journeys by some too domestic scene, flashed out:

> " Keep your wives, children and nurses out of colleges, chapels and cathedral precincts. Those rooms and buildings were raised and enclosed for societies of learned men professing study and prayer, not for families of women and children, for whom they are not fit. If you will not obey, you shall lose your promotions."

She further expressed to her Archbishop regret that—

> " we were thus appointed in office . . . which, being known to all Queen Mary's clergy, they laugh prettily to see how the clergy of our time is handled. . . . I would be sorry that the clergy should have cause to show disobedience with *opportet Deo obedire magis quam hominibus*."

Parker wrote to Cecil, but he meant the Queen to see the letter:

> " I was in an horror to hear such words to come from her mild nature and Christianly learned conscience, as she spake concerning God's holy ordinance and institu-

tion of matrimony. I marvelled that our state in that behalf cannot please her Highness, which we doubt nothing at all to please God's sacred Majesty."

Was it perhaps of this dispute Parker was thinking, when he later wrote:

"I was well chidden at my prince's hand; but with one ear I heard her hard words, and with the other and in my conscience and heart, I heard God"?

Elizabeth, sensitive on the question of marriage, was only partly satisfied by the application of the order to Colleges, while Cathedral clergy continued to live with their families in the precincts; Cox of Ely observing that, if it were not so, "daws and owls may dwell there for any continual house-keeping."

The quarrel with Nicholas Bacon was far more serious, and led to a breach between them. Ill reports reached Lambeth of the state of the diocese of Norwich: "Gehazi and Judas had a wonderful haunt in that country," and Bishop Parkhurst had not "visited" for seven years, because the custom of the place in visitations was septennial. As if the times were so settled that he had nothing to do but follow ancient custom! So Parker visited Norwich, and found things very ill. The choirmaster was inefficient; one canon, reputed to be then in Louvain, had been used to wear a Spanish cloak and rapier in Norwich; and, here was the real trouble, stalls were held by laymen, and of these two at least owed their places to Nicholas Bacon. One was a servingman; the other, though a "mere laybody," was learned enough for Parker to urge him to take Orders. He was unwilling to do this, but eager to resign his stall, if the Church would assure him £5 a year, which Parker found he had promised to pay to Bacon's nephew at Cambridge. Bacon was furious that these two were deprived without his consent, seeing the arrangement merely as one of household economy, while Parker saw it as the black sin of simony. The Archbishop certainly regretted his anger, and asked Lady Bacon to present his case to her husband, but in no spirit of apology:

"I am sorry he can so soon conceive displeasantly against me, not deserved, I say, and to abide thereby not deserved. For I meant not only prudently, but Christianly, godly and friendly, howsoever it be taken. The testimony of my conscience shall make me take this storm quietly to Godward, rather offering him in my prayers to God, than careful of any submission as having offended. If my Lord be angry with me for my plainness, I fear not Almighty God."

The Lord Keeper had been Parker's friend and patron, but there should be an end, in Norwich, of rendering to Cæsar the things that are God's.

Why, with his passion for righteousness and his devotion to the Bible, was Parker so hated by the Puritans? There were two main reasons: he could not conceive of a Church without authority, and he insisted, driven by Elizabeth, on a uniformity which they regarded as un-Biblical and therefore wrong. They were probably further embittered by his attempts to arrive, by discussion, at some understanding of their position, which they mistook for yielding. There was no real understanding possible between the Archbishop, saying in all good faith, during a debate on the Thirty-Nine Articles: " You will refer yourselves wholly to us (the bishops) therein," and Peter Wentworth, replying " No! by the faith I bear to God, we will pass nothing before we understand what it is, for that were to make you Popes."

The breach became manifest on the question of clerical dress. Elizabeth ordered Parker to ascertain " what varieties there are in the clergy," and to enforce " uniformity of order in every church." But when Parker had drawn up the " Advertisements " enjoining the clergy " to be of one decent behaviour in their outward apparel," she refused the support of her authority and even received at Court a cleric in hat and short coat, contrary to the rule ordaining gowns and square caps.

> " I alone they say am in fault. For, as for the Queen's Majesty's part . . . they cease to impute it to her, for they say but for my calling on, she is indifferent. . . . I alone am the stirrer and incenser."

Elizabeth was ingenious in getting her own way while another bore the blame; as Parker understood, for he wrote

" so that my prince may win honour either by standing or relenting, I will be very gladly *lapis offensionis*." He was surprised by the violence of Puritan opposition to " decent apparel," but saw " that they will offer themselves to lose all, yea their bodies to prison, rather than they will yield."

The Queen's continued refusal of support first roused him to protest: " Execution, execution, execution of laws and orders must be the first and last part of good government "; and then left him a prey to depression : " Must I do all these things alone? . . . I only shame to be so vilely reported. And yet I am not weary to bear, to do service to God and to my prince; but an ox can draw no more than he can."

He *was* " vilely reported "; he was nicknamed the " Pope of Lambeth," and as an old man, he nearly lost his life through a Puritan plot to sink his barge in the Thames.

His mind often took refuge from public affairs and their difficulties in memories of Cambridge. He was a thoughtful and generous benefactor of Corpus : it owed him endowments of land, additional buildings and money for the maintenance of the Hall fire. When its ancient arms, of the Guilds of Corpus Christi and of the Blessed Virgin, were attacked as superstitious, he paid for a new grant from the College of Arms, bearing a pelican in her piety, and three slipped lilies. He certainly enjoyed the continuity of symbolism here achieved. By his will, the College received plate and a major part of his magnificent collection of manuscripts. A year earlier, the Cambridge University Library had received a noble gift of his Biblical commentaries, but Corpus has nearly five hundred books. He safeguarded this legacy so effectually, that Pepys, whose Library at Magdalene includes a number of books with the pressmarks of other Colleges, paid him the sincere compliment of imitation; the three different keys for each bookcase, in the hands of Master, Dean and Librarian, and the annual search by another College, to which, were any books lost " by supine negligence," the Library and the plate should pass. Parker also, characteristically, gave the College its own History, which he had caused his Secretary to write. His name is inscribed on the door of the Master's Lodge at Corpus, and his benign spirit broods over the place.

The later years of his life were passed in comparative retirement, his illness increased upon him, and he suffered some disfavour at Court, both for his hatred of the French

Alliance, and for his opposition to the growing influence of Leicester, the friend of the Puritans. The Queen, however, determined in 1573 to show that he still had her countenance and regard, and went to visit him in full state at Canterbury. Two years later he died, and left the control of the Church in less capable hands; but so surely had he guided her policy, and so wisely had he administered her, that the Church of England was strong enough to survive both the Jesuit attempts to undermine her, and the storm of the Puritan attack.

SIR THOMAS GRESHAM

1519–1579

By

R. H. MOTTRAM

SIR THOMAS GRESHAM

by R. H. MOTTRAM

THE name of Sir Thomas Gresham is conspicuous among the number of those who have been an ornament to the land which gave them birth and a blessing to the age in which they lived. His life was at once so actively and so usefully spent that, had he left no other memorial of himself than the space he occupies on the page of the historian, his career would have been far from an uninteresting subject of literary enquiry; but when we consider, besides, how greatly he adorned and enriched the metropolis of this country, he appears to possess a peculiar claim on our attention; and it seems but natural that we should desire to become better acquainted with his personal history and character."

Such are the opening sentences of *The Life and Times of Sir Thomas Gresham, Knt., Founder of the Royal Exchange,* which John William Burgon (whose birth in the Eastern Mediterranean had perhaps led him to notice the effect of English trade on the Levant) finished compiling in Brunswick Square on July 12, 1839. The genesis of the book was in an Essay which won a competition instituted by William Taylor Copeland, Esq., M.P., Lord Mayor in 1836. Burgon's Essay won the " premium " offered, although it exceeded the condition that it should be susceptible of " public recitation within the limits of half an hour." The Rev. George Cecil Renouard, B.D., Rector of Swanscombe, Kent, publicly read " such portions as seemed best adapted, at the Mansion House, on 14th May 1836." At first there seemed no chance of its being published, but the burning of the second Royal Exchange in 1838 revived interest in the subject, and Burgon having added considerably to his original effort, by reference to manuscripts in the State Paper Office, through facilities " promptly as well as very obligingly granted by the Right Hon. Lord John Russell," the book was brought out appropriately by Effingham Wilson of the Royal Exchange.

It remains the most considerable work on the subject, and has to-day the inestimable advantage of showing us Sir Thomas as Burgon saw him. It is not hard to guess why Burgon thought that the vigorous, unscrupulous Elizabethan was an " ornament and a blessing " and an adorner of the Metropolis. Thomas Gresham was one of the figures clearly in the biographer's sight. He stood just where the long flexible stream of English History had turned a corner. He was one of the new men of a time when overseas trade, based on nascent credit and defended by the germ of a strong navy, was beginning to expand. It was still expanding, amid the same conditions, in 1839. We, standing at yet another corner, can see Thomas Gresham in another perspective. Overseas trade has had a shock, from which it may never entirely recover; men are making demands upon credit they never made before, and a strong navy is now an expensive competition. More than his ornamental or blessed qualities, we see the irony that has turned back to his family birthplace so much of the result of his restless energy.

The balance of learned opinion seems now to have tilted toward the conclusion that Thomas Gresham was born in London and not in Norfolk. There is, however, less doubt about the stock from which he came. The Greshams were natives of the village of that name that stands on the high wooded ridge dividing the shallow basin in which the Bure takes its rise from the north coast of Norfolk. It must be one of the healthiest places in the world. The family seem to have been in the employ of the even more celebrated Pastons, who had a manor there. During the fifteenth century, one, John, moved to the neighbouring market town of Holt. Presumably it was by this move that he acquired the surname of Gresham. The move argues a rise in the family fortunes, from a position of dependence to one of owning a manor. James Gresham, eleven of whose letters are in the Paston collection, seems to have succeeded and to have been followed by yet another John, who still further advanced the family fortunes. James was

already writing from London and using the seal engraved
with a grasshopper that has become so familiar in connection, first with the original Royal Exchange, and lately
with Martin's Bank. His son, John, was Lord Mayor of
London and married an heiress, a Blyth of Stratton, who
brought him a fortune. By her he had four sons : William
the eldest, inheriting the Manor of Holt; Thomas, after
whom the greater nephew with whom we are concerned
was named; Richard, the father of our Thomas, and John,
who had the excellent idea of purchasing the family manor
in which they had been born, but which had seemingly
been deserted by them for mansions in London, and turning it into a Free School, endowing it with estates in Norfolk
and London and placing the management in the hands of
the Fishmongers' Company. Thus was laid the train of circumstance that makes Gresham's School at Holt to-day the
most solid memorial of that magnificent but defunct family.

For the Greshams were nothing less. Before the tremendous events of the sixteenth century had ripened, the
Greshams had entered the one sure path to material success
—they were useful to King Henry VIII and his powerful
ministers. The sources of their wealth—apart from the
second John Gresham's fortunate marriage—do not transpire. Perhaps to have been in the service of Sir William
Paston was an introduction to the Court circles into which
they were soon admitted, if they did not regularly move
there. Perhaps the ownership of manors such as East
Beckham made possible an accumulation of coin, or a
participation in the woollen trade that had been firmly
rooted in the villages as well as the towns of Norfolk ever
since Edward the Third had encouraged the immigration
of Flemish weavers more than a century earlier. The
second John Gresham and Richard his son had such an
accumulation at the moment it was wanted. The wars
and foreign policy of Henry VIII had been ruinous. Taxa-
tion by consent was no remedy for the indebtedness revealed
in the correspondence that these two members of the family
carried on with that monarch, his son, and his minister the
Cardinal.

Richard was born at Holt in 1485. By 1507 he was
admitted a member of the Mercers' Company, lived in
London, and visited Antwerp, then at the height of its
mercantile supremacy. In 1511 he was lending money to

the King, and in the succeeding years he, his brothers, and a partner of the name of Copeland were chartering ships from the Crown, or lending it their own. In 1520 he was providing Wolsey with foreign workmen for the tapestry work at Hampton Court. He even advanced money to the artificers. The next year we need not be astonished to find him petitioning Wolsey for licence to carry out foreign transactions the duty on which exceeded £2,000.

But Wolsey was not a very safe friend. His plan of "benevolences" found little favour with the Common Council, and when Richard Gresham spoke in its favour before that body, with only two who agreed with him, it began to look as if the Minister's favour could be too dearly bought. Nor were his troubles confined within the shores of this island. The following year, 1526, found him and his brothers arrested at Nieuport, as hostages, because some of the Emperor's ships were under arrest in England. His friend and customer Hochstetter's safe conduct was valueless and led apparently to a quarrel with the latter. He obtained freedom, but the death of Wolsey was a blow, and an embarrassment in two ways. The great man was no longer popular above or below stairs, and was moreover (so he himself declared on his death-bed) in Gresham's debt. Nor can it have been to his advantage to have been a creditor of Queen Anne Boleyn on the day of her execution. By what manœuvres or wise silences Gresham escaped being involved with his rising fortunes in so many that were falling does not transpire. But he was in favour evidently by 1537, was knighted, and held the office of Lord Mayor of London. It is true that, as Sheriff, he had presided at the burning of heretics, and now set himself zealously to enforce the Six Articles. He dissolved the Monastery at Walsingham, and for one or all of these judicious deeds was in a position to ask Thomas Cromwell to obtain him a doe from the royal preserves for his feast. So that he seems to have righted his fortunes by the time he fell sick and died at his Bethnal Green mansion, from which he had a magnificent funeral at St. Lawrence Jewry. Such was the father, such the family stock and tradition, such the precarious times of our Thomas Gresham.

It is almost fatally attractive to date some great change in human destiny or man's daily habit by the number of a certain year, or to make it the deliberate achievement

of some well-known and picturesque figure. Fortunately
Thomas Gresham will not fit in with any such facile scheme.
He may look very purposeful and profound to Burgon in
1839, but in 1925 Mr. Salter, a fellow and lecturer of
Magdalene College, Cambridge, armed with a modern
knowledge of economics, and still more usefully perhaps,
with a post-war view of human nature, was able to show
Gresham standing at a most exposed spot in the destiny of
English-speaking people, in a more convincing light.

The son Thomas, who was born to Richard Gresham at
his London mansion in 1518 or 1519, was by no means
certainly foredoomed to be a leader of the Protestant
mercantile England that we look back upon, and which
seemed so inevitable to Burgon. True, his father moved
with the times, in religion and foreign policy. That father
and all the boy's uncles were engaged up to the neck, and
sometimes to the danger of their necks, in overseas filibuster-
ing—merchanting—coin-changing adventures that took
them into the perilous Mediterranean and Baltic Seas, and
involved them in transactions with Princes whose lives were
as brief and changeable as their policies. But Thomas
Gresham was a grown man, a member of the Mercers'
Company, Crown Agent, and resident for the purpose in
Antwerp, before the fate of England clarified out from
intricacies of the times. This is not, however, the beginning of his story. The first thing we know of him is that
he was employed at the age of twenty-four in getting together munitions for Henry VIII's attack on Boulogne.
About the same time he married Anne, the widow of Wm.
Read, a member of the Mercers' Company.

By far the most obvious factor in the world in which he
lived his first thirty years was the domination of Europe
and the new world overseas by the great Austro-Spanish
Empire. For some four or five years, during which the old
unity of Catholic Europe, including England, was reaffirmed,
and Mary Queen of England became the wife of Philip
of Spain, there was a chance, and it must have seemed to
Gresham a very fair chance, of the old order, with its inheritance of absolute and centralised power inherited from
Rome, being riveted on the known world. The only indications we catch are his air of caution, his obvious
retirement, the dropping of his formal title of Royal Agent,
in which capacity he appears still to have acted.

Even more can be learned perhaps from his portraits. Is it fanciful to suppose that that splendidly dressed, powerful, and apparently fortunate man has those pursed lips, those indrawn cheeks and sidelong glance, because he had to think furiously and quite uselessly about his fate, that, in the long run, depended on a turn of events as inscrutable, as trivial in issue, as the toss of a coin? He seems not to have been deceived by the rumour of the birth of a son to Mary and Philip, an event that might have changed the history of the race, a canard that caused a solemn *Te Deum* to be sung in Norwich Cathedral, while the incumbent of St. Anne-within-Aldersgate dilated at length on the appearance and beauty of the child. Then in a very short time that must have seemed very long, desolate, ill-matched Mary was dead, and her so dramatically different sister was on the throne, and the world was safe for Gresham and all like him. It may well be that his face never lost the expression that was fastened on it during those years. His fortune, his creed, and therefore, at that time of day, his life, were inextricably involved in what must often have looked like a futile and dangerous experiment. He was much too friendly with the ambitious and tragic Edward Dudley, Earl of Warwick, and subsequently Duke of Northumberland, whose backing of the ill-fated Wyatt's Rebellion cost several lives and made it look as if the Catholic Restoration were a strong and permanent fact.

An analogy might perhaps be drawn with Monmouth's easily suppressed rebellion that for a while only strengthened James II's position a hundred and fifty years later. The connection between Gresham and Northumberland was all too intimate. Before succeeding to the ducal title, the Earl of Warwick had been employed in suppressing what will always be known as Kett's Rebellion, at Norwich, in August 1549. That very considerable and by no means isolated outbreak was symptomatic of the economic and social troubles of those brief ineffective interludes in the stronger tendencies of the development of English life that we know as the Protectorate of Somerset, and the reigns of Edward the Sixth and Mary. There were perhaps twenty thousand ill-provided, but determined and exasperated, Norfolk men, at a time when all such possessed and were used to arms, defeating the Royal forces under Lord Northampton and sacking a city of the importance that Norwich then had.

Warwick, at the head of an army of knights in armour so elaborate that if their horses fell they were helpless until released, plus a substantial contingent of " alemains " or " lanceknechts " armed with pikes and arquebuses, the whole diverted from a Scottish expedition, arrived at Gresham's Manor of Intwood, three miles from Norwich, on his way to suppress successfully the rising. It is thought he met Gresham there, and if so the meeting was more than ordinary, it was almost prophetic. For Warwick was one of the last of that class immortalised by Lytton Strachey in his *Essex*, an ambitious mediæval baron. Gresham was one of the first of the new men, a commoner concerned with overseas trade and national finance.

There are still standing at Intwood, near the site of the hall, great oaks under which the two men, one might almost say the two ages, walked together. This, and the subsequent judicious retirement under Mary, was over and past in 1558 when Elizabeth mounted the throne, and the tide of affairs turned and flowed, at first hesitant, but presently strong and full in a direction it was never seriously to desert for over three hundred years.

Instead of seeing Gresham, as Burgon did, as a great prepotent heroic figure preparing the dramatic change, we may well be inclined to the more enlightened view of Mr. Salter, and see rather a cautious, not over-scrupulous, experimental man, prepared unwittingly by a most alarming series of experiences, for the very eventuality that now opened before him.

He and all his sort, lords of manors, who had come up and dominated the overseas trade of London, now had their chance. To seize it, however, was no easy task. No sooner had the domestic quandary been settled than England became, on account of that fact, a protagonist in a vaster drama. Under Philip and Mary the island was to have been the possible basis of a flank attack on the newly prosperous and united France that was already threatening, and was destined to disintegrate the wide, unwieldy Empire that the almost fabulous Charles VIII had relinquished to his son. Now, by a stroke of dual effect, England became the mercantile opponent of the military power that ruled nearly the whole world. The chain of causation is tied in a series of almost inextricable knots. The bumptious vitality of Henry VIII, the sickly good intentions of Edward VI had

run up debts that could only be satisfied by obtaining coin
abroad. Because Gresham belonged to a family already
for generations immersed in overseas trade, he had been
sent to reside in Antwerp in a semi-public, semi-private
capacity, which enabled him to obtain first-hand knowledge
of continental business complications stretching right away
to the Fuggers' banking house astride the Danubian trade
routes. It had to be Antwerp, the Shanghai of that ancient
world, the only place for such transactions in foreign exchange as he had to undertake. Fatally, without any
foresight on Gresham's part, Antwerp became the centre
of the new Protestant and partly trading and non-aristo-
cratic revolt against Spain. With Elizabeth on the English
throne, the Protestants of Flanders and France felt encouraged, and events drifted into that sanguinary series of
superficially religious wars that ruined Antwerp, and drove
international trade northward to Hamburg and Amsterdam,
into English and northern European hands. Because of
this Gresham conceived, nay, it seems had almost thrust
upon him, the idea of a Royal Exchange in London. Remote and irrelevant events as much as the new ease he
found in the changed atmosphere of his native land thus
drew him home to England, and instead of a kind of
foreign correspondent living abroad he became a great
figure in London, was knighted, and built his house in
Bishopsgate. So now he set on foot that remarkable idea
which was to have such far-reaching effects on the shape
of London, its importance in the scheme of world trade, and
incidentally on the value of the properties that were destined,
centuries later, to transform the old manor-house of the
Greshams, at Holt, into a great modern school.

The idea of joint-stock companies was just taking shape.
The old fixing of " Staples " and granting of full or quasi-
monopolies or licences, such as had been accorded to older
members of the family, were insufficient for the project
Gresham had in view. There is no certainty about the
matter, but Mr. Salter very plausibly suggests that the
death of Gresham's only son left him a little purposeless and
uncertain what to do with his already considerable wealth.
Why Gresham did not devote himself to one of the newly
formed trading companies, that which dealt with Russia, or
those of Africa or the Levant, why still more, if his heart
was set on erecting a permanent building to harbour in

London some transferred portion of the trade he had seen for years transacted in Antwerp, he did not divide the responsibility into shares, we shall never know. In this as in all else, Gresham's mind seemed to move in a mixed atmosphere of prescience and luck. On the one hand, he was slightly better educated than his forbears. They had been crudely magnificent, after the fashion of the time, helping Wolsey with Hampton Court, or re-enacting the ancient city pageant of the " marching watch " with great splendour. Gresham, however, had been at Cambridge under the remarkable Dr. Kaye, or, as his name is generally known in its latinised form, Caius, who had endowed, with Norwich benefices, the college partly named after him.

Gresham himself had apparently talked of doing something for his university. But perhaps there were more insistently present to his mind the grumbles of his fellow-merchants, and doubtless of the smaller fry, about the inconvenience of meeting each other in the transept of St. Paul's, or walking in open, narrow, noisy Lombard Street. Anyhow, the fact is that, in January 1565, he went to the Court of Aldermen, and offered to provide an Exchange building if they would provide a site. One is irresistibly reminded of the custom still prevalent in Norfolk, by which the landlord finds a tree, for posts, a gate, and irons, and the farmer finds the labour. In this case, individual citizens put up £3,532 for the purchase of certain houses on Cornhill and in adjacent alleys. It is difficult to picture the tangle of narrow streets and lanes, with a market standing where we see the Mansion House, and a whole parish with its church and churchyard where we see the walls of the Bank of England. The ground was cleared and handed over to Sir Thomas. On June 7, 1566, he laid the first brick, in company with some Aldermen. In November 1567 the building was covered with slate, and on December 22, 1568, the London merchants took possession. On January 23, 1571, Queen Elizabeth entered the City in state, dined at Sir Thomas Gresham's in Bishopsgate, and after, entered and walked about the new building, and had her herald, with the blast of a trumpet, proclaim it the Royal Exchange.

There can be no doubt that it was a fine handsome building and very adequate for its purpose. A well-known pair of engravings of its exterior and interior show it to have been a quadrilateral arcade, with a gallery above, enclosing a piazza faintly reminiscent of St. Mark's at Venice. A handsome elaborate clock tower is shown as rising above the main entrance, and there is also inserted in the picture a pillar more slender but not less commanding than the subsequent monument on Fish Street Hill, surmounted by a golden grasshopper. It does not seem certain that this was ever put up, but there were gigantic golden grasshoppers on the four angles of the roof. Besides the rooms for exchange transactions, there were a number of shops, and these do not appear at first to have found favour, for we learn that, prior to Elizabeth's formal opening, Gresham was obliged to bribe such tenants as there were to furnish the unfurnished apartments with goods, and light them with wax candles, by the offer of having the use of them without rent for a period. The ruse was successful, and he was able to obtain the rents; but even so, the retail trade carried on was of the cheapest and shoddiest description, and the place became at times a rendezvous for rowdies and idlers, and persons " known to the police " in modern phrase. It was in fact a building and a venture in exact keeping with Gresham's life. It was magnificent with brick, stone, and marble, but the vaults were damp and useless. In less than a century it was utterly burnt out, in the Great Fire of London, Gresham's statue, not that of any of the accompanying kings and queens of England, remaining undamaged. Yet equally characteristic of Gresham was the fact that his main idea was sound, and succeeded. London did inherit the importance of Antwerp in world trade, above all in finance, which was more especially Gresham's care, and about which he knew more than he ever did of handicraft and manufacture. And to-day, on the site which he and no one else could have induced the citizens to obtain and clear and make over to him for the purpose, stands the third Royal Exchange.

Thus, from his fortieth year on, the life of Thomas Gresham straightened out and became, apart from domestic bereavement, happy and successful. There can be no doubt that he, rather than the cautious Cecils, the magnificent and erudite Bacon, the brilliant, noble favourites of the Queen or her daring, piratical sailors, was the central type of his time. Without his peculiar mixture of cunning and fortitude, all the greater men whom Elizabeth seemed to have an uncanny power of calling into activity, and retaining near her, in spite of her capricious treatment of them, might have legislated and philosophised and fought and dared in vain. Gresham died in 1579; he never saw the desperate climax and splendid close of the reign of his royal mistress. But he had done more than anyone else to set finances right, and build up the prosperity of London that was a sure foundation for the self-reliance that the country had to show, when it stood alone against a world in arms.

Next to the Royal Exchange, his name is perhaps most closely linked with the " Law " of Economics, to which it has become attached, and which amounts, for the plain man, to the statement that bad money drives out good. Recent scholarship, notably the work of Mr. Salter, throws some doubt upon the extent to which Gresham can be said to have formulated anything worth calling a law. The voluminous crabbed and involved correspondence can be read in the State papers, but it is not so certain if anyone to-day can divine the real motive, or ganglion of motives, behind the odd archaic Norfolkese of the sometime Royal Agent. For Gresham was that mixed and utterly English thing, a private merchant anxious for private gain, and desperately close, as the letters also show, about his " diet " or expenses allowance, and at the same time, a public servant, capable and devoted as Burghley, determined to reduce rates of interest that foreign lenders were charging, and to see England sound, safe, and independent. Probably the last-named aspiration was a far stronger strain in his Protestantism than any religious feeling for the sanctity of private conscience. And it would perhaps be more fitting if, instead of his somewhat superficial connection with an economic law, more stress were laid on his efforts to help the fishing trade, because the men who conducted it were the recruiting ground for the Navy. It was those very men who, nine years after his death, ill-provided with powder and shot, with little but hardy seamanship to arm them, defeated the Armada, kept England inviolate, and turned her face and her destiny away from Europe, towards the Atlantic, to North America, and Africa, and thus eventually to the East and the Southern Seas. That he was permanently successful in dealing with England's debt is not the case. He seems to have died of apoplexy, falling down in the kitchen of his Bishopsgate house, on a November day, after coming from the Exchange. He was only sixty. On the one hand, he had been lame for nineteen years as the result of a fall from a horse, which he said in one of his letters that complain bitterly of Royal economising at his expense, he incurred in the Royal Service. On the other, he was held up to Burghley, says Mr. Salter, as a "living advertisement of the value of Rhenish wine as a cure for gout." May it not have been that he was worn out with worry and travel and anxiety and danger? His frequent crossings of the North Sea were not merely uncomfortable as they can be to-day. They were dangerous, and he wrote on one occasion at least, of how, setting out from Flushing, he was delayed by storms, then by the appearance of suspicious sail on the horizon, so that the whole company, passengers and crew indiscriminately, looked to their arms. Finally, the ships were found to be none other than English warships. Then again, bad weather intervened. Such were the commonplaces of his business. He saw Antwerp, the seat of his operations and frequently his residence for twenty-five years, gradually become the prey of civil disturbance and finally of military threat. He had some difficulty in getting his own plate and furniture away.

And at the back of all was the fact that for the twenty years of his prime he was the servant, the constant correspondent, in spite of himself, the tool of Elizabeth Tudor. Plenty has been written on the subject these last years to make it easy to understand what such a life must have been. Somerset and Edward may have been visionaries, and futile visionaries; Northumberland and Mary were positive dangers. But none of them lasted twenty years of his life, and had they done so, that would not have been as wearing, one is inclined to think, as a single year of Elizabeth. The sovereign, and such a sovereign, was the nation, then, so far as Gresham's chief preoccupation was concerned, the National, which was the Royal, Debt, and the relationship of the English coinage to that of other countries followed. It might be necessary to support the Protestants abroad. He must provide for it. Then, the Queen might take a fancy to give one of her favourites an expensive jewel, or a still more expensive command, at sea or by land. Gresham must see to that too. He might preach economy as the only possible way of reducing interest, rates, or even providing for maturities, that, if not met, meant increased difficulties in borrowing. She did not contradict. She economised— out of Gresham's personal allowance. Or, he might, and frequently did, write lengthy epistles and disquisitions on financial matters. She was always likely to try to legislate for the foreign exchange as she had for the apprentices, and that he hated and feared as his spiritual descendants to-day hate and fear quotas and tariffs.

If apoplexy is the result of a fretted and over-taxed brain, he had every excuse for dying from it. If the expression of his face in the portraits is to be trusted, it seems to give colour to the idea. The irony almost inevitable to prosperous and practical men whose thoughts and acts are unsanctified by any high ideal or personal sacrifice, pursued him. The correspondence over his dealings with the Crown is the least pleasant expression of himself, and shows closeness, if not actual sharp practice. He left his wife a very wealthy woman, who enjoyed the Bishopsgate mansion until her death, when it became the site of Gresham's College, the foundation he seems to have preferred to one at Cambridge. Here were taught Divinity, Astronomy, Music (Burgon remarks in 1839, " the only instance of an endowed lectureship for the promotion of the divine art "), Geometry, Law, Medicine, and Rhetoric. The professors' lives, especially their salaries, were straitly governed by a joint board of the City Corporation and the Mercers' Company, and the activities of the institution continue, in necessarily modified form, on a neighbouring site, to this day.

For the rest, change worked upon him, an artificer of great changes. He had no direct descendants, and his family stock, some branches of which married into the aristocracy, became extinct in its main line in the eighteenth century. His Exchange, perhaps the finest flower of his imagination, has twice been supplanted. The England he helped to make stands on the point of even greater changes. Perhaps the most lasting thing he did was to fix in London much of the trade he himself had conducted in Antwerp, with the result that, when the leases of the properties his uncle had devised to the School housed in the old Gresham home at Holt, fell in, about 1900, they had so greatly increased in value that the present institution took the place of the humble Free School. Such is the fate of Thomas Gresham.

EDMUND CAMPION, S.J.

1540–1581

By

CHRISTOPHER HOLLIS

EDMUND CAMPION, S.J.

by CHRISTOPHER HOLLIS

THE Catholic priests who had been ordained in Queen Mary's reign would in time die out and thus, argued Cecil, England would be automatically de-Catholicised. To prevent this, in 1568 William Allen, a Lancashire priest, established a seminary at Douai to train new priests to take the places of the old Marian priests. In 1580 Allen persuaded the Jesuits to co-operate with him in this missionary work. Two priests and a lay-brother were chosen to form the first Jesuit missionary enterprise to England. Of the priests one, the Superior, was Robert Parsons, till lately the Dean of Balliol College, Oxford. The other was also an ex-Fellow of an Oxford College, of St. John's, where he had received the Deacon's orders in the Church of England. He had fled from Oxford to Ireland and to the Continent—had renounced his Anglican orders for those of Rome and, when the summons came to him, he was teaching Rhetoric in a Jesuit school in Bohemia. He was Edmund Campion. The name of the lay-brother was Ralph Emerson.

Both to these three religious and to the authorities of their Society the political problems of the day were of secondary importance. The problem of primary importance was to see to it that as many souls as possible should receive the Catholic Sacraments. Therefore their superiors laid upon Campion and Parsons the obligation to take no side in the English politics of the day, and Campion and Parsons willingly accepted that obligation. They asked for, and obtained from the Pope, a ruling that " the declaration of Pius V against Elizabeth . . . should in no way bind the Catholics, while things remain as they are (*rebus sic stantibus*)."

However difficult and disputable may be the interpretation of the conduct of others in those tangled times, the interpretation of Campion's conduct is certain and beyond argument. The complete sincerity of his faith has never been questioned even by those who are unable to share it. We have his own letters, and it is evident from them that he was not a man who took any natural interest at all in secular politics or the quarrels of parties; had he lived in some quiet time in which Conservatives and Liberals or Whigs and Tories alternated in power, there can be little doubt that he would not have troubled to put himself upon either the one side or the other. The argument which compelled him to act as he did ran thus.

Christ, he said, was God. And Christ taught not merely that certain doctrines were true, but also that those truths must be propagated. The Christian Faith was of its nature missionary. It only remained then to decide whether the Elizabethan Church was a part of the Catholic Church, whether one who received the Sacraments according to its rites did in truth receive valid Sacraments or not. The story of Campion's own life was sufficient to show that that was not a question to be answered lightly. He did not answer it lightly, but he answered it in the end, and his answer was negative. From that negative answer followed the necessary consequence that then every risk must be braved in order to introduce the valid Catholic Sacraments into England.

The objector may be inclined to say that the issue was not as simple as all that. There was the Papal Bull. The concession that it was inoperative " *rebus sic stantibus*," was little more than a concession that the enemy would not attack until it suited him to do so, and the Government were entitled to reply to it with a " thank you for nothing." At the very time that Parsons and Campion were crossing to England on their peaceful mission, the Pope was sending Nicholas Sanders to Ireland on a mission of war. There was war between the Elizabethan Government and the Catholic Church, it may be objected, and, however little Campion might be responsible for that war, he could not complain if he should happen to suffer in it.

Campion did not complain of his sufferings; he gloried in them. It might be argued that Elizabeth and Cecil, granted their primary sincerity, were justified in executing Campion. He never troubled himself to argue that they were not justified. All that he was concerned to do was to argue that he was justified in dying—that he could not but do as he did, though the consequence were death.

Campion and Emerson crossed to England from Calais to Dover on June 24, 1580. Parsons had preceded them by a few days and had landed in safety. As soon as he landed, Campion fell on his knees behind a neighbouring rock and commended to God the cause on which he had come. His hope was that he would be able to pass the "searchers" without difficulty. But unfortunately a rumour had come down that Gabriel Allen, the brother of William Allen, was about to attempt to smuggle himself into the country. The authorities were therefore on the alert. Campion was willing to swear that he was not Gabriel Allen, but there was for a short time an inconvenient probability that he would be sent up under escort to be examined by the Council in London. However, in the end they were convinced of his innocence, and let him go.

A certain ardent Catholic, called Thomas Jay, had been told off to wait for Campion at the boat-landing at Hythe. When Campion reached the landing, Jay touched him on the arm and said, " Mr. Edmunds, give me your hand; I stay here for you to lead you to your friends." He led him off to the agreed rendezvous in a house in Chancery Lane, where Campion was furnished with a new disguise, and where he was able to wait until Parsons returned to London from the country.

He had to wait some ten days, during which he preached in a hired hall in Smithfield and took part in several secret conferences. But London was, of course, full of Government agents who posed as pious Catholics, anxious to be told by their co-religionists where they could assist at Mass or where they could hear a sermon. Priests whose coming had been advertised as widely as that of Campion and Parsons could not have hoped to remain long undetected in the capital, and, when the Catholics discovered that one Sledd who had frequented their company was in reality a Government informer, they insisted that the two Jesuits must be immediately got out of London. Parsons and Campion agreed, and rode out together to a house in Hoxton, then of course a country village quite separate from London. There they purposed to separate from one another, but, while they were resting, there overtook them from London a certain eager Catholic of the name of Pounde. Pounde represented to them that they might well be captured and that, if they were captured, their enemies would almost certainly put out libellous accounts of the reasons which had led them to come to England. It would therefore be well that, now that they were still at liberty, they should write out a statement of those reasons which they should leave with Pounde, and which he could keep and later publish if publication should be necessary to refute a libel. Both agreed, and Campion sat down there and then and wrote in half an hour an open letter to the Lords of the Council in which he stated that he was a Jesuit priest, come to England solely to preach and to administer the rites of his religion, that he was forbidden by his superiors to take any part in politics and asked nothing more than to be allowed to debate the religious question in public " before the doctors and chosen men of both universities." He concluded with a prayer to " Almighty God the Searcher of hearts " to " send us of his grace and set us at accord before the day of payment to the intent we may at last be friends in heaven, where all injuries shall be forgotten." One of Campion's greatest heroes was Sir Thomas More, and there was perhaps an intentional echo of Sir Thomas's famous prayer that he and his condemning judges might one day " merrily meet together " in heaven, like St. Paul and St. Stephen.

Campion wrote off the letter and gave it to Pounde, not even troubling to seal it up. Pounde's instructions were to keep the paper secret, unless and until Campion was arrested. But he was not one of those who are capable of keeping a secret. He told a friend; friend passed on the news to friend; copies of the letter were made and circulated among the faithful, with the inevitable result that before long a copy came into the hands of the Elizabethan Bishop of Winchester, and by him was handed over to the authorities.

There was no mention in the letter of the circumstances under which it was to be published, and, read as it was when Campion was a free man and not a prisoner, it sounded like a somewhat arrogant and provocative challenge, and the Government replied to the challenge by a vigorous enforcement of their anti-Catholic laws. They arrested all the prominent Catholics on whom they could lay their hands, and they redoubled their efforts to capture Campion and Parsons.

Meanwhile, the two Jesuits were travelling separately through the country from Catholic house to Catholic house, Campion's journeys taking him through Berkshire, Oxfordshire, and Northamptonshire. Their procedure was to arrive at a house in the afternoon. All the Catholics of the neighbourhood were collected, and the evening was spent in hearing their confessions. Very early in the next morning the Jesuit said Mass, preached, and gave Communion to his congregation. Then, as soon as might be, he rode on his way. It was dangerous to spend more than one night in the same house. " The harvest," wrote Campion, " is wonderfully great," and Parsons claimed that as a result of their mission as many as fifty thousand had refused any longer to conform to the Elizabethan Church. Campion knew very well that it was only a matter of time before he was captured.

" I cannot long escape the hands of the heretics; the enemies have so many eyes, so many tongues, so many scouts and crafts. I am in apparel to myself very ridiculous; I often change it, and my name also. I read letters sometimes myself that in the first front tell news that Campion is taken, which, noised in every place where I come, so filleth my ears with the sound thereof, that fear itself hath taken away all fear. My soul is in mine own hands ever. Let such as you send for supply premeditate and take count of this always. . . . Threatening edicts come forth against us daily; notwithstanding by good heed, and the prayers of good men, and, which is the chief of all, God's special gift, we have passed safely through the most part of the island. I find many neglecting their own security to have only care of my safety. . . . At the very writing hereof, the persecution rages most cruelly. The house where I am is sad; no other talk but of death, flight, prison, or spoil of their friends; nevertheless they proceed with courage. Very many even at this present, being restored to the Church, new soldiers give up their names, while the old offer up their blood; by which holy hosts and oblations God will be pleased, and we shall no question by Him overcome. . . ."

In October of 1580 Campion and Parsons met again at the house of a well-wisher at Uxbridge to compare notes and to decide upon their future programme. It was decided that Parsons should remain in or near London, while Campion, against whom, owing to his letter, the hunt was exceptionally keen, should go up into the distant and strongly Catholic county of Lancashire. It was decided, too, that Campion should follow up his letter with a pamphlet of appeal to the Universities, Parsons meanwhile seeing to the establishment of a secret printing press, where it and similar literature might be published.

This programme was carried through, the pamphlet was written, and on June 27, St. Peter and Paul's Day, every person who attended the service at St. Mary's in Oxford found a copy of the pamphlet lying in his place.

The pamphlet was entitled the *Decem Rationes*. The romantic circumstances of its production give to it a special interest. It is a statement of ten reasons for finding the Roman Church rather than the Elizabethan to be the Church of Christ. The reasons do not differ greatly from those commonly advanced in this controversy—the evidence of the Fathers, the evidence of the Bible, the mutual contradictions of Protestants, their refusal of reason, the difficulty that their very argument compels them to admit the Catholicity of the Roman Church, through which alone can they claim Apostolic Succession, and so on. Able as the work is, and proof as its production under such difficulties is of Campion's thorough competence in his subject, yet it is the romantic circumstance of its production rather than its argument which gives to the *Decem Rationes* its special interest.

The impudence of that production astonished the Government; Campion's chances of evading their officers much longer was small. But those chances, it was thought, were larger the farther he was from London. Parsons ordered him to go first to Lancashire to collect his books and papers and thence to make his way to Norfolk.

On the way to Lancashire he and Emerson, his companion, stopped for a night at Lyford Grange in Berkshire, the home of a Catholic family called Yate. They were received with that jubilation with which they always were received in Catholic houses. Campion heard the confessions of the Catholic inmates, and the next day said Mass and preached. They then rode on. The visit had passed off without mishap. However, that afternoon a party of Catholics happened to call at Lyford. They were distraught with grief to learn that they had just missed the great Campion, and nothing would content them but that a deputation be formed to ride after him and fetch him back. They found him at an inn near Oxford, where he was in conversation with a number of Catholic undergraduates and Dons, who also had heard of his coming. They proffered to him their request. Campion refused, pleading his obedience, for Parsons had appointed Emerson his superior for this trip. When they pressed him, he explained that he was under Emerson's orders; he could not act except at his command. They then turned on Emerson. At first, he too was firm in his refusal, but, in the end, he was persuaded that he would save Campion both danger and trouble if he himself went on to Lancashire and allowed Campion to remain behind at Lyford. As soon as Emerson gave the order Campion obediently accepted.

There was a certain Eliot, a Catholic, a servant of Lady Petre. This man was suspected of murder and of other crimes, and, in order to prevent the charges from being preferred against him, he had promised Lord Leicester to betray the secrets of the Catholics amongst whom he moved. It happened that Eliot was in Oxfordshire at this time. On the next Sunday, July 16, he turned up at Lyford Grange and asked the cook there if he could hear Mass. The cook, who knew him and thought of him as a trustworthy and pious fellow-Catholic, told him that not only could he hear Mass, but that he would have the good fortune to hear it from no less a priest than Father Campion himself. Eliot expressed himself delighted at his good fortune, excused himself for a minute, during which he despatched a message to a neighbouring magistrate, ordering him to come with a hundred men to seize Campion, and then went in with the cook and heard the Mass.

After the Mass the whole household went in to dinner, and, while they were seated there, word came down from the watchman posted on one of the house's turrets, that armed men were closing in on them from every side. There was a secret chamber in the wall above the gateway. Into it Campion and two priests resident in the house, Ford and Collington, were hurried. The " searchers," with Eliot at their head, broke into the house but a few minutes afterwards. They searched and ransacked every room of it, but without result. The neighbouring magistrate and his men, though not Catholics, were yet friends to Mrs. Yate and not at all enamoured of their work. After three hours of ineffectual searching they departed with apologies to Mrs. Yate, and curses on Eliot for having brought them out on a wild-goose chase.

Yet to Eliot it was very probably a matter of life that Campion should be captured. His treachery was the price with which he had bought his life, and, if it should be reported, as it now would be, that he had deluded the magistrate with false information, it would be suspected that he was playing traitor to his own treason. Leicester would argue that there was no advantage to be gained by preventing the law from taking its course in order to preserve such a man in freedom. Besides, he knew well enough that Campion was in the house. He was determined not to be fooled. He therefore turned on the magistrate and asked him what figure he imagined that he himself would cut if it should be told to the Council that he was a friend of Mrs. Yate, and that Campion, the Jesuit, had escaped from Mrs. Yate's house through his negligence. " I myself have seen Campion there," he cried. The magistrate was shaken. There was some force in Eliot's argument, and the methods of vengeance of Elizabeth's Council were not pleasant. He was persuaded to return. After apologies to Mrs. Yate, he insisted on another thorough search of the house. But, though they broke down panelling and broke open walls, they were unable to find the object of their search.

When they at last abandoned this second search, it was too late for the men to return home that night. They had to sleep at Mrs. Yate's house. And, as soon as they were asleep, Mrs. Yate brought the priests out of their hiding-place and insisted on Campion preaching once more to the household. It is hardly believable; nor is it surprising that this business made a noise sufficient to awake and arouse the suspicions of the searchers. However, by the time that they had broken into Mrs. Yate's room, the priests were once more safely hidden. Nor was it until all were departing next morning that it suddenly struck Eliot that they had not searched the wall above the gate. " We have not broken through here," he cried, and calling for a hammer he smashed down the wall. Within were the three priests.

The Sheriff of Berkshire was compelled to deliver Campion

up to the officers of the Council. They tied his elbows behind his back, his hands in front, his legs under the horse's belly. In his hat they stuck a paper on which was written, " Campion the seditious Jesuit." Thus arrayed he was compelled to ride through the London streets, with its jeering Protestant mob and its few sorrowing Catholics, and to the Tower.

Four days later he was brought out and examined before the Queen and the leading councillors. They asked him to tell them the plain truth why he and Parsons had come to England, and he gave them a frank and courteous answer. They told him that they found no fault with him save that he was a Papist, and the Queen offered freedom, riches, and honour, but on a condition—the condition presumably of attendance at Anglican services—which he could not accept. He was sent back to the Tower with orders that he should receive better treatment.

Had the Government been content merely to rely on their own laws against Jesuits and on the fact that there was war between the Catholic Church and the Elizabethan State, and to kill Campion simply for being a Jesuit, their action would have been certainly not dishonourable, and perhaps, granted the premiss that Catholicism was false, justifiable. But they were determined not merely to kill Campion, but also to persuade the world, that, in addition to the crime of his Jesuitism, he had also been guilty of political intrigue. He was therefore to be questioned on his relations with an Irishman called Rochford, who was mixed up in Sanders's rebellion in Ireland, and " in case he continues wilfully to deny the truth "—so run the instructions—" deal with him by the rack." This was done some time in August. Campion was accused of having sent over the £30,000 to the rebels in Ireland and, when he denied the accusation, he was racked.

There was hardly a serious pretence even at the time that this accusation against him was true. Certainly there has been no such pretence since. Indeed, it is quite certain that so far was he from being implicated in the Irish rebellion that he did not even know of it until just before his landing in England, and was then greatly perturbed to hear of its existence. More serious is the question of whether he did under the rack reveal the names of some of those who had given him hospitality. The Government gave out that he had made such revelations and even put abroad a rumour

—which was entirely without foundation—that he was about to turn Anglican. One is naturally suspect of the Government's claims concerning Campion, for it was their whole purpose to discredit him. On the other hand, there are few surely who will not be ready to admit that the version of the story which Campion himself gave is likely to be the true one—in particular, since he does not meet the accusation with that outspoken and unqualified denial with which it would have been to his interest to meet it, had his conscience allowed him to do so. He wrote to a friend—Thomas Pounde—we have not the letter, but we have three independent accounts of it, all substantially similar—" It grieveth me much to have offended the Catholic cause so highly as to confess the names of some gentlemen and friends in whose houses I had been entertained. Yet in this I greatly cherish and comfort myself that I never discovered any secrets there declared and that I will not—come rack come rope." And on the scaffold he " desired all to forgive him, whose names he had confessed upon the rack, for upon the Commissioners' oaths that no harm would come to them he had uttered some names."

It was well known throughout the land that Campion had challenged the Anglican champions to debate with him. It was thought well to accept that challenge. Therefore on August 31 Campion and some other captive priests were brought out to dispute with the Deans of Windsor and St. Paul's in the chapel of the Tower. In the details of its arrangement the debate was most unfairly staged. For the two Deans there was a table with books of reference on it and two seats by its side. Campion, though he was but fresh from the rack, was allowed neither books nor chair nor table. He was allowed only a little stool. The Deans were well prepared for the contest, Campion was given only an hour or two's notice that it was to take place.

It is hard to know where victory lay, but at least the confession of the two Deans, when after Campion was safely dead they published their own version of the proceedings—a confession that " divers gentlemen and others, neither unlearned nor of themselves evil affected," had got the impression that Campion had the better of it—makes us inclined to think that Campion had the victory. One, at any rate, of the audience had no doubt where victory lay—the pleasure-loving irreligious courtier, Philip Earl of

Arundel. " By what he saw and heard then he easily perceived on which side the truth and true religion lay," he wrote years afterwards.

Other debates followed with other theologians. Naturally they were inconclusive, and before September was through, the authorities were coming to the conclusion that they did their cause more harm than good. They must push on with their business. The attempt to connect Campion with Rochford was dropped, as there was no shadow of evidence of such a connection. On the other hand, they were determined to have against him some further charge than that of his religion. Therefore they invented a story of a plot to murder Elizabeth that had been hatched at Rheims, and in which Campion and several priests whom they happened to have in their custody were alleged to be implicated. At the end of October they racked him with the hope of wringing a confession from him, but without success.

On November 14 Campion and seven other priests were brought to Westminster Hall, and there put upon trial for complicity in this plot. So well had the rack done its work that Campion was unable to raise his hand to plead " Not Guilty." Another had to raise it for him. It has never been denied by any serious historians that this plot was entirely fictitious. And Camden who wrote the story of these times from the Government's point of view admits that Elizabeth herself was well aware of Campion's innocence. " The prosecution," writes, for instance, Hallam, " was as unfairly conducted, and supported by as slender evidence, as any perhaps that can be found in our books." It is therefore not necessary to follow in detail the story of the exposure of the paid or blackmailed false witnesses. Campion had no wish to save his own life, nor was he especially concerned to blame the Government for executing him. All that he was concerned to do was to make it clear that the cause for which he was executed was his religion. In this he was by general admission successful. " If our religion do make us traitors, we are worthy to be condemned, but otherwise are and have been as true subjects as ever the Queen had," he was able to say after the verdict of guilty had been brought in.

On a cold and wet December morning they came and fetched out from the Tower Campion and two priests, Sherwin and Briant, who were to die with him. There were two hurdles. To one Campion was bound, to the other his two companions. Each hurdle was tied to the tail of two horses, and thus they were dragged through the filth of the London streets. A jeering mob followed behind them, and lined the streets to the side, though there were some there who were not at all moved to jeer. There was one, for instance, who stepped forward and " either for pity or affection most courteously wiped his face all spattered with mire and dirt."

At Tyburn the crowd was greater than had ever been known at an execution before. They put Campion into the cart and his neck into the halter. He turned to the crowd and repeated what he had already said at his condemnation. " If you esteem my religion treason, then I am guilty, as for other treason I never committed any, God is my judge." They shouted out at him to hold his peace. So he contented himself with saying that he forgave all that had brought him to this pass. After a few more questions they called on him to pray for the Queen. He did so. " For which Queen? " asked one. " For Elizabeth, your Queen and my Queen, unto whom I wish a long quiet reign with all prosperity," answered Campion. And at these words the cart was drawn away from under him. They waited till he was dead, then cut down the body, quartered it and threw the parts into the boiling cauldron. A drop of the horrid mixture of blood and water splashed out on to the clothes of a chance by-stander, a young lawyer named Henry Walpole. He accepted the accident as a call from God, himself joined the Society of Jesus and fourteen years later suffered as Campion had suffered. The executioner turned to one of Campion's companions. " Come, Sherwin, take thou also thy wages," he said to him. Sherwin stooped and kissed the execu-tioner's bloodstained hands and then stepped up into the cart.

It is the ironic glory of the Society of Jesus that among the first of their fathers to land in England should have been one who was, as completely as any who ever lived, a typical English gentleman. Thrown into a world of lying and intrigue, of turmoil and blackmail, he won his way through that world by his sheer and guileless simplicity. He possessed in a pre-eminent degree all those qualities upon which the gentleman most prides himself—courage in adversity, tenderness, humour, simplicity, loyalty, and the love of honour and the love of truth. Like other men, he was not naturally indifferent to success and to the applause of the world, but firmly, though not without a struggle, he put these things behind him when honour demanded that he should do so. He was " one of the jewels of England," as the great Lord Burleigh himself said of him. Yet he possessed one further quality which the English gentleman does not commonly possess. He possessed holiness.

SIR HUMPHREY GILBERT

1539–1583

By

PETER FLEMING

SIR HUMPHREY GILBERT

by PETER FLEMING

HUMPHREY GILBERT was born in 1539. He had three brothers and one sister; Humphrey was the second son. The Gilberts lived in Devonshire, on estates granted to them by William the Conqueror. They were people of substance and position in those parts, though hardly more than country cousins at Court. Greenway, on the river Dart, was the family seat, and it is legitimate to suppose that ships, tall and otherwise, were a fairly constant decoration in the background of Humphrey's childhood. He himself, however, seems to have preferred another of the family estates, a more machicolated and Otrantine residence called Compton; in after-life he often styled himself " of Compton." This predilection has been taken by the more giddily conjectural of his biographers to indicate a romantic streak.

His father, Sir Otho, died in 1547, the same year as Henry VIII. His mother remarried with alacrity, and in due course provided Humphrey with a half-brother in the shape of Walter Raleigh. In spite of the discrepancy of fourteen years in their ages, these two men became close friends and worked well together; they were at times a powerful combination.

Sir Otho's death scattered the family. John, the eldest son, got Greenway, Compton, and most of the land; even the Elizabethans sometimes knew when they were well off, and the eldest Gilbert remained until his death respectable, bucolic, and obscure. Humphrey was billeted on an uncle. Nothing is known of his early years. The reader will be spared a rehearsal of the trite and slender clues whereby the man's greatness is arbitrarily detected in the child.

Humphrey went to Eton at an early age. Eton was under Nicolas Udall, in the history of that great school the only headmaster (I believe) to steal the College plate, and the only headmaster (I know) to be dismissed for doing so. He was also the only headmaster to score a major success in the London theatre: *Ralph Roister Doister* still bears revival. Udall was highly Elizabethan.

What, if anything, his influence was on Humphrey Gilbert we do not know; nor do we know much about Gilbert's Oxford career. He first approaches the centre of the stage when, at the age of fifteen or sixteen, he entered the service of the twenty-year-old Princess Elizabeth, presumably in the capacity of a page, and probably through the influence of his aunt Kate Ashley, who acted as her governess.

Eton and Oxford had equipped him with rather more than the average degree of culture; Nature had given him an eager and speculative mind and a handsome exterior. Elizabeth seems to have valued his company. Hooker noted that " Her Majesty had a special good liking for him, and very oftentimes would discourse and confer with him in matters of learning." Gilbert on his side formed an opinion of the Queen which was to prove a paramount factor in all the enterprises of his life; he often tried to get round her, but he never dreamed of going against her.

She was not, of course, on the throne when he entered her service. Soon after she became Queen she launched an undertaking, comprising the usual elements of buccaneering and humbug, which gave Gilbert his first taste of action in the field.

England was not at war with France, but France was at war with herself. The Huguenots, beleaguered in Rouen, Dieppe, and Havre de Grace, appealed to Elizabeth for help. Ostensibly in the sacred cause of religion, actually on the chance of securing a Channel port to replace lamented Calais, Elizabeth lent 100,000 crowns and 6,000 men for the defence of Havre de Grace. Warwick commanded the force, Gilbert served in it " with great commendation."

The venture, not very nobly conceived, developed ingloriously. The civil war coming to an end with the fall of Dieppe and Rouen, the English forces were invited to withdraw. Warwick would accept no such invitation from a foreigner, and the English stood a siege. But plague swelled the casualty lists to fantastic proportions, and Warwick surrendered, obtaining honourable terms. In 1563 Humphrey Gilbert was back in England. He had fought, he had been wounded. More important, he had acquired at first hand a working knowledge of the ethics and technique of contemporary foreign policy.

At Oxford Gilbert had shown enthusiasm and proficiency in the study of navigation. On his return to England he took it up seriously. He joined the Merchant Adventurers, a company concerned with the development of new trade routes for British ships. He talked to travellers, pored over maps, and invented an instrument for the proving of longitude and a system for the pricking of sea-cards. Geography in those days was very far from being an exact science. The world was a dimly lit stage on which the curtain, rising slowly and by jerks, revealed scenery which, although arresting and diversified in the extreme, was often not very like the real thing. Fresh information was coming in every day, but each country kept its findings to itself, and the common stock of knowledge increased but slowly.

In the race for empire Spain and Portugal had got away to a flying start. They claimed the known parts of Africa and the Americas, and held what they could of them jealously. Eighty per cent. of England's trade was with the Low Countries. For us, commercially speaking, the world was a very small place.

English ships needed, above all, a free-trade route to the East. Until the hour of his death Humphrey Gilbert was obsessed by the belief that he could find it for them, by the North-west Passage. Unfortunately, to find it required more money than a younger son in a period of declining land values could easily raise. Desperate for capital, Gilbert wrote and submitted to his elder brother *A Discourse To Prove A Passage By The North West To Cataia And India*. Though it failed to loosen the family purse-strings, the *Discourse* is a remarkable document.

No practicable passage by the north exists between England and the Orient. But the motto on Gilbert's coat of arms was *Quid Non?* (*Why Not?*), and the fact that no passage exists was not so serious an obstacle to his immediate ambitions as the fact that practically everybody else thought there was a passage by the north-east. Much of the *Discourse* is devoted to attempts to shake the orthodox convictions in this matter of the Merchant Adventurers; the arguments used are typical of the wild logic which is the key-note of the whole document.

Anthony Jenkinson had brought back from the depths of Russia certain particles of evidence supporting the existence of a North-east Passage. A Tartar fisherman, for instance, claimed to have sailed a prodigious distance towards the south-east, " finding no end of the sea." Gilbert retorted that no Tartar had the *nous* to tell south-east from north-east.

Then Jenkinson had heard of a unicorn's horn being picked up on the coast of Tartary, a country to which the creature was notoriously not indigenous. Gilbert once more blamed the natives, saying that it was doubtful " whether those barbarous Tartarians do know an unicorn's horn, yea or no," and suggesting either the *Asinus indicus* or a certain one-horned fish as alternative explanations of the phenomenon. So much for Jenkinson.

And anyhow, Gilbert adds, even if there were a North-east Passage, the other way would be better from the English point of view—shorter, more temperate, and easier to control. Look, he says, at all the people who have asserted its existence! What moved them to assert it he does not, he confesses, know; but they were learned men, and there must be something in it. Gilbert's mind was very true to his motto.

The *Discourse* was not intended for publication, and its style, though workmanlike and urbane, has no particular distinction. The end is a fine kind of buccaneering Amen:

" And therefore to give me leave without offence, always to live and die in this mind. He is not worthy to live at all, that for fear, or danger of death, shunneth his country's service, and his own honour: seeing death is inevitable, and the fame of virtue immortal. Wherefore in this behalf, *Multare vel timere sperno*."

There is one other phrase that sticks in the mind. Gilbert is telling of a startling revelation concerning the existence of a North-west Passage which had been made by a traveller to Charles V. The King of Portugal heard that it had been made, and (according to Gilbert) paid the Emperor 350,000 crowns to forget about it. Now we can hardly suppose, argues Gilbert, that the King of Portugal would have disbursed so considerable a sum for " egges in moonshine."

346

Eggs in moonshine. . . . With how lofty a contempt Gilbert discharges the phrase! And with how pathetic an irony it recoils upon his head! Eggs in moonshine, though he never knew it, were his own stock in trade. They have had no more magnificent or resolute purveyor than the man who tried to change the face of the world by arguing about a unicorn's horn which no one had ever seen.

There is a certain grandeur about Gilbert's misapprehensions, as indeed there is about the aspirations which he based on them. He is Don Quixote with a difference—this difference: that within the limits of even his wildest dreams he was practical, far-sighted, and quite often dead right. The *Discourse* is the work neither of a charlatan nor a fool. It makes shrewd, though not always legitimate use of the available geographical data, and in its less technical passages good sense at least holds its own with the chimerical. It required, for instance, a man of vision and a realist to point out that the navy " should be greatly increased by the traffic ensuing upon this discovery, for it is the long voyages that increase and maintain great shipping." Whereas Gilbert's suggestion that vagabondage and unemployment throughout the realm would be liquidated by " setting poor men's children . . . to make trifles and such like, which the Indians and those people do much esteem " is the sort of suggestion which few men of his ability could have made with a straight face.

The *Discourse* failed of the purpose for which it was written. John Gilbert could not be induced to express more than an academic interest in his brother's scheme, and Humphrey, though he did not forget about it, put the document aside. More will be heard of it later.

In the meantime he had been sent to Ireland, where Shane O'Neil was crying havoc in Ulster. Sir Henry Sidney had reluctantly succeeded the inept Sussex as Governor. He found Ireland a country in which

> " a man might ride twenty or thirty miles nor ever find a house standing, and the miserable poor were brought to such wretchedness that any stony heart would have rued the same. Out of every corner of the woods and glens they came creeping forth upon their hands, for their legs would not bear them; they looked like anatomies of death; they spoke like ghosts crying out of

their graves; they did eat the dead carrions, happy when they could find them. . . ."

Sir Henry, it is clear, would have made a good war correspondent.

Gilbert did well in Ireland (he was appointed Colonel at the age of twenty-eight). But his heart was not in the work; seeing that it was mostly butcher's work, this was perhaps as well. His own methods in the field he described as follows:

" I refused to parley or make peace with any rebels. . . . After my first summoning of any castle or fort, if they would not presently yield it, I would not afterwards take it of their gift but win it per force, how many lives so ever it cost, putting man, woman, and child of them to the sword. . . . Being for my part constantly of this opinion that no conquered nation will ever yield willingly their obedience for love but rather for fear."

This analysis of his own policy reflects the temper both of the man and his age. It reflects also a certain realism of outlook. As the poet Churchyard pointed out, this summary and high-handed technique " made short wars," an important consideration for a commander when " the gaining of time was one of his chiefest cares, because he had no provision of victuals for his people, but pulled as it were out of the enemy's mouth perforce."

To Gilbert's personal bravery in the field several unprejudiced tributes have survived. The Irish, unarmed and undisciplined, did not, it is true, make very formidable foes. But Gilbert, at the head of 150 men, withstood 4,000 of them at Knockfergus, and at Kilkenny, with only 13 retainers, cut his way through a force of 1,200; and these are long odds. It is hardly surprising that " the Irish wondered so much they made sundry songs and rhymes of him and his black curtal horse, imagining himself to have been an enchanter that no man could hurt, riding on a Devil." Nor can their awe have been lessened by Gilbert's habit of lining the approach to his tent, along which suppliants and prisoners must pass, with the heads of their friends and relations. This, he found, had an excellent psychological effect, and " the dead felt no pains by cutting off their heads."

Gilbert left Ireland with a great name as a fighter and an

administrator. He was without question glad to be back in England; complaints about an affliction of his eyes ceased as soon as Ireland was out of sight. In 1570, the year of his return, he was knighted, and about this time he married Anne Ager, a lady of undoubted wealth and alleged beauty. After a year or two in Devon, he settled down in the rural surroundings of what is to-day Limehouse.

For the next few years Humphrey Gilbert is an indistinct figure. He went back to Ireland once, but only for a short time. In 1571 he sat in Elizabeth's fourth Parliament as member for Plymouth. The atmosphere of the house was Puritan and independent, and Gilbert, championing the Queen in all, seems not to have made a favourable impression. On one occasion Peter Wentworth attacked him as " a flatterer, a liar, and a naughty man." " This," observes one of his biographers, " being the only incident of his Parliamentary career mentioned by English historians, we may justly infer that Sir Humphrey did not attain high eminence as a statesman." I think we may.

The address in which Elizabeth prorogued that Parliament is tartly flavoured, but Gilbert had earned her approbation and his reward. It came in the shape of a seven years' appointment as Surveyor-General of " all horses, armour, weapons, munitions, artillery, etc." It was an appointment made in the Chinese manner; it offered, that is to say, in lieu of salary, the power to collect money and retain a large proportion of it. Gilbert's terms of reference included " the suppression of unlawful games, by which archery is greatly decayed ": a clause which had its origin not entirely in sentimental memories of battles long ago, nor in the age's confidence in the bow's superiority over the musket as a weapon of precision. There were commercial interests involved, and it is possible here to detect the first faint echoes of the post-War pamphleteer's favourite target, the Armaments Racket. The best fire-arms were made abroad. The best longbows were made in England. Up, therefore, with archery!

Of Gilbert's activities as Surveyor-General we know nothing. But a characteristic sidelight is thrown upon the man by his sudden, though short-lived, addiction to alchemy. There was a man called Meadley who claimed to be able, by means of vitriol, to transmute iron into copper, at that time a rare and expensive metal in England;

he gave a demonstration of his powers sufficiently impressive to convince Sir Thomas Smyth, a man of substance and shrewdness. Smyth interested Leicester, Burghley, and Gilbert in the process, and the four men, observing a portentous secrecy, incorporated themselves into " The Society of the New Art," rented property containing the necessary ingredients, and advanced Meadley £100.

Then Smyth succeeded Walsingham as our Ambassador in Paris, and Gilbert's connection with the dexterous Meadley became somewhat closer. Distance had lent an enchantment to the experiments which first-hand supervision went far to dissipate. A tremendous row took place; there was vitriol in the retorts on both sides. Gilbert withdrew from the " Society," his fellow-backers followed his example, and two years later Meadley was in gaol for debt.

The interlude of hocus-pocus once more reminds us how well the motto on Humphrey Gilbert's coat of arms was fitted to his speculative and spectacular mind. Copper from iron? Why not?

We see him next on the other side of the Channel. Officially, his presence in the Low Countries with a force of 1,500 men was sheer banditry, for we were not at war with Spain, against whose oppression the Dutch were rebelling; officially, Elizabeth knew nothing of this enterprise undertaken by certain of her subjects to aid their coreligionists. Actually, of course, the expedition had the full approval and support of the Queen, and was a typically backstairs attempt (a) to weaken Spain, and (b) to get Flushing. Gilbert was a pirate on paper only.

He landed at Flushing in July 1572, carrying in his head the Queen's secret orders and an elaborate code whereby they might be supplemented. In Flushing he found a delicate situation. Not only was a force of Huguenots, playing Elizabeth's game for Catherine de Medicis, already installed there, but the Dutch commander was a man with whom Gilbert found it quite impossible to get on. There followed some months of inglorious and uneasy campaigning, clandestinely directed from London, until the St. Bartholomew's Massacres changed Elizabeth's attitude *vis à vis* France and Spain, and Gilbert received a letter recalling him which really meant what it said. In London he went through the motions of being in disgrace for the benefit of the Spanish Ambassador, who was not deceived.

Back in England, he resumed his attack on the North-west Passage. He took counsel with pilots and travellers, capitalists, and men of learning. But all his efforts failed to shake the Merchant Adventurers from their conviction that the North-west Passage was a mare's nest, and that the only wild-goose chase worth initiating was north-east-wards. Since the Merchant Adventurers had a monopoly of the relevant exploration rights, Gilbert's hands were tied; the eggs-in-moonshine market was sluggish.

So he turned his eyes south, and, as usual, they saw rather farther than the eyes of most men. He raised money, found associates, and in 1574 petitioned the Queen for permission to sail to the Americas south of the Equator and plant there an English colony.

The petition was never granted, for what reason we do not know. Gilbert's dream got no farther than a prospectus. It was an ambitious dream, with an unusually (for that age) constructive quality to it. Colonisation was a new idea. Most of the English adventurers had the smash-and-grab, wolf-on-the-fold technique. Humphrey Gilbert discerned the possibilities of Empire.

Several years ago, in Ireland, Gilbert had met Martin Frobisher, a Yorkshireman of great bulk, no culture, and real brilliance as a navigator. It is probable that Gilbert's belief in the existence of a North-west Passage was the original inspiration of Frobisher's famous voyages. The first took place in 1576. Gilbert, with a singular lack of jealousy, invested a considerable sum of money in the theft of his own thunder, and rendered Frobisher notable assist-ance at Court, where Warwick's influence enabled him to override the opposition of the Merchant Adventurers.

Frobisher made three voyages. On the first he reached Resolution Island, off Baffin Land, and returned with geological specimens which included a mysterious black stone, and an Eskimo who was robbed of the social success he deserved by a severe cold, of which he died. An Italian metallurgist converted a fiasco into something very different by inducing the black stone to yield a small but alluring quantity of gold dust. The Queen put up £1,000 and a big ship for the second voyage.

The second voyage produced several hundred tons of the black stone, and it looked as if Frobisher, in spite of an Eskimo arrow-wound in the buttocks, was sitting pretty.

But the third voyage, undertaken by fifteen ships carrying
the personnel and equipment for a sixteenth-century Klon-
dyke, turned out less happily, and Frobisher came home to
find that the auriferous qualities of the black stone had
failed to survive closer inspection; it was being used for
road construction. Frobisher withdrew to Ireland.

This was bad luck on Humphrey Gilbert. His *Discourse*,
published without his consent in 1576 by George Gascoigne,
that turbulent, talented, and attractive figure, had done
much to make England North-west-Passage-conscious; and
now his eggs in moonshine were condemned as addled,
through no fault of his own. Moreover, he had in the
meantime sponsored another though a minor failure.

It does not seem likely that he set much store by *Queen
Elizabeth's Academy*, a memorandum (though he did not call
it that) which he submitted to his sovereign. Nor apparently
did she, for history records no reactions on her part. This is
a pity, for the *Academy* is an extremely enlightened treatise
on educational reform, in many respects far ahead of its
time and in some not yet wholly out of date. Briefly, it is
a plea to Elizabeth to abolish the ineffectual and sometimes
iniquitous systems of Wards (under which the education of
children of gentle birth was scamped in the great houses to
which they were farmed out), and to establish a large
academy in London, in which the young would receive, not
merely book learning, but a sound practical training calculated to make them useful citizens. The total cost Gilbert
estimates, not at all roughly, at £2,966 13s. 4d.

It was a remarkable and intelligent scheme, but nothing
came of it. . . . " Nothing came of it." The words are
beginning (are they not?) to have a familiar ring. Already
it is impossible not to suspect that Humphrey Gilbert had
almost all the qualities necessary for success, except the power
to succeed. He was a man to whom the wages of enterprise
were often due; yet to the end of his life that pay was in
arrears. One cannot help feeling that in a man, so outwardly effective, who had no more than his share of bad
luck, there was something missing somewhere. I shall return
to the point anon.

The *Academy*, of course, never looked like a winner. The
Englishman, of whatever age, has always secretly regarded
education as rather a waste of time, and the Elizabethans
had other matters on their minds. Gilbert's next memor-

andum had a far stronger contemporary appeal. It bore the somewhat euphemistic title *How Her Majesty May Annoy the King of Spain.*

Although *Euphues* was not published until two years later, the style of this document is not uninfluenced by the fashions which Lyly was beginning to found. It is a little more flowery, a little more laboured, than is usual with Gilbert, and we find phrases like " the wings of man's life are plumed with the feathers of death," which is just the sort of clumsy, involved, and indeed practically meaningless result produced by an unskilled Euphuist trying to paraphrase a platitude.

But perhaps the cloak of Euphuism was a disguise. Gilbert's signature to the document is erased, and there are abortive attempts to wrap up its meaning in a code. The *Discourse* is indeed one which might have suggested even to an Elizabethan the advantages of anonymity. It is an elaborate, comprehensive, and strategically sound plan for a big-scale piratical campaign on the high seas, directed against the Spanish colonies and trade routes on a front extending from the St. Lawrence to the West Indies.

Of the reception of this document by the Queen we know nothing. She was not yet as bold against the Spaniards as she became later, and probably she pigeon-holed the underlying idea without accepting the plan in its entirety. Nevertheless, in 1578, a few months after it had been submitted to her, she at last granted to Humphrey Gilbert a six years' charter authorising him to equip a fleet and plant in the New World a colony of which he would be the Governor.

In a remarkably short space of time Gilbert had assembled a fleet of eleven ships and was ready to sail on a preliminary voyage of discovery. The Spanish Ambassador, vigilant, a little apprehensive, and extremely well informed, did what he could to hinder the preparations. There were quarrels among Gilbert's subordinates, and Knollys, his second-in-command, backed out in a huff, taking with him four of the eleven ships.

Gilbert was undeterred. On September 26 he sailed from Dartmouth for an unknown destination with seven ships so heavily armed that it seems likely that the Empire-builder contemplated piracy as a side-line.

The expedition was a complete failure. How or why it

failed we do not know. It returned unobtrusively three months later. Nobody knows where Gilbert went, or what it was that forced him to turn back. Probably it was bad weather. Certainly he lost one ship with all hands. The rest is silence.

The irrepressible man planned a fresh start immediately, but his two ships were ordered to Ireland and his schemes hung fire. He was very near being discredited. It was other men who held the public's—and, more important, the Queen's—imagination; Drake, for instance, had just returned, laden with booty, from a voyage which had put a girdle of destruction round the world. And soon the time-factor began to worry Gilbert; his charter, granted in 1578, had been for a period of six years only. He redoubled his efforts.

It would be tedious to enumerate the obstacles he encountered, or the means by which they were overcome. The former included obstructionism on the part of the Merchant Adventurers, now more euphemistically styled the Muscovy Company: the will of a capricious Queen: the shadow of that earlier fiasco: and Spanish intrigues. The chief props of his ultimate success were probably Raleigh's influence at Court: the support of the English Catholics, who were toying with the idea of founding a refuge for themselves overseas; and his own ingenious methods of attracting the capitalists by granting them large segments of an empire which he had never seen. At any rate, in June 1583, Humphrey Gilbert sailed out of Causet Bay, near Plymouth, and made northwards for the coast of Newfoundland.

His preparations had been elaborate. The Utopia which he was going to found was already planned on paper, down to the last archbishop and the first public library; Gilbert might almost have been one of the models for Gonzalo in *The Tempest*. His ships ranged from the *Bark Raleigh* (200 tons) to the *Squirrel* (8 tons); they carried 260 men. The ships' masters had full sailing instructions, sealed as a precaution against spies; a comprehensive code of signals catered for most of the conceivable emergencies. Much thought had gone to the victualling of the ships, and

" for the solace of our people, and allurement of the savages, we were provided with Music in good variety: not omitting the least toys, as Morris dancers, Hobby horses, and Maylike conceits to delight the Savage people, whom we intended to win by all fair means possible. And to that end we were indifferently furnished of all petty haberdashery wares to barter with those simple people."

Captain Haies was to be the expedition's historian, and Stephen Parmenius, from Buda, its Laureate.

Gilbert's plan seems to have been, not to colonise in Newfoundland or Labrador, but to work south down the Atlantic seaboard and pick the best site that offered itself. The fleet made an auspicious start; but on the third night out, the *Bark Raleigh*, pleading by signals that her captain and many of the crew were ill, incontinently went about and made for home. The expedition had lost almost exactly half its tonnage at a single stroke, and Gilbert was furious. Captain Haies, a man sometimes aggressively philosophical, merely wrote, " I leave it to God."

Thereafter rain, fog, and adverse winds sundered the fleet. Seven weeks out from Plymouth the *Desire* and the *Golden Hind* sighted a barren and forbidding coast, presumably that of Labrador. They worked their way south, were duly amazed by some birds which may have been great auks but were probably penguins, and presently came up with the little *Swallow* (40 tons) off Baccalaos Island. The *Swallow*, whose crew were for the most part professional pirates, had captured two French barques, which Gilbert caused to be released. He found also that the men on the *Swallow* had, by a particularly underhand ruse, boarded a Newfoundland fishing vessel and plundered her of clothes, equipment, and provisions, " not sparing by torture, winding cords about their [the Newfoundlanders'] heads, to draw out else what they thought good." On their way back to the *Swallow* the cockboat capsized; a few of the raiders were drowned, but most were saved by their victims, whom Haies, using the adjective in its antique sense, calls " silly fools." " What became afterward of the poor Newlander," he adds on a slightly more sympathetic note, " God alone knoweth."

On the same day the three ships were reunited with the eight-ton *Squirrel*. She was anchored outside the harbour of St. John's; inside lay a cosmopolitan fishing fleet of thirty-six vessels, in which the English held the balance of power. Gilbert, secure in the knowledge that the land was his on paper, charged his cannon, put up his fighting screens, and prepared to force an entry.

The particular brand of bathos which had taken the gilt off the *Swallow's* gingerbread distinguished the scene that followed. In the mouth of the harbour the *Delight* contrived to run aground on an exposed rock; Haies is guilty of no overstatement when he calls it " a great oversight." She was ignominiously rescued by the boats on which her cannon had been trained. Tripping heavily, like a clown entering the circus ring, Humphrey Gilbert came into his own.

The expedition spent seventeen days in St. John's, and got on well enough with the odd community of fishermen who came there for two or three months in every summer to dry their fish. These men had a rough-and-ready form of government of their own, but they took it quite as a matter of course when Gilbert formally claimed the place in the name of Queen Elizabeth, and duly discharged their cannon when a flag was unfurled and the arms of England erected on a wooden pillar.

Gilbert carried out some superficial investigations of the surrounding territory, a brave new world, the diversity of whose hitherto neglected fauna moved the doughty Haies to chastise " the fault and foolish sloth of many in our nation, chosing rather to live indirectly, and very miserably to live and die within this realm pestered with inhabitants, than to adventure as becometh men."

But of all things Gilbert was " most curious in the search for metals," and it was a great day for him when the expeditionary refiner, a Saxon called Daniel, produced, trembling with excitement, a piece of ore which he alleged to be silver. Only Sir Humphrey's wish to extend his explorations farther south kept him from sailing home immediately. He was completely satisfied.

The ore was taken on board the flagship in an atmosphere of secrecy. The *Swallow* was sent back to England with the sick. The unrulier members of the expedition, whose heads had perhaps been turned by the high living at St. John's, were called to heel from their various unlawful activities. On August 20 the three remaining ships put to sea with Gilbert on board the tiny *Squirrel*, which now carried a superfluity of the *Swallow's* cannon, " more," in Haies' opinion, " to give a show than with judgment to foresee unto the safety of her and the men." Gilbert had transferred his quarters to her so that he could explore in person inlets which would deny an entry to the two heavier ships.

On the following night they reached Cape Race, where they made a prodigious haul of cod. (" The hook," noted Parmenius the poet, " is no sooner thrown out, but it is eftsoons drawn up with some goodly fish.") Thence they headed for Sable Island.

On August 28 they found themselves in threatening weather off a treacherous coast. There was a south wind. Gilbert insisted on a north-westerly course. The masters of the *Delight* and *Golden Hind* objected, but were overruled. The *Delight* sailed onwards with music playing, " like as the Swan singeth before her death." Schools of porpoises on the move portended storm. All seem to have had a sense of doom. " I omit," says Haies, " to recite frivolous reports by them in the Frigate, of strange voices, the same night, which scared some from the helm."

The following day brought mist and a high wind. Early in the morning they took soundings and knew their danger. The *Delight*, drawing 14 feet, was in the lead. She seems to have kept inadequate watch, and took warning only from the two ships astern to beat out for sea. She put about, and struck. Very quickly she was broken up.

Of her crew of nearly 100—two-thirds, now, of the expedition—none were picked up, for the *Golden Hind* and the *Squirrel* had to save themselves, and did so only by a narrow margin. But sixteen men from the *Delight* made for the coast of Newfoundland in her pinnace, and fourteen of them reached it alive, returning at last to Europe in a French ship.

Gilbert's situation was nearly desperate. All the extra supplies, all his papers, and Daniel's lump of ore had gone to the bottom with the *Delight*; the loss of the ore seems to have touched him most nearly. Mutiny threatened on both vessels, and Gilbert, who wanted to go on, had no other choice but to turn back for England. They started home on August 31.

At the moment of doing so the sailors were dumbfounded by an apparition. As the ships were putting about, there passed between them, " sliding upon the water," an undreamed-of beast, " a very lion to our seeming, yawning and gaping wide, with ugly demonstration of long teeth, and glaring eyes "; as he passed, " he sent forth a horrible voice." It was not, however, sufficiently horrible to perturb Sir Humphrey, who took the walrus " for Bonum Omen, rejoicing that he was to war against such an enemy, if it were the Devil."

On the homeward voyage the winds were favourable, but the seas ran high. Gilbert had to visit the *Golden Hind* to have an injured foot bandaged by the surgeon, and he was begged to stay on board the bigger ship for safety's sake. He refused, and went back to weather another sudden storm in his eight-ton cockleshell.

When the weather cleared he was back on the *Golden Hind*, making merry " from morning until night," and discussing, mysteriously, but optimistically, his expeditionary projects for the following year. On leaving, he was again, and still more importunately, urged not to risk his life in the diminutive and overloaded *Squirrel*. He replied, " I will not forsake my little company going homeward, with whom I have passed so many storms and perils."

Haies was not impressed by the gesture. After the fiasco of that first expedition, Gilbert had acquired the reputation of " a man noted of no good hap by sea " (the words are his own) ; and in certain quarters a lack of courage had been hinted at. Haies felt that Gilbert was not unmindful of this when he played Sydney Carton in the cockboat and went back to the *Squirrel*. " This," says Haies, " was rather rashness than advised resolution, to prefer the wind of a vain report to the weight of his own life."

But it is difficult, especially when we remember his daredevilry in Ireland, to believe that Gilbert was not doing the natural thing, was playing to the gallery. If he was, it was for the last time. A frightful—according to Haies an unprecedented—storm struck the two ships almost immediately afterwards. For hour after hour the *Squirrel* hung on the edge of perdition. From the *Golden Hind*, herself in sore danger, fascinated men watched their leader's ship riding the mountainous seas. Sir Humphrey (was this another gesture?) sat on the poop with a book in his hand. Whenever the two vessels lurched within hailing distance of each other, he waved his arm cheerfully to those above him on the *Golden Hind*, crying, " We are as near to Heaven by sea as by land ! " The storm grew worse. Night fell.

About midnight, " the Frigate being ahead of us in the *Golden Hind*, suddenly her lights were out, whereof as it were in a moment, we lost the sight, and withal our watch cried, the General was cast away, which was too true. For in a moment, the Frigate was devoured and swallowed up by the Sea."

That was on September 9. On September 22 the *Golden Hind* limped into Falmouth. The expedition was at an end.

To reconstruct a man's character from almost purely objective and not very plentiful evidence is to play blind man's buff with the truth. Humphrey Gilbert had none of those helpful traits or foibles, was involved in none of those unambiguously revealing situations, which are so helpful to the biographer. The only moment at which we see him clearly, through the eyes of a reliable witness, is the moment of his death. He remains a rather mysterious figure.

It is probable that his contemporaries found him rather mysterious, too. Proud, aristocratic, and quick-tempered, he seems to have cultivated inadequately the essential arts of self-advertisement. Considering the number and variety of his projects, and his own faith in them, it is surprising, not how few of them came off, but how few of them were even put to the test of action. Gilbert must have lacked something. What?

I suspect that it was the ability to get on with his fellow-men. Those who knew him well—Raleigh, for instance, and the Queen—valued him at his true worth; the rest of the world, it seems probable, found it difficult to do so. " Would God," wrote Raleigh in a letter praising Gilbert to Walsingham, " his own behaviour were such in peace as it did not make his good service forgotten and hold him from the preferment he is worthy of." Gilbert's loyalty was above question, and it is unthinkable that his " behaviour " comprised anything which was, so to speak, actionable. Raleigh is referring to something well known to Walsingham and everyone else—at a guess I should say to Gilbert's capacity for putting people's backs up, to the fact that he " didn't go down well."

He may have been a bore, he may have been overbearing; he may have been both, or neither. But certainly there was something about him, some inner angularity, which spoilt his relations with the world at large. Look at the Merchant

Adventurers. Frobisher got round them at his first attempt; Gilbert, a member from his youth up, never did. At Flushing he quarrelled with the Dutch commander, and he quarrelled with his own second-in-command. He quarrelled with Knollys, he quarrelled with Meadley. He made no hit in Parliament. All through his life we have the feeling that Humphrey Gilbert was, in some way that will never be defined, a *mauvais sujet*.

It is wrong to remember him as a Glorious Failure; he failed all his life, but he only failed once gloriously. A surer tact, a happier manner towards his fellow-men might have secured him more and better chances to do or die; for by contemporary standards his eggs in moonshine were far from being unmarketable. But Humphrey Gilbert was no salesman. That, I think, was his tragedy.

SIR PHILIP SIDNEY

1554–1586

By

C. HENRY WARREN

SIR PHILIP SIDNEY

by C. HENRY WARREN

SIR PHILIP SIDNEY has become a legend, but for once the legend and the man are closely akin. Spenser called him " The President of Noblesse and of Chivalree "; and what was right for Spenser, whose flesh and blood friend he was, is still right for us, these centuries later. Not without reason has posterity clung to the Zutphen story as the one thing most rightly memorable about Sidney, the one thing in which all the man stands clearly defined in a sudden flash of divinity.

> " As he was putting the bottle to his mouth," Fulke Greville tells us in his life of Sidney, " he saw a poor soldier carried along, who had eaten his last at the same feast, ghastly casting up his eyes at the bottle, which Sir Philip perceiving, took it from his head before he drank and delivered it to the poor man with these words, ' Thy necessity is yet greater than mine.' "

Those words were written some thirty years after Sidney's death; but, whole or partial as the truth in them may be, they depict a gesture so entirely in keeping with all the known facts of Sidney's life that we need not hesitate to accept them without stint. The whole course of his life, in fact, may be said to have been shaped towards this immortalising moment.

The shaping began at Penshurst, that " goodli Kentish garden " where, on November 30, 1554, Philip was born. There he was instructed in the beginnings of such behaviour as should become a Dudley. At the age of ten he was sent to Shrewsbury. Whatever other instruction he suffered there, we know that " a Virgile " and " Calvines chatachisme " helped to instil that balance between art and morals which the times admired. There were also letters, packed with wisdom, from Dublin Castle, where his father had recently been installed as Lord Deputy of Ireland. From one of these Polonius-like efforts, for instance, we learn that the young Philip was entreated to " tell no untruths; no, not in trifles "; to use prayer " as an ordinary act and at an ordinary time "; to be courteous " with a diversity of reverence according to the dignity of the person "; and, above all, to remember " the noble blood you are descended of by your mother's side; and think that only by virtuous life and good action you may be an ornament to that illustrious family." (How refreshingly different, years later, were Philip's own letters to his younger brother, Robert: " Now, sweet brother, take a delight to keep and increase your music, you will not believe what a want I find of it in my melancholy times. . . .")

From Shrewsbury, at the beginning of 1568, he went up to Christ Church, Oxford. If the instruction proffered there was less worldly wise than his father's had been, no doubt it atoned for the lack by an ample addition of earnestness. For although we know very little of Sidney's life at the University, we do know that his first tutor, Dr. Thomas Thornton, was " a great encourager of learning," that his second, Dr. Thomas Cooper, was afterwards created Bishop of Winchester, and that his third, Nathaniel Baxter, was the author of several volumes of a Puritanical persuasion. There followed a three years' tour of the Continent, with the good and learned (if slightly over-anxious) Languet always somewhere at hand to speed the young nobleman on his way with letters of introduction into the choicest society in Europe and to keep his inquisitive thoughts in check when they seemed in danger of straying too near Rome and the Catholic Church. Sidney was only a few months short of twenty when he arrived back in England, but his reputation was already established as a young man of great physical beauty, keen intellect, and a rare gentleness of spirit. Aubrey said " he much resembled his sister, but his hair was not red, but a little inclining, viz. dark amber colour. If I were to find a fault in it, methinks 'tis not masculine enough; yet he was a person of great courage."

Two years after his return the Queen favoured him by sending him as her ambassador to condole with the Emperor Rudolph on the death of Maximilian. By now there was no longer any need for those sage paternal precepts from

Dublin. Indeed, it was Sir Henry's turn to seek his son's advice. "Good my lord," he wrote to Leicester, when affairs in Ireland had become even more than usually distressing, "send Philip to me. There was never father had more need of his son, than I have of him. Once again, good my lord, let me have him." Neither was there really any need for the continued watchfulness of Languet. But when the old man saw his beloved Philip (his embassy fulfilled) return to Court to languish there in premature disuse, he could not refrain from keeping his self-appointed ward posted in wise recommendations. "The habits of your Court," he wrote, after a visit to England in the train of Casimir, "seem to me somewhat less manly than I could have wished. . . . I fear lest that noble nature of yours may be dulled, and lest from habit you may be brought to take pleasure in pursuits which only enervate the mind." But Sidney was not likely now (if ever he had been) to run amuck among the follies and intrigues of harried courtiers. Within a month or two he was already giving sufficient proof of the extent of his integrity by his famous remonstrance to the Queen on the occasion of her proposed marriage to Anjou.

Nevertheless, Languet's fears were quite understandable. In his youth Sidney had exhibited such extraordinary promise that his friends expected only the utmost of him. There seemed no limits to what he might achieve as well by statesmanship as by scholarship. Scholars of the widest repute had delighted to reason with him, princes had been quick to see the singular astuteness of his judgments. Had not the dying Essex said of him: "He is so wise, so virtuous and godly; and if he go on in the course he hath begun, he will be as famous and worthy a gentleman as ever England bred"? And when Elizabeth chose him as her ambassador to Rudolph he had turned that modest mission to such good account (too good account, for Elizabeth's liking) that, but for her Majesty's vacillations, the Protestant League might have become something more than a dream. Even Walsingham had said: "There hath not been these many years any gentleman that hath gone through so honourable a charge with as great commendation."

But, so far as Languet and others could see, apparently no good was to come of it all. And now Sidney was not even at Court, waiting on the spot to catch the Queen's favours: he was wasting his time and his opportunities away in

Wiltshire. So the Huguenot continued to worry. Could he not see (and if Languet could not, who should?) that Sidney was too exacting in his demands, too honest in all his dealings, too essentially a poet, to qualify for such honours as Elizabeth was likely to bestow? "To what purpose," he had written, "should our thoughts be directed to various kinds of knowledge unless room be afforded for putting it into practice so that public advantage may be the result, which in a corrupt age we cannot hope for. . . ." This was no momentary concession to the fashionable posings of the day. It was not even over-scrupulousness. What Sidney said, he invariably meant; and here, there is no doubt, he meant that he found himself very much out of tune with his times. The first qualification for a successful Elizabethan was an almost boyish excess of spirit which he might "work off" in a life of adventure—whether as a statesman, a courtier, or a discoverer. And in this reckless zestfulness Sidney was quite lacking. Fulke Greville wrote of him: 'Though I lived with him, and knew him from a child, yet I never knew him other than a man; with such staidness of mind, lovely and familiar gravity as carried grace and reverence above greater years." And maybe the worldly wise Sir Henry had in mind a possible handicap for future years when he thus counselled his son: "Give yourself to be merry, for you degenerate from your father if you find not yourself most able in wit and body to do anything when you be most merry." Certainly Sir Henry had done his very best to instil in the boy the rules of a working compromise for a successful life; and school and university had instructed him in that nice balance between art and morality (a "Virgile" and a "Calvines chatachisme") which was the basis of the renaissance humanism.

But though the twig might be bent as it should grow, no amount of bending could dictate what kind of flowers it should finally put forth. And though paternal and academic training had made Sidney enough a creature of his time for him to exclaim upon one occasion, "For my part I would rather be charged with lack of wisdom than of patriotism," and, upon another, "My chiefest honour is to be a Dudley, and truly I am glad to have cause to set forth the nobility of that blood whereof I am descended," his true and lasting temper was betrayed again and again in words of a very different import. Even while Languet was expressing his rather auntish fears, Sidney, in retirement, was discovering himself with no uncertainty. It was as if he had done his best to try to conform with the ideal expected of him and had realised, how soon, it was a folly not to be endured. Let others hang about the Court waiting for the tricksy, wheeling beams of Elizabeth's favour to shine on them: in four years he had had more than enough of that foolish game. Hitherto his motto had been, "I hope": now it should be changed to "I have done with hoping." Two years earlier Languet had written to him: "Beware I do beseech you and never let the cursed hunger after gold of which the poet speaks creep over that spirit of yours into which nothing hath hitherto been admitted save the love of goodness and the desire of earning the goodwill of men. . . ." And now Sidney was so fixed in that love of goodness that nothing could tempt him from it. To his brother he wrote as "one that for myself have given over the delight of the world." His flowers were opening in such secret air that even Languet hardly guessed what kind they were.

Sidney's contemporaries knew him for a noble patron of the arts: poets and learned men from all over Europe did homage to his sensitive intelligence in dedications of unusual sincerity. But that patronage had in it nothing of condescension: rather it was the privileged offering of a more fortunately placed fellow labourer.

> "Gentle Sir Philip Sidney," said Nash, "thou knewest what belonged to a scholar, thou knewest what pains, what toils, what travail conduct to perfection. Well could thou give every virtue his encouragement, every wit his due, every writer his desert, 'cause none more virtuous, witty or learned than thyself.'"

Shyly and almost secretly, for the sole delight of his sister, the Countess of Pembroke, he had been practising the art of words himself, often wasting in prose the finer substance of poetry. In years to come Hazlitt was to think of *Arcadia* as one of the greatest monuments on record of the abuse of intellectual power; but to Sidney's contemporaries such praise as Harvey's came nearer the truth: "Here are amorous courtings (he was young in years), sage counselling (he was ripe in judgment), valorous fighting (his sovereign profession was arms) and delightful pastime by way of pastoral exercises." *Arcadia*, however, was but a beginning, a prelude in prose to a poetry richer than the times either deserved or understood. With such friends as Spenser, Harvey, and Dyer, Sidney was helping to pave the way for "the new poetry." By his enlargements on the famous "Rules" of Dr. Drant, by his experiments in sonnets, canzons, terza rima, sestinas, and other forms, he was endeavouring to mould the standards of a natural English prosody. Spenser put his finger on the main endeavour of these poet-adventurers when he wrote to Harvey: " . . . For why a God's name, may we not, as else the Greeks, have the kingdom of our own language, and measure our accents by the sound, reserving the quantity to the verse? " Examples of Sidney's " patterns " (as Harvey called them) are to be found scattered throughout the pages of *Arcadia*.

But for his real championship of poetry, as an expression of the imagination rather than as a formal art, we must turn to the lively *Defence of Poesie* itself. Though ostensibly written as an answer to Stephen Gosson's violent *School of Abuse* (1579), Sidney's *Defence* was really a declaration of his own belief in poetic inspiration and an appeal to English poets to have done with mere formalism.

> " But truly many of such writings as come under the banner of unresistible love, if I were a mistress, would never persuade me they were in love; so coldly they apply fiery speeches, as men that had rather read lovers' writings, and so caught up certain swelling phrases, which hang together like a man that once told my father that the wind was at north west and by south, because he would be sure to name winds enow,—than that in truth they feel those passions, which easily (as I think) may be bewrayed by that same forcibleness, or *energia* (as the Greeks call it), of the writer."

Here speaks one who looked upon poetry neither as a conceit fit for the pastime of courtiers nor as an art to be redeemed by moral purpose, but as a natural expression of the emotions, teaching, if it teach at all, only by " divine delightfulness." " With a tale forsooth he cometh to you, with a tale which holdeth children from play, and old men from the chimney corner. . . ." The value of the *Defence* is in the creative spirit that informs it: it is the poet speaking.

But if we would test how well the poet puts his theories into practice we must read *Astrophel and Stella*. This sonnet-sequence, which was not printed until five years after Sidney's death, occupies a unique position in Tudor poetry. It is love-poetry, but at its best it is as remote from the " mouth love " of the conventional amorous poems of the time as Sidney's own life was from the lives of most of his contemporaries. Nash, who contributed a preface to the original edition of 1591, summarised the " plot " of the sequence as follows: " The argument cruel chastity, the prologue hope, the epilogue despair."

But Sidney's poems are no classical exercise, after the fashion of the day. They are the fruit of a genius so original and daring that it could shake poetry at one throw from a precious artifice to a flaming sincerity. Most of them—to quote Lamb's familiar appreciation—are " full, material and circumstantiated. Time and place appropriate every one of them." Nevertheless, despite the impassioned outburst in the very first sonnet (" Fool, said my Muse, look in thy heart and write "), it is not until we come to the thirty-third that we find the poet impatiently flinging aside those literary emotions and " certain swelling phrases " scorned in the *Defence*, and embracing that disciplined *energia* the lack of which he deplored in others. From this sonnet onwards the sequence shines almost continuously at white heat: the torments of despised love are communicated as authentically as art can ever hope to communicate them. It is of course always an assumption to suppose that love-poetry is self-revealing; but both from internal evidence and from the very naturalness of the expression there can be little doubt that the " story " of *Astrophel and Stella* is drawn from the poet's own experience; in which case the Stella of the poems is that Penelope Devereux whose marriage with Sidney had been one of the highest hopes of her father, the Earl of Essex.

But Essex's hopes—and Sidney's—were doomed to come to nothing. Penelope (although, against her guardians' wishes, she had secretly become engaged to a boy of her own age, named Charles Blount) married, probably in 1581, Lord Rich. And it was this conclusive answer to Sidney's aspirations, enhanced, maybe, by the fact that Penelope was unhappy in her marriage, which suddenly transformed the literary emotions of the first thirty-two sonnets into the

passionate sincerities of the remainder of the sequence.
Apart from the sonnets we have no reason to suppose that
Sidney's love was ever substantially reciprocated (indeed,
we know that when Penelope was finally divorced from Rich
she returned to the faithful Blount, now become Earl of
Devonshire), and even the sonnets themselves scarcely suggest that Stella ever allowed herself more than an occasional
flirtation with the distraught lover: "Feigning love, somewhat to please me." But Astrophel's love was of the kind
that finds encouragement where no encouragement was
intended: even though it be plunged back again and again
into a resultant despair it could not choose but hope. In
vain did he attempt to seek consolation in the defeat of
desire:

> " *True, that on earth we are but pilgrims made,*
> *And should in soule up to our countrey move:*
> *True, and yet true that I must Stella love.*"

Nothing so direct and natural as these sonnets had been seen
in English poetry since Chaucer. Even when they pay something like lip-service to the verbal dexterities fashionable at
the time, they cannot smother the fire that burns in them—
as the following " question-and-answer " sonnet proves:

> " *Come let me write, and to what end? to ease*
> *A burthned hart: how can words ease, which are*
> *The glasses of thy dayly vexing care?*
> *Oft cruell fights well pictured forth do please.*

> " *Art not ashamed to publish thy disease?*
> *Nay, that may breed my fame, it is so rare:*
> *But will not wise men thinke thy words fond ware?*
> *Then be they close, and so none shall displease.*

> " *What idler thing, then speake and not be hard?*
> *What harder thing then smart, and not to speake?*
> *Peace foolish wit, with wit my wit is mard.*

> " *Thus write I while I doubt to write, and wreake*
> *My harmes on Inks poore losse, perhaps some find*
> *Stellas great powrs, that so confuse my mind.*"

Sometimes the poetry achieves the magic of sheer incantation (" A rosy garland and a weary head "); memorable lines abound (" A kind of grace it is to slay with speed." . . . " And love doth hold my hand, and makes me write "); and occasionally, it must be owned, it descends to conceits as false as any from that exuberant and conceitful age (" Her flesh his food, her skin his armour brave "). The ever-continuing struggle in the frustrated lover between the desires of the flesh and the final emancipation of the spirit runs like a *leit-motiv* throughout the sequence. But the emancipation is prevented by the abrupt conclusion (at Sonnet 108) in a night of " most rude despair." We may assume that more was intended : this is clear both from the unsatisfactory nature of the termination of the sequence and from the fact that two songs and sonnets closely bearing on the theme were printed, with some occasional verses, in the folio edition. Perhaps no more was written after Sidney's own marriage, in 1583, with Frances Walsingham. However that may have been, these two sonnets make it sufficiently clear that the sequence should have ended, not in despair, but in deliverance.

" *Thou blind mans marke, thou fooles selfe chosen snare,*
Fond fancies scum, and dregs of scattered thought,
Bond of all evils, cradle of causelesse care,
Thou web of will, whose end is never wrought.

" *Desire, desire I have too dearely bought,*
With prise of mangled mind thy worthlesse ware,
Too long, too long asleepe thou hast me brought,
Who should my mind to higher things prepare.

" *But yet in vaine thou hast my ruine sought,*
In vaine thou madest me to vaine things aspire,
In vain thou kindlest all thy smokie fire.

" *For vertue hath this better lesson taught,*
Within myselfe to seeke my onelie hire :
Desiring nought but how to kill desire."

And :

" *Leave me O Love, which reachest but to dust,*
And thou my mind aspire to higher things :
Grow rich in that which never taketh rust :
What ever fades, but fading pleasure brings.

> " *Draw in thy beames, and humble all thy might*
> *To that sweet yoke where lasting freedomes be:*
> *Which breakes the clowdes and opens forth the light.*
> *That doth both shine and give us sight to see.*
>
> " *O take fast hold, let that light be thy guide,*
> *In this small course which birth drawes out to death,*
> *And think how evill becommeth him to slide,*
>
> " *Who seeketh heav'n, and comes of heav'nly breath.*
> *Then farewell world, thy uttermost I see,*
> *Eternall Love maintaine thy life in me.*"

Nor is it accidental that the second of these sonnets should be the finest poem Sidney ever wrote: it is the full and perfect utterance of that ideal towards which all his life had been purposely directed, the expression in words of that renunciation of which Zutphen was the expression in deed.

For Sidney was essentially a religious man. It was this, far more than the unusual keenness of his intellect, which bound him to Languet. If Languet was sometimes inclined to be fussy and over-solicitous, Sidney could smile without slackening his very real affection: he knew, only too well, how few they were who could offer genuine encouragement the way he was going.

It was probably also this religious temperament, this invulnerable sincerity, far more than any vacillations of the Queen, which accounted for his continued inactivity when men of much less worth were up and doing. It is quite possible that Elizabeth knew her Philip better than Languet knew him—better even than, at that time, he knew himself. He might seem to chafe at her unwillingness to make any use of him; but she was not looking for men of integrity to fulfil her obscure purposes. Sidney was not only far too influential abroad: he was also too fundamentally honest at home. Looking back a little, she could remember, for instance, that occasion when he had had the effrontery to reproach her publicly for her continued determination (as it then seemed) to marry Anjou: ". . . Carrying no other olive branches of intercession but the laying of myself at your feet, nor no other insinuation either for attention or pardon but the true and avowed sacrifice of unfeigned love, I will in simple and direct terms set down the overflowing of my mind." Simplicity and directness were not exactly the qualities most freely smiled upon by her Majesty. Or she could remember his refusal, in 1581, to take any share of those recusant forfeitures (instituted after an Act had been passed on the recommendation of a Committee on which he himself had sat) whereby fines of £20 a month were imposed for abstention from the Anglican Service. " Truly I like not their persons," he had said, " and much worse their religions, but I think my fortune very hard that my reward must be built on other men's punishments." There was evidently no pleasing such a man. He had all the unhesitating courage of his contemporaries, but nothing would have persuaded him to exploit that courage in a cause out of harmony with his convictions. " For me," he said, " I can not promise of my course . . . because I know there is a Higher Power that must uphold me or else I shall fall."

He finally gave his life, not so much in the service of his Queen, as in an attempt to avert the threatened ascendancy of a Catholic Spain over a Protestant Europe. " If her Majesty were the only fountain I fear that we should wax dry. But she is but a means whom God useth. . . ." Elizabeth would not view too pleasantly such diminutions of her power. No wonder that when the news of his death reached her, her grief sounded a little hollow. It even seemed rather unnecessary that he should have died at all. She complained to Blount afterwards that it was wasteful for a gentleman to let himself get killed like a common soldier. . . . Elizabeth never guessed what a torch she had lighted to flare down the ages. For Zutphen (and she had only made him Governor of Flushing as a sop for having dragged him back from his proposed expedition with Drake) was destined to become the symbol in all men's minds of one " sublimely mild, a spirit without spot." Strange that he, a quiet man in an age of action, should have been the only Elizabethan of noble rank to die in battle. Stranger still that in such a death he should have made his greatest claim to that sublime mildness the poet praised. It had been Leicester's hope, by securing the reduction of Zutphen, to gain control of the Yssel. He took Norris and Sidney (who, incidentally, had already shown the manner of his courage by capturing Axel without a single loss of life) along with him. But his plan of attack was forestalled by Parma, who decided to try to get a three months' supply of provisions into the town. When Leicester learned of this, from a Spanish prisoner, he ordered the interception of the convoy. Some three hundred horse and two hundred foot took up their position a mile and a half outside the town. Through the mists of daybreak, on October 2, 1586, the convoy was heard approaching. It was found to consist of three thousand men. The struggle that ensued was as brave as it was futile. Three times the English broke through the enemies' lines; and in the third charge, Sidney, who had already had one horse shot under him and who, from an exaggerated sense of chivalry, had thrown off his thigh-pieces because he saw the veteran Sir William Pelham riding without any, was struck by a musket-ball three inches above the knee. He was carried to the English camp, and it was while he was being thus painfully conveyed that the immortal gesture was made. But it was in the agonising days which followed that Sidney showed to the full that courage which, in his case, was truly a triumph of the spirit over the flesh.

"When they began to dress his wounds," wrote Greville, " he . . . told them that while his strength was still entire, his body free from fever, and his mind able to endure, they might freely use their art, cut, and search to the bottom. For besides his hope of health, he would make this farther profit of the pains which he must suffer, that they should bear witness they had indeed a sensible natured man under their hands, yet one to whom a stronger Spirit had given power above himself, either to do or suffer."

Some days later he sent for various ministers of religion and requested them to discuss with him the immortality of the soul. Of the last day of all, Gifford, one of these ministers, has left a full and most moving account.

" . . . It was proved to him by testimonies and infallible reasons out of the Scriptures that, although his understanding and senses should fail, yet that faith, which he had now, could not fail, but would hold still the power and victory before God: yes, in that respect all one as if he had his senses and understanding. At this he did with a cheerful and smiling countenance put forth his hand and clapt me softly on the cheeks. Not long after he lift up his eyes and hands, uttering these words, ' I would not change my joy for the empire of the world.' "

And so, some six weeks short of his thirty-second year, he died, of whom his father had written, years before, " In troth, I speak it without flattery of him or of myself, he hath the most rare virtues that ever I found in any man. "

JOHN FOXE

1516–1587

By

HUGH MASSINGHAM

"He must have little spirit who thinks that a spirit is nothing."—St. Bernard.

JOHN FOXE

by HUGH MASSINGHAM

FOXE is famous as the author of *The Book of Martyrs*, once a work to be found in every good Protestant home, but now even more neglected than the Bible. There are, indeed, few things more striking in the history of literature than the popularity Foxe enjoyed in his lifetime and long afterwards, and the neglect with which he is treated to-day. It is not only that he devotes a great deal of space to nice theological points that are no longer of fashionable or popular interest. On the top of his theology, his naïvety, his verboseness, his pages of unimaginative prose, he uses a violence of language that shocks an age which prides itself upon its scientific and accurate interpretation of facts. Foxe is partisan and violently partisan. He is a fighter and not a refined observer looking at a riot from the safety of the drawing-room window.

In the sixteenth century they were not so squeamish. Protestants [1] were neither shocked by Foxe's prejudiced and vigorous way of saying things, nor bored by his long theological discussions. On the contrary, they enjoyed both. They admired his frankness, and found in his theology arguments to answer the contentions of their enemies. Foxe, indeed, stands to the Protestant movement as Tom Paine stands to the American Revolution. He was the great Protestant journalist of the Tudor period; and in a sense he is the first great journalist in English history. Because he wrote books and not for newspapers is no reason why we should hesitate to say that he was a journalist. Like all the great editors of the nineteenth century Foxe thought of himself as a preacher first, a propagandist, and as a literary man second, if he ever thought of himself as a literary man at all.

[1] Puritan is the word that really fits the people I am describing, but unfortunately it does not come into use until very late in the sixteenth century.

He was in many ways like W. T. Stead. He had Stead's sensationalism, Stead's passion for the truth, Stead's furious intention to hit the bull's-eye; and like Stead, he sometimes hit the bull's-eye first time, and he sometimes missed it, not by a yard, but by a mile.

He could not have been the great journalist that he was had he been born rich and a nobleman. Foxe was not born with a silver spoon in his mouth, and all his life he was forced to fight against extreme poverty. He started therefore with the great advantage of knowing what the ordinary man had to contend with. He understood perfectly the fear of poverty and the shadow of unemployment. He did not see these things imaginatively, as something distant and intriguing; he had experienced them himself.

He was, of course, a Protestant. But he was far more than just intellectually sympathetic to the new movement. Although Foxe died in his bed, and although his life seems almost tranquil when compared with the terrible deaths he describes in the *Book of Martyrs*, he suffered for his religion socially as most Protestants did during the Tudor period. He has indeed nothing in common with Thomas Cromwell, whom he so much admires. Foxe praises Cromwell for protecting Protestants and for weakening the power of the Church; but he does not see that Cromwell is only using Protestantism for political ends, and that he has no real understanding of what it means and no sympathy with its objects. Henry VIII and Elizabeth had the same attitude as Cromwell. They protected Protestantism when they found it useful, but they had no intention of giving all Protestant forms complete religious freedom or a proper influence politically. Elizabeth was deeply offended by the democratic speeches of Wentworth and put him in the Tower. The more she perceived how Protestantism exalted the individual by teaching that all men were equal in the sight of God, the more she feared the eruption of this sturdy independence into the political world. " No bishop, no king," said James I shortly after his accession, and his predecessors instinctively felt the democratic spirit in Protestantism, and feared and disliked it.[1] Thus while Pro-

---

[1] The political consciousness of the movement developed very rapidly. Here, for instance, is the remarkable declaration made by a committee in the House of Commons in 1604: " All free subjects are born inheritable, as to their lands, so also to the free exercise of their industry, in those trades whereto they

testantism was growing year by year, especially after the publication of the English Bibles in 1537, and was spreading upwards from the lower classes, where it was strongest, to the rich and the nobility, it was in reality being thwarted and gagged. Protestants had to wait until Oliver Cromwell became Protector before they had a man on the throne who was of their soil and filled with their deepest convictions.

Foxe, however, was Protestant in mind and feeling, and was as much a part of the political and religious revolution of Protestantism as Lenin was of the Russian Revolution.

*　　*　　*　　*　　*

He was born at Boston, Lincolnshire, in 1516, and his father died while he was still very young. Little is known about his childhood, except that he is said to have been a studious youth and very poor. He went up to Oxford when he was sixteen, and he stayed there until 1545, when he resigned his fellowship. We do not know how or when he became a Protestant. He was evidently one at Oxford. He refused to attend the College Chapel with any regularity when he was a fellow, and to proceed to holy orders within seven years of his election to his fellowship. He also objected to the enforcement of celibacy, and his resignation in 1545 seems to have been for religious reasons.

Very little, either, is known about what he did after he left Oxford. He first became tutor to young Thomas Lucy, and towards the end of 1547, the year in which he married, he was appointed tutor to the orphan children of the Earl of Surrey. Between then and the time he escaped to Strasbourg for fear of being persecuted by Mary, he was writing religious tracts and plays, as well as reading Church History with the idea of doing a defence of Protestantism.

According to a book written after his death, under his son's name but almost certainly a fake, he had gone through periods of extreme poverty while in England, and he was desperately poor while in exile. Foxe, indeed, never seems to have had any money. Even later on, after he had returned to England and was famous as the author of the *Book of Martyrs*, he remained poor. He might now have made a career for himself in the Church, for he had always had

apply themselves and whereby they are to live. Merchandise being the chief and richest of all others, and of greater extent and importance than all the rest, it is against the natural right and liberty of the subjects of England to restrain it into the hands of some few."

powerful friends. Cranmer and Tyndale, with whom he was intimate before he left England, and Ridley, who ordained him a deacon in 1530, were all dead. But Parker, under whose patronage he published an Anglo-Saxon version of the Gospels, was Archbishop of Canterbury, while Grindal, Parker's successor, both ordained him priest in 1559–60, and had helped him with part of the *Book of Martyrs* while they were both abroad. Foxe, however, had conscientious objections to the surplice, and because of them resigned a prebendary stall, first at Salisbury Cathedral, and then at Durham. But Foxe was not a narrow-minded person. Although fervently pious, he was a cheerful creature and a great lover of dogs. He was also far more tolerant than his merciless attacks on the Catholics might suggest. He was a moderating influence in the fierce religious quarrels that broke out at Frankfort, and in 1575 he did everything possible to save two Dutch Anabaptists condemned to death for their opinions, although he himself had no sympathy with their views.

*   *   *   *   *

When Foxe fled to Europe he had with him in manuscript the first part of a Latin treatise on the persecutions of reformers [1] from the time of Wycliffe to his own day. This was published while he was abroad, and forms the first part of the *Book of Martyrs*. It is the dreariest part of his work, and is not particularly valuable as history or remarkable as literature. Foxe's book does not come to life until he continues the story of the persecution of the reformers and begins to describe the sufferings of his contemporaries. Knowing from personal experience what hardships Protestants had to undergo, inflamed by stories of the cruelties of the Church and the fortitude of the heretics, he forgot his duties as an historian, and used his pen to immortalise the Protestants and to confound the Church.

The popularity of his book was instantaneous and immense; four editions were brought out in Foxe's lifetime, the first in 1563, the second in 1570, the third in 1576, and the fourth in 1583. A majority of the Protestant clergy, both then and in the seventeenth century, believed Foxe implicitly; they accepted without question his interpretation of Church history, found a boundless source of inspiration in

[1] Foxe included in his book everybody who had ever rebelled against the Church. Any stick was good enough to beat the Catholics.

the sufferings of the early Christians and Protestants, and drew fresh determination from his picture of a tyrannical and merciless Church. Innumerable sermons were preached on texts taken from his pages. The Convocation of 1571 proposed that his book should be placed in the houses of bishops, deans, dignitaries, and in cathedrals, where the *Monumenta Martyrum* was to take second place only to the Bible.

Its popularity was natural. Protestants took their stand upon the Bible, which they believed the Church had both misinterpreted and deliberately prevented Christians from reading. They had nothing else to support their opinion. They had neither centuries of tradition nor a majestic background of history to support them; and while they might not waver in their opinion, they inevitably felt at a disadvantage when arguing with the ablest of their opponents. Ridley felt, and was, the equal of the Catholic Bishop Bonner; but Ridley was an exception. The majority of the men who came before the ecclesiastical courts charged with heresy were ordinary men, with no learning, no knowledge of Greek and Roman authors, and no subtleties in their intellectual equipment. They had only read and re-read the Bible. Foxe both gave them a battery of new facts to support their case and confirmed them in the belief that they were right. He had written what he called a Church History, and there is no reason to suppose that he did not mean to produce an objective account of Christianity from the time that Jesus lived. But the history of Christianity was for Foxe the process by which the true teaching of Jesus had been deliberately falsified or deliberately kept away from the people, and he therefore saw religious development as the struggle of a few enlightened minds against the Church. This was the drama that he emphasised in his work, and that so strengthened his Protestant readers. Other qualities added to its popularity. Foxe gave Protestantism an historical background, an historical justification. Before it appeared, the majority of Protestants inevitably felt cut off from their immediate past, because they had always thought of it as Catholic, and this feeling of loneliness became all the greater when, particularly in Mary's reign, they found that their faith had turned society against them. However strongly they might feel that they were right, however much they might reflect on how the early Christians had been persecuted for their religion just as they were being persecuted now, the feeling of loneliness persisted. Foxe linked the movement up with the past. Protestants no longer felt that it was a sudden contemporary growth, but a movement as old as the Church, with a list of saints and martyrs as long and as noble as the Catholic Calendar of Saints. Foxe, when he thought of compiling a Protestant Calendar, an idea that has shocked Catholics both then and since, was prompted by an instinctive under- standing of the craving of his contemporaries to feel that the big battalions were not all Catholic ones.

*   *   *   *   *

Foxe, of course, wrote up his history, and had he stopped at putting magnificent language into the mouths of people incapable of saying the things that he records, his critics would not have found it so easy to attack him. Foxe, how- ever, sometimes juggled with facts, and both during his life and since he has been charged with being inaccurate and falsifying his evidence. His most famous critic is F. W. Maitland, who accused Foxe of being biased, copying manu- scripts hastily and inaccurately, muddling his dates, borrow- ing without acknowledgment, being vague in his references, magnifying trivial incidents into events of the utmost importance, and including among his martyrs people con- demned for secular offences. Maitland is by far the ablest and most scholarly of the critics, but before Maitland and in Foxe's lifetime, people severely criticised the accuracy of the work. Foxe himself seems to have been greatly irritated by the charge that it was " as full of lies as lines," and he made some effort to correct mistakes after Mary was dead and he was back again in England. The effort was not very thorough, and Maitland points out one glaring instance where Foxe does not correct a statement even after he found it to be untrue. Maitland's list of mistakes is a long one, but considering the difficulty under which Foxe wrote and the colossal scope of the work, it is surprising that there were not more inaccuracies. Foxe was certainly slapdash (he even forgets the date of the act of the Six Articles), and we have a right to ask a higher standard of scholarship from a man who proudly quoted Cicero's remark that " Historie is the witnesse of truth, the glasse of times."

At the same time Maitland goes too far when he tries to

suggest that Foxe is valueless as an historian. He was a most industrious worker, collecting a greater number of original documents from the bishops' registers, and preserving the stories of men who had actually seen the burnings which he describes. The pity is that he was not able to sift evidence and to reject stories that were mere malicious gossip. Foxe had not a historical mind. He had none of the objectivity of the unimaginative historian who feels that all facts are equal in the sight of God and sees events almost as if they were a row of Chinamen, alike in size, feature, and colour. He was a man of imagination; but his imagination was untrained, and he was unable, like the great historians, to use it in order to project his mind into the being of somebody whose views he might detest. Foxe was aware of his failings:

> " I heare what you will saie," he wrote to a Mr. Cope who had taxed him with inaccuracy, " I should have taken more leisure, and done it better. I graunt and confesse my fault; such is my vice, I cannot sit all the daie (Mr. Cope) fining and mincing my letters and combing my head, and smoothing myself all the daie at the glasse of Cicero. Yet notwithstanding, doing what I can, and doing my good will, me thinkes I should not be reprehended."

Maitland goes much farther than saying that Foxe was a bad historian. He attacks the whole tone of Foxe's writing, and gives as an instance of bad taste this description of St. Fráncis:

> " The order of the Minors, or minorite friars, descended from one Francis, an Italian, of the City of Assisium. This Assisian ass, who, I suppose, was some simple and rude idiot, hearing, upon a time, how Christ sent forth his disciples to preach, thought to imitate the same in himself and his disciples, and so left off his shoes. . . . He left, in writing, to his disciples and followers, his rule, which he called ' Regulum Evangelicum,' the rule of the Gospel. As though the gospel of Christ were not a sufficient rule to all Christian men, but it must take its perfection of the frantic Francis. And yet, for all that great presumption of this Francis,

and notwithstanding this his rule, sounding to the derogation of Christ's gospel, he was confirmed by this Pope Innocent. Yea, and such fools this Francis found abroad, that, not only he had followers of his doltish religion, both of the nobles and unnobles of Rome, but also some there were who builded mansions for him and his friars."

There are plenty of instances of this offensive language in the *Book of Martyrs*, and it is not all written by Foxe. The martyrs themselves are sometimes even more vigorous. For instance, a man called Filmer, who was charged with heresy, said that if the sacrament were no more than a sign, then he had eaten twenty gods in his lifetime. Another attacked a priest who was holding the chalice and struck him on the head with a wood knife. A third wrote to Bishop Bonner, who was not the bloody tyrant that Foxe makes him out to be, telling him that—

" You are the common cut-throat and general slaughter-slave of all the bishops of England ; and therefore it is wisdom, for we and all other simple sheep of the Lord, to keep us out of your butcher's stall as long as we can."

These remarks, together with Foxe's description of St. Francis, should not be judged without reference to the age in which they were spoken. Men naturally expressed themselves more vituperously in the sixteenth century than they do now. The present generation is more scientific, and we are so self-conscious in our empirical attitude to life, that we have lost the power to believe in any particular case passionately. We are like the cautious professor who, when asked if a certain sheep were white, replied, " It is white on this side." We feel easier with a footnote to support every statement. At the same time our passion for objectivity has really given us an understanding of the other man's case, and therefore we instinctively dislike hearing anyone abused. No modern person can read Foxe without immediately reacting against his consistent unfairness, and without feeling that there is a case for the Church which Foxe has not put. Indeed, the reports of the trials that Foxe gives show how humane the judges were, how anxious to save the accused. We do not have to know the Catholic Bishop Bonner was not the monster that Foxe says to prove that the *Book of Martyrs* gives only one side of the picture.

Foxe had every reason to feel strongly about the Catholics. He not only hated the Church intellectually. He felt that it had prevented people from understanding what Christianity really was, as revealed in the Bible. He hated it because of what it had done to himself and his friends. Foxe had gone in fear of his life. He had been forced to live in exile. His friends had been burnt at the stake. He had no certainty that the Church might not yet be triumphant, that the same scenes might not be re-enacted, and that he himself might not be one of the victims. Foxe felt about the Catholics as we feel about Hitlerism, and a man filled with forebodings, who was a participant in the struggle, and not an aloof spectator of it, could not be expected to take up such a commendable attitude of objectivity as the tolerant and comfortable Protestants and atheists of the twentieth century.

The offensiveness of some of the accused during their trials was not solely because they were uneducated men who would naturally express themselves more outspokenly than Foxe. The reports suggest that their most objectionable phrases were spoken, partly out of defiance, partly out of contempt for what they considered the sophistry of their opponents; but sometimes the heretics seem to have been deliberately insolent in order to break a kind of net that they felt the Catholics were drawing round them. Foxe calls the Catholic judges " subtle," and they were certainly subtle in the sense that they supported their case by reference to a wealth of knowledge that the accused lacked. It is no reflection on the sincere humanity of the judges to say that their reluctance to condemn heretics was not disinterested; their great object was to win them back to Catholicism, and the accused being well aware of this intention, saw in this kindness only a Machiavellian method of seduction. The offensiveness of a man like Filmer is a kind of defence and a way to avoid being drawn, step by step, into an intellectual position where a denial of his faith was inevitable. The accused purposely insulted their judges so that they could cut short their trials and avoid long intellectual argument in which they might have to acknowledge with their minds what their hearts told them was false. Hence the brutality of their language and their relief at seeing the stake.

*   *   *   *   *

If Foxe was a bad historian, he had great qualities as a propagandist, and he did more than he is given credit for in bringing the people of England out of the old churches and into the new. He was a single-hearted creature. He loved few things and he loved them passionately. He wrote at all times about the things that afflicted men's hearts, and he wrote of them in a language that everybody could understand. But he did more than write simply. Foxe wrote about simple people for simple people. Kings, bishops, prelates, and aristocrats move indeed through his pages, and the records of their sins or achievements take up much of his space. But in the main, the *Book of Martyrs* is the story of how the ordinary man defied his oppressors, revealed unsuspected heroic qualities, and eventually won immortality. The butcher, the baker, the labourer, the carpenter, these are the heroes of the *Book of Martyrs*, just as they are the important characters in the gospels. No one who read Foxe felt out of his depth. No one could feel that he was reading about unreal people who moved in an orbit infinitely remote from the reader's. No one could feel that his stories were just romances. Everybody knew Foxe's martyrs. They were not like the remote St. Cecilie, whom Chaucer describes as " hevenes lilie," " of noble kinde," and on whose behalf heaven intervened at the moment of trial. They were simply the people that the reader met every day of his life, and angels never intervened to save them from the torment of the stake. They were reassuringly earthy. Just as everybody can understand St. Peter and very few people can sympathise with Herod, so the man that read the *Book of Martyrs* felt instantly that he knew all about the characters who are the heroes of Foxe's narrative. They were actually his father and his mother, his brother and his sister, his friends and his beloved.

There are other reasons why the *Book of Martyrs* became so popular. Like Bunyan, indeed, like a great deal of the teaching of Jesus, the book appealed both to men's sense of excitement and drama as well as to their religious nature. The *Book of Martyrs* is a wonderful book, not only because it is the record of man's suffering and a picture of his nobility in the moment of passion and trial, but because it also contains stories just as dramatic as the stories chosen by a novelist. Foxe was a born story-teller. He was verbose, ribald, and cantankerous in his argumentative passages, but when he came to description he wrote with great power, and great simplicity. Take, for instance, this well-known and moving description of the death of Dr. Taylor, the Vicar of Hadleigh :

" Now when the sheriff and his company came against St. Botolph's church, Elizabeth cried, saying, ' O my dear Father! Mother! mother! here is my father led away.' Then cried his wife, ' Rowland, Rowland, where art thou? '—for it was a very dark morning, that the one could not see the other. Dr. Taylor answered, ' Dear wife, I am here,' and stayed. The sheriff's men would have led him forth, but the sheriff said, ' Stay a little, masters, I pray you, and let him speak with his wife.' . . . Then came she to him, and he took his daughter Mary in his arms, and he, his wife and Elizabeth kneeled down and said the Lord's Prayer. At which sight the sheriff wept apace, and so did divers other of the company. After they had prayed he rose up and kissed his wife and shook her by the hand, and said, ' Farewell, my good wife, and be of good comfort, for I am quiet in my conscience. God shall stir up a father for my children.' And then he kissed his daughter Mary, and said, ' God bless thee and make thee his servant ' : and kissing Elizabeth, he said, ' God bless thee.' . . . All the way Dr. Taylor was joyful and merry as one that accounted himself going to a pleasant banquet or bridal. . . . Coming within a two mile of Hadleigh he desired to light off his horse, which done he leaped and set a frisk or twain, as men commonly do in dancing. ' Why, master Doctor,' quoth the sheriff, ' How do you now? ' He answered, ' Well, God be praised, master sheriff, never better; for now I know I am almost at home. I lack not past two styles to go over, and I am even at my father's house.' "

No one can read this simple account of Dr. Taylor's martyrdom without being profoundly moved, and there are a thousand Dr. Taylors in Foxe's pages. The reading of these stories, most of them showing the spotless virtue of Protestants and the monstrous villainy of Roman Catholics, inevitably inflamed men's passions, increased the hatred of Protestants for the Church, and thus helped to delay the coming of religious toleration. At the same time they taught men something about Protestantism that was not to be found in more learned and profound treatises. They taught him the power of the spirit to redeem man. Unlike Calvin, who wanted to take men out of one ecclesiastical pen only to shepherd them into another ruled by himself, Foxe instinctively knew that Protestantism is an affair of the spirit, and nothing but an affair of the spirit. It is simply what George Santayana calls in another connection the " weather of the soul." Other beliefs have their dogmas and their creeds, landmarks by the aid of which the spiritual traveller can find his way; Protestants have nothing but the word of the Bible, and the promptings of their conscience. This inner light needed to be nourished, not only by constant meditation and prayer, but also by the study of the lives of the saints, and the early Protestants found in the records of the innumerable martyrs in Foxe's pages a source both of inspiration and comfort. They were amazed afresh by the immense power of spiritual passion, they longed to be given a similar opportunity of " witnessing to the truth," and as they read of the sufferings of the martyrs they determined to endure the persecution that they themselves had to contend with.

Constant study of the Bible led them to believe that they had discovered the real intention of God, and in consequence they arrogated to themselves an infallibility that they denied to the Pope. There are plenty of instances of arrogance in Foxe's work, for the *Book of Martyrs* records the faults as well as the virtues of Protestantism. But if a conviction that we must live as our hearts tell us to live led some Protestants to fall into spiritual arrogance, it also gave them the most amazing fortitude and transformed ordinary men into heroes and saints. Take, for instance, the case of Rawlins White. White was a poor devil of a fisherman who became a Protestant in the reign of Edward VI. According to Foxe he was " altogether unlearned," and had to get his son to read the Bible to him. During Mary's reign, he was seized, and after spending a year in Cardiff Castle, he was eventually brought to trial and condemned to be burnt. When the day of execution came, White put on what he called his " wedding garment," which was his shirt, and protested against the large troop of guards that had been sent to carry him to the stake, for, he said, he had no wish to escape and thanked God that " He hath made me

worthy to abide all this." The poor man broke down when
he saw his wife and children weeping in the street, and it
was some minutes before he could muster up his courage to
go on. When he came to the stake he fell down on his knees
and kissed the ground, and on finding that some earth
remained on his face, he cried out, " Earth unto Earth, and
dust unto dust; thou art my mother, and to thee I shall
return." He then went " very joyfully and set his back very
close unto the stake," and waited for them to burn him.
Just before his time came, he grew afraid lest his courage
should desert him, and catching sight of a friend in the
crowd he called out:

> " I feel a great fight between the flesh and the spirit,
> and the flesh would very fain have his swing; and there-
> fore I pray you, when you see me anything tempted,
> hold your finger up to me, and I trust I shall remember
> myself."

Nor did Protestantism manifest itself only in militant
examples of martyrdom. The detractors of Protestantism
have so underlined the Puritan sense of sin and so exaggera-
ated the number of works of art that a small minority of
Ironsides destroyed that many people have come to believe
that Protestantism was on the whole a bad influence,
oppressing men's hearts and twisting their imagination.
For instance, everybody knows Bunyan's cry of the soul
when he thinks his sins have eternally cut him off from God,
whereas fewer people know of what George Fox felt when,
sitting by the fire, he was " beset " by " a great cloud " of
temptation:

> " And as I sat still under it and let it alone, a living
> hope rose in me, and a true voice rose in me which
> cried: There is a living God who made all things. And
> immediately the cloud and temptation vanished away,
> and the life rose over it all, and my heart was glad, and
> I praised the living God."

The *Book of Martyrs* is essentially the story of how " the life
rose over it all " to refresh men's faith in their own goodness.
Foxe, of course, is not primarily concerned with the gentler
side of Protestantism, and he makes no particular effort to

bring it out in his narrative. He is concerned with the way
Protestants behaved when given the choice of death or the
renunciation of their convictions; he uses all his power to
bring out the tremendous heroism they showed in the
supreme trial of their lives. Foxe is perfectly right to stress
the sterner side, for had Protestantism not been a militant
force it could never have triumphed, Charles I would not
have lost his head, and the subsequent history of England
would have been very different. But Protestants did not—
as we might think after reading Foxe—spend all their time in
being martyrs, in defying bishops, and in thinking of their
souls. They thought of the goodness of God as well as of
the punishment of being "secluded eternally, eternally,
eternally from the sight of God." Read again, both for the
beauty of the language and the calm assurance of its spirit,
the conversation Ridley wrote shortly before he died and
which Foxe quotes. It is remarkable first of all for his
scrupulous fairness to the Catholic point of view. It is
remarkable for the warmth and moderation of his language.
And finally it is remarkable for a humility and tenderness
that comes out most forcibly at the end in the moving words
of Latimer:

> " Pardon me, and pray for me, I say. For I am
> sometimes so fearful that I would creep into a mouse-
> hole; sometimes God doth visit me again with his com-
> fort. So he cometh and goeth, to teach me to feel and
> know my infirmity, to the intent to give thanks to him
> that is worthy, lest I should rob him of his due, as many
> do, and almost the whole world. Fare ye well."

These are the passages that suddenly illuminate Foxe's
pages. The *Book of Martyrs* is in many ways an ugly book
with its story of intolerance and cruelty. But it is also an
invigorating one. Read it again for the light it throws upon
the feeling of his time. But read it above all for the unforgettable picture it gives of the fortitude of man. Because of
this it is more than an interesting historical document; it is
a book for all ages and conditions of men. And it may
perhaps have more to say to this generation than we imagine.

" The present time," says Mark Rutherford in *Miriam's
Schooling*, " is disposed to overrate the intellectual

virtues.   No matter how unselfish a woman may be, if she cannot discuss the new music or the new metaphysical poetry, she is nothing and nobody cares for her. Centuries ago our standard was different, and it will have to be different again.   We shall, it is to be hoped, spend ourselves not in criticism of the record of the saints who sat by the sepulchre, but we shall love as they loved."

MARY STEWART,
QUEEN OF SCOTLAND
1542–1587

By
MARJORIE BOWEN

MARY STEWART, QUEEN OF SCOTLAND

by MARJORIE BOWEN

MARY STEWART was not in herself a very remarkable woman, but her circumstances made her appear so. There is no indication in her character that she would have become notable by reason of her own personal qualities. Fair, high-spirited, indiscreet, and ardent women were common enough in the aristocracy of the Renaissance, have been common enough in any sheltered, idle, luxurious class. Of political acumen, of elevated patriotism, of selfless, far-seeing devotion to a cause or to an ideal, Mary Stewart showed no trace. Her little accomplishments of verse-making, lute-playing, dancing, fine needlework, have largely to be taken on trust, and at best, could have been matched by any well-bred lady of her time. Her seductive charm has become largely fabulous; the authority for it rests in great part on the studied eulogies of courtiers, or the tributes of men like Brantôme, writing in their old age of youthful memories. Her few authentic portraits give us no more than that " pleasing face of a gentlewoman " which was John Knox's description of his sovereign's countenance.

But because she was placed in such an extraordinary situation, because her story contains the crude elements of apparent romance, love episodes, murders, imprisonments, escapes, plots, a violent death, legends have clustered thickly round her personality; she has been dramatised and sentimentalised until it is extremely difficult to see her even with that small degree of truth that is the most we can hope for when looking back at the great figures of history.

The most important parts of her story are obscure, and will always be matter for controversy among the many, and for fanatic bitterness and acrid partisanship among the few.

Mary Stewart was, politically, of importance because of her position, and not because of her character or attainments. As queen of one country and heiress to another she was, all her life, of great interest to European statesmen, and during the last years of her imprisonment she became a very powerful factor in the Roman Catholic effort to effect a counter-reformation in England; it has been said, probably without exaggeration, that the whole of Elizabeth Tudor's policy revolved round Mary of Scotland. It has also been said, with equal truth, that Mary's failures—her almost incredible misfortunes—rested within herself; she had not the qualities necessary for success in a position of bewildering and intricate difficulty. We may admit as much, but we should also concede that very few women indeed would have been able to succeed where Mary failed. It is indeed doubtful if any Roman Catholic girl of nineteen, foreign-bred, without disinterested advisers, could have achieved the task of ruling well and wisely the Protestant Scotland which Mary found when she landed at Leith in 1561. It is perhaps not likely that many women in Mary's position would have made the terrible mistake of marrying a man implicated in the murder of a husband, but, on the other hand, it is extremely unlikely that any woman, trying to queen it in Holyrood, would have escaped some amorous entanglement, some snare of bloody violence that would have brought her to ruin as swiftly as the Rizzio, Darnley, Bothwell imbroglio brought Mary to disaster. If her imprudence seems startling, it is probably because we do not sufficiently realise her background or the atmosphere in which she moved. This typical woman of the late Renaissance is too often viewed either in the fairy-tale light of legend, or through the sentimental pages of nineteenth-century refinement.

The first step towards understanding Mary is to understand her period; she was neither the heroine of a ballad, nor a Victorian lady in distressing circumstances. Nor was she that poetic conception, an ethereal creature seeking an ideal lover and continuously betrayed by love. Her choice of husbands seems stupid beyond belief, until we consider the men who surrounded her, the men who were offered to her as possible lovers or consorts. Her actions were those of a woman always tormented, often desperate, driven by circumstances and her own temperament into horrible difficulties, and extricating herself by the wit, courage, and falsehood born of necessity. Stripped of the trappings given it by fiction writers and poets, her story is not noble or beautiful, nor, in the true sense of the word, romantic. The motives of all concerned in her downfall, and as far as we know them, her own, were too brutal and sordid for her tragedy to have real dignity or pathos. Even if she were as brilliantly innocent as her most fanatic admirers would have us believe she was, her conduct during the crisis of her fortunes was too wilful, foolish, and opportunist to be really admirable or moving. Her royal position demanded an impossible virtue, a self-respect, a self-control, a fortitude, and a dignity that no young woman could have been expected to possess, but Mary's behaviour fell disastrously below even a moderate standard of queenly decorum. It was the old story of Cæsar's wife; what did it matter if she was really spotless?—she gave *cause* for a blaze of scandal in Europe and was cast out of her own country, despoiled of everything, to the last shred of reputation. Nor was she wholly the victim of the lies of her rivals and enemies; even the impartial observer, the friendly well-wisher, might in all honesty have thought that it was a murderess, an adulteress, a treacherous liar who fled across the Solway after the Langside defeat in 1568. Du Croc, the French ambassador, who was desirous, from every point of view, of championing Mary, observed that her personal appeal to the King of France would be of little avail—" since the unhappy facts are too well known." Those then who had cause to dislike or to fear the Queen of Scots, had plenty of excuse for violently decrying her, and the plain man and woman every reason for regarding the discrowned ruler with doubt and suspicion.

Imprisonment and death were, in this age, the results of political failure—they were also the punishments for domestic crime. Mary had not succeeded in ruling Scotland, and she could hardly have hoped to escape the penalty her ancestors had paid for failure in the same task. As a woman she had recklessly misjudged and mishandled her affairs, and could, as a private person, not have expected to escape censure and punishment. Her only chance of escape from being damaged by embarrassing charges would have been in her strength as a ruler; a Sophie of Anhalt, with a Potemkin by her side, might have lived down or glossed over a scandal like Kirk o' Field. But Mary was a weak, a dethroned, sovereign, and therefore could not afford to disregard conventional standards of morality. What protection, what measure of safety she had, she owed to her sole possession—the name of queen. If, like Alice Arden, she had been arraigned with her lover for murder of her husband before an English jury, her fate would surely have been the same as that of the murderous wife of Faversham. She was fortunate that, as a queen who made a headlong failure of politics, she escaped by flight the instant vengeance of her enemies, and fortunate that, as a woman, she was never put on trial for her supposed crimes, but allowed to die when these were almost forgotten and changed circumstances had given her the dignity of a martyr.

So much warm sympathy and tender sentiment has been expended over Mary Stewart, the facts of her long imprisonment and violent death seem in themselves so atrocious, there is something so touching in the slow wearing away of her youth and beauty in hopeless pining, that to consider her case logically is to be adjudged hard, or prejudiced in favour of Protestantism and Queen Elizabeth. If, however, any attempt is to be made to present an even partially true portrait (the whole truth will surely be for ever concealed) of this much-discussed character, the pity allowed to the poet, the championship permitted to the novelist, must be discarded. Mary's appeal, of femininity, of beauty, of misfortune, is wholly to the heart, and the heart is a bad guide for the historian.

Mary's life was, from first to last, dramatic and unfortunate; she was born in 1542, a week before her father, James V, died at the age of thirty in Falkland Castle, overwhelmed by the disastrous relationship with England that had culminated in the defeat of the Scots at Solway Moss, November 1542. James V was directly descended from Robert the Steward (reigned 1371–90); the Kings of this House had all been able men, quite the equal of contemporary sovereigns; their misfortunes, the violent deaths of many of them, might rather be ascribed to long minorities, the power of the Barons, the fiery independent spirit of the Scots, and the rudeness of the times, rather than to any marked incapacity of their own. James IV (reigned 1488–1513) was a notable Prince, under whose rule Scotland flourished in what was afterwards regarded as a Golden Age; he was a great builder, a founder of three Universities, a patron of Literature, an ambitious ruler. He married

Margaret, daughter of Henry VII (1503), and was slain fighting against the forces of his brother-in-law at Flodden (1513). This King was Mary Stewart's grandfather; from his wife, Margaret Tudor, Mary derived the dangerous claim to the English throne, which was the root of most of her grandeur and most of her troubles. During the minority of James V (1513–42) this Queen-Mother Margaret complicated the claims to the Scottish succession by marrying and then divorcing the turbulent Earl of Angus, to whom she bore a daughter, Margaret, afterwards married to Mathew Stewart, Earl of Lennox.

James V married in succession two French Princesses; the "Auld Alliance" with France was a strong element in Scottish policy, and the menacing attitude of Henry VIII did much to strengthen this ancient connection. Mary Stewart was the only child to survive infancy of the second marriage, that of James V with Mary of Guise, daughter of the great House of Lorraine and widow of the Duc de Longueville.

The dispute that had led to Solway Moss was caused by an attempt on the part of Henry VIII to force his nephew to set up the tenets of the Reformation in Scotland, to defy the Pope and despoil the monasteries, which had absorbed an enormous share of the country's wealth. James V, however, was a sincere Roman Catholic, and his principal adviser was David Beaton, the Cardinal Archbishop of St. Andrew's. This strong and able prelate was the principal adviser to the widowed Mary of Guise, and crowned the infant Queen a year after her father's death. The Regent was the heir-presumptive to the throne, the head of the Hamiltons, the Earl of Arran. This nobleman was inclined to Protestantism and the English alliance, and Mary, despite her mother's opposition, would have been betrothed to Prince Edward (Edward VI) had not King Henry's terms been couched in a manner completely insulting to the proud Scots. Upon the breaking off of the marriage treaty (1543) Henry VIII invaded and devastated Scotland; for six years (1544–50) the war (continued after Henry's death, 1547, by the Protector Somerset) harried the Scots with every horror of fire and sword. The little Queen, in the safe retreats of Inchmahome and Dumbarton, lived peacefully in the midst of these turmoils; her mother and Beaton leaned naturally to the French alliance, and in 1548 Mary, with an elegant

15

retinue and the little playmates who bore her name, was sent to France to be educated by her maternal grandmother, the austere and virtuous Antoinette de Bourbon, and her celebrated uncles, the soldier Prince and the Cardinal Prince of the powerful and ambitious House of Guise.

Mary was warmly received by the King of France, Henri II, and from what we know of the childhood that she spent mostly on the fine estates of Joinville, it was happy, uneventful, and full of promise. The child who was in such an exalted and strange position was praised by all as lovely, charming, docile, and accomplished. Two lessons, at least, her Guise relations taught her—a firm adherence to her hereditary faith and an intense pride of birth.

While the young Queen was growing up under the influence of the haughty members of the House of Lorraine, her mother was endeavouring to stem the rising forces of Protestantism in Scotland. Lutheranism had for some years begun to attract the sturdy spirit of the Scottish commoner, and the nobles looked with greedy eyes on the swollen possessions of the Church. The Government was weak, and outbursts of fanaticism roused and focused popular discontents. Cardinal Beaton had been murdered (in revenge for the death of the Protestant, George Wishart) in his own castle two years before Mary went to France; John Knox was with his murderers, who were sent to the galleys in 1548; after nineteen months of this slavery he was released by English intercession, resided for a while at the court of Edward VI, then retired to Geneva and the counsels of Jean Calvin. By 1555 Knox, a furious firebrand of a man, was back in Scotland rejoicing over the rapidly increasing power of Protestantism. To counteract this English Protestant tendency, Henri II induced Arran to accept a French Dukedom (Châteauheralt), and to resign the Regency to the loyal, brave, and single-minded Mary of Guise. In 1558 Mary Stewart married François, the Dauphin, with great pomp in the Cathedral of Notre Dame, Paris. The bride was admired for her beauty, sweetness, and amiable grace; the bridegroom, a swart lad of nineteen, bore pitiful marks of degeneracy—stammering, frail, in constant pain, he was already a victim to the tuberculosis that was in a short time to kill him. Mary seems to have been fond of her unhappy husband; she was kind and affectionate with him, and nursed devotedly his increasing illness.

On this occasion of her marriage she entered politics with an act of treachery which showed either the foolishness of a girl or the double-dealing of a false nature. She signed Scotland away, by a secret document, to her father-in-law, while the Scottish Commissioners who had come to France to protect their country were fobbed off by a sham undertaking which Mary privately promised not to honour. Doubtless the young bride acted under the influence of her relations; but in thus endeavouring to reduce her kingdom to an appanage of France, like Brittany, in thus, as the first act of her reign, deliberately tricking her subjects, she gave no indication of either the brilliant intellect or the generous heart she was supposed to possess. In 1559 Henri II was killed in an accident, and Mary and François became joint sovereigns of Scotland and France. Her father-in-law had done her one disservice in advising her to adopt the style, arms, and liveries of Queen of England on the death of Mary Tudor in 1558. Elizabeth was, in the opinion of all Roman Catholics, illegitimate, and Mary Stewart was the rightful sovereign of England; but to assert these claims was a meaningless flourish on the part of Henri II, and roused a bitter resentment and a deep suspicion in Elizabeth Tudor that she never overcame.

The return of Knox to Scotland in 1559 was the signal for a Protestant rebellion that Mary of Guise was powerless to repress; when she died in 1560 (a great personal grief to her daughter), the triumphant Protestants established the Reformed Church, and " the Lords of the Congregation " assumed the government of the country, with only a technical acknowledgement of the sovereignty of Mary and her husband. This was the end of the Roman Church and the French alliance in Scotland; the Lords, chief among whom was James Stewart, Mary's half-brother, gorged themselves with Church lands, and looked to Elizabeth for support, money, and counsel.

The death from tuberculosis of the young François II in 1560 left Mary in a desolate position; the new King, Charles IX, was a child, the power of the House of Guise was in eclipse, and Catherine de Medicis, the Queen-Mother, disliked her daughter-in-law. The Queen of Scots, who had won golden opinions by her beauty, meekness, discretion, and dignity, refused to ratify the treaty of Edinburgh, made between England and the rebel Lords, thereby

incurring the increased enmity of Elizabeth, and returned to
Scotland, August 1561. She had refused an invitation
from the Earl of Huntly, Cock o' the North, brought by
Leslie, Bishop of Ross, to attempt to restore her faith by force,
but acquiesced, probably on the advice of her Guise kinsmen
in the Protestant establishment; she made the able and
avaricious Lord James, her half-brother, her principal
adviser, and submitted to a state of affairs that punished
with death a second attendance at Mass. She could barely
obtain a reluctant consent for the private exercise of her own
worship in Holyrood, and signed decrees banishing monks
and nuns under severe penalties. Her figure is here
shadowy; she seems to have been passive in the hands of the
Lord James and his party, very willing to please her Protestant subjects, eager to court Elizabeth, full of high spirits
and pretty ways. She had brought a French retinue with
her, and their luxurious elegance and her own frivolous
amusements proved ample material for the eloquence of
John Knox to embellish into a picture of " Venus and all her
crew." The fiery reformer was probably half-insane, and
there is no evidence whatever that Mary had learnt any
vices in France or that her diversions in Holyrood were not
wholly innocent. So far did she go in complacence to her
half-brother and the Lords, that she rode herself against her
rebellious subject and co-religionist, the Earl of Huntly, and
appeared to rejoice at the ruin of the Gordons and the
Roman Catholic North. She gave the Lord James the title
of Earl of Moray (Murray) and endured patiently perpetual
schemes and counter-schemes for her second marriage.
Her nerves were galled raw by the intricate disputes as to her
future husband; the same question as that which was also exasperating Elizabeth almost beyond endurance. With these
speculations was joined that of the successions to the two
Kingdoms: would Elizabeth die unwed or childless, and
Mary and Catholicism inherit England, or would Elizabeth
and Protestantism swallow up, one way or another, Scotland? Moray, and even more definitely Sir William Maitland, most brilliant of Scottish politicians, were working
towards England and the tenets of the Reformation; Mary,
passive though she seemed, was in everything vowed to
France and the Pope, who had sent her the Golden Rose,
sadly naming her—" Rose among Thorns."

It is not known how many Roman Catholics remained in

Scotland, nor how far the desolation of the country, the ruin of abbeys, convents, churches, and church property was due to the zeal of the Reformers, and how much to the brutality of Somerset's armies, but it cannot be disputed that Mary found her faith cast out and insulted, her way of life reviled, and her conduct exposed to the fanatic insolence of John Knox and his followers. She kept her temper admirably, but she suffered in spirit, and her health failed; she was subject to frequent fainting fits and bouts of melancholy. Among the turbulent, lawless, greedy, and often dishonest nobles who surrounded the lonely girl, there was not one on whom she could rely in any way. Even Moray, well as he served her, was Elizabeth's pensioner, and no one could be sure of Maitland.

Mary showed some interest in a brilliant French bred chieftain, James Hepburn, Earl of Bothwell, her mother's loyal servant, but he had to flee the country for misconduct and Mary appears at this period not to have had any favourite, man or woman.

It is impossible, here, even to hint at the complexity of European politics which formed Mary's background; her own one political idea was to be recognised as heiress to the English crown and, ultimately, to bring back the two Kingdoms under Roman Catholicism. She was even pre-pared to consider Elizabeth's own favourite, the Earl of Leicester, as a possible husband, if that Queen would promise her the English succession; but Elizabeth and Burghley's intricate schemes were developed in an endless procrastination. Mary's conduct, never yet blamed for more than feminine frivolity or youthful lightness, was the subject of gossip during the Chastelard affair, when a young Frenchman was beheaded (1562) for the audacity of twice concealing himself in her bedroom; she, however, passed the first years of her reign without provoking any censure more serious than the unseemly diatribes of the fanatic Puritans. Her elegance and beauty, her taste and sweet manners, were much extolled; she was affable to all, and seemed to have triumphed in a difficult position when she made the marriage that was, literally, fatal to all her fortunes.

Henry Stewart, Lord Darnley, came to Scotland in 1565; he was the elder son of Mathew Stewart, Earl of Lennox, who had taken service with the English, and Margaret, daughter of Margaret Tudor and the Earl of Lennox; he was, after Mary, the heir to the English throne. Through his father's side he could claim royal blood, for Lennox was descended from James II through his daughter Mary. Darnley had been educated as an Englishman, trained and pampered by an ambitious mother, and came to Scotland an arrogant, wilful, passionate boy of nineteen. He was instantly disliked by the Scottish nobles and instantly infatuated Mary. All the accounts that we have of him are so unfavourable that it is difficult to understand how a brilliant, witty, ardent woman could have become so enamoured of him. It is to be supposed that he possessed exceptional good looks; Randolph, the dry, English ambassador, thought that no woman could resist " that fair face."

Mary's sudden passion was headlong; despite the Tudor claim, Darnley was not—especially by Moray and his party —thought to be a worthy match, but Mary married him secretly in March and publicly in July of 1565.

The Queen's behaviour during the next few years of her life has been the subject of such acrid dispute, and is in itself so obscure, that only the mere outline of her story can be described in a limited space, and this with the greatest reserve.

The marriage gave the Queen a sudden spirit of independence—she cast herself into the Romish party, neglected Elizabeth and Moray, showed energy, restless self-assertion, and a disposition for foreign intrigue. She raised to authority and her intimacy one David Rizzio, a confidant of her husband, and made him her foreign secretary, an honour the Italian bore with insolence and one that outraged both the nobles and the King. Moray was stung into rebellion and rose in arms at Ayr; Mary, gathering five thousand men, chased him from pillar to post, and finally out of the kingdom. Meanwhile, her marriage had fallen to pieces; Darnley, weak, bewildered, young, and undisciplined, clamoured for the crown matrimonial, and spent his time in field sports, and invectives against all who opposed him.

Mary's passion for the fair youth soon flared out, and such was her indiscretion that when her pregnancy was first known, the English envoy noted his conviction that the child had been fathered by Rizzio. Darnley also took the extreme step of jeopardising the succession of the child by asserting that the Italian was his wife's lover, while the nobles took advantage of Darnley's fury to plan the murder of Rizzio. This scheme was known at the English court, but Mary seems to have been in utter ignorance of the storm that her folly had provoked, until it broke in her presence, March 1566. By Darnley's express wish Rizzio was dragged from Mary's supper table in Holyrood and murdered in her ante-chamber. The Queen was made a prisoner, but had, under these fearful circumstances, the address to detach her husband from his fellow-conspirators, and to induce him to escape with her from Holyrood. Moray returned to Scotland, and though Mary probably knew of his share in the Rizzio outrage, she received him in friendly fashion. Also, until the birth of her son (June 1566), she affected good terms with Darnley, who had publicly repudiated any share in the murder of the Italian. But Mary had received from the other conspirators proof of his complicity. Soon after the birth of her son (Darnley tacitly accepted the paternity) Mary made the Earl of Bothwell conspicuous by her favours, and did not disguise her frantic desire to be rid of her wretched husband. Darnley had been doomed from the moment he had so foolishly betrayed his fellow-murderers, and the Lords (the guiding spirits being probably Moray and Maitland) decided to use Bothwell as a catspaw in removing him, as they had used Darnley as a catspaw in removing Rizzio. Bothwell was " a lewd man, blinded by ambition," violent, brave, and vicious; he had earned Mary's gratitude by helping in her escape from Holyrood and, used to success with women, was confident of winning her, and through her, the crown. The Lords seem to have promised him Mary as a bribe for murdering (or organising the murder) of Darnley; but this is all matter for endless controversy. Certain it is that Mary and Darnley quar-relled bitterly, that he threatened to leave the kingdom, that she showed open favour to Bothwell, newly married to Jane Gordon, sister of the Earl of Huntly. It was believed by many that Bothwell was her lover soon after the birth of the child, as they believed that Rizzio had been her lover soon after her love match with Darnley. It is certain that she knew of a deep conspiracy against her husband when she went to fetch him, a sick man, from Glasgow, where he was safe with his father, to Kirk o' Field, a lonely house out-side Edinburgh. This was blown up, and Darnley's dead body found in a nearby field, February 1567.

Seldom has a crime caused greater scandal. The explosion in Kirk o' Field echoed throughout Europe, and the death of this young man, despised and hated, important only by the accident of birth, was a political rallying cry and an excuse for political and personal revenge for years. It is not certain how many people, instigators and hired bravoes, were implicated in this clumsy murder, but most, if not all of those known to be concerned in it, perished by murder or on the scaffold. Mary was instantly suspected and instantly had her defence ready—the plot had been intended to destroy her also and she had escaped by accident. This was not tenable, and was held as futile as Bothwell's explanation—" that thunder (*sic*) from heaven had consumed the King's dwelling."

No one seemed to doubt that Bothwell was the leading spirit in the taking off of Henry Darnley, and Mary was warned by friends and foes (notably by Elizabeth) that she could only save her reputation by bringing the murderers to justice. It is doubtful if she could have done this, as there were probably few indeed among the Lords who had not had some hand in the crime. But she made no show of wanting to; Bothwell, under pressure from England and Lennox, was brought to a farcical trial, where some of his fellow-murderers were among the judges, and acquitted. Mary, disregarding all warnings and threats, continued to show him open favour. On her return from a visit to her son in Stirling Castle, April 1567 (this was the last time she saw him), she was abducted by Bothwell at a bridge over the Almond and taken to Dunbar Castle. It was at once believed by many that this outrage was committed with her connivance. Bothwell, with scandalous haste, hurried a divorce from his innocent wife through the courts, and brought the Queen to Edinburgh on May 3rd, the day that the decree of divorce was pronounced. Mary made no protest, offered no explanation, and made no effort to escape. Bothwell forced the fiery and reluctant John Craig, Knox's deputy, to announce his approaching marriage to the Queen, which the minister did on May 9 in St. Giles's Church, calling " Heaven and earth to witness that the proposed union was odious and scandalous to the world." On May 12 Mary went to the Chief Court of Justice and declared that she acted of her own free will and bore no offence against Bothwell; the same day she created him Duke of

Orkney, and on May 15 she married him, by the rites of the Reformed Church, in Holyrood Palace.

Her reasons for this ruinous marriage have been variously given: some argue that she had a romantic infatuation for Bothwell and did not believe he was concerned in the Darnley murder, and so acted with all the good faith a woman in love is capable of; others suppose that she had been the Earl's mistress for some time, and had urged on the murder and the divorce and arranged the abduction to save her honour; and the third opinion is that she was a wholly innocent woman, overpowered by Bothwell, and forced to marry him after he had violently outraged her in Dunbar Castle. The common feeling at the time, and apparently one shared by Elizabeth, the French and English ambassadors, was that the wretched marriage was owing to Mary's desperate attempt to save her reputation. It should be noted that a woman of Mary's wit, spirit, and courage was hardly likely to be tricked by a ruffian without some attempt to save herself or some appeal for help. On the other hand, she had long been in miserable health, was tormented by pain, fainting fits, and hysterical attacks, while her appearance and manner showed the utmost anguish of mind. Bothwell was detestable to all, a personal enemy of England, of a bad reputation, offensive to Mary's French relations as a Protestant and a commoner, hopelessly compromised in the murder of a man whose widow he had married three months after the crime. Mary lost the good opinion of all; the Pope, Spain, and France tacitly repudiated her, her subjects were shocked and angry, the Lords—who had edged Bothwell on to destroy Darnley—now had a good excuse to raise their standard against a murderess and a murderer. The Queen and Bothwell gathered what army they could together, and met the Lords at Carberry Hill seven miles from Edinburgh, June 1567. A day's wearisome negotiation, when Du Croc tried to act as mediator, ended in the Queen's men straggling over to the Lords, Bothwell fleeing the field, and Mary being brought back a prisoner to Edinburgh, where the people greeted her with cries of "Murderess!" She was ignobly treated and lodged roughly in the Provost's house, where she might be seen at the window in a state of violent emotion, dishevelled and half-naked, shrieking for help. Mary feared the death of an adulteress and murderess at the stake, and with reason. The Blue Blanket, the famous banner of the Trades Guild, had to be brought out to protect her from the mob when the Lords moved her to Lochleven, the island home of Moray's mother, Margaret Douglas. Moray's return to Scotland and the skilful intervention of Elizabeth's envoy, Thockmorton, saved Mary's life and avoided her trial for murder, but she was forced to abdicate in favour of her son, who was crowned as James VI.

The following year she contrived to escape from Lochleven and to raise a force against her half-brother, Moray, then Regent for the little King. At Langside her medley of supporters were defeated, and Mary fled for her life as fast as a horse could carry her, to England, crossing the Solway with a few followers in May 1568. She has been blamed for this flight into England as for a great blunder, but it is difficult to see what else she could have done. She certainly hoped that Elizabeth was her friend, because that Queen had helped her against the rebel Lords, and even hoped she might find an English army to lead against Moray, but even though she was here grievously deceived, she had no reasonable alternative to a flight into England. Elizabeth played her usual game of shuttlecock; she detained Mary in honourable captivity, set up a Commission to enquire into her position and guilt, and meanwhile refused to see her or to allow her to come to London or to plead her cause in person. Moray, to justify his rebellion, put in the famous " casket " letters, which he declared had been found under Bothwell's bed. These were love letters supposedly written by Mary to Bothwell before their marriage, and one, the Glasgow letter, afforded damning proof of her active agency in Darnley's death. Mary declared the letters to be forgeries and Elizabeth broke up the Commission with a verdict of " not proven," but continued to support Moray and to keep Mary in prison.

The question of the " casket " letters is one of the mysteries of history; if they were forged (and this was an age of forgery and the Lords were completely unscrupulous), some very cunning hand must have done the work, so exactly do they fit into Mary's story. Mary, fretting desperately against a captivity she regarded as an act of base treachery and injustice, intrigued with the Roman Catholics for her release (1569), agitated for her divorce from Bothwell, who had fled to Denmark, where he was a prisoner, and schemed to marry the Protestant Duke of Norfolk. The rebellion was promptly crushed by Elizabeth, and Norfolk finally put his head on that " wooden pillow " against which the English Queen had warned him. A small party in Scotland— " Queen's men "—struggled for Mary, but with their ultimate defeat her last hopes of returning to her throne vanished.

The rest of Mary's life is a dismal and monotonous chronicle of the rapidly ageing, restless, ambitious, and sick woman's attempts to regain freedom and power. It is easy to understand both her attitude and that of Elizabeth. It was quite natural for Mary to use every weapon of intrigue, deceit, and guile in order, not only to escape from an English prison, but to gain her lifelong ambition, the English throne, and it was quite natural for Elizabeth to watch and thwart these schemes and to regard Mary as a source of grave potential danger, not only to herself, but to her faith and the liberty of her people. The English Protestants profoundly mistrusted and feared Mary, and Elizabeth was continually urged by Parliament and people to do what her instinct forbade her to do, get rid of a fellow-woman and a fellow-sovereign.

As Elizabeth aged, the question of the English succession became of increasing interest to Europe, and as thus Mary's political importance increased, Pope, Spain, and France alike forgot her tainted reputation, which years of imprisonment might be supposed to gloss over. France, however, abandoned Mary by the Treaty of Blois, and the desperate captive willed her rights in England to Philip of Spain in return for his assistance in obtaining her freedom. This letter was intercepted by the vigilant Walsingham, and it was then decided by Burghley, if not by Elizabeth, to destroy Mary. An elaborate scheme of judicial murder was evolved; Walsingham patiently spun the web of the Babington conspiracy, and Mary, too ill, hopeless, frantic, and shut away from public affairs to be prudent, fell into the trap. She dictated a letter to Babington, which gave consent to a rising on her behalf, and tacitly agreed to an attempt on the life of Elizabeth (1586).

Mary, so ill that she could not walk alone, was brought before an imposing Commission of Elizabeth's peers. The forlorn and helpless woman defended herself with spirited skill, but without evoking compassion from the judges determined to destroy her. She was found guilty and sentenced to die by the axe. Elizabeth, ill from emotion, tried to put off the execution, or at least to evade responsibility for it, but Burghley was resolute in the pursuance of his policy. There is no reason to believe that Elizabeth was animated by vindictive feelings, nor that her reluctance to put Mary to death was feigned. The Queen, Burleigh, and the majority of the nation honestly saw Mary as a murderess, a wanton, a liar, and a woman continuously plotting to murder Elizabeth and restore the tyranny of Rome by the force of foreign arms.

With formal ceremonial Mary was beheaded in the great Hall of Fotheringhay, February 7, 1587. Her noble dignity, her touching farewells to her devoted servants, her lofty fortitude and unshaken fidelity to her faith, her splendid appearance—all infirmities and blasted beauty being disguised by rich attire and artful feminine devices—moved the spectators of this awful scene to respect if not to sympathy. But the news of the death of the Scottish Queen was received with bell-ringing and bonfires in London and with great rejoicings all over the country. It was generally believed that the newly won and not wholly consolidated liberty of England had been rescued from a great peril.

The Protestant James VI assented to his mother's death in his eagerness to become King of England. When that ambition was achieved (1603) he had his mother's body (1612) brought from Peterborough Cathedral, where her coffin had lain near to that of Catherine of Arragon, and placed under a handsome monument near to that of Queen Elizabeth in Westminster Abbey.

Mary, Queen of Scots, died without having, by a single word, thrown any light on any of the mysteries of her life which have been subjects of such keen controversy for so long. There will always be painful and probably fruitless debate as to Mary's conduct as a woman and a queen. Immediately after her death she became a martyr in the eyes of many of her own Faith, and as such was elevated almost to the position of a saint. Even to those who do not invest her with mythical qualities, her charm, her suffering, her famous name, and most of all, the tragedy of her death, will always give her a romantic importance which is enhanced by the apparently insoluble puzzles presented by her conduct during her brief reign. This is, from the historian's point of view, a mere episode in the story of Scotland that did not affect the development of that nation one way or another; neither the Queen herself, nor Rizzio, nor Darnley, nor Bothwell, was more than a passionate child of chance and circumstance. None of them believed in, or strove for, large issues, or for any but selfish aims, but because this woman was Mary Stewart and because these men were singled out by her regard they have a certain but brittle immortality, the useless brilliancy and the guarded permanency of a jewel in a shrine, that in itself is nothing but a lustrous shining, but which may be symbolic of anything that the spectator chooses to invoke.

Mary, in herself, was something less than a queen, yet is something more than a figure in the history books; she is always doubled by her legend, as a flower or a star may be doubled in water or glass. Not the least fascinating part of her story is the wonder of it, the sense of exasperation that it raises in the mind; the tantalising possibilities, the bewildering questions provoked by the two murders and the two marriages, the lovely figure of the woman whom so many praised and whom none helped, who had no weapon beyond her tears and no buckler beyond her pride, and who was fortunate in nothing save in the cruel death that dimmed all her faults.

SIR FRANCIS WALSING-HAM

Circa 1536–1590

By
CONYERS READ

SIR FRANCIS WALSINGHAM

by CONYERS READ

SIR FRANCIS WALSINGHAM was one of the most distinguished statesmen who served Queen Elizabeth. In the order of greatness he certainly ranks below Sir William Cecil and possibly below Cecil's son Robert, but he is an easy third. The other conspicuous figures at the Elizabethan court, men like Hatton and Leicester and Essex and Raleigh, were courtiers rather than statesmen, and though they played their part in the shaping of public policy, their pre-eminence was due rather to the royal favour than to any outstanding skill in statecraft. Possibly a remote connection with the Boleyns may have commended Walsingham to Elizabeth's attention in the first place, but he was never in any sense a favourite. If for no other reason, he lacked the essential physical attributes. It was the robust, dashing, military figure like Essex, or the graceful, dancing gentleman like Hatton, that caught the Queen's fancy, and Walsingham was a frail, sickly, studious type. He was no soldier, no dancer, no coiner of fine phrases, and apparently never aspired to be. Neither for that matter was William Cecil or Robert. But both of them were of a nature much nearer akin to Elizabeth's own. Both of them were politicians, opportunists, quite ready to trim their sails to whatever wind that blew. Walsingham, on the contrary, was a man of strong convictions and definite purposes, firm in his beliefs and apt to state them in unvarnished prose. One gets the impression that of all those in her immediate *entourage* Elizabeth liked him least. At times she vented her dislike upon him in rather a violent form. Nevertheless, he remained in her service for over twenty years. In fact, he never left it from the day when he entered it until the day of his death. Elizabeth had use of his competency, and she never doubted her ability to control his enthusiasms when they ran counter to her own. But she kept him always in what must be regarded as a subordinate place. He never advanced beyond the position of principal secretary; he never attained to the peerage. Cecil indeed was the only one of her great commoners who did. Elizabeth in this respect was wiser than her father, who allowed his Wolseys and his Cromwells to mount so high that they almost over-shadowed the throne itself and had to be levelled down at last with the executioner's axe.

Walsingham, like Cecil, was of the new gentry. His recorded family history begins with a London shoemaker early in the fifteenth century, and proceeds by easy gradients through the craft gilds to the trading gilds, and so to a country seat in Kent. At the beginning of the sixteenth century the Walsinghams had firmly established themselves among the country gentry, and had acquired a pedigree which ran back to the Volsungs of Norse legend. Sir Francis himself was of a cadet branch of the family. His father was a London barrister, his mother a sister of Sir Anthony Denny, one of the more radical Protestants at the court of Henry VIII, his step-father, who very likely was responsible for his upbringing, a brother of the Cary who married Ann Boleyn's sister. Here then were influential connections, a tradition of public service, some flavour of the new religion on the distaff side and apparently adequate means. The education of Sir Francis was that of a gentle-man's son, culminating at King's College, Cambridge, with a year or two of foreign travel to follow. Somewhere along the line, possibly from his mother, more probably at King's, he became an enthusiastic Protestant, "of the Austerian embracement" as Sir Robert Naunton quaintly puts it; so much so, that he fled to the Continent shortly after the accession of Mary the Catholic. There he read law for a time at Padua and later sojourned with other English Protestant refugees in Germany or in Switzerland. He returned to England shortly after Mary's death, a young man in the middle twenties singularly well equipped for public service, notably for foreign service. He had estab-lished many personal connections abroad, particularly among the Protestant leaders in Germany and France, had mastered both French and Italian, and had mastered also at first hand in Italy the new Machiavellian school of state-craft. In more than one respect he conformed to the type currently condemned in England as Italianate. It revealed itself in his dress, in his manners, in the cut of his beard. It revealed itself perhaps most of all in his cosmopolitan outlook. What differentiated him, however, was his zeal for the Protestant faith. Like the Jesuits in the other camp, he was ready to apply his mastery of Italian craft to the uses of his religion.

All these characteristics were apparent in him from the very beginning of his public service, which we may perhaps date from 1570 when Elizabeth sent him as her resident ambassador to France. Before that time he had established himself in England, had married and lost one wife and married a second one, both of them widows of some substance, had sat twice in Parliament, and had done some casual secret service work for the government. Of his wives we know virtually nothing, still less about his love affairs, if he had any. The records of the man's human, private contacts are nearly all of them lost. He had one daughter, who later married Sir Philip Sidney. As to his parliamentary career we know little more than that he sat, first as a borough, later as a county member in virtually every parliament that met during the term of his official life. How much he did there under cover it would be dangerous even to guess about. But he was pretty clearly not of the stuff of which great commoners are made.

Walsingham's despatch to France coincided in point of time with the termination of the third religious war there, and the return of the Huguenot leaders to the French court. That may explain in part Elizabeth's choice of an ambassador already well known as a rather too zealous Protestant. Her relations with Spain were strained almost to the breaking-point and the need of a *rapprochement* to France rather pressing. In any event Walsingham's first two years of foreign service really laid the foundation for something like a diplomatic revolution by which the old Anglo-Spanish entente was more or less dissolved, and the old Anglo-French hostility more or less amended. It began, as so many of Elizabeth's diplomatic adventures began, with a courtship, the brother of the French King being the rather unresponsive suitor, but it found definite expression in a defensive alliance and a commercial treaty in the spring of 1572. As to the courtship Walsingham encountered there for the first time the problem of keeping on friendly terms with the two leaders in the English Privy Council who were sharply at variance about the matter. Cecil favoured a French marriage as likely to solidify Anglo-French relations, give Elizabeth a husband which he felt quite sure she ought to have, and the English people, as he hoped, an heir apparent. Leicester opposed the marriage, privately because he had his own fish to fry, publicly because he feared that Elizabeth's marriage to a Catholic would jeopardise the cause of Protestantism in England. We may perhaps note here the beginning of Leicester's zeal for the Protestant faith which grew stronger as time went on and which made him eventually the leader of the Puritan party at the English court. Caught between these two opposing fires Walsingham was hard put to it to avoid partisanship. Not the least of his triumphs in France was his success in preserving the friendship and goodwill both of Cecil and of Leicester. Certainly he breathed more freely when the marriage project was finally abandoned and he could turn to the simpler business of a defensive alliance. He got the alliance, for what it might be worth. Unfortunately, so far as French internal politics were concerned, it registered the triumph of the Huguenot leaders at the French court and did much to advance Admiral Coligny to a dominating place in the counsels of the French king, and Catherine de' Medici, the Queen-mother, would brook no rival in that position. And so the Treaty of Blois in April was followed hard by St. Bartholomew's Massacre in August.

To Walsingham the massacre spelt the destruction of all that he had striven for two years to attain. More than that it shook his faith in the wisdom of attempting to develop a foreign policy on the basis of a balance of power. He came to the conclusion that the fundamental issue in Europe was not that between nation and nation but that between creed and creed. He decided that Spain and France were secretly planning a crusade for the destruction of protestantism everywhere, and from that day forward he advocated a policy of regarding all Catholics as potential enemies and all Protestants as potential friends. This conclusion was partly reached because he believed that the Protestant cause was even more important than the cause of England and he had rather have seen England perish in support of the reformers than flourish by alliance with the powers of Rome. But he really believed that religion was as potent a factor in determining the policy of princes as it was in determining his own, and that all alliances with Catholic powers were broken reeds to lean upon. Christ and Belial, as he put it, could hardly agree. That was where he made his fundamental mistake. In point of fact nationalism was far stronger and the influence of religion on policy far weaker than he took it to be. That was where both Elizabeth and Cecil were wiser than he. Nevertheless, so he was, and his influence in shaping English foreign policy was steadily exerted towards the formation of a grand Protestant alliance under English leadership to confront the menace of a holy Catholic league. Reduced to practical terms, this meant English support to Protestant rebels in France and in the Spanish Low Countries, in combination with protestant Germany and protestant Scotland if it could be managed.

It may be that this attitude was natural to him, it may have been for him as for so many other Englishmen that it was the product of his religious exile during bloody Mary's reign. But there can be no reasonable doubt that the grim experience of St. Bartholomew's accentuated it and deepened it.

After St. Bartholomew's, Walsingham's one idea was to get home, but it was not until the following spring that he was finally relieved. So far as positive achievements were concerned he had little more to show for three years in Paris than a sadly depleted purse. The Anjou marriage had failed, the treaty of alliance had been knocked into a cocked hat by the massacre. The Huguenots, England's friends in France, were rebels in arms against the French crown. All the prospects which had seemed so fair in the midsummer of 1570 seemed very remote indeed. Nevertheless, he had proved to be a very competent ambassador, certainly the most competent in the Elizabethan diplomatic service. His despatches were regarded as a model of their kind and were among the earliest of Elizabethan State papers to find their way into print. Perhaps the most expressive tribute to his skill lies in the fact that whenever again during his lifetime Elizabeth had a diplomatic mission to be performed which called for exceptional astuteness, she chose Walsingham for the place.

In December 1573 Elizabeth appointed him one of her principal secretaries, and in that position he remained almost until the day of his death some seventeen years later. It was an office without precise definition. One of his own secretaries wrote of it later :

> "Among all particular offices and places of charge in this State there is none of more necessary use, nor subject to more cumber and variableness than is the office of principal secretary, by reason of the variety and uncertainty of his employment, and therefore with more difficulty to be prescribed by special method and order."

And his successor in office observed:

> "Only a secretary hath no warrant or commission in matters of his own greatest peril but the virtue and word of his sovereign. For such is the multiplicity of occasions and the variable motions and intent of foreign princes, and their daily practices, and in so many points and places as secretaries can never have any commission so large and universal to assure them."

Wolsey and Cromwell both had discovered this to their sorrow and Walsingham's own associate, William Davison, the man who passed on Mary Stuart's death warrant to her executioners, had opportunity to reflect bitterly upon it in the Tower. It is at once a tribute to Walsingham's ability and to the Queen's loyalty that he was never called to account for anything he did in office, or out of office either for that matter, though he was virtually the managing director of Elizabeth's government during the most critical years of her reign.

Outside of public finance, which was Cecil's province, and the administration of justice, which was left to the Chancellor and the Chief Justices, Walsingham was what we should call to-day secretary of state for all departments. Mostly he was busy about foreign affairs, but since foreign affairs included matters so diverse as the hunting down of seminary priests, the guarding of Mary Stuart, the muster of soldiers to meet the Spanish invasion, and the organisation of expeditions to Ireland, to the Low Countries and to France, not much of moment escaped his attention. The actual bulk of his official correspondence was enormous and it increased steadily. His fundamental conception of the rôle of England in European affairs he had defined in France and he never deviated from it. Whatever Elizabeth chose to do, Walsingham always knew what should be done. " I wish first God's glory," he wrote, " and next the Queen's safety." God's glory was for him the advancement of the Protestant cause. That was the centre of his purpose and by that simple and convenient yard-stick he measured every issue. Spain, the arch enemy, was to be smitten by land and sea, her enemies supported, her friends attacked.

> " The proud Spaniard, whom God hath long used for the rod of His wrath I see great hope that He will now cast him into the fire, that he may know what it is to serve against God."

Walsingham wrote these words in 1572 and though he often later grew sick at heart as the visitation of divine justice was again and again postponed, he always nursed that unconquerable hope. It made of him the recognised champion of the war party at court, of Henry of Navarre in France, of the rebellious Dutch in the Low Countries, of Hawkins and Drake on the high seas. It made him also the determined enemy of the captive Scottish Queen and the untiring detective of conspiracy among the Catholics in England.

In every aspect of his public policy his pre-occupation with religion is apparent. And yet he was no bigot. Had he been he could hardly have remained in the Queen's service as long as he did, for she herself was as far as possible from bigotry. There can be little doubt about the intensity of his Puritan sympathies. Camden speaks of him, " as a most sharp maintainer of the purer religion." But he was shrewd enough to recognise that if English protestantism was to develop its fighting strength it must avoid internal dissensions. He drew the line sharply between Protestant and Catholic, but within the Protestant camp he would admit no right of rebellion.

> " I would have all reformation," he wrote, " done by public authority. It were very dangerous that every private man's zeal should carry sufficient authority of reforming things amiss."

And again :

> " The time requireth an unity and perfect agreement
> rather in them that maketh profession of that truth
> which is elsewhere so impugned and hath no mighty
> enemies and so cruel wars kindling against it in these days
> amongst our fellow members abroad. Our unity might
> be a strength to ourselves and an aid to our neighbours,
> but if we shall like to fall to division among ourselves,
> we must needs lie open to the common enemy and by
> our own fault hasten, or rather call upon ourselves, our
> own ruin."

It was perhaps this disposition to compromise differences
among the faithful which led James of Scotland to say,
when someone commended Walsingham for his zeal in
religion, that he was, " not withstanding his outward profession, a very Machiavel."

The one quality which was noted in him by all his contemporaries was that he saw much and said little. *Video et
taceo.* We shall therefore never know how much he had to
do with the efforts of the Puritans at the court, in the House
of Commons, and in the City to influence the royal mind.
It must be remarked however, that Peter Wentworth, the
most vigorous of Puritan commoners, was his brother-in-law
and that Puritans great and small looked upon him as their
certain, though necessarily very discreet, friend. It cannot
have been merely a coincidence that the vigorous persecution of them was deferred until after his death.

The English Catholics, then and since, have always
regarded him as their chief persecutor. In fiction and in
fact they almost invariably single him out as the villain of
the piece. We may ascribe this in large measure to the
methods he employed in hunting them down. Spy systems
are never popular institutions and spies are rarely remarkable for their high moral standards. When the hunter is a
rogue, as he is apt to be, and the hunted a saint, as he is
almost bound to be assumed to be when religion is in
question, the setter-on can hardly hope to escape defilement.
It is besides so very easy to damn spy systems because so
little is really known about them. This much we do know,
that Walsingham's secret service, though probably nothing
like so elaborate as it has been represented to be, was fairly

efficient and largely instrumental in preventing what it was designed to prevent. There is no sound evidence to show that Walsingham himself got any fiendish satisfaction out of harrying and torturing Catholics. He regarded them as a dangerous political menace, much more so probably than in fact they were. That they could at once be loyal to their Queen and loyal to the Church which had excommunicated their Queen was unbelievable to a man of his clear convictions; though it is patent enough now to have been true of the great majority of them. They were to him traitors, actual or potential, all of them. He was not concerned about the welfare of their souls, but he wanted to put them out of harm's way. It is to be remarked that he thought it bad policy to make martyrs of them. Detention, surveillance, deportation, were his preferred methods of dealing with them. At one time he interested himself in a plan to establish a colony of them in America. That he employed torture as a means of extorting information from those implicated or thought to be implicated in conspiracy against the Queen, is undoubted. But such was the general practice of the times, and if Walsingham in this respect was no better he was certainly no worse than his contemporaries. The picture of him in the torture chamber turning the rack and writing down the faltering words of his writhing victim is pure fiction. Those grim details were left to subordinates.

Walsingham did believe, and rightly, that the situation was critical; he did believe, rightly too, that some of the Catholics were conspiring actively against the Queen, and he was determined to wring the truth from them any way he might. It is easy enough to say now that Elizabeth was safe, but that fact was very far from apparent to Walsingham. What he saw was a whole network of intrigue and conspiracy against her supported by a formidable party in England, by Philip of Spain, by the Guises in France, and by the forces of the Counter-Reformation throughout Europe. It was no time for him to be over nice about his methods. It was better, he said, to fear too much than too little. Let those happy few who did not succumb to the war psychology of 1914–18 cast the first stone!

The focal point of all the active plotting against Elizabeth was the captive Scottish queen. It does not follow that she was herself cognisant of this plotting or that she actively participated in it. But she was, she could not help being,

16   *425*

the competitor, and those who designed to get rid of Elizabeth designed almost inevitably to set Mary in her place. So it was that Walsingham was particularly curious about Mary's channels of information with her friends. It was obviously the place to look for important revelations. Furthermore he believed that Mary's presence in England, indeed her presence on earth, constituted one of the greatest menaces that faced Protestant England.

" So long as that devilish woman lives," he wrote to Leicester fifteen years before her death, " neither her Majesty must make account to continue in quiet possession of her crown, nor her faithful servants assure themselves of safety of their lives."

But the problem was to get rid of her. England at large was agreed that she should be got rid of. The obstacle was Elizabeth herself, who could not be induced to take the final necessary step against a sister sovereign. Imprisonment, yes, close imprisonment, perhaps, but trial and execution, no. The precedent was too dangerous a one. Elizabeth perhaps remembered how close a call she herself had had during her sister's reign. Walsingham's problem, therefore, was not only to secure information about conspiracy from Mary's correspondence but also if possible to secure conclusive proof that she herself was an active conspirator. The temptation was strong to manufacture evidence and he has been charged with having done so, but the proof of this is not convincing. Mary had every incentive to plot for her own release and the destruction of her rival and a very good will to do so. Given the opportunity, the plot almost inevitably followed. A group of hare-brained young Catholics supplied the plot; a carefully supervised channel of communication enabled Mary, as she thought with safety, to confer her blessing upon it. In due season the trap was sprung and the catch laid before Elizabeth's eyes. She was convinced. Mary was brought to her trial. Her condemnation was a foregone conclusion; England had condemned her fourteen years before. If the evidence in the particular case had been far less conclusive than it was the result would have been the same. But the conventions had to be maintained, though there were those who thought it would have been more discreet to have had her quietly murdered. Walsingham's part in it was merely formal, though of course he supplied the prosecuting attorneys with the documents in the case. He managed to avoid, by sickness real or pretended, the difficult business of securing Elizabeth's signature to the death warrant and the responsibility of having it executed. Possibly he foresaw that she would presently be looking for a scapegoat. It is to be noted that when she handed the warrant to his colleague, William Davison, she bade him show it to Walsingham, " the grief thereof," she added, " will go near to kill him outright."

With Mary's death Walsingham breathed easier. Matters really seemed to be working out at last as he had hoped. The year before he had seen an English army sail to the support of the Dutch. The year after he was to see the Spanish Armada shot-riddled and storm battered, limp back to Spain a hopeless failure. The organisation of English forces by land and sea to meet the Spanish attack had been largely his doing.

> " You have fought more with your pen," Drake wrote to him, " than many here in our English navy fought with their enemies."

After nearly thirty years of peace England was, in short, at war. Everyone in England almost was prepared to admit that, except the Queen herself. And Walsingham was in large measure responsible. We must certainly regard Leicester as the leader of the war party in the Privy Council, but Walsingham was equally certainly its organising genius. It was one thing, however, to lead Elizabeth to war and quite another thing to induce her to wage war with any degree of vigour or enthusiasm. The problem which Walsingham had to face during the short residue of his life was to keep her hand to the plough after she had started the furrow. He succeeded only indifferently well. That exhilaration which comes with the consciousness of success after long sustained effort was never to be his. Neither were the temporal rewards. Elizabeth was more generous to him than she has been represented to be. She made him in fact many commercial concessions which might have been valuable had war not completely disorganised the normal courses of trade. As it was they did not prove to be particularly profitable. Certainly he died poor; so poor that he gave instructions just before his death for an unpretentious funeral in the interests of his creditors. Of worldly honours, outside a bare knighthood he received none. Perhaps this mattered less to him because he left no son to succeed him. In any event he tried to be philosophical about it.

> " Let a man," he wrote, " by doing worthy acts deserve honour and though he do not attain it, yet he is much a happier man than he that gets it without desert. For such a man is beforehand with reputation. And the world still owes him that honour which his deserts cry for and it hath not paid."

It will never do to think of him as a Puritan in the conventional sense of the term. Few men at the Elizabethan court displayed a keener interest in almost every aspect of the renaissance culture. Sir Philip Sidney was his son-in-law as well as his close friend, lived with him and gathered about him the choice spirits in the Court literary circle. Edmund Spenser speaks of him as the great Mæcenas of his age. If he apparently knew nothing and cared nothing about the rather shabby playwrights who gathered at the Mermaid Tavern, he does not seem to have shared the Puritan antipathy to the stage. He established a chair of international law at Oxford. No man in his time, unless perhaps Raleigh, did more to encourage exploration and discovery. Richard Hakluyt dedicated to him the first edition of his *Voyages*. Drake and Frobisher and John Davis all owed much to his bounty. We may ascribe this in part to his inveterate hostility to Spain, in part also to a definite inclination towards speculative enterprises which was characteristic of the time. But he had no vision of Empire. The world beyond the seas was for him as it was for almost all his contemporaries, simply an alluring way to wealth. It proved to be a mirage so far as he was personally concerned, and yet we find combined in him the two elements out of which the foundations of the British Empire were compounded, religious zeal and commercial enterprise.

Walsingham comes close to being the conventional Elizabethan, much closer than the canny, provincial Cecils, much closer than the Queen herself. He had the broad cosmopolitan outlook, the essential sanity, the literary and artistic interests combined with the practical common sense. Where he deviated from the type was in his resolute religious purposes and in his lack of any strong national feeling. Neither Elizabeth nor the Cecils could have been anything else but English; Walsingham might have belonged to any Christian country. England was for him simply an instrument in a greater cause. His fundamental loyalties were to the culture of the Renaissance and above all to the gospel of the reformed religion.

SIR RICHARD GRENVILLE

Circa 1542–1591

By

JAMES A. WILLIAMSON

SIR RICHARD GRENVILLE

by JAMES A. WILLIAMSON

SIR RICHARD GRENVILLE was a wealthy land-owner of Cornwall and Devon, a servant of the State in various civil and military employments, a projector of empire-building undertakings, a Channel privateer in the irregular warfare of the Counter-Reformation, the leader of the first colonising expedition to Virginia, a planter of English colonists in Ireland, and finally, in the last year of his life, an officer of the Queen's Navy. In all these activities until the Virginia voyage of 1585 he is for us a type rather than an individual. He represents the careers of a large number of Englishmen of his time, the alert, venture-some, public-spirited gentry and merchants who formed the backbone of Tudor England. Then in his later years we begin to know more about him, and he is seen as an individual of strongly marked character, making a deep impression on friend and foe, and ending in a blaze of valour that will never die as long as Englishmen sail the seas.

He was born about 1541–3, the son of Sir Roger Grenville, who served Henry VIII in the wars and was drowned in 1545 when the *Mary Rose* foundered off Portsmouth as she was sailing out to fight the French. Of the boyhood and education of Richard Grenville nothing is known.[1] The ordinary course for a youth of his rank was attendance at the grammar school until the age of fourteen or thereabouts, then the University until seventeen, followed by two or three years of reading law at the Inns of Court, and lastly a tour of continental travel in the train of some ambassador or of service under some great commander in the fashionable

---

[1] There is at present no full biography of Grenville. The *Dictionary of National Biography* contains a brief outline, and many additional particulars on parts of the career are collected in " New Light on Sir Richard Grenville," by R. Pearse Chope, *Transactions of the Devonshire Association*, 1917.

war of the moment. So was the young man of wealth fitted for his duties in the condition to which it had pleased God to call him. When at length he entered into his estate he was expected not only to mind his private affairs, but to do justice among his humbler neighbours, to represent them in Parliament and lead them in arms, to do for the Government all manner of jobs that are now performed by paid civil servants, and to mould the public opinion upon which the monarchy leaned for its support. Most likely Grenville went through some such training, but all we know of it is the final stage. In 1566, according to Camden, he served the Emperor in Hungary against the Turk. To serve the Emperor was then the correct thing to do, for the time-honoured Anglo-Spanish-Imperial alliance still held good. But a few years later the favoured services for training young Englishmen were those of the Huguenots and the Dutch. Raleigh, ten years younger than Grenville, learned his soldiering under Coligny and Louis of Nassau.

Grenville's personal adventures in Hungary are unknown, but he did not long remain there. In 1569 he was in Ireland, and by that time he was married, for his wife had a narrow escape at the hands of the Munster rebels. Next year he was back in Cornwall, where, on April 28, he made before the Justices at Bodmin a declaration of his submission to the Act of Uniformity for common prayer and service in the Church. In 1571 he sat as member for Cornwall in the Parliament summoned during the excitement of the Ridolfi Plot. His next public employment was as Sheriff of Cornwall in 1577. In the course of his duties he arrested the Jesuit Cuthbert Mayne, and according to Cardinal Allen it was for this piece of service that he received knighthood later in the year. Probably the promotion was on more general grounds, but its date certainly was 1577, as appears from the *Book of Knights*.[1]

Meanwhile, an empire-building project was taking shape, and Grenville bore a part in it. The spice trade with the Moluccas and the silk trade with China had long been the object of commercial ambitions. Portugal was the actual monopolist of the first-mentioned, and Spain was hoping to engross the second by means of her Philippine colony, which attracted Chinese merchants. The Portuguese trade-route was by the Cape of Good Hope and the Indian Ocean.

[1] Edited by W. C. Metcalfe, London, 1885, p. 130.

That of Spain ran across the Isthmus of Panama and thence westward to Manila. From the beginning of the sixteenth century Englishmen had been thinking of a passage to the Pacific by the north-west (round North America) or by the north-east (round northern Asia). Such a passage, if found, would be considerably shorter, but unfortunately it had not been found, although half a dozen attempts had been made before the opening of Elizabeth's reign. Hope had not been abandoned. Sir Humphrey Gilbert, Martin Frobisher, and Michael Lok were seeking means of equipping new expeditions for the north-west. The Muscovy Company was rather lethargically pondering another push by the northeast—it actually made one in 1580. There was yet another means of access to the Pacific, by way of the Straits of Magellan, known for half a century, but never regularly used.

In the early 1570's certain geographical studies brought this Straits of Magellan route or South West Passage once more into prominence, for they promised, not only a commerce with China and the Spice Islands, but also the discovery of desirable countries, hitherto unknown, in the South Pacific. The book of Marco Polo's travels, although not yet printed in English,[1] was well known to men of learning, and from it they drew information of rich lands in the South Pacific—Malaiur, producing spices and drugs; Pentam, an island covered with aromatic trees; and, more interesting still, " Beach, *provincia aurifera*," sometimes called Locach, and surmised to be the land of Ophir and King Solomon's mines. The general position assigned to these countries was " south of the equinoctial " and in the longitudes where Australia actually lies. John Dee, England's most eminent man of science, was convinced of great possibilities in this quarter, and so also were the Flemish geographers Gerard Mercator and Abraham Ortelius. The latter published a world-map in 1570 showing a vast continental coast stretching from Beach (placed south of Java) south-eastwards all the way to Magellan's Tierra del Fuego. According to this conception a navigator needed only to pass the Straits and skirt this great southern continent to reach lands and peoples worth discovering. Moreover, a man of action had already contributed a promising addition to these

[1] The first English translation was made by John Frampton and published in 1579.

studies. In 1567 Alvaro de Mendaña sailed from Peru far out into the Pacific. In seas previously untraversed he found a group of large islands in which he thought (erroneously) that he saw indications of gold. He returned to the west coast of Mexico and announced the discovery of King Solomon's Islands, a name which the archipelago bears to this day. English merchants in Mexico heard the story and reported it to their countrymen at home.

In 1573–4, a syndicate of Devon men sought means of opening trade and founding an empire in the South Sea.[1] The first name on the list is that of Richard Grenville, and with him were associated Piers Edgcumbe, Arthur Bassett, William Hawkins, and several others. It seems that Grenville was to have been the leader of the enterprise, for on one of the documents there is an endorsement in Lord Burghley's handwriting, "Mr. Grenville's voyage." The associates petitioned for a patent of incorporation empowering them to discover and possess for the Queen any lands in the southern hemisphere not already subdued by European princes. Their statement shows that they intended to voyage by the Straits of Magellan, and therefore that their aim was the South Pacific. A patent was actually drafted to the above effect, but seems never to have been completed or issued. There were reasons of state to suggest hesitation. Drake and others had already attacked the Spanish treasure route where it crossed the Isthmus of Panama, and Englishmen in the South Sea would be tempted to attack it between the treasure ports of Chile and Peru, as Drake did a few years later. In 1574 Elizabeth was seeking to patch up her damaged relations with Spain, and did not wish to give further provocation. The Netherlands were in full revolt, and promised to give Spanish armies sufficient occupation to preclude any plan for an invasion of England. The situation suited the Queen's instinct for a watchful, defensive policy, and she was content not to change it. This probably accounts for the dropping of the South Sea project. Moreover, in 1575 Frobisher and Lok set about their North West Passage enterprise, which offered hopes of rich trade with Asia by a perfectly unprovocative route. Grenville put in a last appeal in 1576, elaborating the advantage of the South West Passage, and after that there is no further

[1] The chief documents on this project are in Lansdowne MSS., 100, ff. 52–4, 142–6, and State Papers Domestic, *Eliz.*, vol. 235, No. 1.

record of his participation. The matter passed into the hands of Drake, and how he dealt with it in 1577–80 is well known.

Grenville and his friends had undoubtedly taken the South Sea project seriously, and had made some preparations in anticipation of the Queen's consent. In May, 1574, a letter of intelligence on English affairs was sent to Don Luis de Requesens in the Netherlands. It states that Grenville, " a great pirate," and others had fitted out seven ships on pretext of a voyage to Labrador, but really, it was suspected, to help the Huguenots in Normandy. That plan having fallen through, the letter continues, they now assert that they are going to the Straits of Magellan, but the writer suspects that they mean to attack the plate fleet from the Indies. They have recently acquired three more ships, including the *Castle of Comfort* of 240 tons.[1] This Spanish correspondent was evidently ignorant of the negotiations for the South Sea enterprise, and did not attach importance to the rumours of it which he had picked up.

Whether Grenville's squadron did attempt the plate fleet is unknown, but he and William Hawkins carried out a stroke that smacks of piracy nearer home. In 1575 the *Castle of Comfort* captured a ship of St. Malo called *Le Sauveur* with a lading from the Levant valued at 60,000 crowns.[2] Guillaume Le Fer, the owner, complained that she was taken into Baltimore on the Irish coast and there gutted, the goods being probably distributed in small vessels to various ports. He asserted that Hawkins and Grenville were the owners of the *Castle of Comfort*. This, to the aggrieved parties, was sheer piracy, but to the aggressors was perfectly legal. The explanation lies in the revolt of the Netherlands and the religious wars in France. The Prince of Orange and the Queen of Navarre claimed the status of sovereigns, and issued letters of marque to seamen of all nations " to attack the enemies of God called Papists." Brittany was a Catholic province, and its shipping was held to be fair game for the possessors of a Huguenot commission. That was the view conveniently taken in the Cornish and Devon ports. Elizabeth's Government at first endorsed it, but when the resulting complaints became serious, authority grew hesitant and began to take legal

---

[1] *Calendar of Spanish State Papers, Eliz.*, vol. II, p. 481.
[2] *Calendar of Foreign State Papers, 1575–7*, p. 215; *ibid., 1577–8*, p. 478.

advice on the validity of the Orange and Huguenot letters of marque. Characteristically it went on taking advice for years without ever coming to a conclusion, until the outbreak of regular war in 1585 shelved the question.

Guillaume Le Fer did what he could to secure restitution. In 1576 he took action against William Hawkins and Grenville in the High Court of Admiralty.[1] Grenville attended to answer for himself and partner. He admitted that they had fitted out the *Castle of Comfort* and engaged the officers and crew, intending to make a lawful voyage to Newfoundland. But they had then sold her as she lay to one Captain Jolliffe, a Frenchman, who had a commission from the Prince of Condé, and it was under Jolliffe's command that she had captured the Breton ship. Grenville went on to explain that the *Castle of Comfort* did not attack the *Sauveur*, but was attacked by her, " and after a number of the *Castle of Comfort* were hurt, and one slain, they of the *Castle* did prevail against the said ship, and boarded and apprehended the same, and brought her to the port mentioned." The triple line of defence was ingenious. The *Castle* sailed under a Condé commission. If that was not valid, the defendants were not her owners. If that was not accepted, she acted only in self-defence and meritoriously " apprehended " an evildoer. In 1578 the King of France wrote to Elizabeth that the wrongs of Guillaume Le Fer were still unredressed.

For the next few years Grenville's name occurs frequently in the performance of a variety of public duties. He was Sheriff of Cornwall, as has been noted, in 1577. Next year he and others were preparing a force for service in Ireland in case the renegade Thomas Stukeley should succeed in landing there. Then we hear of him enquiring into piracies at Padstow and Falmouth, reporting on the condition of Tintagel Castle and the rebuilding of Boscastle quay, and going to Dover as one of the commissioners for the harbour improvements at that place. In 1584 he signed the Instrument of Association for the defence of Her Majesty, consequent upon the detection of Throgmorton's assassination plot, and in the same year he was M.P. for Cornwall for the second time.[2] Similar affairs for the same part of the

---

[1] High Court of Admiralty, Examinations, No. 22, 1576, July 19.
[2] References for these affairs are in *Calendar of Domestic State Papers, 1581–90*, pp. 29, 53, 140, 178, 181–6, 194, 209, 211, 228. Star Chamber Records, Eliz., G. Bundle VI, No. 4, contains details of a lawsuit in 1579–80.

country occupied much of Sir Walter Raleigh's attention, and the two men must have been well acquainted. Hence arose their association in the Virginia enterprise.

Since the 1570's English colonial ambitions had been modified. The Straits of Magellan were no longer regarded as the gateway to empire-building in the South Sea. Drake had made them the approach to the treasure-route, and his dazzling success made it certain that with whatever instructions an English expedition should enter the South Pacific, its actual procedure would be to raid the Peruvian coast. The North West Passage also had been revealed by Frobisher's voyages as a difficult undertaking, although it was by no means despaired of. By the 1580's the colonial party held that the first move in empire-building should be the founding of colonies on the Atlantic coast of North America. Such colonies would sell English goods to the natives, gather their commodities in return, discover gold mines, and serve as an advanced base for the penetration of the Passage to the Pacific, which last thus became an ulterior instead of a primary motive. To such views Gilbert became converted before the voyage of 1583, in which he lost his life, and after that tragedy Raleigh took up the promotion of the enterprise.

This is not the occasion for a full account of the Virginia colony. Grenville's first part in it was to lead the important expedition of 1585, which followed the reconnaissance made by Amadas and Barlow in the previous year.[1] On April 9 Grenville sailed in command of seven ships with over a hundred colonists in addition to the crews. Ralph Lane, an experienced officer, was to be the resident governor of the colony, and among the captains were Philip Amadas and Thomas Cavendish. Grenville went by way of the Canaries and Dominica to Porto Rico, where he made a fortified camp and constructed a pinnace whilst waiting for the arrival of Cavendish, who had parted company in bad weather. From Porto Rico he passed on along the north coast of Hispaniola, where he also landed and had friendly communications with the Spaniards. It is evident that he was looking about him with more in mind than the enterprise of Virginia; and indeed an English colonisation of the Greater Antilles would have been a feasible undertaking, for there were extremely few Spaniards in these vast islands, and

[1] The narratives of the Virginia voyages are printed in Hakluyt. See also A. Brown, *Genesis of the United States*, London, 1890.

a resolute exercise of sea-power might have ensured their conquest. Grenville, however, moved on, examined the Bahamas, and reached Wokokon in Virginia (now North Carolina) on June 26. He stayed two months, during which time he examined the mainland and adjacent islands. The colonists complained that he made things difficult for them by quarrelling with the Indians. The savages stole a silver cup. The chief of the offending village promised to restore it, and when he failed to do so, Grenville burned his huts and crops. We have only a bare outline of the story, without details, but on the face of it Grenville's conduct may not have been unreasonable. These Indians, as we know from later history, were not altogether the mild innocents they were reported to be by Amadas and Barlow, and Grenville may have considered it in the best interest of the colony to inspire respect for the white man's property.

In other ways things had not gone smoothly during the voyage and the planting of the settlement. Lane and some of the others were intensely indignant with Grenville's methods of command. Lane wrote to Raleigh and Walsingham complaining of Grenville's tyrannical conduct throughout, of his intolerable pride, insatiable ambition, and harsh proceedings towards all.[1] Again we have no details, and can only surmise whether all this heat arose from the enforcement of discipline among a party of headstrong gentlemen-adventurers. At any rate Grenville " performed the action directed " and did actually plant the settlers at the designated spot. He must have had before him the warning furnished by Gilbert's failure two years before, when indiscipline ruined the whole project and a seaman's death in mid-Atlantic saved the commander from having to answer for complete inadequacy as an administrator. Raleigh, whose money and credit were embarked in Virginia, showed no dissatisfaction with Grenville, and remained his friend in life and death.

On his way home Grenville captured a Spanish ship of 300 tons bound from Santo Domingo to Seville. Having no boat, he boarded her in a makeshift contrivance of sea-chests lashed together, which fell to pieces as he mounted her side. This prize was of considerable value. Grenville, in his report to Walsingham, said merely that she was laden with sugar and ginger, and added that the report that the

[1] *Calendar of Colonial State Papers, 1574-1660*, pp. 2, 3.

Spaniards brought gold, silver, and pearls from Santo Domingo was untrue. He had his reasons for a modest statement, as appears from a passage in a memorandum to the Queen written by one " W. H." a few weeks after his return. This informant stated that, according to letters from Seville, the prize contained registered treasure worth 600,000 ducats, besides as much more unregistered, " which is no treasure for private persons to usurp, seeing that her Majesty hath need thereof for the peace of the land." Bernardino de Mendoza, also, the Spanish ambassador lately resident in England and thence transferred to France, wrote to Philip II that the ship had a large treasure in gold, silver, pearls, cochineal, sugar, ivory, and hides, and that Raleigh had personally gone down to the port to take possession of her and prevent plundering.[1] W. H.'s hint was of the sort that the Queen was apt to take, but Raleigh was then a prime favourite, and so it is possible that he and Grenville saved their booty.

In 1586 Grenville sailed again for Virginia with supplies and reinforcements. He arrived in August to find that Lane and the colonists had all deserted the place two months before, having been given a passage home by Drake. In order to maintain possession Grenville left fifteen men with stores for two years, but when the next English fleet arrived in 1587, these men had been killed by the Indians. On his way home Grenville raided the Azores, " making spoil of the towns and there taking divers Spaniards." As with so many actions of his, we have no details. But he made a name of terror in the islands, as Linschoten recorded years afterwards. In respect of this 1586 voyage Mendoza sent from Paris an amusing piece of news to Spain, to the effect that Richard Grenville with seven ships had been captured by five Spanish vessels. Philip wrote on the margin, " I do not believe it." It was not by such odds that Grenville was to be caught.

The approach of the invasion menace in 1587 prevented Grenville from taking any further part in the Virginian enterprise. On March 8 the Council wrote to the Lords-Lieutenants of Devon and Cornwall that the Queen had appointed Sir Richard Grenville to survey the maritime defences and review the trained bands of those counties. In

[1] *Colonial Calendar, 1574–1660*, p. 4; *Foreign Calendar, Eliz.*, vol. XX, p. 230; *Spanish Calendar, Eliz.*, vol. III, p. 599.

December of the same year Raleigh reported to Burghley that Grenville was active in training the Devon militia. This was undoubtedly his command in 1588, and it is certain that he did not serve at sea against the Armada. In the spring he was preparing a fleet for Virginia, but it was forbidden to sail, and the ships were taken into the naval service. That Grenville did not accompany them we may be sure by the absence of his name from the records of the campaign, although we have no actual evidence of his doings until September. In that month the Queen directed him to stay all shipping on the north coasts of Devon and Cornwall because some of the retreating Spanish vessels had been driven to the west coast of Ireland.[1] The implication is that it might be necessary to transport troops to Ireland in case the Spaniards should have landed in force. It turned out not to be necessary, for the Irish massacred the unhappy castaways. During the two following years, 1589-90, Grenville seems to have been engaged mainly in Ireland, where he was associated with Raleigh in the plantation of Englishmen in Munster. It was a natural sequel to his previous activities, for in the view of that time the settlement of Ireland was regarded as a work of colonisation equally with that of Virginia, and Raleigh and Grenville were obviously the men to take the lead in it.

Grenville was a coloniser and a soldier, but he was also a seaman, and it does seem a little curious that he found no opportunity of taking part in the great sea campaigns of 1587, 1588, and 1589. These were the years of Drake's ascendancy, and the explanation may be that he was not on good terms with Drake. A Spanish report of 1587 points to this. On June 20 Mendoza wrote to the King that the English Government had decided not to make Grenville subordinate to Drake (in the expedition which singed Philip's beard), because " it was necessary to send some person who would not raise questions, but would obey Drake unreservedly."[2] Mendoza is a very unreliable informant, but there may be some truth in this. Grenville had been accused of pride and ambition, and perhaps entertained some social prejudice against submitting to the humbly born Drake. Perhaps also there was a grievance over the return of the Virginia colony in 1586. At any

---

[1] *Domestic Calendar, 1581-90*, pp. 393, 445, 544.
[2] *Spanish Calendar, Eliz.*, vol. IV, p. 110.

rate, it is not until after Drake has been placed in retirement that Grenville at last comes forward as an officer of the Navy.

In the summer of 1591 Lord Thomas Howard was sent to the Azores with six fighting ships to intercept a great Spanish convoy expected from the West Indies, while the Earl of Cumberland cruised with an armed squadron on the Spanish coast. It was vital to Philip to get this convoy through, and he equipped a strong force under Alonso de Baçan to go to the Azores and drive Howard away. Baçan had over fifty vessels, of which more than a third were of serious fighting value. Howard's six were attended by one or two privateers and a few victuallers. In the *Revenge*, as vice-admiral of the English squadron, sailed Sir Richard Grenville. Cumberland, learning of the departure of Baçan, sent off Captain Middleton in a pinnace to warn Howard, and Middleton arrived only a short time before the Spaniards themselves appeared.

Howard found himself surprised in an awkward situation. He had been several months at sea, sickness had reduced his crews to half strength, his ships were foul with weed and therefore slow, and within board they had become intolerably dirty. The remedy for the sickness was the routine known as " rummaging." That is to say, the sick were taken ashore to recover in camp, the stone ballast into which the refuse of food and cookery had percolated was thrown overboard, new ballast was collected from the beach, and all the interior of the ship was scrubbed and fumigated with vinegar. If a suitable sheltered coast and tidal range were available, the ships were also careened and the weed and barnacles scrubbed off their bottoms. Howard was in the anchorage of Flores in the act of rummaging when the Spaniards caught him. His sick were ashore together with working parties, and his foul ballast had been thrown out. But he had not taken in new ballast nor had he careened. His ships were thus undermanned, foul under water, and unable to carry their full sail area for lack of ballast. Moreover, in their light condition they would heel unduly in a breeze and be unable to use their heavy guns on the lee side for fear of swamping through the open ports.

For what occurred we have the following contemporary authorities, none of whom was present at the action : (1) Sir Walter Raleigh, who wrote a few months afterwards, from the testimony of survivors, a nobly worded vindication of

Grenville and Howard. His work was intended for the general public and gives the personal details and heroic incidents which have rendered the fight immortal, but it omits the vital facts of times and distances which are necessary to a true understanding of what took place between the first alarm and the envelopment of the *Revenge* in the midst of the Spanish fleet; (2) the Dutchman, Jan Huyghen van Linschoten, who was resident in the islands and talked with Spanish and English survivors of the battle. Linschoten makes no attempt at a critical reconstruction of the position, and credulously retails idle gossip, notably the ridiculous story that Grenville was in the habit of chewing and swallowing wine-glasses. A man who could swallow that is not to be taken very seriously; (3) Sir Richard Hawkins, who included a brief account in his *Observations*, written in 1602–3. He approved of Grenville's conduct, and had some right to express an opinion, since he had passed through the same experience himself, of a hopeless fight against odds to the bitter end of the surrender of a sinking ship; (4) Sir William Monson, a naval officer of the period, who wrote in his old age some thirty years afterwards. He decries Grenville, as might be expected, since the general tone of his voluminous writings reveals him as a mean-minded man who could never appreciate the merits of anyone better than himself. His historical facts are also frequently inaccurate.[1]

Such are the authorities. Between them they give no information of the actual position of the anchorage, the distances of the English ships from each other and the shore, the direction and force of the wind, the direction from which the Spaniards approached, the time occupied in the various movements, or the true extent to which the *Revenge* and other vessels were handicapped by want of ballast. Lack of these particulars would seem to discount positive criticisms, and to the present writer it seems best to confess ignorance and to suggest rather than assert explanations.

The first suggestion must be that Grenville was possibly not a mad fanatic, but a man who found himself in a tight place

---

[1] Sir W. Raleigh, " *A true report of the fight about the Isles of the Azores,*" etc., printed in Hakluyt ; *The Voyage of John Huyghen van Linschoten to the East Indies,* Hakluyt Society, 1885, vol. II, pp. 308–13 (extracts also in Hakluyt, but with omissions and mistranslations) ; *The Observations of Sir Richard Hawkins,* Argonaut Press, 1933, pp. 16–17 ; *The Naval Tracts of Sir William Monson,* edited by M. Oppenheim, Navy Records Society, 1902, etc., vol. I, pp. 253–68.

and acted upon calculation. Consider his career, his employments of trust, his good relations with his fellow magnates and the Queen's ministers. He was a disciplinarian undoubtedly, and discipline was generally resented in maritime circles in his day. This may account for the statements that he was a man very unquiet in his mind, of nature very cruel so that his own people hated him for his tyranny and feared him much, and that he rounded off his meals with broken glass—all of which are tavern talk and emanate from Linschoten. Perhaps he did rush on his death in an access of devilish pride, but one cannot be certain.

When the Spanish fleet appeared, Howard quitted the anchorage in haste. Grenville, in the *Revenge*, was left behind. In the reason for his delay lies the crux of the discussion about his conduct. Raleigh says that he remained " to recover the men that were upon the Island, which otherwise had been lost." Hawkins had probably read Raleigh's tract, and quite as probably had discussed the matter with other officers; and he was in the habit of forming independent views. He says: " Sir Richard Grenville got eternal honour and reputation of great valour and of an experimented [i.e. experienced] soldier, choosing rather to sacrifice his life and to pass all danger whatsoever than to fail in his obligation, by gathering together those that had remained ashore in that place, though with the hazard of his ship and company. And rather we ought to embrace an honourable death than to live with infamy and dishonour by failing in duty; and I account that he and his country got much honour in that occasion."

Monson gives a different explanation: " But Sir Richard Grenville, being a stubborn man and imagining this fleet to come from the Indies and not to be the Armada of which they were informed, would by no means be persuaded by his master or company to cut his cable to follow his admiral, as all discipline of war did teach him." Linschoten, in dealing with this part of the action, says only, " the cause why could not be known." At that we must leave it, for there are essential facts that we do not know. Was the *Revenge* nearer to the shore than the other ships? Did Grenville assume that someone had to take off the men on the island, and that the duty fell upon him? It was a matter for instant decision, and he could not consult

Howard; the signalling of detailed messages was then unknown. In Hawkins's view Grenville performed his obvious duty. In Monson's he violated all discipline of war. Hawkins was at least as good an authority as Monson, an officer of greater experience, and a man of infinitely higher character.

Howard with five ships weathered the Spanish fleet by a narrow margin, and maintained the windward position. Grenville was cut off. Up wind lay the great armada, and beyond them his friends. The master's first impulse was to set the mainsail and run for it, before the wind and away from both fleets. Grenville forbade it. Under easy sail he stood to windward in the desperate hope of pushing through the Spaniards and rejoining Howard. Here lies the accusation of insane pride. Is there no alternative? The critics say, on the suggestion of Linschoten, that the *Revenge* could have got away, being one of the fastest ships of her time. No doubt she was, but in her then condition she was as light as a cask and as foul as a half-tide rock. Could she have outsailed every one of the Spaniards in a general chase in which only one would need to catch her to pin her until the rest came up? We do not know, but Grenville did. There were good vessels in Baçan's fleet. Several of them, we are told, were Dutch, and the Dutchmen did not build sluggards. Was it fury or reason that forbade the setting of the great mainsail, half the total area in those ships, as their pictures show us? Without it the *Revenge* had no chance of getting away. With it perhaps Grenville judged she risked capsizing and an ignominious end. Just so had his father died in the *Mary Rose*, not indeed in running away, but in hastening too eagerly to fight. Such things stick in a man's mind.

These are all suppositions, but so also are those cold, shallow judgments in the *D.N.B.* and the *Cambridge Modern History*. It is a national habit to belittle our heroes. Perhaps it is sounder than blind adulation, but an occasional speech for the defence is not out of place. The maritime history of the sixteenth century is an unsuitable theme for confident criticism, for the evidence is nearly always defective.

What followed the reader knows.[1] Tennyson's *Revenge*

[1] The present paper is limited to the biographical aspect, which Tennyson expressed with genius. His poem should be re-read by those who do not know every line of it, and no less should they read Raleigh's prose. For modern interpretations of the campaign and the battle, see Oppenheim's analysis in his *Monson, ut supra,* and Professor Geoffrey Callender's *The Battle of Flores*, in *History*, July, 1919.

gives the essence of Raleigh's *True Report*, from which the poet drew all his details except the dying speech, which comes from Linschoten. That, by the way, is probably fictitious. No Englishman, prisoner or not, seems to have heard of it. If Raleigh had, we may be sure he would have placed it on record. Linschoten says that it was spoken in Spanish and admits that his version is partly imaginary—" these or such other like words." Raleigh ends the story thus:

" Sir Richard died, as it is said, the second or third day aboard the General, and was by them greatly bewailed. What became of his body, whether it were buried in the sea or on the land, we know not. The comfort that remaineth to his friends is that he hath ended his life honourably in respect of the reputation won to his nation and country, and of the same to his posterity; and that, being dead, he hath not outlived his own honour."

CHRISTOPHER MARLOWE
1564–1593

By
ALFRED NOYES

CHRISTOPHER MARLOWE

by ALFRED NOYES

THE name of Christopher Marlowe has become almost a
symbol of a certain aspect of the Elizabethan period—
its full-blooded grasp of life; its intellectual and spiritual
voyages of adventure into the unknown; and its devil-may-
care desire to " batter the shining palace of the sun." He
was fortunate in the moment of his birth; for, like most
other men whose names have become symbols and a convenient means of focusing a period into sharpness, he owes
his place in the history-books, neither to the stars nor to any
peculiar depth in his own nature, but simply to the fact that,
with one peculiar talent, he walks into the picture, and is
easily and vividly focused there at exactly the right con-
juncture. Like Diego Valdez, who became a High
Admiral because, at the right moment, " the dawn-wind
brought his top-sails," Marlowe was at the mercy of wind
and wave in most things. His galleon was a somewhat
gaudy affair and, to the critical eye, very far from seaworthy.
But it appeared at a crucial moment; and, when it was
finally carried away, it was washed up and broken on the
coasts of an El Dorado that he did not live to explore.

Nothing is more difficult than to measure and assess
his real achievement. The re-examination of traditional
literary values is usually limited to those of our immediate
predecessors, and contemporary rebels are often meekly content to follow the merely contemporary changes of fashion.
There is no question that, in an age when additions to
the shelf-room of famous libraries are measured in miles, a
more severe process of re-examination will soon be imposed
upon us, if not by our critical faculties, then, certainly by
the laws of time and space. The scholars who deal with
literature from an historical point of view do occasionally
fall into the specialist's besetting sin. They help us to " know

more and more about less and less "; and incidentally tend—sometimes out of mere curiosity—to counteract the valuable principle of the " survival of the fittest " in literature, very much as the humanitarian, on higher grounds, may interfere with it in real life. Lowell, though he confessed to an early hero-worship of Marlowe, uttered a salutary warning against the vague habit of regarding all Elizabethan dramatists as minor Shakespeares, or Shakespeares that might have been if time and fate had been kinder. Sir William Watson's fine quatrain is equally just and true:

> " I close my Marlowe's page, my Shakespeare's ope.
> How welcome, after gong and cymbal's din,
> The continuity, the long s low slope
> And vast curves of the gradual violin."

This may be coupled with Ben Jonson's reference to Marlowe, in his great tribute to Shakespeare,

> " How far thou didst our Lily outshine,
> Or sporting Kyd, or Marlowe's mighty line."

In this reference to the power of the line in Marlowe's work, Jonson lays his finger on the one outstanding talent which Marlowe possessed; and on one of the oddest phenomena in literature. He associates him with Lyly and Kyd. Readers of the *Spanish Tragedy* may well exercise themselves as to whether Jonson himself were not a little sportive in his application of " sporting " to its almost farcical horrors. But it is the line, the single end-stopped line, that he picks out as the leading characteristic of Marlowe's work. Sometimes, it is true, we get two of these lines in succession, each complete in itself. Once or twice we get a series of about a dozen. They bear little or no relation to the structure of the play, or to the character who speaks them. Bajazeth, Tamburlaine, Faustus, the Pope, the Jew of Malta, and even Edward the Second all use them in the same exalted vein:

> " Batter the shining palace of the sun . . .
> And ride in triumph through Persepolis. . . .
> Adding this golden sentence to our praise
> That Peter's heirs should tread on emperors."

In this kind of way it would almost be possible to link all the memorable lines of Marlowe together into one passage, with as much or as little real coherence as they actually have in his plays, and—in some ways—with a more essential harmony. For some of his single lines which, like blank cheques, are capable in detachment of being filled up for any amount of emotion, denote in their context—if character counts for anything—a most strictly limited liability. The line,

" *Infinite riches in a little room,*"

has been quoted scores of times to express a thousand subtleties. It has been used to suggest the way in which great art, for instance, represents much in little, by a kind of sacramental symbolism. But, as spoken by the Jew of Malta, gloating over a diamond, the line can be made to include the greater meaning only by doing violence to the character that Marlowe is depicting. This is not to say that the line does not deserve the praise that has been lavished upon it. But it is a fact that Marlowe had a gift for writing fine single lyrical lines, which express in themselves the heights of a lyrical ecstasy, and bear no relation to the characters who utter them, since almost all his serious characters use them in turn, and each line seems to be dictated by exactly the same ecstatic emotion, whether it arises from a diamond, the sacking of a city, a decree from Rome, or the vision of the phantom Helen.

" *Was this the face that launched a thousand ships*
And burnt the topless towers of Ilium ?"

This last passage is curiously illustrative of the way in which Marlowe's ecstasy could detach itself. None of the critics (so far as I know) has touched upon the fact that it is almost a translation of a passage in Lucian; or that this passage has a Shakespearean quality and a real ground entirely lacking to the circumstances of Marlowe's dream.

In Lucian, as in Shakespeare's *Hamlet*, the observer is looking, not at a phantom of the living, but at the skull of the dead, and this, as it seems to me, gives the real ground of the emotion, which is exactly that of the famous cry of Hamlet, over the skull of Yorick.

These are the original words in Lucian:

HERMES: Τουτὶ τὸ κρανίον ἡ Ἑλένη ἐστίν.
MENIPPUS: Εἶτα αἱ χίλιαι νηες δια τοῦτο ἐπληρώθησαν ἐξ ἁπάσηζ τῆς Ἑλλάδος, καὶ τοσοῦτοι ἔπεσον Ἕλληνές τε καὶ βάρβαροι, καὶ τοσαῦται πόλεις ἀνάστατοι γεγόνασιν.

The passage is thus rendered in the fine version by H. W. and F. G. Fowler:

HERMES: This skull is Helen.
MENIPPUS: And for this a thousand ships carried warriors from every part of Greece; Greeks and barbarians were slain, and cities made desolate.

But the whole deep ground of the emotion in the phrases " for *this* " and " was *this* " is lost in the reproduction of the living Helen and doubly lost when Faustus desires her kiss. Here again Shakespeare seems by native power to give the authentic ground. " Here hung those lips which I *have* kissed."

But there is no need to dwell on this particular instance, though Marlowe directly or indirectly was influenced in other ways by the sceptical spirit of Lucian, as were many other men of the Renaissance; notably, and in a far less crude and slap-dash fashion, Erasmus and Sir Thomas More. The colloquies of the former point to a literary delight, not in Luther, but in Lucian, as the source of their iconoclasm. Many of the " irreligious " remarks attributed to Marlowe by tradition strike one as naïve schoolboy imitations of the witty author of the *Life of Peregrine*; but the chief value of the comparison is perhaps in the light which it reflects upon what may be called the historical standard of literary criticism. Whether there be any absolute æsthetic standard or not, it seems to be generally accepted that there must be a double standard for literature; and that though Falconer's *Ship-wreck*, æsthetically regarded, may be an absurd piece of clap-trap, we must still, on historical grounds, encumber our shelves with the " unrivalled strains " in which he set out to " deplore ":

" *The impervious horrors of a leeward shore.*"

There may be some truth in this: but we ought not to forget that " history " is not confined to our own country;

and that, in any complete view, the earlier masterpieces of other nations may justly constitute a standard. In his notes to Jonson's *Underwoods*, Gifford says that " it is not just to consign Marlowe to ridicule. He and his contemporary, Peele, were produced just as the chaos of ignorance was breaking up : they were among the earliest to perceive the glimmering of sense and nature, and struggled to reach the light."

The truth of this is obviously relative only to our own literature, and even then it is only a half-truth. Marlowe had been preceded by Chaucer in his own language. He had translated some of the classics ; and, in a world that had already produced an Æschylus and a Sophocles, it is difficult to see how he can be counted among " the earliest to perceive the glimmering of sense and nature." Even more difficult is it to reconcile this point of view with the remarks of a critic like Charles Lamb, that, in Marlowe's *Edward the Second*, " the death scene of Marlowe's king moves pity and terror beyond any scene ancient or modern with which I am acquainted."

If this is true, we can only suppose that Lamb was un-acquainted with the Lear of Shakespeare, and the Œdipus of Sophocles. But it is not true. It is merely an instance of the fact that English criticism has for the most part been wildly impressionistic, capricious, or merely declamatory. A large part of the criticism of poetry is based upon vague recollections of isolated passages, and sometimes isolated lines, torn out of their context and enshrined in textbooks. I suppose that at least ten thousand school-books could be found in which two lines of Faustus about Helen would be unintelligently quoted and re-quoted, not from the original, but from other textbooks, and the in-finite riches of Marlowe would be taken for granted on the strength of that isolated jewel.

And now I have a personal confession to make. My own admiration for the verbal splendours of Marlowe was once immense. But, on carefully re-reading him, my chief im-pression is that no English poet is so essentially a poet of immaturity. It is a glorious immaturity in many ways ; for it is the immaturity of genius ; but, both in its virtues and its vices, it is the work of an uproarious schoolboy, at one of the crudest stages of intellectual development. All these invitations to—

> *" Batter the shining palace of the sun "*

and

> *" Slice the dark sea with sable-coloured ships,"*

are magnificent in sound as isolated lines, though not in long passages where they become monotonous. They are just the kind of thing that a literary Tom Sawyer loves to bellow out of sheer physical exuberance on a windy day at the seaside. The bridled kings, drawing the coach of Tamburlaine, are simply school-fags drawing the coach of the school-dictator. The dungeon of King Edward, into which all the drains of the castle empty themselves, is just the kind of thing a schoolboy would design for the unpopular master. The extraordinary devices of the *Jew of Malta* for murdering his enemies, his friends, the entire population of a convent, and his own daughter are not, in any way, subtilised by the isolated

> *" Infinite riches in a little room."*

Indeed, many of the beauties of Marlowe (and the beauty of these isolated lines is undeniable as far as it goes) appear to have been inserted more or less at random, to provide a fine speech for a quite unsuitable speaker. The famous passage on " beauty " and " all the pens that ever poets held " is utterly out of place in its context. What on earth it has to do with the impossible creature to whom it is attributed, or how anyone can take that impossible creature seriously for a single moment, except as a schoolboy cheats himself into a belief in the melodramatics that schoolboys love, I am unable to conceive. In many passages, even of *Edward the Second*, one encounters a note of sheer silliness. The infatuation of the King for Gaveston is not a subject that can easily support the weight of a tragedy, as it is handled by Marlowe. The king " love-sick for his minion," as Marlowe depicts him, is too feeble and contemptible to arouse the feeling upon which tragedy depends.

> *" My Gaveston!*
> *Welcome to Tynmouth! welcome to thy friend!*
> *Thy absence made me droop and pine away;*
> *For, as the lovers of fair Danaë*
> *When she was locked up in a brazen tower*

> *Desired her more and waxed outrageous*
> *So did it fare with me; and now thy sight*
> *Is sweeter far than was thy parting hence*
> *Bitter and irksome to my sobbing heart."*

So says the king, and Gaveston replies in these simple, and unaffected words:

> *" The shepherd, nipt with biting winter's rage,*
> *Frolics not more to see the painted spring*
> *Than I do to behold your majesty."*

And, in another passage, the king himself expresses a similar manly sentiment:

> *" Make several kingdoms of this monarchy*
> *And share it equally amongst you all*
> *So I may have some nook or corner left*
> *To frolic with my dearest Gaveston."*

On my own mind, this sort of stuff—and the whole of the belauded *Edward the Second* is tainted with it—has an effect of slightly nauseating silliness. The best excuse that can be made for it is that it is the crude work of an adolescent mind that never arrived at maturity.

We are left, then, with Marlowe's " mighty line," as his real contribution to the literature of the drama; and it was one of the chief tasks of Shakespeare, on the technical side, to show how this mighty line could run on, and be modulated into the period, so that it was no longer an isolated unit, but the norm by departure from which the really great and subtle effects were to be achieved. But this is not quite all. It is a long way from

> *" Batter the shining palace of the sun "*

to

> *" When you do dance, I wish you*
> *A wave of the sea."*

But, strangely enough, it is not so far to

> *" The light that never was on sea or land "*

or

> *" A sound like thunder, everlastingly."*

And here, I think, we have the clue to most of the bewildered praise of Marlowe. He was, first and foremost, a lyric poet groping for his medium. His mighty line was not only mighty. It had all the mysticism of the romantic movement in it, though, as he used it, the mysticism was out of place. " Infinite riches in a little room " might have been the perfect close to a sonnet by Wordsworth in the vein of his " narrow convent room," or by the poet who wrote of " laborious orient ivory, sphere in sphere." And so, with Marlowe's one almost unqualified success—his *Hero and Leander*—we find ourselves almost at once in the company of Keats. There are one or two lines that are too florid, in the artificial manner of Sidney's *Arcadia* (the description of Hero's chirruping buskins, for instance). There is what we may call a Gaveston passage which, again, is merely a symptom of immaturity. But, apart from these very brief passages the poem is one long delight, and may well rank with the masterpieces of Keats. The amazing difference in quality between this poem and the plays can only be explained by the fact that, in the lyrical narrative, Marlowe had drawn nearer to his true medium, while in the drama he was laying heavily about him, like a man in a fog. It is not without significance that Shakespeare himself made the ranting spirit of Pistol use Marlowe's " mighty line," in some of his superbly humorous passages of critical parody.

> " *A foutra for the world and worldling's base!*
> *I speak of Africa and golden joys.*"

It is all there—the far horizon, and the vague high-sounding ecstasy. And again—

> " *Shall pack-horses*
> *And hollow pampered jades of Asia*
> *Which cannot go but thirty miles a day*
> *Compare with Cæsars and with Cannibals ?* "

But he does not laugh at *Hero and Leander*, or the " dead shepherd " who wrote it. At the same time, it is a mistake to underrate Chapman's continuation of the poem. If it be true, as our moderns appear to think, that Donne is a greater poet than Waller, and that " Go and catch a falling star " is a finer lyric than " Go, lovely rose," then I can see no reason why Chapman's intellectual subtleties—some of them extremely beautiful in form—should not rank higher than the expression of physical beauty, exquisite as it is, in the earlier section of the poem. I will not say that it is so; for I am by no means sure of the premises. But those who accept the premises should find it difficult to confirm the traditional view of the superiority of Marlowe's verse.

> " *His body was as straight as Circe's wand.*
> *Jove might have sipt out nectar from his hand.*"

Beautiful as this undoubtedly is, I cannot feel sure that there is any passage in Marlowe's section of the poem that is superior (by the modern standard, if that be valid) to Chapman's fine passage in the third sestiad.

> " *Then thou most strangely intellectual fire*
> *That proper to my soul hast power to inspire*
> *Her burning faculties, and with the wings*
> *Of thy unsphered flame visit'st the springs*
> *Of spirits immortal; now (as swift as time*
> *Doth follow motion) find the eternal clime*
> *Of his free soul, whose living subject stood*
> *Up to the chin in the Pierian flood,*
> *And drank to me half this Musæan story*
> *Inscribing it to deathless memory:*
> *Confer with it, and make my pledge as deep*
> *That neither's draught be consecrate to sleep. . . .*"

I will not attempt to decide; but I know which comes the nearer to just those qualities in Donne which induce the moderns to rate him above the simpler lyrists. Strangely enough, too, the latter passage has striking affinities with certain passages in Keats; and there is a certain fitness in the fact that Marlowe having expressed the physical beauty as perfectly as he could, Chapman should complicate the theme with intellectual and spiritual motives.

The poem of *Hero and Leander* may almost be taken as a parable of Marlowe's own life and quest for the ideal beauty.

His own story ended in disaster, as he was struggling through a darker sea; and, on reading all the later evidence in the case, I still believe that—like most " evidence " of this kind—it obscures rather than reveals the true history;

that the latest account of his death has many weak spots in it; and that, on several points, Sir Bernard Spilsbury would make short work of it in a modern court of law. *Suppressio veri* has left obvious gaps in the tale of his death at Deptford; and for me it is still best told in parable, as I tried to tell it long before the newer evidence was discovered. I cannot understand why the festive gathering at the Deptford Inn with only two companions should have begun at ten o'clock in the morning, or why they should have been still at it so late in the afternoon of the same day. They had to make a longish journey to get there. The festivity—according to the evidence—seems to have consisted chiefly of a seven hours' conversation with two not particularly congenial friends; and the thinnest part of the story is that which describes how Marlowe, reaching behind one of those friends, drew that friend's dagger out of its sheath, stabbed him in the back, and then—in the ensuing tussle for the dagger, ran his eye upon the point and died in a way that modern doctors say is impossible. The probabilities of character and psychology are all against the literal truth of that story, as well as other probabilities. Moreover, the story is badly worked out. As a novelist might say, it is " not properly realised." Indeed, it is not realisable, not quite picturable by the imagination. On the other hand, I cannot trace the origin of the legend that Marlowe's death at Deptford took place at a festal gathering on the deck of the *Golden Hind* which had been drawn up there for public display. But I can imagine *that*, as a reason for his visit to Deptford, at ten o'clock in the morning. I can imagine a festal occasion *there* of some duration. And, again, like all good legends, this tale was a parable, representing a little more of the truth than could be expressed by tongue, or pen, or legal evidence of interested " witnesses." There may be a certain truth in all the accounts, in the balladmonger's tales of " Archer," and the quarrel over a woman, for instance. But whether Marlowe died in the back-parlour of an inn or not, this vagabond child of genius died at the same moment on a nobler stage, for which no symbol would be more fitting than the deck of the *Golden Hind*, the *Pelican* of the great Elizabethan adventure, the ship that sacked the Spanish Main, and plying out into the unknown ocean-sea came to its home in amazement, simply by sailing on.

SIR JOHN HAWKINS

1532–1595

By

PHILIP LINDSAY

SIR JOHN HAWKINS

by PHILIP LINDSAY

UNDER the portrait of Sir John Hawkins in Holland's *Herωologia* are engraved the words: *Advauncement by dilligence*, and a brief reading of Hawkins's life might perhaps lead one to accept this statement as fitting him perfectly. Most historians have accepted it. Yet, diligence alone cannot explain the greatness of his achievement, nor the vision behind his actions. He acted nothing that he had not carefully planned, making certain that success would mean glory for England, or at least, for English trade. He was diligent, without doubt, and he was cautious; but he was also subtle, patient, and courageous. His historical proximity to his kinsman, Drake, has obscured his fame, relegating him to a disproportionately small place in the history of English seamanship. Just as Shakespeare's brilliance shadows the lesser Elizabethan dramatists, so does Drake's glory dim the quieter, steadier, subtler genius of Hawkins. The two were often together, and their last, most tragic voyage shows them in contrast, revealing pathetically the human weaknesses of each.

Hawkins, to the average Englishman, is merely the man who started the slave-trade. A certain associative sense of shame attaches to his name, and because of that few have troubled to study him. Few, therefore, have understood or appreciated his greatness. The famous slave-trading expeditions are by no means the important passages in his life. They have no connection with his really great achievement, and their chief interest is that they reveal Hawkins as a man of action and that they show us the first glimpse of his cautious desire to keep always on the right side of the law.

Hawkins was a merchant as well as a sailor, and these trading expeditions were the outcome of a definite ambition. They were not reckless, daredevil, piratical exploits. He was not out for plunder, he robbed no man. All his actions were entirely legal, for at the period of his first voyage in 1562, England and Spain were not enemies. It is of course impossible to know for certain what Hawkins intended, because he was far too wary a man to commit his schemes to paper, yet Mr. J. A. Williamson very plausibly suggests that he was offering armed service to Philip II of Spain in return for a permission to trade in the Indies.[1] Hawkins hoped to force trade on Spain. Accordingly he sent two ships to Spanish ports on his return voyage, to test the Spanish attitude by pretending friendliness and trust. He was not long in doubt. Only one of the ships reached Spain, and it was instantly seized by Philip. The other went to Portugal and was seized there. Neither of them actually belonged to his fleet. One was a Spanish ship chartered in Hispaniola; the other was possibly but not certainly a Portuguese vessel brought over from Guinea. Hawkins could well afford to let both of them go; yet it is probable [2] that he journeyed, with great courage, to the Spanish court to plead his case in person in an effort to recover them. He was never a coward, being always sustained by a sense of the justness of his actions, but at the same time, he was not reckless. In the story of this first voyage, we see him clearly. We see the breadth of his ambitions, in the vision of such a trade, in the care he took to appear to be acting legally, in the courage that urged him to travel afterwards to the country he had wronged.

The second voyage took place in 1564–5; and the third, in 1567, although described in many books, must in part be treated again here. It ended in tragedy, yet it shows Hawkins's sagacity and courage, and it includes a strange incident, apparently to Drake's discredit, which has never been explained. "The *Judith* [Drake's ship]," said Hawkins, "forsook us in our great misery." Drake made no explanation that has survived, so that we have one side of the case only; but Hawkins was evidently quite certain that Drake had deserted him in a moment of peril.

Hawkins had six ships when he set sail from Plymouth,

---

[1] J. A. Williamson's *Sir John Hawkins: The Time and the Man* (Oxford, 1927), is the definitive life of Hawkins, and it is of great interest. I might add that the quotations in the following article are all from contemporary letters or from the accounts of eye-witnesses.

[2] See Williamson's book. Professor J. E. Neale puts up a strong argument against the journey to Spain in his review in *History*.

and he was almost immediately caught in a violent storm that separated his fleet, and that nearly sank the flagship, the *Jesus of Lubeck*. Hawkins was something of a puritan, and it is not surprising that he called his crew together and made them pray while the winds tore down upon them, tugging at the masts and flinging the vessel from side to side, from giant wave to wave:

> " The weather was very extreme, and brought the *Jesus* in such case that she opened in the stern aft, and leaks broke up in divers places in her. But where she opened in the stern the leak was so great that into one place there was thrust 15 pieces of baize to stop the place . . . the which when our general saw he began to enter into prayer and besought them to pray with him, the while indeed he yet letted not with great travail to search the ship fore and aft for her leaks. Thus we passed the fourth day at the mercy of God."

He succeeded in stopping the leaks, the winds withdrew, and the *Jesus* eventually staggered to Teneriffe, which Hawkins had appointed as a meeting-place for such an emergency.

His troubles were not over. Two of his officers, Edward Dudley and George Fitzwilliam, lost their tempers, and decided to fight a duel ashore. Hawkins tried to put a stop to this nonsense, and while arguing with Dudley, he struck him. Dudley drew his rapier, Hawkins drew his, and there was a brief skirmish, in which both were slightly wounded. The sailors would have murdered Dudley for his mutinous violence if Hawkins had not restrained them. In a crisis such as this a commander shows the measure of his genius, for he should be neither weak nor unjustly harsh. Hawkins took a middle course. He said that he would pardon Dudley for the harm done to himself, but that he could not pardon him for the injury done to the Queen through her representative, nor for the danger in which he had placed the expedition by such disobedience. Then he took up an arquebus, loaded it with two bullets, and told Dudley to prepare to die. The wretched man fell to his knees, crying that he deserved death, while the crew gathered round, and implored Hawkins for mercy. Hawkins raised the gun. Then, as if overwhelmed by sudden pity, he put the weapon aside and commanded the irons to be struck from Dudley. He had no further trouble after that.

If he had no more trouble with the crew, he found plenty on the Main. The trading part of the voyage was over, and all Hawkins needed was a stock of victuals, when he put into the port of San Juan de Ulua. While there, collecting food and repairing the flagship, the Seville plate fleet arrived. Thirteen ships rose from the skyline, bearing down on the port where the English fleet lay. Hawkins dared not risk a fight, for England and Spain were at peace, and he had no delusions about the swiftness of Elizabeth's justice towards a reckless servant. She would not raise the arquebus in order to fling it aside. In this perilous corner, with the enemy in the open sea outside, himself snug in port, what was Hawkins to do? He could keep the Spaniards in the open and let the winds batter them to pieces; but that would be as dangerous as open battle, and as unforgivable. As usual, cautiously he took the middle course and sent sailors to man the batteries on the island, drawing up his fleet to bar the mouth of the port. Although he could not fight, he could threaten and demand terms. The new Viceroy of Mexico was aboard the Spaniards, and he swore that he would enter San Juan, let who would try to stop him. This was the first cry of outraged dignity; but soon he calmed enough to give in, to swear to keep the peace, and to promise not to land armed men, while Hawkins could gather victuals and man the batteries. Then he entered, and the English and Spanish fleets lay side by side at anchor with only a few yards between them. Hawkins must have known that he could not trust the Viceroy, but the oath and promise of safety placed legal right on his side. He was in a difficult position, in which it was essential not to give any excuse for charging him with piracy, and in which also his only hope of a favourable outcome was that the Spaniards would respect the solemn agreement. If the Viceroy showed opened hostilities, he would be in the wrong and Hawkins would be in the right, while he possessed the paper bearing his enemy's signature. Yet he was alert for the first sign of treachery, being in hostile waters, and his men scarcely numbered a third of the Viceroy's.

It was not long before the Viceroy acted. Hawkins was at dinner, when a trumpet-call brought him to his feet and on to the deck. The Spaniards had attacked the batteries

and were boarding the English ships. " God and St.
George! " cried Hawkins, " upon these traitorous villains! "
The batteries, the key position, had fallen, and Hawkins
could only fight with his ships. He cut the mooring lines,
drew clear of the enemy and opened fire. It took terrible
effect. The Spanish admiral sank, the vice-admiral blew
up. Hawkins, in this perilous situation with the land-
batteries pounding at him, with the larger Spanish ships
training their guns upon his *Jesus*, showed no fear. He

> " called to Samuel his page for a cup of beer, who
> brought it to him in a silver cup, and he, drinking to all
> men, willed the gunners to stand by their ordnance
> lustily like men. He had no sooner set the cup out of
> his hand, but a demi-culverin shot struck away the cup
> and a cooper's plane that stood by the mainmast, and
> ran out on the other side of the ship; which nothing dis-
> mayed our general, for he ceased not to encourage us,
> saying, ' Fear nothing! for God, who hath preserved us
> from this shot, will also deliver us from these traitors
> and villains.' "

Most of the fleet was lost. The *Jesus* was smashed beyond
hope of rescue and was surrounded by shattered and burning
vessels. In the midst of the fight, while repelling boarders
and commanding the gunners, Hawkins did not forget the
treasure he had aboard. He ordered it to be moved from
the *Jesus* into the *Minion* and into Drake's vessel, the
Judith. Fireships were loosed upon him, and these flaming
vessels, the horror of seamen, ended the battle. The *Jesus*
was deserted. Hawkins, with his men, leaped into the
Minion, which was at that moment creeping away; he was
nearly left behind, for he remained until the last moment,
until it was useless to stay longer and when no further
treasure could be shifted.

The fight had been fierce, and it showed that Hawkins,
besides being sailor and merchant, was a general. More than
that, the fight became as a battle-cry to the English, for they
never forgot the Spanish treachery. From this time on, the
English turned pirates like the French. They were inspired
by the lust for vengeance and they had a fierce and terrible
memory to urge them forward. Hawkins himself, except for
his last ill-fated voyage, never again sailed for the Indies;

but others followed where he had led, and chief amongst them was his kinsman, the great Sir Francis Drake, who so mysteriously had crept away from the fight in San Juan.

Hawkins now entered upon a different stage, the stage of politics. It is with surprise at first that we find him involved in Ridolfi's plot to rescue Mary Stuart and to aid a Spanish invasion. There is no evidence that Hawkins had communication with Ridolfi himself, but he dealt with Gueran de Spes, the Spanish Ambassador, and seems definitely to have become a spy. Briefly, he went to de Spes in the first place to ask for the release of the men imprisoned at Seville, and finding the Spaniard inclined to talk unguardedly he tempted him by abusing his own country and his Queen. The conversation developed into an arrangement by which Hawkins swore to assist a Spanish invasion, in return for which his men were to be released, and he was to be paid for his treachery. He was meanwhile reporting this to Burghley and was acting under his instructions. The men were released, and the rest of the plan came to nothing, because Burghley obtained full information of the plot (only in a minor degree from Hawkins) and arrested the Duke of Norfolk. It is very unlikely that Hawkins actually received any money from Philip; but the incident shows that the sailor had become not merely a spy but an able intriguer.

The really important achievement of Hawkins's life was the building of the English Navy. The Admiralty was then in its normal state of corruption, matching the corruption of other departments of Tudor government. Hawkins stopped this; he swept aside the wholesale graft, he built a policy of honour, and placed the administration on a decent basis unknown before, although upon a basis that was soon to be undermined by the terrible corruption under the Stuarts. It was a thankless and a painful task. He naturally infuriated his colleagues, and he had continually to fight lying scandal. Without Burghley to stand beside him, he could never have succeeded. His enemies were many and powerful. Yet he did succeed and his success ensured the defeat of the terrible Armada.

His father-in-law, Benjamin Gonson, had been Treasurer of the Navy, and on his retirement, Hawkins, on January 1, 1578, took his place. " I shall pluck a thorn out of my foot and put it into yours," said old Gonson, and it was not long before Hawkins found that this was " too true "—his own words. The corruption of the previous members of the Navy Board must have been known to Burghley and the Queen, for Hawkins soon told them about it. Yet not a man was removed from office. Hawkins was thus in a worse than awkward position, for he had to work with men whom he had exposed and who therefore naturally hated him and were eager to frustrate any attempt at reform. It shows much for his charm that these men eventually admitted the greatness of his achievement.

Hawkins's first report stated that the keeping and refitting of ships in harbour cost £6,000 when it should have cost £4,000, that the building of new ships cost £4,000 when £2,200 would have been sufficient; that out of 900 loads of timber, 400 were taken by the officers for their own use. This reveals how insidious the corruption had been. It has been said that Hawkins was no better than the men he superseded, and that one grafter merely took the place of another. The other officers were of course eager to swear that he was stealing and over-charging, but these slanders were never proved. Before the Armada arrived, Howard swore that the fleet was in splendid condition.

"I have been aboard of every ship that goeth out with me," he wrote, "and in every place where any may creep, and I do thank God that they be in the estate they be in; and there is never a one of them that knows what a leak means."

Again and again, he repeated the substance of this statement. Surely his testimony is enough to prove that Hawkins's administration was honest and patriotic. Even his enemy, Winter, the most corrupt of the old board, cried triumphantly before the Armada's arrival: "Our ships do show themselves like gallants here."

There is no actual proof or certainty, but circumstantial evidence gives a likelihood that the new build of ship must be placed to Hawkins's credit. It seems to me more than coincidence that the ships should have a new build immediately he takes command, and this new type was to give England the supremacy of the seas and was to defeat the great but old-fashioned Armada. Hawkins cut down the enormous poops, and he built smaller, more agile vessels. He realised that the days were gone when the Navy was nothing but an army at sea and when grappling and boarding were the only methods of winning a sea battle. Less men, and more guns, became the rule of the Admiralty. With more guns, you could stand off and smash the enemy without harm to yourself; and less men meant less stores. Food was the great problem in those days of scurvy, and it was partly the lack of food among the English that saved the Armada from complete destruction. Food could not be kept save when it was salted; and salt meat is not healthy. The Armada would have been completely destroyed but for this fact. Elizabeth, with the optimism of fear, refused to believe that Philip would dare to fight; she had been niggardly with stores. It was impossible, for financial and political reasons, to lay up quantities of food at great cost, when it might be left merely to decay, therefore the English, in the hour of need, were badly short of rations and also of powder.

Besides, by having checked corruption and by having built better and swifter ships, Hawkins also helped to defeat Spain in the decisive and glorious battle by personal fighting. Howard was Admiral, Drake Vice-admiral, and Hawkins Rear-admiral, but his noblest part was in creating a sea-worthy fleet. In the actual battle there was no individual exploit that can be mentioned, he did his duty as many another seaman did. Neither he nor any of the others distinguished themselves, for they were all equally as brave and as adroit. But on Friday, July 26, during a lull in the battle, Howard summoned six men, including Hawkins, aboard his flagship, and the old sailor knelt on his admiral's deck to arise Sir John Hawkins. He was fifty-six at the time and had waited long for recognition. Rarely has man better deserved the honour of knighthood, given for merit and in the hour of danger. It was not a bought title, nor a reward for bribery, it was an honour given by an admiral to one of his bravest and most loyal captains.

After the battle, after the great winds had helped to break up the mighty Armada, there came the horrors of starvation. Boat-loads of English seamen were rowed ashore dying of hunger and wounds. Hawkins had to see that these men were paid, for he was Treasurer of the Navy. He was unfortunately a treasurer with no money. Desperate letters to Burghley, footnoted by Howard, only brought angry responses. The Queen was hampered by considerations of finance and politics, and could not spare money even for the men who had saved England. Hawkins answered Burghley sadly:

" I trust God will so provide for me as I shall never meddle with such intricate matters more, for they be importable for any man to please and overcome it. If I had an enemy, I would wish him no more harm than the course of my troublesome and painful life; but hereunto, and to God's good providence we are born."

In another letter he wrote of his task that " God, I trust, will deliver me of it ere it be long, for there is no other hell." Old Gonson's words were truly proved: " I shall pluck a thorn out of my foot and put it into yours! "

Hawkins would have liked to retire; he was feeling old, and years of responsibility, of fighting slanderous jealousy, had made him weary. He hoped to put to sea again, away from the intrigues of the Naval Office, but he was too useful a man for the Queen to let slip. He was tired and feeling old after his " careful, miserable, unfortunate, and dangerous " life, for diplomacy was not his real trade. He was a sailor and the sea invited him. He was sixty, and still showed plenty of vitality, yet he was condemned to a chair, to worry about little expenses, about the cost of this and of that. He must worry about rigging, food, and the building of ships for other men, for Drake and Frobisher, while himself remained in England, watching others set out to the lands beyond the skyline, the lands of his youth, which now he feared never to see again. Soon, he felt, he would be fit for nothing but his chair in the Navy Office. The Queen dared not let him go. He wrote imploring letters to her Ministers, and at last his opportunity came. Elizabeth realised that the danger from Spain was over, and decided that defence should be succeeded by aggression, and that Hawkins and Drake, England's greatest living seamen, should sail together to the Indies.

Nothing more idiotic could have been conceived than to make these men co-commanders. They were both courageous, they were both excellent sailors and soldiers. But Drake was reckless while Hawkins was cautious, and each of them undoubtedly was jealous of the other's greatness. The plan given to them was, roughly, to attack Nombre de Dios, and then to march across the Isthmus and capture Panama, but the expedition was delayed again and again, for some unexplained reason. The Queen blamed both captains, but it seems that the fault was really Drake's, as he made careless preparations, and both he and Hawkins were beginning to show signs of jealousy—Maynarde tells us "that whom the one loved, the other smally esteemed." Both were evidently bickering about small matters even before beginning, and this bickering already doomed the adventure. It was impossible that these two men should sail together successfully, although the name of each was an inspiration to England's youth and a terror to Spain. They were alike in heroism, but most unlike in the small points that are essential to friendship—Drake was courageous, reckless, he relied on the opportunity of the moment, and often he succeeded by sheer audacity, but Hawkins did nothing without careful forethought, his every action was reasoned, and he examined every detail of victualling and manning with amazing patience. It is not known who was the instigator of this absurd combination of opposites, although the conception is said to have been Drake's. In that case, he should have been the sole leader, and Hawkins ought never to have gone with him. Much of the blame must rest with Elizabeth, who should have understood the dangers, but, great as she was, and with her splendid diplomatic vision, she never really understood her servants because she thought of them only as servants. They were automatons of her will, men who must have no feelings apart from her commands, they must exist only to obey. A few years before, when Hawkins had been driven back by winds from an encounter with the Spaniards, he had written to Burghley, quoting scripture. Impatiently and cruelly Elizabeth had cried " God's death! This fool went out a soldier and is come home a divine! " She did not comprehend Hawkins's character, with its mixture of piety and need for action, the type of many of England's greatest men like Henry V and Cromwell. She took no account of subtleties of character. Drake and Hawkins were great sailors; therefore, together, she thought, they must be unconquerable. The opposite was true. Separate, they were inconquerable; together they were broken before they started. Drake was in many ways the greatest of the Elizabethan seamen, yet the failure of this expedition was his fault. Hawkins had seen to the ships and victualling, but Drake delayed the date of sailing, probably from lack of foresight. He left everything until the last moment, with the result that Spain learned exactly what was intended.

After the fleet had set out, Drake's carelessness was even

more apparent. During a council aboard Hawkins's ship four days after leaving port, Drake announced that he was short of provisions. The amount of rations needed had been thoroughly investigated, and it was inexcusable that he should be deficient in provisions after a mere four days at sea. Contrary to all Hawkins's ideas of sea-fighting, Drake had signed on three hundred men more than were necessary, thus overloading his ships. Hawkins lost his temper, and Drake did the same. Maynarde, who was present, tells us that if he had been " entreated," Hawkins would have softened, but to apology " Sir Francis's stout heart could never be driven." The quarrel temporarily calmed down, only to flare up more violently than ever, and this time on deck. Hawkins completely forgot himself and his position in his rage, he shouted out the secret orders of the adventure so that the whole crew could hear. Perhaps the memory of San Juan de Ulua rose before him and he recalled how Drake had, as he believed, crept treacherously away against his master's orders.

Drake's position was now desperate, for his crews were eating everything and would soon be starving. A week later, he told Hawkins that he could not go on without additional stores, and suggested that they should raid Madeira or Grand Canary. At this, there was another quarrel, Hawkins refusing to take action unless Drake would confess that he was in the wrong, but Drake's obstinate pride prevented him acknowledging any blame. The next day, however, his need became too great for his pride and he confessed his fault. Hawkins instantly agreed to the raiding plan.

The attempt on Las Palmas was a complete failure. No food was presumably captured, and much harm was done by thus warning the Spaniards of the English proximity. Nothing further is heard of any food scarcity, and probably the provident Hawkins had taken even more than his correct complement. Nevertheless the expedition was doomed already, for the Spaniards knew where the English were, and the Main and the Indies were warned, with the consequence that all gold was hidden, and no treasure-ship would venture out while these two notorious demon Englishmen were scouting the ocean.

The objective of the expedition was Porto Rico, and it was there that Hawkins died. He lay in his cabin on November 12, 1595, until the very last gasp beseeching his officers to remind the Queen of his loyal service, " and forasmuch as, through the perverse and cross dealings of some in that journey, who, preferring their own fancy before his skill, would never yield but rather over-rule him, whereby he was so discouraged, and as himself then said his heart even broken, that he saw no other but danger of ruin of the whole voyage." " In a codicil as a piece of his last will and testament," he " did bequeath unto Your Highness two thousand pounds, if Your Highness will take it; for that, as he said, Your Highness had in your possession a far greater sum of his, which he then did also release." This appears to have been the £7,000 due to him as profits from Drake's circumnavigation, and probably there were other sums, for Elizabeth did not like paying debts.

This man, who even in his last moments was honest and loyal, has been decried as the creator of the African slave-trade. Some have called him a pirate. His exploits, except for San Juan de Ulua, are not of the type to live in men's memories. They are not dazzling as Drake's adventures are dazzling. They are not reckless, they are cautious, but nevertheless, they are heroic. Without Hawkins, it is more than likely that Philip's enormous Armada might have won through the English lines. Hawkins's caution and honesty built the ships that could not spring a leak; his years of planning, of parsimony and loyalty, made the little English vessels such that Howard could not speak of them without pride. Too long Hawkins has been forgotten, ignored or dismissed contemptuously. He deserves his place as one of the very greatest of the Elizabethans.

PETER WENTWORTH

1524–1597

By

HUGH ROSS WILLIAMSON

PETER WENTWORTH

by HUGH ROSS WILLIAMSON

I

" MR. SPEAKER, I find written in a little volume these words : ' Sweet is the name of liberty, but the thing itself has a value beyond all inestimable treasure.' " So, on February 8, 1576, " the unconquerable Peter Wentworth " began before the Commons of England his memorable speech which they " out of a reverent regard for her Majesty's honour " did not allow him to finish. In addition, it cost him his own liberty, but that was a consequence he had foreseen.

The speech was not unpremeditated. In the years which had elapsed since the previous Parliament, he had pondered over it in the quiet of his Oxfordshire manor; he had rehearsed its indictment of the Queen's persistent attempts to suppress the Commons' freedom of debate and the bishops' avidity for ecclesiastical tyranny; and, being not without worldly wisdom, he had tried " to have it put out " of his mind for fear that it should carry him to the Tower. The Tower, under the despotism of a sovereign who made no secret of her dislike for him and his opinions, was an unpleasant prospect for an ageing country gentleman of fifty. Yet when, at the opening of Parliament, his decision could no longer be delayed, there was no hesitation despite circumstances even more adverse than he had anticipated. For in the interval between the Parliaments, the Crown had not been idle and, by reviving many extinct boroughs under its influence, had packed the new House with an anti-Puritan majority. So, ironically, it was the Commons themselves, on whose behalf Wentworth was pleading, who sent him to the Tower. They answered his appeal to them to show themselves " neither bastards nor dastards, but as

477

rightly-begotten children sharply and boldly reprove the enemies of God, our Prince and the State " by sharply reproving him.

He was unrepentant. That same afternoon, in the Star Chamber, he told the committee which was examining the matter :

> " The consideration of a good conscience and of a faithful subject did make me bold to utter it in such sort as your Honours heard. With this heart and mind I spake it, and I praise God for it; and if it were to do again, I would with the same mind speak it again."

In Peter Wentworth's voice is heard unmistakably the accent of the great Puritan constitutionalists who, in the next century, were partially to fulfil his ideals. He was, in fact, an earlier Sir John Eliot. He had the same quick temper and untamable tongue, the same gift of oratory and vivid phrase, the same unquestioned courage, the same loyalty to the person of the sovereign even when most vehemently reproving misgovernment. Like Eliot, he insisted that the final guarantee for the liberty of the subject was the freedom of the Commons from Crown interference. Like Eliot, he died in prison, his health shattered by rigorous imprisonment, his pathetic appeals for fresh air ignored by an angry tyrant and the ideals for which he strove hopelessly in eclipse.

Since those ideals—springing from a stark logic which ill suits the English genius for compromise—have not even yet been fully realised, it is no accident that in the Elizabethan mythology, which is the epic of England, the name of Peter Wentworth is seldom mentioned and scarcely known. He was too far ahead of his time. He, like Eliot and Hampden later, stood for the rule of law, in opposition to the Crown's effort to enforce the dictatorship of the executive. Also, by ante-dating the millennium, he made the mistake of all the Puritans in supposing that the average sensual man was interested in ethics. The age was concerned with prin-cipalities and powers. The Puritans had another vision. As one of them put it in the House :

> " This cause is God's. The rest are all but terrene; yea, trifles in comparison. Call you them never so

great or pretend you that they import never so much: subsidies, crowns, kingdoms, I know not what they are in comparison of this. This I know, whereof I thank God: ' Seek ye first the kingdom of God and all things shall be added unto you.' "

Or, as Peter Wentworth himself wrote to Elizabeth, tempering his analogy to her Erastian intelligence:

" The most safe and profitable way for you to preserve your person and honour is by all good means to keep the King of Kings on your side. He that hath a good farm and hath none other hold thereof but at his landlord's pleasure, the best policy for him, we would think, is to please his landlord. And this is the case, Madame, betwixt you and God in respect of your kingdom."

This preoccupation with things of the spirit inevitably infected secular affairs. Elizabeth, within politic limits, deplored the incompetence and unworthiness of her clergy, but when the Archbishop explained to her that a reformation would necessitate thirteen thousand reputable ministers, she dismissed the idea with the astonished *non possumus*: " Jesus! Thirteen thousand! It is not to be looked for! " To Wentworth and his fellow-Puritans, on the other hand, it was not only to be looked for, but imperative to be found. And the means were ready to hand. Though the theological hatred of the Puritans for the Catholics passed all reasonable bounds, the two sects were in fundamental agreement on the deeper question of the relative values of the spiritual and the temporal. Few proposals caused Elizabeth and Whit- gift more annoyance than the Puritans' demand that the confiscated revenues of the Church of Rome, the tithes and the Abbey lands, should be used for religious purposes and administered by non-secular bodies to train and equip a learned and devout ministry. This arrangement would have provided more than enough for more than thirteen thou- sand, but it would have brought down in ruins the edifice of Elizabethan statecraft whose foundation was the payment of the ecclesiastical plunder as blackmail to secular supporters.

Less catastrophic, but hardly less revolutionary, was the Puritan denial of the hierarchic nature of the Church

(Wentworth, speaking of bishops, told the House bluntly: "It is an error to think that God's Spirit is tied only in them") and their consequent assertion of the layman's right to discuss doctrine. Unforgivably they attempted to revise the Thirty-Nine Articles and suppress, among others, that which put a premium on the indolence of an already sufficiently ignorant clergy by permitting the reading of homilies in place of the preaching of sermons.

It was, however, the constitutional implications of Puritanism which were finally intolerable. The theory that the sole justification of a ruler was the welfare of the ruled was incompatible with the Tudor (and, later, the Stuart) conception of Kingship. In practice, the struggle between Elizabeth and the Puritans on this matter resolved itself into an unceasing defensive fight for individual freedom against the encroachments of an arbitrary prerogative, and an offensive skirmish to compel her to secure the safety of England by overcoming her fear and her vanity and naming her successor.

Wentworth, citing the appointment of Joshua and Solomon, told her, with his accustomed lack of tact:

> "Think therefore (most gracious Sovereign) that these acts of Moses and David are thus recorded in the holy story, not only that you should know that God's magistrates thus governed, but especially that you may learn to govern for the safety of your subjects, as they did. . . . You see that neither peril to their persons nor fear of eclipsing their own present honours could stay either of these from governing for the safety of their people."

These rude words were too near the truth to be palatable, but even worse was his Parliamentary declaration of the supreme rights of the Commons:

> "It is perilous always to follow the prince's mind, for the prince may favour a course perilous to himself and the whole State, and then to follow the prince were to be unfaithful to God, the Prince and the State —for we are chosen of the whole realm, of a special trust and confidence by them reposed in us, to foresee all such inconveniences,"

with its offensive corrollary:

> " Certain, is it, Mr. Speaker, that none is without
> fault, no, not our noble Queen, since her Majesty hath
> committed great fault, yea, dangerous faults to her-
> self. . . . It is dangerous in a prince unkindly to abuse
> his or her nobility and people, to oppose or bend her-
> self against her nobility and people . . . and could any
> prince more unkindly entreat, abuse, and oppose herself
> against her nobility and people than her Majesty did in
> the last Parliament? "

Small wonder that the faithful Commons stopped his
eloquence in full flight! Small wonder that Elizabeth,
furious at his repeated calls for liberty, his unabashed
meddling with the Church settlement and his ingenuous
impertinence in demanding the nomination of her heir,
" heartily disliked " Mr. Peter Wentworth.

II

Very little is known of Wentworth's early life. Even the
date of his birth, 1524, is only a deduction from his last letter.
His father, Sir Nicholas Wentworth, was knighted by Henry
VIII at the siege of Boulogne and given the office of Chief
Porter of Calais, and Peter himself allied the family
tenuously with the reigning house by marrying a cousin of
Henry's last queen. Sir Nicholas, however, survived into
Mary's reign and some time before his death in 1557, his
eldest son had married again, this time Elizabeth, sister of
Sir Francis Walsingham, an ardent young Puritan who took
refuge abroad during the Marian persecutions. Thus when
Elizabeth became queen, Peter Wentworth at the age of
thirty-four had inherited his father's manor of Lillingstone
Lovell, and was committed by both sympathy and alliance
to the party of the Left. But it was his younger brother,
Paul, who first sprang into prominence as a Puritan spokesman in the second Parliament of the reign.

Four years after her accession Elizabeth was so critically
ill that the Court mourned her as dying. The shock was
sufficient to inspire the Parliament which met on her recovery in 1563 with a single thought—the necessity of
nominating her heir. An unsettled succession might mean

18   *481*

civil war. To the Puritans especially was it a vital question, lest the Catholic Mary of Scotland should become a second Mary of England, and on this subject Paul Wentworth, in the words of a scandalised chronicler, " used so great liberty of speech as (I conceive) was never used in any session before or since." His excesses, however, sprang from commendable zeal, and in the following year he was certified by the bishops' commission of enquiry as " one earnest in religion and fit to be trusted."

In the autumn of 1565 both Peter and Paul were in trouble. Peter's first recorded emergence from obscurity was the appearance of his name, with his brother's, on a writ received by the Sheriff of Essex from the Justices of the Peace requiring the production of Peter and Paul Wentworth at the Epiphany sessions on an indictment " for transgressions and contempts." Two yeomen from the Lillingstone Lovell estate were indicted with them, and it may be presumed that the four, at the time of their transgressions, were on a visit to Peter's manor of Westhall in Essex. The nature and the consequences of their faults are unrecorded.

Paul was back in the Parliament of 1566, still urging the settlement of the succession question. To the Queen's order that the Commons were not to discuss the matter further, he moved that her command was against the liberties and privileges of the House. The ensuing debate was of such proportions that the Commons had resort to the innovation of an adjournment. Paul Wentworth had made history at least to that extent. More importantly, he wrung a measure of victory from the Queen who, realising the opposition she had aroused, withdrew her order.

The Wentworths might be troublesome, but their loyalty remained unquestioned. Indeed, in so far as the main danger to Elizabeth threatened from the Catholics, their Puritanism made them eminently trustworthy. Three years later, Elizabeth paid Paul the undoubted, if expensive, honour of committing to his charge the Duke of Norfolk on one stage of that nobleman's journey to Court to explain his treasonable activities.

It was in an atmosphere of plots and rumours of plots and under the shadow of the Northern Rebellion that, in 1571, Parliament again met and Peter Wentworth, as Member for Barnstaple, took his place in the Commons as the ally of his younger brother. He was forty-seven, and henceforth for twenty-two years he was to bear the brunt of the battle.

III

Peter Wentworth first attracted attention to himself on April 20, 1571, by a biting attack on Sir Humphrey Gilbert. A few days earlier Gilbert had attempted to defend the royal prerogative in the House. What was worse, he had made use of his intimacy with the Queen to misinform her of the Commons' proceedings. Wentworth deprecated his " disposition to flatter and fawn upon the Prince," and suggested that, like " the chameleon which can change himself into all colours save white, even so this reporter can change himself into all fashions but honesty." He called him a liar to his face, quoted the words of David: " Thou, O Lord, shalt destroy liars," and embellished his remarks on liars in general by additional references to Holy Writ. In his peroration he " requested care for the credit of the House and for the maintenance of free speech, to preserve the liberties of the House and to reprove liars." Three times Sir Humphrey tried to speak in self-defence, and three times " had the denial of the House." The Commons were with Wentworth.

Having clarified the constitutional issue, he turned to the religious. This time his opponent was the Archbishop of Canterbury. Wentworth, who was a member of a committee on a bill examining the Thirty-Nine Articles, was appointed with five others to interview the Primate on the matter. Inevitably he was the spokesman of the group. When the Archbishop enquired why they had omitted from their draft " the article of the homilies, and that for the consecration of the bishops and some others," Wentworth informed him: " Because we were so occupied in other matters that we had no time to examine them how they agreed with the Word of God."

The Archbishop, taken aback, replied: " Surely you mistake the matter. You will refer yourself wholly to us therein."

At that Wentworth exploded: " Know, by the faith I bear to God, we will pass nothing before we understand what it is. For that were to make you popes. Make you popes who list, but we will make you none."

Elizabeth, however, agreed with the Archbishop, announced that she disliked Wentworth as much as she did his bill, and ordered the Commons to refrain from meddling with ecclesiastical matters. The House, undeterred, continued to debate three ecclesiastical measures, and were incontinently dissolved by their angry sovereign.

Between the dissolution and the calling of the next Parliament in April 1572, another Catholic plot against the Queen's life had been discovered. Sponsored by the Pope, and aiming at securing the throne for Mary, Queen of Scots, it provoked in Wentworth a combination of hatred and fear which roused him, at best a " hot gentleman," to a paroxysm of fury. In the joint committee of the Lords and Commons to consider the best line of action, he described Mary as " the most notorious whore in all the world "; and, when Elizabeth tactfully refused to be guided by the too-violent recommendations of the committee, he opposed the Commons' vote of thanks for her confidence in them by announcing bluntly that she deserved no thanks at all.

Nor were ecclesiastical matters more satisfactory than formerly. The prolonged discussion of the bills of rites and ceremonies was stopped, and the Commons told once more to confine themselves to secular topics. They were to consider no bills concerning religion unless the clergy had first approved them. This was even more insulting than an unadorned prohibition. Wentworth, after his experience with the Archbishop, not unnaturally attributed that " doleful message " to episcopal machinations. At the end of the short session he left London, his " whet and vehement temper " unsweetened, to prepare his great speech.

IV

That summer England was profoundly moved and shocked by the news of the massacre of Saint Bartholomew. Had there been a Parliament the following spring, there is little doubt that the intensity of feeling would have found expression in a sweeping victory for the Puritan extremists against the moderating influence of the Crown. Wentworth was brought into closer contact than most with the crime by the fact that his brother-in-law, Walsingham, as ambassador in Paris, was an eye-witness of it. Needless to say, it increased his apprehensions. In view of this proof of the lengths to which the Papists were prepared to go, Elizabeth's refusal to adopt energetic measures for her safety or to safeguard the Protestant succession, as well as her obvious leanings towards episcopacy on the Catholic model, assumed a more sinister aspect. As Wentworth considered it, he remembered the words of Elihu: " Behold, I am as the new wine which hath no vent and bursteth the new vessels in sunder," and decided: " I will speak that I may have a vent. I will regard no manner of person; no man will I spare."

Nor did he. The three and a half years which the politic Queen allowed to elapse between the massacre and the summoning of a new Parliament diminished neither his memory nor his bitterness. And when, as Member for Tregony, he rose to risk the Tower, his speech—even what he was allowed to deliver of it—was a comprehensive catalogue of grievances. Even the five-year-old episode of Sir Humphrey Gilbert was glanced at in his exhortation to " hate all tale-carriers; yea, hate them as venomous and poison to the Commonwealth." But, above all, harm was done by rumours of the Queen's displeasure and messages from her to avoid certain subjects in debate. " I would to God, Mr. Speaker, that these two were buried in Hell—I mean rumours and messages. The Devil was the first author of them."

Next day, February 9, 1576, Wentworth was committed, by a Commons' committee, a close prisoner to the Tower, " there to remain until such time as this House should have further consideration of him." There he remained for a month. On March 12, on Elizabeth's recommendation, he was released and brought to the bar of the House, where he admitted his fault.

The enforced meditation in prison may have cooled his heat, but it did not affect his ardour. Rather it decided his future course of action. He had time to disentangle the essence from the accidents, and his enunciation of principles was to gain weight from a comparative moderation of statement. He became so much the more dangerous in consequence. That month in the Tower was only a foretaste of three further and increasingly rigorous imprisonments, though the next and sharper skirmish was not to begin till ten years later.

In the 1581 session, Peter remained in the background and Paul came once again to the fore. His motion for a public fast and the institution of a sermon " every morning at seven o'clock before the House did sit, that so, they beginning their proceedings with the service and worship of God, He might the better bless them in all their consultations and actions " was carried by the Commons, but vetoed by the Queen. She admitted that their action sprang from excess of zeal, but at the same time attributed it " partly to her own leniency towards a brother of that man which now made this motion," and reminded them that last session Peter Wentworth " was by this House for just cause reprehended and committed, but by her Majesty graciously pardoned and restored again."

The House submitted, withdrew Paul's motion and next day, January 25, appointed Peter on a congenial and uncontroversial committee to enquire how " evil-affected subjects " might best be restrained. He gave no further occasion for comment, and in the 1584 Parliament, both he and his brother were absent.

V

The next attack was on the subject of the liberty of the House. Wentworth was decisively beaten, but not before he had formulated questions so pertinent that they largely defined the issues of the Civil War. It is probable that he did not realise their full implications, but he foresaw— and said so—that the " true, faithful, and hearty service of our merciful God, our lawful Prince, and this whole and worthy realm of England, will much consist hereafter upon the answer unto these questions." The paradox of his position was that he could never see himself other than as an ultra-Royalist. His sense of personal loyalty to Elizabeth was so great that once, when a colleague suggested that, to save time, the clerk should be permitted to write an unadorned " Queen Elizabeth," he reproved him with his accustomed heat: " What! Shall we not acknowledge her to be our Sovereign Lady? This is well indeed! I think some of us are weary of her. I am not weary of her for my part, and therefore I will have it set down: ' Our Sovereign Lady.' "

Nevertheless when, on March 1, 1587, his Sovereign Lady

ordered the Speaker to interpose in one of the perennial (though more than usually revolutionary) ecclesiastical debates, Wentworth—now Member for Northampton—desired to know " whether the Speaker may overrule the House in any matter? " This was only one of the questions which he handed to the Speaker, who asked him to withhold them at least until the Queen's pleasure on the bill under discussion were known. " But Mr. Wentworth would not be so satisfied, but required his articles might be read."

The two most vital points were " whether this council be not a place for any member, freely and without constraint of any person or danger of laws . . . to utter any of the griefs of this commonwealth whatsoever? " and " Whether there be any council which can make, add to, or diminish from the laws of the realm but only this council of parliament? " But the questions were never put. That afternoon he, with four of his supporters, was sent to the Tower.

On his release he returned to Lillingstone Lovell with his thoughts momentarily diverted to that other burning topic—the succession. The matter was more pressing than ever. Elizabeth's ill-health was chronic, she had now definitely abandoned any idea of marriage, and the execution of Mary, Queen of Scots, while it had removed a Catholic heir, had given a sharper edge to Catholic plots. Wentworth succinctly summed up the situation: " Delay breeds danger, and the Crown of England is a jewel of too great a price to continue in peril one hour upon so weak a string as the life of one person." But recent experiences had suggested that any speech he might make on the matter was likely to be robbed of its conclusion, even had there been, at that moment, a parliament to listen to it. This time he would write what he had to say.

He set to work and composed *A Pithy Exhortation to her Majesty for establishing her successor to the Crown*. From a multitude of examples in classical story, the Hebrew Scriptures and English and Scottish history, he deduced the horrors which would follow on a disputed succession. There would be chaos and bloodshed at home and, " what help we may look for from other nations, it will be just none at all—rebellion in Ireland, all in arms in Scotland, God knoweth what in Wales." Moreover, in the event of such catastrophe, it was probable that Elizabeth's own noble person would lie upon the earth unburied as a doleful spectacle to the world, to say nothing of the fact that she would find on her deathbed " ten thousand hells in her soul for perilling the Church of God and her natural country." He reiterated: " You, our Sovereign Lady, know that the eyes of all England are on you to the end, that you should tell them who shall sit on your throne after you," and pointed out that by naming James of Scotland " not only should you make the heart of every true Protestant like the heart of a lion, but you should . . . break the neck of the Popish hope of their golden day."

No doubt he had a persuasive pen and was notably erudite and logical, but he had learnt, too, the value of summaries. Lest Elizabeth should lose track of his argument, he epitomised it for her in ten " short questions to be considered of by you and answered between God and you in your secret chamber."

But the real difficulty was to ensure that she read it. Wentworth considered the idea of asking Essex, the reigning favourite, to present it to her, but before anything so tactful could be arranged, a manuscript copy had found its way into her hands. So it came about that at the beginning of August, 1591, Wentworth received a missive from the Privy Council ordering him immediately to present himself at Court, bringing his son with him. On the 15th he appeared before the Council, and was sent to the Gate House " to be kept close prisoner in some convenient place in such careful sort as he be not suffered to write or to have conference or speech with any manner of person whatsoever, without special direction to the contrary."

Write, however, he did. He wrote a defence of his *Pithy Exhortation* against those who argued that it would be impolitic to name James of Scotland as heir. And he wrote to Burghley, asking his help to persuade the Queen to listen to his *Exhortation*. He quite realised that her Majesty might be offended at first, but on reflection she would surely understand the spirit in which it was written. Solomon had said that " the wounds of a lover are faithful, but the kisses of an enemy are deceitful," and Wentworth had .but wounded in good faith.

Elizabeth merely commented that Mr. Wentworth had a good opinion of his own wit, but Burghley, who was a statesman, wrote that " he had three several times perused it and found nothing but what he thought to be true and was assured would at last come to pass, but her Majesty had determined that the question should be suppressed as long as she lived."

Wentworth's spirit might be unquenchable, but his body was unable to bear the close confinement. On September 8, his punishment was mitigated and, because he was found " by reason of his close imprisonment to grow (with his age) weak and diseased," he was granted the liberty of the prison. On September 27 he was released " upon bonds to be first taken of him to remain at the house of the parson of Whitechapel."

VI

It might have been thought that, at the end of his third imprisonment, Peter Wentworth would have learnt wisdom. Yet, at the beginning of the 1593 Parliament, he moved a petition asking his Sovereign Lady to entail the succession. This time her patience was exhausted. Next day, Sunday, February 25, he was sent to the Tower, where he was to remain for nearly five years till death released him. In this last long silence, only a word or two reached the outer world.

That same spring his brother Paul died, an event which must have further helped to shatter his health. On May 29 he was so ill that he was granted a certain degree of liberty and allowed to be visited by his sons, his friends and physicians, and to have a servant continually in attendance. His wife came to share his lot, and for three years remained with him. Then death claimed her also. She was buried in the Chapel of St. Peter ad Vincula on July 21, 1596.

Four days after her funeral, his rooms were searched secretly for copies of his offending book. One was found and confiscated, but " upon his soul's pain " he denied that he had others. But the rigour of his imprisonment increased once more.

Another year dragged by. Then, in the summer of 1597, he pleaded for himself to the extent of admitting that he would " be glad of whatsoever liberty her Majesty may grant him," asking only that he might not return to Lillingstone Lovell, since " no place will be so uncomfortable to him as that house in regard of the want of his wife whom he so dearly loved, whose memory will be always renewed thereby to his great grief." He was asked to give an unconditional guarantee of good behaviour, but he refused to find sureties until he had seen the conditions, " for otherwise I may not with honesty entreat any sureties to enter into bonds for me."

On July 29 he wrote:

> " I am the more earnestly enforced to entreat a speedy discharge for that I have been this three months weekly troubled with sickness in this place of prison; only for want of air, exercise, and liberty. It would pity your heart to see my oftener than weekly sickness, and some compassion, I trust, will be carried towards me in regard of my old years, being above 73."

There was no compassion. He died in the Tower on November 10, 1597.

VII

The Lieutenant of the Tower said: " If the gentlemen of England were honest, there would be five hundred more in prison for Mr. Wentworth's opinion before long." That may stand for his epitaph. And on the fiftieth anniversary of his death, King Charles the First signed the death-warrant of the monarchy by escaping from Carisbrooke Castle, where he had been detained by a new generation of the gentlemen of England whose honesty matched their courage.

SIR FRANCIS DRAKE
1538–1596

By

ARTHUR PERCIVAL NEWTON

SIR FRANCIS DRAKE

by ARTHUR PERCIVAL NEWTON

THE proverbial fickleness of fame makes it rare in
history to find a man whose celebrity remains consistent
throughout the ages. Most men are forgotten, however
renowned they may have been in their own days, and of the
rest most look smaller to their descendants than they did
to their contemporaries. Especially among men of action
reputation quickly fades and their glory seems hollow and
tawdry to later generations. Among the Elizabethans,
however, there were one or two whose fame has never been
dimmed, and especially the seaman who was regarded in
his own day as the boldest and most fortunate of leaders and
the greatest champion of the national idea. Later generations have admired him as the founder of British sea-power
and, somewhat uncritically, as the earliest builder of the
British Empire beyond the sea.

To common men on both sides of the Atlantic in his own
day Francis Drake's exploits were of almost legendary audacity and worthy to be placed with the stories of the paladins,
while in every subsequent age his name has been a household
word and his career a theme of high romance. Even to the
prosaic scientific historian Drake has made a special appeal
as a protagonist in the Elizabethan struggle for national
security and maritime leadership, and he has been painted
in almost invariably glowing colours. His principal biographer has admired him, not only as a consummate man of
action, as he most certainly was, but also as a profound
thinker and statesman with schemes of national policy that
were thwarted and brought to naught by the malice and
incompetence of jealous rivals or the pusillanimity of those in
high places. Uniform admiration tends nowadays to arouse
the professional detractor whose vogue as a biographer is
measured by the belittlement of his subject, but luckily

Drake has so far escaped. Some scholars profoundly versed in the Elizabethan period have doubted Sir Julian Corbett's interpretation of his hero's ideas and motives, and have tried to place the great seaman in a more balanced setting among his contemporaries.

They have been aided in their task by the revelation in recent years of much fuller material from the archives both of Spain and England than was available when Corbett was making his researches into the history of the Tudor navy some forty years ago. All the contemporary English accounts of Drake and his exploits were filled with a strongly nationalist and Protestant bias against his Spanish enemy and the ambitions of the Papacy of the Counter-Reformation. Some of this propaganda found its way even into Corbett's scholarly pages, while the romantic Froude, in his portrait among the *English Seamen in the Sixteenth Century*, unashamedly gloried in his patriotic colouring. Now we can see Drake through other eyes, as he appeared to his Spanish prisoners or the local officials in the Indies, and the romantic glamour of Kingsley is parted to let the truth appear. In a brief study it is impossible to attempt even a cursory survey of the evidence for a more sober estimate of Drake's real contribution to the history of his time. All that we can do is to afford some indication of what may be the outlines of the full-scale appreciation that we still await. Such a biography cannot detract from the real greatness of its subject, but it will show him as a more human product of his rough upbringing, as he was to his friends and rivals, his patrons, and his chivalrous Spanish enemies, an essential contributor to the Elizabethan age.

The England of the first half of the sixteenth century gave little promise of her future maritime greatness. It is true that the first two Tudors were the founders of the fighting navy, for they realised how the essential defence of their new-won realm lay on the sea; but Englishmen had no particular repute as sailors, and most of their merchant ships were cumbrous, slow-sailing vessels carrying cargoes of raw materials across the North Sea or lumbering down to Gascony to fetch wine. The boldest seamen and the best-sailing English ships had an evil reputation, for they were the dreaded pirates of the West Country who had their hunting-ground at the mouth of the Channel and found their richest prey among the Portuguese carracks that brought their cargoes of Eastern goods to be dealt with at Antwerp.

The borderline between criminal piracy and legitimate sea-war was very indistinct, for by age-long custom ship-owners were permitted to recoup themselves for their losses at the expense of any compatriot of those who had plundered them. Letters of reprisal and commissions of marque were very common in that time of constant war, and so the Narrow Seas were filled with little seafights in which it was hard to distinguish between attackers holding lawful commissions and sea-robbers whose hand was against every man. Those who had rich cargoes to guard, like the Portuguese or the Spaniards, naturally held stricter notions of what constituted piracy than did the sailors of the northern nations whose fortunes were still to make. Thus it was possible to hold sincerely differing views about maritime morality in England and the Peninsula—a fact of real importance for our under-standing of the mental attitude of one like Drake, who was brought up among the traditions of the conservative county that still regarded wrecking as comparatively venial and all foreign ships as fair game.

In the reign of Henry VIII a particularly able and enter-prising citizen of Plymouth, William Hawkins, was breaking away from traditional lines and building up a new trade with Andalusia and Portugal and as far south as the Canar-ies, besides occasional voyages to Brazil. Like other mer-chants', his ships suffered depredations at the hands of sea-rovers, and he took out letters of reprisal to recoup himself. But Hawkins to avoid damage to his merchant trade, was scrupulous in observing the maritime conventions and the men-of-war employed were true privateers and no pirate outlaws. There grew up round him in Plymouth a well-disciplined and well-trained maritime community that depended for its success upon its good seamanship and gunnery, and it was from this group that the great Devon sailors of Elizabeth's time sprang with all their nice conven-tions of what could and could not be legitimately done at sea. There was naturally some differentiation between those who were mostly employed in peaceful trade and those who were more often employed in voyages for reprisals.

It was into this circle that there were born under Henry VIII two cousins, John (1532), second son of William Hawkins the elder, and Francis Drake (1542), who were destined to be the typical protagonists for these differing views during the age of England's rise to sea-power. The ideas and conventions of the community from which he sprang had more influence in shaping Drake's career than has sometimes been acknowledged, and they go far to explain some of his apparent inconsistencies. All through his life he had the mentality of the fighting privateer, while John Hawkins was more of the merchant and the organiser.

Francis was the eldest of the twelve sons of Edmund Drake, a yeoman client of the great Russell family who profited so greatly by the dissolution of the rich Abbey of Tavistock. Edmund was a fanatical supporter of the Protestant Party, and when a Catholic insurrection broke out at Tavistock in 1549, he was forced to flee and found refuge with his young family at the naval port of Chatham in Kent. There for some years he earned a meagre living by reading prayers and preaching to the sailors and was allowed to live aboard a hulk in the Medway. Thus Francis spent the formative years of his boyhood in a strongly Protestant atmosphere and was familiar with ships and seamen from his infancy. Both his Protestantism and his intuitive understanding of the sailor's mind were to play vital parts in his later career. With such an upbringing it was entirely natural that when the boy had to go out to earn his living, he should take to the sea. At the age of fourteen he was apprenticed on a small coasting bark plying round the Kentish coast and across to the ports of northern France and the Low Countries wherever cargo could be found. It was a hard training, but one of the utmost value for a boy with a keen eye and a retentive memory, for it familiarised him with the navigation of difficult and uncharted shallows where quickness of decision and an intuitive knowledge of dangerous tides and currents were essential. His master came to love him for his cheery humour and, when he died, he left the little vessel to Drake as his own property. Thus before he was twenty he was his own master and learning the habits of command.

For a few years he continued in the coasting trade, but in the middle of the 1560's he took employment in the service of his cousins, the Hawkins brothers. They were engaged in a bold attempt to extend their usual trade with the Spanish colonies in the Canaries across to the settlements in the West Indies, where the trade was strictly reserved for Castilian subjects under royal licence. Hawkins's first two voyages were profitable and made employment in the service of the firm attractive. Drake had been voyaging backwards and forwards in the Narrow Seas, but John Stow, who knew him well, tells us that at eighteen he went as purser in a ship to Biscay and at twenty on a voyage to Guinea. It was probably in the Spanish trade that he was mostly employed, for he picked up a fluent knowledge of Spanish and a familiarity with Spanish customs that were to serve him in good stead. As yet he had made no mark, and it is hard to trace his adventures, but when he was twenty-four and took part in the third West Indian voyage, he comes more into the light.

We may pause a moment to look at the young shipmaster after his ten hard years of training. Drake was rather below the middle height, broad breasted, with strong limbs and round head covered with a profusion of wavy, light-brown hair that grew low over his forehead. He had a pointed, close-cropped beard of lighter colour than his hair, and a fair, ruddy complexion, set off by a pair of extraordinarily large, clear eyes that showed unmistakably his abundant vitality. Though short and thickset, he was extremely active and quick in his movements, and his long apprenticeship had made him apt at all the tasks of the mariner. His schooling was of the briefest and he had little power with the pen. His writing was crabbed and almost illiterate, and his power to express himself on paper was sadly lacking, but he made up for it when he had to use his tongue. He had complete confidence in himself and a natural gaiety and good humour that carried off his often boastful speeches about himself and his achievements by their vivid and fluent phrasing. On occasions he was explosive and violent of temper and harsh and trenchant of speech, but he wound up his most cutting censures with some whimsical turn of phrase or a jest that let his natural good humour shine through and left the culprit still his devoted admirer. Of all admiration and even of flattery he was inordinately fond, but none could deny his natural charm, his indomitable pluck, and a capacity for work that demanded the last ounce of effort from all who followed him. He had, in fact, a natural genius for leadership in action that made him an awkward companion-in-arms for his equals and a touchy subordinate, but intoxicated those who served under him and keyed them up to audacious deeds that were almost unique, even in that age of daring.

It is only among the Spanish *conquistadors* that we can find his like, and he was a fitting enemy for the power that had won the New World.

Such was the man who, at the age of twenty-four, made his entrance upon the stage of history as one of the subordinate officers in the expedition of Captain John Lovell, equipped in November 1566 by the Hawkins brothers to follow up the success of their first two voyages for the sale of negroes to the colonists in the Spanish Indies. But the authorities in every port were now on the alert to prevent breaches of the express royal prohibitions that forbade the commerce of the Indies to all but Castilians. At Rio de la Hacha, on the Spanish Main, Lovell was compelled to abandon almost all his negroes and sail away discomfited and with serious loss. Hawkins blamed him and Drake for having been the victims of Spanish duplicity, and the latter, who never forgot an injury, began to tot up a long score that called for reprisals. In his voyage he had met many French corsairs, and they could give him skilled advice as to how best to undertake those reprisals, for their countrymen had been practising West Indian raids for forty years, ever since Francis I loosed a *guerre de course* against the commerce of his enemy, Charles V. Though France was now officially at peace with Spain, her Huguenot men-of-war were busier than ever, and it had already become a familiar maxim that there was "No peace beyond the line." It was from such French experience that Drake stored up in a prodigiously retentive memory details about the intricacies of West Indian navigation that were to serve him well in his quest of revenge.

Undeterred by Lovell's losses, Hawkins fitted out another slaving voyage in 1567, and this time Drake had command of a little ship of his own, the *Judith*. In the familiar story of the voyage his first appearance is again at Rio de la Hacha with an attack upon a Spanish coaster, much to Hawkins's disgust, for such violent action endangered his elaborate make-believe of legitimate trading. But this was the last voyage in which such a pretence could be maintained, for on September 22, 1568, Hawkins, who had taken shelter from the Caribbean storms in the harbour of San Juan de Ulua, was overwhelmed by what he held to be the basest Spanish treachery, and less than half his men escaped. Drake and the *Judith* came off best, for they were able to slip away before the end of the fight, and they were the first to bring home the disastrous news. It was Drake's first contact with high authority when he journeyed up from Plymouth to tell his story to the Council, and it was fitting that the turning-point in his career should be the same as that in national affairs. San Juan de Ulua marked the opening of a new period in Anglo-Spanish relations, and Drake was to be the star in the new drama of war.

He spent the following summer at home, and married a girl, Mary Newman, of whom, like so much of his private life, we know practically nothing. His stay with her can have been but short, for he was soon off quietly to the Caribbean again to serve among the French corsairs, who were creating a veritable reign of terror along the Spanish Main. In 1570 the great Spanish commander, Pero Menendez, drove them out, but in 1571 they swarmed back again with bolder designs than ever. No longer were they content to snap up their booty along the coast; they planned now to raid the main route of Spanish communications across the Isthmus of Panama itself. Drake was among them, learning and beginning to plan separate action. By the end of the year he was home again with sufficient plunder in his pockets to make him independent of his cousins. He could fit out and arm a small privateer of his own, and he did not bother much about a commission, for he was insignificant enough to risk the penalties of piracy if he were caught, and he had no great patron to help him. He was resolved to attempt for himself the design he had heard talked of among his French associates, to tap the Spanish treasure where it came to be loaded aboard the annual galleons at Nombre de Dios.

The plan was audacity itself, for Drake could afford to fit out no more than seventy men, and he was proposing to raid the central point of the Indies just when it was strongest, because only then would it hold the treasure he coveted. From the start his adventure was dogged by ill-luck, but we can see therein the rise of his outstanding qualities. His resource and inventiveness, his skill in extracting his little band from the jaws of danger, his high-humoured courage which cheered on the faint-hearted or depressed among the trials of the disease-filled rains of the tropical jungle—all combined to fill his men with a passionate belief in his leadership. Bold to utter rashness, his first dash succeeded, and Nombre de Dios fell to a night assault, where bluff masked the fact that he had but a handful of Englishmen behind him. The treasure house lay open to make an ineffaceable impression on the minds of the wondering raiders and to start the marvellous legend of the riches of the Indies that was to inspire the rest of his life. The sight of that mountain of silver bars was never forgotten by those who saw it and those they told, but it was in the later stages of the adventure that Drake first showed his supreme capacity for leadership. The story of how, with the maroons he so much impressed, he crept through the woods until, first of all Englishmen, he looked out over the Great South Sea, and how he took the treasure train from Panama has been retold a thousand times. His joyful return to England laden with plunder has become a legend, but it has only been of recent years, with the revelation of the details of the story from the long-hidden reports of the Spaniards he despoiled, that we have learned how it was that his inborn qualities won through and brought his tiny band through their perils. The truth is more astonishing than the legends, and the real Drake, as seen through the eyes of his enemies, is greater than the theatrical swashbuckler the writers of romance have painted. From failure after failure his magnetic personality and indomitable persistence and resource had snatched success. The bravado that was part of his character was perhaps never more pardonable than when, gorged with plunder, he passed " hard by Cartagena in the sight of all the fleet with a flag of St. George in the maintop, with silk streamers and ancients down to the water, sailing forward with a large wind."

Drake had " made his voyage " and made himself, for the news of his exploit was told throughout Western Europe. The King of France sent for his portrait, and Englishmen rejoiced at the spoiling of the Papists. But it had been done without a commission and in the company of notorious French pirates, so the best way to avoid such restitution as the Spanish ambassador legally demanded was for Drake to lie quiet. But the war-party in the Council and their merchant associates kept him in mind, and when a new enterprise of the greatest importance for the extension of English commerce was planned in the utmost secrecy, it was upon him that their choice for leader fell.

There has been much dispute about the purpose of the celebrated voyage of circumnavigation, but it now seems certain that the design was twofold—first, to search for the rich kingdoms that geographers believed to lie to the south-east of Asia in the Great South Land, and, second, to open up relations with the Spiceries of the Moluccas, despite the monopoly that the Portuguese had held there for three-quarters of a century. Incidental to these purposes was the plan to establish an English base or half-way house on the unoccupied Pacific coast to serve as a victualling station both for the south-west route or by the North-west Passage for which Frobisher was searching. The expedition was wholly English in its conception and equipment, but it is impossible to say how much of the plan was Drake's; in all probability it was not much, but the carrying-out was all his own. In the oft-told story we can note again the unremitting persistence and determination and the power of getting loyal service from his subordinates for which he was remarkable. In the tragic affair when Thomas Doughty strove to rouse his fellow-gentlemen against their low-born leader and suffered the extreme penalty, Drake showed himself greater than the " pirate " they had called him in the West Indies. But he still had all his old corsair instincts. They were governed and restrained by a new-won fitness for high command, but they were still there. His raids all up the Pacific coast from Peru to Mexico wrought a far worse injury to Spanish confidence than the tip-and-run affairs in the Caribbean, but we can see in their own newly published evidence that the Spaniards found in him an enemy more worthy of respect than a mere freebooter.

The return of the *Golden Hind* after her wonderful voyage round the world was in a sense the climax of Drake's career. Henceforward he was the most celebrated of English seamen, but still he could not be accorded official recognition. The Council and the leading merchants attached the highest importance to his treaty with the Sultan of Ternate, which for generations was looked upon as the first title deed of England's power in Asia, but the public at large knew little of such far-sighted plans; it was the booty he had taken that attracted their admiration, and the sailors and the privateering shipowners were inspired to emulate his exploits. The Spanish ambassador called Drake the " arch-pirate " to the Queen's face, and infinite care and dissimulation were necessary to avoid the open breach that she was still anxious to defer. Thus it was long before she could reward his services, and her ultimate action in knighting the circumnavigator on the deck of his own *Golden Hind* was a bold declaration that she was almost ready for a national war. Despite all his popularity and renown, Drake was but a pawn in a vast game of diplomatic chess, to be used or left unacknowledged as policy dictated.

For five years he was suffered to enjoy his new-won wealth as Mayor of his native Plymouth and a squire among the lesser Devon gentry, but his chance came at last, and the "arch-pirate" was launched again into the Caribbean. This time it was no more as a mere privateer, but as an admiral of the Queen's ships with navy captains under his command. It is greatly to be doubted whether, as some writers have maintained, Elizabeth was willing to attach much importance to his advice as a strategist and to confide to him the planning of campaigns. Such matters were reserved for men of higher rank and the narrow group of statesmen who served her in Council. Drake was the man of action employed to carry out their designs, and though his advice might be sought on their detailed execution, he had little influence on policy.

So Drake, the audacious free-lance, passes into Sir Francis Drake, admiral of the Queen's ships, and his career becomes merged in the history of the Elizabethan naval war, whither we cannot follow him. His great Caribbean raid in 1585–6 shows his powers at maturity. He was entrusted with the command of twenty-five sail and four thousand men, and the expedition was a very different affair from what he had accomplished with seventy followers only twelve years before. At Cartagena and Santo Domingo he carried off his triumphs with the same bravado, and again he could flaunt the flag of St. George with superb assurance. A year later he won even wider acclaim from his countrymen. He rejoiced with boisterous glee as he sailed backwards and forwards off Cadiz under the eyes of his helpless enemies on land, while he poured broadside after broadside from his new Sussex guns into the outranged and outmanœuvred galleys of the *armada* that King Philip had prepared for the invasion of England. The action ushered in a new era of naval tactics derived directly from the lessons that had been learned by the Devon privateers. Good gunnery and rapid sailing manœuvres were henceforward to replace the galley tactics that had won their last victory at Lepanto.

So long as Drake was entrusted with expeditions for definite objectives under his sole command, he was dazzlingly successful. From his first West Indian voyage with a tiny ship under his independent command to his triumph at Cadiz, his exploits were one long *crescendo*, and he and most Englishmen came to believe that their colossal enemy could be beaten into the acknowledgment of defeat if those exploits could be repeated on a larger scale, and if they were not hampered in delivering their rapier thrusts where they would. But Burghley and the Queen saw farther into the truth, and they knew that Philip's still vast power needed deeper and heavier blows. The later years of the war proved that they were right. To deliver such blows needed combined effort, and Drake was not fitted to work with others. He was an individualist who quarrelled with equals and fumed against the restrictions of the national leaders who would not give him a free hand. He put it down to the machinations of his enemies, and some of his biographers have believed him, but in truth the authorities, while they appreciated his capacities as a fighting commander, did not trust his powers of organisation or of attention to the numberless details that are necessary for operations of war on a great scale. He was never able to repeat what he did at Cadiz, and in the crowning victory against the Spanish Armada of 1588, where he was but one among the many captains who did well, he showed some serious defects.

The legends that have gathered round him at that time have more romance in them than truth, and they have tended to attribute to him a greater position on the stage than he really filled. His failure to obey the explicit orders of the commander-in-chief was notorious, and his fellow-captains believed that his readiness to leave his appointed station to capture rich prizes was a manifestation of his old passion for booty and might have led to disaster. Frobisher proclaimed it openly, and the scandal of the quarrel sadly marred the rejoicings after the victory. The whole incident is an illustration of Drake's character, and its defects appeared even more clearly in the amphibious expedition with Sir John Norreys as commander of the land forces against Lisbon in 1589. The plan was over-ambitious and ill-conceived, and the preparations were slapdash and neglectful of necessary precautions. Its carrying out revealed what Drake had not realised, that attacks against the centres of Spain's power were not like raids upon her out-lying possessions. Quarrels between the commanders and terrible mortality among the men were the marks of a lamentable fiasco, but Drake's reputation suffered most by a patent decay in that decision in action for which he had once been so remarkable. At the official enquiry he was able to clear himself of anything culpable, but it was more than the machinations of his many enemies that forbade his further immediate employment in high command. He retired to the lands in Devon that his second wife, Elizabeth Sydenham, had been managing since their marriage in 1585, and there he stayed for three years.

The war went badly, for though England had been saved in 1588, she could not be certain that there would not be another Armada, and she could find no way to do anything decisive. In many ways Spain was less vulnerable at sea than she had been ten or twenty years before, for she had learned how to defend herself against the type of attack of which Drake had been master. But the English statesmen, not only of that day, but for a century afterwards, failed to realise that fact, and they tried again and again to win a decisive victory with inadequate means. The last act of Drake's life was played out in such an effort, in which ironically he was linked with the man under whom he had begun his active career thirty years before.

John Hawkins was now an old man who had for many years been absorbed in the details of shore administration. He was no longer fitted for the onerous demands of West Indian warfare, while Drake's imperious self-confidence and impatience of contradiction made him a most awkward colleague. The failure was tragic. None of the successes of the Caribbean raid of 1585 came to grace the more amply fitted expedition of 1595, but ill-fortune dogged it from the start. Its story belongs to naval history, and here all that we can note is Drake's decline from his pristine vigour. The romantic biographer may attempt to disguise it and blame all the fault on the more prosaic Hawkins, but it is hard to deny that a good deal of the trouble was the fault of Drake's petulance or perhaps even of his conceit. His own end came after Hawkins was gone, and as all through his life his actions had been touched with the high colours of the picturesque, so the manner of his death was darkened to an almost theatrical effect. When all the plans of the venture had failed, and the Spaniards at San Juan had shown that the treasure of which he was in search would never be his, Drake determined to make a last desperate throw. He would return to renew at Nombre de Dios the triumphs of his first exploit. But all had changed, save the conditions of tropical nature. The Drake of fifty-five could not recapture the volcanic energy of his youth, and the Spaniards were prepared. Baffled, deceived and repulsed, first at Rio de la Hacha and Santa Marta, and at last at Nombre de Dios itself, Drake came back to his ships. The miasma of the tropical jungle demanded its toll and the deadly Chagres fever had seized him. His once buoyant spirit had gone for ever, but before he passed Drake added a last touch of the *bravura* that is almost the characteristic note of his life. When he knew that he was dying, he commanded that he be dressed with his armour and girt like the fighter he had always been. And so the end came on shipboard in the waters of his early triumphs.

Fame has never forgotten him, for the maritime legends of England's power derive one of their main sources from his career. He has often been credited with being what he never was and hardly could have been, a great strategist and a profound thinker. But, when all allowances have been made and all has been subtracted, there remains the certainty that Francis Drake was one of the greatest of all English men of action, a splendid figure of high adventure, and one of the most typical of the Elizabethans.

WILLIAM CECIL—LORD BURGHLEY

1520–1598

By
HILAIRE BELLOC

WILLIAM CECIL—LORD BURGHLEY

by HILAIRE BELLOC

WILLIAM CECIL, LORD BURGHLEY, is one of the very greatest figures in the history of European statesmanship. He stands for power of intrigue, of tenacity, and, by the fruits of his efforts, on the same plane with Bismarck and Richelieu. But he did more than Bismarck, and on the whole more than Richelieu. Bismarck destroyed the unity of the Germans, dividing the Catholic Germans into two bodies with separate political regions. He rendered impossible, perhaps for ever, the creation of a German State. He canalised and controlled everything towards the creation of the most powerful Prussian State possible. He in part succeeded, but only in part, as we all know; though it was not his fault that his scheme was ruined by the stupidity of the Prussian General Staff and their determination upon war in 1914.

Richelieu did much more than Bismarck. He finally consolidated the French State. He brought the monarchy to the pinnacle of its power, and left that power as an inheritance to the various experiments which have come after, republican and imperial. He left as a model for succeeding generations the conception of a strong, well-organised, central government, dealing with a very large national unity. It was the first thing of the kind since Byzantium. Richelieu's work endures in all its essentials after the test of three centuries. Yet Richelieu did not transform the society in which he lived; he only helped it on the way it was naturally going and presided over its last maturity.

William Cecil did more than Richelieu; he transformed the religion of the nation which he indirectly, but most really and effectively, governed. With the transformation of its religion he transformed its culture, and yet he achieved this great task without civil war or serious conflict. It is further to be remarked that he was the deliberate architect and planner of the whole thing. That is in its way as astonishing as his tenacity in carrying out his scheme. The greater part of men, especially what are called "men of action," move from accident to accident. They neither know how far they are going nor why fate is taking them as it does. That is in the main true of Napoleon. It is obviously true altogether of Oliver Cromwell. But William Cecil set out deliberately to do what he did. He made his plan at the beginning of his effort, carried it out patiently, secretly, and triumphantly over a space of thirty years—thirty years of unremitting industry and watchfulness. He is the chief creator of all that is called to-day " England."

If Great Britain is to-day one nation, if England is a Protestant country (which she is, to the marrow of her bones), a commercial country, a country boasting continuity, not so much of institutions as of their names—so that the institutions themselves can be modified indefinitely; these characteristics she owes much more to William Cecil than to any other man.

It is of course a question which can be debated for ever how much one man ever is the creator of any considerable human thing, especially of anything so complicated, organic, and deep-rooted as a State. But when we consider what the place was which bore the name of England when Cecil's efforts began and what England has been within memory of all men now living; when we further consider that this modern England which we know, has been as to the central principles of it unchanged, not indeed since Cecil's death, but since not more than a lifetime after the death of his son; and when we find him presiding over every step that was creative and decisive in the formative years of that change, we must give to his personal effort a very high place indeed. He was of course working upon a certain national temperament without which he could not have achieved his result. He was working in favour of a large group of men whose interest it was to preserve the great fortunes they had made out of the Reformation before Cecil himself came into power. He had further on his side the enthusiastic support of a religious minority, which, though at first very small in numbers, had high driving power behind it; the intense anti-Catholicism of the Calvinist-minded among the official reformers. Allow for all this, and yet William Cecil stands up above all the other forces which made modern England as does an isolated mountain out of a plain.

Contrast the conditions which he found with those which he left, remembering all the while that the newer conditions were foreseen by him, designed by him, often written down in so many words, years before they were realised.

He was born the son of a well-to-do government official, what we should call to-day, a man with some hundreds a year, but not with some thousands a year; a man, however, who both saved and invested well, so that, towards the end of his life, having faithfully served Henry VIII's government, he was in a substantial position so far as property went. Cecil was thus of the middle class, and by his immediate ancestry something not very high in this middle class—provincial inn-keepers. His father looked forward to putting him in his turn into the Civil Service, and he had his wish. The young man was destined under such conditions to at least an honourable and perhaps a fairly lucrative official career. Before he entered it he was sent to Cambridge, associating with the small clique of Protestant-minded men in that University (which had so much to do with the propagation of the religious revolution in England).

He married rather humbly, the sister of a great scholar, but a woman of very narrow means—luckily for him he lost her early in life. He went on his destined way, attaching himself, through the favour of his father's traditions and standing, through his own energy, industry, and reputation for aptitude in affairs, to the man who was, upon Henry VIII's death, the chief of the gang in power: the dead king's brother-in-law, Seymour. Cecil was a young man twenty-seven years old when he thus appeared, not as yet very conspicuous to the people, or even to the inner circle of politicians, as Seymour's secretary and factotum. He was in that position when Seymour made himself Protector and began to use royal power and the royal " we." He was still in that position when, at the age of thirty years, he saw his all-powerful master overthrown by enemies and he himself for a moment imprisoned; a man of no presence or physique, small, quiet, more talked about than he had been, but no one yet outside a small circle even beginning to appreciate his powers.

Note the next step, for it is the explanation of all. The men who had overthrown Seymour (known at the time as the Protector Somerset) were headed by Dudley, who had given himself the title of Warwick. They were like all the rest of the clot who usurped power during the minority of the child, King Edward VI, unscrupulous and greedy public robbers. But they were also unused to business and, most of them, to any habits of industry at all.

When they had overthrown Seymour they found that there was this one man, young Cecil, through whose hands had passed all Seymour's papers. He knew all about his late master; he knew all about his master's enemies, the people who were now governing. He was indispensable. They took him over and made him secretary to the Council.

When he had been secretary to Somerset he had already seen all the State Papers, for Somerset was virtually King of England. Now as Secretary of the Council, he saw everything in the regular way of business, and with his precision, his enormous powers, not only of work but of organisation, with his tenacity of purpose and of memory even for details, he was the one man in England without whom his new masters could not rule.

There was one question of overwhelming importance to those new masters and indirectly to Cecil himself; that question was the survival of the religious revolution.

There had been proceeding in Europe for about as long as Cecil's own lifetime, that is, for the last thirty years, or rather more, a religious revolution the consequences of which were bound to be of the first moment if the fruits of that revolution could be maintained. It was primarily a revolution against the ancient organisation of society on a united Catholic basis, the corruption of whose officers, coupled with the growth of debate and the weakening of central authority, had provoked the explosion.

By the middle of the sixteenth century, when Cecil becomes secretary, the natural Catholic reaction against the first enthusiasm of the zealous reformers was beginning to take shape; and, meanwhile, not only in places where the attack on the old religion had succeeded, but elsewhere, the vast wealth of the clergy had been seized on all sides. This had happened on an especially large scale in England, where there was a group of new millionaires having among them many men of long inheritance who had only grown

richer through the new loot, but composed in the main of
new men whom that loot had suddenly brought up out of
nothing, or out of very little. They had leaped from the
position of small squires or less, into the position of millionaires.

Sooner or later the vast new interests thus created by the
rifling of Church wealth would be ruined if the old religion
should permanently return to power. That was the great
problem of those critical years when William Cecil was
entering the thirties and beginning to enjoy the maturity of
his powers.

Now the great mass of the English people naturally lived
in the tradition of their old customs, religious as well as lay.
All men save a few exceptional enthusiasts are in that position at the beginning of any great change or revolution.
Pretty well all England was Catholic in tradition during
Edward VI's nominal reign. Paget, one of the chief men
in the clique that governed, and one of the principal beneficiaries by the religious revolution, one of the men who was
interested to make the Reformation as successful as possible,
estimated that hardly a twelfth was opposed to the old
religion, and of that tiny minority the greater part were
in London. Up and down the country as a whole Protestantism as yet (1550) had no hold.

How then could William Cecil hope to succeed in con-
firming his colleagues in their new-found wealth and
incidentally enriching himself by his services to them?

He had three things in his favour—first, that the Catholicism of the English people, though taken by them as a
matter of course, inherited through centuries of habit, was
not fervent. It had not been aroused by opposition. There
was no strong feeling for the Papacy; the Latin Mass and
the usual religious habits had not been destroyed, but presumably most people were slack in their practice as men
nearly always are in a Catholic community where the
Church has for very long suffered no active persecution.
We must remember that there had been no active opposition
to Catholicism as the ordinary man understood it, for Henry
had only separated from the Papacy without interfering
with ordinary Catholic religious habit; on the contrary he
enforced it by special laws.

Secondly, at a time when so much was controversy and
nothing yet fixed, men were confused. Translate the Mass

into English, for instance, and it might still seem to them to be the old Mass though in a new form. This or that particular doctrine might be attacked without an individual whose religion was sound feeling it to be particularly important : and so on.

The third factor in favour of Cecil's tremendous attempt was King-worship. In the generation to which he belonged all men had for the Prince a feeling which to-day we have for the nation. To disagree with one's monarch, to disobey his commands or the commands which came to one under his or her name, still more to question his or her title to authority and to the right of government in *all* things was, to the Englishman of the mid-sixteenth century, what treason to the nation and being false to his patriotism is to the Englishman of the twentieth century.

To have upon the throne a monarch, even a child like Edward VI, a monarch duly anointed and crowned who should lean towards the new religious practice rather than towards the maintenance of the old religion was half the battle.

Before little Edward VI died an attempt had been made to impose the English Prayer Book and its essentially Pro-testant ritual and ideas upon the mass of the people. This attempt led to violent rioting and insurrections on all sides, except in the north, which had been cowed by the fearful cruelty following upon the suppression of the Pilgrimage of Grace only a few years before. The insurrections were put down, but it was clear that the attempt to change religion so suddenly and by force was premature.

When the child died his half-sister Mary was received with enthusiasm, largely because it was known she would restore the old popular religion. There had been an attempt to usurp her throne to the profit of the Dudley family, and William Cecil had joined in that attempt, but he was for-given, and though Mary did not take him into her council she used him because he was still indispensable.

He knew all there was to be known about everybody and nobody else was in that position. Mary's early popularity was tarnished, in London and the home counties at least, by the religious persecution which raged in her name—though not over the whole country. Her popularity was also weakened by the Spanish marriage.

The result was that the six years of her power left things

still very confused and the anti-Catholic faction stronger than it had been. Her young half-sister Elizabeth was *nominally* the figurehead of the reforming party. She herself had no sympathy with the religious revolution, but she was determined to be Queen.

William Cecil was the man who understood the situation most thoroughly when Mary was sinking. He became sponsor for and protector of the Princess Elizabeth in the interval of waiting, acting hand-in-glove with Philip the King of Spain, Mary's husband, whose whole object it was to put Elizabeth on the throne in order to prevent Mary Stuart, the legitimate heiress, being made Queen of England; because Mary Stuart represented French influence, and French influence, especially in the Netherlands, was the nightmare of the Spanish power.

Elizabeth was thus enthroned, anointed, and could be used by the revolutionary faction, though she disliked it. She accepted reluctantly the new policy of Cecil, and soon found herself bound to give way on all points to his superior skill and knowledge. She had to accept a married clergy, the New Prayer Book, and the rest of it. She promised to send Bishops to the Council of Trent and was then prevented from doing so. On one point she did stick out—she refused to be called " Head " of the Church. She took the vague title of Governor. But that made no practical difference. A new establishment had appeared with a new hierarchy of its own, and the tone and character of that establishment were Protestant.

The genius of Cecil was never more apparent than in the ten years which followed (1560–70); he rushed nothing, he avoided all friction as far as it could be avoided, he worked for all it was worth the intense desire of Philip of Spain to keep Elizabeth on the throne, no matter what should happen to religion, although he was himself a champion of Catholicism in Europe.

Cecil did not force the Oath of Supremacy at once even upon all clerics, let alone the laity. He did everything by steps. If ever there was a man who understood the modern hybrid word " gradualness," it was Cecil. If ever there was a man who understood the factor of time in achievement, it was Cecil. He kept his goal steadily before him, like a lighthouse on a clear night. He knew his task would take many more years. He knew that it would need all his individual genius, but of that he had no doubt; he had tested it in power.

As the first ten years of the new experiment drew to their close, it was clear that the reliance on Spain was less and less necessary, because the French were embroiled in the beginnings of violent civil dissensions over the new religion. Spain, freed from the French menace, might become hostile; for she was, after all, the leader of the Catholic side in Europe, and it was by this time clear that Cecil's experiment was more and more acutely anti-Catholic. Just before the ten years were over Cecil played that masterstroke which will always testify, beyond any other individual event, to his supreme judgment and calculation of values.

Violent revolutionary troubles had broken out in the Spanish dominion of the Netherlands—what to-day we call Holland and Belgium. There had been widespread tortures and burnings and anarchic robberies carried on by mobs and inspired by the zeal of a few Calvinistic leaders who made up in vigour and action and feeling what they lacked in numbers. The insurrection was put down with the utmost severity through the use of the highly trained Spanish soldiers of Alva. Nothing the rebels could bring against them counted. They were by far the best military force in Europe, but that force was a mercenary force which needed high pay. Philip of Spain was sending round that pay in the shape of gold coin by sea, to be landed in the ports of the Netherlands. His ships took refuge in the ports of the English southern coasts from the pirates in narrow seas, and the Spanish Ambassador asked Elizabeth to be allowed to convoy the money to the Straits of Dover by land; a request which she of course at once granted; for revolution against a lawful sovereign was horrible to her (as to nearly everyone of that time), and also because the Spanish Government was still a friendly, and virtually allied, government.

Then it was that Cecil did what no other man would have dared to do, took a risk which no other man would have dared to take, and piloted the thing through to success by the breadth of a hair. He forbade the movement of the gold, holding it up in spite of the Queen's decision. The pretext was to discover who the gold really belonged to, for it had been advanced by certain Italian banks to the King of Spain, and its ultimate ownership might have been debated. But the pretext did not matter; the point was to prevent

Alva getting the money. If Alva's soldiers were not paid they would mutiny and lose their value as an instrument of Spanish government in the Netherlands. Spain would be irretrievably weakened.

But would not Spain declare war on the seizure of the gold ? If she did, Cecil and all his efforts were ruined. His Government was intensely unpopular, the Queen would certainly not support him when the peril came; even the threat of war would be enough. It was here that Cecil's highest genius appeared. He calculated the exact odds, and he had calculated right. It was still just necessary for Spain not to break with the English Government. There was no breach. Cecil's triumph had depended upon the precise judgment which had proved by a very narrow margin to be right.

Meanwhile, Mary Stuart, the Queen of Scotland (the rightful Queen of England by strict legitimacy, but an alien in English eyes), having lost in her struggle against revolutionaries in Scotland, had to take refuge in England, trusting to the promise of Elizabeth, for she, like the Pope and pretty well everyone else, except the keenest observers in London itself, thought that Elizabeth was the government and Cecil no more than Elizabeth's servant; whereas in reality it was Cecil who governed and Elizabeth who was driven and guided by him. He held the reins.

The evident determination of Cecil to prevent Mary Stuart from returning to her kingdom, his secret support of those who rebelled against her, his treatment of her more and more as a prisoner, brought on the crisis of the reign. The next months may be compared to the passage of a ship through a tumultuous " race " at sea. The vessel is with difficulty labouring in stormy water when it comes upon a special patch of confusion and violence of waves, worse than what had gone before and worse than what was to come after. In that turmoil it might have foundered, and Cecil was certainly in grave danger. The Spanish power had lost its temper and might move at any moment. The individual piracies of English seamen were known to be winked at by the English Government at the expense of Spain, and the virtual imprisonment of the Queen of Scotland was the last straw. The north of England rose against Cecil, but the rising was defeated. A plot against Elizabeth's life was exposed. The power of the old nobility was paralysed, not only by the destruction of the leaders in the north, but by the execution of the Duke of Norfolk, the head of them all. He was a strong Protestant, but it was none the less necessary for Cecil to make an example of him in order to show that the new millionaires, of whom he was the type and the leader, were now in full possession of power and that the old feudal tradition had been conquered by them.

The Pope in the midst of all this had committed the blunder of publishing a bull excommunicating Elizabeth and of publishing it too late after the northern rising had failed. The King of Spain refused to publish the bull in his dominions, so did the King of France. The Pope's action had done nothing but weaken very gravely the Catholic cause in England and make certain the triumph of the new Government and the new religion. At the end of a dozen years after the beginning of Cecil's direct power in government, that power was confirmed for good. He was now Lord Burghley, and admittedly the English Government incarnate.

The difficult task still remained to him of getting rid of Mary Stuart. She was a sovereign and amenable to no tribunal. It was difficult to have her murdered, though the plan very nearly succeeded once when Cecil's allies in Scotland had promised to kill Mary if she were sent back over the frontier. The plan failed because the man who was to have executed it was dead by the time the assassination should have taken place.

Mary, therefore, was kept in domestic imprisonment, but it was impossible to get Elizabeth to accede to the policy of putting her cousin to death. The thing was worked at last—not till more than a dozen years after Cecil's triumph over his various enemies, domestic and foreign. It was worked by involving Mary in a plot got up once more by Cecil, through his agents, and notably through Walsingham, the head of his special spy system. Of the secret agents such as are used for provoking others to crime in order that the Government might act against them, one was despatched to France. He, and those working with him, egged on, in France and in England, men who ultimately determined to rescue Mary Stuart.

The money was provided by a young enthusiastic gentleman called Babington. He was the chief dupe in the affair, and therefore the plot, which was really Cecil's, is known in history as " Babington's plot." The letters that passed between Babington and Mary Stuart were of course opened unknown to the Queen of Scots, read, copied, and only after that process had been gone through, conveyed to her by what she believed was the trustworthy channel of communication chosen by and known only to Babington. At last a letter written by Babington to Mary Stuart proposed her rescue and the forcible capture of Elizabeth. In that letter, if we are to trust the version which the Government issued (for they never produced the original drafts which were in their possession), it was further proposed to kill Elizabeth if she resisted capture. There already existed a widespread organisation in England for killing Mary Stuart if there were danger of her accession.

Whatever was in the original letter of Babington (and he admitted the chief part under peril of torture), Mary Stuart replied agreeing to his efforts at release. Cecil, in possession of this letter, or rather a copy which had been made of it, and into which an attempted forgery had been interpolated (with what other interpolations we do not know), procured a trial of the Queen of Scotland, and, at last, with great difficulty got Elizabeth to sign the warrant for the execution of the prisoner. Mary asked in vain for the original evidence against her to be produced. The sentence of the Commissioners, that is, of Cecil's Court, was a foregone conclusion; but the putting of Mary to death was another matter. Elizabeth would have none of it. She had signed the warrant under Cecil's pressure, but she refused to take the last step and be responsible for Mary's death before all Europe. Then came the final and supreme example of Cecil's power and of Elizabeth's impotence in face of that power. Cecil acted on the warrant in spite of Elizabeth and had Mary beheaded.

The shock of that axe reverberated throughout Europe. It led, as everyone knows, to an attempt at invasion by the Spanish, which invasion was to have joined up with a Catholic movement in England. Presumably, if the invasion had succeeded, Elizabeth would have made terms with it. That would have been the end of Cecil and of all that he had accomplished. Though Catholic numbers had lessened and the whole Catholic position had become more confused and weakened than ever through the disappearance of Mary Stuart, there was still a formidable opposition which could have set alight the whole country. But the Spanish invasion failed through the combination of adverse weather and the superior seamanship and gunnery of the fleet organised by Cecil to meet it under the headship of one of the most violent anti-Catholics of the day, Lord Howard of Effingham.

Cecil was now a man in extreme old age, especially as old age was counted in those days. His personality hardly weighs in future, but it is characteristic of him that his spirit continued to preside over the final triumph of the institutions he had created, fostered, and established. He had trained his son—his second son, Robert (an intelligent little dwarf with a hump on his back)—in all the arts of government which he himself, Burghley, knew now from a long lifetime of successful practice. Thus through the son the Cecil dynasty extended for nearly ten years after Elizabeth's death. It was that son who worked the gunpowder plot, nursed it, exposed it with the final effect of making Protestantism secure in England for good.

But great as Robert Cecil was we must always see him in the light of his greater father.

By the early seventeenth century, with Spain now beyond all hope of recovering the Northern Netherlands, with the French power in chaos through religious war and its consequent assassination of Henri IV, with the Empire on the brink of the worst religious war Europe had ever known, William Cecil had created a new England, not indeed united —there was to be violent dissension, a civil war and perpetual conflict for another lifetime, but a new England which was destined to achieve the complete destruction of the old religion within its boundaries and to enjoy thereby that moral unity which has been increasing ever since.

EDMUND SPENSER

Circa 1552–1599

By

W. L. RENWICK

EDMUND SPENSER

by W. L. RENWICK

"MR. BEESTON sayes he was a little man, wore short haire, little band and little cuffs." That is all the inquisitive Aubrey could record of Spenser's person. Of the two portraits that go by his name, one shows him in his bravery as a courtier, smiling; the other "more solemne sad" in dark doublet and plain falling band. Each has its truth—or at least our fancy can carry into them an image derived from the poems—in one, the deliberate decorative intention of the fantastic costume, in the other a brooding melancholy. In both, the sensuousness of nose and mouth, rather like Ronsard's, seem to belong rightly to the poet of *The Faerie Queene*. Yet they are not revealing as the portraits of Leicester and Ben Jonson are revealing. There is nothing in them to perturb Hazlitt, who preferred to exclude Spenser from among the "Persons one would wish to have Seen," because "he was (to our apprehension) rather 'a creature of the element, that lived in the rainbow and played in the plighted clouds,' than an ordinary mortal." Hazlitt had adopted Spenser as his symbol of airy romance, and refused to consider him in any other wise; yet Spenser was an ordinary mortal, troubled with business, with the problem of daily bread and butter, with the conduct of life and the thought of death.

He was born in London in the latter part of Edward VI's reign, and attended the new Merchant Taylors' School, where, under Richard Mulcaster, he would learn Latin, French, perhaps the elements of Greek, and an unusual respect for English. He would be given some bodily exercise—unlike some contemporary schoolmasters, Mulcaster believed in football, provided a referee was present—some music and singing, and what Mulcaster called " loud speaking," which culminated in the acting of plays before the Queen's Majesty herself. When in later life Spenser said

> " *And for I was in thilke same looser yeares* . . .
> *Somedele ybent to song and musicks mirth,*
> *A good olde shephearde,* Wrenock *was his name,*
> *Made me by arte more cunning in the same.*"

I believe he was commemorating his old headmaster.

Mulcaster may indeed have had something to do with Spenser's first publication, for his opinions owe much to Joachim du Bellay, and Spenser was still under his care when there appeared, in a compilation by one van der Noodt, certain translations from du Bellay which reappeared, twenty years later and in revised form, in Spenser's *Complaints*. The promising lad was sent, with charitable assistance, to Pembroke Hall in Cambridge, where we may believe he was happy, in spite of bad health and the bad graces of the Vice-Chancellor, and where he made a friend, Gabriel Harvey, a young don who, though socially impossible, had a restless mind, a taste for rhetoric, a modern outlook, and an omnivorous gluttony for books. Harvey encouraged him, and criticised. Both services were useful, for if to us, looking back, the criticism seem inept, it probably stiffened Spenser's back, and that was valuable, for part at least of the poet's ill-luck in life was probably due to his own defect of temperament.

According to Aubrey, " he misst the fellowship there which bishop Andrewes gott "—friendship with the unpopular Harvey may not have advantaged him in the election—and that was, I fancy, a disappointment, the first of many. All his life Spenser desired independence, peace, and learning.

> " *What more felicitie can fall to creature*
> *Then to enjoy delight with libertie?* "

His own notion of felicity was the kind of life Milton led at Horton and Gray in his own College. He envied Harvey as one " That Paradise has found, whych *Adam* lost," " the happy above happiest men," " like a great Lord of peerless libertie," who

> " *as one carelesse of suspition,*
> *Ne fawnest for the favour of the great :*
> *Ne fearest foolish apprehension*
> *Of faulty men, which daunger to thee threat.*"

To such a life he never attained. Like Marlowe, Greene, Lyly, and Peele, he left the University with poetry for his profession, but unlike them he did not try to make it his livelihood. The old days were gone, when the Church might have sheltered these clerks, and the service of the State, the modern substitute, was difficult of entry and precarious in tenure, for it depended too much on the favour of the great. What he did after leaving Cambridge in 1576 is not clear. He was in Limerick in 1577, secretary to the Bishop of Rochester—formerly Master of his own College— in 1578, and in Leicester's entourage in 1579–80. But he faced the world with misgiving. Diffident and sensitive, he hesitated to dedicate *The Shepheardes Calender* to Sidney, for fear of a rebuff, and he published it without his name. It may be partly convention that in his first book he appears as the lovelorn shepherd rejected of Rosalind : his amorous nature found speedy consolation. But always he expresses fear of envy, detraction, and misconstruction : in the epilogue to the *Calender*, in the sonnet to Harvey quoted above, in dedicating *Colin Clouts Come Home Againe* to Raleigh, whom he prays " with your good countenance protect against the malice of evill mouthes, which are alwaies wide open to carpe at and misconstrue my simple meaning," up to the end of the Sixth Book of *The Faerie Queene*, when one might consider him sufficiently established in reputation. Certain unlucky happenings may have helped to fix that diffidence in his character. As a partisan of Leicester he could hope for little from Burleigh, who was not tender to poetry at best and against whose ill-will he had occasion to protest in after years, and just as things were going well, when he was discussing the latest poetic theories with Philip Sidney and his friend Edward Dyer " in some use of familiaritie," urging Harvey to come to London and take advantage of the time, enjoying the success of *The Shepheardes Calender*, and planning new publications, some well-meant indiscretion lost him the favour of Leicester.

He found another employer in Arthur Lord Grey of Wilton, the newly-appointed Lord Deputy of Ireland, a man who, however unpopular with the Irish, was admired, loved, and trusted by those nearest him, and in the summer of 1580 Spenser sailed for Dublin as his secretary. It has become traditional among Irish historians to describe any Elizabethan Englishman who crossed St. George's Channel as a fortune-hunting adventurer seeking to enrich himself at the expense of the native Irish. Some such there were indeed —Raleigh is a conspicuous example—but there were readier ways to fortune, as Raleigh soon decided, and many Englishmen, if not most, were there on the Queen's business rather than their own. Many of them acquired lands which were forfeited for rebellion by Anglo-Irish lords, because that was the simplest way of paying the services, customary, and least strain on the depleted treasury, and it placed reliable tenants in strategic positions; also it was the most desirable, for men learned only too well that *Service n'est pas Héritage.* To this category Spenser belonged, and among such men he lived. He did not go to Ireland as to a Promised Land, but because he had to earn his living, and had to follow his employer in paths which neither of them liked. Grey returned in a couple of years; Spenser had nothing to return to, and had picked up one or two odd jobs which kept him alive in the meantime. His work was that of a minor Civil Servant: letter-writing—he wrote a beautiful hand—attesting copies of documents, organising and paying the messenger service, taking down attestations and examinations of suspected persons; in another capacity recording documents in the ecclesiastical Court of Recognisances; again, checking the (often fraudulent) muster-rolls of county militia; then back to the mixed duties of Clerk to a provincial Council at Limerick. It may not have been so dull at headquarters, but it was no great occupation, not highly remunerated, and it entailed long journeys in frequent peril and constant discomfort. After ten years' service he acquired the lands of Kilcolman, in County Cork, a domain he called "Hap Hazard," surrounded by mountain, forest, and bog, but fortunately provided with a defensible tower. Later on he added some richer land by purchase, he could see the beauty of some of its surroundings—that limestone country abounds in the clear running streams he loved—and it grew dear to him by association. But it was always a dangerous region, an outlying tower, and if its possession gave him some small measure of independence, "this salvage soyle, farr from Parnasso mount," did not permit much indulgence in the studious peace in which he placed his felicity. He never rose to high place in the service, holding even his Clerkship to the Council of Munster as deputy to his friend Ludovick Bryskett, partly because (we can believe) his gifts did not lie that way, partly because his personal attachments were too strong to suit him to the frequent changes of command, but he knew enough about Irish administration to write down, in clear-cut English prose, a trenchant criticism of it and a lucid plan of reform.

This *View of the Present State of Ireland*, which he wrote in 1596, is not a poetic dream of an ideal commonwealth, but a realistic survey drawn up by an official, embodying, I believe, the information and the opinion of a group of officials—the usual old headquarters set—and possibly written at their instigation. We can glean from it something of the writer's personality, his loyalty to his old master, dead these three years, his horror of destructive warfare, and the wide range of his curiosity. We find that he shares the limitations of his kind: the Londoner's inability to appreciate alien modes of life; the Englishman's assumption that English law is eternally just and universally applicable, and his self-dramatisation as God's policeman; the official's tendency to regard the population as a card-index to be reshuffled at will; the colonist's instinct to look upon the natives as inferior beings with some good points of their own. Spenser does not rise above his kind. Nor, despite the traditional horror with which the *View* is regarded (especially by those who have not read it) does he fall below it into mere indiscriminate hatred of the Irish and a policy of massacre. Some of his suggestions are ill-judged, and, like everyone else, he thought of government as resting upon force and requiring the exercise of force as a preliminary to reform. It was necessary to put down the warrior castes that lived by raiding and fighting, and to subject all Ireland to a uniform rule. On the other hand, Spenser, like many of his colleagues, wished to improve the status of the peasants, and even showed some care for the rights of the native landlords. The book is a spirited attempt to work out a plan covering the entire field of law, administration, police, defence, and finance. It is clear-sighted and courageous, for it attacks the English as fiercely as the Irish—Anglo-Irish lords, Government officialdom, the administrative system, and, by implication, the central government in England; it faces the difficulties, and it recognises that the solution proposed is not ideal. The *View* is a series of practical suggestions for the improvement of a dangerous state of affairs; for as Spenser's life in Ireland began in war, so it was ending in war. Trouble was looming, not only in Ireland, where Tyrone was growing in strength and ambition, but in Spain, where another Armada was preparing. The Spanish threat was dissipated by Raleigh and the sailors; the Irish trouble grew worse and worse, until in 1598 Tyrone made his desperate bid for the command of all Ireland. In that affair Spenser's personal fortunes were soon involved, his house burned, and with it, according to Ben Jonson's gossip, one of his children. He himself was sent to London to report on the situation, and died in Westminster in January, 1599. So he saw neither the debacle of Essex nor the recovery under Mountjoy when the Celtic chiefs collapsed with Celtic suddenness, nor the return of his family to Kilcolman, but died in misery, all his fears come true.

From *Colin Clouts Come Home Againe* we can gather what Raleigh thought of Spenser and of his situation in 1589:

> " *He gan to cast great lyking to my lore,*
> *And great dislyking to my lucklesse lot:*
> *That banisht had my selfe, like wight forlore,*
> *Into that waste, where I was quite forgot.*"

And Spenser dedicates the poem to Raleigh " That you may see that I am not alwaies ydle as yee thinke, though not greatly well occupied, nor altogither undutifull, though not precisely officious." It would be easy to reconstruct the conversation between a diffident, discouraged Spenser settled down into his loneliness, and the energetic Raleigh who dragged him from that obscurity and brought him to London to publish his masterpiece and gain the Queen's countenance. It was close on ten years since Spenser had been in London, and ten years, less four days, between the entry of his first publication and his second on the Stationers' Register. Yet *The Shepheardes Calender* had been a success, and was now in its third edition. Diffidence, discouragement, and the pressure of affairs might be the causes of delay; but not the whole cause. For, however uncertain of himself in the world of business, Spenser lacked neither energy nor confidence in the sphere of poetry. In his early days he deferred to Harvey in other matters, but in poetry he took his own line. When he was smitten with the quantitative versification which was the latest fashion in the

Leicester circle, he argued it hotly—though Harvey, who derived a similar theory from other sources, had a better notion of it—and he took no notice of Harvey's advice to drop *The Faerie Queene* and follow up a project of writing comedies. His views on diction traversed those of all the English critics, including those that might have been expected to weigh most with him, from the Cambridge masters Cheke, Ascham, and Wilson, to Philip Sidney himself. For he knew his own strength. The proem and epilogue of the anonymous *Shepheardes Calender* are humble enough, but in the eclogues themselves the poetic skill of " Colin Clout " is well advertised, and it is made quite clear who Colin was.

Poetry was Spenser's vocation, and he knew it. The ways of Ireland were difficult and dangerous, but—

> " *The waies, through which my weary steps I guyde,*
>   *In this delightfull land of Faery,*
>   *Are so exceeding spacious and wyde,*
>   *And sprinckled with such sweet variety,*
>   *Of all that pleasant is to eare and eye,*
>   *That I nigh ravisht with rare thoughts delight,*
>   *My tedious travell doe forget thereby;*
>   *And when I gin to feele decay of might,*
> *It strength to me supplies, and chears my dulled spright.*"

In this land he enjoyed delight with liberty. When Swinburne divided the poets into the Gods and the Giants, he forgot the third category, and the title given to Spenser in his epitaph, the title Ronsard bore—of all poets the likest to Spenser—" The Prince of Poets in his Tyme." This title he held, not by favour of the great, but by the grace of God. His friend E. K., who annotated the *Calender*, was quoting him when he claimed poetry to be " no arte, but a divine gift and heavenly instinct not to bee gotten by laboure and learning, but adorned with both : and poured into the witte by a certaine ἐνθουσιασμὸς, and celestiall inspiration," and he tells us that on this theme " the Author . . . at large discourseth, in his booke called the English Poete," which he meant to publish but unfortunately did not. By right of this heavenly gift, Spenser held his vocation in princely security. Even the problem that haunted him all his life, the problem of Mutability, the uncertainty and vicissitude of human things, was solved in a way, for the grace of God gave to the poet—and to the poet alone—an immortality of his own.

> " *For deeds doe die, how ever noblie donne,*
> *And thoughts of men do as themselves decay,*
> *But wise wordes taught in numbers for to runne,*
> *Recorded by the Muses, live for ay;*
> *Ne may with storming showers be washt away,*
> *Ne bitter breathing windes with harmfull blast,*
> *Nor age, nor envie shall them ever wast.*"

He not only recognised his vocation, but had faith in it. Worldly reward might be poor and uncertain, but that of faithful service to poetry was magnificent and sure.

This contrast between his employment and his vocation could be developed at length. Even when we catch him at his most businesslike, in the *View of Ireland*, he scarcely hides the fact that he is more interested in the history and antiquities of Ireland—the proper study of an epic poet—than in its administration. Yet the contrast must not be overstressed. The airiest fancy must have something to work upon, and Spenser's poetry, like any other, is made out of his experience. Also, his great poem had—as, according to the doctrine current long before his time and long after, it should—its triple meaning, and if the first meaning is the pure fancy in which Hazlitt delighted, the second is a reflection of, and upon, contemporary affairs. The notion of Spenser as dwelling aloof in an ivory tower of poetry is as false as it is derogatory: every book he published contains some discussion of the public issues in which his time was involved. In three of the eclogues in *The Shepheardes Calender* he handles the one quasi-political question on which public opinion existed, the quarrel between the Puritan and High Church parties. In *Mother Hubberds Tale* he satirises labour conditions, the High Church Party, the Court, and some highly-placed personages—indeed, this last section was evidently too bold, for he revised it before publication, and there was a rumour that the poem was suppressed. And these belong to his early days, before he went to Ireland or was personally concerned with government. But this is usual with poets. Like other poets, again, he lived in the world of action and in the world of books, and counted what he derived from each as equally valid experience. The difficulty with Spenser is, that he drew upon each kind of experience with equally conscious intention, used one or other as suited the purpose of the moment, and worked them up to the same kind of surface. Thus the *September* eclogue begins with a literary imitation from Mantuan, and continues in a discussion of the clergy easily paralleled in contemporary pamphlets. We know that one of the protagonists in the dialogue is Gabriel Harvey; the arguments of the other are precisely those of William Harrison, vicar of Radwinter, near Harvey's home, in his Description of England contributed to Holinshed's Chronicle. But the first part will not fit Harrison's life. Is it then merely "literary"? Perhaps. But *Virgils Gnat,* a straight translation of the *Culex,* was addressed to Leicester in deprecation of his wrath. *Muiopotmos* reads like a flight of artistic fancy, but men will persist in suspecting a personal story behind it. The elucidation of Spenser's allusions to personal and public affairs thus provides endless entertainment for the sportsman critic, but the results are often insecure, and the finest tact cannot always discriminate.

Beyond the secondary meaning, again, lay the third, the "anagogical" or spiritual. The divine gift of poetry brought its responsibilities as well as its privileges, and Spenser accepted the well-understood duty of teaching. He was a good Protestant Christian, but not a religious poet. His early Puritanism was a vague anticlericalism picked up at Cambridge, as a modern undergraduate might pick up a vague socialism; in the *View of Ireland* he confesses "Lyttle have I to saie of relidgion, both because the partes thereof be not manie, yt self beinge but one, and my self have not bene much conversant in that callinge," but he repudiates the objections of "our late too nyce fooles" to the comely order of the Church. His anagogical meaning is not mystical, but ethical, for our airy romancer is consistently practical. The aim of *The Faerie Queene* is "to fashion a gentleman or noble person in vertuous and gentle discipline" —to teach men to live the good life. Nor are his allegorical figures static metaphysical entities, but active energetic fighting principles. His conception of the good life is positive, the normal, central conception of Western European moralists. For one thing, speculation was not his concern. When he indulges in it he philosophises as a scholar, not as a metaphysician, and is content to share the duty of his time, the gathering together and spreading abroad of all the diverse ideas of the ancients, the task the Renaissance had to accomplish and consolidate before thought could travel in the new direction for which Bacon laid out the landmarks. But though wisdom was to be sought in all the schools, Spenser found his real guide in the teaching in which he was brought up, the ethics of Christianity as interpreted by the Church of England. There is no need to search far for the sources of his ethical and religious ideas: they are contained in the Bible, the Prayer Book, and the Catechisms, and in the social teaching of his time, that tried to combine the personal virtues of the mediæval knight with the intellectual enlightenment of the cultivated mind, and the artistic sensitiveness of cultivated senses. It is an unusually comprehensive ideal, but neither aberrant nor obscure.

We can trace, then, a whole series of interests: the poet's personal surroundings, his views on public affairs and contemporary events, his moral ideas, and his religious beliefs. These are the things Hazlitt would dissuade us from trying to understand. Yet if on his advice we disregard the allegory, we disregard a great deal that Spenser meant us to observe and to ponder. No great poet writes merely for our amusement, but for the improvement of human life. It was long before serious poets learned to trust their readers and to trust the intrinsic beauty and interest of their poetry, and the allegory is but a crude attempt to combine the attractiveness of beautiful rhythm and imagery with effective guidance to good. The glory of earth and the hope of heaven had been set in opposition by centuries of preaching, and Spenser, desiring and believing in both, made use of all the expedients—parable, personification, myth, *exemplum* —that promised their unification. Only the great humanists, Chaucer and Shakespeare, realised the eternal value of plain humanity, and Spenser was not a great humanist in that sense. We must accept the allegory, since Spenser made it so; but Hazlitt insists overmuch on the obstructiveness of the allegory. The way to read *The Faerie Queene* is to take it as it comes, in all its variety; enjoy the romance, savour the delight, recognise the imitations and literary allusions as far as we can, and grasp as much of the personal, historical, and moral allegories as strikes at the time or clarifies in the memory; and read slowly, to give ourselves time. The various interests are of unequal value. Spenser meant the obscure personal allusions—the *roman à clef*—for his friends; they are valuable to the later reader only as gossip, and Spenser was content to leave them obscure. The allusions which are now historical and were then topical, he meant for his contemporaries; they are usually easy enough to anyone who knows anything about the period. The ethical teaching is broad and simple, to be gathered in the by-going. On this understanding, Hazlitt's advice, however exaggerated, is sound. Do not trouble about the allegory: it will come.

Hazlitt's advice is sound in another sense. Whatever Spenser made his poetry out of, he made it poetry, and as good poetry as he could make it. It was pleasant to insert in the Third Book of the *Faerie Queene* an adventure of Raleigh's which happened in Spenser's own county, to give little portraits of friends and patrons, as Florentine painters did in their frescoes, and it was strictly correct according to the best critics. But the thing that mattered, first and last, was not the sources, but the poem, the " wise wordes taught in numbers for to runne " which men would read long after sixteenth-century deeds and thoughts, however absorbing and important, were dead and decayed. For the first and last responsibility of the poet was to cultivate his heavenly gift and use it well. The princely title does not come by accident: there must be ambition as well as faith, and if poetry is " not to bee gotten by laboure and learning," it must be " adorned with both." The ambition was there, certainly. *The Shepheardes Calender* was not the only set of poems Spenser had written by 1579. Though E. K. hoped he would " put forth divers other excellent works of his, which slepe in silence, as his Dreames, his Legendes, his Court of Cupide, and sondry others "; though the Dreames were ready, down to the illustrations, in 1580; it was only after he had published the first part of *The Faerie Queene* that he vouchsafed to put forth a volume of minor poems, the *Complaints*, some new work, some old. The cause may be, as I have suggested, diffidence and discouragement. The Dreames may have been held up by that unknown trouble that occurred between April and June, 1580, and Spenser too busy in Ireland, and perhaps too dejected, to recover them. But he had begun an epic-romance called *The Faerie Queene* by that date, and the ten years of silence, though longer perhaps than had been anticipated, may well have been caused by growing ambition and a plan of campaign. The plan is clearly hinted at by E. K. It was an emulation of the career of Virgil—first the *Bucolics*, then the *Æneid*, with some of the lost poems taking the place of the *Georgics*. For this New Poet was no common rhymester, but a learned and serious poet who followed the highest example the humanists set before educated Europe. The success of the first venture, and acceptance in the larger world outside the academic precincts of Cambridge, would encourage the adventurer. The plan seems to us rather solemn and pedantic, but among the notions we have to revise is that of relative chronology. In sixteenth-century England, Virgil was modern. It was as natural for a young poet to model himself on Virgil as for a present-day novelist to learn from Stendhal or Dostoievsky, and if Spenser had the trick of looking back to an ideal past, he was well up in the latest criticism. Nor was Virgil his only master. He studied all the acknowledged poets, Latin, Italian, and French, from Ennius and Lucretius to Desportes and du Bartas. It was his task, as he conceived it, to bring to England not only the wisdom of the philosophers and the learning of the historians, but the fine flower of poetic art.

He was unlucky in his exile. It removed him from the sources of learning, it absorbed time and energy, it lost him the encouragement his nature required, and it kept him out of the current of thought and art. On his tomb his birth was dated at least forty years too early, and the error is significant, for he belonged to an earlier epoch than that of the lively crowds that thronged round Marlowe and Shakespeare and Ben Jonson. For political, social, philological, economic, and many other reasons, England's period of production came late, and " Elizabethan " literature traced nearly the full curve of the " Renaissance " in some forty years. Spenser was its first great master, and he was away from the centre of activity, out of sight, for most of his life. That decade of Spenser's first residence in Ireland was indeed crucial. When he returned in 1589, the Spanish Armada had been defeated, Mary Queen of Scots executed, and English politics reoriented; Leicester and Sidney were dead, and Walsingham dying; Captain Raleigh—a helpful wellwisher and a good poet, but no substitute for Sidney— was Sir Walter and a great man; and Lyly, Marlowe, Greene,

Peele, Shakespeare, Daniel, and a score of new poets were at work. The theatre, again, was making poetry a possible profession. If he had stayed in England, Spenser might have anticipated Lyly with the projected *Nine Comedies*; he and Gabriel Harvey certainly enjoyed *The Merchant of Venice* when they saw it: as things fell out, he had no share in the great literary invention of the age, into which the brightest spirits poured their energy. We instinctively connect him with the Cambridge humanists and the Sidney coterie; and rightly, for his ideas were formed by 1580, and the rest was but the working-out. To the young men of that swiftly-moving time, he must have seemed almost ancestral. Ireland, indeed, was no bad training-ground for a romantic poet, and the hard life may have saved him, as the Civil War saved Milton, from mere luxurious poetising. We cannot tell; he had too much of it, perhaps, but we must take what the gods give. It is doubtful, even, whether the rush of London life, the literary squabbles, the melancholy that beset the later years, the new ideas and directions, the distractions that would inevitably have arisen, would have allowed him any more time than he had at Kilcolman—still more, whether they would have allowed his early acquirement to remain uncontaminated to ripen into the perfect homogeneity out of which grew *Epithalamion*, and would not have clouded the eye that gazed upon so much loveliness. It was in dangerous loneliness, but in perfect artistic security and happiness that the Shepherd Colin companied with the Muses and the Graces:

> " *Unto this place when as the Elfin Knight*
> *Approcht, him seemed that the merry sound*
> *Of a shrill pipe he playing heard on hight,*
> *And many feete fast thumping th' hollow ground,*
> *That through the woods their Eccho did rebound.*
> *He nigher drew, to weete what mote it be;*
> *There he a troupe of Ladies dauncing found*
> *Full merrily, and making gladfull glee,*
> *And in the midst a Shepheard piping he did see. . . .*

> " *There he did see, that pleased much his sight,*
> *That even he him selfe his eyes envyde,*
> *An hundred naked maidens lilly white,*
> *All raunged in a ring, and dauncing in delight. . . .*

535

" *Such was the beauty of this goodly band,*
   Whose sundry parts were here too long to tell :
   But she that in the midst of them did stand,
   Seem'd all the rest in beauty to excell,
   Crownd with a rosie girlond, that right well
   Did her beseeme.   And ever, as the crew
   About her daunst, sweet flowres, that far did smell,
   And fragrant odours they uppon her threw ;
  But most of all, those three did her with gifts endew.

" *Those were the Graces, daughters of delight,*
   Handmaides of Venus, *which are wont to haunt*
   Uppon this hill, and daunce there day and night :
   Those three to men all gifts of grace do graunt,
   And all, that Venus *in her selfe doth vaunt,*
   Is borrowed from them.   But that faire one,
   That in the midst was placed paravaunt,
   Was she to whom that shepheard pypt alone,
  That made him pipe so merrily, as never none.

" *She was to weete that jolly shepheards lasse,*
   Which piped there unto that merry rout,
   That jolly shepheard, which there piped, was
   Poore Colin Clout (*who knowes not* Colin Clout?)
   He pypt apace, whilst they him daunst about.
   Pype jolly shepheard, pype thou now apace
   Unto thy love, that made thee low to lout :
   Thy love is present there with thee in place,
  Thy love is there advaunst to be another Grace."

That is a supreme example of the decorative fancy in which Hazlitt delighted.   It is also allegorical, for " who knowes not *Colin Clout?* " and who can fail to recognise the allusions to *Epithalamion,* in which Edmund Spenser claimed the right to celebrate, for once, his own happiness?   The anagogical meaning of the Graces is explicit, and inseparable, though developed at length later in the Canto.   The style is that of a trained rhetorician, and the whole Canto is constructed out of Claudian, Politian, the commentators on Horace, and so on, just as *Epithalamion* is solidly based on Catullus.   And it is also Spenser's supreme and rapturous vision of himself, the Poet, and his declaration of independence, his challenge to the successful men of affairs around him.   He had received the celestial inspiration.   He had gathered learning and had not stinted his labour.   And he had his reward.

RICHARD HOOKER

1554?–1600

By

CHRISTOPHER MORRIS

RICHARD HOOKER

by CHRISTOPHER MORRIS

"BEFORE the world was God" and "After God came Christ his Son": such were the watchword and the countersign of the fleet in which Frobisher set sail to find the North-west Passage. And the Admiral's orders began, "Imprimis to banish dice, card-playing, swearing and filthy communication, and to serve God twice a day." Religion and even theology then played a bigger part in most men's lives than they do now. Queen Elizabeth herself was something of a theologian. No doubt she kept her powder very dry, but it is probable that she feared God as well. The exact colour of her religious beliefs may be uncertain, but we can be fairly sure that the Church over which she ruled was something more to her than a mere instrument of worldly policy. Many political issues were involved, but the new Church was, after all, a new road to heaven; and the exploration of it was one of the more exciting adventures that her subjects undertook. There were times when she felt herself responsible for the eternal safety of their souls.

When the Queen entered upon the last decade of her reign, she must have been anxious about her religious experiment. Everything depended upon the new generation, and too many of the young men were losing their hearts to the old religion or catching fever from the new sectarians. At the beginning of her reign the Queen had known that she could only wait. The Catholic clergy were politically disloyal and had to be discarded. The only able or learned men to take their places were the returning exiles who sought to bring England into line with the Protestant "International" in Switzerland. A vaguely Zwinglian doctrinal settlement had been devised to satisfy the Reformers. A vaguely traditional liturgy and system of Church government had been provided to appease the

Catholics. Neither party had been pleased. For some time there were only three " Anglicans " in England—the Queen herself, William Cecil, and Archbishop Parker—and Cecil was half a Puritan, while Parker was not a strong man. The Queen had to put her trust in two things only, education and the fertility of English soil. Perhaps the Universities could train recruits; perhaps a religion suitable for Englishmen would somehow grow—instinctively the Queen left much to the *genius loci* : but, after waiting for more than thirty years, she might well have suspected that she had sown on stony ground.

The Universities had failed her. Oxford, strange to relate, had produced the first of the Puritans, and was now sending many of her best young men to join the great Cardinal Allen and his Jesuits. Cambridge had produced the arch-puritan Cartwright and remained a Calvinist stronghold. The Catholic North had actually risen in arms; while London, the Home Counties, and the East were honeycombed with Puritan organisations. The life of the established Church was at its lowest ebb. Its morals were bad, its administration corrupt, its creed amorphous, its learning meagre, its propaganda ineffectual, its discipline lax. Archbishop Grindal had been lodged in the Tower for neglecting to act against the sectaries. The new Archbishop Whitgift, whom the Queen called " her little black husband," though a stern disciplinarian, was himself a Calvinist in theology. The Jesuits were everywhere and still threatened the Queen's life, the blood of martyrs pleading eloquently for their cause. The House of Commons rang with Puritan demands; and the reading public regaled itself with the Marprelate tracts.

Just when the Anglican Church appeared to be withering, parched by the long drought, there came a small cloud no bigger than a man's hand, promising gentle and life-giving rain. An Oxford don, now rector of the parish of Boscombe in Wiltshire, had published the first part of a learned work.

Richard Hooker's treatise *Of the Laws of Ecclesiastical Polity* is probably less read than any work of equal merit in our literature. It is known to a few scholars and, doubtless, to a few more clergymen. And yet it is perhaps the finest sustained piece of Elizabethan prose, the foundation of the English " Classical " style, besides being the first and by no means the least of the many splendid mansions which philosophy has built in England. It was once, deservedly, a best-seller, for there was a time when this book alone had saved the Church of England from intellectual and perhaps from spiritual sterility. Even the ranks of Tuscany had applauded: Walton says that Allen and Stapleton, the leaders of the English Catholics at Rome, went and " boasted to the Pope that, though he had lately said he never met with an English book whose writer deserved the name of an author, yet there now appeared a wonder to them, and it would be so to his Holiness, if it were in Latin; for a poor obscure English priest had wrote four such books of laws and church-polity, and in a style that expressed so grave and such humble majesty, with clear demonstration of reason, that in all their readings they had not met with any that exceeded him." The first book was translated for the Pope, who declared,

> "There is no learning that this man hath not searched into; nothing too hard for his understanding. . . . His books will get reverence by age, for there is in them such seeds of eternity that . . . they shall last till the last fire shall consume all learning."

The author was indeed obscure, the darkest of dark horses. He was a man of almost pathological bashfulness— he could not look people in the eyes—and cut a fabulously poor figure in the world. Even his appearance was unprepossessing, for he was " of a mean stature, and stooping," his eyes myopic and peering, " his face full of heat pimples, begot by his inactivity and sedentary life." So self-effacing was his disposition that for long the ordinary facts of his life were hard to come by. Indeed, his first biographer, a certain Bishop Gauden, praised him for his saintly devotion to the celibate life; whereas in truth he had married his landlady's daughter, " a clownish, silly woman, and withal a mere Xanthippe," as Anthony à Wood will have it.

Hooker was born, probably in 1554, in Exeter, of good burgess stock—his grandfather had been mayor. The family was almost Puritanical in religion, and his uncle, John Hooker, was the editor of Holinshed, who added insertions of his own which are in excellent prose and have a highly Protestant flavour. His father was poor, but the uncle, impressed by the boy's progress at the local grammar school, secured him the good offices of Bishop Jewel, who got him into Corpus Christi College, Oxford, at the age of fourteen, first as a chorister and later as a clerk. At nineteen he was a scholar of the college and at twenty-three a fellow. His academic career was by no means meteoric, although he once was deputy for the Professor of Hebrew.

In 1581, just after he had taken orders, he came to London to preach at Paul's Cross. The lodging provided for the preacher, called the Shunamite's House, was kept by a draper called Churchman who had fallen on evil days. Hooker arrived ill and travel-worn and displaying anger, for the only time recorded in his life, against a friend who had provided him with a bad horse. Mrs. Churchman nursed him into a fit state to preach his sermon, persuaded him that he stood in need of a wife, and provided her own not too eligible daughter to fill the bill.

Marriage involved the resignation of his fellowship, and Hooker became Rector of Drayton Beauchamp, near Aylesbury, in 1584. It was there that two pupils

> " found him with a book in his hand (it was the *Odes of Horace*), he being then tending his small allotment of sheep in a common field; which he told his pupils he was forced to do, for that his servant was then gone home to dine and assist his wife to do some necessary household business. When his servant returned and released him, his two pupils attended him unto his house, where their best entertainment was his quiet company, which was presently denied them, for Richard was called to rock the cradle."

The two pupils were influential—one was the son of Archbishop Sandys—and reported the state of affairs in high quarters. In consequence Hooker became Master of the Temple—a stop-gap appointment, since other candidates with stronger backing had cancelled out—and his career as a controversialist began. He was already opposed to Presbyterianism, probably as the result of his own unaided reflections, for the atmosphere of his college had been Puritanical. The Presbyterian leader, Walter Travers, who had been Burleigh's candidate for the Mastership as well as tutor to the Cecil children, was the Temple lecturer in the afternoons. Hooker refuted Presbyterianism in the mornings. Half London came to listen and Hooker made a name.

Eventually Whitgift suspended Travers, but the strain had been too much for Hooker: he could not stand publicity, competition, or conflict with a person. The *Ecclesiastical Polity*, which he had begun, made little progress until he was allowed to retire to the quiet rectory of Boscombe in 1591. The first four books, with a syllabus of the four to come, were printed in 1594, the fifth in 1597. Whitgift and Burleigh himself were constantly consulted, for the obscure country parson was already the official apologist of the Anglican Church. For the last five years of his life he was Vicar of Bishopsbourne, near Canterbury, where he died in 1600. The remaining three books were finished, but the manuscripts fell into the hands of Puritan relatives, were mutilated, rescued with difficulty, and have only survived in an imperfect form.

As a parish priest Hooker was assiduous and saintly, kind and rather charming: he tried manfully not to preach above the heads of village audiences—without very much success, it has to be admitted. He was of course too virtuous to escape the assaults of the ungodly, and was once blackmailed by a woman of ill-fame. He was able to leave a hundred pounds as dowry to each of his four daughters. His wife allowed him four months of rest before she joined him in the grave.

Writing must have been to Hooker as a healing draught. With his pen in his hand, the world, so often too much for him in real life, could be subjected to his will. Its seeming waywardness and confusion could be reduced to order. Everything fell into place in his great intellectual system. There were no excrescences, no pimples, in his scheme or in his style: all rough places were made smooth. His " mane stature " vanished as he measured and bestrode the universe. There were no longer people staring: only ideas were left, and these could be dominated, these could be outfaced. His virility flowed back to him, because in that interior world he found a household where he could be master. There logic brooked no tiresome interruptions, and there truth prevailed against the speciousness of error and, doubtless, against slander also. Besides, he was preaching to the learned, to an audience who could understand, and no hostile preacher was to follow in the afternoon. He was writing something classical and formal, and, in so doing, he was "escaping" just as much as any writer of romantic poetry.

Thus reassured, Hooker in his writings became a new man. His meekness vanished, but fortunately not his tolerance. He could hit very hard, though always above the belt. Even a certain knowledge of the world and shrewdness came to him, and, more remarkable still, a sense of humour. Nor was the temptation to be erudite too much for him. He marshalled incredible masses of learning, but always with relevance, always to the best tactical advantage. His style is somehow not pedantic, and, for all his polish and urbanity, he never quite lost the countryman's rough, trenchant pithiness; he could drive in his nails with something of a homely touch. The prose is built up in long, imposing periods, the unit being the paragraph rather than the sentence. It is rhetoric, though of course it is not ranting. Unity is given to the whole structure by the inevitable movement of the logic, by the governing idea. Occasionally the book becomes a little flat and lifeless but, taken as a whole, it is less monotonous and stirs more emotions than other English classical façades of the same order, Gibbon's for example. Hooker's style, says Fuller, "was long and pithy, driving on a whole flock of clauses before he comes to the close of a sentence"; but the clauses do not go far astray, and the emphatic word is inevitably found in the emphatic place. Few English ears have been more sensitive to rhythm or to cadence.

Writing to reassert himself against his own humility, Hooker was doing a great service to his fellow men. For part of his humility was intellectual and came from his Protestant environment; and it was from the rather dangerous self-abasement of Protestant thought that Hooker rescued English religion and English speculation. He saved the Renaissance from undergoing total immersion at the hands of the Reformers.

Justification by Faith, the central doctrine of the Reformation, means roughly that you are saved by a sense of your own inferiority. By reason, it was argued, of the fallen state of man, by reason of his total depravity and original sin, you cannot hope to keep God's Law, you cannot put your trust in conduct or in Works. Nor can you be saved by obeying any set of rules drawn up by earthly churches. All human effort being doomed to fail, you must rely only upon the Merits of Christ to turn away God's wrath. To understand this process of Atonement is not given to the human mind. Reason is of no avail, and may be dangerous. Faith is not the intellectual acceptance of a certain creed; it is a matter of the heart, of the emotional acceptance of God's Word; it is a spiritual mood in which you acknowledge your sinful state, your human impotence, and throw yourself unfeignedly upon God's grace and mercy. No estimate of man's moral and intellectual capacity could sink lower.

From the intolerable burden of the sense of sin the Puritan had found one way of escape. After saying, " God be merciful to me a sinner," he noticed that other men were not acknowledging their sins, and so he went on to say, " God, I thank thee that I am not as other men are." The publican had become a Pharisee. The sense of sin had been replaced by a sense of being Elect.

Hooker discovered, or rather rediscovered, a more excellent way. He accepted the theological framework of Protestantism, and defended it in his *Learned Discourse of Justification*, but found room in it for other things. " God," he wrote, " is no favourer of sloth : and therefore there can be no such absolute decree touching man's salvation as on our part includeth no necessity of care and travail." Ultimately, he admitted, everything depends on Grace and Faith; but much remains to be done by conduct, much by reason, much by law : man need not lose his self-respect. Besides, even if salvation itself is not attained by obedience to the discipline of a Visible Church, there is still a wide field in which tradition, order, and authority are of value.

In Hooker's time the health of a society was not thought to depend upon its economic system, but upon its system of Church government. Social justice was bound up with the service of God, and sixteenth-century minds would no more think of separating religion from politics than we should think of separating politics from economics. " So natural," says Hooker, " is the union of Religion with Justice, that we may boldly deem there is neither where both are not. For how should they be unfeignedly just, whom religion doth not cause to be such; or they religious, which are not found such by the proof of their just actions? " It is this which makes it impossible to say whether Hooker is writing about theology or politics. His enemies were drawing their weapons from the great armoury of Calvin's *Institutes*, a gigantic system which embraces every social as well as every religious question, and Hooker had to produce something on the same scale.

The Calvinists were advocates of the Presbyterian system, on the grounds that it alone carried the warrant of scriptural authority, and Hooker replied that scriptural authority was not enough. In one of his flashes of worldly wisdom, he noticed what gave the Puritans their popular appeal. They impute, he said, " all faults and corruptions, wherewith the world aboundeth, unto the kind of ecclesiastical government established. Wherein, as before by reproving faults they purchased unto themselves with the multitude a name to be virtuous; so by finding out this kind of cause they obtain to be judged wise above others." They " propose their own form of church-government, as the only sovereign remedy of all evils. And the nature . . . of the people . . . is to imagine that anything, the virtue whereof they hear commended, would help them; but that most which they least have tried." The Puritans must have been very like the Marxists.

Hooker chose to appeal, not to the multitude, but to reason, and reason led him to appeal to history and to all human experience. For, he argued, in these things as well as in Scripture is the will of God revealed.

> " The general and perpetual voice of men is as the sentence of God himself. For that which all men have at all times learned, Nature herself must needs have taught; and God being the author of Nature, her voice is but his instrument. By her from Him we receive whatsoever in such sort we learn. . . . By force of the light of Reason, wherewith God illuminateth every one which cometh into the world, men being enabled to know truth from falsehood, and good from evil, do thereby learn in many things what the will of God is; which will Himself not revealing by any extraordinary means unto them, but they by natural discourse attaining the knowledge thereof, seem the makers of those laws which indeed are his, and they but only the finders of them out."

We should not rely on Scripture alone, he argued; we must avail ourselves of " all the sources of light and truth with which man finds himself encompassed." All our faculties should be used, for all are given us by God. Besides, he asked, how should we know that Scripture is the Word of God, unless the Church had told us so? Nor is the authority of the historical, Catholic Church to be lightly set aside. That authority we must accept—not blindly, but simply because it is the reasonable thing to do. Hooker was not one of those who " do not ask to see," who find in the bosom of Mother Church the lost delights of infancy or of the womb. " For men to be tied," he thought, " and led by authority, as it were, with a kind of captivity of judgment, and though there be reason to the contrary not to listen unto it, but to follow like beasts the first in the herd, they know not nor care not whither, this were brutish." His emotional needs demanded the assertion of his manhood, not denial of it.

The function of the reason, as Hooker saw it, was to discover laws—the laws of God, the laws of Nature, the laws that should govern society on earth. The pattern of the *Ecclesiastical Polity* consists of a great hierarchy of laws, ranging from " the Law which angels in heaven obey " down to the positive laws of Church and commonwealth. This was important at a time when the universe was thought to be governed by divine caprice. The God of Protestants was constantly liable to interfere: He had not wound things up and left them to work by their own laws. Hooker's universe is graded, rising from sphere to sphere, each governed by the law of its own being, and each striving after some more perfect law. God alone is perfect and a law unto himself.

When he descends again to the sphere of terrestrial politics, Hooker is still thinking of the laws. The Rule of Law indeed is the *primum mobile* of his political philosophy. " The public power of all societies is above every soul contained in the same societies. And the principal use of that power is to give laws to all that are under it; which law in such case we must obey. . . . Because except our own private and but probable resolutions be by the law of public determinations overruled, we take away all possibility of sociable life in the world."

From the need for law Hooker is led on to the need for a

sovereign power. Jurisdiction " must have necessarily a
fountain that deriveth it to all others and receiveth it not
from any." All political power, he says, belonged originally
to the whole community; but, once delegated to a sovereign,
it cannot be taken back. " When the multitude have once
chosen many or one to rule over them," then the right of the
people is " derived into those many or that one which is so
chosen; . . . that which they did, their rulers may now do
lawfully without them." Nevertheless, Hooker did not
want despotic government, nor did he believe in the divine
right of kings. God, he said, does not positively command
" that the Christian world should be ordered by kingly
regiment." Besides, " what power the king hath, he hath
it by law: the bounds and limits of it are known "; yet it has
to be admitted that Hooker is a little vague as to how the
ruler is to be kept obedient to the rules.

He can be called Erastian for putting the laws and
government of the Church under the control of Crown and
Parliament. Without that, he feared, there would be no
sovereignty. He defended too the right of a nation to deter-
mine its own form of Church government. Yet Hooker can
also be called a High Churchman in that he held a high view
of the place in society which the Church should take. He
pours scorn on the idea that " regal power ought to serve for
the good of the body and not of the soul, for men's temporal
peace and not for their eternal safety; as if God had ordained
kings for no other end and purpose but only to fat up men
like hogs and see that they have their mast." His view of
Church and State was simply that they were two aspects of
the same body, the Christian Commonwealth, identical in
membership and personnel. He joined issue both with
Catholics and Presbyterians, largely because their doctrines
implied the separation into two bodies of what ought to be
one. He was defending not only the established Church,
but the principle of establishment itself.

When he finished his work Hooker had given to the
Church of England a doctrine of its own. As early as 1562
his patron, Bishop Jewel, had written an official *Apologia* for
the national Church, but that had only been negative
criticism and not a positive creed. Jewel had explained
why Englishmen could not be Papists; Hooker explained
why they could and should be Anglicans. Henceforward
Englishmen could know what was meant when their Church

claimed to be Catholic although not Papal, and what was meant when it was said to be " by law established."

The *Ecclesiastical Polity* is comprehensive without being inconsistent. Whig and Tory political thinkers, High Churchmen, Low Churchmen, Broad Churchmen, Erastians, and Rationalists have all found in Hooker what they wanted. Hobbes owed much to him, and so did Locke the enemy of Hobbes. So also did Laud the champion of authority and Hume the champion of reason. It is said too that King James II was converted, by reading Hooker, to the Roman Catholic faith. The story is attractive, for, though it pays a doubtful compliment to the author's clarity, it does confirm our worst suspicions of the king's intelligence. Moreover, it suggests the pleasing thought that, without Hooker, there might well have been no Revolution.

Hooker is Catholic, it is true, but quite clearly not a Roman Catholic. His front is very wide, but his command is only of the centre, and a centre, by definition, excludes the wings. His right flank is no nearer to Rome than his left is to Geneva.

More catholic and comprehensive still is Hooker's range of subject: there are few things on which he has not something valuable to say. He can be found explaining incomparably well the effects of music on the mind, when ostensibly he is only defending Church music against Puritan attacks. Or again he can be found explaining that " no truth can contradict any other truth," a maxim still quoted by logicians.

Hooker's philosophy covers the full range of man, all man's activity, all man's thinking, all man's striving after what may lie beyond activity and thinking.

> "Man doth seek a triple perfection: first a sensual, consisting in those things which very life itself requireth either as necessary supplements, or as beauties and ornaments thereof; then an intellectual, consisting in those things which none underneath man is either capable of or acquainted with; lastly, a spiritual and divine, consisting in those things whereunto we tend by supernatural means here, but cannot here attain unto them. . . . For man doth further covet, yea oftentimes manifestly pursue with great sedulity and earnestness, that which cannot stand him in any stead for vital use; that which exceedeth the reach of sense; yea, some-

what above capacity of reason, somewhat divine and heavenly, which with hidden exultation it rather surmiseth than conceiveth ; somewhat it seeketh, and what that is directly it knoweth not, yet very intentive desire thereof doth so incite it, that all other known delights and pleasures are laid aside, they give place to the search of this but only suspected desire."

We are reminded of a more familiar passage in Elizabethan prose: "What a piece of work is a man! How noble in reason! How infinite in faculty! in form and moving how express and admirable! in action how like an angel! in apprehension how like a God!" But Hooker would not have added, as Hamlet did, "And yet, to me, what is this quintessence of dust? Man delights not me."

ROBERT DEVEREUX, EARL OF ESSEX
1566–1601

By

A. L. ROWSE

" Tan hidalgo no he visto entre herejes."—Philip II.

ROBERT DEVEREUX,
EARL OF ESSEX

by A. L. ROWSE

IT is perhaps a little difficult to understand, still more to explain, why Essex should have made such an extraordinary impression upon his age. During the last decade of the century, he occupied, in the popular estimation, a position only less brilliant than that of Elizabeth herself. At a time when the monarchy was at a higher eminence than before or since, and when there was no Royal family to distract attention from the more than human glory and isolation of the Queen, Essex was sole, at any rate, upon the steps of the throne. But, after all, he was no Napoleon, he was not a Henry V—nor even a Robert Cecil. He was neither a great warrior, nor a politician. Yet all the poets sang his praises, from the divine poet downwards:

> " *The courtier's, soldier's, scholar's eye, tongue, sword,*
> *The expectancy and rose of the fair state,*
> *The glass of fashion and the mould of form,*
> *The observed of all observers* ";

and when he appeared in the streets, the people cried, " God save him "; he was the man most beloved by all the nation, so that after he died his name remained a name to conjure with. How was it done?

It would be easy to say that the people were, as usual, deluded, and that popularity is no index to intrinsic worth or real political importance. And it is true that there is no answer in terms of ability or anything tangible or lasting that he achieved.

The clue to it all, to my mind, lies in this : that there were in his character all the elements which would endear him to the age. He was the man it chose for its own, *l'homme représentatif*. He was above all adventurous—without being an adventurer: that came later when he had vanished from the scene: the era of the Stuarts. His whole career was an adventure from his first action before the gates of Zutphen, to its glorious apex with his planting his standard upon the citadel of Cadiz and its end in the mirage of a popular rising in the city against the Queen's Government. There is something unreal in his life as there was in his mind. Then he was gallant and honourable—he was the soul of honour and chivalry; extremely courteous (unlike Raleigh) to all his inferiors socially—and nearly everybody was; upright and altogether straight with his equals. Indeed, he was a good deal too straight for that environment, the quick changes and shoals of the Court, " being," as Camden said, " not easily induced to any unhandsome Action . . . and one that could not conceal himself, but carried his love and his hatred always in his Brow." He was extremely generous, to the point of forgetting what he had done for others, an attractive trait in the man, which boded ill for his success as a politician; as Francis Bacon said when Essex insisted on giving him an estate to console him for not becoming Solicitor-General:

> " His Lordship's offer made me call to mind what was wont to be said when I was in France, of the Duke of Guise, that he was the greatest usurer in France, because he had turned all his estate into obligations; meaning that he had left himself nothing, but only had bound numbers unto him. Now, my Lord, I would not have you imitate his course, nor turn your estate to us by great gifts into obligations, for you will find many bad debtors."

Bacon was, of course, the worst debtor of the lot; when the time came, he was the most relentless and the most effective of the Crown lawyers whom Essex had to face at his trial.

With all this, Essex was very much gifted by fortune. He was talented, had great charm of mind and body, was handsome, and had the romantic appeal, at his start in life, of being the orphan son of a father who died worn-out and wellnigh ruined in serving the Queen in Ireland. It may have been this that early attracted Elizabeth's attention to him; she had ill-requited his father's devotion; perhaps she would make it up to the son.

It was not only this: there were other attractions for her in the fine, long-limbed youth who was brought to Court, which only grew stronger as he grew to maturity and into manhood. "There was in this young Lord," Sir Robert Naunton wrote, "together with a most goodly person, a kind of urbanity or innate courtesie, which both won the Queen, and too much took upon the people, to gaze upon the new adopted son of her favour."

This, however, would be to accept too simple a view of their relations, relations which were as complex as any in Elizabeth's extraordinary mental life. Essex was not so much her adopted son as her adopted lover; and yet not that entirely either. She was attracted by him, by his youth, his freshness, his brave enthusiasm; she fastened upon it, and—a woman of fifty-five now grown old in the ways of men and in the knowledge of affairs—perhaps she battened a little upon it, reinvigorating herself with the ardour of his flame. Life became delightful again for her in these early days of his at Court; the melancholy gap left by Leicester's death he had come to fill:

"When she is abroad, nobody near her but my Lord of Essex; and at night, my Lord is at cards, or one game or another with her, that he cometh not to his own lodging till birds sing in the morning."

But she could not have had any illusions at the bottom of her heart; she must have known. There is something pathetic, too, in the need she had of him—and so rarely is the attempt made to see their relations from her point of view. She had made, when she was young, the great renunciation, for the sake of politics; she sacrificed her normal life as a woman when she resisted the temptation to marry Leicester whom she really loved, for the sake of political success. Mary Stuart had married her Darnley and it brought her to disaster; but she lived through it the full life of a woman. Elizabeth sacrificed herself for the sake of her country; and as she succeeded in the long-drawn-out game, astonishing the world by her triumph, becoming more and more gorgeous, a living legend to her people, so her inner life shrank, the natural emotions of the woman dried up, her nature denied. That was Elizabeth's inner tragedy; it was what makes her so mysterious and pro-

foundly exciting a being; it is the clue to the strained artificiality, the nervous unnaturalness of her relations with the
young men of the new generation.   She had got everything
except the one thing essential to a woman's life, and it was
now too late.   Deep down in her being there must have been
a feeling of *schaden-freude*, a determination to have her own
back upon the handsome young men of the Court who
wanted to make use of her to rise to power, to exact the last
ounce from their protestations (so easy to see through!) of
their love for her.   In the end, I believe that Essex, hopelessly entangled and on the verge of ruin, came to realise
that when he cried out that "the Queen's mind was as
crooked as her carcase."   Elizabeth, on her side, seems to
have recognised its truth, that the hand of a man had at last
laid a brutal finger upon the raw place in her heart; she
never forgave him, but giving him plenty of rope, went on
to ruin him.   But before that he had already ruined himself.

It is not even a matter for irony that in this tragedy
Elizabeth, on her side, should have been absolutely right,
politically.   She was determined, in all this struggle, to rule
herself; after all, she had ruled for forty years with signal
success, and had come through all the trials and dangers that
beset her reign in triumph.   No doubt she felt that she could
afford to risk the attractive restiveness of the young man; but
it is clear that she was a little mistaken in him, and had for
once over-estimated her powers.   It seems as if her idea
was to carry on in the new generation, with Robert Cecil and
Essex, the kind of balance between the professional politician
upon whom she really relied for governing the country and
the brilliant favourite who might perform special services
and give her personal support, the combination which had
worked well with Burghley and Leicester.   But Essex was
not the man to play this kind of rôle; he was too noble a
nature to do as his step-father had done and "put all his
passions into his pocket"; he was out for power.   The
trouble was that he was not really fitted for it; Elizabeth
knew that, and yet in her partiality for him she allowed him
to go much farther than her judgment of his ability really
warranted.

However, he had so many other gifts.   He had been
brought up as child in the country, mostly at Chartley, along
with his brilliant sister Penelope—Sidney's Stella; and there,
as afterwards at Cambridge, he grew up studious of habit,

fond of books, of the society of poets and the intelligent, himself well educated. He began his public career, after being kept by the Queen's side all the summer of the Armada, by running away from Court the next year to join the great Expedition of Drake and Norris against Lisbon. It was the kind of thing that endeared him to the hearts of the people; the Queen was very annoyed—but he had not much difficulty in making his peace this first time. In 1591 he was permitted to go at the head of an expedition to Normandy to the relief of Henry of Navarre, who was very hard-pressed. Here he behaved with very great gallantry and equal foolhardiness, creating a large number of superfluous knights and riding a hundred miles across enemy country in a small troop to make a spectacular entry, in orange velvet, into Compiègne. It was all very dashing and wanton, a sort of Dumas version of the heroic age; and perhaps he was in his way a d'Artagnan, only much grander and more superb.

What soon afterwards gave him a political importance out of all proportion to his ability was his association with the Bacons, the brilliant brothers Anthony and Francis. Though nephews of Burghley, they were both kept out of office or even employment in the interest of his son Robert, so they transferred their services to the rising favourite. Installed at Essex House, overlooking the Thames, Anthony established an intelligence service which brought him information from all over Europe, superior to that of Cecil's, while Francis directed his immense abilities to drafting state-papers for the Earl and planning his political course. The Queen was much impressed, finding him always so well-informed and taking politics seriously; he was admitted to the Privy Council and became one of the inner governing circle; he seemed to be settling down.

But no! there was that in him which would never be content with mere politics. He is to be seen at his best, and as he fain would be, as the acknowledged leader in the famous exploit of the taking of Cadiz in 1596. It was England's reply for the Armada, and there was something still more complete and satisfying about the action than even the great victory (as much due to the winds and waves as to English seamanship) in 1588. The capture of Cadiz was the most striking episode in the whole war, and Essex was the hero of it. Within the twelve-month Drake had died at sea and was buried off Nombre de Dios in the Spanish Main; there was nobody now to rival Essex: he had stepped into Drake's place in the hearts of the people. Stories reached home of his throwing his hat into the sea crying, "Entramos! Entramos!" when they came into Cadiz Bay, of his being the first to land, always at the head of the attack; of his chivalrous protection of the nuns and women of the sacked city, which wrang a word from the taciturn Philip that ran through all Europe.

His name was made, if only he could have been content with that; but—and in this he could not have been more truly Elizabethan—he was still looking for fresh worlds to conquer. He had set his heart upon being the ruling influence in the State; and here he came up against a rock far more difficult to assail than the citadel of Cadiz. It was not merely that he came up against rivals like Raleigh— they were merely the outworks, or the entrenched Cecils; in time he came to realise that the resistance came, not so much from his rivals and enemies, as from the Queen herself. She was determined to resist the pressure that he constantly put upon her to fill all the offices of State with his nominees. First the Attorney-Generalship was refused to Francis Bacon, then the Solicitor-Generalship; while Essex was away on the Cadiz Expedition, Robert Cecil was made Secretary of State; Essex had pushed for the restoration of Davison, and failing him Bodley; then he resisted the appointment of Mountjoy as Lord Deputy of Ireland, nor would he have his uncle Sir Francis Knollys sent over, since that would be to diminish the number of his supporters at court. The situation became impossible; the old happy relations between the Queen and him were broken by it, they became rasping "like an Instrument ill-tuned, lapsing to discord"; they got on each other's nerves; neither would give way to the other. She was the Queen and determined to rule as she had ruled; moreover, she was right politically, she had far greater experience, and an incomparable judgment. But there was that in her which made her delight in humiliating the man, leading him on, half-yielding and encouraging him with the flattery of power (there was nothing else she had that he wanted, save her name and power; other women, her own maids-of-honour, had his love; there lay the bitterness). But since he was a man, and not a puppet, he would never wholly yield; and though in the end it brought about his ruin, he would not ask her pardon to save his life, and died, without any message for her or submission, in his pride.

The struggle came to a head over Ireland. There had been frequent quarrels and reconciliations, and some scenes. On one occasion, when he had retired sulking to Wanstead, the Queen determined not to ask him back, and said that he had " played long enough upon her, and that she means to play awhile upon him, and to stand as much upon her greatness as he hath done upon stomach." On another occasion she sent him a message that she " valued herself at as great a price as he valued himself." To which Essex replied with a melancholy dignity, and quite truthfully, in one of the exquisite letters he knew so well how to write : " I was never proud, till your Majesty sought to make me too base." Certainly as far as dignity was concerned, he came off best; for all her ability and political sense, he reduced her to her essential coarseness, scolding like a harridan, hoity-toity like a fish-wife.

It was at this time that he wrote the charming poem— in those days there was so much genius in the air that a politician might also be a poet, a brilliant lawyer both philosopher and scientist, an actor a painter in his spare-time, while they all wrote (and died) like angels :

> " Happy were he could he finish forth his fate
> In some unhaunted desert, where, obscure
> From all society, from love and hate
> Of worldly folk, there should he sleep secure;
> Then wake again, and yield God ever praise;
> Content with hip, with haws and brambleberry;
> In contemplation passing still his days,
> And change of holy thoughts to keep him merry
> Who, when he dies, his tomb might be the bush
> Where harmless Robin resteth with the thrush;
>   —Happy were he! "

Alas, it was not to be. The posture of affairs in Ireland moved on to a crisis. O'Neill in the North was leader of a national rebellion; then came swift news of a dreadful defeat of the English forces, Sir Henry Bagenal the Commander and 1500 men being slain in a battle on the Blackwater; meanwhile there was no Lord Deputy to take command, because of the divisions at Court. Essex had manœuvred himself into a position in which the only thing was for him to go over and take command himself.

Yet, in his heart, he was averse to the service. His father had come to grief and to an early death in Ireland; it was the grave, rather than the seed-bed of fame and fortune. Nevertheless, he was bound to go, and his whole career was staked upon his making a success of it. He was given a large army, some 15,000 men, and larger powers than any Lieutenant before him; so that there could be no excuse for failure. He arrived in Dublin in April 1599, and to fill up the time before the rains had abated and he could undertake the campaign against O'Neill's northern fastnesses, he went on a minor campaign into Munster. The summer months drew on, his resources were being wasted, precious time lost, and his whole confidence in himself undermined by sickness and recriminations with the Government at home. Elizabeth wondered why nothing was being done after such an expenditure of money and effort; she wrote him in her sharpest vein:

> " If sickness of the army be the reason, why was not the action undertaken when the army was in better state? if winter's approach, why were the summer months of July and August lost? if the spring were too soon, and the summer that followed otherwise spent? if the harvest that succeeded were so neglected, as nothing hath been done, then surely we must conclude that none of the four quarters of the year will be in season for you and that Council to agree of Tyrone's prosecution, for which all our charge is intended."

The reply that came back from that country of illusions and despair was this:

> " From a mind delighting in sorrow; from spirits wasted with travail, care and grief; from a heart torn in pieces with passion; from a man that hates himself and all things that keep him alive, what service can your Majesty reap? Since my services past deserve no more than banishment and proscription into the most cursed of all countries, with what expectation or to what end shall I live longer? No, no, the rebel's pride and successes must give me means to ransom myself, my soul

I mean, out of this hateful prison of my body. And if it happen so, your Majesty may believe that you shall not have cause to mislike the fashion of my death, though the course of my life could not please you.

"From your Majesty's exiled servant

"ESSEX.

ARDBRACKEN, *the 30th August.*"

What did it mean? Was the man mad? He certainly had lost all grip upon his actions. But this was not good enough for Elizabeth; he was hounded into some show of action which could justify the campaign and its expense. Too late, and with an inadequate force, he marched into Ulster; and here, after a prearranged feint at a battle, he met O'Neill at a ford of the river Lagan, riding into the water up to their horses' bellies, and agreed to a truce.

It was the most ignominious and the most dangerous of all possible conclusions to the much-heralded campaign. Elizabeth was rightly furious when she heard of it, incredible as the news seemed. It would have been better if the Lord-Lieutenant had been defeated in battle and slain at the head of his troops; it would not have been so contemptible: this utter fiasco, as she said, made her Government a laughing-stock in Europe. But there may have been something worse behind it; the question of the succession was looming near, and Essex was gambling upon that; he was already in touch with James in Scotland, and it may be that he was not unwilling to allow O'Neill to retain his army in Ireland for future purposes that should be unspecified.

It was clear that there would be no home-coming for him such as the leading dramatist, who was the friend of his friend Southampton, hoped:

> " *Were now the general of our gracious empress,*
> *As in good time he may, from Ireland coming,*
> *Bringing rebellion broached upon his sword,*
> *How many would the peaceful city quit,*
> *To welcome him!* "

There is already a note of anxiety observable in the lines. On a day towards the end of September, unable to bear the situation any longer, he suddenly left his charge, embarking from Dublin with a handful of his closest friends, hurried

21

across the country before a soul knew of his movements, and arrived at Nonsuch, where Elizabeth was, early in the morning of Michaelmas Eve. She was completely taken by surprise, and may, in the subtle recesses of her mind, have suspected some attempt to force her hand. But no, he was too innocent for that, until it was too late. She received him kindly, perhaps was genuinely moved by his presence, for the last time; and then, her political judgment asserting itself, he was placed in confinement while the examination into his doings in Ireland went slowly forward.

His political career was irretrievably wrecked; but he might have saved himself by going into retirement. There was something in him which made it impossible for him to do the one safe thing—a sort of confused nobility of mind which held him back from throwing over those whose fortunes and careers depended upon him. It made it all the worse. In the months of his confinement and afterwards, as he began to recover from the serious illness that at this time threatened his life, he began to collect together a party around him. He had always been the leader of the party of action, of all the high-spirited young men in society who—the intolerable fools!—wanted an interminable war with Spain; neither he nor they had the subtlety to understand what was in the far superior brains of the Queen and the Cecils—that the country was becoming as exhausted as Spain in the struggle, that trade was being strangled, the merchant classes discontented, the financial deficits mounting up—that, in short, we stood to gain more by peace than by prosecuting an endless war. They could not understand such calculations; such fools never do, with their insensate cry for Action, Action, always Action! no matter whether the action leads to disaster, so long as it is action.

It was the men of action, as might have been expected, that ruined him. All through that summer and autumn of 1600, they drew in around him and came and went at the great house in the Strand. There was Sir Gilly Merrick, a Welsh adventurer who was steward of Essex's Welsh estates; as the time drew near, Sir Christopher Blount, that military man, came up from the country and Sir Ferdinando Gorges from Plymouth, where he was Governor; there was Sir Charles Danvers and the extraordinary Cuffe, with his genius for subterranean intrigue, who became Essex's Secretary in place of Anthony Bacon. Then there was the young Earl of Southampton, young and so beautiful of countenance, to whom the incredible fortune had happened of being loved by Shakespeare, a young man who was the darling of fortune and yet, in the end, was good for nothing. And there were other sympathisers and supporters among the young peers, the Earls of Rutland and Bedford, Lord Sandys, and Lord Monteagle. Such were the men upon whose counsel Essex now depended.

By the New Year of 1601 there was plainly something astir. On Saturday, February 7th, the Council sent for Essex—a calculated move to precipitate whatever was afoot before plans were complete; the next day a deputation from the Council was sent to Essex House. This was the final touch; they were put under lock and key, while the mob of armed men with whom the great courtyard was full burst into the City by Ludgate to raise the City against the Queen, Essex at the head of them. It was a day of confused turmoil and shouting and disillusionment; Essex and his friends found that the safe citizens and merchants who had regarded him with so much favour for his patronage of Puritanism were not the kind to risk their skins for mere friendship's sake. He was driven back into Essex House and there forced to surrender.

The Queen, at a moment of crisis like this, revealed the stuff she was made of, the iron beneath all the exterior arts and graces, the artificiality, the affectations. When she heard that the conspirators had paid the actors at the Globe Theatre to put on *Richard II*, to put the citizens in mind of the deposition of Kings, she was in a towering rage: " I am Richard the Second: Know ye not that? " she shouted at the terrified courtiers. She declared that she would go out to meet the rebels face to face, and see if any of them would withstand her. If Essex House had not been surrendered, she was prepared to have it blown up by gunpowder.

This was the end to which the curious story of their relations, their friendship and intimacy, had come. There remained only for him to pay the penalty; which he did with all the grace possible: nothing became him in life so well as his actions in leaving it.

There was a great trial by his peers in Westminster Hall, where he defended himself skilfully, and with great dignity and candour.

The trial at first went very much in his favour, save that

the conclusion was inevitable; until, in fact—of all people—Francis Bacon, who had been briefed by the Government, brought him down and confused him with his remorseless logic and utter inhumanity.

Afterwards, in the Tower, he broke down in anguish at the horror of his fate, protesting all the while that he had never meant any violence to the Queen's person; but still he would not sue for her mercy, great as he confessed his crime to have been. Even if he had, it seems that Elizabeth would not have been moved; she had borne with him past all endurance for ten years, he had become an unmitigated nuisance, there was nothing now that could be done with him; alive he was a living danger to her and to the peace and well-being of the country. Mr. Lytton Strachey concludes:

> " Like her other victims, he realised too late that he had utterly misjudged her nature, that there had never been the slightest possibility of dominating her, that the enormous apparatus of her hesitations and collapses was merely an incredibly elaborate façade, and that all within was iron."

When Essex was brought to the scaffold within the court-yard of the Tower, on February 25th, Sir Walter Raleigh, his enemy, was looking on from a window of the White Tower, the tears streaming down his face—he was just thirty-four years old. They buried him within the narrow enclosure of the chapel of St. Peter-ad-Vincula—" the saddest spot in Christendom "—by the side of Elizabeth's mother, who had died by the axe, as he did.

But this was not the end. Elizabeth had screwed herself up to the point of making the great and necessary decision; but as time went by and the tension relaxed, the absence of that charming youthful figure came more and more home to her. It was noticed that she took what chance she could to speak of him and bring him back to mind, sometimes her great spirit giving way, and she crying a little the while, as she recalled who knows now what memories of glad days that had been, what vain dreaming of days that were to come and now could never be ?

JOHN LYLY

1553?–1606

By

H. J. MASSINGHAM

JOHN LYLY

by H. J. MASSINGHAM

JOHN LYLY, the King of the Précieux, as Jusserand called him, lived all his life in a museum. The biographical details of his career are uncertain. In his family relationships he has been confused with the grammarian of the same name, the pedagogue of literature making a dual personality with the scholar. Little enough can happen to the museum hermit, so that all we hear of Lyly is that he left one department of his museum for another, the university for the court. He was born in 1553 or 1554, became an alumnus of Magdalen College, Oxford, in 1569, and took his degree four years later. A Latin epistle of his to Lord Burghley is extant, the year before he took his M.A. in 1575, and it was perhaps through the offices of the great man that he received an appointment at court. In 1579, he published *Euphues*, and its sequel, *Euphues and His England*, a year later. For the next ten years, during which he wrote a number of courtly pastoral and courtly mythological plays, all written in prose and following the same literary convention, he was as much the idol and dictator of letters as he appears to have been the curled darling of the maids of honour. In 1590 and 1593 he wrote begging letters to the Queen, decorated in this kind of wallpaper design:

"Most gratious and dread soveraigne, tyme cannot worke my peticions, nor my peticions the tyme. After many years service yt pleased your Majestie to except against Tents and Toyles, I wish that for Tents I might putt in Tenements, so that I should be eased of some toyles. Some lande some good fines, or forfeitures that should fall by the just fall of these most false traitors, that seeing nothing will come of the revells, I may pray upon the Rebells. Thirteen years your highnes servant

567

but yet nothing. . . . A thousand hopes but all nothing, a hundred promises but yet nothing. Thus casting upp the inventory of my friends, hopes, promises and tymes, the summa totalis amounteth to just nothing."

This letter, wherein complaint and compliance fight an even battle, means more than that Lyly had failed to obtain the Mastership of the Revels to which his literary successes had temerariously caused him to aspire. The Queen turned a deaf ear to his supplication. His reputation was ebbing. He wrote two or three more plays, the last in 1601, and died in poverty and neglect five years later.

Fashions in literature are as eternal as are some of its beauties. But it is difficult for us who catch the same morbus as past golden, silver, or copper ages have handed down to us, to realise the extent of Lyly's divinity as arbiter of the literary mode. For that we have to go to his contemporaries. There were five editions of *Euphues* in seven years, but only ten in fifty-six years. The "University Wits," Lodge, Greene, Peele, and Nash, were profoundly influenced in their non-dramatic writings by whom Francis Meres in *Palladis Tamia* called "eloquent and wittie John Lillie." William Webbe's *Discourse of English Poetrie* (1586) discharged a volley of commendations:

"Whose works, surely in respect of his singular eloquence and brave composition of apt words and sentences, let the learned examine and make tryall thereof thorough all the parts of Rhethoricke, in fitte phrases, in pithy sentences, in gallant tropes, in flowing speeche, in plain sence and surely in my judgement, I think he wyll yeelde him that verdict, which Quintillian giveth of bothe the best Orators, Demosthenes and Tully, that from the one, nothing may be taken away, to the other, nothing may be added."

The smiting pedant, Gabriel Harvey, called Nash the "ape of Greene" and Greene "the ape of Euphues." Lodge spoke of him as "famous for facilitie in discourse." But since idols attract iconoclasts alike with ministrants, as good manure makes a rich bed for slugs and leather-jackets, we expect and hear contrary voices to the chorus of acclamations, and they are as we had hoped, good yeomen of letters, Drayton and Ben Jonson. At the end of the folio edition of Drayton's poems, published in 1627, occur these plain lines:

> " *Sidney . . . did first reduce*
> *Our tongue from Lillies writing then in use*
> *Talking of Stones, Stars, Plants, of fishes, Flyes,*
> *Playing with words, and idle Similies,*
> *As th'English, Apes and very Zanies be*
> *Of every thing, that they doe heare and see,*
> *So imitating his ridiculous tricks,*
> *They spake and writ, all like meere lunatiques.*"

In *Every Man Out of His Humour*, Ben Jonson introduced Fastidious Brisk, " a neat, spruce, affecting courtier," whom Edward Arber, in his 1868 edition of *Euphues*, conjectured to be an embodied parody of some of the stylistic mannerisms of Euphuism. The parallel, however, is not at all precise, and Brisk was a composite portrait, spotty with Euphuism but not dyed in it. But this is clear enough: " O Master Brisk (as 'tis in *Euphues*), ' Hard is the choice, when one is compelled either by silence to die with griefe or by speaking to living with shame,' " and in his noble lines to Shakespeare Ben had no doubt how far his supreme rival did " our Lily outshine."

Shakespeare's indebtedness to Lyly was considerable, and did him some harm.

Lyly wrote eight plays, three of them pastorals, four with a mythological theme, and one a comedy. These divisions are largely conventional, not only because *The Woman in the Moon* is more of a masque than a pastoral and *Midas* has comic scenes intermingled with pastoral and allegorical elements. The main reason is that all the plays present courtly characters disguised in classical fancy-dress and relating, quite undramatically, some familiar theme filtered down through a European sieve from Greek legend or Latin comedy. *The Woman in the Moon*, for instance, is a series of conversations revolving round the Pandora motif. *Gallathea* is modelled upon the story of Andromeda with a happy ending, as the virgin is not considered beautiful enough for the offended god to accept. There is a byplot of Cupid playing truant to Venus, and wounding two nymphs with his darts. They fall in love with each other, and one of them is changed into a man. *Love's Metamorphosis* represents the love of three foresters for three of Ceres' nymphs who disdain them. In *Endimion*, the hero is thrown into a deep sleep by the enchantments of Tellus, whose love he rejects in the cause of his Neoplatonic devotion for Cynthia (Queen Elizabeth). Sir Tophas, the bragging warrior who falls in love with a witch, is the comic underplot. Cynthia restores the sleeper by a kiss, and he dedicates himself to her service. *Midas* gives the same story as Ovid's in the *Metamorphoses*, with variations borrowed from the Italians. *Campaspe* is captured by Alexander, who commissions Apelles to paint her portrait. They fall in love and Alexander abandons her to the painter. *Sappho and Phao* is the classical tale with Sappho as a Queen of Syracuse rivalled by Venus in her love for Phao, the ferryman. *Mother Bombie* shows young couples resisting the marriages arranged for them by their old parents and assisted by the crafty servants of the four old men.

Some of Shakespeare's earlier plays were strongly influenced by these closet exercises. The grouping of people round one theme, the paramount importance of love, the analysis of different styles of courtship and (in *Love's Labour's Lost*) the mechanism of construction were all signposts of which he availed himself. Lyly's clowns, serious like Sir Tophas and consciously comic like Robin in *Gallathea*, were too obviously Robots of crude and pedantic humour to influence anybody, and it is not true, as some writers assert, that Launce and the Gobbo were included in Lyly's academy. But the verbal influence was temporarily powerful, and the young Shakespeare did go down with an attack of Euphuistic measles. He soon recovered, but in the period of convalescence his attitude was two-faced.

There is no question about Falstaff's

> " There is a thing, Harry, which thou hast often heard of, and it is known to many in our land by the name of pitch: this pitch, as ancient writers do report, doth defile; so doth the company thou keepest: for, Harry, now I do not speak to thee in drink but in tears; not with pleasure, but in passion; not in words only, but in woes also."

This is the Euphuistic dodge of antithesis-cum-alliteration to the life. But Shakespeare was by no means so detached in the earlier plays. Don Armado and Holofernes are Euphuistic specimens, but their comedy does not yield a certificate of immunity to their creator. Five of the plays—*Love's Labour's Lost, The Two Gentlemen of Verona, The Merchant of Venice, Twelfth Night,* and *As you Like It* are in the mode, and *Love's Labour's Lost* is a conversation piece which reveals how studiously the lion had gone to school of the lap-dog. Amorous discussions seasoned by verbal fence, classical allusion, quasi-erudite conceit, punning and sententious simile are veritable Euphuism, and Shakespeare's strong vein of fantasy drawn from a source of pure imagination found Lyly's technical quiddities in style highly congenial to it. Shakespeare's early work owes a great deal more to Lyly's preciosity than to Marlowe's mighty line, and it is not greatly to his credit that he was so easy a victim to its prolix ornament and frigid pseudo-intellectuality. Perhaps it is natural that a young man of such complexity of mind and abnormal sensitivity should have preferred the Neoplatonic niceties and refinements of Euphuistic thought to the extravagances of the blood-and-thunder school of Kyd and Marlowe. Between the two a gulf was fixed, and not to be bridged, for, if we can guess one domestic certainty without evidential warrant, it is that John Lyly never once ordered a pint of sack at the Mermaid. Even the lyrical numbers hymned between Romeo and Juliet are as over-sugared with affectations of speech and the mental rule-of-thumb rigidly ordained by the Euphuistic convention as is Polonius's advice to Laertes. Most of what is tediously mechanical in the early Shakespeare, particularly his passion for verbal jigsaw, was derived from Lyly, and the influence was altogether vicious. There is not one good word to be said for it, but Marlowe and genius were his guardian angels and, once we hear Falstaff, we know that the laboured Euphuism of *Venus and Adonis*, spiced with juvenile sensuality, has been shed. But Shakespeare did not break out of the greenhouse before he had inhaled large draughts of its fumes. The best thing that Lyly did for Shakespeare was in introducing the sub-plot to him as in *Twelfth Night* and *As You Like It*, whereby the emotions of the aristocrats are reflected and burlesqued in those of their social inferiors.

By the time that Blount in his 1632 reprint of Lyly's *Six Court Comedies* had written, " The spring is at hand, and therefore I present you a Lilly, growing in a Grove of

Laurels," Lyly's ghost though not its Euphuism had declined from courtier to clown. The opinions of later editors were almost unanimous. Whalley's edition of Ben Jonson in 1756 refers to *Euphues* in much the same terms as Berkenhout in *Biographia Literaria* (1777), " a most contemptible piece of affectation and nonsense." Gifford (1816) says: " The chief characteristic of his style, besides its smoothness, is the employment of a species of fabulous or unnatural natural philosophy, in which the existence of certain properties is presumed, in order to afford similes and illustrations." This, with a few exceptions, has been the common literary and editorial verdict. Charles Kingsley called *Euphues* " as brave, righteous, and pious a book as man need look into," which reads like damning a man with the wrong kind of praise, and Arber himself felt wounded at the many derisive comments he met in preparing his edition of *Euphues*. But though Lamb and Longfellow quoted our dusty author and Malone and Hazlitt praised him, literature in the large has inevitably forgotten him, and Saintsbury disposed of the fallacy that Sir Piercie Shafton in Scott's *Monastery* was a walking parody of *Euphues*. Every periphrastic and pretentious style is in some measure an unconcious descendant of Euphuism, but the thing in itself has been dead these three hundred years.

The Euphuistic style is a courtesy title, for Lyly's peculiar mode of expression is not idiom but formula. No writer in the history of English literature has so reduced the art of writing to a mathematical canon. It is machine-made throughout, and has actually been tabulated in algebraical terms—" As the A is B, so the C is D and the more E is F, the more G is H." This series of balanced antithesis, oiled and polished by alliteration's artful aid, works with the precision of a steam-hammer, so that you can time the beats and calculate the stresses almost as accurately as in a factory. It is incredible to us nowadays that the two parts of *Euphues* could ever have secured a single reader, when so arid a method must and does destroy all life and spontaneity, any trace of feeling, every wayward grace, the unexpected felicity, the charm of accident, the force of intuition, the natural rhythm, the flights of poetry, the terse home-thrust, the condensed appeal of flowing line, all the arts of literature together with its personal spirit. Euphuism, indeed, bears no more resemblance to literature than M. Coty's perfumeries to a garden. Words are so many metal parts for putting the clockwork toy together and, though the figure itself may be of an elephant or a camel, it always performs the same antics in the same way. Tick-tock, dickery-dock it goes, and what may amuse us for a few sentences becomes, when repeated for little short of five hundred pages, a form of mental torture.

That Lyly was not only read by the Elizabethans but was the most fashionable writer of his day, imitated by incomparably better writers than himself and made the pattern and exemplar of art, taste, and elegance in letters throws a light upon Renaissance art which hardly brings to our lips the *cliché* of the spacious days. One is dumbfounded by the fact that Lyly was read not by crabbed old men and the then votaries of word-problems and puzzles, but by cavaliers, by peacocking young courtiers, by ardent pioneers in the fashioning of a new literature worthily expressive of the adventurous times, by these and more especially by brilliant and beautiful young women who spent all their time in parties, functions, dressing, and thinking about love. " All our ladies were then his Schollers," wrote Blount in his 1632 edition of some of the plays and the Grand Enchanter himself:

> " It resteth, Ladies, that you take the paines to read it (' Euphues '), but at such times as you spend in playing with your little dogges, and yet will I not pinch you of that pastime, for I am content that your dogges lie in your laps, so ' Euphues ' may lie in your hands, that when you shalle be wearie in reading of the one, you may be ready to sport with the other. . . . ' Euphues ' had rather lye shut in a ladies casket than open in a Scholler's studie."

The Sylvias of the period read *Euphues* with as much avidity as the rather more bourgeois Clarindas of a later epoch devoured Richardson's *Pamela*. " She who spake not Euphuism," wrote a contemporary, " was as little regarded at court as if she could not speak English." Lyly was the gallant of the entire feminine portion of the court and surely not an eye closed in the boudoirs of the palace, but some honeyed sentence from the pillow was the last of its waking sights.

Depending as he did upon a shell of formal architectural

stresses and counter-stresses in verbal structure, Lyly adopted the device of fleshing his anatomy by ransacking current literature for parallels, similes, and analogies. A recent critic has made the discovery that Coleridge wrote *Kubla Khan* and *The Ancient Mariner* from intermingled memories of the books he had read. Lyly's method, more laborious and innocent of imagination, was the same. Most unfortunately for the survival of his works, he chose classical mythology and the natural history which he gleaned from Pliny, the mediæval bestiaries, herbals, and such examples of the contemporary observation of nature as Topsell's *Four-Footed Beasts* and *Serpents* (1607). He was thus able to illustrate and, as he and his readers believed, to vivify the Neoplatonic sentiments and refinements springing from his themes of love, friendship, and morality by reference to the magical properties, functions, and attributes of plants and stones and animals and mythical beings. Jusserand, in *The English Novel in the Time of Shakespeare*, has entertained us with an account of this outrage upon science in the cause of literature. The cockatrice which devours a man and then laments him all his life scores a point against the cruelty and vain regrets of an obdurate feminine heart. The wickedness of the whale which allows sailors to light a fire on its back and forthwith dives and drowns them brings home a similar point. Even the dragon which feeds on elephants' blood (which all the world knew to be the coldest in the world) in order to cool it of its feverish humours, lumbers upon the shadowy stage as an actor in the amorous conflict or hortatory dialogue upon the civilities of taste or correctitudes of behaviour. The rhinoceros with its equine neck breathes air to kill a man, and such is the disdain of ladies. The cockatrice, in spite of being a man-eater, is the king of the serpents on account of its "stately face and magnanimous mind," and so coquetry may relent and be the mask of fidelity. The Mantichora and the Sphinga, the Papio and the Lamia swell the muster of the Noah's Ark which embarks upon the uncertain sea of human passions, and, even if the animal be not fabulous in itself, its habits are more outrageous than if it were. In the opening pages of *Euphues and his England*, the travellers, Philautus and Euphues, land in England partly in order to extend the area of their interminable conversations and partly to carry the flattery of Queen Elizabeth, who is likewise the deified heroine of the masque-like *Endimion*, to still loftier hyperbole. They meet an old man named Fidus near Canterbury. Fidus enters upon a dissertation on the manners and customs of bees. If any of the subject bees disobeys his " King's " commandments, " hee kylleth himselfe with his owne sting, as executioner of his own stubbornesse." " The King himselfe not idle, goeth up and doune, entreating, threatning, commanding, using the counsell of a sequel, but not loosing the dignitie of a Prince, preferring those that labour to greater authoritie, and punishing those that loyter, with due severitie." Observe how nicely the antithesis of the last two lines is supported by a corresponding alliteration. Extracts like the following are showered over the whole of the two parts of *Euphues*:

> " Gentlemen, you make me blush as much for anger as shame that seeking to praise me and proffer yourselfe, you both bring my good name into question, and your ill-meaning into disdain: so that thinking to present me with your hand, you have thrust into my hands the Serpent *Amphisbaena* which having at each ende a sting, hurteth both ways."

Such was the mosaic of Lyly's style. Granted his verbal weights and scales and his dilution of the Petrarchan love-convention to suit English tastes, his bestiaries and mythological dictionary were at his elbow for inexhaustible padding.

Up to recent years, the claim for Lyly as the creator of the novel-form which broke with the epic, the metrical romance and tales of chivalry to found the psychological novel of manners remained undisputed. The publication of Violet Jeffery's *John Lyly and the Italian Renaissance* six years ago deprived him of the title and superseded Warwick Bond's contention of his originality in the 1902 edition of the *Works of John Lyly*. Before her exhaustive researches, it was generally accepted that the sources of *Euphues* were Pettie's *Petite Pallace of Pettie His Pleasure* (1577), Guevara's *Diall for Princes* (1529) and *Marcus Aurelius His Golden Book*, translated by Berners in 1532 and Sir Thomas North in 1557. Pettie and Berners are markedly Euphuistic in style (*alto estilo*), and Guevara's Platonism inspired the spirit. Violet Jeffery, however, supplied overwhelming testimony of

Lyly's slavish adherence in theme, in treatment, and verbal artifice to the Italian pastoral convention of the Cinquecento. Lyly never travelled in Italy and the bead-roll of Italian translators (Painter, Fenton, Fortescue, Smythe, Wolfe, Turbeville, Geoffrey Whitney, and others) was lengthy enough to furnish him with a complete literature. His theories about love, learning, education, morals, and philosophy were ready-made to his hand. His " Questions and quirks of Love " were hardly even a modification of the " Questioni d'Amore " rhetorically provided by Castiglione, Tasso, Boccaccio, Bembo, Ariosto, Boiardo, Straparola and their school, who in the moral treatise and novella set the high cultural fashion not only for Italy but for the upper classes of European society. Violet Jeffery's analysis reveals that Lyly inherited, not merely a courtly art of writing but its minutiæ. Such pretty problems as " what sort of love would you choose? Is beauty, wit, or virtue to be preferred? Should the perfect courtier excel in arms or letters? Which is the best or worst, the fair fool, the witty wanton, or the crooked saint? Is love good or evil? " are provided for the author of *Euphues*, both question and answer, in Lando's *Quesiti Amorosi* (1552), who in his turn manufactured them from the mediæval Courts of Love. Lyly's introspective response to Shakespeare's careless warble, " What is love? " was elaborately documented for him by a host of Englished foreigners faithfully marching to the discipline of a fixed literary tradition. Lyly, like Florio, " ransacked Italian gardens to adorn English orchards," and his stock was delivered by English middlemen. Both in love and in manners he was acting as an interpreter of continental good breeding. He became a best-seller simply as an ambassador of the fashionable code. Even the tirades against Italian vices echo one of the conventional points scored by the Italians themselves.

As the " novel," so the plays. The plot of *Gallathea* is the sacrifice of a virgin to appease a god, and Lyly has adopted the same variations as Ariosto in his divergences from the classical legend of Andromeda. The girl who falls in love with her friend believing her a man was a well-worn theme of Italian Renaissance comedy. The punishment of disdain by metamorphosis occurs among other sources in Boccaccio's *Filocolo*. The pastoral court-masque was not only introduced by the Italians, but acted by them on its first appearance in 1573. Gascoigne's Italianate *Kenilworth Festivities* of 1575 was an accepted pattern. The same influences crowd in upon such mythological plays as *Midas* and *Campaspe* as upon the pastoral. Olympus is a court, not a pantheon, and the stylised, bloodless beings assemble to tell the same type of intricate tale as in *Euphues* and the Italian remodelling of classical texts. Lyly's plays do not contain a single dramatic element or scene, and the characters saunter in and out of the acts and their arbitrary subdivisions in the same desultory fashion as in *Euphues* they wander from one conference room to another. The Italian Marinists and Petrarchists drew up the same regulations for the subsequent Euphuistic style as the Italian comedy and novella exported subject-matter and spirit for the form and treatment of *Euphues* and the Plays. Even Lyly's inveterate punning of atheist with Athens, liver with lover, nature with nurture, and in hundreds of other examples is derived almost verbatim from his English-Italian schoolmasters. So obsequiously are the specialised tricks of Euphuism copied from Bembo's, Boccaccio's, and others' use of the parallel clause, the rhetorical question, the cluster of similes, the alliterated antithesis and the rest, and so frequently does the Euphuist employ terms and phrases that are meaningless except in their Italian sense, that *Euphues* itself and the Plays with it become little more than compilations from Italian sources. Their structure, mentality, choice of theme, and verbal technique make such trifling divergences from their originals that it would be hard to find a single mutation in the whole body of Lyly's work. He was loaded with repeated commendations from his disciples for his classical learning. But his reader is too often struck by the flourish with which he uses Latin speech (" summa totalis " for " sum total " in the letter to Queen Elizabeth, is an example), not to be suspicious of the length and breadth of Lyly's erudition. The probability is that he knew no more Latin than Shakespeare himself, who made considerably less parade of what he did know. He got his classics from the Italians, and he got his Italian from the English translators. Give him all and more than his due; say that his characters are abstract and lifeless because they are idealised; that it is illegitimate to demand action and movement from a world of manners or a discussion play; that literary inventors are second-rate and Shakespeare took all his stories at second-hand; that he raised the status of women by making his female characters converse on the same intellectual terms as the men; that he helped to purge the English court of its grosser Tudor legacy; that he anticipated, not only Richardson, but even Freud by his secretaryship in the court of love, his science of the soul and diagnosis of the emotions. It is still no longer to be questioned that Lyly was simply the loud-speaker, installed at the Court of Elizabeth, for rendering a convenient digest of Italian literary elegance.

When Lyly is not anatomising the nature of love, piling up the similes and showing off his classical knowledge like a sailing-boat at a regatta, he sometimes indulges in comic characters like Sir Tophas in *Endimion*, presumed to be the prototype of Don Armado, or comic scenes like the baiting of Diogenes in *Campaspe*. Here are a few lines from the latter:

" GRANICUS: *What beast is it thou lookest for?*

DIOGENES: *The beast my man, Manes.*

PSYLLUS: *He is a beast indeed that will serve thee.*

DIOGENES: *So is he that begat thee.*

GRANICUS: *What wouldst thou do, if thou shouldst find Manes?*

DIOGENES: *Give him leave to doe as he hath done before.*

GRANICUS: *What's that?*

DIOGENES: *To run away.*

PSYLLUS: *Why, hast thou no neede of Manes?*

DIOGENES: *It were a shame for Diogenes to have neede of Manes, and for Manes to have no neede of Diogenes.*

GRANICUS: *But put the case he were gone, wouldst thou entertaine any of us two?*

DIOGENES: *Upon condition.*

PSYLLUS: *What?*

DIOGENES: *That you should tell me wherefore any of you both were good.*

GRANICUS: *Why, I am a scholler and well seene in philosophy.*

PSYLLUS: *And I a prentice, and well seene in painting.*

DIOGENES: *Well, then Granichus, be thou a painter to amend thine ill face; and thou Psyllus a philosopher to correct thine evill manners.*"

I do not say it would be impossible to parallel so crude and jejune a piece of humour from the popular dramatists who possessed no court privileges. But assuredly the theatre of the man in the street was incapable of its peculiar brand of insipid pedantry. Such passages no less than his themes, his effeminacy of treatment and an artificiality supreme over the whole range of English literature, clearly reveal that Lyly is the grand example of the coterie writer, plying his painted skiff in a backwater, safeguarded from criticism and walled from the lightest breeze of reality. He is the only dramatist among them all who had no contact whatever with his fellows and so produced a type of drama unique in its remoteness from that rough and violent but essentially human nature of the true Renaissance theatre. He enables us to see with better eyes how original that theatre was in going its own way and breaking the mould of the old and foreign forms, and how preferable were the worst excesses, the most childish melodrama of Kyd and Marlowe to the sham elegancies of a Lyly. The court itself was ultimately drawn into that great resurgence of life of which the Elizabethan drama was the most intense expression, a resurrection from dead forms which has few parallels in the history of civilisation. That drama escaped from the tutelage prescribed for it much as Hellenism freed itself from the bonds of Egyptian formulæ and gave the world a new vision. These mighty movements have been all too rare in the records of nations, but the Renaissance English Drama is one of them, and once its fringes brushed the more exclusive circles, Lyly was doomed. He is one of the very few English writers who has never either at the caprice or just estimation of later generations been raised from the grave. It is certain that he never will be.

Perhaps the most interesting fact about this super-fop of literature is that he did know how to write. The graceful songs in *Campaspe*, especially " Spring's Welcome " with its Shakespearean lines :

> " *Now at heaven's gate she claps her wings,*
> *The morn not waking till she sings,*"

are so true to the lyric mind of the age that, occurring as they do within the chilly wastes of the play, they seem the inspiration of another hand, as though some gay little flowering weed had managed to seed itself in an ambitious plot of carpet bedding.

Lyly wrote two or three songs to each one of his plays, but, oddly enough, they do not appear in the Quarto edition, only in Blount's 1632 reprint. It is interesting that the others are not markedly inferior to the *Campaspe* songs. The " Fairies Song " in *Endimion*:

> " *Pinch him, pinch him, black and blue,*
> *Sawcie mortalls must not viewe*
> *What the Queene of Stars is doing*
> *Nor pry into our Fairy wooing.*"

is as lively a warble as any of the lyrics in Beaumont and Fletcher, while Daphne's Song in *Midas* (" My Daphne's hair is twisted gold . . .") reads uncommonly like " the first streaks, the early dawn " of the specific Carolean lyric and to pass over the technically Renaissance lyric altogether. Lyly's songs, indeed, if not so good as the best of his contemporary's, Greene, are so just in sound and free in movement that it was an outrageous paradox for him to make prose his chief medium. The felicity of the natural lyrist was his. In poetry, he forgot his library and discarded his wearisome literary etiquette. In poetry, he shut up his books and walked in the garden. Too brief the spell and soon he was conscientiously back in the reading-room and the rustling of bough was exchanged for that of page.

But even in his prose Lyly could now and again write a happy sentence. In the two parts of *Euphues* I have found two examples ; none, alas, in the Plays : " Issyda, the water standing in her eyes, clasping my hand in hers, with a sadde countenance answered me thus." The action itself was in the proper convention of the Italian novella, where tearful ladies were always clasping hands as preliminary to a dissertation in which they demonstrated that grief in the Petrarchist's or Marinist's or Euphuist's breast was never known to overcome the power to voice it. But there is melody in the words and in the other sentence, something more. There is beauty. " Gentlemen and Friends, the longest Summer's day hath his evening, Ulisses arriveth at last, and rough windes in time bring the ship to safe Road."

WILLIAM SHAKESPEARE

1564–1616

By

ALFRED W. POLLARD *and* J. DOVER WILSON

WILLIAM SHAKESPEARE

by ALFRED W. POLLARD *and* J. DOVER WILSON

SHAKESPEARE was England's amazing, but not undeserved reward for having kept her head amid the rival distractions of the Renaissance and the Reformation. With the latter her success had been only partial, and to some extent temporary; but Shakespeare maintained the spirit of the decade in which he was born, in which the queen was not yet excommunicated and Catholics not yet regarded as potential traitors. Up to the very end of the reign he largely retains the atmosphere of the old faith, while acquiescing in that which claimed to be "reformed" and being sturdily English in his attitude to papal aggression. The evil side of the Renaissance, which did little harm in England and from which Shakespeare himself wholly escaped, was that which put style and form above character and matter, reducing the richness and colour of the Middle Ages to a thin elegance. Shakespeare was so free from this that outside the Bible there is no plenteousness in literature comparable to his. He complied with the law of the development of English literary genius, that it needs to be fertilised by some touch of foreign influence to produce its best. But it was mainly plots and localities that he borrowed from abroad; he himself is English to the core and his art is English also. He has been contemptuously called "the man from Stratford" by those who believe that, whichever peer may be selected, only a peer of the realm could have written his plays. These plays themselves bear abundant witness (more especially as Professor Spurgeon has pointed out, in their imagery) that whoever wrote them was country-bred, had had keen eyes in boyhood for every aspect of country life, and in the inner depth of his consciousness had stored memories which give life and colour to his work, whenever it is most characteristically his.

Our subject in this paper is not the complete Shakespeare whose powers at the height of his experience of life produced the four great tragedies of *Othello, Macbeth, King Lear*, and *Antony and Cleopatra*, and whose final romances are now somewhat more curiously criticised than they used to be, but the Tudor Shakespeare who, by the time the England of Elizabeth became the England of Stuart James, had twenty-five plays to his name, as well as two of the most popular poems of the age and the *Sonnets* passing in manuscript from hand to hand " among his private friends." It is these plays and poems with which we have to deal.

We know nothing of the date when he first took to acting, of the company or companies for which he played before 1594, of the number and titles of the plays he had written by that year, or of the plays drafted by other dramatists he may have rewritten. All we know is that in 1585 the man of Stratford became the father of twins and that seven years later the eye of history discovers him in London, a man of twenty-eight, and already successful both as a player and as a dramatist, so successful that he was exciting the jealous anger of the unsuccessful Robert Greene.

Yet though these years are blank, it is easy to guess how he employed them from the character of his early plays. Variety of production and readiness to learn from others are outstanding features of Shakespeare's work to the end of his career, but never more so than in his first attempts. This Johannes factotum, as the chagrined Greene called him, took pains to show he could better the instruction of his predecessors in every kind of drama they had hitherto brought on to the London stage. *Henry VI, Richard III, Richard II, Titus Andronicus, Romeo and Juliet, The Comedy of Errors, The Two Gentlemen of Verona, A Midsummer Night's Dream*, and *Love's Labour's Lost* are generally reckoned his earliest plays, and it would be difficult to catalogue a more heterogeneous collection of types. Call to mind, however, the inventions of Peele, Marlowe, Kyd, Greene, and Lyly, and it at once becomes apparent where the types came from and what dictated their choice. The pupil took each master in turn, showed him with effortless ease what he had painfully striven to attain, and added thereto " the play, the insight, and the stretch " of which he had never dreamed. All five laurels met and grew fresher upon his victorious brow. Peele, Greene, and Kyd, busy plotters of plays, had predigested many a novel and chronicle story for his use, but had been unable to transfuse the blood of life into character or the blank verse of dramatic speech. Marlowe, with a command of character and poetry far exceeding theirs, lacked their industry and constructive ability. Shakespeare was a better poet than Marlowe, a better dramatic craftsman than Peele, Greene, or Kyd, a better wit than Lyly; and from the first he spoke through the lips of men and women beside whom their puppets squeaked or bellowed like ghosts in vizards.

He had the pull in something else than native genius. They were dramatists writing for " common players " whom they despised; he was a player writing for his fellows, whom he knew and studied as a modern sports captain knows and studies the individuals of his team. There is plenty of evidence of his loving care in this matter. About the end of the century, for example, he was making capital out of a small boy with a very lively personality, who played Maria, " the youngest wren of nine," in *Twelfth Night*, Robin the " eyas-musket " in *The Merry Wives*, and the page before whom Falstaff walked in 2 *Henry IV* " like a sow that hath overwhelmed all her litter but one." Then there was the tall thin-faced man whose comical figure and profile give point to a score of allusions, who is in turn Pinch, Holofernes, Slender, Aguecheek, and whom we see most clearly perhaps in *King John*, where he is given the part of the Bastard's legitimate brother in the opening scene, in order that his face like " a half-faced groat," his legs like " riding-rods," and his arms like " eel-skins stuffed " might serve as a foil to the mighty limbs and " large composition " of Cœur-de-Lion's son. In the latter we may, no doubt, catch sight of Burbadge himself, the chief actor of the company, who excelled as the bluff soldierman or whimsical rudesby, and for whom Shakespeare created Berowne and Petruchio, Benedick and Henry V, all rough wooers. To him also may probably be assigned the part of Bottom in *The Midsummer Night's Dream*, of Sir Toby in *Twelfth Night*, and of Falstaff himself, parts which likewise go well with a great frame and a roistering manner.

But intimacy with his fellows taught Shakespeare much more than the theatrical possibilities of their physical idiosyncrasies. From them also he caught the trick of character-making. For it is noteworthy that, apart from the " cards " which Burbadge loved, the most lifelike of the early characters are clowns, which were played by William Kempe. In other words, Shakespeare first learnt to create men of flesh and blood by giving the two principal players of his company parts in which they were best able to express their own personalities. Kempe quarrelled with the Chamberlain's men about 1599, and leaving them was superseded by a subtler clown in Robert Armin. But in the early 'nineties Shakespeare was greatly in his debt. And Kempe on his side must have been grateful to a dramatist who gave him jests and stage-business very different from the patter and horse-play which Tarleton had made famous and, before his death in 1588, was probably making a little tiresome. The delicious Lancelot Gobbo is one fruit of the collaboration between Shakespeare and Kempe: a country yokel, slow of wit, dimly aware of a conscience, but very much alive to his own interests. Pompous Master Constable Dogberry is another. Both are mere English, and the humour of both largely consists in tripping themselves up, not physically upon the stage as Tarleton would do, but linguistically, because their tongues become constantly entangled in the intricacies of the English language.

Word-play, indeed, of all kinds forms a very large portion of Shakespeare's comic stock-in-trade. Mistress Quickly, who accompanies Falstaff through three plays and survives him into a fourth, has a breathless way of misusing speech all her own, though to some degree anticipated by her prototype Juliet's Nurse. As for the deliberate quibbling and repartee of young men and mocking wenches belonging to the upper classes, that is almost endless. Shakespeare devotes a whole play to it in *Love's Labour's Lost*, a play which probably seemed to his contemporaries the most brilliant of all his comedies, and which, it is interesting to note, was one of the first selected by Cecil and Southampton to be acted before James's consort, Queen Anne, upon her arrival in London. Such " fine volleys of words " and " sets of wits well played " must have taxed to the utmost the intellectual as well as the histrionic qualities of the performers. They demanded a new kind of acting which had never before been seen upon the English stage. And the company rose to the occasion, as is proved by the fact that, so far from relinquishing his subtleties after his first experiments with them, Shakespeare went on developing and elaborating them until, in *Twelfth Night* and *Hamlet*, they reached a pitch beyond which it was impossible to soar.

From these generalities we turn to consider briefly Shakespeare's Tudor output, paying most attention to the Histories and Comedies, which reach their climax at this period of his career.[1]

We take the Histories first, since, so far as our evidence shows, it was with the three parts of *Henry VI* that Shakespeare commenced playwright. Based as a rule closely upon the chronicles of Halle and Holinshed, these plays of English history must be regarded as forming a class by themselves and therefore to be judged by the standard of what their author tried to do and did, and not by the rules which underlay the great Greek tragedies or the Latin plays

---

[1] It may be well here to use a footnote to call over the roll of the Tudor plays, premising that in the space at our disposal we must needs accept as Shakespeare's those ascribed to him in the First Folio without entering into controversial questions either of earlier forms of them or of the possible share of other writers as collaborators. As we cannot in a footnote set forth and defend an independent chronology, we tie ourselves for the occasion to that of Sir Edmund Chambers in his *William Shakespeare* (pp. 270–1), only deserting him as regards the *Sonnets* for which we must prefer the guidance of the late J. A. Fort (*A Time Scheme for Shakespeare's Sonnets*, The Mitre Press, 1929). We thus get as Shakespeare's first seven plays, four histories, the three parts of *Henry VI* and *Richard III*, followed by two comedies, *Errors* and the *Shrew*, and the crude Senecan tragedy, *Titus Andronicus*, which personally we should like to put earlier. This brings us to 1593–4, the years during which Shakespeare made his reputation as a poet with *Venus and Adonis* and *Lucrece*, both dedicated to Southampton, and began the *Sonnets* with the series exhorting the young Earl to marry. It is predominantly as a poet that he writes the five plays which follow, *The Two Gentlemen of Verona*, *Love's Labour's Lost*, *Romeo and Juliet*, *Richard II*, and *A Midsummer Night's Dream*. In 1596–7 we have the full-blooded rhetoric of *King John*, and it is useful to ask what evoked it. Accompanying it comes *The Merchant of Venice*, most triumphant of tragi-comedies. Then the new cycle of histories, begun with *Richard II*, is continued in 1 and 2 *Henry IV* (with the dynastic interest a little overshadowed by Sir John Falstaff), and *Henry V*. On these follow another tragi-comedy, *Much Ado about Nothing*, with Beatrice and Benedick guaranteeing a happy ending, and the two delightful unshadowed comedies, *Twelfth Night* and *As You Like It*. About the same date tragedy is resumed in *Julius Cæsar* with the philosophic conspirator Brutus as its real hero, whatever we may think of him, and from this Shakespeare rises to the greatest achievement of his Tudor art, the beauty and mystery of *Hamlet*. Thanks to the command of Queen Elizabeth that Falstaff should be shown " in love," it may be right to regard *The Merry Wives of Windsor* as following *Hamlet*, like the farce which followed a Greek tragic trilogy, but we hold to our old belief that the fortnight the legend allows him for writing it was spent in introducing Falstaff into an older play.

The end of the century has been reached and here we should like to close our catalogue of Shakespeare's Tudor plays, but the Queen's reign had still two unhappy years to run, and to 1601–2 is ascribed *Troilus and Cressida*, and to 1602–3 *All's Well that Ends Well*, to be followed by a year's silence, and then in the new reign by a like-minded tragi-comedy *Measure for Measure*.

of Seneca. They offered occasions for splendid tragic passages and also for interludes of comedy, and Shakespeare availed himself of both; but their course was governed by the complicated facts of history. When, as in 1 *Henry VI*, the playwright not merely foreshortened these (as to get the story of a reign into a play he was often bound to do), but misrepresented them, he clearly fails. But in itself to show the course of history on the stage was no unworthy effort. As we have said above, Shakespeare did not invent this form of drama. It had been practised before him by Peele in his *Edward I* (very poorly), while Marlowe's *Edward II*, though it has been overpraised, offers a much worthier example of the same class. The growth of this class in England may have been fostered by memory of the Miracle plays, one cycle of which, that played at Chester, was still being performed as late as 1594. Just as spectators of the Miracle plays knew the main incidents of the gospel story from reading their Bibles and expected to find them represented also in the cycles, so also many of the spectators of the English history plays had read their Halle and their Holinshed and would expect to find not merely the major but the minor incidents duly acted. When the play we know as 2 *Henry VI* was first published (in a mangled version) its attractions were itemised on the title page of the edition of 1594 (the year, it will be noted, of one of the last performances of the Chester plays) as:

> " The first part of the Contention betwixt the two famous houses of York and Lancaster, with the death of the good Duke Humphrey: And the banishment and death of the Duke of Suffolke, and the Tragical End of the prowd Cardinall of Winchester, with the notable Rebellion of Iacke Cade: And the Duke of Yorkes first clayme to the Crowne."

That and no less was what the spectators came to see, and in fact they were shown not only these major incidents, but a good many minor ones as well, such as the fight between the armourer and his apprentice who had appeached him of treason, and the detection of the impostor who pretended to have been born blind, first recorded by Sir Thomas More.

Such multiplicity of incidents tended to incoherence, but there can be no question of the skill with which the incidents are told. In 1592 the lyrical farewells of the brave John Talbot and his son, as they lay dying on the field of battle in 1 *Henry VI*, according to Thomas Nash in his *Defence of Playes*, evoked " the teares of ten thousand spectators " during the season it was being played, and form a gallant interlude in a play which otherwise has some claim to be the worst in the Folio. Originally written independently, it was linked on to 2 *Henry VI* by additional scenes which defy chronology; and the addition of *Richard III* (made impressive by the appearance of Margaret of Anjou in the royal palace to utter curses which the recipients duly recall when being led to their respective executions) turns the three plays into a loose tetralogy. The triumph of *Richard III* is achieved in the audacious first scene, in which Richard woos and wins the Lady Anne as she is following the bier of Henry VI whom he has murdered; a subsequent flyting towards the end of the play is much less successful. The highest point in the cycle is touched in 3 *Henry VI* originally called *The True Tragedy of Richard, Duke of York*, when the earlier Richard is mocked and murdered. But *Richard III* is the only one of the four which has any hold on the modern stage. When produced they all had the interest of comparatively recent history, as recent as that of George IV to the subjects of George V. As political propaganda for the House of Tudor they could hardly be more effective. To exhibit on the stage the havoc wrought by the feuds of York and Lancaster was the best possible advertisement of the blessings brought by the Tudor peace.

In *Richard II* Shakespeare started a new tetralogy to show how the feuds of York and Lancaster arose. In style and temper it is the most flawless of the histories, with no undocumented episode save the conversation between the Queen and the philosophic gardener. A splendid note of patriotism and love for England is struck in the speech of the dying Gaunt, which renders more despicable the callous rapacity of Richard. Nevertheless, the political teaching of the play is clear: that not only Richard's murder, but his deposition was a sin destined to bring " disorder, horror, fear, and mutiny " on the land, and that the usurper and his supporters would of a surety soon be warring against each other. These prophecies are recalled in each of the three succeeding plays of the new tetralogy, with much more effect than Margaret's curse in *Richard III*, but the history of Henry IV of England was temporarily made uninteresting by the need of supporting Henry IV of France, and on the lines of an older play on *The Troublesome Reign of King John*, Shakespeare, to suit the mood of the hour and possibly to aid recruiting, depicted the French invasion of England to support the revolting barons against the King. It is generally reckoned a bad play, but it is full of effective rhetoric, ending with the lines:

> " *This England never did, nor never shall,*
> *Lie at the proud foot of a conqueror,*
> *But when it first did help to wound itself.*
> *Now these her princes are come home again,*
> *Come the three corners of the world in arms,*
> *And we shall shock them. Nought shall make us rue,*
> *If England to itself do rest but true.*"

Having supported the government in *King John*, Shakespeare produced the two *Henry IV* plays for audiences who had had time to count the cost of their own war and were keenly alive to the scandals which had attended it. Thanks to Falstaff, the first part is one of his unforgettable successes, a success by no means repeated in Part II, which alone among the Histories published in early quartos failed to reach a second edition. Playgoers love the characters who make them laugh, even when they are clearly warned that the characters are not respectable, and Prince Hal's cold-blooded humiliation of the disreputable friend whom he had used for his own recreation, though good enough for the chroniclers, is not good enough for the stage. In his own play, *Henry V*, the King does much better and wins back the sympathy of any audience, not only by his gallantry but by making it feel how hard and lonely a life a king must lead. The whole trend of this later written cycle, *Richard II*, *Henry IV*, *Henry V*, is to exalt the kingly office, as that of the earlier-written, though historically later one, 1–3 *Henry VI* and *Richard III*, is to illustrate the miseries brought about by dissension and rebellion. The reverence which Shakespeare shows for the throne may have been obligatory in a Tudor theatre, but to judge from the frequency with which he recurs to the theme (with a chain of ideas so closely linked that one of them can hardly appear without the others) in his contribution to the play of *Sir Thomas More*, in *Troilus and Cressida*, and in *Coriolanus*, there was no belief which he held more strongly than that which associates order with respect for " degree," and thus makes the sovereign hold his headship, not by the will of the people, but by the will of God.

In the politics of the History-plays Shakespeare is serious; he almost, as the nineteenth century would say, has a message, though he knew of course that it would sound gratefully in the ears of both people and sovereign. In the Comedies he is frankly and entirely the entertainer; and never has the world of men been more subtly and deliciously entertained, with a feast, moreover, at which Beauty, Wit, and Humour are all servitors together and by turn. Yet the Comedies reflect the Tudor regard for " degree, priority, and place " no less than the Histories, though from a different angle. What is declared in the one to be essential to social stability, is in the other shown as a very human condition of affairs, compatible with the utmost possible good feeling and affection between members of the different classes. There is not a note of snobbery in Shakespeare, despite the accusations of some modern democratic writers; for snobbery is the product of a democratic society.

Further, the Tudor social hierarchy to a large extent determines the form of the dramas. Apart from the humours of low life which we have already spoken of and which the high-brow insolence of Marlowe condemned as " such conceits as clownage keeps in pay," two main patterns run through the stuff of Shakespearian comedy: the romance of high life, and middle-class domestic realism. The loves and friendships of high-born ladies and gentlemen form the more obvious and familiar element. Against an appropriate background, generally somewhere in Italy, though the forest of Arden or a wood near Athens serves equally well, four figures, two men and two women, move in stately comic minuet. In the early plays the quartet tend to have fixed and traditional rôles: there is the hero and heroine, destined of course to marry, there is the hero's friend (who falls in love with the heroine), and there is the lady he has forsaken. *The Two Gentlemen of Verona* gives us the complete scheme, and here the claims of male friendship are shown in conflict with those of love. It is much the same in *The Dream*, though in this case it is the friendship of the women which is disturbed by rivalry. In *Much Ado*,

Twelfth Night, and *As You Like It* the pattern varies without much change in the general design; the four figures are still present, and in two of the plays one of the ladies is forlorn. The disguise-motive, a trick of which Elizabethan audiences never seemed to tire and which was of course made more piquant by the fact that women's parts were taken by boy-actors, is a frequent feature of the same scheme; and when, in *Twelfth Night*, her rival is made to fall in love with the disguised forlorn lady the possibilities of dramatic entanglement are even further exploited than they had been under the influence of Puck's mischief-making.

Less attention has been paid to the merchants of Shakespeare's comedies than to his courtly lovers, though the one are as traditional as the other, and *The Comedy of Errors* is a tacit admission of his debt to Plautus and Terence. *Errors* gives us the basic type here, as *The Two Gentlemen* does with romantic comedy. The whole play, the scenes of which are set in the streets, the market-place, and the private houses of a seaport town, is concerned with the doings of merchants, their wives, and their servants; the male characters (apart from the Dromios, Dr. Pinch, the scarecrow schoolmaster, and the Duke) comprising no fewer than seven representatives of the merchant class. *The Taming of the Shrew*, again, contrasts the opulence, comfort, and culture of a well-to-do city merchant's house with the rude cheer and down-at-heels service at Petruchio's grange in the country. In this connection it is hardly necessary to mention *The Merchant of Venice*, which opens magnificently upon the quayside with talk of " argosies with portly sail " and "ventures " upon the ocean, and which introduces the usurer, a stock Terentian figure. Nor must we overlook the comic scenes in *Romeo and Juliet*, especially those in the house of the Capulets, which let us into a middle-class kitchen and servants' quarters. But the most perfect comedy of this genre is laid not in Ephesus, or Padua, or Venice, or Verona, but in England; and if we read " Stratford " for " Windsor," we discover the secret of Shakespeare's interest in merchant life, seeing that the Fords and Pages of *The Merry Wives of Windsor* might be the Quinys and Sadlers and Shakespeares of his native town. So close is the parallel that it gives us Master Justice Lucy complaining of deer-stealing in the first scene and devotes a later one to a *viva voce* examination in Latin grammar of little William himself.

Thus the very age and body of the Tudor time, its form and pressure, are to be seen in the mirror which the Tudor Shakespeare held up to nature. And never does the mirror shine brighter or the showman's wit dance more lightly than in the three great comedies which bring the century to a close. But *Much Ado*, *As You Like It*, and *Twelfth Night* represent something more than the highest flight of Shakespeare's comic muse. They are the greatest utterance of that Tudor gaiety of spirit which was first heard in the interludes of John Heywood and in the laughter of Sir Thomas More. And they mark the end of an age. The fine careless rapture, the unclouded self-confidence, the unquestioning faith in the splendour and dignity of human nature, which we associate with the Renaissance, are here expressed for the last time. The melancholy of Jaques, the wistfulness of Feste, even the seemingly unanswerable question: "Dost think because thou art virtuous, there shall be no more cakes and ale?" are hints of what is to come. But the heavy-hearted Dane, ill-concealing a mysterious spiritual distemper beneath his antic mask of bitter merriment, is the earliest spokesman of the new dispensation.

There is no bitterness in the preceding tragedies. The imagery of *Romeo and Juliet* is predominantly drawn from many kinds of light, and the rapture of light and beauty transcends the tragedy. In *Julius Cæsar* Casca has his caustic speeches and the mob rages when Antony has played on it; but Brutus has no quarrel with Cæsar for what he was, only for what he might be, and though sarcasm had been latent in Antony's catchword "For Brutus is an honourable man," there is none in his eulogy which begins "This was the noblest Roman of them all." There had been bitterness in some of Shakespeare's sonnets, but it is personal to himself, the fruit of an unequal friendship and misplaced love. Even in *Hamlet* bitterness is for the most part overborne by the grace of language and verse. As we hear or read it the main impression, as in *Romeo and Juliet*, is still of beauty, though Shakespeare's inmost judgment reveals itself in the imagery drawn from cancers and festering sores. In *Troilus and Cressida* these break out; and Cressida, for whom Chaucer had had such ruth, is stripped bare. Even if we regard the last play of our period, *All's Well that Ends Well*, as Shakespeare's vindication of the right of a woman to pursue a man, as men pursue women, the plot is bizarre.

22 593

It would be idle here to seek for explanations. We only note that to Hamlet, through whom Shakespeare himself perhaps speaks more often than through any other character, he assigns the speech which we quote from the text of 1605:

> "What a piece of work is a man; how noble in reason; how infinite in faculties, in form, and moving; how express and admirable in action; how like an angel in apprehension; how like a god: the beauty of the world; the paragon of animals; and yet to me, what is this quintessence of dust?"

With these words the majestical roof and brave o'erhanging canopy of the Renaissance universe become the baseless fabric of a dream, and we find ourselves in the world of Ben Jonson and John Webster, of Robert Carr and George Villiers, of Strafford and Cromwell, of Burton and Thomas Hobbes. The Tudor age is over; and the English spirit leaving the happy harbour into which the Virgin Queen had magically directed its helm, puts forth once more upon the high seas.

SIR WALTER RALEIGH

Circa 1552–1619

By

WYNYARD BROWNE

SIR WALTER RALEIGH

by WYNYARD BROWNE

AS a prophet of Empire and a pioneer of British expansion, Raleigh has been made a hero by men who would have disliked and distrusted him if they had been his contemporaries. He was not a man whom fools could suffer gladly. Although his patronage and pursuance of exploration set the ball of our dominion rolling, he was not befogged by patriotic emotions until he imagined his services to be of inestimable value to all mankind. The intention of his first expedition to Virginia was to give the Queen " a better Indies than the King of Spain hath any." But the Queen, like God, was to Raleigh nothing more venerable than a rewarder of them that served her. " To what end were religion," he wrote, " if there were no reward ? " And this strain of sensible, personal materialism runs through all his conduct. But modern business men who have more cause to be grateful to him than the Queen ever had, if they were to discover what kind of man he was, would find their obligation embarrassing. For he was neither sentimental, which they can admire, nor merely avaricious, which they could understand, but a man of imagination and fine intelligence.

A poet and a friend of poets, an associate of cranks and intellectuals, and probably a founder of that bohemian haunt *The Mermaid Tavern*, Raleigh cannot easily be associated with Empire Day. John Dee, who knew him well enough to become a shareholder in one of his commercial ventures, was a spiritualist, and wrote as madly as those *surréalistes* in Paris. An Italian æsthetician dedicated a book to him; and Spenser discussed with him the technique of poetry. Of course, in Elizabethan England poetry had not yet been reduced to the status of a secret sin. To be a good poet was almost as gentlemanly then as to be a good shot is now. But even for that spacious age, Raleigh's mind was too active and too free. Conversations with a disreputable young man called Kit Marlowe and a close friendship with Thomas Hariot, a mathematician who had dared to suggest that some parts of the Old Testament were not literally true, laid him open to a charge of heresy.

" Rawe *is the reason that doth* lye *within an Atheist's head*
 Which saith the soule of man doth dye, when that the boddies dead."

Free thinking, as in some modern countries, was punishable by death, and the charge was thought serious enough to necessitate the appointment of a commission of enquiry which sat ineffectually at Cerne Abbas, like something in a limerick. Raleigh was acquitted, but, though the Digbys can console themselves that Sherborne Castle was never a " schoole of Atheism," no one can claim, in spite of the constant references to religion in his writings, that Raleigh's faith was complacent or unquestioning. That splendid curiosity for which we have been taught to admire the Greeks was equal with personal ambition as a motive force in his life. Two hours of even the busiest day he devoted to reading, and he never went abroad without a chest full of books. During his long imprisonment in the Tower he built a shed in the garden for a laboratory in which he hoped to discover nothing less than a panacea, and on homeward and boring voyages he would conduct chemical experiments to pass the time. Even the voyages themselves, dangerous and expensive, were prompted nearly as much by curiosity as by desire for gold or fame. He was convinced that the world contained " stranger things than are to be seen between London and Staines," and he did his utmost to discover for himself those men who were reported " to have their eyes in their shoulders and their mouths in the middle of their breasts." With as much enthusiasm as Herodotus, he recorded in detail the customs and manners of the strange nations with whom he came in contact; and much of his fame rests upon a history. Like Socrates, but less persistent, he speculated upon the nature of the soul. Like Æschylus, but less profound, he was a poet who took a conspicuous part as a soldier in the events of a great period.

It is remarkable that a man to whom such impressive comparisons may be made, and of whom so much praise may be spoken, should dwindle to a minor figure, however romantic. For it is impossible, even for those who, like myself, admire him immoderately, to claim that he was a great man. His expeditions were unsuccessful; his panacea was never found; his history is unfinished; his speculations were intermittent, and most of his poetry is lost. There is plenty of evidence that he might have been any kind of great man, but not enough to show that he was. He has been called a *poseur*, and the word has been supposed to solve the problem. Actually, it merely restates it and confuses it by a sneer. The question, " Why was Raleigh not a great man ? " can be equated with the question, " Why was it necessary for him to be a *poseur* ? " And the answer is still obscure. I suggest that it was because his personality was divided. He was, in something like Mr. Wyndham Lewis's sense, a split man. In *The Lion and the Fox* Mr. Lewis has said: " It is impossible to be both a poet and a man of action; both Homer and Hector." But Raleigh was both; or, rather, he tried to be and very nearly succeeded. The two parts of him were evenly matched, and though they combined in a magnificent effect, they incapacitated each other. He was too busy with action ever to do more than display his potentialities as a poet; and being a poet he was too contemplative and self-conscious to make his actions more than play-acting. His poetry was hurried and occasional; his action haphazard and histrionic. These two sides of his nature, perpetually at war or striving to combine, kept him in a turmoil. Cecil noticed the contrast between the reflective and the active in him. For, when Raleigh was first in the Tower, he wrote: " His heart is broken, as he is extremely pensive, unless he is busied, in which he can toil terribly."

The fate of all such men is that, if they cannot be despised, they are disliked. Imagination and intelligence in men of action, though they help to provide material for posthumous romantic reputations, always tend to make their possessors unpopular while they are alive. They are tolerated or admired only in those who are content to take a back seat as public tutors or entertainers, and to keep their fingers out of the pie of practical affairs. Raleigh was not so content, and he quickly became the most hated man in England.

He went up to Oxford when he was fifteen, and even at that age he apparently became celebrated for that kind of

wit which is more a weapon than an ornament. The steel
and flint of thought and action struck dangerous sparks. If
his primary ambition had been poetic and not political,
academic rather than active, this wit would have made him
fewer enemies. But in competition or co-operation with
soldiers and sailors, still more in court intrigue, which was
carried on for the most part by people with slower and less
incisive minds than Raleigh's, it was certain to alienate those
whom it enabled him to supersede. For he had little or no
humour. Except possibly during the short, uproarious time
in his youth when he stopped the mouth of a talkative
acquaintance with sealing-wax, he could not easily be
trapped into a comfortable guffaw. His wit was always the
servant of deliberate purpose, and his attitude therefore
quickly became aggressive. His poem *The Lie*, too long to
quote in full, written probably when Elizabeth had put him
in the Tower for being insolent enough to marry, shows perfectly this aggressiveness, which had been induced at first by
close contact and competition with men to whom he felt
himself superior, and grew, when he was cut off from them,
into melancholy and cynicism:

> " *Say to the Court it glowes,*
>   *and shines like rotten wood,*
> *Say to the Church it showes*
>   *whats good, and doth no good.*
> *If Church and Court reply,*
>   *then giue them both the lie.*

> " *Tell men of high condition,*
>   *that mannage the estate,*
> *Their purpose is ambition,*
>   *their practise onely hate:*
> *And if they once reply,*
>   *then giue them all the lie.*

> " *Tell age it daily wasteth,*
>   *tell honour how it alters.*
> *Tell beauty how she blasteth*
>   *tell fauour how it falters*
> *And as they shall reply,*
>   *giue euery one the lie.*

> " *Tell wit how much it wrangles*
> *in tickle points of nycenesse,*
> *Tell wisedome she entangles*
> *her selfe in ouer wisenesse.*
> *And when they doe reply*
> *straight giue them both the lie.*"

And the first verse of one of the replies to it shows equally clearly the hostility which his attitude provoked in his acquaintances and rivals:

> " *Go, Eccho of the minde,*
> *a careles troth protest;*
> *make answere that rude Rawly*
> *no stomack can digest.*"

But he could use his wit to charm as well as to attack, and his eloquence probably did as much as his good looks to attract the Queen. She certainly enjoyed his conversation immoderately, and " Raleigh the witch " did not take long to convince her that he had oracular powers. His early and spectacular success in Ireland had made a certain Captain Appesley so jealous as to write to Walsingham: " For mine own part, I must be plain: I neither like his carriage nor his company; and therefore, other than by direction and commandment and what his right can require, he is not to expect at my hands." His sudden omnipotence at court, the ease with which this clever but penniless upstart seemed able to twist the Queen round his little finger, enraged many more important people. But for a time they could do no more than mutter that he was a charlatan, an accusation which no one versatile has ever escaped.

Raleigh suffered more from it than most men, perhaps only because he was more versatile. Elizabeth herself may have been influenced by it never to appoint him to any of the more responsible offices of State. The public was certainly convinced, as it always is when a man of exceptional talent and intelligence appears, that he was a sham. When, on his return from the first voyage to Guiana, no great enthusiasm was displayed, he found that the cause of the general apathy was a report, circulated by his enemies and easily believed by a credulous public, that he had never gone abroad at all, but stayed hidden in Cornwall, while his ships went to buy gold ore in Barbary which they could bring back to England triumphantly as though it had been discovered in Guiana. To this malice and credulity we owe his account of the voyage, *The Discoverie of the Large, Rich and Bewtiful Empyre of Guiana, with a relation of the great and Golden Citie of Manoa which the Spanyards call El Dorado*, one of the most fascinating travel-books that have ever been written. For he was compelled to write it in his own defence. Oddly, or perhaps if we are cynical, naturally enough, the defence itself has given rise to further similar slanders. Not only at the time was it considered cowardly of him to have turned back if he had really got as close to El Dorado as he said, but later historians have accused him of wilfully inventing wonders which he had never seen. Neither of these accusations is difficult to answer. It would have been ridiculous and not brave to proceed any farther during the floods, in an unknown and difficult country, particularly since he knew the disasters which had overtaken previous visitors: and anyone who reads his account attentively will notice that he is careful to distinguish between what he heard from others and what he saw for himself. But, arising out of these, a more insidious accusation was made against him: that, though most of his actions were futile or selfish, he relied upon supple eloquence and cunning argument to magnify or justify them. This may have been true. Certainly his narrative prose was persuasive. His account of the last fight of the *Revenge*, written to defend and commemorate his cousin Sir Richard Grenville, was so vivid that Tennyson could turn it into a melodramatic poem by a few tricks and jingles without any effort of the imagination. But it has to be remembered that, in England, anyone who can talk or write at all well about his own schemes or actions is apt to be regarded with suspicion or described with a sneer as plausible.

Like that of most other intelligent men who have dared to be also men of action, his confidence increased his unpopularity. " He was a tall, handsome, and bold man," says the inestimable Aubrey, " but his næve was that he was damnable proud." To-day it is a commonplace that those who do not allow their sentences to lumber and trail off into nonsense or embarrassment are called conceited; but even in Elizabeth's day, when a good address was not so rare, there were plenty of people to resent a man who always knew before he spoke exactly what he meant to say. It can scarcely be doubted that this was part of the reason why there were always men like Lord Henry Howard and Sir "Judas" Stukely to libel and betray him. But we have to admit that Raleigh's blemish was more than a justifiable confidence. His passion for fine clothes, that "humour of rags" as he called it, was so extravagant that he carried a fortune on his shoes, though his pearls, Aubrey says, were not so big as they were painted in his portraits.

If his fondness for display labelled him proud, it also labelled him greedy. His rich look constantly reminded poorer men of the vast fortune which his wits and charm had so quickly won him. Elizabeth had given him estates at Sherborne, forty thousand acres in Munster, and a "palace" in London. She gave him exclusive licences for exporting certain cloths and for selling wines throughout the whole country. In 1585 she made him Lord Warden of the Stannaries. This was a lucrative position at the head of the West Country tin mines, and his appointment called forth a complaint to the Lord Treasurer that the wardenship should have been given to someone "whom the most part well accounted of . . . whereas no man is more hated than him, none more cursed daily of the poor, of whom in truth numbers are brought to extreme poverty through the gift of the cloths to him; his pride is intolerable, without regard for any, as the world knows. . . ." Yet, if he was greedy, he spent money more freely in national enterprise than any other man of his time. The plantation of Virginia alone cost him £40,000, and he was always ready to finance expeditions of exploration. When he was "enlarged from the Tower" to go his last and fatal voyage to Guiana, he invested £10,000 of his own money in the exploit, and Lady Raleigh, "deare Besse," parted with a house and lands of her own inheritance to help him, so that before his death he had reduced himself and his family to penury by his enterprise.

His rivals disliked him through jealousy, but their supporters detested him. During the Islands voyage an incident took place which was typical of their attitude towards him. Essex, who was in command, was darting about the seas after rumours of the Plate Fleet and failing to keep appointments. Raleigh waited for him for three days at Fayal, whither he had been ordered, and then decided to attack the next objective, the town of Horta, without him. Sir Gelly Meyricke and Sir Christopher Blount, two of Essex's supporters, refused to follow him. Horta was captured without their assistance, but when Essex arrived at last, Sir Gelly and his friends did their best to persuade him to court-martial Raleigh and sentence him to death. Fortunately, his charm and the tact of Lord Thomas Howard saved the situation. Raleigh was always in danger from such nonentities. Later on the same Sir Christopher Blount fired four shots at him during a parley on the Thames. The greater part of the population of England would have done him an injury if they could. The carriage in which he drove to his trial had to be protected by armed guards from the fury of the crowd. But he had a proper contempt for them: " As we see it in experience, That dogs doe alwaies barke at those they know not; and that it is in their nature to accompany one another in those clamours: so it is with the inconsiderate multitude."

The monstrous trial for High Treason against King James the First was the climax of all the hatred which his double power inspired. No Soviet or Nazi injustice has been more shameless. Communists and Fascists have principles to excite them and pervert their judgment. Raleigh's judges and jury were swayed only by personal animosity. On the Bench were the very Privy Councillors who had planned the prosecution, including Lord Henry Howard who, for some time even before James had left Scotland, had been poisoning his mind against Raleigh. Gawdy himself, one of the judges, said before his death that English justice had never been so debased as by Raleigh's trial and condemnation.

Many of the charges were ridiculous, and there was practically no evidence except a statement by the weak-witted Lord Cobham which he had already recanted. Raleigh was allowed no counsel nor was he allowed to speak until the whole case for the prosecution had been completed.

The trial is interesting, if only because it provides another example of the fury which an intelligent man can unwittingly provoke from the stupid. The more skilful and the wiser Raleigh's answers were, the more the Attorney-General became enraged.

" I do not hear yet that you have spoken one word against me; here is no treason of mine done. If my Lord Cobham be a traitor, what is that to me ? "

This was too convincing for the Attorney to tolerate, and he broke into abuse.

"All that he did was by thy instigation, thou viper: for I thou thee thou traitor."

"It becometh not a man of quality and virtue to call me so, but I take comfort in it. It is all you can do."

"Have I angered you ?"

"I am in no case to be angry."

If Raleigh had been fool enough to lose his temper or relax his pride, the tide of his unpopularity might never have turned. As it was, his composure and his wisdom so impressed his contemporaries that, as soon as he was condemned to death, the public enmity changed to admiration. Towards the end of the trial, he spoke a sentence that has now an irony which he can hardly have suspected nor intended. The Attorney was still blustering.

"I want words sufficient to express thy viperous treason."

"I think you want words indeed, for you have spoken one thing half-a-dozen times."

"Thou art an odious fellow. Thy name is hateful to all the realm of England for thy pride."

"It will go near to prove a measuring cast between you and me, Mr. Attorney."

Throughout the trial Raleigh displayed in its most impressive form that despised power of gesture and self-dramatisation which only a split man can have. A contemporary who described the trial in a letter seems to have noticed how much the poet in him enjoyed inventing and controlling the words and behaviour of the man of action who was now a prisoner: "Save it went with the hazard of his life, it was the happiest day he ever spent."

Far more has been written of Raleigh as a man of action than as a poet; so much indeed that there is little more to be said and no need for repetition. His expeditions to Virginia and Guiana, the attack on Cadiz, the Islands voyage are known at some time in some detail to most school-boys. His bravery and resource as a soldier have been praised and discussed only less than his naval strategy which during his life "a great many malignant fooles despised," though perhaps it is not generally known that he was apt to be seasick and disliked the sea. So little of his actual poetry is left, so confused and uncertain are the texts, that it is easily excusable that those who have not noticed or not been especially interested in the division of his personality, those who have regarded him exclusively as an Imperial hero or merely as a romantic figure, should have neglected it or under-emphasised its importance. It is, however, not negligible. Contemporary critics—Gabriel Harvey, Francis Meres and George Puttenham—recognised him as one of the best living poets, though they were apt to classify him casually among that " crew of Courtly makers, Noble Men and Gentlemen of her Maiesties owne seruants who haue written excellently well." But Spenser in his dedicatory sonnets to the *Faerie Queene* distinguishes Raleigh from the rest. Of Essex's poetic abilities he makes no mention. To the Earl of Oxford, for whom some people wish to make fantastic claims, he says only that he loved " th' Heliconian ymps " and they him. To the Earl of Ormonde he says that he had a mansion on every Parnassus and Helicon that was still left for the Muses. Only Lord Buckhurst, who, Puttenham says, wrote well when he was young, is told that his golden verse is " worthy immortal fame ". All these praises are formal and expressed in classical imagery. All, except Lord Buckhurst's, are incidental, hardly more than polite references to the noble gentlemen's Muses, and even the sonnet to Buckhurst begins dully with the lines :

> " *In vain I thinke, right honourable Lord,*
> *By this rude rime to memorise thy name.*"

But the sonnet to Raleigh begins vividly and vigorously :

> " *To thee, that art the sommers nightingale,*"

and its imagery is not formal but natural and spontaneous. The whole tone of the sonnet shows that Spenser quite genuinely and seriously regarded Raleigh as a poet. The difference between a nightingale and a noble Lord with a mansion on Helicon is precisely the difference between Raleigh and the other courtly makers. There is more in the word " nightingale " than meets the eye. Raleigh's poetry came as naturally as a bird's song or the leaves on a tree. It fulfilled Keats's requirement. He never found it necessary to assume an artificial diction, and was seldom pleased to elaborate trivial conceits. Though he often used his poetry for a purpose, to persuade Queens to show him favour or let him out of prison, he did not produce, even on these occasions, sets of forced verses.

The Boockes of the Oceans Love to Scinthia, of which only one out of eleven remains, were written when Raleigh had first fallen into disgrace with Elizabeth and were his longest poem. Because here and there a verse is not finished or has an extra line waving loose at its end, the extant book has been called careless and straggling. Because the meaning is sometimes obscure or the expression intricate, it has been called confused. But even if these censures are justified, the poem cannot be dismissed as an unimportant fragment. More than any other, it suggests what Raleigh's contribution to English poetry might have been, if he had not spent so much time in other pursuits; or what it actually may have been, though it has been lost. Apart from a private music which could be mistaken for no one else's, Raleigh was actually doing something in *Scinthia* which at that time no English poet had done. He was making poetry directly about his own intimate emotions. For this reason, like some of Shakespeare's sonnets and very unlike the *Faerie Queene*, which is remote and impersonal, *Scinthia* has a strangely modern air.

> " *I hated life and cursed destiney*
> *the thoughts of passed tymes like flames of hell,*
> *kyndled a fresh within my memorye*
> *the many deere achiuements that befell*

> " *in those pryme yeares and infancy of love*
> *which to discribe weare butt to dy in writinge*
> *ah those I sought, but vaynly, to remove*
> *and vaynly shall, by which I perrish liuing*

> " *And though strong reason holde before myne eyes*
> *the Images and formes of worlds past*
> *teaching the cause why all thos flames that rize*
> *from formes externall, can no longer last,*

> " *then that those seeminge bewties hold in pryme*
> *Loves grovnd, his essence, and his emperye,*
> *all slaues to age, and vassals unto tyme*
> *of which repentance writes the tragedye.*"

It seems that he had formed that relation between the poet's own life and his poetry which attracts and baffles so many of our contemporaries. He did it apparently without difficulty and at a time when no one else had done it in English. For the conjectural dates make it improbable that Shakespeare's sonnets had even been written, much less read by Raleigh, at the time when he was engaged upon *Scinthia*. The loss of the other books then seems to have been another of those cruel accidents which were always smashing the impressive pedestals upon which Raleigh might have stood. Like an Atlantic flight, his probable achievement was something which, when it has once been done, can be done more easily again. The first to do it should be especially remembered. But just as he has overshadowed Drake and others in tobacco and potatoes, so in poetry Shakespeare and Donne have snatched his peculiar glory.

The great mass of the imagery he uses in *Scinthia* is not, like Shakespeare's, detailed and specific, but simple and universal—rivers, mountains, the sun, the dew, and the seasons—but he chooses and uses his images with such skill that they have a variety of meanings almost comparable to the variety of appearance in nature itself. And what he loses in precision, he gains in valuable ambiguity. The passage already quoted could be, perhaps even is, a description of his attitude to the whole history of the world as well as to those early days with the Queen.

We have already seen that *The Lie* expressed with vigour and wit the scorn which one half of him felt for the world which the other half loved too much. But how personal the poem is we are apt to forget, because the emotion is so neatly externalised and made into a song. We have become accustomed to lyric poetry being an intimate affair. But to Raleigh's credit it must be remembered that most Elizabethan lyrics were like carved jewels, the matter fetched from another country and only decorated in England. He dug his treasures out of his own experience.

The anonymous stanzas which are obviously Raleigh's in *The Phœnix Nest*, a sixteenth-century anthology " full of varietie, excellent invention and singular delight," are an example of the melancholy reflection on time and the passing of life which was characteristic of his thought. The man of action in him, as soldier, politician and explorer, fought and intrigued and navigated strange rivers: then when he was suddenly checked, the poet in him, coming uppermost, saw how all these actions, which had seemed so delightful and so real, were vanished.

> " *Like truthles dreames, so are my ioyes expired,*
> *And past returne, are all my dandled daies:*
> *My loue misled, and fancie quite retired,*
> *Of all which past, the sorow onely staies.*
>
> " *My lost delights, now cleane from sight of land,*
> *Haue left me all alone in vnknowne waies:*
> *My minde to woe, my life in fortunes hand,*
> *Of all which past, the sorow onely staies.*
>
> " *As in a countrey strange without companion,*
> *I onely waile the wrong of deaths delaies,*
> *Whose sweete spring spent, whose sommer wel nie don,*
> *Of all which past, the sorow onely staies.*
>
> " *Whom care forewarnes, ere age and winter colde*
> *To haste me hence, to finde my fortunes folde.*"

Death and memory were much in Raleigh's mind: memory because " wee haue no other keeper of our pleasures past," and because we can learn by it the wisdom which he most valued and to teach which he wrote his history, that unless, like " those few blacke Swannes," we have had " the grace to value worldly vanities at no more than their owne price," we can draw from our past actions " no other vapour than heavie, secret and sad sighes "; and death, which he had often faced so closely that its aspect had become familiar, because it would bring, he hoped, a reward for any good a man might have done. It was natural that such a man should be able to write a poem like *The Passionate Man's Pilgrimage*, which has the simplicity and clarity of George Herbert, combined with a use of wit which we associate with Donne and the other metaphysical poets of the next century.

> " *Giue me my Scallop shell of quiet,*
> *My staffe of Faith to walke vpon,*
> *My Scrip of Ioy, Immortall diet,*
> *My bottle of saluation:*
> *My Gowne of Glory, hopes true gage,*
> *And thus Ile take my pilgrimage.*

" *And by the happie blisfull way*
More peacefull Pilgrims I shall see,
That haue shooke off their gownes of clay,
And goe appareld fresh like mee.
Ile bring them first
To slake their thirst,
And then to tast those Nectar suckets
At the cleare wells
Where sweetnes dwells,
Drawn up by Saints in Christall buckets.

" *From thence to heauens Bribeles hall*
Where no corrupted voyces brall,
No Conscience molten into gold,
Nor forg'd accusers bought and sold,
No cause deferd, nor vaine spent Iorney,
For there Christ is the Kings Atturney:
Who pleades for all without degrees,
And he hath Angells, but no fees."

It was natural, too, that such a man should be able to die well. On the morning of his execution, fifteen years after the sentence against him had been passed, when he had received the Communion, breakfasted and smoked a final pipe, carefully dressed in velvet, satin and taffeta, he acted consciously and magnificently what he himself would have called the last scene of his tragedy. As in all well-constructed tragedies, death was the solution of a conflict. The two warring halves of the split man were at last united. For this was an action bolder than any cruel fighting in Irish bogs, than any boarding of galleons at Cadiz or bribing of Indians near El Dorado; but it was also an action which could not have been so magnificently performed without the wisdom and imagination of a poet. The poet in Raleigh was needed to say to the executioner who suggested that he should face towards the east, " What matters it which way the head lie, so the heart be right? " The man of action was needed to give the order for his own death, " What dost thou fear? Strike, man, strike! "

RICHARD BURBAGE

Circa 1567–1619

By

NIGEL PLAYFAIR

RICHARD BURBAGE

by NIGEL PLAYFAIR

THE poets, or at least those who have attacked their typewriters or flourished their quills during the last hundred years, have paid very little attention to actors, largely, no doubt, because actors, unfortunately, have paid very little attention to them. It is true that a very respected Victorian, more at home in a highly idealised eighteenth century than in either the sixteenth or his own, wrote a rondeau to celebrate Burbage himself, but he was more concerned with the accuracy of his French verse-form than in any attempt to translate into rhyme the atmosphere of an Elizabethan stage.

There is only one set of verses dedicated to the sad story of the player which every schoolboy used to know. I refer to Henley's, written as a ballade this time, and carrying the refrain " Into the night go one and all." The pessimism of its burden is perhaps due to the fact that the author had a brother, a reputable but not very successful professional actor, who probably was never able adequately to contribute toward the exigencies of the family exchequer. Its sentiment few will be found to deny, but of course it is not intended precisely to be illuminating. To a biographer it sounds a note of warning as to the difficulties of the task which he has rather rashly undertaken, though, writing as an actor, I am not really greatly concerned with its implications. I can hold my head bloody but unbowed before a fate which, after all, I shall share with many a well-graced jutebroker, and I think that many a greater man than Burbage might well envy his chances of immortality, who undertook his dark journey into the unknown, having been chosen as the first actor to play upon an English stage the part of " Hamlet," and that too under its author's direction. One cannot doubt that this direction survives to the present, seeing that the traditions and methods of English acting have persisted from that great day to this, in spite of incredible difficulties and vicissitudes.

From this point of view alone it may be held worth while to set down again the outline of the life of this much-favoured man, as far as it can be deduced from the very insufficient material that survives from contemporary report and appreciation. It is tragic but true that there was no man of genius to set himself the task of reporting with vividness the quality of any of the actors of Shakespeare's period—and indeed such men have existed in very few periods of the theatre's long history. What would we not give to discover a Hazlitt in the Elizabethan age? For that matter there is no Hazlitt in our own, though music has its Newman.

"Into the night" went Edmund Kean as well as Burbage and Garrick and Henry Irving. But can we not realise something—a great deal—of the personality of Kean and his majestic effect upon those who saw him when we read this?—

> "In a word Mr. Kean's acting is like an anarchy of the Passions, in which each upstart terror or frenzy of the moment is struggling to get violent possession of some bit or corner of his fiery soul and pigmy body, to jostle out and lord it over the rest of the rabble of short-lived and furious purposes."

I am afraid that I can give no such passage or anything approaching it from anyone who had seen Burbage upon his stage. Shakespeare himself was grateful, in moderation, to his actors; their personalities, no doubt, had some influence upon the form in which his plays were written, but playwright, and skilled playwright though he was, his passionate rebellion against the limitations imposed by *their* limitations, and that of the theatre generally, is evident. He was, if I may say so without irreverence, too big for his buskins.

I write purposely "of the theatre generally." One hopes that the complacent Victorian theory, that had Shakespeare been graciously permitted to have been born in the middle of the nineteenth century, his attitude would have been a far more contented one, with its theatre's neatly interchangeable scenery and its conscientious study of heraldry and the correct costumes that were worn in different periods, has been finally scotched. I do not think that his mind would have been set at rest with a larger O or that a double or treble number of supers would have realised for him "a puissance" without imagination. I do not believe that Shakespeare or the Elizabethan dramatists had any contempt for the resources of their theatres as such, whatever they may have thought of the possible resources of any theatre. But it was the fault of the later Victorian critics, and for the most part the audiences following them, to imagine that the art of the theatre and especially its mechanical and scenic arts, are steadily progressive, and to pour the balm of their pity on the memory of Shakespeare in that he could not, through natural circumstances, take advantage of that advance. How often, for example, have we not read of the sad shortcomings of the eighteenth-century stage decorators compared to those employed by Irving and by Tree? To anyone who still believes this comfortable doctrine I would give this advice. It is that he should look at two pictures now in the Garrick Club and compare them. One is by the late John Collier, and depicts a scene from *The Merry Wives of Windsor* with Tree and Ellen Terry and Dame Madge Kendal. The other is a scene from Otway's *Venice Preserved*, presumably, at least, inspired by a memory of a stage presentation, with all its archæological inaccuracies, painted by Zoffany. If he has any taste I fancy the contrast will surprise him out of his complacency.

* * * * *

Burbage was born, theatrically speaking, in the purple and about the year 1567. He was the second son of James Burbage, whom you can spell Burbadge if you prefer it. His father was a builder, an actor, and a theatrical manager in the days when the latter two professions were not particularly troubled by competition.

James Burbage built the first regular playhouse in London, known as "The Theatre," modelled from the form of a platform on wheels within the courtyard of an Inn, as nearly as the first motor-cars were designed on an imitation of the horse-drawn carriages. He built afterwards another theatre, "The Blackfriars." He died in 1597, and both of these passed into the hands of his two sons, Cuthbert and Richard. It is reasonable to suppose that Richard made his first appearance at one of them, though his father had also an interest in "The Curtain."

At any rate by 1588, when still a very young man, Richard

was recognised as a considerable tragedian in his father's
company, now known as the Lord Chamberlain's Players,
though formerly as the Earl of Leicester's. A year or two
later this company and the two theatres were both for
practical purposes under the direction of the two young
brothers, for James Burbage retired some seven years before
his death.

Shortly after his retirement there arose a quarrel between
Richard and one Giles Allen, an actor, over the payment of
the ground rent of " The Theatre " in Shoreditch, with the
result that with the help of a carpenter, Richard himself
pulled down the flimsy structure and in 1599 built " The
Globe," Bankside, largely out of its materials, and the share-
holders of the new theatre were mainly its company of
actors, of whom William Shakespeare was one. In 1613
this Globe Theatre was burnt down, but rebuilt with the aid
of various subscribers.

Meanwhile the second theatre, owned by Burbage himself,
and intended to be used as a winter playhouse, was leased to
the " Queene Majestie's Children of the Chapell." They
became the rage of the town, and it is to be remembered that
the fashionable craze for the acting of children is a recurring
catastrophe which adult players have through the ages been
called upon to face. It is amusing to trace the thread from
that speech of Rosencrantz :

" But there is, sir, an eyrie of children, little eyases, that
cry out on the top of question and are most tyranically
clapped for't: these are now the fashion, and so berattle
the common stages—so they call them—that many wearing
rapiers are afraid of goose quills, and dare scarce come
thither "—through " their own succession," Master Betty—
to see whose performance of *Hamlet* Pitt moved the adjournment of the House of Commons—down to Master Jacky
Coogan of our day. It is at least a fairly safe surmise that
Shakespeare was considering the lease by Burbage of his
theatre to his own detriment when he put this speech into
Hamlet.

It would indeed be gratifying if we could find some passages from Shakespeare in which the poet really told us how
highly he regarded the help of the more intelligent actors,
such as Burbage must most certainly, from all the evidence,
have been, towards the interpretation of his plays. To him,
or to his like, he must undoubtedly have referred in his line

about the " well-graced actor," but it does not get us very
far, and his most famous references to actors, including of
course his own apparent regret that he was ever one himself,
though not, if tradition speaks fairly, a very good one, are
largely to their shortcomings. In this connection, I may
possibly make one tiny contribution to Shakespearean
Scholarship, if that is not too bumptious a claim. It is in
regard to Hamlet's advice to the players. To most critics it
has appeared either that Shakespeare was leaving Hamlet,
the Prince, alone for the moment, and using him as a mere
mouthpiece for his own sentiments, or that he was allowing
himself to be swayed by a rather snobbish instinct in suggesting that Hamlet, because he was a Prince, was entitled to lay
down the law to experts who must have known a great deal
better than he did what the rules that govern acting are, or
ought to be. This second theory was very amusingly
supported by W. S. Gilbert in his skit of *Rosencrantz and
Guildenstern.* But those who hold either of these views have
forgotten the possibility that the great noblemen who owned
these early companies of players might have pursued their
hobby and taken advantage of their position to the extent of
training themselves to be, shall I say, the unpaid Granville-
Barkers or Basil Deans of their day, like the Duke of Saxe-
Meiningen in an earlier period. They can quite reasonably
be portrayed as knowing very well what they were talking
about, and I am sure Hamlet had at least been President
of his University Dramatic Society.

I may in this connection quote a passage from a later playwright than Shakespeare, Richard Brome (" the Gipsy-
led ") who gives what is, no doubt, an imitation of Hamlet's
speech to the players, but with some interesting differences:

> " NOBLEMAN: *My actors
> Are all in readiness, and I think all perfect
> But one, that never will be perfect in a thing
> He studies: yet he makes such shift extempore,
> (Knowing the purpose that he is to speak to)
> That he moves mirth in me 'bove all the rest,
> For I am none of these Poetic Furies
> That threats the actor's life, in a whole play
> That adds a syllable or takes away.
> If he can thribble through and move delight
> In others, I am pleased.*"

Probably Shakespeare, and small blame to him, is alluded to as one of these " Poetic Furies," and perhaps here we have the germ of the quarrels between the Author and the Producer that have continued to this day. At any rate there is not the slightest reason to suppose that Burbage was the actor here referred to, indeed clearly he was not, for Burbage was, one may deduce, a serious-minded worker and in any case the whole scene belongs to a later period than his as the following passage proves :

> " PLAYER :
> *That is the way, my Lord, has been allowed*
> *On elder stages, to move mirth and laughter.*
>
> "NOBLEMAN :
> *Yes, in the days of Tarleton and of Kemp,*
> *Before the Stage was purged of barbarism,*
> *And brought to the perfection it now shines with.*
> *Then Fools and Jesters spent their wits, because*
> *The Poets were wise enough to save their own*
> *For profitable uses."*

Tarleton and Kemp were, of course, contemporaries and co-workers with Burbage. Does not this passage explain much of the comic Interludes of Shakespeare's plays, so often quoted in detriment of their alleged author, or worse still, excused as having lost the savour of their yet inevitable wit, because of the changing fashion of language?

I often hope that the Spirit of Shakespeare sometimes and somewhere enjoys its quiet amusement over all the learned comments upon passages of whose authorship he was completely innocent or those completely misprinted. Perhaps the spirit of Burbage joins him in discussing the " fat and scant of breath " phrase which is supposed by many to allude to the adiposity of the actor. Whether " fat " may or may not be a misprint for " faint " I do not know, but it is clear that even if " fat " it is, it does not mean " fat " in its pure Pickwickian sense.

There is evidence to prove that Burbage was short of stature :

> " *His stature small but every thought and mood*
> *Might throughly from the face be understood;*
> *And his whole action he could change with ease*
> *From ancient Lear to youthful Pericles* ";

but it is unlikely that he would have been cast for all the tragic parts of his day if he had been physically unfitted. And when he played " Hamlet," on that first thrilling afternoon, he was a young man of roughly thirty-five.

" Hamlet " was about the seventh of Shakespeare's heroes played, and dare I say in modern parlance " created," by Burbage. He had previously acted Shylock, Richard III, Prince Hal, Romeo, Henry V, and Brutus, and was to follow Hamlet with Othello, Lear, Macbeth, Pericles, and Coriolanus.

His most famous part, Richard III, was acted first in the days of his bachelorhood, and thereby may be recalled the anecdote, *ben trovato* perhaps, but at least in his lifetime, of Shakespeare anticipating him at some gallant rendezvous and making the excuse that " William the Conqueror came before Richard the Third." All the same, I have the odd instinct that though Will Shakespeare fits well enough into that anecdote, Burbage does not. At any rate Richard married Winifred in the year succeeding the production of *Hamlet*, and of his eight children, only one, christened appropriately " William," survived him, so I think that even if the anecdote is true, all was forgotten and forgiven. Richard Burbage died on or about March 16, 1619, leaving behind him, as did many actors of that blessed time, a considerable fortune, though not of course comparable with that, for example, left by Edward Alleyn.

Acting and theatre management was, in those days, an exceeding lucrative profession, enjoying, comparatively speaking, a boom somewhat similar to that of the film to-day. They were, like the film to-day and popular journalism at the beginning of this century, the excitement of the people, to which their pence were easily contributed. This may be gathered from the " review " called *The Return to Parnassus*, in which Burbage and Kemp were impersonated *in propria persona*. Here Kemp gives his advice to the Cambridge students in these words : " Be merry, lads, you have happened on the most excellent vocation in the world, they come North and South to bring it to our Playhouse." One can imagine Douglas Fairbanks addressing the Union in similar words, amid ringing cheers, and perhaps with equally disastrous results.

I must write a little more of this *Return from Parnassus*, because the scene from it to which I refer does throw some light upon the character of Burbage, though more " lime-light," if I may use the anachronism, upon that of his friend Kemp. It was, as I have said, " a review," performed at Cambridge by its scholars, at Christmas time, and just before the death of Queen Elizabeth. Mr. Oliphant Smeaton maintains, and I am sure rightly, that it was the work of different pens. As a whole, though its allusions cannot help being interesting, it is a pretty poor affair, certainly no better than the average " Footlights " reviews of these days, which indeed do not follow its faults that " smell too much of that writer Ovid and that writer Metamorphosis and talk too much of Proserpine and Jupiter."

But the scene in which Kemp and Burbage make their appearance is good, and I should not be the least surprised to learn in Elysium that Kemp himself had lent a friendly hand and written it, on one of his visits to Cambridge. If he did he was wise enough to give himself the best part. I suspect it was well acted, for it is likely that Cambridge undergraduates, with a taste for the Playhouse, then as now, studied pretty accurately the characteristics of their favourite players. At any rate the dramatised visit of Kemp and Burbage to the students has an authentic ring about it. It is much as a visit to Cambridge of Irving and Toole might have been, Irving allowing his comic friend to shine and pretending to take himself with modesty and perfect serious-ness, or it might be as a visit of Henry Ainley and Leslie Henson at a later day. Throughout it is most interesting to observe that Kemp, though he does nearly all the talking, yet suggests an intense admiration and respect for his " honest Dick," just as Toole had for Irving, and Henson, I am sure, has for Ainley.

Says Kemp, discussing Ben Jonson, " but our fellow Shakespeare hath given him a purge that made him bewray his credit." To which Burbage answers, " It's a shrewd fellow indeed " and then quickly changes the subject. " I wonder these scholars stay so long, they appointed to be here presently that we might try them." Is there a hint here of Burbage's occasional and fleeting resentment at Shake-speare's sometimes rather trying insistence upon detail or at least that upon this occasion he was on holiday, and didn't want to talk too much about him? It looks to me very much like it.

Then Burbage to the scholars, " Master Philomusus and Master Studioso, God save you," to which parodies the comedian (could Leslie Henson resist the chance?) " Master Philomusus and Master *Otioso*, well met." [The italics are mine, and his, I am sure.]

Follows the respectful and the light greeting of the Under-graduate—" The same to you, good Master Burbage. What Master Kemp, how doth the Emperor of Germany? " And even so would the present President of the A.D.C. differenti-ate his greeting between Mr. Ainley and Mr. Leslie Henson.

But the real character of Burbage, the honour in which he was held by the world and by his fellows, is illustrated by the following speech of Kemp's. To get the effect of just what I mean (and to prove that I am right in my deduction) it must be read aloud and jauntily, and, most importantly, after each " Burbage " must be a comedian's pause and a heavy stress on the " and," the stress growing firmer as he proceeds : " And for honours, who of more report than Dick Burbage— *and* Will Kemp? He is not counted a gentleman that knows not Dick Burbage—*and* Will Kemp: there's not a country wench that can dance " Sellenger's Round " but can talk of Dick Burbage—*and* Will Kemp." The punctuation and italics are again mine and again I feel sure his, or rather, his impersonator's.

It is not always easy to defend the stage's contribution to the better understanding of the classics, though as an actor I should like to. But occasionally, perhaps even more often than occasionally, one can show the value that a careful actor may bring to the task.

Perhaps it would not be irrelevant (or irreverent) to give as an example a passage from Bradley's great work on Shakespearean tragedy when he writes thus of Hamlet's lines :

" *There are more things in Heaven and Earth, Horatio,*
Than are dreamt of in your philosophy."

" Of course ' your,' " writes the Professor, " does not mean Horatio's philosophy in particular. ' Your ' is used as the Gravedigger uses it when he says that ' Your water is a sore decayer of your . . . dead body.' " The omission is Bradley's (and Queen Victoria's). But Burbage could have shown Bradley that for once he had tripped, by reciting the lines in the only way they can be correctly recited, thus proving that Hamlet was referring to Horatio in his character as a student of Philosophy. I want to put this quite plainly. If the " your " was intended to have a generic application, it would have to be pronounced shortly, and if it were, it would destroy the beat and rhythm of the line which would stumble thus, " Than are dreamt of in y'r philosophy."

Whether his wife succeeded in keeping Richard's fortune intact to her end, history does not relate. There was trouble about a lease a little later, and in a petition in regard to it, we find allusion to " the great desert of Richard Burbage for his quality of playing that his wife should not starve in her old age," but that was very possibly merely a picturesque way of making assurance doubly sure. It is an odd circumstance, but explainable by the fact that legal documents, however dull, are set out on good parchment, that the lives of all Elizabethans, fully and conscientiously undertaken, appear to be one long succession of quarrels about leases, but I do not think it is necessary for me, or in the least interesting to my readers, that I should set any of them out.

The tributes to Burbage's acting were mostly paid after his death, and some of them a considerable time after, but it need not be suggested that they did not represent a very general feeling. Indeed, that any poets should make such tributes after a lapse of time surely suggests the strength of a well-founded tradition. The tributes also need not be held to be less sincere because they were frequently written in very indifferent verse. It must, however, be stated in fairness that the making of valedictory odes throughout the seventeenth century was a very favourite form of metrical exercise, and cannot therefore be regarded as an unassailable witness to sentiment, let alone truth. More than one specimen would be wearisome to read, but this that follows has its interest, not only in itself, but because it alludes to Burbage's hobby of painting, in which he was followed by a distinguished actor of our own day, Forbes Robertson. An authentic picture by Burbage is to be seen in the Dulwich Gallery. It is an amusing coincidence that Dr. Johnson followed the same train of thought as the author of these lines in using the word " eclipsed " in his fine epitaph on another great actor, David Garrick.

" On the death of that Master in his Art and Quality, painting and playing, R. Burbage."

" Astrologers and Stargazers this year
Write out of four eclipses: five appear.
Death interposing Burbage and Time staying
Hath made a visible eclipse of playing."

And here is a better tribute in prose:

> " Never more delighted than when he spoke, nor more
> sorry than when he held his peace. Yet even then he
> was an excellent actor still, never failing in his part when
> he had done speaking but with his looks and gesture
> maintaining still into the height."

A great actor, then, this Burbage was, with heaven-sent
opportunities, but with great difficulties too. Shakespeare
saw to that and perhaps Shakespeare, all too conscious, as
undoubtedly he must have been, of the limitations of the
actor's capacity as interpreter, did not make his task any
lighter. But can one reasonably doubt that as I have suggested and in spite of these limitations, between them they
fashioned this fine tradition of English acting that has been
passed down a great line? Burbage, Betterton, Garrick,
Kean, Phelps, Irving, Martin Harvey, to name but a few,
have made it possible to convey through acting some interpretation of the grandeur of the poet's mind, which need not
offend the too refined, and can give much pleasure to simple
people.

Can one guess any further, through the haze of ages, what
Burbage was like as a man? He suffered in his lifetime at
least no ill report. He must have been a tireless and stupend-
ous worker. One thinks of him somehow, and I have given
some evidence to support the theory, as a silent man amidst
the chatter of the tiring-room, overburdened perhaps by the
tasks he has undertaken, half conscious perhaps of their
importance to future generations. One thinks that he did
not overrate his own position: he took no conscious steps as
Alleyn did to secure his name and fame after his death. One
can but guess what he thought of his fellow-workers; there
is, at least, no trace of quarrelling over his work, but only
over his business affairs. I do not believe he complained at
all about the means of the presentation of the plays in which
he acted. The enthusiasm for this pioneer craft must have
been ample compensation for the draughty stage and for the

fickleness of his audience—ever ready, as they are to this day, to wander across to the bear-garden next door, a fact of which Alleyn again took the fullest advantage, founding Dulwich College with the doubtfully earned proceeds! He did not complain that his leading ladies were of his own sex —nor very much did anyone else at the time. It is true that Shakespeare, who considered everything, made Cleopatra lament the prospect of the day when

> " *The quick comedians*
> *Extemporarily will stage us and present*
> *Our Alexandrian revels: Antony*
> *Shall be brought drunken forth, and I shall see*
> *Some squeaking Cleopatra boy my greatness,*
> *I' the posture of a Whore."*

It is too intricate a question to enquire into now, but following the law of supply and demand, it is, I think, probable that little or nothing was missed in the art of acting as far as that art can go, by the custom of boys and men playing women's parts. Indeed, something was probably gained, in that acting requires criticism of character as well as impersonation. I have seen a modern actor play " a heroine," not only convincingly, but giving a suggestion of pathos and even tragedy and yet without the faintest suggestion of " effeminacy." He practised his odd craft, of course, in a war concert party. His name is Mr. Reg Stone, and you could learn a great deal about women from him.

Of Burbage, as of Kemp and Tarleton and even of Dick Robinson, of whom it was written that he had " the gait, the gesture, the voice, the passions of a woman " it may be said, in the words of Heywood, " Though they be dead, their deserts yet live in the remembrance of many." An actor need ask for no better epitaph.

FRANCIS BACON
1561–1626

By
H. C. O'NEILL

FRANCIS BACON [1]

by H. C. O'NEILL

"WHO can see worse days," wrote Francis Bacon, in the longest and noblest of his essays, " than he who yet living doth follow at the funerals of his own reputation? " It is the supreme irony of his life that the words, little as he thought it, were to find their fullest application to himself. His reputation as a statesman did not survive his cession of the seals. Harvey, his great contemporary, gave the epitaph of his philosophy in the words " he wrote philosophy like a Lord Chancellor." His punishment for bribery buried his title to fame as a lawyer. To Charles and his ministers he had become, long before his death, merely a troublesome old gentleman.

He was too massive a figure to rest quiet in his grave. Pope and Macaulay tore his character to shreds, despite the gallant defence of Spedding and Montagu. His admirers have raised such a monument to his memory that it is the mausoleum and not the man that survives. The Encyclopædists regarded him as the discoverer of experimental science and inductive philosophy. Even in the last century there were those whose difficulty was merely whether he were a new Aristotle or a Socrates. And, by contrast, De Morgan found him a fit subject for laughter and Nettleship for scorn. He has even been accused of ignorance of Latin, though this would have been something of a feat in a household so famous for classical scholarship even on the distaff side. His reputation as a writer of essays, generally more read about than read, appears to have performed the last obsequies on his other careers. And, thus, Bacon rises upon

[1] It seems wiser to maintain his original name than the incorrect " Lord Bacon " which is apparently an ellipsis. He was, at the end, " Lord St. Albans." His full description would be " Francis Baron Verulam, Viscount St. Albans," and, though he signed " Fr. Bacon " in earlier life, he used some variant of the full description towards the end.

the jaded eyes of the twentieth century as a sort of evil wraith, trailing clouds of Shakespeare in his train, declaiming in unimpeachable though unfamiliar English sentiments that seem boring to a weary generation, and wearing a nimbus, very shadowy and uneven, of natural philosophy.

*   *   *   *   *

" He sold justice," says Macaulay; and it is undeniable that he fell on the charge of accepting bribes as Lord Chancellor. But the paradox of his position is that he would not have fallen if he had accepted bribes. The satisfied purchaser does not object. Aubrey, Egerton, and Lady Wharton, the petitioners against him, had lost their cases. It is true that either directly or indirectly he took gifts from litigants; but no one has been able to show that his judgments were unjust. Bacon himself, an old man at the time and all too well aware that the end of his public life had come, pleaded guilty and cast himself on the mercy of his judges. But to take this as evidence against him, on the plea that if he had admitted so deep a guilt without deserving it he were mean indeed, argues too great a zeal to pass judgment. He knew that it was his own and his friends' importunities and not his gifts which had won his position; and Buckingham's behaviour in the matter of his brother and Coke's daughter, when Bacon's action had the fullest justification, showed how slack was his grasp upon the Great Seal. He had witnessed the ruin of many another in an age dominated by capricious majesty. He attempted to make the best bargain he could; and, in fact, he achieved his aim.

Throughout his life Bacon had been short of money. He was not bred to penury. The son of the Lord Keeper, acquainted with the Court from his boyhood, he never came to terms with the actual conditions of his life. Elizabeth called him her " little Lord Keeper "; but though, in later years, he kept the Great Seal, he could never keep accounts. He was twice imprisoned for debt. Once he was seized as he left the Tower, where he had been engaged on the Queen's business; and his perversity saw in this only a subject of grievance against his debtors. At his marriage he would have been accounted a rich man even on modern standards. But he loved to live sumptuously. He gave lavishly. In fact, he never lived within his means; and the consequent slavery persisted even when he was Lord Chancellor. He accepted presents. In the *New Atlantis* he makes an official who is offered a gift protest that he " must not be twice paid for one labour." No such scruple weighed with Bacon; and in the end he paid for his looseness by his downfall.

He paid even more, since that terrible disgrace put a lifetime of public service into eclipse. It was hard service, almost forced on the Government, rarely sought, for long ill-rewarded and never wholly welcomed. At sixteen he had left Cambridge, and was already at the Paris Embassy, turning his opportunities to good account. Three years later his father died, and he found himself compelled to earn his living. He importuned Burghley for some post such as his birth and gifts deserved; but Burghley had a son and saw no point in launching so talented a rival. At twenty-one he was admitted at Gray's Inn as an utter barrister, and two years later he began his long connection with Parliament.

There are memoranda from his pen during these years, which show how seriously he took himself and how great a loss it was to the kingdom that he had no position to compel consideration for his counsel. His " Letter of Advice to Queen Elizabeth " and his " Advertisement touching the controversies of the Church of England " are stamped with a wisdom in advance of his time. The Queen was at first favourably disposed towards him; but the clash came early. He began to catch the ear of Parliament He was appointed to Committees; and in 1593 he led the opposition to an expedient which seemed to diminish the privilege of the Commons. A little later he directly opposed Sir R. Cecil on the distribution of the subsidies. This was fatal. Burghley informed him of the Queen's displeasure, and Bacon could not have been the man he was not to have appreciated the full meaning of that event. There was no question of his seeking popularity. Bacon never courted it. Under the conditions of the time he could never have won it by speeches in Parliament. And, as he said later, he did " not love the word people." Elizabeth never forgave him. When the Attorney-Generalship fell vacant the following year, it was kept dangling before him for the words of apology which never came from his lips. The next year he had another chance. The Solicitor-Generalship rose in prospect. Bacon remained impenitent. At thirty-two he had already a glittering future behind him.

* * * * *

Bacon's new friend Essex had done all he could to secure first the higher, then the lower, post for him. He spent himself in vain; he doubly spent himself in vain, for he seems even to have failed to win Bacon's gratitude. The Essex episode is less creditable to Bacon than any of his long life. It is impossible, bearing in mind his defence of Parliament with its known and measured risks, to pass the easy judgment with regard to his treatment of Essex. He was no mere place-seeker or money-snatcher. There is not the slightest reason to doubt that he welcomed the championship of Essex, as he did later of Buckingham, more to secure the platform necessary to urge the reforms he saw were necessary than for the mere sake of position. His principles were his interest. He was always a parliamentarian. Even when, later on, he felt constrained by office to defend measures that tended to support autocracy, it is on record that his advice was frankly given for wiser action. Gardiner maintains that " he was the one man capable of preventing a catastrophe by anticipating the demands of the age." But he could not secure the acceptance of his views. " The House of Commons would take part of them and James would take another part, whereas it was only in their entirety that they could exercise a healing influence." To have carried out his programme would have been " to avert the evils of the next half century."

Is it possible to regard such a man as a mere sycophant? Yet the Essex episode remains, like one of those " inevitable and stubborn facts " which Bacon was to set in their proper value. It remains to do the same service for his behaviour towards Essex. He had been Bacon's patron. On his side, at least, there is evidence of true loyalty, deep respect, and affection. On Bacon's part there was certainly no affection. Indeed, it is one of the strangest, one of the inexplicable features of his life that, from beginning to end, there is no sure evidence that he gave real affection to anyone. His brother Anthony, bright, irresponsible spirit, seems almost his exact antithesis. There is no evidence that Francis was even capable of an adventurous, unstudied action. Even his marriage was carried out like a purchase in a bargain basement. He seems to have been utterly cold and calculating. But he had the qualities of his defects. When he accepted a generous gift from Essex, he made a significant reservation : " Always it is with a saving of his faith to the

King and his other lords; and, therefore, my lord, I can be
no more yours than I was, and it must be with the ancient
savings." In his next letter to Essex he says: " I reckon
myself as a common—and as much as is lawful to be enclosed of a common, so much your lordship shall be sure to
have." There is, moreover, in one of his most ambiguous
letters of advice a pointed warning to Essex that " obedience
is better than sacrifice."

It is intelligible, therefore, that he should have dis-
sociated himself from Essex when the latter plunged to
disaster. There might even be an excuse for his taking part
in the trial of Essex, if he had thought that by so doing he
could the better prevail upon the Queen to be lenient to her
old favourite. But he did not so much take a part as actually
conduct the trial. When Coke floundered and, in his
ardour, lost the thread of his argument, Bacon intervened
and, in deadly words and taunts, brought Essex to judgment.
He went further. He allowed himself to be made the
mouthpiece of the Government's justification. The terms
in which he wrote are not known, since the text was finally
edited by others. But what he did earned as full a condemnation from his contemporaries as it has from posterity;
and his apologia written later, skilfully worded as it is, fails
to acquit him.

* * * * *

There is more evidence as to character. In the month of
July 1608 he seized upon a free week to take an inventory of
his position. This private note-book, *Commentarius Solutus*,
surely one of the most amazing documents of history, bears
intrinsic evidence of being one of a series. He is forty-seven,
married, Solicitor-General. He feels his feet, at last, on the
rungs of the ladder, and sets himself to take stock of his aims,
his assets, and his chances. Day by day, throughout the
week, he puts down notes, sometimes in English, sometimes
in Latin; sometimes clear, frequently cryptic, always frank
and often cynical. There are reflections on his health and
case-notes of his bouts of indigestion. There is a careful
plan for his garden. There are estimates of his capital and
income. There are suggestions as to how he may improve
his delivery. A long memorandum deals with the " Greatness of Britain," and how it may be established and
increased. There is a section dealing with the reform of
philosophy, how it may be achieved by the help of patrons

(with names) and by the endowment of schools of research at the Universities. And there are reflections as to the better establishment of his own position; and these are devastating in their frankness as to the King and the figures who count with him:

> " To set afoot and maintain access with His Majesty, Dean of the Chapel, May, Murray. Keeping a course of access at the beginning of every term and vacation with a memorial. To attend sometime his repasts or to fall into a course of familiar discourse. To find means to win a conceit, not open but private, of being affectionate but assured to the Scotch, and fit to succeed Salisbury in his marriage in that kind; Lord Dunbar, Duke of Lennox, and Daubiny: secret."
>
> " To correspond with Salisbury in a habit of natural but no ways perilous boldness, and in vivacity, invention, care to cast and enterprise (but with due caution), for this manner I judge both in his nature freeth the stands, and in his ends pleaseth him best and promiseth more use of me . . .
>
> " To furnish my L. of S. with ornaments for public speeches. To make him think how he should be reverenced by a Lord Chancellor, if I were; Princelike."
>
> " To prepare him for matters to be handled in Council or before the King aforehand, and to show him and yield him the fruits of my care."

There are notes as to how he may advance himself by disparagement of the Attorney-General: " To have in mind and use the Attorney-General's weakness " (there follows a list). " Too full of cases and distinctions—Nibbling solemnly; he distinguisheth but apprehends not." " No gift with his pen in proclamations and the like." In the margin he notes: " Solemn goose. Stately, leastwise nodd, crafty."

Here are magnificent projects and mean expedients, spacious dreams and narrow aims, splendid ideas and petty shifts. Bacon's admirers urge, quite soundly, that habit and custom are not set down: it is the unfamiliar. They suggest that Bacon would not have needed to remind himself of such ambiguous courses if they had been natural to him, if, in fine, he had not to school himself to them. It is certain that the reader, coming upon this strange document, and reading

Bacon's plans to worm himself into power, will be more disturbed than when he realises, on analysis of the characters of the time, that they were the common currency of the successful. It is unjust. Bacon conceived himself pledged to, because inspired by, a great mission, and experience shows that idealists are not infrequently coarse feeders, little apt to look askance at garbage that would revolt men of commoner clay.

*　　*　　*　　*　　*

It is pleasanter to turn to Bacon's true passport to the Commonwealth of ideas. Men die, ideas fructify. In sending to Sir Thomas Bodley (1605) his *Two Books of the Advancement of Learning*, Bacon wrote:

> " I think no man may more truly say with the Psalm *Multum incola fuit anima mea.* For I do confess since I was of any understanding my mind hath in effect been absent from that I have done; and in that absence are many errors which I acknowledge; and, among them, this great one which led to the rest; that knowing myself by inward calling to be fitter to hold a book than to play a part, I have led my life in civil causes for which I was not very fit by nature and more unfit by the preoccupation of my mind. Therefore, calling myself home, I have now enjoyed myself."

These words which recur in his letters, in one form or another, give the key to his life. He wrote a few years later: " Itaque magis videor cum antiquis versari quam cum his quibuscum vivo." He was out of his time, out of his place. When quite young he had written to Burghley: " I have taken all knowledge to be my province "; and, in the preface to a work on the " Interpretation of Nature," written about the first year of the reign of King James, he wrote:

> " For myself, I find that I was fitted for nothing so well as for the study of Truth; as having a mind nimble and versatile enough to catch the resemblance of things (which is the chief point) and, at the same time, steady enough to fix and distinguish their subtle differences; as being gifted by nature with desire to seek, patience to doubt, fondness to meditate, slowness to assert, readi-

633

ness to reconsider, carefulness to dispose and set in order; and as being a man that neither affects what is new nor admires what is old, and that hates every kind of imposture. So I thought my nature had a kind of familiarity and relationship with Truth."

It would be unwise to take these words at their full face value. Something must be allowed for weariness in the pursuit of power which could only have seemed at times a will-o'-the-wisp. To conclude that Bacon was a mere misfit would be to misjudge his dimensions completely. If he did not leave the same mark upon polity that he did on philosophy, it is owing to the fact that his public life was at the mercy of autocratic monarchs who never failed to find counsellors to present the easy course even when it was perilous. Gardiner holds that his policy would have prevented the Civil War with all its attendant evils; and in his legal life there is such evidence of a grasp of essentials that it is clear there, too, his service might have been memorable if he could have had his way. His words imply a sort of nostalgia for another life for which he felt himself supremely fitted.

Of the much that he wrote, three main streams may be selected. There are his historical works represented by his *History of Henry VII*, and *In felicem memoriam Elizabethæ*; his *Essays*, the best known of his writings; and his philosophical work, *The Great Instauration*. There are also some religious works, among which may be noted the prayers he wrote towards the end of his life. Of one of them Addison said: "For elevation of thought and greatness of expression, it seems rather the devotion of an angel than of a man."

His historical work would have received more attention if he had left no other monument to his memory. Throughout it all, indeed, in all his work, there is evidence of a mind that in his time and country had no peer. He draws attention to the significant and his purpose went no farther.

The *Essays*, issued and reissued during his life, remain his most widely known and popular work. The final edition, published the year before his death, contains sixty essays, including the fragment on fame and the noble reflections on death. They are written with an easy mastery of language, with an extraordinary repertoire of apt illustrations, with the severest compression, and with an inimitable style.

With an opening sentence he is in the heart of his subject and has riveted the attention. "Virtue is like precious odours, most fragrant when they are crushed." "Men in great place are thrice servants." "He that hath wife and children, hath given hostages to fortune." "We take cunning for a sinister or crooked wisdom." "As the births of living creatures at first are ill-shapen: so are all innovations, which are the births of time." "Suspicions amongst thoughts are like bats among birds, they ever fly by twilight." "Nature is often hidden, sometimes overcome, seldom extinguished."

It is astonishing what a quarry they form for clichés and quotations. Some of his *bons mots* might have been made by the Wilde young men of a generation ago: no doubt they were. "There be not two more fortunate properties, than to have a little of the fool, and not too much of the honest." "Wives are young men's mistresses; companions for middle-age; and old men's nurses." But whether they are wise or cynical, his phrases are always apt, and represent the finest economy in the use of words. For the most part the essays are short. They take up a thought, develop it, illustrate it, and clinch it either by some telling quotation (or misquotation) or by some illuminating epigram. The first ten, issued at a comparatively early age, read more like a code for courtiers. They abound in sage advice, written tersely, almost like notes. It was on finding them popular that he took them in hand to prune and perfect them. In their final form they give a reflection of the world as he saw it, and provide a sure though incomplete insight into his own life. What can be more significant than his warning against love: "By how much the more men ought to beware of this passion, which loseth not only other things but itself." Or this: "Fame is like a river, that beareth up things light and swoln, and drowns things weighty and solid." Or this: "The errors of young men are the ruin of business; but the errors of aged men amount but to this, that more might have been done or sooner."

This, at least, will be admitted of the *Essays*, that, from beginning to end, there is scarcely a sentence that is not significant, hardly a superfluous word, rarely a dead one, much that is pointed and wise, a great deal that is noble.

* * * * *

But it is by his philosophical and scientific work Bacon will be remembered; and, in effect, he wrote but one book, *The Great Instauration*. On this theme his mind did not so much advance as revolve. He completed now one part, now another, writing and re-writing: " And, after my manner, I alter when I add so that nothing is finished till all be finished." Of the *Novum Organum* there were at least twelve drafts, and it remains the most carefully written of his philosophical works. But all of his scientific writings fall into the scheme, either as an instinctive or as a deliberate draft of some part of the *great restoration of knowledge*. The *Novum Organum* has for its title *Francisci de Verulamio . . . Instauratio Magna*, with a sub-title, *Pars secunda operis quæ dicitur Novum Organum sive indicia vera de interpretatione naturæ.* There were, in fact, six sections of *The Great Instauration;* and four separately published studies form part of the third section. The *Sylva Sylvarum*, with its conspectus of the odd and, at times, the absurd, was one of these, as was the *Historia Veterum* which, during his life and for many years after, was, after the *Essays*, the most popular of his works. *The Advancement of Learning* (1605) does not appear to have been written as part of the great work; but the *De Augmentis*, the revised and enlarged Latin edition (1623), was designed as an integral part of it.

No just measure of Bacon's genius—and it was generously admitted by Leibnitz, Hume, and Kant—can be gained unless this fact is borne steadily in mind. Though he scolds the Schoolmen, it was from them he inherited the magnificent insolence to set about a reasoned survey of all knowledge. The *Novum Organum* (in contradistinction to the Aristotelian *Organum*) is merely the most famous chapter of the tremendous whole he set out to produce, though lack of strength and opportunity prevented the completion of more than part.

There is an arresting modernity about his declared aim. It is, perhaps, natural that one who, born in the Strand, on the fringes of the Court, lived all his life at the centre of practical affairs, should have conceived it as severely practical. But it is none the less remarkable, since his own mind was essentially speculative and stamped with an insatiable curiosity. He lays it down definitely that the only appropriate end of scientific enquiry is *to enlarge the empire of man over nature*. The words he wrote then might have been written to-day or to-morrow. He saw in the womb of nature a life for everyone incredibly richer, fuller, and freer; and his labour was devoted to its surest and speediest delivery.

This new dominion was to be acquired by a more whole-hearted and universal attention to "irreducible and stubborn facts." Harvey was at that very moment building such observations into one of the cardinal generalisations of physiology. But to Bacon's outlook that would have been almost a parochial affair. His vision saw facts being collected on all sides, in every branch of knowledge. He saw them being placed in systematic order with the main attention on the essential natures of things; and carefully analysed with a mind, liberated from the four tyrannies (idola) which tend to lead it astray. The tyranny of the tribe; the tyranny of training; the tyranny of terms, and the tyranny of theories—all fetter the mind so that it cannot judge freely. His new method was to be a " true induction," and Bacon is at pains to make it clear that he is advocating a *new* method, " by means never hitherto attempted."

His actual contribution to philosophy is his insistence upon experiment, the requisite attention to " irreducible and stubborn facts," and a true induction from observation. Around each of these points a fable has grown which tends to obscure Bacon's contribution. He lays down elaborate rules for inductive logic, and most of the criticisms that have been urged against his suggestions appear to be founded upon the examination of some small part of his work without taking into consideration the whole to which it is subordinate. " Inductive logic," says Fowler, at the time professor of Logic at Oxford, " that is the systematic analysis and arrangement of inductive evidence, as distinct from the natural induction which all men practise, is almost as much the creation of Bacon as deductive logic is that of Aristotle." This statement will stand the test of time.

It is urged that induction was actually practised before Bacon's time, and was being used independently of him while he lived. The same may be said of deduction and Aristotle. It is urged, with more force, that induction is a more complex process than Bacon thought. He appeared to hold that if there were a sufficiency of observations the generalisations would become evident of themselves. It is mainly appearance; but in so far as his words are ambiguous it is well to remember that he also wrote: " We, who regard the mind, not only in respect to its own faculties, but also in its relation to things, ought to hold that the art of discovery may advance as discoveries advance." This statement seems to forestall the caustic commentary of De Morgan that it is the prime function of observations to test theories and not to advance them. Bacon has some harsh things to say of that method as it was applied in his day. It was not the instrument of advancing science so much as of raising pseudo-science to a position in which it merely stifled enquiry.

He has been challenged for his advocacy of " random " experiment and observation. The passage from the *New Atlantis* upon which this criticism is founded gives no ground for objection. A careful reading suggests that the critics have read into the words the meaning they expected to find. The actual words, making due allowance for the necessary changes of usage, might serve as the general prospectus of a universal research laboratory. And much nonsense has been written about " random " observation. It is, in fact, almost impossible to carry out a series of completely random experiments. Anyone conversant with scientific research knows this from experience. Men can no more divest themselves of reason than they can of the tendency to fatigue. Each is a purely human attribute. Reason seeks coherence, seeks to follow a thread. Moreover, the uselessness of " random " observation is exaggerated, since it is obvious that the evidential character is the end and not the beginning of research. And finally, such a theory as evolution must owe much to what is strictly called " random " observation. There is but one point which appears to support the suggestion that Bacon advocated completely random experiment. He certainly differentiated the rôle of the observer from that of the maker of theory. Actual experience verifies that distinction every day.

What Bacon set out to do was to indicate a method— the *Novum Organum*—and to provide a conspectus of knowledge which had some sanction of authority. The *Sylva Sylvarum*, despite its obvious errors and limitations, was almost certainly the best summary of the kind in existence at the time. It is true that he depreciated pure mathematics; but there are at least some eminent philosophers of to-day who would enthusiastically approve his relegation of the science to a purely ancillary rôle. He saw quite correctly the promising field physics offers to " mixed," or as a modern would say " applied mathematics." This is the more remarkable, since he was ignorant of Kepler's work, which was being published at the time. He was unsympathetic to the Copernican theory, which was launched some years before his birth. He shows no knowledge of Harvey's great discovery, and he knew apparently only the less significant parts of Galileo's work, though both men were his contemporaries.

It is evident there were gaps in his knowledge and defects in his reaction. But the admission would be superfluous in a lesser man. The factor of *quantity* seems strangely absent from his work, though there is internal evidence in his writings that he was not ignorant of mathematical analysis. In casting off the trammels of deductive philosophy, he depreciated the value of hypothesis. He was dealing with its actual use at the time; and the great discovery of the age which followed was the discovery of how to make discoveries. It came, as he had suggested, through the aggregation of discoveries. Indeed, scattered about his writings, there is a sufficient number of flying sentences to make the fame of a generation of philosophers. But, in the end, he may be best remembered by the vision he drew from Albertus Magnus of an ordered universe of knowledge which the " generalist " shall evolve from the narrow concentration of the specialist. Some such integration is the work of to-morrow; and there are numerous signs that the thinkers of to-day are as alive to its practical as to its speculative importance. Bacon, in that respect, was a path breaker.

His mental energy never flagged. Yet he was sickly from his youth, and, in maturity, suffered much from bouts of indigestion which sometimes incapacitated him. At fifty he was already finding " this muscovia weather . . . a little too hard for my constitution." He died of bronchitis. He was driving near Highgate, towards the end of March, when he left his coach to gather up some snow in order to stuff a fowl to see how far he might thereby arrest putrefaction. He caught a chill; and so died as the result of an attempt to satisfy his insatiable curiosity.

Bacon was always extremely honest with himself. In sending his *Cogitata et Visa* to Bishop Andrewes, whom he calls his Inquisitor, he wrote:

" And though for the matter itself my judgment be in some things fixed, and not accessible to any man's judgment that goeth not my way: yet even in those things, the admonition of a friend may make me express myself diversely."

This is the secret thought of every man of ability; the admission merely argues more honesty on Bacon's part. He was no better and no worse than many idealists, ever less careful of the means than of the end. But he left a greater legacy to posterity.

* * * * *

" *Death* hath this also, that it openeth the gate to good fame, and extinguisheth envy: *Extinctus amabitur idem.*" [From the *Essay* on Death.]

BEN JONSON

1572–1637

By

ENID GLEN

BEN JONSON

by ENID GLEN

MORE is known about Ben Jonson than about any other Elizabethan dramatist, many details of his life, his way of writing, his appearance, given to us by his own self-assertiveness, and by the hatred, devotion, and awed respect of his contemporaries; and the impression they leave is the one most men have of him to-day, powerful and un-sympathetic—the too energetic reformer, the critic and dictator. The memorial verses collected six months after his death speak for the most part of the strictness and learning of his Muse, and of his service to English, many of them timidly written, as if he might rise to reproach the poets for their unpolished verses; the traditions which spring up a little later, with still more details of his brave swaggering, his slow and laborious writing, his learning, strengthen the impression; Dryden in the next age, it is true, writes of his work with understanding and care; but most later criticism covers up the man and the artist under the qualities of "strong sense and painful industry."

He is the last of the great Tudors; certain Elizabethan precepts are to him living principles, and this accounts for the seriousness and austerity, and the energy, of his work; its splendour and sombreness, and its curious method, are peculiarly part of the mood and manner of writing of the end of the Elizabethan age and the beginning of the Jacobean.

He devotes his life and work to the Renaissance belief in the dignity and immortality of poetry, "fit to be seen of none but grave and consecrated eyes"; like Sidney he believes that poetry has to do with virtuous action, and not only that its aim is to teach and delight, but that the man who writes must be worthy, that the whole effort of his spirit and mind must be "laboured and distill'd" into his work so that those who read it "may breathe his spirit out of him"

24*   643

and use it to live well. So he rejects the romantic and unnatural writing of his time, hates the servile imitation of other poets he finds in it, and tries a new, more truthful vein ; he is exasperated by " doubtfull writing " and will have nothing easily done—he blames the man who writes all he can, and prefers in poetry what he finds in Bacon's oratory : " No man . . . suffered less emptiness, less idleness, in what he uttered "—a style from which " you can take nothing away without loss, and that loss . . . manifest."

His ideal in man is the Renaissance " Senecal man," standing square, self-controlled, unmoved by circumstance because he has, with the help of learning (in this function of learning Sidney and Bacon also believed), complete self-knowledge. He says : " I know no disease of the soul but ignorance, not of the arts and sciences, but of itself " and speaks of the " true measure of oneselfe that everie man ought to make " ; he had by heart and quotes in part several times in his plays Sir Henry Wotton's verses of the man who is " lord of himselfe " and " whose passions not his masters are." He would like to be such a man himself, and most vigorously maintains his all roundness and self-control at the times when he is most in danger of losing them, as in the portraits of himself as Crites and Horace in the Stage Quarrel plays. He watches himself : he writes to Sackville

> " I have a list of mine own faults to know
> Look to, and cure."

and

> " Men have been great, but never good, by chance."

He is impatient of those who misspend their time, who live trivial unconscious lives, of the modern who believes that " nought that delights is sinne," of the man who is " a mere impertinent " in conversation. It is true that like many men with a high intellectual and moral standard, and insufficient love, he sees men's failings more clearly than their virtues ; and true, too, that sometimes the severity of his judgment is exaggerated against men who have failed to understand him, have accused him of not being what he most wishes to be ; but there is always a basis of truth in his criticism. That he could justly distinguish truth from falsity is clear from the fine and careful discrimination in the whole tone of his work ; it comes out sometimes in the exactness of his descriptions of men—the " heroic ample thoughts " of Digby (" Other soules, to his, dwelt in a lane ") and the grave and high Camden; and no one has perceived and described casuistry more acutely than he. His rare praise is the more valuable: his saying of Shakespeare that " there was ever more in him to be praised than pardoned "[1] is seen in its right proportion, and his love of Bacon is made still more moving:

> " I have and do reverence him, for the greatness that was only proper to himself, in that he seemed to me ever, by his work, one of the greatest men, and most worthy of admiration, that had been in many ages. In his adversity I ever praied that God would give him strength: for greatness he could not want. Neither could I condole in a word or syllable with him, as knowing no accident could do harm to virtue, but rather help to make it manifest."

Two of the better known of his statements to Drummond are particularly characteristic: that " of all stiles he loved most to be named honest, and hath of that ane hundreth letters so naming him "; and that " he heth a minde to be a churchman and so he might have favour to make one sermon to the King, he careth not what hereafter sould befall him, for he would not flatter, though he saw Death ": he was sensitive to opinion, and in his desire to be appreciated often explained aggressively what his virtues were—virtues he truly possessed; and he was impatient to share his moral convictions.

In the earlier years of his life, he spent in action the vigour and decision he put later into his writing and the maintaining of his critical opinions. After the death of his father, the " grave minister of the gospel," he was brought up poorly, but fortunately put to school by a friend at Westminster, where the great antiquary Camden was second master. His devotion to Camden, " most reverend head," lasted all his life; Jonson owed him " all that I am in arts, all that I know "; he was Camden's " alumnus olim, aeternum amicus." Camden was present on at least two great occasions of his later life: when at the time of the

---

[1] The fact that the phrase is a translation from the elder Seneca does not make it the less Jonson's own; and I have used the *Discoveries* so throughout.

plague he saw the vision of his eldest son with a bloody cross on his forehead and was persuaded by Camden that it was " ane apprehension of the fantasie," though it was proved a true prophecy; and at the banquet he gave to his friends on his release from prison in 1605.

He was taken from Westminster to work for his stepfather as a bricklayer; it is worth recording again, because his critics were apt to remember it: when twenty years after his success as a dramatist, in the city and at court, is certain, one of his Masques is considered poor, " divers thinke fit that he should returne to his ould trade of bricklaying again." He escaped from the craft he " could not endure " to take service in the Flemish wars, and he remembered with pleasure his exploit there, when in face of both the camps he killed an enemy in single combat and stripped him of his arms.

He returned from war to his "wonted studies"; contemporary allusion and later tradition say that he earned his living as a strolling player, acting mad Hieronimo's part, and then played at Paris Garden " Zulziman," a part probably full of the " scenical strutting and furious vociferation " he later wrote that he hated in Tamburlaine. Aubrey says that he was never a good actor; he always liked to declaim, as his enemies remember: " 'Tis cake and pudding to me to see his face make faces, when he reads his songs and sonnets " ; but the Duchess of Newcastle remembered that he read excellently and Overbury praised the grace of his reading.

In 1597 he was writing for Henslowe, collaboration and hackwork, but three plays of his own, and he could be praised by Meres in the next year for his work in tragedy. At this time he suffered imprisonment as maker of part of the *Isle of Dogs*, the " lewd plaie " begun by Nashe; and in 1598 he was put in prison again, on a more serious occasion which brought him " almost at the gallows," when he fought in Hoxton fields with Henslowe's actor Gabriel Spenser, and killed him: " Gabrell . . . is slayne by the hands of Bengemen Jonson bricklayer," Henslowe spitefully remarks, while Jonson remembered with pride that his sword was ten inches shorter than his adversary's.

It was during this imprisonment that " by trust of a priest " he became Roman Catholic. Twelve years afterwards he was to turn Protestant again, drinking off the full cup of wine " in token of true reconciliation "; but there are no signs of a serious conflict in his mind about the two churches; his final attitude, after years of making " humble gleanings of Divinity " for his library, was in favour of

> *" those wiser guides*
> *Whom Faction had not drawne to studie sides."*

His first great comedy, *Every Man in His Humour*, produced by the Lord Chamberlain's Company at the Curtain, was a success; but in his next three plays he was involved in the Stage Quarrel, the mainspring of it his hatred of Marston, who admired and envied him, and had dared to compare their work, and who must have appeared to Jonson a hideous parody of himself, so unlike and so like, writing in the " stalking straine " Jonson detested, a satirist, " a pretty Stoic too," and given to preaching. The gibes at his poverty and his learning roused Jonson to angry arrogance, made clear to him his beliefs and the seriousness of his work; and the wrath of London and the threat of prosecution strengthened his resolve to withdraw himself:

> *" Something . . . must . . . be sung high and aloof*
> *Safe from the wolf's black jaw, and the dull ass's hoof."*

He retired from his home to write his tragedies, to accept the hospitality of Sir Robert Townsend and of d'Aubigny.

With the accession of James his reputation was at its height: his fame as a scholar, as a maker of Masques, and from the time of the production of *Volpone* before both Universities, as a dramatist. His " conversation " was now " with men of most note "; he was acquainted with the Sidney family, with Pembroke and Salisbury, and among men-of-letters with Drayton, Donne, and Chapman; he was leader of " the right worshipful fraternite of Sirenical Gentlemen that meet the first Fridaie of every Moneth at the signe of the Mere-maide in Bread Street in London." In these years occurred the two interludes when he left England—once journeying to the Continent as tutor to Raleigh's scapegrace son, once to Scotland on foot, to be entertained in Edinburgh " with much respective love " by " Gentlemen that know his true worth," and to visit Drummond of Hawthornden.

After the death of James, his prosperity declined, with the indifference of the court, the production of poor and unsuccessful plays, the death of his friends, and the growth of " Disease the enemy." In his house at Westminster, he spent his last years in learned pursuits, collecting foreign grammars and writing letters on minutiæ of scholarship; he wrote the *Discoveries*, which " flowed out of his daily readings "; and received the visits of devoted younger " sons."

He was followed to the Abbey after his death by " all or the greatest part of the nobilitie and gentry then in the town," and he was mourned with honours greater than those accorded to any earlier English poet except Sidney.

Every Man in his Humour put into practice the Renaissance doctrine of Comedy, " a thing throughout pleasant and ridiculous, and accommodated to the correction of manners," having decorum in action, and congruity in character. Its subject was the " humours," men whose characters were thrown out of perfect balance by the predominance of one trait or quality, which wholly possessed them and influenced all their actions. In London society at the time the word was used as a term in psychological jargon, or more lightly, to describe affectations; the writing of character sketches in the manner of Theophrastus, the pictures " all . . . heightened by one shaddowing," was a literary fashion; but this more severe categorising of men, and its use in serious drama, was exactly fitted to the temper of the time.

The literature of the late fifteen-nineties to about 1614 is full of melancholy and doubt, of revolt against the age, against life itself, and the writers' troubled selves. The mood is first fully expressed in Donne's *Satires*, written from 1593 to 1597, and in Marston's *Satires* and *Scourge of Villanie* in 1598; it continues in Marston's plays, later to some extent in Chapman's, and as late as the work of Webster and Tourneur. The objects of the satire are the old ones—women and lawyers, clergy and courtiers; the melancholy figures in the plays are based on types made familiar in the psychological and pseudo-psychological writings of the time, and become sometimes a convention handed on from one dramatist to the next; at times the adoption of melancholy is a pose; but the prevalence of the mood is extraordinary, and on the whole it is bitterly sincere. There are reasons for it probably in the uncertain political and economic state of the country, the depression in trade after the wars, the difficulty, especially for educated men, in getting employment; or partly perhaps in the unsettling and disconcerting new discoveries in science, the Copernican theory which removes earth from the centre: " The new Philosophy calls in doubt . . . the Sun is lost and th'Earth . . . tis all in peeces." But whatever the reasons in the contemporary world, there is nothing in earlier or later literature stronger, more vivid, and more complex than the treatment at this time of the themes of disillusion, of evil, and death.

The writers hate especially hypocrisy, and see it everywhere: in conventions and fashions, everywhere " painted jays with a deal of outside," in the false presumption of rank—for " we are all the sons of heaven though a tripe-wife be our mother,"—and where it should least be, in the church, " that publike place of much dissimulation." They furiously search for truth in themselves, too, always with self-consciousness and scepticism, the intellect meddling at every turn: it is no exaggeration, or romantic hypothesis, to see in Marston's plays the evidence of his long personal struggle with self-distrust, his restless fear of being consoled by what may be only partly true; and there is the same tormented honesty and self-insight in certain of Donne's *Songs and Sonets* and his divine poems.

The mood is often one of disgust at the futility of life, Hamlet's " What is the quintessence of dust? man delights not me "; or a detached and passionate view of the whole of life, the procession of its miseries, the mood of Shakespeare's sonnet " Tir'd with all these," of Hamlet's catalogue of the " whips and scorns of time," of Marston's description of the world as a dunghill, and of Webster's plays with their atmosphere of the " shaddowe or deep pit of darkenesse " in which mankind walks.

The Malcontent of the plays, sometimes seriously, sometimes mockingly, presented, stands self-consciously apart from life to comment on it, alternately despising and pitying men, analysing their motives ruthlessly, but unable to solve his own conflict: " The elements struggle within him: his owne soule is at variance within herselfe." He has been a libertine, and a scholar; he tries the life of the senses, but is quickly disillusioned by the decay of beauty and the blunting of the mind; he surveys the field of learning, but finds nothing permanently true there. His ideal is often the unfeeling, unknowing fool—Feliche and Malevole and Jaques delight in him; while others praise with Hamlet the Senecal man:

> " bless'd are those
> Whose blood and judgment are so well commingled
> That they are not a pipe for fortune's finger
> To sound what stop she please."

Sometimes even Stoicism will not bear their scrupulous examination: Marston's Malcontent cries of Seneca:
" Out upon him, he writ of Temperance and Fortitude, yet lived like a voluptuous Epicure, and died like an effeminate coward."

Pyrrho's " opinion " and the scepticism of Montaigne they find more acceptable:

> " There's nothing good or bad but thinking makes it so,"

Hamlet says; and Donne

> " There's nothing simply good, nor ill, alone,
> .   .   .   .   .
> The onely measure is, and judge, opinion " ;

and the conclusion is that of Chapman's hero, that chance rules the world. Marston rejects even this: it is praised as a way of life in the *Dutch Courtesan,* but in the later *Fawn and Sophonisba* only the villains reason in Montaigne's manner.

Hamlet is the perfect type of the Malcontent: his tragedy is partly that he sees too truly in a world of ordinary unthinking people who live by commonplaces; and partly that he confounds the particular and the general: " Frailty thy name is woman." It is a common error of the Malcontent; its comic aspect is seen in Jaques, who, on the hint of the Duke's sympathy with the " woful pageants " of the world, reduces all the varieties of mankind to seven ages.

In personality and temperament, Ben Jonson is unlike these writers; he expresses his resolve, in words as vehement as theirs,

> " to strip the ragged follies of the time
> Naked as at their birth,"

650

and once begins, in Macilente, the portrait of a Malcontent; in the Stage Quarrel plays there is anger and querulousness which makes strange disproportion in the form, and *Every Man Out of his Humour* is a curiosity of self-consciousness; but his real resemblance to these contemporaries is in the tone of his work, the brutal, direct, and unsentimental representation of all the shades of knavery, and the closeness to the life of the time, not only in his "deeds and language such as men do use," but in the completeness of the satire, impregnating every detail of the plays. His thoroughly conscious intellectual control makes his work in a way greater than most of theirs, though it is not as moving.

In much of the contemporary writing there is a new intellectual stiffening; it is epigrammatic, or the imagination is controlled by the intellect:

> " *Man is a tree that hath no top in cares*
> *No root in comforts.*"

The relation of intellect and emotion is interesting; it is finest in the metaphysical style, where strong feeling speeds up the intricate mental processes, driving on the mind so that the obvious links between associations are lost, and the images can be disentangled only by painful thought, though the imaginative meaning of the whole is instantly felt, with an added thrill of pleasure from the adumbrated movements of the mind: such are Donne's

> " *and all your graces no more use shall have*
> *Than a Sun Diall in a grave.*"

and Webster's

> " *how long have I beheld the devil in crystall?* "

In drama, sometimes the intellect is most strongly at work, as in Chapman's plays, where the people and the action are in the background, and only their shadows move across the nearer world of ideas; or intellect and feeling work on each other with fine imaginative and dramatic effect: a passion is not expressed headlong, lyrically, as in Marlowe, but the chief delight is in the anatomising of it, as in the

careful unfolding of Beatrice-Joanna's descent into depravity in Middleton's *Changeling*.

The distinction between comedy and tragedy is often
lost; in Marston's plays the result is a curious and unpleasant anomaly; but often a kind of play new in the
Elizabethan age, and very great, is produced : the method
is that of comedy, the final effect is decided from the outside,
or sometimes the whole based on an idea ; and the characters
and situations are consciously grouped according to the plan
or the idea ; yet the whole is steeped in tragic feeling, and the
effect is terrible and superb. *Measure for Measure* is one of
these plays, and *Volpone* another.

All Jonson's plays are full of a great vigour and delicacy of
the mind, the smallest detail worked on, and surely and
wittily placed in its right proportion to the whole. His
comedies are not like Shakespeare's, related to the whole of
life, with their final meaning as inconclusive as life, but each
is self-contained and is perfectly proportioned within its set
limits. Even in the matter of superficial unity, Jonson's
difficulties were great, given his subject of many different
" humours." When Shakespeare gives *As You Like It* the
theme of " All nature in love is mortal in folly," he places
Rosalind in the centre as the embodiment of normal love,
and everyone in the play, ranging from the extreme of
Jaques, who despises love, through the romantic Orlando
to the nadir of common sense in Touchstone's love, is
confronted and tested by her standard. Jonson can have
no such embodiment of a standard. But he solves the
difficulty by his settings in the atmosphere of contemporary
London, by his use of the Unities—the excellent choice of a
situation and a moment in the *Alchemist*—and in *Volpone*,
where his method is superficially nearest Shakespeare's, by
colouring the whole play with a single passion, the lust for
gold, all characters partaking of it in different degrees.

In *Every Man in his Humour* the background is not rich
enough yet, the light over the whole is bleak. The movement of the play is too slow at first, with soliloquy and
sparse scenes, for the briskness of the end, and too staccato,
and the high spirits are unevenly divided. But Jonson
is mature and certain here in his best contrivance, the
grouping and contrasting of the " humours " so that each
gives life and meaning to the other; the shallow fools throw
into relief the men deeply deceived by their folly; Matthew

and Stephen, with their affected melancholy, take tobacco with the soldier Bobadil, who ruminates in lofty gloom on the details of his past exploits, and Cob's loud honest and absurd outburst of jealousy follows immediately on Kitely's jealous fit, and shows how seriously comic and comically serious it is.

And even this most neatly, barely planned of Jonson's plays is far from being merely " a scholar's excogitation of the comic." It has the taste for nonsense, for inconsequentiality, that is in all his comedy, and his fine ear for the exact turns of speech of different kinds of men—only Chaucer has a finer; and it has one of the best examples of the imaginative understanding for which Jonson is too seldom given credit—when he makes Kitely argue with painstaking, unhurried logic within the increasing storm of his jealousy.

In *Epicœne* and in *Bartholomew Fair* the atmosphere is the whole action. For craftsmanship, *Epicœne* is perhaps, as Dryden thought, Jonson's greatest work; but the skill with which episodes and humours are manœuvred in their places is lost sight of, dissolved, like every other element in the play, in the perfectly sustained atmosphere of light-heartedness. The effortless witty talk, Jonson's " very good conversation," goes on and on, with no apparent selection: Morose sits up in a " whole nest of nightcaps " and devises ingenious ways of preventing noise, he and Truewit antiphonally curse the barber, Truewit discourses on the thousand miseries of marriage. It is as dexterous and as thorough in detail as the writing of the Elizabethan pamphleteers, and much smoother and gayer. Nothing sensible or of the real world disturbs this atmosphere, and any absurdity is possible in it : a nonsensical theme which in any less fluent environment would have the sharp lines of farce, and humours which apart from the setting would lean too far towards grotesqueness.

Bartholomew Fair is in the spirit of the coarse practical " jests " Jonson told to Drummond, and the energy and virility of Jonson's personality, his tremendous love of life, are poured out in the confusion of the Fair. Every detail is so distinct and sharp that the canvas appears almost too crowded, too brilliant. A little knot of people moves in the foreground, the citizen and his wife and mother-in-law, drawn in the natural humorous manner of mid-Jacobean comedy, like the citizen and wife in the *Knight of the Burning*

Pestle; the rest of the men and women are vigorously alive in the world of the Fair; not one of them, though none is a type or two-dimensional only, could survive outside it. Among them are the kinds Jonson rejoiced in most, the vapid complete fool, the Puritans who love to hear their own voices, and the man who affects learning: " Of all beasts I love the serious ass; he that takes pains to be one."

The richness and unity of the *Alchemist* is more difficult to account for. It is written with great zest and enjoyment, from the violent beginning with the rogues' quarrels to the downfall of common sense in Surly, and the triumph of knavery; with a romantic delight in the realistic details which is like Dickens'; and with a mind working at great speed, through the ingenuities of the villains, their quick turns to meet quickly contrived difficulties. The effect of closeness and compression is entirely Jacobean; every figure, the druggist, the woman of the town, the gallant, is of great size and distinctness in a small world; the real humours are wholly interdependent and at every encounter cast on each other deeper shades of meaning. Mammon has the humour of Marlowe's Jew of Malta, the lust for riches; beside the superficial humours he is as powerful and harsh as the Jew, by contact with the subtle hypocrisies of the Alchemist and the Puritan, he is seen to be naïve and very near to madness. Three hypocrites meet, and there is a nice study in casuistries and in Puritans: Tribulation Wholesome piously splitting hairs, Ananias breaking in with his idiotic obstinacy, and Subtle answering their scruples with wickedly apt argument.

The poetry in which Mammon describes the splendours of his desires is Jacobean: in Marlowe the imagination is diffused in patterned lyrics, here it is penetrating, with full sensuous enjoyment of every detail:

> " *Dishes of agat set in gold, and studded*
> *With emeralds, sapphires, hyacinths and rubies.*
> *The tongues of carps, dormice, and camel's heels,*
> *Boil'd in the spirit of sol, and dissolv'd pearl.*"

And instead of the broad savagery of the Jew:

> " *I walk abroad o' nights*
> *And kill sick people groaning under walls,*"

there is **Mammon's** bitterness:

> *" I'll have no bawds*
> *But fathers and mothers; they will do it best*
> *Best of all others."*

So in the whole of *Volpone* the evil and luxury of Renaissance Italy is shown from the inside; the characters emerge from its darkness, Volpone, the closest embodiment of the passion of greed, looming largest; and the play progresses within it from one great scene to the next. Some scenes have the contrivances, the ingenious logic, of comedy: the first, in which avarice gradually takes on a darker shade with the succession of the characters, from Voltore, to Corbaccio, then to Corvino who will not stop at murder, has a doubling and trebling of hatred and deception, Volpone mocking the suitors, they mocking each other, Mosca mocking Volpone to his face and behind his back; and in the splendid confusion of the last court scene there is narrow intricate order, as betrayal follows betrayal. The sharp horror of the attempted rape is purely tragic, the atmosphere of the play at its highest point; the making of the will is like a scene in Balzac, its cold depravity and its detail—the crowding in of the suitors, and Corbaccio, " old glazen eyes," waiting his turn.

The poetry of the play is magnificently appropriate, with its conjuror and devil, jewels and starlight, the Ægyptian Queen and Lollia Paulina. And Volpone's

> *" milk of unicorns and panther's breath*
> *Gathered in bags ",*

like Chapman's " Armenian dragons " and " mooncalves with white faces," is more " strange and farre removed " than anything in Marlowe.

Volpone and the part of Kitely in *Every Man in his Humour* make it seem entirely possible that Jonson wrote the additions to Kyd's *Spanish Tragedy* for which he was apparently paid, but which are usually thought to be too much in the vein of high tragedy to be his. Kyd's chiming, artificial lines are broken up into abrupt naked words, the painted passion of his tragedy, its lack of dimension, gives place to intensity of feeling, despair, and terror. It is the best of the many contemporary studies of madness, showing its swift changes of mood, from apathy to violence, its repetitions and irrelevancies, and the dreadful foundation of all the moods, to which they always return—the vision of the tree with the hanged man on it. The completeness of the treatment is like Jonson's work; the slow, thorough, bitter discourse on what a son is, is like his writing, and so is, in the prose, the rapidity and the spareness.

His own two tragedies he wrote with the Renaissance aim of " dignity . . . gravity and height." They are on a large simple scale, which is Elizabethan rather than Jacobean. In *Sejanus* the movement is slow and grave, straightforward through simple incident and repetition of incident. Everything is heightened, but not in the lyrical rushing manner of Marloweian tragedy; Silius, Sejanus, Tiberius, are equally colossal; the changing treacheries of Tiberius are arabesques in the stone; there is no sudden downfall, but Sejanus, accumulating power, topples over with his own weight. *Catiline* is greater; it has the size and sweep of epic. The places, the customs, the riches of Rome, are packed into little space; there is epic clearness of outline and strength in the moving orations before battle, and in the third act, where Cicero on one side, Catiline on the other, tower above their minions, directing, seeing and judging all. Nowhere, except occasionally in Milton, has learning been more magnificently used in art; the Ancients are so loved and understood that they are completely absorbed and assimilated, and Jonson speaks with their voice and his own, with the elaborate care and sobriety of Cicero, and Cæsar's even directness.

The style of both plays is rhetorical, more like Elizabethan Senecan than Jacobean tragedy; but it is the voice of the orator, not, as in Marlowe's rhetoric, of the actor, that one hears. Sometimes the height and simplicity convey a tragic heaviness of import:

> " *Shake off the loosen'd globe from her long hinge*
> *Roll all the world in darkness* "

and

> " *Slaughter bestrid the streets and stretch'd himself*
> *To seem more huge;* "

and in the beginning of *Catiline* when Sylla's ghost speaks, a powerful sense of dread:

"Dost thou not feel me Rome? not yet! is night
So heavy on thee?"

The verse of the tragedies is at times, like that of the comedies, a direct, plain, and sufficient style, with the tones of the speaking voice in it. There is richer compression and a more austere rhythm in Jonson's prose than in the verse of his plays. In the *Discoveries* he writes:

" Have I not seen the pomp of a whole kingdom, and what a foreign king could bring hither? Also to make himself gazed and wondered at, laid forth as it were to the shew, and vanish away in a day? . . . The bravery was shewne, it was not possessed, while it boasted itself, it perished."

In the *Staple of News* this becomes:

" Say, that you were the emperor of pleasure,

And had the pomp of all the courts, and kingdoms,
Laid forth unto the shew, to make yourself
Gazed and admired at; you must go to bed,
And take your natural rest: then all this vanisheth.
Your bravery was but shewn, 'twas not possest:
While it did boast itself, it was then perishing."

It is exactly the reverse of what Webster does when he points and heightens in his dramatic verse the prose of Montaigne or of Sidney.

In lyric poetry Jonson particularly admired, besides those verses which he chose for their meaning—Southwell's *Burning Babe* and Wotton's poem—some of the *Shepheardes Calender,* Donne's lines in the *Calme,* and his *Lost Chaine,* and he wrote a few of his own Elegies in the neat, involved, quick style of this poem. But he is rarely metaphysical in his lyrics; some are purely Elizabethan: those written for music, the Echo Song in *Cynthia's Revels* and the three songs to dance to in the Masque *Love Restored,* with the sound of the instruments in the words; his last piece of poetry, the *Sad Shepherd,* spontaneous, gentle, and romantic, with its " span-long elves that dance about a pool " and English country scenes ; verses like

" Have you seen but a bright lily grow,
Before rude hands have touched it?
Have you marked but the fall of the snow
Before the soil hath smutched it?
Have you felt the wool of the bever
Or swans down ever?
Or have smelt o' the bud of the briar?
Or the nard in the fire?
Or have tasted the bag of the bee?
O so white, O so soft, O so sweet is she "

with its Elizabethan use of the concrete word, clear, hard, and delicate. *Drink to me only with thine eyes*, a poem he himself liked very much, his best lyric, his finest mosaic of translation, has not the Elizabethan graceful artificiality, but rather a seventeenth-century solidity and grave directness.

Like all his poetry, even the most formal, like every piece of his work, it bears a strong impression of his personality, its ardent sincerity, its earnestness and integrity of mind and purpose.